Business Marketing Management

Frank G. Bingham, Jr.
Bryant College

Barney T. Raffield, III
Lebanon Valley College

SOUTH-WESTERN College Publishing
An International Thomson Publishing Company

Acquisition Editor: Randy G. Haubner
Sponsoring Editor: Robert B. Jared
Production Editor: Peggy A. Williams
Production House: Matrix Productions
Cover Design: Lorus Wittkopf
Internal Design: The Book Company
Cover Photographer: Thomas K. Leighton©
Marketing Manager: Scott D. Person

SN60AA

ISBN: 0-538-83678-4

1 2 3 4 5 6 7 8 9 D 2 1 0 9 8 7 6 5 4

Printed in the United States of America

I(T)P

International Thomson Publishing
South-Western Publishing Co. is an ITP Company. The ITP trademark is used under license.

Library of Congress Cataloging-in-Publication Data

Bingham, Frank G.
Business marketing management / Frank G. Bingham, Jr., Barney T. Raffield III.
p. cm.
Rev. ed. of: Business to business marketing management, c1990.
Includes bibliographical references and index.
ISBN 0-538-83678-4
1. Industrial marketing—Management. 2. Industrial procurement—Management. 3. Industrial marketing—United States—Case studies. 4. Industrial procurement—United States—Case studies.
I. Raffield, Barney T. II. Bingham, Frank G. Business to business marketing management.
HF5415.1283.B56 1994
658.8—dc20 94-4271
CIP

For their patience, love, and understanding,
this book is dedicated to
Caryl and Sherrie

Preface

We are experiencing a tremendous expansion in the teaching of business marketing. Trade magazines and scholarly journals are giving ever more space to the special issues and concerns of business marketers and students of business marketing. The recent focus on these markets reflects the recognition that the largest part of American business is not driven by consumer business methods, but has its own practices and complexities. What's more, students are also realizing the variety of career opportunities in business marketing and are eager to prepare themselves with the practical information and theoretical principles of business marketing practices.

Business marketing is also in a period of transformation, reflecting the changing face of American business in general: less growth in heavy industry and more in service, the evolution of information as a product, and the increasing prominence of international opportunities. A few years ago this text would have been called "Industrial Marketing Management," but smokestack industries are on the decline, and course and text titles are changing to reflect the broader range of enterprises that rightfully fall under the umbrella of business marketing. Almost every available product or service is either aimed at business users or has a business marketing facet. Financial services, company car fleets, construction cranes, trade magazines, industrial lubricants, corporate jets, convention services: the list is vast.

The business-to-business information boom has led to a parallel rise in the number of textbooks devoted to business marketing. But quantity has not always proven to be quality. When it came time to teach this course ourselves, we were dissatisfied with the available texts, new and old. All seemed to lack either a practical grounding in the real-world activities of business marketers, or a full integration of the newest developments and insights into the study of this evolving discipline. So it became our custom to prepare lengthy, detailed lecture outlines to fill in the gaps with which every text seemed to be riddled. These notes, in time, became *Business Management Marketing*. We think that we have produced a text worthy of our high aspirations. We hope that you will think so, too.

The Intended Audience for This Book

The business marketing course, often called business marketing or industrial marketing, is taught at trade schools, two- and four-year colleges at the junior or senior level for undergraduates, or as an MBA-level course. *Business Management Marketing* is aimed at those students with a foundation in basic marketing principles. It builds upon this knowledge and focuses on the special elements and requirements of business markets.

What to Look for in Our Book

While the business market has undergone rapid change, the textbooks have been slow to do the same. We have included a number of special features and pedagogical aids in *Business Management Marketing* to add structure and depth to the learning process, many of which will be new to this market.

Chapter Outlines. These are simply a supplement to the table of contents, enabling the student to see at a glance the chapter structure and content, without having to turn to the front of the book. They also reflect the way in which various topics are related, serving as a sort of "road map" to the chapter.

Learning Objectives. Each chapter begins with a listing of the major topics of the chapter and some indication of what the students should be able to glean from their coverage in the text. These are perhaps the primary points of interest in the chapter "road map."

Concept Questions. Concept Questions occur two or three times within each chapter, and are designed to give students a chance to test their recall of the preceding material. They are a simple and effective way for the student to check retention of concepts before getting to the end of the chapter.

Business-to-Business Marketing in Action Boxes. Each box contains a brief story of real business dilemmas or tactics that illustrate a major concept in the chapter.

Enumerated Summaries. The summary recaps the chapter contents point by point, rather than in a cluttered paragraph format, and is numbered for easy reference.

Chapter Cases. Unlike any other book on the market, *Business Management Marketing* provides two cases at the end of each chapter. The cases are generally short in length, and give a more focused examination of the chapters topics and issues than do the lump of long cases provided at the back of other textbooks. The shorter length of the chapter cases allows the instructor a number of options for their implementation, such as homework or in-class assignments, test questions, or group study. Each case is followed by two or more discussion questions that help the student to probe the case scenario for causes, solutions, and lessons.

Part Cases. We fully recognize the usefulness of longer cases, and therefore, we end each part division with one or more extended cases. These cases enlarge upon the material covered in the preceding part, focusing on the attendant issues and often drawing on topics covered in previous parts. The last section of the book contains two extensive comprehensive cases.

Unique Content

Buyers and Sellers. We have arranged *Business Management Marketing* to give a strong emphasis to the unique elements of the buyer-seller dyad. Following Part One, the Introduction, we move to two chapters in Part Two that examine the buying function and business buyer behavior, from fundamentals of purchasing management to management of the buying function and buyer-seller relationships. This approach brings forward the factor that most clearly shapes business marketing: the unique needs and processes of the business buyer. It is the buyer, after all, that distinguishes consumer marketing from business marketing, a point we feel should be made early and maintained throughout the course.

Personal Selling and Sales Management. Unlike most other texts, we recognize the inescapable importance of personal selling in the business marketing process by devoting separate chapters to the selling process and the management of the process and sales force. The multitude of issues surrounding both sides of the person-to-person sales contact deserve comprehensive treatment, rather than being squeezed into one chapter.

Marketing of Business Services. As America's economy becomes more service oriented, the emphasis on this topic is going to grow. We think that students should be made aware of the unique problems and concerns that face marketers of services, as well as the newest practices and scholarly findings.

International Business Marketing. In addition to a complete chapter on international marketing (Chapter 14), we have taken care to introduce global concepts and examples whenever possible and logical. Indeed, international business marketing is covered in all but Chapter 1. The benefit of this arrangement, we think, is that the student, exposed numerous times to the global focus of business, will learn to look for the international facets in all areas of business.

Ethics. If there is one change that we are proud to take a lead in, it is the increasing illumination of ethical perspectives in business textbooks. All businesses and business people must face their social and legal responsibilities.

Students will take their leads from the actions of business people, their professors, and their textbooks. Therefore, we find it essential to end our discussion of business marketing practices with a thorough overview of the various social ramifications of business practices.

Appendix. We are fortunate to have a unique appendix on future trends in business marketing. The appendix provides material found in no other business marketing text.

Instructor's Manual

The instructor's Manual for *Business Management Marketing* consists of several features:

Chapter Teaching Materials are comprised of (1) an overview/outline of the chapter contents to facilitate lecture preparation; (2) answers to review questions; and (3) end-of-chapter case discussions.

Part-Ending Case Materials provide an overview of the issues presented in each section of the text, and a discussion of the case outcome.

The Test Bank for each chapter includes multiple choice, true-false, fill in the blank, and essay questions. Questions are of varying degrees of difficulty.

Transparency Masters are numerous, consisting of the most important tables and charts from each chapter, along with several that are not highlighted in the text itself.

Acknowledgments

Although *Business Management Marketing* was the brainchild of the authors, it would not have come to pass without the abundant help and support of our colleagues, relatives, friends, and editors. First, we would like to thank the reviewers who provided their time and expertise to help us refine our various manuscript drafts into a smoother, more cohesive whole. Those patient and hardworking individuals are:

John Henke
Oakland University

Valerie Kijewski
University of Massachusetts—Lowell

Jay L. Laughlin
Kansas State University

J. David Lichtenthal
Baruch College

Richard E. Mathisen
Kennesaw State College

David Reid
University of Toledo

We cannot overlook the contributions of our Acquisition Editor, Randy Haubner, Editorial Assistant, Pamela M. Person, and our Production Editor, Peggy Williams. Their savvy and energy gave use inspiration and guidance. We thank them for their patience. We also owe a special thanks to both Sherrie Raffield and Jean K. Murray, a Bryant College graduate student, for the long hours worked over the past many months helping the authors with this monumental task. Without their help, this undertaking would have taken several more months to complete. There are always numerous others who should be thanked for providing small but necessary doses of assistance or criticism. We send our thanks to all of you.

Despite all of the above contributions, we acknowledge that some errors and infelicities will insist on creeping into the final product. For these we assume full responsibility. Any comments or suggestions would be most welcome and can be sent to us in care of South-Western Publishing Co., 5101 Madison Road, Cincinnati, Ohio 45227, Attention: Acquisitions Editor, Marketing.

Frank G. Bingham, Jr.
Barney T. Raffield, III

Contents in Brief

Preface iv

PART ONE INTRODUCTION 1

Chapter 1 The Business Marketing Environment 2

PART TWO HOW BUYERS BUY 31

Chapter 2 Fundamentals of the Purchasing and Materials Management Function 32
Chapter 3 Management of the Business Buying Function 79

PART THREE IDENTIFYING THE CUSTOMER 129

Chapter 4 Business Marketing Research and Information Systems 130
Chapter 5 Market Segmentation, Positioning, and Demand Projection 168

PART FOUR MAKING AND MOVING THE GOODS 217

Chapter 6 Product Development, Management, and Strategy 218
Chapter 7 Business Price Planning and Strategy 261
Chapter 8 Business Marketing Channel Participants 300
Chapter 9 Business Physical Distribution Management and Strategy 340

PART FIVE PROMOTING AND SELLING THE GOODS 393

Chapter 10 The Personal Selling Function in Business Marketing Strategy 394
Chapter 11 Business Sales Management 435
Chapter 12 Advertising and Sales Promotion Strategy in Business Markets 476

PART SIX TRENDS IN BUSINESS-TO-BUSINESS MARKETING 525

Chapter 13 Marketing of Business Services 526
Chapter 14 International Business Marketing 563
Chapter 15 Ethical Considerations in Business-to-Business Marketing 601

PART SEVEN COMPREHENSIVE CASES 641

Case Study Branford and Sons, Inc. 642
Case Study Leykam Mürztaler 648

Index 664

Contents

Preface iv

PART ONE INTRODUCTION 1

Chapter 1 The Business Marketing Environment 2

Business Marketing: An Overview 4
 The Business Market 4
Why Study Business Marketing? 5
How the Business Market Differs from the Consumer Market 7
 Greater Total Sales Volume 8
 Larger Volume Purchases 8
 Fewer Buyers 8
 Larger Buyers 8
 Geographically Concentrated Buyers 8
 Close Supplier-Customer Relationship 9
Business-to-Business Marketing in Action 10
 More Direct Channels of Distribution 10
 Professional Buying 10
 Multiple Buying Influences 11
 Complex Negotiation 11
 Reciprocity 11
 Leasing 12
 Emphasis on Personal Selling 12
Concept Questions 12
Characteristics of Business Demand 13
 Derived Demand 13
 Inelastic Demand 13
 Fluctuating Demand 13
 Joint Demand 14

The Nature of Business Buying Behavior 14
A Classification of Business Goods and Services 14
  Major Equipment 15
  Accessory Equipment 16
  Fabricated and Component Parts 16
  Process Materials 16
  Maintenance, Repair, and Operating (MRO) Supplies 16
  Raw Materials 17
  Business Services 17
Concept Questions 17
Business Customers 17
  Commercial Enterprises 18
  Governmental Organizations 18
  Institutions 19
International Customers 19
Business Marketing Planning and Strategy Formulation 20
Concept Questions 21
Format of This Text 22
Summary 22
Key Terms 23
Review Questions 24
Case 1-1 *The Fabric Studio* 25
Case 1-2 *The Merck-DuPont Joint Venture* 26
Suggested Additional Readings 28
Endnotes 28

PART TWO HOW BUYERS BUY 31

Chapter 2 Fundamentals of the Purchasing and Materials Management Function 32
Basic Policies and Procedures of Purchasing 34
The Business Buying Process 35
  Recognizing the Need 36
  Developing Product Specifications 37
  Soliciting Bids from Potential Suppliers 37
  Making the Purchase Decision 37
  Issuing the Contract 38
  Inspecting Delivered Goods for Quality 39
  Evaluating Vendor Performance 39

Concept Questions 39

Evaluating Potential Vendors 40
- Basic Considerations in Evaluating Potential Vendors 40
- Vendor-Rating Approaches 41

Concept Questions 47

The Changing Role of the Buyer 47
- Relationship Marketing 47
- Profile of a Business-to-Business Buyer 49

Business Buying Motives 50

Purchasing Organization 53
- Organization Related to Size of Company 53
- Centralization versus Decentralization of the Buying Function 54

Concept Questions 55

The Materials Management Concept 56
- Alternative Approaches to Materials Management 57

Business-to-Business Marketing in Action: Features and Implications of JIT 58
- Reasons for Adopting the Materials Management Concept 61

Business Buying Situations 62
- New-Task Buying 63
- Straight-Rebuy Buying 65
- Modified-Rebuy Buying 66

Purchasing and the Law 66
- Law of Agency 67
- Law of Contracts 68

Concept Questions 68

Summary 68

Key Terms 69

Review Questions 70

Case 2-1 *Morlock Manufacturing Company* 71

Case 2-2 *Manufacturers Hanover Corporation* 72

Suggested Additional Readings 74

Endnotes 76

Chapter 3 Management of the Business Buying Function 79

Objectives of Efficient Business Buying 81
- Objectives of Business Buyers 81
- Seven Rights of Business Buyers 81
- Purchasing Costs 82

The Buying Center 82

Concept Questions *85*

Quality in Business Buying and Selling 85
  Responsibilities of the Purchasing Department 87

Service in Business Buying and Selling 88
  Differentiation through Service 88
  Service as a Competitive Effort 89

Price in Business Buying and Selling 90
  Perceived Value 90

Value Analysis 91
  Development of Value Engineering 92
  Appropriate Tests Used 92

Concept Questions *94*

Make-or-Buy Analysis 94
  Ascertaining Profitability 94
  Reasons to Manufacture 95
  Participants in Make or Buy 96

Negotiation 96
  Analyzing Both Buyer and Seller Strengths 98

The Small-Order Problem 99
  The Centralized-Stores System 100
  The Petty Cash System 101
  The Blanket-Order System 101
  The Electronic-Ordering System 101

Environmental Forces and Buying Decisions 102
  The Economic Environment 103
  The Physical Environment 103
  The Competitive Environment 104
  The Technological Environment 104
  The Legal-Political Environment 105
  The Ethical Environment 105

Business-to Business Marketing in Action: Tech-Type Buyers Are Needed to Keep the Lid on Inflation *106*

Purchasing's Impact upon Company Profit 107

Concept Questions *109*

Summary *109*

Key Terms *110*

Review Questions *110*

Case 3-1 *Northern Chemical Company* *112*

Case 3-2 *Conner Peripherals* *114*

Suggested Additional Readings *116*

Endnotes 117

Case Study *Trus Joist Corporation 119*

PART THREE IDENTIFYING THE CUSTOMER 129

Chapter 4 Business Marketing Research and Information Systems 130

Differences between Business and Consumer Marketing Research 132
    Focus of Business Marketing Research 132

Major Tasks of Business Marketing Research 134
    Market Potential 134
    Market-Share Analysis 134
    Market Characteristics 136
    Sales Analysis 136
    Forecasting 136
    Other Applications 137

Marketing Research versus a Marketing Information System 137

Business-To-Business Marketing in Action: Quiz Customers for Clues about Competition 138

    Five Basic Elements of Future Marketing Information Systems 139
    Primary Uses of a Marketing Information System 140

Concept Questions 142

The Business Marketing Research Process 143
    Planning the Research Design 143
    Preparation 144
    Field Operations 144
    Processing 144
    Tabulation, Analysis, and Interpretation 144
    Reporting 145

Using Outside or Inside Research Specialists—Make or Buy? 145

Developing Information Sources 146
    Secondary Data Sources 146
    Primary Data Sources 156

Concept Questions 158

Organization of Business Marketing Research 158

Conducting International Marketing Research 159

Concept Questions 160

Summary 160

Key Terms 161

Review Questions 161

Case 4-1 *Arlington Chamber of Commerce 163*

Case 4-2 *International Marketing Research: An Entirely Different Animal 164*

Suggested Additional Readings 165

Endnotes 166

Chapter 5 Market Segmentation, Positioning, and Demand Projection 168

Segmentation, Positioning, and Demand Estimation: An Overview 170

General Market Segmentation Strategy 171
 The Nature of Business Market Segmentation 171

Strategies for Business Market Segmentation 172
 Undifferentiated Marketing Strategy 172
 Differentiated Marketing Strategy 173
 Concentrated Marketing Strategy 174

Approaches to Market Segmentation 174
 Macro/Micro Segmentation 175
 The Nested Approach to Market Segmentation 175
 Other Approaches to Business Market Segmentation 177

Concept Questions 178

Segmenting Business Markets 178
 Type of Economic Activity 178
 Size of Organization 178
 Geographic Location 178
 Product Usage 180
 Structure of the Procurement Function 180

International Segmentation 180

Evaluating Potential Market Segments 181
 Market Profitability Analysis 182
 Market Competitive Analysis 182

Concept Questions 184

Product Positioning Strategy 185
 Perceptual Mapping 185

Business-To-Business Marketing in Action: Inmac's Creative Approach to Positioning 186

 Positioning Business Products 187

Business Demand Projection 193
 Strategic Importance of Forecasting in Decision Making 193
 Definition of Some Basic Terminology 194
 Common Forecasting Problems 195

Selecting Forecasting Methods 196
 General Approaches to Forecasting 196

Qualitative Approaches to Forecasting 197
Quantitative Approaches to Forecasting 199

Concept Questions 204

Summary 204

Key Terms 205

Review Questions 206

***Case 5-1** AST Research, Inc. 207*

***Case 5-2** The Gallo Wine Company 208*

Suggested Additional Readings 209

Endnotes 210

***Case Study** Tuttle Corporation 213*

PART FOUR MAKING AND MOVING THE GOODS 217

Chapter 6 Product Development, Management, and Strategy 218

Product Strategy in Business Marketing 220
Effective Product Management and Strategy 220

Business New-Product Development 221
Types of New-Product Approaches 222
The New-Product Development Process 223

Organization of the New-Product Effort 230
Product Manager 230
New-Product Committee 230
New-Product Department 231
New-Product Venture Team 232

Concept Questions 232

The Product Life-Cycle Analysis 233
An Application of the Product Life-Cycle Model 234
Business Life Cycles and Experience Curves 234

Determinants of the Product Mix 237
Technology 237

Business-to-Business Marketing in Action: Yes, But What Does It Do? 238

Competition 240
Changes in Levels of Business Activity 241
Operating Capacity 241
Market Factors 241

Concept Questions 242

The Business Product Adoption-Diffusion Process 242
Stages in the Adoption Process 242

Factors Influencing the Rate of Adoption-Diffusion 243

Business Product Portfolio Classification, Analysis, and Strategy 244
What Is the Product Portfolio? 244
Diagnosing the Product Portfolio 245
Product Portfolio Strategies 246

Business Product Deletion Strategy 248
Harvesting 249
Line Simplification 249
Total-Line Divestment 249

International Product Strategy 250

Concept Questions 251

Summary 251

Key Terms 252

Review Questions 252

Case 6-1 *Cincinnati Milacron* 254

Case 6-2 *Abbott Laboratories* 255

Suggested Additional Readings 257

Endnotes 258

Chapter 7 Business Price Planning and Strategy 261

Business Pricing: An Overview 263

Major Factors Influencing Price Strategy 264
Competition 264
Cost 264
Demand 265
Pricing Objectives 265
Impact on Other Products 266
Legal Considerations 267

Pricing Methods 268
Marginal Pricing 268
Economic Value to the Customer 270
Break-even Analysis 271
Target Return-on-Investment Pricing 271

Demand Assessment and Strategy 272
Price Elasticity of Demand 272
Cost-Benefit Analysis 274

Concept Questions 274

Pricing Across the Product Life Cycle (Life-Cycle Costing) 275
Introduction Phase: New-Product Pricing Strategies 275
Growth Phase 277
Maturity Phase 277

Decline Phase 278
Price-Leadership Strategy 278
Competitive Bidding In The Business Market 279
Closed versus Open Bidding 280
Business-to-Business Marketing in Action: Conjoint Analysis Can Explain Why Some Business Bids Are Rejected 281
A Probabilistic Bidding Model 281
Concept Questions 285
Leasing in the Business Market 285
Advantages of Leasing for the Buyer 286
Advantages of Leasing for the Seller 286
Types of Lease Arrangements 287
Types of Business Leases 287
Pricing Policies in Business Pricing Strategy 288
Trade Discounts 288
Quantity Discounts 288
Cash Discounts 289
Geographical Price Adjustments 289
International Marketing Pricing Policy 289
Concept Questions 291
Summary 291
Key Terms 292
Review Questions 293
Case 7-1 *American Excelsior 294*
Case 7-2 *Hudson Valley Tree Company 295*
Suggested Additional Readings 297
Endnotes 298

Chapter 8 Business Marketing Channel Participants 300
Functions of the Channel Intermediary 302
Buying 303
Selling 303
Storage 304
Transportation 304
Sorting 304
Financing 304
Risk Taking 305
Market Information 305
The Nature of Channel Decisions 306
Concept Questions 307
Direct Channels 307

Sales-Volume Base 307

Indirect Channels 308

The Business Products (Industrial) Distributor 309

Business-to-Business Marketing in Action: Creating a Team of Distributors for Epson Products 312

The Manufacturers' Representative (Agent) 314

Sales Agents and Brokers 317

Facilitating Agencies 318

Combining Direct and Indirect Channels 318

Concept Questions 319

Channel Cooperation 319

Methods of Channel Cooperation 320

Channel Conflict 321

The Nature of Channel Conflict 323

Conflict Management and Resolution 323

A Legal Perspective on Channel Conflict 324

Typical Problem Areas in the Manufacturer-Intermediary Relationship 324

Intensive, Selective, and Exclusive Distribution 327

Intensive Distribution 327

Selective Distribution 328

Exclusive Distribution 329

International Channel Decisions 329

Types of Indirect-Channel Intermediaries 330

Concept Questions 331

Summary 331

Key Terms 332

Review Questions 332

Case 8-1 *Perrier Limited 334*

Case 8-2 *Merisel, Incorporated 335*

Suggested Additional Readings 337

Endnotes 338

Chapter 9 Business Physical Distribution Management and Strategy 340

Physical Distribution in the Business Market 342

The Nature of Physical Distribution 342

Business-to-Business Marketing in Action: Physical Distribution as the Artery of Hospital Service 344

Traffic Management: An Overview 345

Functions of Traffic Management 345

Mode and Carrier Selection 345

Routing 348
Claims Processing 349
Operation of Private Transportation 349
Concept Questions 349
Deregulation 349
Customer Service 351
Customer-Service Standards 352
Examination of Cost Trade-Offs 352
The Impact of Logistical Service on Business Channel Members 356
Warehousing 356
Private or Public Warehouses? 358
Concept Questions 359
Inventory Control 360
Electronic Data Interchange 360
The Just-in-Time Concept 361
The E.O.Q. Model 364
Order Processing 366
The Order-Processing Cycle 366
Shortening the Order-Processing Cycle 366
Vendor Stocking 368
International Distribution 368
Concept Questions 368
Conclusion 369
Summary 369
Key Terms 370
Review Questions 370
***Case 9-1** Itel Distribution Systems 372*
***Case 9-2** A-P-A Transport Corporation 373*
Suggested Additional Readings 375
Endnotes 377
***Case Study** McIlhenny Company—Producers of Tabasco Brand Products 380*
***Case Study** Crinshaw Company 388*

PART FIVE PROMOTING AND SELLING THE GOODS 393

Chapter 10 The Personal Selling Function in Business Marketing Strategy 394

How Personal Selling Differs between Business and Consumer Markets 396

A Profile of Personal Selling 397
    Selling 398
    Cooperative Relationships with Channel Members 398
    Planning 399
    Decision Making 399
    The Management of Communication 399
The Cost of Personal Selling 401
    The Cost to Close a Business Sale 402
Concept Questions 402
Understanding Buyer Behavior 402
    Understanding Buyer Needs 403
    Methods Used to Uncover Important Buyer Needs 404
The Selling Spectrum 406
    Approaches to the Business Sales Presentation 406
    Types of Sales Positions and Selling Styles in the Business Market 408
Some Contemporary Trends in Business Selling 412
    The Importance of Systems Selling 412
    The Importance of Telemarketing 413
    The Emergence of the Saleswoman 414
    The Usage of Terminals and Laptop Computers 417
    The Rapid Growth of Audio-Visual Aids 418
Concept Questions 418
The Personal Selling Process: A Business Salesperson's Perspective 418
    Preliminary Activities 419
    Face-to-Face Activities 419
Business-to-Business Marketing in Action: Humor Can Be Your Best Sales Tool: Salespeople Say the Key Is Knowing Your Customers 420
    Follow-Up Activities 422
International Business Selling 424
Concept Questions 425
Summary 425
Key Terms 426
Review Questions 427
Case 10-1 *Clemson Meat Company 428*
Case 10-2 *The Saturn Division of General Motors Corporation 430*
Suggested Additional Readings 432
Endnotes 433

Chapter 11 Business Sales Management 435
Business Sales Management: A Leadership Challenge 437

Selecting the Sales Manager 437
Perspectives 438
Goals 438
Responsibilities 438
Satisfaction 439
Job Skill Requirements 439
Relationships 439
Basic Types of Sales Organizations 439
The Line Organization 440
The Line and Staff Organization 440
The Functional Organization 440
The Centralized versus Decentralized Organization 441
Organizing by Specialization 442
Concept Questions 444
Staffing the Business Sales Force 444
Determining Sales-Force Size 444
Recruitment and Selection 447
Recruitment 447
Selection 448
Training and Developing the Business Sales Force 450
Purposes of Sales Training 450
What the Training Program Should Cover 451
Who Should Do The Training? 453
Evaluating Sales Training 455
Concept Questions 457
Directing and Motivating the Business Sales Force 457
Providing Leadership 457
Business-to-Business Marketing in Action: Building a Sales Staff into a Team 458
Sales Quotas 459
Compensation 461
Sales-Force Analysis and Evaluation 462
Why Analyze and Evaluate Salespeople? 462
Who Should Analyze and Evaluate Salespeople? 463
When Should Analysis and Evaluation Be Done? 464
Managing U.S. Salespeople in International Markets 464
Selection 464
Orientation and Training 466
Compensation 466
Concept Questions 467
Summary 467
Key Terms 468
Review Questions 469

Case 11-1 *Custom Wheel Lights, Incorporated 470*

Case 11-2 *Coke Gets Off Its Can in Europe 471*

Suggested Additional Readings 473

Endnotes 474

Chapter 12 Advertising and Sales Promotion Strategy in Business Markets 476

An Overview of Business Promotion 478

Creating a Promotional Plan for Business Markets 479

Setting Objectives for a Promotional Plan 479

Developing the Promotional Budget 480
  Prioritizing the Promotional Expenditure 481

Concept Questions 482

Determining and Implementing the Promotional Mix 483
  Business Advertising 483
  Business Publicity 495

Business-to-Business Marketing in Action: In-House Advertising Is Causing Agency Concern 496

  Business Sales Promotion 499

Concept Questions 505

Measuring the Effectiveness of the Business Promotion Campaign 506
  Pretesting and Posttesting 506
  Responses to Business Advertising 506

Following Up and Modifying the Business Promotion Campaign When Necessary 507

Promotional Strategy for International Markets 507
  International Advertising 507
  International Publicity and Sales Promotion 508

Concept Questions 509

Summary 509

Key Terms 510

Review Questions 511

Case 12-1 *U.S. Companies Learn to Deal with the Japanese Media 512*

Case 12-2 *Cause-Related Promotion 513*

Suggested Additional Readings 514

Endnotes 515

Case Study *Northern New Jersey Manufacturing Company 518*

Case Study *Robertshaw Controls Company 520*

PART SIX TRENDS IN BUSINESS-TO-BUSINESS MARKETING 525

Chapter 13 Marketing of Business Services 526

The Marketing of Business Services: An Overview 528

The Environments for Business Service Firms 529
- The Economic Environment 530
- The Societal-Cultural Environment 530
- The Competitive Environment 531
- The Technological Environment 531
- The Political-Legal Environment 532

Important Characteristics of Business Services 532
- Intangibility 532
- Perishability and Fluctuating Demand 533
- Simultaneity 533
- Heterogeneity 534

Concept Questions 534

Business Service Marketing—Challenges and Opportunities 535
- Service Marketing versus Product Marketing 535
- Positioning Strategy 536
- Bundling of Services 537
- Service Strategy and the Marketing Mix 537
- New-Service Development 541

Business-to-Business Marketing in Action: Information Retailers: A Potential Not Yet Realized 542

Concept Questions 544

Classification of Services 544
- Seller-Related Bases 544
- Buyer-Related Bases 545
- Service-Related Bases 545
- Classifying Services by Clusters 546
- People-Based versus Equipment-Based Services 548

International Marketing of Business Services 549
- The Risks of International Marketing for Service Organizations 550
- Problems of Adaptation to and Operation in Overseas Markets 551
- Barriers to Trade in Services 551

The Future for Business Services 552

Concept Questions 553

Summary 553

Key Terms 554

Review Questions 554
Case 13-1 *SAS: A Leader in Profitable Customer Service* 556
Case 13-2 *The Case of the Squealing Tax Accountant* 557
Suggested Additional Readings 559
Endnotes 560

Chapter 14 International Business Marketing 563

The Scope and Challenge of International Business Marketing 565
The Market 566
Stages of Economic Development 566
The International Business Environment 567
The Buying Process 568
Cultural Dynamics 568
The Political and Legal Environment 571
Concept Questions 575
International Law 575
Tax Treaties and Treaties of Friendship, Commerce, and Navigation 575
IMF and GATT 576
UNCITRAL 576
International Standards Organization 576
Domestic Laws in Foreign Markets 576
Differing Legal Systems 576
Foreign Laws and the Product 576
Foreign Laws and Pricing 577
Foreign Laws and Promotion 577
Entry Strategies for the International Business Market 577
Exporting 577
Licensing 578
Joint Ventures 578
Manufacturing 578
Assembly Operations 578
Franchising 579
Turnkey Operations 579
Product Strategy in the International Business Market 579
International Product and Service Positioning Strategy 580
Adaptation versus Standardization 581
Marketing Services Internationally 581
Concept Questions 582
Managing the International Promotion Effort 582
Business-to-Business Marketing in Action: Advertising Agencies Adjust to Demands of Global Clients 583
Global Sales Promotion 584

Global Publicity 585
Global Trends in Direct Marketing 585

Managing the International Distribution System 585

Pricing in the International Business Market 587
Company Factors Affecting Pricing 588
Market Factors Affecting Pricing 589
Environmental Factors Affecting Pricing 589

Concept Questions 591

Summary 591

Key Terms 592

Review Questions 593

Case 14-1 *Trading Again with the Iranians? 594*

Case 14-2 *International Trade without Direct Pricing 595*

Suggested Additional Readings 597

Endnotes 598

Chapter 15 Ethical Considerations in Business-to-Business Marketing 601

Business-to-Business Marketing Ethics and the Future: An Overview 603
Examples of Corporate Social Responsibility 604
The Individuality of Ethical Standards 607

Strategy and Ethics in the Business-to-Business Marketing Environment 607

An Ethical Issue: The Organizational Buying Function and Buyer-Seller Relationships 608
Business Ethics Is Not a One-Sided Proposition 609

Concept Questions 610

Ethical Issues in Business-to-Business Marketing Research 610
Society's Rights 611
Clients' Rights 611
Researchers' Rights 612

Ethics and the Management of the Business Pricing Function 612
Setting a Fair Price 613
Altering Product Quality without Changing Price 613
Practicing Price Discrimination with Smaller Accounts 613
Price Fixing 614
Using a Competitor's Quote to Requote or Rebid 614
Reciprocity 614

Concept Questions 615

Ethics and the Management of the Business Sales Force 615
Ethics in Dealing with Customers 616

Ethics in Dealing with Employers 617
Ethics and Business Advertising Strategy 618
Truth in Advertising 619
Comparative Advertising 619
Ethics and International Business-to-Business Marketing 620
Ethics from Country to Country 620
The Complexity of International Ethical Issues 622
Concept Questions 622
Business-to-Business Marketing in Action: An Ethical Problem in South Africa for U.S. Marketers 623
Summary 624
Key Terms 625
Review Questions 625
Case 15-1 *Coke Battles for French Bottling Contracts 626*
Case 15-2 *Phoenix Laser Systems, Incorporated 627*
Suggested Additional Readings 628
Appendix 15-1 Future Trends in Business-to-Business Marketing 629
Technology 629
Competition 630
Government 631
Global Events 631
Telemarketing 631
Materials Management 632
Continued Development of the Buyer-Seller Relationship 632
Endnotes 633
Case Study *National Peach Council 636*

PART SEVEN COMPREHENSIVE CASES 641

Branford and Sons, Inc. 642
Leykam Mürztaler 648

Index 664

Part One

Introduction

1 The Business Marketing Environment

Learning Objectives

After reading this chapter, you should be able to:

- Discuss the differences between business and consumer marketing.
- Describe the characteristics of business demand.
- Understand the nature of business-buying behavior.
- Distinguish among the basic types of business goods and services.
- Differentiate among the various kinds of business customers.
- Appreciate the increasing importance of international customers in business markets.
- Explain the pivotal importance of planning and strategy formulation to the business marketing effort.

Chapter Outline

Learning Objectives

Business Marketing: An Overview
- The Business Market

Why Study Business Marketing?

How the Business Market Differs from the Consumer Market
- Greater Total Sales Volume
- Larger Volume Purchases
- Fewer Buyers
- Larger Buyers
- Geographically Concentrated Buyers
- Close Supplier-Customer Relationship
- More Direct Channels of Distribution
- Professional Buying
- Multiple Buying Influences
- Complex Negotiation
- Reciprocity
- Leasing
- Emphasis on Personal Selling

Characteristics of Business Demand
- Derived Demand
- Inelastic Demand
- Fluctuating Demand
- Joint Demand

The Nature of Business Buying Behavior

A Classification of Business Goods and Services
- Major Equipment
- Accessory Equipment
- Fabricated and Component Parts
- Process Materials
- Maintenance, Repair, and Operating (MRO) Supplies
- Raw Materials
- Business Services

Business Customers
- Commercial Enterprises
  - Indirect channel members
  - Original equipment manufacturers (OEMs)
  - User-customers
  - Overlap of categories
- Governmental Organizations
- Institutions

International Customers

Business Marketing Planning and Strategy Formulation

Format of This Text

Summary

Key Terms

Review Questions

Cases

Case 1-1

Case 1-2

Suggested Additional Readings

Endnotes

BUSINESS MARKETING: AN OVERVIEW

In one way or another, most large firms sell to other organizations. Companies such as Xerox and DuPont sell the great majority of their product mix to organizations. Even large consumer products companies engage in "organizational or business marketing." For example, General Mills manufactures and distributes a number of well-known products to consumer markets, such as Gold Medal flour, Betty Crocker cake mixes and frostings, Cheerios cereal, and Parker Brother games. Yet, before these products reach the final consumer, General Mills must first sell them to the trade, wholesale, and retail organizations that serve consumer markets. General Mills also manufactures and distributes other products, such as specialty chemicals, that are marketed only to the business market.

Business-to-business organizations, such as Xerox, DuPont, and to a more limited degree, General Mills, constitute a vast market consisting of over thirteen million organizations that buy more than $3 trillion worth of goods and services each year. This market will continue to grow. In a striking finding, 96 percent of leading U.S. corporate marketing executives who were recently surveyed believe their firms will have higher business sales in the next twelve months.[1] Companies that sell to other organizations must do their best to understand organizational buying behavior and the buyer needs, resources, motivations, and buying processes that shape such behavior. Business marketing must be tailored to meet diverse needs that can vary enormously from one market segment to another.[2] In addition to understanding the business buyer and the related buying process, the marketer must have a firm grasp of how some of the traditional marketing tools and techniques studied, used, and written about for many years present major opportunities and challenges in the business marketing environment.

The Business Market

Business marketing can be defined as those activities that facilitate exchanges involving products and customers in business markets. A *business marketing transaction* takes place whenever a good or service is sold for any use other than personal consumption.

Basically, the business market consists of individuals and organizations that acquire goods and services that enter into the production of other products and services that are sold, rented, or supplied to others. This market includes buyers from many types of industries: manufacturing; construction; transportation; communication; banking, finance, and insurance; agriculture, forestry and fisheries; mining; and public utilities. The growing importance of highly technical business products, the significant changes in the pattern of final demand, the rapid pace of technological change, the increasing size and complexity of the business firm and its customers, the growing impact of the computer and management services, and the success of foreign competition—all have highlighted the need for innovative business marketing strategies. All formal organizations, public or private, profit or not-for-profit, participate in the buying and selling of business products and services. The study of this process is what this book is all about.

WHY STUDY BUSINESS MARKETING?

Traditionally, business marketing has been a distant cousin of the mainstream of marketing thought. However, the employment opportunities, along with the growing importance of high-technology business products and the success of foreign competition, have highlighted the need for increased business marketing study.

The increasing size of the business market warrants the study of this sector. In 1986, there were more than 350,000 manufacturing establishments in the United States, employing over twenty million people. These firms were responsible for $2.5 trillion in sales. Another 300,000 firms provided services to businesses and other organizations, while over 400,000 firms served as assemblers, resellers, wholesalers, manufacturers' agents, and brokers. Table 1-1 provides comparative sales figures for manufacturing, wholesaling, and retailing establishments

TABLE 1-1 **U.S. Manufacturing and Trade Sales for 1985 (in Millions of Dollars)**

Manufacturing	$2,341,220
Durable goods industries	1,243,793
Nondurable goods industries	1,097,427
Retail Trade	$1,373,941
Durable goods stores	514,207
Nondurable goods stores	859,734
Merchant Wholesalers	$1,373,926
Durable goods establishments	626,749
Nondurable goods establishments	747,177

Source: 1986 Survey of Current Business.

in the United States; Table 1-2 is a general breakdown of the major manufacturing industries, a $2.3 trillion market. These totals point out the unlimited career opportunities available for students of business marketing.

Other reasons for the increased study of business marketing are the significance of the international interdependence for many business-to-business firms, along with the importance of the service sector of the economy, which in the United States is more than twice as large as the manufacturing sector. Deregulation, changes in professional association standards, and the application of computer technology combine to produce dramatic changes in the environment of many service industries. The increasingly competitive nature of both the international and service sectors of the business market requires a new emphasis on marketing for such diverse industries as airlines and accounting, hotels and hospitals, banking and real estate brokerages, and manufacturing. Both international business marketing and business service marketing are covered in this text.

Finally, the bulk of academic research has focused on consumer goods marketing, which relegated business marketing to the sidelines. However, the situation is changing. This rather cavalier attitude overlooks the distinct differences between the two fields, while emphasizing their similarities. The attractiveness of the opportunities in the business marketing field will continue to grow because the majority of students graduating with bachelor's and master's degrees begin their careers with business-to-business firms, rather than with consumer goods companies.[3] More and more of the over fifteen hundred schools of business in the United States today are offering business marketing courses, because a typical business recruiter is often faced with a pool of applicants lacking even a basic comprehension of what the world of nonconsumer goods is like. The study

TABLE 1-2 **U.S. Manufacturers' Sales for 1985 (In Millions of Dollars)**

Stone, clay, and glass products	$ 57,255
Primary metals	125,777
Fabricated metal parts	168,953
Machinery, except electrical	212,620
Electrical machinery	185,514
Transportation equipment	313,427
Instruments and related products	56,743
Food and kindred products	296,142
Tobacco products	20,606
Paper and allied products	97,565
Chemicals and allied products	214,345
Petroleum and coal products	194,030
Rubber and plastic products	48,246

Source: 1986 Survey of Current Business.

and understanding of business marketing management, out of necessity, will continue to grow.

HOW THE BUSINESS MARKET DIFFERS FROM THE CONSUMER MARKET

Many differences can be found between the marketing of business goods and the marketing of consumer goods. Paper Mate,[4] a division of Gillette, has traditionally manufactured and distributed medium-priced ballpoint pens to consumer markets. As this particular market became increasingly segmented into lower-priced and premium-priced offerings, Paper Mate decided to provide products at both ends of the price continuum.

The firm entered the business market by catering to the office-supplies field as well. Paper Mate created a special commercial sales force to market its pens to business buyers. It also acquired Liquid Paper, an established brand name in office supplies. Top management viewed the business marketing strengths of Liquid Paper as complementary to Paper Mate's specialization in consumer markets. Paper Mate was fully aware that business markets differed from consumer markets and that the characteristics of business markets necessitated the design of new marketing strategies, which would not be appropriate for use in consumer segments.

Business markets have specific characteristics that differ significantly from consumer markets.[5] These characteristics are discussed below, and are summarized in Exhibit 1-1.[6]

EXHIBIT 1-1 **Characteristics of Business Markets as Compared to Consumer Markets**

The following is a summary of the characteristics of business markets when compared to consumer markets:

Characteristic	Business Market	Consumer Market
Sales Volume	Greater	Smaller
Purchase Volume	Larger	Smaller
Number of Buyers	Fewer	Many
Size of Individual Buyers	Larger	Smaller
Location of Buyers	Geographically concentrated	Diffuse
Buyer-Seller Relationship	Closer	More impersonal
Nature of Channel	More direct	More indirect
Nature of Buying	More professional	More personal
Nature of Buying Influence	Multiple	Single
Type of Negotiations	More complex	Simpler
Use of Reciprocity	Yes	No
Use of Leasing	Greater	Smaller
Primary Promotional Method	Personal Selling	Advertising

Greater Total Sales Volume

Total dollar sales in the business market are greater than total dollar sales in the consumer market, even though there are far fewer business buyers than final consumers. An automobile bought by a final consumer is viewed as one sale in the consumer market. Yet, numerous sales transactions occurred in the process of manufacturing that automobile. Iron ore was mined and sold to a steel producer who, in turn, sold steel to the automobile manufacturer. A great many other business transactions also occurred before the automobile came off the assembly line.

Larger Volume Purchases

Business marketers also sell to customers who buy in larger quantities than do final consumers. While consumers buy new sets of tires for their cars, Ford Motor Company buys several hundred thousand tires from several major tire manufacturers. Additionally, the consumer buys home heating oil by the gallon (no. 2 oil), while the electric company will be buying thousands of barrels (approximately forty-two gallons per barrel) of no. 4, no. 5, or no. 6 oil under a long-term contract with the distributor.

Fewer Buyers

A business marketer generally deals with far fewer buyers than does the consumer marketer. Firms that sell to manufacturers usually have less difficulty identifying prospective customers than do firms that sell to final consumers. Allegheny International sells its specialty metals and electronics for jet engines to a very few airplane manufacturers, while its Oster and Sunbeam Divisions sell appliances for the consumer market through thousands of distributors and retail stores.

Larger Buyers

Unlike final consumer markets, a few large buyers account for most of the purchasing in many business markets. In the telephone and telegraph, aircraft engines and engine parts, cigarette, motor vehicles, and organic fiber industries, the top four manufacturers account for over 70 percent of total production.

Geographically Concentrated Buyers

Business buyers are geographically concentrated, whereas final consumers are found virtually everywhere. As shown in Table 1-3, over two-thirds of the business firms in the United States are located in the Middle Atlantic, East North Central, South Atlantic, and Pacific states. Over half of U.S. business buyers are located in just seven states: New York, Pennsylvania, New Jersey, Ohio, Michigan,

TABLE 1-3 **The Geographic Distribution of U.S. Manufacturing Plants Based on Selected Criteria**

Region	No. of Plants	Thousands of Manufacturing Employees	Value added by Manufacturing*	Value of Manufacturers' Shipments*
Northeast	26,393	1,350	$ 78,908	$ 136,989
Middle Atlantic	61,894	3,007	180,165	346,759
East North Central	69,756	4,186	266,248	590,487
West North Central	24,513	1,322	84,891	196,637
South Atlantic	53,476	3,104	179,075	373,181
East South Central	19,718	1,303	74,296	164,862
West South Central	31,304	1,432	101,009	262,832
Mountain	16,479	596	35,822	73,554
Pacific	65,362	2,650	165,503	330,371
TOTAL	368,897	18,950	$1,165,917	$2,476,071

*In millions of dollars.

Source: U.S. Department of Commerce. *Statistical Abstract of the United States 1991,* 10th ed. (Washington, D.C.: U.S. Government Printing Office, 1991), p. 747.

Illinois, and California. The aircraft and microelectronics industries are concentrated on the West Coast, and many of the firms that supply the automobile manufacturing industry are located in and around Detroit. Most agricultural output also comes from a relatively few states.

Close Supplier-Customer Relationship

There is a close relationship between sellers and customers in business markets because of the smaller customer base, the greater volume and cost of the average sale, and the importance and power of the larger customers over the suppliers. A very curious development is reshaping the competitive business marketplace—a trend to increased buyer-seller cooperation.[7] Sales are typically made by those suppliers who closely cooperate with the buyer on technical specifications and delivery requirements. An increasing number of U.S. manufacturers and suppliers are moving from adversarial to cooperative exchange attitudes that focus on long-term relationships. The just-in-time (JIT) supplier-customer exchange concept is a recent operational philosophy thought to epitomize the relational model.[8] As world markets become increasingly competitive, firms have discovered that close partnership relationships with important suppliers can produce managerial, technological, and financial benefits.[9] The box entitled "Business Marketing in Action" describes the benefits derived from the close relationship that General Motors has with its suppliers.

BUSINESS-TO-BUSINESS MARKETING IN ACTION

General Motors (GM), the U.S. steel industry's largest customer, buys thousands of tons of numerous types and gauges (thickness) of steel. At the beginning of each year GM traditionally awarded each of a dozen or so suppliers a certain percentage of its requirements for particular types and gauges of steel at specific plants.

More recently, GM has made some basic changes in the way it buys steel. The firm now concentrates larger purchases on a smaller number of suppliers. GM's management figured the firm would be able to work more closely with fewer suppliers, ensuring that the suppliers deliver the types and quality of steel GM needs. By placing larger orders with fewer suppliers and entering into multiyear contracts, GM may benefit in another way: it may pay lower prices because the suppliers enjoy lower production costs through economies of scale. Closer long-term relationships with its suppliers should also enable GM to lower reject rates on steel shipments received, gain manufacturing efficiencies because of the greater reliability of the steel, and operate with less inventory.

In selecting its suppliers GM ranks them in terms of traditional criteria such as product quality, ability to deliver on time, and price. But because it wants to develop closer long-term relationships with its suppliers, GM also looks at their limitations with respect to producing various widths and gauges of steel, financial strength, and commitment to remaining in the steel-making business and modernizing their facilities.

Sources: Steven Flax, "How Detroit Is Reforming the Steelmakers," *Fortune* (May 16, 1983), pp. 127–129; and Amal Nag, "GM Is Said to Seek Long-Term Accords with Steelmakers," *Wall Street Journal* (May 6, 1983), p. 2. Reprinted from William F. Schoell, *Marketing* (2d ed.), Boston: Allyn and Bacon, Inc., 1985, p. 633.

More Direct Channels of Distribution

In consumer markets, the great majority of goods are sold through a complex structure of wholesalers and retailers who serve as intermediaries between the producer and the consumer. Frozen foods, for example, are sold to several types of wholesalers or food brokers. In turn, these distributors will sell the frozen foods to supermarkets and institutional users. In the majority of business markets, however, sellers and buyers are more directly linked. When dealing with very large purchasers, marketers can make direct sales rather than go through industrial distributors or other intermediaries. However, some products sold to business buyers are commonly sold through one or two levels of wholesalers.

Professional Buying

Business buyers normally take a more formalized approach to buying than do final consumers. A salesperson who is selling portable typewriters in a Sears store generally deals with only one prospect at a time; yet, an IBM computer salesperson may have to give product demonstrations to a firm's purchasing manager, office manager, and secretaries. The professional training of purchasing personnel has resulted in a professional certification program whereby the individual earns the designation of Certified Purchasing Manager (CPM). This distinction comes after several years in the field, or a degree from a recognized college or university, in addition to three years of vocational training. Such individuals must then pass a series of examinations before they can place CPM after their names. Business buyers are professional buyers, and selling to them requires professional salespeople. Successful salespeople keep a vast inventory of information on their customers.[10]

Multiple Buying Influences

More people typically influence business buying decisions than consumer buying decisions. Buying committees composed of technical experts and senior management are common in the purchase of major goods. This phenomenon, coupled with the cross-functional nature of these influences, complicates the marketing communications process. Therefore, business marketers must employ well-trained sales representatives, and marketers often use sales teams to deal with highly skilled buyers.

Complex Negotiation

Although there are a few consumer goods, such as automobiles and real estate, in which negotiation commonly takes place, considerable buyer-seller negotiation exists in the purchase and sale of more expensive business products. In many cases, buyer representatives will meet with seller representatives several times to negotiate sales contracts; and this process may continue over several months.

Reciprocity

Business buyers often choose suppliers who also purchase from them. For instance, a paper manufacturer may buy the chemicals for its production process from a chemical company that buys large amounts of its paper. General Motors buys engines for use in its automobiles and trucks from Borg Warner, which, in turn, buys many of the automobiles and trucks it needs from GM. Reciprocity is considered to be illegal if there is a coercive use of pressure by one of the parties, which results in reduced competition. Noncoercive reciprocity is legal, provided it is supported by elaborate records of purchases and sales to and from other parties.[11] Governmental investigations are currently being conducted into the possibility of illegal influence in procurement in governmental organizations.

Leasing

Many business buyers lease their equipment rather than buy it. Businesses may find that leasing equipment offers several advantages. Leasing allows for greater use of capital. Lease payments are entered on the books as current operating expenses, rather than as liabilities; as such, they do not reduce a company's credit line or ability to borrow. The major advantages of leasing are decreased capital outflow, easier cost forecasting, and protection against equipment obsolescence. A 1989 study by the Gallup Organization for the American Association of Equipment Lessors reports that seven of ten companies lease equipment and that 48 percent of those that do not lease have considered it.[12] Computers, packaging equipment, heavy-construction equipment, machine tools, and sales-force automobiles serve as examples of this phenomenon. The lessee is able to conserve capital, acquire the seller's latest products, receive better servicing, and gain tax advantages. The lessor often receives a larger net income and has the opportunity to sell to those customers who could not afford to purchase the equipment outright.[13] For example, General Electric leases personal computers, manufactured by IBM, Apple, and Hewlett-Packard, along with related equipment and software programs, to business customers.[14]

Emphasis on Personal Selling

Because of each of the characteristics discussed above, business marketers emphasize personal selling more than advertising in designing and implementing their marketing mixes. A good salesperson can tailor presentations and highlight different product features for those individuals involved in the product purchase. The cost of a business sales call can be justified because of the size, complexity, and sales volume per account of most business products, as compared to a typical consumer product. The use of personal selling, in contrast to advertising, provides immediate customer feedback, and business sales representatives can adjust their promotional messages on the spot.

CONCEPT QUESTIONS

1. What is a business market?
2. Why is personal selling, rather than advertising, more commonly used in business marketing?

CHARACTERISTICS OF BUSINESS DEMAND

Business demand can be described as being derived, inelastic, and fluctuating in nature. There is even joint demand for some business goods. These characteristics are different from consumer product demand, and each will be discussed briefly.

Derived Demand

All demand for business goods is derived from the demand for consumer goods and services. *Derived demand* can be defined as the demand for a business product that is linked to demand for a consumer good. The marketer must closely monitor the buying patterns of the final consumer and those environmental factors that affect them.[15] In the long run, no business demand is totally unrelated to the demand for consumer goods.

Inelastic Demand

Because of the derived demand for business products, there is less opportunity for business marketers to stimulate primary demand (demand for a product category) through price cuts than there is for consumer goods marketers. Therefore, the primary demand for business products is more price inelastic than that for consumer products. For example, automobile manufacturers purchase headlights as component parts for automobiles. If the price of headlights goes down, the automobile manufacturers are not very likely to greatly increase their purchase of headlights. If, however, they expect the price increase to be temporary, they may do some stockpiling; but this action actually results in a change in the timing of orders and not an increase in the long-run purchase volume. The cost of headlights accounts for a very small part of the total cost of manufacturing an automobile, and a reduction of a few cents in the selling price of cars is unlikely to stimulate new car sales. Also, the price of headlights could increase significantly before it would have much effect on the sales of headlights.[16]

Fluctuating Demand

The demand for business goods and services tends to be more volatile than the demand for consumer goods and services. This is especially true of the demand for new products and equipment. A given percentage increase in consumer demand can lead to a much larger percentage increase in the demand for plant and equipment necessary to produce the additional output. This phenomenon is often referred to as the *acceleration principle*. An increase in consumer demand of only 10 percent can result in as much as a 200 percent rise in business demand in the next period; and a 10 percent decrease in consumer demand can cause a total collapse in the demand for investment goods. This demand volatility has caused many business marketers to diversify their product lines and markets in order to achieve more balanced sales over the business cycle.

Joint Demand

The demand for a number of business products, such as raw materials and component parts, is affected by joint demand. *Joint demand* occurs when two or more items are used in combination to produce a product. For instance, a firm that manufactures hammers needs the same number of handles as it does hammer heads; these two products are demanded jointly. If the supplier of handles cannot furnish the required number, and the hammer producer cannot obtain them elsewhere, the producer will stop buying hammer heads.

THE NATURE OF BUSINESS BUYING BEHAVIOR

On the whole, it is generally thought that business buyers tend to be more cautious than do final consumers. They generally make a conscious and deliberate effort to act rationally and to do what is best for their companies. Table 1-4 illustrates how business customers and final consumers might view the same product differently. Business buyers, however, are not totally rational in their buying behavior. In fact, according to many marketing practitioners, selling to business buyers is very frequently a personality-oriented sales situation, as is typically the case in final consumer transactions. Though it is true that the demand or need for business products is usually economically motivated and rational, this should not be confused with the actions taken to satisfy that need, or the behavioral aspects of the business purchaser.

Most business marketers and sales managers go to great lengths to differentiate their products. Yet, no matter how favorably they may present their offering, unless the buyer is convinced of the integrity of the seller and of the adequacy of post-sale support, it is unlikely that the purchase will be made from that seller. This convincing is largely subjective in nature, and subjective judgments are seldom entirely rational in the economic sense.[17]

A CLASSIFICATION OF BUSINESS GOODS AND SERVICES

Business goods and services can be classified in a variety of ways. Business goods are generally classified according to tax treatment and end use. In order to appreciate the differences in demand represented by different types of products, a useful scheme for classifying business products might include at least the

TABLE 1-4 **Business Users and Final Consumers Evaluate the Same Products**

Product	Questions Asked by Typical Business Users	Questions Asked by Typical Ultimate Consumers
Typewriter	Will it increase office efficiency? What is its capital investment value? Does it have special features that will help improve our company image?	Will it help my son prepare better school reports? Will it improve my correspondence? Is a portable electric machine worth the extra cost?
Automobile	How efficient is the vehicle to operate? Would it be more economical to lease or purchase it? What is the expected working life span of the car?	How does it enhance my status? What is its potential trade-in value? Will I get reasonable gas mileage?
Telephone	Will expanded service lower the cost of communicating with our customers? Should our intercom system be separate from or connected to the telephone system?	How long will it take to have one installed? Can I get three jacks and two telephones? What colors and styles are available?

Source: Figure from *Marketing Today*, Fourth Edition, by John T. Mentzer, copyright © 1985 by Harcourt Brace & Company, reporduced by permission of the publisher.

following: major equipment; accessory equipment; fabricated and component parts; process materials; maintenance, repair and operating supplies (MRO); raw materials; and business services. Each of these is discussed below.

Major Equipment

Major equipment, also frequently referred to as installations, consists of machinery, computers, machine tools, stamping machines, and robots, among other things. The demand for *major equipment* is considered inelastic, and in addition to the expenditure involved, it is charged to a capital account because of the intent of the purchase and the nature of the product. Because of price and technical requirements, the purchase of major equipment will usually require close cooperation between the technical and sales staff of both the business buyer and seller. Installment payment schedules and leasing arrangements are common because of the large investment involved, and they highlight the significant financial involvement for the buyer. It is also entirely possible that major equipment for one company may be a piece of accessory equipment for another. The seller's marketing strategy would include a strong personal selling effort, exposure to multiple buying influences in most cases, and strong engineering and service support by the business salesperson or sales team.

Accessory Equipment

Accessory equipment is used to facilitate production, administrative, clerical, or marketing activities. Some examples are calculators, office equipment, and fire extinguishers. In general, accessory equipment tends to be standardized and is less costly than major equipment. The demand for accessory equipment would exhibit an elastic demand curve. Less technical service is required on the part of the seller, and price is lower than that of major equipment. The purchase may be considered routine, distribution channels are usually longer, and fewer buying influences are involved in the purchase decision.

Fabricated and Component Parts

Fabricated and component parts are purchased for inclusion into the final product. Although they typically become part of another product, fabricated and component parts can often be identified and distinguished easily. Spark plugs, timing devices, and switches are all examples of fabricated and component parts. Business buyers purchase such items according to their own predetermined specifications, or by standards common within an industry. In purchasing component parts, buyers expect the parts to meet a specified quality level consistently and to be delivered on time so that production is not slowed or stopped.

Process Materials

Process materials differ from fabricated and component parts in that most of them cannot be identified or regrouped in the finished product. Examples of products in this classification are chemicals, plastics, cement, asphalt, and steel bar stock. Most processed materials are marketed to original equipment manufacturers (OEMs)—or to distributors, who, in turn, sell to the OEM market—because very few of these materials have a replacement market. Process materials are generally bought per specifications prepared by the user, or bought according to standards developed by a particular trade. Certain grades of lumber and some chemicals would fit such a category. Generally, there is considerable emphasis on price and service in the sale of process materials.

Maintenance, Repair, and Operating (MRO) Supplies

MRO supplies do not become part of the finished product but do get used up in the production process. MRO items facilitate the production operation, have a relatively short life, and are generally less expensive than most business goods. MRO supplies are usually standardized, involve longer channels of distribution, expose the seller to fewer buying influences, and exhibit a more elastic demand curve than even accessory equipment. Examples of maintenance supplies are brooms, nails, paint, cleaning compounds, and light bulbs. Repair supplies include bearings, gears, and filters. Typing paper, ink, paper clips, pens and pencils, greases, and lubricating oils are types of operating supplies.

Raw Materials

Raw materials are often considered to be the basic lifeblood of industry and are supplied primarily by the agriculture, lumber, and mining and fishing industries. Raw materials are bought to become part of a manufactured product, are generally bought in large quantities, exhibit an inelastic demand curve, and are usually bought on the basis of recognized standards expressed in terms of either grade designations or sets of specifications. Channels of distribution can be either long or short, and multiple buying influences are involved in the purchase, at least in the initial stages of the procurement cycle.

Business Services

Services provided to firms by banks, insurance companies, advertising agencies, CPA and law firms, employment agencies, and management consultants are *business services*. Mead Corporation's Lexpat service is a computer-assisted patent search. Attorneys, business executives, and engineers who use this service can conduct patent searches from their own offices instead of having to do so at the U.S. Patents Office in the Washington, D.C., area.

Business services are expense items that do not become part of the final product. The buyer has decided that buying the service from outside specialists is less costly than having company employees perform it. Multiple buying influences may be present when the cost of a service exceeds a preestablished amount.[18]

CONCEPT QUESTIONS

1. How is the demand for business goods based on the demand for consumer goods?
2. Why is the demand for business goods said to be inelastic?
3. When does joint demand occur in business markets?

BUSINESS CUSTOMERS

A study of business marketing would not be complete without an attempt to examine the customer type within this broad category. Business customers are classified into three types of commercial enterprises, each of which buys goods and services differently; thus requiring a thorough understanding of how marketing strategy differs with the customer type being pursued. Business customers are usually classified into the following three types: (1) commercial enterprises, (2) governmental organizations, and (3) institutions.

Commercial Enterprises

Commercial enterprises would consist of the following: (1) indirect channel members; (2) original equipment manufacturers (OEMs), and (3) user-customers.

Indirect channel members. The indirect channel category consists of firms that are engaged in reselling business goods in basically the same form to commercial, governmental, or institutional markets. Some, most notably business distributors and dealers, take title to the goods. The functions, scope, and limitations of the channel intermediary will be discussed in detail in Chapter 7.

Original equipment manufacturers (OEMs). OEMs typically buy business goods, which, in turn, they incorporate into the products that they produce for eventual sale to either the business or consumer market. Thus, a tire producer, such as Firestone, Goodyear, or Michelin, that sells tires to Ford Motor Company would consider Ford as an OEM.

User-customers. The user-customer generally buys products to support a manufacturing facility. Ford Motor Company would buy stamping equipment to form auto parts made from metal, plastic-injection molding machines to produce parts made from plastic, and milling machines to produce precision tooling for use in conjunction with the metal stamping operation. These purchases do not become part of the finished product; they only help to produce it.

Overlap of categories. The preceding classifications center on how products are used by the business customer. A manufacturer can be a user, purchasing goods to support a manufacturing process; or an OEM, purchasing goods for inclusion into a manufactured product. A manufacturer of machinery can be a user, purchasing raw material to support a production process; or an OEM, purchasing gear assemblies to incorporate into the machinery being manufactured. Again, the classification would depend on product use or intended purpose.

Governmental Organizations

Governmental organizations include thousands of federal, state, and local buying units, and alone account for about 20 percent of our Gross National Product.[19] All levels of government in the United States comprise what is considered to be the largest single market for goods and services in the world.[20] Much government procurement is done on a bid basis, with the government advertising for bids, stating product specifications, and accepting the lowest bid that meets these specifications. Such a procedure sometimes results in the rejection of the lowest bids. For example, the Board of New York City's Metropolitan Transportation Authority must provide toilet paper in the more than one thousand restrooms included in the services of the system. When deciding whether or not to accept a toilet paper purchase in the amount of $168,840, which was higher than three other bids, the Authority Board asked the following question of management: "Why did you reject the lower bids?" The president responded that the Authority had rejected one supplier because there was insufficient tissue on the roll, while two other suppliers were ruled out because their tissues were somewhat like sandpaper and obviously not soft enough. In light of this explanation, the Board approved accepting the higher bid.

Although the governmental market could be a lucrative market for some astute business marketers, many make no real effort to sell to the government, not wanting to bother with the red tape involved. Dealing with the government to any significant extent usually requires specialized marketing techniques and information.[21]

Institutions

Some long overdue attention is now being paid to the multibillion dollar market consisting of *nonbusiness or not-for-profit institutions*. This potentially lucrative market would include such diverse institutions as colleges and universities, museums, hospitals, labor unions, charitable organizations, and churches. These organizations have real marketing problems and spend billions of dollars buying products and services to run their organizations.

Business marketers who desire to sell to the institutional market must be aware of the diversity of this market and tailor their marketing programs to meet the particular needs and wants of prospective customers. For instance, suppose that Acme Foods, a small food products marketer, wanted to market its products to hospitals and nursing homes in smaller communities. Acme's primary focus would more than likely be on the chief dietitian, who must approve food products before the hospital or nursing home's purchasing director can contract for their purchase. However, if Acme also desired to sell its products to larger health-care institutions in metropolitan areas, it would likely need to target its marketing program to a diverse group of individuals (the institution's administrator, business manager, purchasing director, and chief dietitian), each of whom influences the buying decision.[22]

INTERNATIONAL CUSTOMERS

The time has long passed when most business organizations could safely ignore international influences: the potential threat to a firm's domestic market has forced many to reassess their role in the world market, as well as nationally. Major

U.S. corporations are exporting millions of dollars of American goods to international markets, and such exports are representing increasingly greater percentages of such companies' total sales. The emphasis on foreign business operations has caused increased attention in business marketing to the management of information systems for multinational organizations.[23]

Many firms are finding that to be competitive nationally they must be competitive internationally. A number of factors are causing a growing variety and quantity of foreign goods to enter the American market, destroying the isolation from foreign competition that U.S. firms had previously enjoyed. Some of these factors are increasing affluence, greater sophistication of consumers and business buying personnel, improved communication with the rest of the world, better transportation, lower tariffs on imports, and increased aggressiveness of foreign business.[24]

Some examples will illustrate how even small firms can be successful in exporting.[25]

> Starting his seed company in 1974, New Yorker Mithra Newman had sales of $7 million by 1980. Over half was export, including $3 million with China.
>
> Tatus Farms of Georgia began exporting hatching eggs and baby chicks through an export broker. Subsequently, the firm sold some 70 percent of its production abroad.
>
> After a trade show in Tokyo, Gudebrod Brothers of Philadelphia began to export its dacron fishing thread to Japan, averaging $4,000 per month.
>
> EPI, Inc., a Virginia-based maker of aerators for waste water treatment plants, had one-third of its $1.1 million sales in exports with only thirteen employees.
>
> Scientific Radio Systems, a Rochester manufacturer of high-frequency radio transmitters and receivers, exported 60 percent of its $6.5 million in sales.

To compete in the foreign market involves different kinds of problems and different approaches to problem solutions because of what may happen when a business crosses national boundaries. The international marketplace could be characterized as one with the possibility of rapid change, shifting power bases, and lack of political stability in many parts of the world.

BUSINESS MARKETING PLANNING AND STRATEGY FORMULATION

Marketing planning and strategy begins with an analysis of changing environments, both the internal and external macro and micro environments. The environments within which the business marketer works represent a "dynamic" rather than a "static" model—things are always changing. As a business marketer, the one thing you can depend on is continuous change!

Central to the analysis of a constantly changing environment is an assessment of the organization's strengths and weaknesses in relation to the competition, along with a matching of the strengths with unsatisfied customer needs in the marketplace. Many leaders in industry believe that business marketing strategy evolves in close association with information technology (IT) planning.[26] Effective business marketing strategy must continually monitor product, price, promotion, and distribution, making sure that all are consistent with one another and that there is "synergy," wherein the impact of the whole is greater than the sum of the parts. As an example, if the marketing manager decides to lower price, increase a particular promotional outlay, or both, it would be nice if he or she let the sales department know of these plans. Also, if members of the sales department learn of minor product faults, they should bring this information to management's attention. If all members of the marketing team "sing off the same sheet of music," so to speak, then there will indeed be synergy. If one (or more) members of the team sing off-key, the firm will be out of tune and problems may occur. Again, this must be done while still paying attention to other internal activities, as indicated earlier.

The significance of the aforementioned business goods and services classification system (major equipment, accessory equipment, etc.) might illustrate how planning and strategy differ by category of goods. A marketing strategy deemed appropriate for one category of goods or services may be entirely unsuitable for another. Entirely different promotion, pricing, and distribution strategies might be required for each, along with more or less attention being paid to other internal activities, such as manufacturing, technical service, and engineering. For example, producers of sophisticated aerospace and defense equipment place more emphasis on the product and pricing facets of the marketing mix and less emphasis on the sales and distribution effort than other types of business goods producers. A manufacturer of a standard industry widget, on the other hand, might emphasize sales and distribution, giving less emphasis to product and price.

Marketing planning takes the best information about customers and competitors, analyzes the information, generates alternatives (taking into account the organizational issues), and finally proposes a blueprint that best suits the organization at a specific moment. These are the steps that must be taken to ensure that customers, competitors, and organizational issues are covered. Figure 1-1 can be a useful guide in identifying some stages in this process.[27]

CONCEPT QUESTIONS

1. How can the three major categories of commercial enterprises overlap?
2. Why are an increasing amount of international goods coming into the U.S. market?
3. What is meant by "achieving synergy" in the business marketing mix?

FIGURE 1-1 **Stages Involved in Marketing Planning**

INPUT → TRANSFORMATION OF INPUT → OUTPUT
(Generic Process Model)

INVESTIGATION → ANALYSIS, ALTERNATIVES → PROPOSAL
(Marketing Planning Process)

Source: Mary E. Kulpinski, "The Planning Process—Continuous Improvement," *Journal of Business and Industrial Marketing,* Vol. 7, Spring 1992, pp. 71–76.

FORMAT OF THIS TEXT

In comparison with most other business marketing textbooks, the material covered in this text is organized quite differently. For example, this text attempts to make the student aware of the special buyer-seller relationship early in the text, concentrating on the role of purchasing and materials management, along with the general management of the business buying center. Purchasing procedures, organizational considerations, purchasing systems, source selection, quality determination and control, social responsibility, ethical considerations, and international issues are either covered in depth, or are referred to frequently early in the text so that the student gets a feel for the language and the interaction that takes place in the buyer-seller exchange.

Then, the focus of the text turns to the traditional tools and techniques employed in the marketing of goods and services to the business sector. The remainder of the text exposes the student to market segmentation strategy, product strategy, product development and product failure, pricing strategy, distribution strategy, systems selling, promotional strategy, business services marketing, international business marketing strategy, and a host of other activities to which the marketing student is typically exposed. An attempt is made, early in the text, to focus the thinking and attention of the student on the major differences between consumer and business markets—dissimilarities that, while using the same basic marketing tools and techniques, can spell the difference between success and failure in the contemporary business marketing environment.

SUMMARY

1. Business marketing can be defined as those activities that facilitate exchanges involving products and customers in business marketing. A business marketing transaction takes place whenever a good or service is sold for any use other than personal consumption.

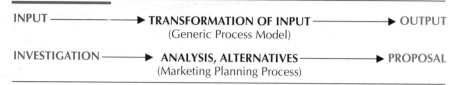

2. Differences between business and consumer marketing are many and varied. Business marketing, as opposed to consumer marketing, is characterized by a greater total sales volume, larger volume purchases, fewer buyers, larger buyers, geographically concentrated buyers, a close supplier-customer relationship, more direct channels of distribution, professional buying, multiple buying influences, complex negotiation, reciprocity, leasing, and an emphasis on personal selling.
3. The demand for business goods is derived from the demand for consumer goods and services. Business demand is relatively inelastic because demand is not likely to change significantly in the short run and tends to be less volatile than the demand for consumer goods and services. There is a joint demand for some business products when two or more items are used in combination to produce a product.
4. It is generally thought that business buyers tend to be more cautious than do final consumers. However, they are not totally rational in their buying behavior. Selling to business buyers is frequently a personality-oriented sales situation, as is true in consumer transactions.
5. Business goods can be classified in a number of ways. One major classification system uses the categories of major equipment, accessory equipment, fabricated and component parts, process materials, MRO supplies, raw materials, and business services.
6. Business customers are usually classified into three broad categories: commercial enterprises which include indirect channel members, original equipment manufacturers, and user-customers; governmental organizations; and nonbusiness and not-for-profit institutions.
7. The time has long passed when most business organizations could safely ignore international influences, as the potential threat to a firm's domestic market has forced many to reassess their role in the world market as well as nationally. Many firms are finding that to be competitive nationally, they must also be competitive internationally.
8. Marketing planning and strategy formulation begins with an analysis of a firm's environments. Central to this analysis is an assessment of the organization's strengths and weaknesses in relation to the competition, along with a matching of its strengths with unsatisfied customer needs in the marketplace.

KEY TERMS

Accessory equipment
Acceleration principle
Business services
Business marketing
Business marketing transaction
Commercial enterprises
Derived demand
Fabricated and component parts
Governmental organizations
Joint demand
Major equipment
Marketing planning and strategy
MRO supplies
Nonbusiness or not-for-profit institutions
Process materials
Raw materials

REVIEW QUESTIONS

1. How is business marketing defined? What constitutes a business marketing transaction?
2. What are the reasons for studying business marketing? Prepare a profile of the contemporary U.S. business sector.
3. Detail the major differences between business and consumer marketing. Create examples to show your understanding of derived demand, fluctuating demand, inelastic demand, and joint demand.
4. Why is business buying behavior not purely rational in nature? Give an example of a situation in which a business buyer might be more influenced by a marketer's use of emotional appeals.
5. Identify and define five major categories of business goods and services. Is there an alternate classification system that can be used? If so, what are the major categories included in such a classification system?
6. What are the three fundamental types of business customers? Identify three types of commercial enterprises. How can these categories overlap?
7. What is the relevance of international customers in the contemporary business marketing environment? Why are there so many international goods and services available in American markets?
8. How are an organization's strengths and weaknesses important for the business marketer to know and utilize in marketing planning and strategy formulation?

Cases

CASE 1-1 The Fabric Studio

The Fabric Studio is a fabric design business that services the furniture-finishing industry. The business is a partnership owned by two women, Carol and Janice, who met while working for another fabric design house. Their scholastic backgrounds are in fine arts, and they both have several years of work experience within the fabric design industry. While working for other large design houses, they became aware that they could be making significantly more money and enjoying more autonomy and artistic freedom by simply eliminating the middleman, the companies they had been working for.

Although the Studio is a small start-up firm, in business for only five years, it is nevertheless relatively successful and has been growing at a rate of about 10 percent per year. Although Carol and Janice—the owners, and sole employees, of the Fabric Studio—have strong design backgrounds, they are admittedly weak in the business planning and marketing portion of the business. Their current dilemma is how to increase business and become better known throughout the industry given the following:

Restrictions

- Very limited finances—approximately $5,000 allocated to promotion
- No strategic planning or marketing knowledge or experience
- Little time to spend on planning and marketing
- Limited personnel

Strengths

- The ability to generate unique, creative designs
- Strong working relationships with current clients
- In-depth knowledge of the fabric manufacturing industry
- A solid customer base; currently designing for most of the major home-furnishing fabric manufacturers

The Fabric Studio owners realized and understood their weaknesses. Therefore, their first course of action was to enlist the help of a marketing/business consultant to help them assess the available channels of action open to them to solve their marketing problem. Their hope was that this professional would bring to their organization the missing planning and marketing components. There was only one restriction that the Studio placed on this consultant. This person's advice and guidance would have to be made within the parameters of the company's given constraints.

Currently, the company has no formal marketing department. They do not advertise and they have no formal sales force. All sales contacts are made through trade shows or cold calls, which the two owners make when not designing products.

Creating a design is a lengthy process that entails significant research and creative studio time. Carol and Janice must first determine what the marketplace demands. Once they know this, they usually make several attempts at painting and sketching the designs until they achieve the look that they want. From this painting, they develop a blueprint of sorts, which shows how the loom must be set up to actually weave the given design into a finished material. After they design a collection (two collections per year), they pack their portfolios and make a tour of their customers. Inevitably, they receive generous orders from their existing customers for their designs.

Of the twenty or so major fabric manufacturers, the Fabric Studio is currently selling to fifteen. While touring their existing customers, Carol and Janice often cold-call on other companies not yet buying their designs. They are firmly entrenched with their existing customer base and cannot expect to bring their business to the next level by trying only to increase their workloads or by capturing the remaining five players. In the long run, they want to expand into other areas besides furniture, perhaps apparel. What they need now, however, is an immediate short-term plan to help increase their business.

DISCUSSION QUESTIONS

1. What is fundamentally lacking at the Fabric Studio?
2. How can the owners increase their customer base?
3. What promotional tools are available?
4. How might they penetrate other markets?

Source: Case contributed by Maria L. Andreano, Consultant, Andreano and Associates, Warwick RI, 1994. Used with permission.

CASE 1-2 The Merck-DuPont Joint Venture

The drug industry has undergone many changes in the past few years. As companies merged, the number of competitors got smaller, and the size of each competitor became larger. Edgar S. Woolard, Jr., DuPont's chairperson and chief executive officer, says, "The rules are changing very fast. Because of all the recent consolidations taking place, the risk of going it alone is much, much higher than five years ago." Merck and Company, an industry leader, needs to expand its product line faster than its research and development (R&D) operation will allow in order to sustain its growth.

In order to maintain high profitability, pharmaceutical companies are forced to develop breakthrough medicines that bring premium prices. The cost of developing these new drugs is astronomical. It is imperative that companies team up to reduce the increasing financial risks associated with R&D.

Merck and Company needs to help sustain its growth. Company growth has leveled off due to the need for funds to increase R&D. Through a joint venture with DuPont, Merck gains access to DuPont's R&D team, including access to DuPont's experimental drugs. Dr. Roy Vagelos, Merck's chairperson and chief executive officer, is convinced of the need to increase R&D to expand the company's product lines. Vagelos feels that expanded product lines will be necessary in dealing with hospitals and insurance companies in the future. Deeper discounts can be offered to hospitals and insurance plans that team up for larger purchases if the firm has a broad product line. Unfortunately, outright acquisitions of competitors are too costly, so mergers are becoming everyday occurrences in the pharmaceutical industry. DuPont will gain some needed capital and access to international distribution.

Dr. David W. Martin, Jr., has been selected to head the new company. Martin said that the joint venture interested him "with the breadth of technology and the long-term commitment of the venture partners." The new company, DuPont-Merck Pharmaceuticals Company, is willing to take aggressive action to maintain its growth in the drug industry. The company will have estimated sales of $700 million, six hundred salespeople, $230 million in R&D expenditures, and fifteen hundred R&D employees.

DISCUSSION QUESTIONS

1. Do you think that the government should be concerned with the decreasing number of pharmaceutical companies? Why or why not?
2. What competitive structure would you say the pharmaceutical industry best represents? Why do you think the pharmaceutical industry represents this competitive structure?
3. Discuss what changes would be necessary for this structure to change to another specific structure? How would this change affect consumers?
4. What effect on prices do you think a merger of this sort will have in the market? Why?

Suggested Readings

Koenig, Richard. "DuPont, Merck Recruit Ex-Head of Genentech R&D." *Wall Street Journal,* 1 September 1990, B4.

Waldholz, Michael. "Merck-DuPont Venture Certain to Stir Drug Industry." *Wall Street Journal,* 26 July 1990, B1, B3.

Source: C. Lamb, J. Hair, and C. McDaniel, *Principles of Marketing,* 1st Edition (Cincinnati, OH: South-Western Publishing Company, 1992) pp. 69–70.

Suggested Additional Readings

Abratt, Russell. "Industrial Buying in High Tech Markets." *Industrial Marketing Management* 15 (November 1986): 293–298. **A survey of 54 South African firms showed that technical personnel dominated in the decision process for medical instruments.**

Berkowitz, Marvin. "New Product Adoption by the Buying Organization: Who Are the Real Influencers?" *Industrial Marketing Management* 15 (February 1986): 33–43. **Telephone survey concerning the decision-making process, product assessment, and the purchasing manager's role.**

Hlavacek, James D. "Business Schools Need More Industrial Marketing." *Marketing News* 13 (April 4, 1980): 1. **Reasons offered as to why schools of business should focus more attention on business-to-business marketing.**

Kuehn, A. A., and R. L. Day. "The Acceleration Effect in Forecasting Industrial Shipments." *Journal of Marketing* 27 (January 1963). **Theoretical discussion of sales and inventory implications of business-to-business derived demand. Applications are provided.**

Matthyssens, P., and W. Faes. "OEM Buying Process for New Components: Purchasing and Marketing Implications." *Industrial Marketing Management* 14 (August 1985): 145–157. **Model development from eight in-depth case interviews, emphasizing mapping the buying process, buying criteria, and interactions of purchasing with other departments.**

Schurr, Paul H., and Bobby J. Calder. "Psychological Effects of Restaurant Meetings on Industrial Buyers." *Journal of Marketing* 50 (January 1986): 87–97. **A survey undertaken to determine the effects on buyer's evaluations stemming from buyer-seller meetings in ordinary and fancy settings.**

Webster, Frederick E., Jr. "Top Management's Concern About Marketing: Issues for the 1980s." *Journal of Marketing* 45 (Summer 1981): 9–16. **Survey of industrial executives found that they see increased marketing competency as a key priority for the 1980s and that they realize that lack of marketing expertise has been a historical weakness in business-to-business firms.**

ENDNOTES

[1]Jan Jaben, "Executive Survey: Is Economy Poised for a 'Big Boom'?" *Business Marketing* 77 (June 1992): 18–19.

[2]Denise F. Winokur and Ravi Venkitaraman, "Simulator Software Avoids Costly Market Tests," *Marketing News* 25 (March 4, 1991): 28.

[3]Peter La Place, *Journal of Business and Industrial Marketing* 3, no. 1 (Winter 1988): 3.

[4]The Paper Mate example is from David L. Kurtz and Louis E. Boone, *Marketing*, 3d ed. (New York: Dryden Press, 1987), 248–249.

[5]However, for an argument that consumer marketing and business marketing do not differ significantly, see Edward F. Fern and James R. Brown, "The Industrial/Consumer Dichotomy: A Case of Insufficient Justification," *Journal of Marketing* (Spring 1984): 68–77.

[6]This section is from Philip Kotler, *Marketing Management: Analysis, Planning, Implementation, and Control*, 7th ed. (Englewood Cliffs, N.J.: Prentice-Hall, 1991), 196–198; William F. Schoell, *Marketing: Contemporary Concepts and Practices*, 2d ed. (Boston: Allyn and Bacon, 1985), 642–643; and William M. Pride and O. C. Ferrell, *Marketing*, 8th ed. (Boston: Houghton Mifflin, 1993), 729–738.

[7]B. G. Yovovich, "Hand in Glove Relationships," *Journal of Business Marketing* (April 1991); 20–21.

[8]Charles R. O'Neal, "JIT Procurement and Relationship Marketing," *Industrial Marketing Management* 18 (February 1989): 55–63.

[9]Lisa M. Ellram, "A Managerial Guideline for the Development and Implementation of Purchasing Partnerships," *International Journal of Purchasing and Materials Management* (Summer 1991): 2–8.

[10]Bernard Goldberg, "Relationship Marketing," *Direct Marketing* (October 1988): 103–105.

[11]See Louis W. Stern and Thomas L. Eovaldi, *Legal Aspects of Marketing Strategy* (Englewood Cliffs, N.J.: Prentice-Hall, 1984).

[12]Glenn A. Endicott, "To Rent or Not to Rent...," *Equipment Management* (December 1989): 25–28.

[13]See Russell Hindin, "Lease Your Way to Corporate Growth," *Financial Executive* (May 1984): 20–25.

[14]"GE Sets Business Rentals of Personal Computers," *Wall Street Journal*, 30 March 1983, 23.

[15]See William S. Bishop, John L. Graham, and Michael H. Jones, "Volatility of Derived Demand in Industrial Markets and Its Management Implications," *Journal of Marketing* (Fall 1984): 95–103.

[16]*Ibid.*, 178–179.

[17]This section is taken from W. S. Penn, Jr., and Mark Mougel, "Industrial Marketing Myths," in *Dynamics of Marketing Principles: A Reader*, ed. Thomas C. Kinnear and Kenneth L. Bernhardt (Glenview, IL: Scott, Foresman, 1983), 51.

[18]Schoell, *Marketing*, 260.

[19]Kenneth H. Bacon, "A Repeat of '29 Depression in '87 Is Not Expected," *Wall Street Journal*, 20 October 1987, 1, 24.

[20]C. Cleveland, "Selling to the Government Markets: Local, State, and Federal," *Government Product News* (1991): 1.

[21]See Warren H. Suss, "How to Sell to Uncle Sam," *Harvard Business Review* (November-December 1984): 136–144; and David E. Gumpert and Jeffrey A. Timmons, "Penetrating the Government Procurement Maze," *Harvard Business Review* (September-October, 1982): 14–23.

[22]Schoell, *Marketing*, 638–639.

[23]Lexis F. Higgins, Scott C. McIntyre, and Cynthia G. Raine, "Design of Global Marketing Information Systems," *Journal of Business and Industrial Marketing* 6 (Summer/Fall 1991): 49–58.

[24]Vern Terpstra, *International Marketing*, 4th ed. (Dryden Press, 1987), 8.

[25]*Ibid.*, 8–9.

[26]Kenneth Andrew, "Bank Marketing in a Changing World," *International Journal of Bank Marketing* (UK), (1990): 2–56.

[27]Mary E. Kulpinski, "The Planning Process—Continuous Improvement," *Journal of Business and Industrial Marketing* 7 (Spring 1992): 71–76.

Part Two

How Buyers Buy

2 Fundamentals of the Purchasing and Materials Management Function

Learning Objectives

After reading this chapter, you should be able to:

- Discuss the steps involved in the business buying process.
- Describe the process by which potential vendors are evaluated.
- Appreciate the changing role of the business buyer.
- Discern various types of buying motives.
- Explain the reasons behind using various forms of purchasing organization.
- Understand the materials management concept.
- Differentiate between types of business buying situations.
- Appreciate the implications and ramifications of purchasing and the law.

Chapter Outline

Learning Objectives

Basic Policies and Procedures of Purchasing

The Business Buying Process
- Recognizing the Need
- Developing Product Specifications
- Soliciting Bids from Potential Suppliers
- Making the Purchase Decision
- Issuing the Contract
- Inspecting Delivered Goods for Quality
- Evaluating Vendor Performance

Evaluating Potential Vendors
- Basic Considerations in Evaluating Potential Vendors
  - Performance considerations
  - Plant visits
  - Geographic location
  - Capacity
- Vendor-Rating Approaches
  - The categorical plan
  - The weighted-point plan
  - The cost-ratio plan

The Changing Role of the Buyer
- Relationship Marketing
- Profile of a Business-to-Business Buyer

Business Buying Motives

Purchasing Organization
- Organization Related to Size of Company
- Centralization versus Decentralization of the Buying Function

The Materials Management Concept
- Alternative Approaches to Materials Management
  - Traditional approach
  - "Just-in-time" (JIT) approach
- Reasons for Adopting the Materials Management Concept

Business Buying Situations
- New-Task Buying
- Straight-Rebuy Buying
- Modified-Rebuy Buying

Purchasing and the Law
- Law of Agency
- Law of Contracts

Summary

Key Terms

Review Questions

Cases
Case 2-1
Case 2-2

Suggested Additional Readings

Endnotes

BASIC POLICIES AND PROCEDURES OF PURCHASING

One of the first questions often asked is why business marketers must be concerned with the *policies and procedures* established by a typical purchasing department. Many will say that only experience will really teach us that there are other facets to a purchasing or buying center (those persons in a buying organization who are related directly to the purchasing process) than those that are most obvious. A buying firm's policies and procedures will determine how the typical business marketing manager markets the product or service to that firm. Policies and procedures alert people to and emphasize the goals that the organization is striving to reach. Policies and procedures actually outline what is to be done, in that they define responsibilities and detail delegated authority and to whom it is assigned. Policies and procedures indicate the intrafirm relations between subsidiaries, divisions, departments, and employees. In short, policies and procedures tell external marketing managers much of what they need to know to market the business product or service effectively. Salespeople are encouraged to request statements of policies and procedures to help them in their sales efforts and to promote good supplier-customer relations. Purchasing policies and procedures are often written as papers or manuals and issued to appropriate parties to ensure that all participants, both internal and external, understand the "rules of the game."

Every transaction involving the transfer of a property between a buyer and seller is a contract. While some contracts are simple, others in the business sector are lengthy written agreements defining in technical terms the nature of the material or service, the method of payment, and other contractual conditions. Because of the contractual arrangement, the authority and responsibility of buying materials and services rest with the purchasing department. This delegation or assignment of duties places the responsibility on those who have the interest and the skill to do the work properly and whose primary concern is the performance of this highly important task. Such a business practice permits the establishment of uniform policies with respect to seller relationships and assumes adequate controls over expenditures. An example of a brief but clear outline of purchasing policy is that of Hunt-Wesson Foods. The firm's policy is divided into twelve broad categories:[1]

(1) Purchasing policy and objectives
(2) Supplier contacts
(3) Negotiations with suppliers
(4) Matters of security relating to purchasing
(5) Suppliers' quotations
(6) Purchase commitments
(7) Selecting sources of supply
(8) Purchase order specifications
(9) Purchasing contracts
(10) Vendor relations
(11) Trade relations
(12) Gifts and gratuities

Further, Hunt-Wesson's policy on supplier contacts states briefly:

> All contacts with suppliers regarding negotiation of price, quantity, delivery, etc., are handled by purchasing. When the needs of a particular group (e.g., research and development or engineering) are for information of a technical nature, and where discussions with a supplier may continue over a considerable period of time, it is not necessary for a buyer to become involved in these purchasing discussions with a vendor. However, there must be no commitment to buy on the part of these other departments, and purchasing is to be kept informed by copies of written communications between other departments and suppliers.[2]

Judging from this type of policy, it is in the best interest of the selling firm to have a firm grasp on the appropriate policies and procedures deemed important by the buying organization.

A key point to keep in mind in a discussion of purchasing policies and procedures is that they are not ends unto themselves; rather, they are means to an end. Policies and procedures should make the accomplishment of a task easier. They should facilitate communication and should help coordinate the efforts of one group with another. Policies and procedures should clearly designate responsibility for the accomplishment of each step in a process. Finally, policies and procedures must permit *management by exception*, or the pushing down of routine decision making to as low a level as possible within the organizational hierarchy.

THE BUSINESS BUYING PROCESS

A buying situation is created when some member of the organization perceives a problem that can be solved through the purchase of a product or service. Their perception of a buying problem can occur at any place in the organization, and at almost any stage in the work of the organization. Since there are wide variations among industries, companies, products, and personnel, it would not be feasible to establish a single set of procedures that would apply to all cases. The essential steps, however, must be taken, in one way or another, to complete a buying transaction. Each of these steps is shown in Figure 2-1 and is discussed below, using the General Electric Company as a hypothetical example.[3] Suppose GE decides to design and build a new line of clothes dryers and needs an electric motor as a key component in the dryer. Let us track each of the stages in this purchasing process.

Recognizing the Need

Following the top management of GE's appliance division's decision to introduce a new line of clothes dryers, engineering and R&D personnel create a workable design that is tested and approved. They confer with the purchasing executive to reach a make-buy decision—an evaluation of whether a product or part will be purchased from outside suppliers or be manufactured by the firm itself. The group decides that the electric motor in each dryer should be bought rather than made.

FIGURE 2-1 **Outline of the Steps in the Business Purchasing Process**

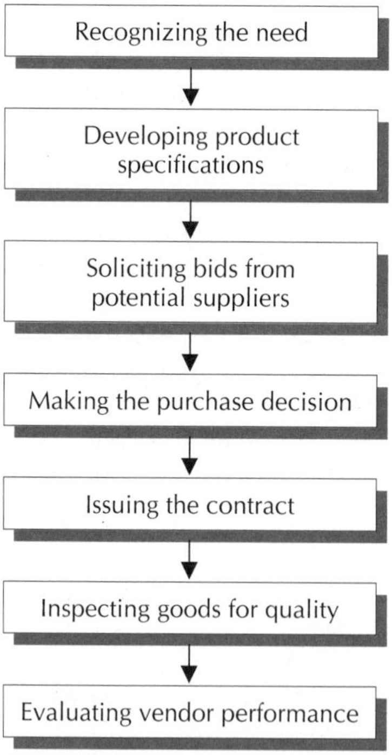

Developing Product Specifications

The engineering and R&D personnel develop product specifications for the electric motor, which include detailed technical requirements the motor must meet, such as its horsepower, life in hours, and ability to operate at a stated temperature and humidity. Members of the purchasing and production departments then do a systematic appraisal of the design, quality, and performance requirements of the product to reduce purchasing costs. For example, suppose the GE engineers conclude that at least a one-eighth horsepower motor is needed to power the dryer. The purchasing department might recommend buying a one-quarter horsepower motor, which must be made to order at a higher cost.

In determining the exact product specifications needed, the purchasing department also relies on the technical expertise of vendors in developing appropriate design specifications. Specifications are generally stated in terms of material, dimensions, and performance characteristics, rather than brand name, to maximize the number of qualified vendors available and to ensure genuine competition among bidders.

Members of the buying center must develop the necessary buying criteria for the electric motor, which in this case are (1) quality requirements, (2) on-time delivery, and (3) price, in that order. The purchasing manager is given the responsibility to select the supplier and negotiate a contract for the motors.

Soliciting Bids from Potential Suppliers

The next step in purchasing is soliciting bids from potential suppliers. This involves selecting the names of vendors from a list of firms believed to be qualified to supply a given item and sending each vendor a quotation request form, describing the desired quantity, delivery date, and specifications of the product. A vendor analysis is typically performed so that all potential suppliers can be objectively evaluated on rating sheets according to the criteria or standards determined as important by purchasing personnel. Figure 2-2 presents such a vendor rating sheet.

Most purchasing departments maintain a separate bidders list for each general class of items they order. These lists are updated continuously by adding the names of potential new vendors and deleting the names of unsatisfactory vendors. To ensure competition even further, many firms require that at least three bids be solicited for purchases exceeding a specified dollar amount.

Making the Purchase Decision

Unlike the short purchase stage in a consumer buying decision, such as buying a six-pack of soft drinks, in organizations the purchase stage covers the period from vendor selection and placing the purchase order until the product is delivered, which often takes months or years. In this period, the GE purchasing manager would perform vendor follow-up, set up an order routine, expedite the

FIGURE 2-2 **Vendor Rating Sheet**

Vendor Rating Sheet
Beach Bums, Inc.
San Francisco, California

Supplier: Beachwear Fashions, Inc.
Location: La Jolla, California
Product(s) Purchased: T-shirts
Stores Served: San Francisco, Berkeley, Palo Alto, Monterey, and Carmel-by-the-Sea

	Excellent	Good	Fair	Poor
Overall quality of merchandise	X			
Distinctiveness of merchandise	X			
Availability of different designs	X			
Variety of styles available	X			
Speed of routine shipments			X	
Speed of back orders			X	
Service provided after the sale		X		
Amount of defective merchandise shipped	X			
Handling of defective merchandise	X			
Conditions of sale		X		
Wholesaler profitability		X		
Retailer profitability		X		
Retail customer satisfaction	X			

Comments: Very pleased with this supplier, particularly in terms of quality and variety of merchandise shipped and overall retail customer satisfaction. Supplier needs to improve upon speed of routine and back-order shipments, and wholesale and retail profitability could be slightly better.

November 2, 1993 — Date

Director of Purchasing — Signed

order, and renegotiate the contract terms if specification changes are made after the initial contract is awarded.

Issuing the Contract

The contract stage of the purchasing process is the crucial part, in which GE and the seller enter into an agreement that is binding on both of them. On the one hand, the seller must supply the electric motors at the agreed-upon price and terms; and, on the other hand, the GE purchasing manager must accept and pay for the motors if they are received in good condition. While the purchase-order forms vary tremendously as to their setup and how they are routed through the organization, the importance of issuing the purchase contract, no matter how involved or detailed, is more important than the actual format and style of the form itself.

Sometimes contracts are awarded directly to vendors based on the data they provide in quotation request forms. At other times, the purchasing manager may wish to negotiate with one or more bidders, particularly on high-volume, high-dollar items. Eventually, the GE purchasing manager selects two vendors and awards each a contract in the form of a purchase order, which is an authorization for the vendor to provide the items under the agreed-upon terms and to bill the purchasing firm.

Inspecting Delivered Goods for Quality

When the electric motors are delivered, the quality control department tests them to ensure that they meet specifications. Shortages, tampered merchandise, and goods damaged in transit must be accounted for prior to the payment of an invoice. If the motors had been unsatisfactory, the purchasing manager would have negotiated with the supplier to rework the items according to specifications or would have arranged for an entirely new shipment.

Evaluating Vendor Performance

Experienced buyers realize that evaluation of purchase decisions is essential. GE's purchasing manager will evaluate the vendor's performance after final delivery of the purchased items. This information is often noted on the vendor rating sheet discussed previously and is used to update the bidders list kept by the purchasing department. Performance on past contracts determines a vendor's chances of being asked to bid on future purchases, and poor performance results in a vendor's name being dropped from the list.

CONCEPT QUESTIONS

1. Why are the policies and procedures of the buying firm a means to an end, rather than ends in themselves?
2. How is a buying situation created?
3. Why is the contract stage of the buying process so crucial?

EVALUATING POTENTIAL VENDORS

Basic Considerations in Evaluating Potential Vendors

The use of business suppliers with whom there is no previous experience requires, at the least, some initial work by the buyer; and, in many instances, if the supplier is to provide a significant part or material, the evaluation may be rather an exhaustive process. In vendor analysis, organizational consumers systematically assess the strengths and weakness of current or new suppliers in terms of such factors as merchandise quality, customer services, reliability, and price.[4] Four basic considerations used by many buyers for this process are discussed below.

Performance considerations. A prospective supplier's total prospective ability to fulfill the requirements of a purchase contract as it relates to price, delivery, quality, and service must be predicted. These points generally revolve around the vendor's financial capabilities. An independent analysis of a potential vendor's financial statements may be in order. A buying executive must be able to obtain information regarding a particular prospective supplier's financial stability, pricing cushion, and general operating efficiency, by applying the tools of ratio analysis to the balance sheets and income statements of that vendor.

Plant visits. A business buyer will learn a great deal by a plant visit to a potential business supplier. Insight into the type of facilities, personnel, housekeeping, and procedures will reveal the level of efficiency that is maintained, as well as provide an indication of potential problems that could affect the prospective supplier's ability to provide necessary presale and postsale services. Care must be taken to ensure that the plant visit did not simply provide the potential supplier with an excuse to "clean up the plant." Usually, a superficial plant cleanup will be obvious, since a team with cross-functional members will perform a relatively comprehensive audit of the plant and its operations.

Geographic location. Shipments from distant suppliers are subject to more and greater risks of interruption from accidents, strikes, and acts of God, thus making the geographic location of the supplier important in many buying situations. Most geographical disadvantages can be overcome by creative marketing, to include special transportation arrangements, inventory make-and-hold service, and the like. The increased adoption of the just-in-time (JIT) philosophy is making geographic location of the supplier a much more important consideration.

Capacity. Production capacity available to the business buyer becomes an important consideration, especially during times of high business activity. In evaluating reserve facilities, the supplier's technical and managerial skills, as well as physical plant and facilities, must be considered. Therefore, in comparing suppliers, it is important to analyze in detail the facilities that the various potential suppliers have to offer as a criterion for the service that they will supply.

Continued potential vendor evaluations are critical in the development of effective long-term relationships and performance. Organizational purchasing is being influenced more by long-term strategic considerations than by short-term operational ones.[5] Purchasing managers are discovering the necessity for new buyer-seller relationships that are long term, that require close interaction among different functions in the two firms, and that provide mutual benefits to both buyers and sellers.[6] A total cost approach (one that is significant to long-term sourcing decisions and ultimately to bottom-line profitability) recognizes that the purchase price is only a fraction of the cost associated with the receipt of materials. The buying focus must shift from primarily a unit-price-oriented evaluation to a cost-based-performance evaluation of potential suppliers, incorporating quality, delivery, and other related costs as measurable factors that must be included when evaluating the total purchase costs of buying from various suppliers.[7] If a supplier fails to meet delivery, quality, and price requirements, additional costs are incurred by the buying organization to correct these deficiencies. These excess costs, both direct and overhead, have an immediate impact on the buying firm's available resources.

Vendor-Rating Approaches

The purchasing department performs an economic function and, as noted earlier, is a vital profit-enhancing unit for the company. Its services disseminate advanced technological techniques, methods of manufacturing, and other pertinent data from vendors to proper echelons within the company. As an economic function, purchasing has a responsibility through its delegated authority from management to evaluate properly both potential and active vendors through all phases of the procurement cycle. Computer assistance allows for a thorough evaluation of vendors on a regular basis, as actual performance must be evaluated. Buyers rate supplier performance in assessing the quality of past decisions, in making future vendor selections, and as a negotiating tool to gain leverage in buyer-seller relationships.[8] As can be seen in Exhibit 2-1, purchasing managers will frequently prepare a rank-ordered list of the desired supplier attributes and their relative importance.

The real test of vendor selection is, of course, the test of experience, or satisfactory performance by the vendor once the order has been placed. It is most often the deciding factor in whether the selected vendor will continue to receive the buyer's business, or be replaced by another source.[9] Figure 2-3 offers a vendor visitation report, and provides evaluation data when it has been some time since the last rating of a particular supplier.

Vendor rating systems generally involve three basic considerations: quality, service (delivery), and price. The most common methods used to evaluate suppliers are (1) the categorical plan, (2) the weighted-point plan, and (3) the cost-ratio plan.[10]

The categorical plan. In the *categorical plan,* buyers keep notes on their dealings with suppliers as events occur. At monthly buyer meetings (or at some other

EXHIBIT 2-1 **Ranking of Factors Motivating Purchasing Managers in Choosing Vendors of a Standard Product**

Accounting Department

1. Providing volume discounts
2. Achieving quality specifications consistently
3. Responding promptly to all communications
4. Offering competitive prices
5. Dealing with product rejections equitably
6. Providing necessary information when requested (e.g., bids)

Production Control Department

1. Rapid delivery in times of emergency
2. Shipping products when desired
3. Achieving quality specifications consistently
4. Cooperating willingly in face of unforeseen problems
5. Providing assistance in emergency situations

Purchasing Department

1. Achieving quality specifications consistently
2. Counseling about potential trouble
3. Using honesty in dealings
4. Supplying goods in shortage periods
5. Cooperating willingly in face of unforeseen problems
6. Shipping products when desired
7. Providing necessary information when requested
8. Providing assistance in emergency situations

Manufacturing/Engineering Department

1. Delivering goods as promised
2. Using honesty in dealings
3. Supplying goods in shortage periods
4. Achieving quality specifications consistently
5. Delivering rapidly in times of emergency

Quality Control Department

1. Achieving quality specifications consistently
2. Using honesty in dealings
3. Giving credit for scrap
4. Supplying goods in shortage periods
5. Providing low percentage of rejects

Specialty Machinery/Engineering Department

1. Supplying goods in shortage periods
2. Achieving quality specifications consistently
3. Providing low percentage of rejects
4. Delivering goods as promised
5. Using honesty in dealings

Tool Design Department

1. Using honesty in dealings
2. Offering technical ability and knowledge
3. Dealing with product rejections equitably
4. Giving credit for scrap
5. Invoicing properly
6. Supplying goods in shortage periods
7. Responding promptly to all communications

Source: Stanley D. Sibley, "How Interfacing Departments Rate Vendors," *National Purchasing Review* 6 (August-October 1980), p. 11.

time interval that is convenient), notes are compared, and suppliers are categorized as being in the good, neutral, or unsatisfactory category. This method is highly subjective, but it is easy to understand and to use. The simplicity of the plan is its most desirable feature. Its simple recording, reporting, and analytical techniques also allow evaluation at a minimum cost. As is shown in Table 2-1, this approach involves a list of significant performance factors that were developed for evaluation purposes, with the buyer assigning a "grade" in simple categorical terms, such as *good*, *neutral*, and *unsatisfactory*. These grades indicate the vendor's actual performance in each area. In this example, Vendor B appears to have generated the best performance record.

The big disadvantage of this approach is that it is largely an intuitive process, relying heavily on memory, personal judgment, and the experience and ability of the buyer.

FIGURE 2-3 **A Vendor Visitation Form Providing Data for Vendor Evaluation**

Company visited: Date:

Purpose of visit:

Representatives contacted:

Survey: If vendor has not been surveyed in 12 months, acquire following information:

a. Size of plant (square feet):
b. Equipment (acquire facility list, if available):
c. Housekeeping:
d. Labor situation:
e. General atmosphere:
f. Product lines:
g. Shipping—Mode:
h. Organization (acquire organization chart, if available):
i. Growth plans:
j. Purchasing—Cost evaluation:
k. Quality Control—Q.C. manual: Organization chart:
l. Research & development:
m. Exchange cost-cutting ideas:

Observation:

Suggestions:

If you go there:

Reported by:

Source: Frederick E. Webster, Jr., *Industrial Marketing Strategy,* 2d ed., p. 46. Copyright © 1984, John Wiley & Sons, Inc. Reprinted by permission of John Wiley & Sons, Inc.

TABLE 2-1 **Illustration of the Categorical Method of Vendor Performance Rating**

	Performance Characteristics			
Vendor	**Cost**	**Product Quality**	**Speed**	**Total**
A	Good (+)	Unsatisfactory (–)	Neutral ())	0
B	Neutral (0)	Good (+)	Good (+)	++
C	Neutral (0)	Unsatisfactory (–)	Neutral (0)	–

Source: Table reprinted with permission from the publisher, the National Association of Purchasing Management, Inc., "An Approach to Vendor Performance Evaluation," by Ed Timmerman, D.B.A., *Journal of Purchasing and Materials Management,* Vol. 22, No. 4, Winter 1986.

The weighted-point plan. With the *weighted-point plan,* quality, price, and service (or other relevant criteria) are assigned weights. Quality might be assigned a weight of 40 points, price 35 points, and service 25 points. This point offering must be adjusted to fit a particular organization's needs. Flexibility is an important feature of this plan, as point values can be changed to suit special requirements, without changing the workings of the plan.

Sellers are rated on each factor, with the resulting ratings changed to a composite, which becomes a portion of 100 percent. One seller will have a composite closer to 100 percent than the others will.

Table 2-2 shows the relative simplicity of arriving at the quality portion of the rating. In Table 2-3 the price factor is illustrated as being more complex, since one must first determine delivered cost, as shown in Part A. Then the buyer must

TABLE 2-2 **Quality Rating Under the Weighted-Point Plan**

	Quality				
(Insert drawing and part number)	**Lots Received**	**Lots Accepted**	**Lots Rejected**	**Percentage Accepted × Factor**	**Quality Control Rating**
Supplier A	60	54	6	90.0 × 40	36.0
Supplier B	60	56	4	93.3 × 40	37.3
Supplier C	20	16	4	80.0 × 40	32.0

Note: To rate lots closer, a system of fractional lots can be used. Thus, if an unacceptable lot is only one-half or one-tenth bad, it could be said that 0.5 or 0.1 lots were unacceptable, etc. This would distinguish between suppliers with a total lot unacceptable and those with only a small part of the lots unacceptable.

Source: Douglas V. Smith, "Vendor/Supplier Evaluation," *Guide to Purchasing*, vol. 1, Article 1.6 (Tempe, Ariz: National Association of Purchasing Management, 1967), p. 1.6.15.

TABLE 2-3 **Price Rating Under the Weighted-Point Plan**

Part A

	Price					
	Unit Price	*– Discount*		*+ Transportation Charge*	*=*	*Net Price*
Supplier A	$1.00	10%	($ .90)	$.03		$ .93
Supplier B	1.25	15%	($1.06)	.06		1.12
Supplier C	1.50	20%	($1.20)	.03		1.23

Part B

	Lowest Price	*÷*	*Net Price*	*=*	*Percentage*	*×*	*Factor*	*=*	*Price Rating*
Supplier A	$.93		$ .93		100%		35		35.0
Supplier B	.93		1.12		83%		35		29.1
Supplier C	.93		1.23		76%		35		26.6

Source: Douglas V. Smith, "Vendor/Supplier Evaluation," *Guide to Purchasing*, vol. 1, Article 1.6 (Tempe, Ariz: National Association of Purchasing Management, 1967), p. 1.6.15.

convert this cost into a merit value, as shown in Part B. Here, the lowest cost is rated as 100 percent, and the others are rated relative to the lowest cost.

In Table 2-4, the service factor has been tabulated as in the quality rating. By combining these factors, as in Table 2-5, an optimum choice of suppliers can be made (Supplier A). Table 2-6 provides an example of supplier evaluation with the weighted-point plan. The majority of buyers are satisfied with the simple but effective weighted-point plan, which can be modified to suit specific conditions.

The cost-ratio plan. With a *cost-ratio plan*, all activities regarding a supplier's performance are valued in terms of dollars and cents. The *total cost of buying* is determined, including the cost of such things as letters, telephone calls, visits, and the like. Business buyers can then select future vendors on the basis of the lowest total cost incurred. The total (real) cost of the same item from several sellers will vary with the skill and dependability of the seller. This method evaluates supplier performance by using the tools of standard cost analysis. The

TABLE 2-4 **Service Rating under the Weighted-Point Plan**

Service	Promises Kept	×	Service Factor	=	Service Rating
Supplier A	90%		25		22.5
Supplier B	95		25		23.8
Supplier C	100		25		25.0

Note: As in the quality factor, a closer or finer evaluation of service can be used. Fractional lots delivered on time can be so reported; for example, the final percentage might be based on 11.5 lots of 14 received on time, etc.

Source: Douglas V. Smith, "Vendor/Supplier Evaluation," *Guide to Purchasing*, vol. 1, Article 1.6 (Tempe, Ariz: National Association of Purchasing Management, 1967), p. 1.6.16.

TABLE 2-5 **Composite Rating under the Weighted-Point Plan**

Composite Rating Rating	Supplier A	Supplier B	Supplier C
Quality (40 points)	36.0	37.3	32.0
Price (35 points)	35.0	29.1	26.6
Service (25 points)	22.5	23.8	25.0
Total rating	93.5	90.2	83.6

Source: Douglas V. Smith, "Vendor/Supplier Evaluation," *Guide to Purchasing*, vol. 1, Article 1.6 (Tempe, Ariz: National Association of Purchasing Management, 1967), p. 1.6.16.

TABLE 2-6 **Weighted-Point Method of Supplier Evaluation**

Factor	Weight	Actual Performance	Performance Score
Quality	40	90% acceptable	40 × .9 = 36
Delivery	30	90% on schedule	30 × .9 = 27
Cost-reducing suggestions	20	% of total received = 60	20 × .6 = 12
Price	10	125% of lowest price 100/125 = .8	10 × .8 = 8
			Total composite score = 83

Source: Adapted from Gary J. Zenz, *Purchasing and the Management of Materials.* Copyright © 1981 John Wiley & Sons, Inc. Reprinted by permission of John Wiley & Sons, Inc.

total cost of each purchase to be evaluated is calculated, as is selling price plus the buyer's internal operating costs associated with the quality, delivery, and service elements of the purchase.[11] The calculation methodology involves a four-step approach. Table 2-7 illustrates the use of the technique in comparing the various elements of cost for four competing vendors.

In the cost-ratio plan, the first step is to determine the initial costs associated with quality, delivery, and service. Next, each is converted to a cost ratio, which expresses the cost as a percentage of the total value of the purchase. The third step is to sum the three individual cost rates to obtain an overall cost ratio. Finally, the overall cost ratio is applied to the vendor's quoted unit price to obtain the net adjusted cost figure. As can be seen in Table 2-7, any costs of doing business with a vendor are assessed as a penalty, which has the effect of raising the overall price and making it less attractive.

TABLE 2-7 **Cost Comparison Utilizing the Cost-Ratio Method of Vendor Rating**

Company	Quality Cost Ratio	Delivery Cost Ratio	Service Cost Ratio	Total Penalty	Quoted Price/ Unit	Net Adjusted Cost
Abraham, S.	1%	3%	–1%	3%	$86.25	$88.84
Winston Inc.	2	2	3	7	83.25	89.08
Plough Co.	3	1	6	10	85.10	93.61
Barron	2	1	2	5	85.00	89.25

Source: Table reprinted with permission of the publisher, the National Association of Purchasing Management, Inc., "An Approach to Vendor Performance Evaluation," by Ed Timmerman, D.B.A., *Journal of Purchasing and Materials Management,* Vol. 22, No. 4, Winter 1986.

Operationally, this approach is complex, requiring a comprehensive cost-accounting system to generate the precise cost data needed. Further, it assumes the ready availability of such data to the purchasing department.

CONCEPT QUESTIONS

1. Why does the presence of both personal and organizational goals complicate the business marketing effort?
2. What are the four sources of inputs that business buyers can utilize in evaluating suppliers that they have not used before?
3. Under what types of conditions do organizational buyers rate potential and/or current vendors?

THE CHANGING ROLE OF THE BUYER

The role of the business buyer is constantly changing in a dynamic marketplace. The historical trend toward profit planning results in a great amount of pressure being placed on the purchasing executive by the buying organization. Effective business marketing is dependent on an understanding of markets, a particularly important factor being the understanding of organizational buying behavior.[12] The search for better methods of rating and dealing with business suppliers is in the forefront of purchasing problems today, just as it has been for decades. A further problem is the trend toward decentralization and group decision making, both of which affect the purchasing function today and, more than likely, will affect it well into the future. Many U.S. industries spend resources for materials, direct production labor, and energy. Purchasing is directly involved in the decision to acquire materials and energy. This involvement is a key reason as to why business sellers and buyers must work closely together, and why they must establish and maintain an enduring relationship, if both buyer and seller are to survive.

Relationship Marketing

Relationship marketing, sometimes called alliances or strategic partnerships, refers to what we can expect future buyer-seller relations to reflect. When a supplier and a buyer develop a working partnership over a period of time, the supplier practically becomes a part of the buyer's organization. The phenomenal growth of relationship marketing between purchasers and suppliers over the past few years reflects a notable example of a silent revolution affecting members in the buyer-seller DYAD exchange. Alliances are redefining the fundamental role of both buyers and sellers. Suppliers are making major adjustments in their thinking, management styles, and methods of responding to purchaser's standards and operational requirements. This alliance or relationship is not driven by a faddish trend but by a combination of four strong business forces: quality, speed, cost-effectiveness, and new design techniques.

The combination of these four forces has fostered closer working relationships between purchasers and suppliers. This trend is accelerating rapidly, particularly among high-tech manufacturers. These companies have learned that strategic partnerships are more than just important—they are critical. Suppliers are cutting their vendor lists and treating the remaining vendors as allies, sharing strategic information freely and drawing upon supplier expertise in developing new products that can meet the quality, cost, and delivery standards of the marketplace.

Early in the decade, Stamford, Connecticut–based Xerox began changing its vendor relationships in an effort to enhance the quality of its reprographic equipment and the company's competitive standing.[13] To continue as a leader in the reprographics industry, Xerox's management realized that the company had to "include suppliers as part of the Xerox family," says Steve Tierney, vice-president of materials management with Xerox's Reprographics Business Group in Webster, New York. "The new approach has yielded a 50 percent improvement in 'factors critical for success,' including lead times, cost, and quality," he adds. "If we can become a more significant part of our supplier's customer base, that will help us become an important part of his world," adds Jim Barden, Xerox's manager of the Plastics Commodity Team in Webster, New York. In forging long-term relationships with a limited number of vendors, Xerox brings in suppliers for consultation very early in the product design cycle, during what Mr. Tierney calls the "concept phase."

Despite the plethora of research done on salesperson effectiveness, very few studies have dealt with the performance of purchasing personnel. A recent study found that buyers who were highly motivated, satisfied with their jobs, and certain of job expectations were more successful.[14] Business marketing managers must keep in mind that adversarial and exploitative buyer-seller relationships are the exception rather than the rule. Partnerships and strategic alliances are interfirm linkages, designed to attain joint cost savings, product enhancements, and competitive services.[15] The erroneous adoption of the adversarial perspective can only impede the development of productive relationships with buyers. Creative business marketers are aware of the profit-making potential available to buyers, and they use this knowledge accordingly. The purchasing function expects to play a greater role in cost reduction projects of all types in the future.[16] Busy buyers who become accustomed to regular and timely assistance from creative sellers will not change sources of supply very readily. Marketing research has largely neglected the relationship aspect of buyer-seller behavior, while tending to study transactions as discrete events.[17] The lack of attention to antecedent conditions and processes for buyer-seller exchange relationships is a serious omission in the development of marketing knowledge.[18]

Profile of a Business-to-Business Buyer

In January 1992, a survey was conducted by the Organization and Planning Committee of the National Association of Purchasing Management (NAPM) in order to update the profile of the typical purchasing executive. This survey not only profiles the purchasing executive but also provides an indication of developing trends as both buyers and sellers prepare to face evolving challenges as we move through the decade of the 1990s and beyond. These survey results indicated that the typical NAPM member is a 36- to 45-year-old Caucasian male who holds a bachelor's degree in business. He has been in the purchasing profession for nine to fifteen years and has the title of Purchasing Manager or Purchasing Agent. His employer is a manufacturer for whom he spends approximately $10 million annually and supervises two to three additional buying personnel. His purchasing department actively makes use of computers, and he has access to an on-line data base. His annual salary falls in the range of $25–$55 thousand.

The most notable data derived from the 1992 survey is the continued rapid rise in female membership. Female membership as a percentage of total membership rose from 16 percent in 1986 to 25 percent in 1989 to 29 percent in the 1992 survey. While the 1992 response rate for men of 71 percent still indicates a predominantly male organization, it must be noted that the rate of new female memberships outpaces that of males by five to one. Cheryl Grigsby, an Arizona State University graduate and purchasing manager for Westinghouse Electric Corporation of Pittsburgh, Pennsylvania, entered the purchasing profession fifteen years ago. She is currently responsible for the Westinghouse Purchasing Development program, the Minority Business Enterprise program for the corporation, and the corporate contracting of electro-mechanical components. Dee S. Johnston, CPM. and vice president of O'Sullivan Corporation, a plastics manufacturing firm in Winchester, Virginia, has put together all the right ingredients to achieve a top management position. This trend will continue as we move through the 1990s.

The marketing implications of the findings of these studies are enormous. The status of the purchasing individuals within the organization seems to be rising, which is reflected not only in the title of the chief purchasing officer, as previously noted, but also in the functions that typically report to the purchasing executive. Table 2-8 provides the functions reporting to purchasing by organization size, and Table 2-9 provides the job titles to which purchasing reports by organization size. Business sellers cannot avoid interaction with the purchasing person on most buying decisions, so a clear understanding and appreciation of this person's duties and responsibilities is a must. Additionally, purchasing executives are opting for more long-term buying contracts, and they will continue to buy from fewer sources. This will force many vendors (or potential vendors) to assume more responsibility for the inventory burden, which coincides with the trend toward JIT buying in many industries. Thus, make-and-hold

TABLE 2-8 **Functions That Report to Purchasing (By Organization Size)**

	Total Organizations		Under $500 million		$500 million to $1 billion		$1.1–5 billion		$5.1–10 billion		Over $10 billion	
	#	%	#	%	#	%	#	%	#	%	#	%
Inbound traffic	29	10	14	17	2	4	8	7	2	6	3	11
Outbound traffic	2	1	0	—	0	—	2	2	0	—	0	—
Both inbound and outbound traffic	91	31	18	21	16	36	32	29	13	42	12	44
Warehousing or stores	102	34	31	37	14	31	40	36	8	26	9	33
Inventory control	111	37	29	35	21	47	43	39	8	26	10	37
Scrap/surplus disposal	169	57	54	64	24	53	62	56	13	42	16	59
Receiving	77	26	24	29	15	33	29	26	4	13	5	19
Incoming inspection	48	16	12	14	5	11	24	22	1	3	6	22
Other*	81	27	20	24	14	31	32	29	10	32	5	19
Number organizations responding	297		84		45		110		31		27	

*Under *Other* are included fleet management (11), personnel travel (9), production scheduling and control (6), contract administration (5), minority programs (5), office services (4), printing (4), material planning and forecasting (4), property administration (4). The following functions were indicated by three or fewer organizations: expediting, pattern shop, aircraft, security, demolition, asset recovery, agriculture, engineering standards, equipment specifications, hydrocarbon trading, packaging engineering, engineering, project management, international trading, and industrial sales.

Source: Harold E. Fearon, *Purchasing Organizational Relationships* (Tempe, Ariz.: Center for Advanced Purchasing Studies, National Association for Purchasing Management, 1988), p. 38.

arrangements via long-term buying contracts, strong negotiation skills, and increased awareness of such factors as the small-order problem will put the astute seller or potential seller in a commanding position. These buying strengths, accompanied by buyers' trend toward single sourcing, put additional pressure on the vendor and sales executives.

BUSINESS BUYING MOTIVES

Several different approaches are found in the literature that reflect different behavioral schools of thought applied to understanding and explaining the buyer behavior and motives of business purchasing personnel. It is not unusual to find purchasing, engineering, manufacturing, and marketing personnel involved both individually and jointly at various phases in the buying decision process, particularly in a new-task or a modified-rebuy buying situation.

TABLE 2-9 **To Whom Purchasing Reports (By Organization Size)**

Number of Organizations and Percent of Organizations in Category (Percent may not add to 100 due to rounding)

To Whom Purchasing Reports	Number of Organizations Responding		Under $500 million		$500 million to $1 billion		$1.1–5 billion		$5.1–10 billion		Over $10 billion	
	#	%	#	%	#	%	#	%	#	%	#	%
President	47	16	11	13	7	16	18	17	10	32	1	4
Executive vice president	54	18	10	12	10	22	17	16	9	29	8	31
Financial vice president	21	7	7	9	1	2	7	6	1	3	5	19
Mfg/prod/opns vice president	71	24	27	33	16	36	22	20	3	10	3	12
Materials mgt vice president	22	8	9	11	3	7	8	7	1	3	1	4
Engineering vice president	3	1	0	—	0	—	2	2	0	—	1	4
Administrative vice president	38	13	4	5	4	9	24	22	4	13	2	8
Other*	35	12	13	16	4	9	10	9	3	10	5	19
	291	99	81	99	45	101	108	99	31	100	26	101

*The 35 shown as reporting to *Other* includes division vice president (6); director of materials (3); materials manager (3); vice chairman (3); board of directors (2); vice president, logistics (2); director of support services (2); and one each to director of administration; manager of administration; director of manufacturing; director of operations; vice president, trading; vice president, systems; vice president, human resources; vice president, engineering and materials; division controller; vice president, law and public affairs; vice president, technical; vice president, marketing; assistant vice president; and manager, planning and distribution.

Source: Harold E. Fearon, *Purchasing Organizational Relationships* (Tempe, Ariz.: Center for Advanced Purchasing Studies, National Association for Purchasing Management, 1988), p. 27.

If uncertainty is involved with a purchasing decision, research studies have found that decision makers will avoid as much risk as possible by remaining loyal to existing business suppliers whom they know and trust. For instance, a number of business observers credit IBM's success in marketing personal computers to this tendency of business buyers. Many purchasing directors who were considering the purchase of personal computers in the early 1980s seemed to be overwhelmed by having more than 150 different computer manufacturers competing for their business. Therefore, to minimize their risk level, many turned to IBM as a trusted name with consistently reliable products.[19] A large number of purchasing managers frequently utilize one or more of the following activities in an effort to reduce or remove perceived risk:

(1) *Reduce uncertainty.* Uncertainty can be reduced by gathering additional information, such as consulting with other influencers, or visiting potential suppliers' plants.

(2) *Play the odds.* Sophisticated quantitative methods of vendor analysis and selection, involving expected value analysis and considering both the probability and magnitude of consequences, are available for use; the industrial buyer will often *play the odds* by selecting the supplier with the most favorable expected value.

(3) *Spread the risk.* The consequences of choosing the wrong supplier can also be reduced through *multiple sourcing,* which enables buyers to choose the proportion of risk to be assumed by allocating it among different suppliers.[20] For example, Loctite holds an 85-percent market share in anaerobic adhesives. A number of other companies have entered the industry by taking advantage of the hesitancy of Loctite's customers to depend solely on a single source of supply.[21]

Unlike consumer products, business products do not necessarily make anyone look or feel better, and they generally do not have significant aesthetic value. Business products are bought to help the users manufacture, distribute, or sell more effectively so that their respective economic and competitive positions can be improved. As such, business firms tend to emphasize price and quality checks and balances in the buying process that are often nonexistent in the typical household purchase situation. Examples of exceptions to this practice would be the business buyer with the latest newly installed computer system (signifying a position of power within the organization) and a company salesperson with a new Acura Legend as a company car (signifying status within the organization). In developing marketing strategy, both existing and potential business suppliers should be aware of buyers' decision strategies in reducing uncertainty and of how such strategies affect supplier choice.

Using another perspective, final consumers buy for their own use or for use by people close to them. As such, personal goals are important to consumers in making their purchasing decisions. Business buyers purchase for their organizations, not for themselves. However, since people are still doing the buying in organizations, both personal and organizational goals may play a role in buying.[22] The presence of both types of goals can somewhat complicate the marketing effort. A vendor's sales representatives can have difficulty in ascertaining whether personal or organizational goals hold more importance for the buyer. For example, a buyer of metal cans, a product that does not greatly differ from one vendor to another, considers organizational goals such as cost control, package safety, and delivery time when choosing a supplier. Simultaneously, that buyer also considers personal goals, such as the desire for power and job security, when making a buying decision. Exhibit 2-2 compares personal and organizational goals.[23] As can be seen from this illustration, personal goals and organizational goals are not usually the same. A business vendor has little choice but to recognize and respond to both types of goals.

EXHIBIT 2-2 **Goals Influencing Buying Decisions**

Personal Goals	Organizational Goals
Want a feeling of power	Control cost in product use situation
Seek personal pleasure	Few breakdowns of product
Desire job security	Dependable delivery for repeat purchases
Want to be well liked	Adequate supply of product
Want respect	Cost within budget limit

PURCHASING ORGANIZATION

The *purchasing function* includes the whole process of deciding and specifying what to buy—in what quantities, at what time, from what sources, and by what procedures; as well as the implementation of these decisions and procedures by requisitioning, authorizing, ordering, receiving, and paying for the purchases. It is convenient to refer to this process as the purchasing function, but it should be noted that parts of it are cross-functional in the sense that other areas, such as design, production, and using departments, not only participate in the process but may also carry the prime responsibility for elements in it. As such, organizations can be thought of in two dimensions. One dimension deals with motivating the individuals and subgroups of the total organization enough to get them to contribute optimally. The other deals with the pattern of formal interrelationships that tie the members of the group together. These dimensions often find expression in organization decisions—an aspect of the organization of purchasing that will be emphasized here.

Organization Related to Size of Company

In a small company with a limited sales volume and variety of purchases, the purchasing department may consist of only the purchasing manager and a clerical assistant.[24] In some very large companies, the department will have several hundred employees. In some companies, purchasing is under the jurisdiction of the production or manufacturing division, and the purchasing manager reports to the manufacturing manager. In other companies, the department reports to a top executive officer, such as the president, executive vice president, or general manager.

In some large companies, and within some diversified industries, the purchasing operation is separated into both the operational and managerial phases of purchasing. Separate buying departments are set up at the divisional level as part of the division organization plan. A *general purchasing department* at company headquarters serves the entire organization as a staff facility. It counsels top management on broad purchasing and materials policies, conducts general and specific purchasing research programs that are made available to all buyers, sets policies for the guidance of divisional purchasing departments, coordinates purchasing policies and activities throughout the company, and gives assistance on specific purchasing problems, where needed. Such a centralized purchasing department does little or no actual buying and has no responsibility for the details of procurement beyond evaluating purchasing performance at the various divisions and pointing out means for improvement. In most cases, it has no jurisdiction over the hiring or firing of divisional purchasing personnel, although it usually sets up the buyer-training programs and has decisive influence in the transfer of individuals with superior buying talent to other company divisions and to positions of greater responsibility and opportunity.

Centralization versus Decentralization of the Buying Function

We need to address the question of whether the buying firm decentralizes purchasing activities in each plant of a multiple-plant firm or employs the concept of centralization at the home office of the firm. In practice, virtually every company answers this question differently. Some companies centralize the activity completely, doing the buying for all plants at a central headquarters office. Others decentralize the function entirely, giving each plant full authority to conduct all its purchasing activities. Still other firms—the majority of them— develop an organizational buying structure somewhere between these two extremes. Both decentralized and centralized approaches offer significant benefits and should be understood by the marketer.

The reasons for having a separate plant purchasing department can be summarized as follows:[25]

(1) The plant or division manager is responsible for the profitable operation of that unit. He or she should have jurisdiction over purchasing as well as production, because a large part of costs and a major factor in the efficiency of production are represented in procurement.

(2) If the division is large enough to be considered a profit center, it is usually large enough to buy in volume at favorable prices.

(3) Each division may have some unique requirements and differences in operating conditions that affect material needs.

(4) The public relations aspect of purchasing locally is important. Goodwill can be fostered by purchasing from nearby sources or through local distributors.

However, the advantages of centralized purchasing are so great in comparison with decentralized purchasing that almost all but the smallest of firms are centralized. Prior to centralizing its purchasing function and realizing substantial savings, General Motors spent millions of dollars each year, with more than one hundred buying locations purchasing twenty-four million pairs of work gloves in 225 styles from nearly one hundred different vendors.

In centralized purchasing, a separate individual or department is established and given authority to make all purchases (except the very unusual buy, such as a new company aircraft). The advantages to be gained from centralized purchasing are as follows:

(1) The standardization of purchased parts is easier, as all decisions go through one central control point.

(2) Administrative duplication is eliminated or reduced. Instead of each department head writing a separate purchase order for a product or part, the purchasing department writes only one order for the firm's total requirement.

(3) By combining requirements from several departments, order quantities can be increased. This will provide faster delivery, quantity discounts, or other concessions. There may also be freight savings, because shipments now can be made in carload quantities.

(4) This form of organization is cost-effective for vendors, since they need not call on several people within a particular buying firm. This also provides better control over purchase commitments.

(5) Centralized purchasing also enables the development of specialization and expertise in purchasing decisions.

As noted earlier, the purchasing organizations of some multiplant firms are found at both ends of the centralization-decentralization continuum.

CONCEPT QUESTIONS

1. Why are contemporary purchasing personnel different from their counterparts of only a few years ago?
2. What are three activities that remove or reduce perceived risk in purchasing?
3. How might the purchasing organization differ between smaller and larger organizations?

THE MATERIALS MANAGEMENT CONCEPT

Materials management is the grouping of functions involved in obtaining and bringing materials into a production operation. (Often, this concept is referred to as logistics, which would incorporate materials management and physical distribution.) A description of the concept offered by several leading scholars in the purchasing management field illustrates the point:[26]

> An organization which has adopted the materials management organizational concept will have a single manager responsible for planning, organizing, motivating and controlling all those activities principally concerned with the flow of materials into an organization. Materials management views material flows as a system.
>
> The specific functions that might be included under the materials manager are material planning and control, production scheduling, material and purchasing research, purchasing, incoming traffic, inventory control, receiving, incoming quality control, stores, in-plant materials movement, and scrap and surplus disposal. Not all functions are necessarily included; the ones often excluded are production scheduling, in-plant materials movement, and incoming quality control.

Because 90 percent of a typical product's cost at the Gillette Company is in the materials that compose it, the materials management team supervises inventories, warehousing, and the shipping of goods and assists research and development personnel in developing substitute materials.

A materials management approach, in one form or another, has been implemented by over 75 percent of all U.S. manufacturing firms. Larger firms, both those geographically dispersed domestically and those on an international level, are able to integrate centralized and operational materials management activities. This linkage, along with on-line computer systems, allows the integration of all aspects of the materials management function.

The continued adoption of the materials management concept will force many business marketing managers to coordinate activities that affect the materials management function of their customers. Suppliers who can manage their own production, inventory, and distribution system, so as to match their customers' requirements, have the best chance to establish long-range business relationships. The materials management approach to business buying and selling will continue to expand into the areas of raw materials, component parts, and inventory control, along with being an important tool in planning and forecasting future supply needs. The organizational buying function must be directly involved in this continued trend toward integrated materials management. The buyers initiate this movement of goods into the buying firm for use by production. As a result, the purchase timing, cost, and specific products chosen will impact the performance of this system.

Alternative Approaches to Materials Management

Critics of the materials management form of organization emphasize that it is difficult, if not impossible, for one person to coordinate and control the many variables involved in materials operations and that effective coordination is too difficult to achieve merely by establishing a new organizational structure. Furthermore, recent literature contains much contrasting information on various approaches utilized in materials management. Some alternative approaches have been suggested.

Traditional approach. Traditionally, inventory has been used to buffer transportation, production, distribution, and sales imbalances, when availability and demand occur at differing rates. This situation is intensified with the great product variety that has been created and, therefore, expected in our economy. Consequently, U.S. firms have emphasized materials delivery systems, and business marketers have reacted accordingly. The business sector has long been the leader in U.S. growth productivity, the wellspring of innovation, and the generator of a rising standard of living.[27] Also, traditionally, inventory has been built into an operation to cover problems. Despite advanced control systems and the realization that inventory tied up capital, the relationship between inventory and its effects on manufacturing methods or measurement systems was seldom analyzed.

As American firms continue to transplant their operations overseas, foreign producers are developing production capabilities in the United States. Low wages in South Korea, Taiwan, and other Asian countries clearly are part of the attraction, but all too often it appears that American companies are simply giving up on the United States as a suitable place to make their goods. Akio Morita, Sony's chairman and cofounder, states, "We are not taking away your manufacturers' business. They are giving it up. If they move out of factories and depend on the Far East, that means the hollowing of American industry."[28] In many cases, this phenomenon has proven costly, as has been reflected in the delivered price of some business goods.

Just-in-Time (JIT) approach. Another form of business exchange, commonly referred to as the just-in-time (JIT) exchange relationship, has been adopted and implemented by many original equipment manufacturers (OEMs) and suppliers of component parts and materials during the past several years.[29] A 1988 survey of JIT practices in the United States found that 45 percent of the companies contacted had formal JIT purchasing programs. Another 22 percent planned to implement JIT purchasing within the next few years.[30] The just-in-time supplier-customer exchange concept is a recent operational philosophy thought to epitomize the relationship marketing model.[31] The box entitled "Business Marketing in Action" discusses the major features and implications of JIT.

BUSINESS-TO-BUSINESS MARKETING IN ACTION

FEATURES AND IMPLICATIONS OF JIT

Over the past two decades, American markets have been bombarded with foreign products. Japanese market-share gains have been especially pronounced in such industries as steel, office equipment, electronics, and automobiles. As American business started studying the reasons for Japanese success in manufacturing, it discovered several concepts, including just-in-time (JIT), early supplier involvement, value analysis, quality circles, total quality control, and flexible manufacturing.

JIT in particular promises to produce significant change in the relationship between suppliers and their business to business customers. The goal of JIT is zero inventory with 100 percent quality. It means that materials arrive at the customer's factory exactly at the time they are needed. It does not mean that the customer shifts inventory to the supplier, as this would not reduce total system costs; instead it calls for a synchronization between supplier and customer production schedules so that inventory buffers are unnecessary. Effective implementation of JIT should result in reduced inventory and lead times and increased quality, productivity, and adaptability to changes.

In a survey of two thousand purchasing executives in 1986, 59 percent indicated that their firm had used or planned to use JIT. General Motors, through its JIT programs, reduced inventory-related costs from $8 billion to $2 billion.

Business marketers need to be aware of the changes that JIT will bring about in the purchasing practices of organizations. They must position themselves to exploit the opportunities that JIT will create. The following are the major features and implications of JIT:

- *Strict quality control.* Maximum cost savings from JIT are achieved if preinspected goods are received by the buyer. The buyers thus expect that suppliers have strict quality-control procedures such as SPC (statistical process control) or TQC (total quality control). This means that suppliers need to work closely with the business customer and satisfy the latter that they can ship products that meet the quality standards.
- *Frequent and reliable delivery.* Daily delivery is frequently the only way to avoid inventory buildup. Increasingly, customers are specifying delivery dates rather than shipping dates, with penalties for not meeting them. Apple even penalizes for early delivery, while Kasle Steel has around-the-clock deliveries to the General Motors plant in Buick City. This means that suppliers must develop reliable transportation arrangements.
- *Closer location.* Since JIT involves frequent delivery, a location closer to the customer can be an advantage for the supplier. A close location results in more efficiency in delivering smaller lots and greater reliability in inclement weather. Kasle Steel set up its blanking mill within Buick City to serve the General Motors plant there. This means that a marketer may have to make large commitments to major customers.
- *Telecommunication.* New technologies of communication permit suppliers to establish computerized purchasing systems that are hooked up to their customer. One large customer requires that suppliers make their inventory figures and prices available on the system. It allows for just-in-time on-line

ordering as the computer looks for the lowest prices where inventory is available. This reduces transaction costs but puts pressure on marketers to keep prices very competitive.

- *Stable production schedules.* Under JIT, customers provide their production schedule to the supplier so that the delivery is made on the day the materials are required. International Harvester provides one of its suppliers with a six-month forecast and a firm twenty-day order. If any last-minute changes are made, International Harvester is billed for the additional costs. This will help reduce the uncertainty and costs faced by the business to business suppliers.
- *Single sourcing.* JIT implies that the buying and selling organizations work closely together to reduce costs. This often translates into the customer's awarding a long-term contract to only one supplier who can be trusted. This makes payoffs high for the winning supplier, and very difficult for other competitors to subsequently get the contract. Contracts are almost automatically renewed provided the supplier met delivery schedules and maintained quality. Single sourcing is increasing rapidly under JIT. Thus while General Motors still uses more than 3,500 suppliers, Toyota, which has totally adopted JIT, uses less than 250. In the United States, Harley Davidson reduced its supplier base from 320 to 180 in two years.
- *Value analysis.* The major objectives of JIT are to reduce costs and improve quality, and value analysis is critical to accomplishing those objectives. To reduce costs of its product, a customer must not only reduce its own costs but also get its suppliers to reduce their costs. Thus some large manufacturers hold VA seminars for their suppliers. Suppliers with a strong VA program have a competitive edge, as they can contribute to their customers' VA program.
- *Early supplier involvement.* Business buyers are increasingly realizing that marketers are experts in their field and should be brought into the design process. Marketers must have qualified personnel who can participate in customers' design teams. In 1986, a survey of one thousand purchasing executives found that the major criteria for selecting suppliers to participate in design teams were quality, prior delivery performance, recommendations by the customer's engineering department, and prior value-analysis assistance.
- *Close relationship.* All the above features of JIT help to forge a close relationship between the customer and the marketer. To make JIT successful, they coordinate their efforts to maximally satisfy the customer's needs. Under JIT, the supplier is viewed as a work station that is located away from the customer's manufacturing site. To be successful, the supplier has to customize its offering for the particular customer. In return, the supplier wins the contract for a specific term. Because of the time invested by the parties, locational decisions, and telecommunication hookups, the transaction-specific investments are high. Since switching costs for the customer are high, these customers are extremely selective in choosing suppliers. A major implication is that U.S. business marketers must improve their skill in *relationship marketing* as compared with *transaction marketing.* Profit maximization over the entire relationship rather than over each transaction should be the objective. Otherwise the supplier may lose the customer for good.

Source: Philip Kotler, *Marketing Management: Analysis, Planning, Implementation, and Control* (7th ed.), Englewood Cliffs, NJ: Prentice-Hall, Inc., 1990, pp. 204–205.

The objective of the JIT concept is to eliminate waste of all kinds from the production process. It requires the delivery of the specified product at the precise time and in the exact quantity needed. Variations in any of these three dimensions are considered wasteful. In theory, the product must conform to the customer's specifications every time. It must be delivered when needed—not earlier and not later; and it must be delivered in the exact quantity needed—not more and not less.[32] In the JIT operating environment, a critical role of purchasing is to locate, evaluate, and select suppliers able and willing to support the JIT process.[33]

Just-in-time was neither a creation of the academic community nor a development of a consulting firm. This approach was Toyota's response to managing its own internal operations and its relationship with its suppliers. The creation of JIT was driven by the vision and leadership of Taiichi Ohno (first a plant manager and later the vice president of manufacturing at Toyota), along with Shigeo Shingo (head of the industrial engineering consulting branch of the Japan Management Association).

In the United States, just-in-time is an approach to production and inventory management that reduces inventory. The approach is similar in terms of objective, and to a large extent in terms of practice, in the United States, Japan, and Western Europe. Thus, descriptive expressions such as "stockless production" or "zero inventories" are often used. Alternatively, just-in-time is defined in terms of the coincidence in time of the movement of completed work from an upstream operation to the start of work at the successive downstream operation. Two examples illustrate this approach:

> One such concept of an ideal production system is most commonly called Just-in-Time production, a name which emphasizes producing exactly what is needed and conveying it to where it is needed precisely when required.[34]
>
> The Just-in-Time concept appears to be the core of Japanese production management and productivity improvement. The JIT idea is simple: Produce and deliver finished goods just in time to be sold, subassemblies just in time to be assembled into finished goods, fabricated parts just in time to go into subassemblies, and purchased materials just in time to be transformed into fabricated parts.[35]

The basic idea of JIT is that carrying any inventory is undesirable because it ties up capital. JIT inventory management ensures that each person involved in the manufacturing process receives what they need just in time.[36] For example, a Bendix plant recently adopted a JIT system and was able to convert ten thousand square feet of floor space from storage to manufacturing usage.[37] Black and Decker, IBM, Firestone, General Motors, Harley-Davidson, and other firms are experiencing decreasing costs and higher quality with the system. General Motors claims to have saved $2 billion in one year with the use of the JIT system.[38]

To be effective, just-in-time purchasing and production scheduling require very careful managerial monitoring. Undoubtedly, the most important single factor to success in JIT is top management's commitment both to providing necessary resources and to an understanding of the philosophy involved. High levels of cooperation and coordination are called for between suppliers and producers, and then between production and marketing people within the manufacturing firm.[39] Also, JIT is not appropriate for all business buyer's operations. Therefore, it will never totally replace traditional systems, relying on inventory back-up.

The terms *JIT* and *Kanban* are often used interchangeably, whereas in fact, Kanban is a subset of JIT. (*Kanban* actually means marker.) The goal of Kanban is to produce required units on time and only in the quantities necessary. The Kanban system controls production by the use of markers or cards, with the flow of materials being dependent on the Kanban cards. The "pull" card pulls work from previous work centers based on a production schedule. This "pull" system works by controlling the sequence of job activities in a manufacturing facility.

When the just-in-time philosophy takes place within a buying firm, the alert and knowledgeable business supplier may serve in the role of a change agent in facilitating this transition. This will require a very thorough understanding of the JIT philosophy and its translation into marketing, purchasing, and manufacturing practice.[40] Suppliers who have adopted JIT have the advantage of using their system's capabilities as a marketing tool and taking the role of advisor in working with reluctant adopters. This should put the supplier or potential supplier in an excellent position to become a preferred supplier. It should also be noted that JIT purchasing concepts can provide competitive advantages to firms in nonmanufacturing industries, as well as to those in manufacturing industries. Preliminary results obtained from research conducted by Guinipero and Keiser, using a large firm in the communications industry, indicate significant benefits—improved internal and external communications, improved supplier performance, and reduction in the requirement for warehouse space.[41]

Reasons for Adopting the Materials Management Concept

There are many reasons for the adoption of the materials management type of organization, with the greatest advantage being the improved communication and coordination between departments that such an organizational structure permits. Materials management provides a central administration where conflicting functional or departmental interests can be balanced out in the overall interests of the company. Centralized responsibility and control also make for a smoother, faster flow of materials from the time they are requisitioned by using departments, to the time they are shipped out to customers as finished products.[42]

Among the more specific ways in which a centrally controlled materials organization has helped a number of companies to improve efficiency and to reduce cost are easier and simpler control of inventories, reduced clerical work, and fewer problems with delivery scheduling and emergency orders.

BUSINESS BUYING SITUATIONS

Understanding buyer behavior (organizational versus consumer) becomes easier if the task is divided into phases, and these phases are then analyzed under different buying situations. This procedure enables the marketer to identify critical decision phases, the information needs of the buying organization, and various criteria that buyers consider when making a buying decision.[43] The steps in the business purchasing process presented in Exhibit 2-3 are useful in analyzing the buying process over several different buying situations. Three types of buying situations have been delineated: (1) new-task buying, (2) modified-rebuy buying, and (3) straight-rebuy buying.[44]

Figure 2-4 provides common examples of business goods and services purchased in these three types of buying situations. Each type of buying situation must be related to the seven-stage buying process as presented in Table 2-10. The exact same purchase in two very different buying situations can be quite

EXHIBIT 2-3 **Characteristics of Three Buying Situations**

New Task	Straight Rebuy	Modified Rebuy
A requirement or problem that has not arisen before. Little or no relevant past buying experience to draw upon. A great deal of information is needed. Must seek out alternative ways of solving the problem and alternative suppliers. Occurs infrequently—but very important to marketers because it sets the pattern for the more routine purchases that will follow. May be anticipated and developed by creative marketing.	Continuing or recurring requirement, handled on a routine basis. Usually the decision on each separate transaction is made in the purchasing department. Formally or informally, a "list" of acceptable suppliers exists. No supplier not on the "list" is considered. Buyers have much relevant buying experience, and hence little new information is needed. Appears to represent the bulk of the individual purchases within companies. Item purchases, price paid, delivery time, etc., may vary from transaction to transaction, so long as these variations do not cause a new source of supply to be considered.	May develop from either new task or straight rebuy situations. The requirement is continuing or recurring or it may be expanded to a significant larger level of operations. The buying alternatives are known, but they are *changed.* Some additional information is needed before the decisions are made. May arise because of outside events, such as an emergency or by the actions of a marketer. May arise internally because of new buying influences, or for potential cost reductions, potential quality improvements, or potential service benefits. Marketers who are not active suppliers try to convert the customer's straight rebuys into modified rebuys.

Source: P.J. Robinson, C.W. Faris, and Y. Wind, *Industrial Buying and Creative Marketing* (Boston: Allyn & Bacon, 1967), p. 28. Reproduced with permission.

FIGURE 2-4 **Goods Purchased Using Three Different Types of Buying Situations**

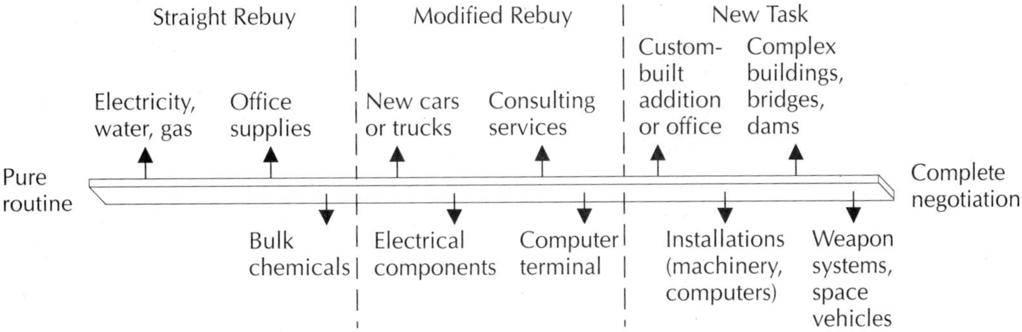

TABLE 2-10 **Linking the Industrial Purchasing Process to Industrial Buying Situations**

Steps in the Industrial Purchasing Process	**Buy Classes** New Task	Modified Rebuy	Straight Rebuy
1. Recognizing the need	Yes	Maybe	No
2. Developing product specifications	Yes	Maybe	No
3. Soliciting bids from potential suppliers	Yes	Maybe	No
4. Making the purchase decision	Yes	Maybe	No
5. Issuing the contract	Yes	Maybe	No
6. Inspecting goods for quality	Yes	Yes	Yes
7. Evaluating vendor performance	Yes	Yes	Yes

Source: Adapted from Patrick J. Robinson, Charles W. Faris, and Yoram Wind, *Industrial Buying and Creative Marketing* (Boston: Allyn & Bacon, 1967).

different. Therefore, marketing strategy must begin with identifying the type of buying situation that the purchasing firm is facing.[45]

New-Task Buying

When confronting a *new-task buying* situation, organizational buyers operate in a stage of decision-making that might be referred to as an extensive problem solving stage, where the buyer is faced with a buying situation that is new and very different than anything that has been faced in the past. A new type of machine, part, material, or service is needed, and the purchaser is faced with a buying situation to which he or she has not yet been exposed. This buying situation presents the marketer with a chance to participate in the early stages of the procurement process (thus increasing the probability of making the sale). The astute marketer anticipates and recognizes a problem even before it has been recognized by the present or potential customer and is prepared to respond to the needs of new-task buyers.

As an example of new-task buying, consider a hospital's purchase of a computer-aided tomography (CAT) scanner—a device that x-rays tiny slices of body structures and then combines the thousands of shots into a composite picture. The scanner can pinpoint stroke-induced brain damage and also provide valuable diagnostic information about vascular structures and other soft-tissue organs. Central General,[46] the largest of three hospitals in a medium-sized midwestern city, plans to share the CAT scanner with other local institutions. The need has been recognized: The hospital can vastly improve its diagnostic work and make it available to the entire community. Moreover, the need has been generally identified: a third- or fourth-generation scanner, with high resolution and thin-sectioning capabilities.

To characterize and write specifications for so important a purchase, the chief of staff and the hospital administrator appoint a committee under the direction of the senior radiologist. One of the members, Central General's purchasing agent, will record all the information that the group gathers and will summarize it prior to a final decision. Each member has assigned tasks. Some will canvass the hospital services (other than radiology) that will use the scanner or refer to its output: neurosurgery, cardiology, orthopedics, neurology, ophthalmology, oncology, and so on. Others will identify the CAT units available, set up interviews with potential vendors, and check out the reputation of each manufacturer with several hospitals in Chicago.

After eight weeks and as many committee meetings, several units are rejected as too difficult to service and too crude in imaging capability. Positron tomography, a technologically different option, has also been ruled out. Three units remain in contention, with marketing representatives and technical specialists invited to make formal presentations to the committee. Marketers from General Electric will present the advantages of GE's model 8800; those from Varian will promote its model 360; and the group from Siemens will push for its Somatom 2.

Owing to its wide range of functions and convenient service provisions (and because the model received high marks from current users), the committee votes, with only one dissent, for the GE CT/T 8800. The chief of staff and the head radiologist, who share the burden of the final choice, concur in this decision. At a subsequent lunch hosted by GE's regional sales manager, the purchasing director talks through the details of shipping, billing and servicing. That afternoon, the purchasing director meets with the GE technical staff and the hospital's chief of building maintenance to plan the subcontracting needed to build a suitable room for the new equipment.

The cost of the CAT scanner is between $3 and $4 million; typically, such expensive purchases are made through the kind of deliberative and collective process described above. The better informed that marketers are about the customer's buying procedures and decision makers, the better the marketers' chances for a successful sales effort.

Straight-Rebuy Buying

A *straight-rebuy buying* situation is the most common purchasing situation in business buying and requires little or no new information on the part of the buyer. The buyer simply purchases a routine part, material, or service, with little thought or effort going into the buying process. The marketing job required of the business marketer is to become a supplier for these relatively routine types of purchases. This job can be difficult because of buyer time constraints and previously established relationships. Testing, evaluations, and approvals will be viewed by buyers as costly, time-consuming, and perhaps unnecessary. Present suppliers strive to maintain product and service quality, while potential suppliers attempt to sell through the provision of better quality products, more reliable and efficient service, and lower prices. Table 2-11 shows the strategies of present ("in") suppliers vs. potential ("out") suppliers in responding to different business buying situations.

TABLE 2-11 **Reacting to Various Buying Situations: Profiling Essential Marketing Strategies**

Buying Situation	The Supplier Who Is "In"	The Supplier Who is "Out"
New Task	Keeping track of evolving purchasing needs in the organization	
	Recognizing specific needs	Recognizing specific needs
	Engaging actively in early phases of buying process by supplying information and technical advice	Engaging actively in early phases of buying process by supplying information and technical advice
Straight Rebuy	Strengthening the buyer-seller relationship by achieving organization's expectations	Showing organization that the potential benefits of reexamining requirements and suppliers exceed the costs
	Adapting to evolving needs of the customer	Trying to position yourself on an organization's preferred list of suppliers even as a second or third choice
Modified Rebuy	Correcting problems with customer	Determining and reacting to the organization's problem with existing supplier
	Analyzing and meeting customer needs	Persuading organizations to try alternative offerings

Source: Patrick J. Robinson, Charles W. Faris, and Yoram Wind, *Industrial Buying and Creative Marketing* (Boston: Allyn & Bacon, 1967), pp. 183–210.

Suppose that Central General's purchasing director buys hundreds, perhaps thousands, of items every month. Articles such as surgical gloves, rubber tubing, electronic thermometers, and paper cups are routinely reordered without approval from the hospital management.[47]

Modified-Rebuy Buying

With *modified-rebuy buying*, the business decision makers have well-defined criteria but are uncertain about which suppliers can best fit their needs. Buyers will speculate that gains to be derived from reevaluating alternatives are significant relative to the expended effort involved. The distinctive element here is the reevaluation of alternatives—after the consideration of new ones—prompted by the conviction that it is worthwhile to seek additional information and alternatives before a decision is reached. The nature of the buying requirements have changed so that the relatively routine buy or purchase is no longer routine. The needs have changed, so the business marketing effort must be changed in response to the revised aspects of the customers' requirements.

Let us suppose that Central General is opening a new intensive-care ward in three months and will need additional help and rigorous cleaning procedures. Indeed, the chief of staff has already complained about poor hygiene in the maternity and postsurgical wards. At just this time, the hospital's contract for janitorial services comes up for renewal. This situation transforms what might have been a straight rebuy into a modified rebuy. Although the purchasing director knows about janitorial services, the new requirements of the intensive-care unit and the complaints about the current vendor suggest that the contract should be reopened for bids. The chief of staff, the hospital administrator, and the head nurse in the new intensive-care unit must be consulted. The purchasing director will search for new suppliers while urging the present supplier to upgrade performance.[48]

PURCHASING AND THE LAW

The *purchasing-sales interchange* creates legal and binding commitments, with the primary legal areas involved being those concerned with the laws of agency and those of contracts. Legal considerations afford protection and, in many instances, monetary recompense for nonperformance by the business buyer or seller. Legal constraints exist regarding buyer-seller relationships, pricing, product liability, policies regarding the use of small companies and minority-owned firms, transportation, hazardous waste movement and disposal, storage, and potential personal liability of both the buyer and the seller.

Law of Agency

In buying and selling situations, the buying and selling personnel involved are acting as agents for their employing firms. An *agent* is any individual authorized to act on behalf of another and yet not be subject to the other's control. Because the law of agency enters into all forms of business activity, business buyers and sellers must understand the rights and duties of all parties involved, as these rights and duties create a series of potential lawsuits.

It would be difficult to find two purchasing executives who would agree on how closely they should attend to the legal aspects of the position. One survey, for example, revealed that 40 percent of all manufacturing firms do not bother to include any terms on purchase contracts, that they do not worry about legal fine points, and that they feel that any misunderstandings that might arise with industrial suppliers can be worked out by friendly negotiations.[49] Some buyers and sellers might blanch at such viewpoints, realizing that it is entirely possible for buyers and sellers to involve their respective companies unwittingly in legal hassles that can be catastrophically costly in terms of both money and prestige. Obviously, a working knowledge of the most important laws affecting the buyer-seller exchange is essential. Consider each of the following examples of potential legal issues.

You buy a machine from a reputable manufacturer, but the machine breaks down after an hour's work. Do you have to give the manufacturer time to remedy the situation before you can demand your money back? If so, how much time must you give? Are the answers different if every minute of the machine's downtime is costing your company thousands of dollars? Would the answers be different had the salesperson promised you that the machine would work for twenty years?

Your company needs a critical part immediately, or there is a chance that a large account will be lost. A supplier promises that the part will be on your doorstep the next morning, so you wipe your brow and sit back. The part shows up three weeks later. Can the supplier be held liable for your company's lost profits? Can the supplier be held liable at all? Are the answers different, depending on whether you talked with a sales manager or a sales representative?

You order equipment with a purchase order that says that the supplier's liability is unlimited. The equipment arrives accompanied by a sales form that says the supplier has no liability. Within minutes of installation, the equipment blows up, causing a fire that costs your company millions of dollars. Who pays for the damage—you or your supplier?

Your company refuses to pay for goods you ordered two months ago because you quit last week. So, the supplier sues you personally. Can you be forced to pay for the goods out of your own pocket?[50]

Simple answers to these questions are not readily available. Although a legalistic approach to buying and selling is in most cases unnecessary, all buyers and sellers must nevertheless protect their company against potential legal problems.

Law of Contracts

The major responsibility of buyers and sellers in contractual situations is to ensure that the purchase contract is satisfactorily drawn and that this contract is legally binding on both parties. To be valid and enforceable, a purchase contract must contain each of the following basic elements: (1) agreement ("meeting of the minds") resulting from an offer and an acceptance, (2) consideration or obligation, (3) competent parties, and (4) a lawful purpose.

The law is a vast subject. Fortunately, most industrial buyers and sellers subscribe to ethical standards of business, making it unnecessary to conduct daily business in an atmosphere of constant legal danger. Buyers and sellers are well advised to limit application to legal principles to preventive law and recognize problems and situations that should be referred to professional legal counsel.

CONCEPT QUESTIONS

1. What is the greatest advantage in a firm's adopting the materials management concept?
2. How does dividing the understanding of buyer behavior into different phases aid the marketer?
3. What is created by the purchase-sales interchange?

SUMMARY

1. A buying firm's policies and procedures, along with the buying process, should be understood by the business marketer, as these usually define responsibilities and detail both the buying authority that is delegated and to whom it is delegated. Salespeople are encouraged to examine prospects' statements of policy, plants, analysis of possible vendors' geographic locations, and study of the production capabilities of various potential suppliers.
2. As part of its economic function, purchasing has a responsibility through its delegated authority from top management to evaluate both potential and present vendors through all phases of the procurement cycle. Three models of vendor analysis are presented.
3. Marketers are increasingly confronted today by a well-educated, more sophisticated purchasing executive. Relationship marketing may well be the way of future relationships between buyers and suppliers. Relationship marketing (also called strategic partnerships) is driven by four strong forces: quality, speed, cost-effectiveness, and new design techniques. The combination of these has fostered closer working relationships between purchasers and suppliers. In light of the

strong competition present within the business sector, marketers need to make every effort to learn as much about their customers as possible. Buyer profiles are very useful in this endeavor and enable the marketer to tailor strategy to particular buyers and markets more easily and effectively.

4. In developing marketing strategy, both existing and potential suppliers should be aware of buyers' decision strategies in reducing uncertainty and of how such plans affect the choice of suppliers. Purchasing personnel will often develop a rank-ordered list of desired supplier attributes so as to facilitate comparisons among competing vendors.
5. The purchasing organization varies from one firm to another, with some purchasing managers working out of corporate headquarters and others operating at the divisional or plant level. In large companies, the purchasing operation is often separated into both operational and managerial units. Further, the question of whether the buying organization decentralizes buying activities in each plant (or division) of a multiple-plant firm or centralizes the activity at headquarters—or uses a combination of both organizational methods—must be understood by the business marketer.
6. The materials management concept advocates the grouping of all materials activities into a single department. Typically, materials management includes materials planning and control, production scheduling, materials and purchasing research, purchasing, incoming traffic, inventory control, receiving, incoming quality control, stores, in-plant materials movement, and scrap and surplus disposal. Alternative approaches to materials management include both the traditional approach and the just-in-time (JIT) approach.
7. Understanding business buying situations—specifically new task, modified rebuy, and straight rebuy—allows the business marketer to identify critical buying decision phases, the information needs of the buying organization, and criteria that the buyers consider when making a buying decision.
8. The purchasing-sales interchange creates legal and binding commitments, with the primary legal areas involved being those concerned with the laws of agency and contract.

KEY TERMS

Agent
Categorical plan
Cost-ratio plan
General purchasing department
Management by exception
Materials management
Modified-rebuy buying
Multiple sourcing
New-task buying
Play the odds
Policies and procedures
Purchasing function
Purchasing-sales interchange
Relationship marketing
Straight-rebuy buying
Total cost of buying
Vendor rating systems
Weighted-point plan

REVIEW QUESTIONS

1. What is the role of basic policies and procedures in carrying out purchasing tasks? Of what value are contracts in the purchasing function?
2. Identify each of the steps in the business buying process. How is a buying situation created? Create an example to show your own understanding of how a business-to-business firm goes through the business buying process.
3. Discuss the four basic sources of input that purchasing managers frequently utilize in evaluating vendors with whom they have had no previous experience.
4. Why is the evaluation of vendor performance referred to as an economic function? Identify the major features of the categorical, weighted-point, and cost-ratio plans of vendor evaluation.
5. Describe the typical purchasing professional. In what areas of the purchasing executive's job have the major changes occurred? What is relationship marketing? What role does it play in fostering purchaser-supplier relationships?
6. Identify three methods by which buyers attempt to minimize or avoid risk in selecting suppliers. How can personal and professional goals of organizational buyers create conflict for the marketer?
7. How does the organization of the purchasing department differ in regard to the size of the firm?
8. Discuss the reasons for having either a centralized or decentralized purchasing organization. Which form of organization is more commonly used by purchasing departments?
9. Define the materials management concept. Discuss the reasons why a company would adopt a materials management approach. Identify and explain two alternative approaches to materials management.
10. Identify and discuss three types of business buying situations. How are these types of buying situations related to the various stages of the procurement process? Create your own examples of business buying situations that correspond to each of the three types of buying situations.
11. Explain how contracts and the law of agency are applicable to the purchasing-sales interchange.

Cases

CASE 2-1 Morlock Manufacturing Company

Morlock Manufacturing Company is a medium-sized manufacturer of precision measuring instruments. Its product line includes a wide variety of mechanical and digital devices sold to major manufacturers of transportation, electronic, and biomedical equipment. Sales over the past three years have averaged $693 million with a 6 percent growth rate.

Historically, Morlock has maintained a high inventory level of major materials and components in order to meet delivery to primary customers. Recently, in an effort to reduce costs and to remain competitive, Mike Hammer, the materials manager, has been reviewing inventory policy. Initial attention is being given to high-usage, purchased components that comprise the major dollar portion of material inventory. Among these are a switch assembly that is used in over 50 percent of their mechanical and electronic instruments, a servomotor, and a digital display device. Hammer has gathered the following data from the purchasing and sales departments:

Purchased Component	1992 Purchases (units)	Average Unit Cost	End Item Sales (units)
Switch assembly	7,000	$ 7.35	5,750
Servomotor	5,400	37.50	4,353
Digital display	3,900	103.95	3,240

Purchasing records also indicate that lead time for reorders has recently been reduced to approximately twenty days. This is primarily due to emphasis on value analysis, improved vendor relations, and changes made to incoming traffic policy. The ordering cost in 1992 for straight rebuys was $45 per purchase order. Modified rebuys run between 20 percent and 30 percent higher.

The controller has provided information related to materials holding costs:

Materials inventory (average)	$35,000,000
Storage and handling costs	4,375,000
Interest and taxes	1,750,000
Insurance	2,650,000

Once purchased component inventories have been optimized, Hammer plans to shift the emphasis to manufactured components.

DISCUSSION QUESTIONS

1. What role should purchasing play?
2. What other suggestions could be made to reduce inventory costs?
3. What should the company do about safety stock?

Source: Case contributed by Robert J. Mahoney, Adjunct Professor of Marketing, Bryant College, 1994. Used with permission.

CASE 2-2 Manufacturers Hanover Corporation

At Manufacturers Hanover, vice president Arthur Block is responsible for all computer purchases. The sheer volume of computers purchased by Block constitutes opportunities and major problems for the computer distribution channel. Block prefers to deal directly with the manufacturer. Computer manufacturers prefer that customers purchase the product through existing computer dealers. Manufacturers Hanover believes that better prices come from buying directly from the manufacturer. Better product support is obtained when buying from the retail stores. This type of problem requires a closer working relationship between all three parties—manufacturer, retailer, and customer. Large companies often do not need extensive product support for one of two reasons. First, many firms have their own internal computer support capabilities. Second, after having bought several hundred machines, firms do not need support with additional machines.

Block influences not only the choice of vendor but also the actual product purchased. Manufacturers Hanover purchases 80386-based machines almost exclusively. Block prefers products with open architecture (third-party vendors have access to all necessary information to manufacture peripheral devices to connect to these types of computers). For this reason, Block did not consider the new IBM PS2 machines. Block buys Zenith, Wang, and AST computers. IBM courted Block heavily, but the design was only a small problem. IBM sells all of its 80386-based machines with a hard disk drive. Block only buys machines without a hard drive. All of the Manufacturers Hanover machines are connected to a network, and backup and lost data would be big problems if every machine had a hard drive.

Manufacturers Hanover is dependent on software companies offering license agreements to large corporations. License agreements allow large companies to reduce investments in software packages. By buying a site license agreement, companies like Manufacturers Hanover can allow several users in one location to have access to the same software packages. Without license agreements, companies would have to buy one copy of each software package for each individual in the company. The benefit to software developers comes in not having to actively police these large corporations to verify that they are maintaining all the legal requirements associated with using the software packages.

In addition to working closely with several user advisory councils, the company actively participates in several open-exchange forums. Manufacturers Hanover is considered an early adopter of personal computer hardware and software and as such is a coveted account for many computer companies.

DISCUSSION QUESTIONS

1. What role would you consider Arthur Block to play in the purchase-decision process?
2. How important would it be for a company selling computer products to Manufacturers Hanover to get the company to buy a nonstandard machine? What process would they have to go through to make this purchase?

Suggested Reading

Calderbank, Allison. "The Tough User." *Computer Reseller News* (November 12, 1990): 143.

Source: C. Lamb, J. Hair, and C. McDaniel, *Principles of Marketing*, 1st Edition (Cincinnati, OH: South-Western Publishing Company, 1992) p. 133.

Suggested Additional Readings

Anderson, Erin, Wujin Chu, and Barton Weitz. "Industrial Purchasing: An Empirical Exploration of the Buyclass Framework." *Journal of Marketing* 51 (July 1987): 71–86. **Study of the buyclass framework by querying the managers of sales forces about the behavior their salespeople encounter on the part of their industrial customers.**

Bates, Bryan. "Buying-Decision Research: A Case." *Industrial Marketing Digest* (UK), 11 (Third Quarter 1986): 107–116. **Survey of European buyers focusing on supplier characteristics, quality, service, delivery, and price.**

Bilborough, C. A. M., and B. G. Dale. "The Role and Influence of Factory-Level Purchasing Within a Corporate Structure," *International Journal of Physical Distribution and Materials Management* (UK), 15, No. 1 (1985): 39–48. **Case studies and comparisons of corporate purchasing departments and factory purchasing departments.**

Bingham, Frank G., Jr. "When, How, and Why Suppliers Consider Price Moves." *Journal of Purchasing and Materials Management* 25 (Fall 1989): 2–8. **A discussion of the strategic pricing decisions made by business suppliers.**

Carusone, Peter S. "Buying Extractive Products: Criteria and Influences." *Journal of Purchasing and Materials Management* 21 (Winter 1985): 28–36. **Survey of purchasing behavior, decision processes, buying constraints, environmental considerations, and marketing strategy formulation of purchasers of natural resources.**

Celley, Albert F., William H. Clegg, Arthur W. Smith, and Mark A. Vonderembse. "Implementation of JIT in the United States." *Journal of Purchasing and Materials Management* 22 (Winter 1986): 9–15. **Comparative analysis of the just-in-time approach to materials management in Japan and the United States.**

Dale, B. G., and R. H. Powley. "Purchasing Practices in the United Kingdom: A Case Study." *Journal of Purchasing and Materials Management* 21 (Spring 1985): 26–33. **A comparative analysis of U.S. versus British purchasing organization, performance measurement, materials management, and vendor selection.**

Dillon, Thomas F. "Vendor-Rating System Boosts On-Time Delivery." *Purchasing World* 30 (July 1986): 62–64. **Case study of a vendor performance record related to delivery service.**

Farmer, John Haywood, and Michael R. Leenders. "Psychological Need Profile of Purchasers." *Journal of Purchasing and Materials Management* 22 (Winter 1986): 23–29. **Survey of purchases, high-level and low-level needs, negotiations, and purchasing behavior trends among industrial buyers.**

French, Warren A., Jan W. Henkel, John S. Kanet, and John B. Ford IV. "MRO Parts Service in the Machine Tool Industry." *Industrial Marketing Management* 14 (November 1985): 283–288. **MRO parts survey to include postpurchase parts and replacement policies.**

Ghingold, Morry. "Testing the 'Buygrid' Buying Process Model." *Journal of Purchasing and Materials Management* 22 (Winter 1986): 30–36. **Study of decision making in various stages of the industrial buying process.**

Grassell, Milt. "What Purchasing Managers Like in a Salesperson . . . and What Drives Them Up the Wall." *Business Marketing* 71 (June 1986): 72–77. **Survey of purchasing managers as to their perceptions of both positive and negative attributes exhibited by industrial sales representatives.**

Gregory, Robert E. "Source Selection: A Matrix Approach." *Journal of Purchasing and Materials Management* 22 (Summer 1986): 24–29. **Case study of Texas Instruments' approach to supplier evaluation and selection.**

Jackson, Donald W., Jr., Richard K. Burdick, and Janet E. Keith. "Purchasing Agents' Perceived Importance of Marketing Mix Components in Different Industrial Purchase Situations." *Journal of Business Research* 13 (August 1985): 361–373. **Systematic role-playing study of 254 industrial purchasing executives, using five product types and three types of buyclasses.**

Jackson, Ralph W., and William M. Pride. "The Use of Approved Vendor Lists." *Industrial Marketing Management* 15 (August 1986): 165–169. **Vendor analysis and background checks of various-sized firms in five industries.**

Krapfel, Robert E., Jr. "An Advocacy Behavior Model of Organizational Buyers' Vendor Choice." *Journal of Marketing* 49 (October 1985): 51–59. **An experiment using a causal model to explain information diffusion, attributed source credibility, and source factors.**

Kriger, Ruth Haas, and Jack R. Meredith. "Emergency and Routine MRO Parts Buying." *Industrial Marketing Management* 14 (November 1985): 277–282. **Survey of purchasing criteria and sources utilized in MRO parts buying.**

LeBlanc, Ronald P. "Insights into Organizational Buying." *Journal of Business and Industrial Marketing* 2 (Fall 1987): 5–10. **Research suggesting that the decision rules used to select buyers for consideration are independent of the decision rules used to make the final purchase choice.**

Mast, Kenneth E., and John M. Hawes. "Perceptual Differences Between Buyers and Engineers." *Journal of Purchasing and Materials Management* 22 (Spring 1986): 2–6. **A study of how industrial buyers and engineers differ in how they rate the importance of various attributes in the purchasing process.**

McWilliams, Robert D., Earl Naumann, and Stan Scott. "Determining Buying Center Size." *Industrial Marketing Management* 21 (February 1992): 43–49. **A study of organizational buying behavior to include an assessment of various purchase situations and phases.**

Meredith, Lindsay. "Developing and Using a Customer Profile Data Bank." *Industrial Marketing Management* 14 (November 1985): 255–268. **Discussion of the decision-making task, daily sales decisions, buyer mix analysis, and on-line information systems.**

Moller, K. E. Kristian. "Research Strategies in Analyzing the Organizational Buying Process." *Journal of Business Research* 13 (February 1985): 3–15. **Review and integration of strategic approaches to analyzing the organizational buying process to include decision system analysis, role analysis, information processing analysis, multiattribute choice paradigms, and social influence theory.**

Monczka, Robert M., Ernest L. Nichols, Jr., and Thomas J. Callahan. "Value of Supplier Information in the Decision Process." *International Journal of Purchasing and Materials Management* 28 (Spring 1992): 20–30. **A comparison of purchasing behavior according to type of purchase, size of purchasing firm, and company position of purchaser.**

"MRO Buyers Are Getting Better, Tougher." *Purchasing World* 30 (November 1986): 53–54. **Analysis of trends in the purchasing of maintenance, repair, and operating supplies, with a look at systems contracting and the role of the industrial distributor.**

Narasimihan, Ram, and Linda K. Stoynoff. "Optimizing Aggregate Procurement Allocation Decisions." *Journal of Purchasing and Materials Management* 22 (Spring 1986): 23–30. **Model development and applications using mixed-integer programming.**

Perdue, Barbara C. "Material Cost Sensitivity: Some Consequences and Antecedents." *International Journal of Purchasing and Materials Management* 28 (Summer 1992): 26–32. **A survey of purchasing managers as to the impact and implications of material costs.**

Quigley, Charles, and Charles McNamara. "Evaluating Product Quality: An Application of the Taguchi Quality Loss Concept." *International Journal of Purchasing and Materials Management* 28 (Summer 1992): 19–25. **A discussion of supplier selection issues is included.**

Schroeder, Gary D., Gary D. Scudder, and Michael J. Pesch. "Approaches to Managing the Cost of Materials." *International Journal of Physical Distribution and Materials Management* (UK), 16, No. 3 (1986): 57–69. **Guidelines and case studies for purchasing and supplier relations as they relate to materials management.**

Shealy, Robert. "The Purchasing Job in Different Types of Businesses." *Journal of Purchasing and Materials Management* 21 (Winter 1985): 17–20. **Survey of job task similarities among industrial buyers in various types of manufacturing concerns and service specialties.**

Smith, David, and Rob Taylor. "Organisational Decision-Making and Industrial Marketing." *European Journal of Marketing* (UK), 19, No. 7 (1985): 56–71. **Guidelines for, and discussion of, strategic decision-making in organizational buying behavior.**

Wilson, David T., J. David Lichtenthal, and Arno J. Rethans. "Grounded Theory in Organizational Buying Behavior: Back to the Past." *Proceedings*, Consumer Psychology, Division 23, Joel G. Saegert (ed.), Washington, D.C. (1986): 13–16.

ENDNOTES

[1]Paul V. Farrell and George W. Aljian, *Aljian's Purchasing Handbook,* 4th ed. (Mc-Graw-Hill, 1982), 3–21.

[2]*Ibid.,* 3–22.

[3]The General Electric example is taken from Eric N. Berkowitz, Roger A. Kerin, and William Rudelius, *Marketing,* 2d ed. (Homewood, Ill: Richard D. Irwin, 1989), 128–129.

[4]Richard Germain and Cornelia Droge, "Wholesale Operations and Vendor Evaluation," *Journal of Business Research* 21 (September 1990): 119–129.

[5]Louis J. DeRose, "How Industrial Markets Buy Value Selling: A Strategy for Dealing with Changes," *Journal of Business and Industrial Marketing* 7 (Winter 1992): 65–69.

[6]S. Joe Puri, "Industrial Vendors' Selling Center: Implications for Sales Management," *Journal of Business and Industrial Marketing* 7 (Summer 1992).

[7]Robert M. Monczka and Steven J. Trecha, "Cost-Based Supplier Performance Evaluation," *Journal of Purchasing and Materials Management* (Spring 1988): 2–7.

[8]David Bonneville, "Vendor Analyzers Pack a Punch in Negotiations," *Purchasing World* 27 (March 1983): 32–34.

[9]Stuart F. Heinritz, Paul V. Farrell, and Clifton L. Smith, *Purchasing: Principles and Applications,* 7th ed. (Englewood Cliffs, N.J.: Prentice-Hall, 1986), 103.

[10]The following discussion is based on Farrell and Aljian, *Aljian's Purchasing Handbook,* 6–24 – 6–28, 1982; also based on National Association of Purchasing Management, *Guide to Purchasing,* 1.6.10–1.6.18.

[11]E. Timmerman, "An Approach to Vendor Performance Evaluation," *Journal of Purchasing and Materials Management* (Winter 1986): 2–8.

[12]Simon Knox and Tim Denison, "Purchasing Behavior in Local Government in the United Kingdom," *European Journal of Marketing* (UK) 23 (1989): 31–42.

[13]Kate Bertrand, "Crafting 'Win-Win' Situations in Buyer-Supplier Relationships," *Business Marketing* (June 1986).

[14]Peter M. Banting and Paul A. Dion, "The Purchasing Agent: Friend or Foe to the Salesperson?" *Journal of the Academy of Marketing Science* (Fall 1988): 16–22.

[15]Joseph L. Cavinato, "Identifying Interfirm Total Cost Advantages for Supply Chain Competitiveness," *International Journal of Purchasing and Materials Management* (Fall 1991): 10–15.

[16]Lisa M. Ellram, "The Role of Purchasing in Cost Savings Analysis," *International Journal of Purchasing and Materials Management* 28 (Winter 1992): 26–33.

[17]For a related discussion, see Frank G. Bingham Jr. and Paul A. Dion, "Are Buyers Misled by Their Perceptions of Salespeople: An Empirical Investigation," *Journal of Marketing Management* (Winter 1991): 43–50.

[18]Robert F. Dwyer, Paul H. Schurr, and Sejo Oh, "Developing Buyer-Seller Relationships," *Journal of Marketing* (April 1987): 11–27.

[19]"Computer Shock Hits the Office," *Business Week,* (8 August 1983), 46.

[20]Robert R. Reeder, Edward G. Brierty, and Betty H. Reeder, *Industrial Marketing: Analysis, Planning, and Control* (Englewood Cliffs, N.J.: Prentice-Hall, 1987), 113. See also T. W. Sweeney, H. L. Mathews, and David T. Wilson, "An Analysis of Industrial Buyers' Risk-Reducing Behavior," *Proceedings of the American Marketing Association* (Chicago: American Marketing Association, 1973), 217–221; and David T. Wilson, "Industrial Buyers' Decision-Making Styles," *Journal of Marketing Research* 8 (November 1971): 433–436.

[21]"Loctite: Ready to Fend Off a Flock of New Competitors," *Business Week*, (19 June 1978), 116, 118.

[22]Thomas V. Bonoma, "Major Sales: Who Really Does the Buying?" *Harvard Business Review* (May/June 1982): 116.

[23]David W. Cravens, Gerald E. Hills, and Robert B. Woodruff, *Marketing Management* (Homewood, Ill.: Richard D. Irwin, 1987), 160–161.

[24]Heinritz, Farrell, and Smith, *Purchasing: Principles and Applications*, 71–86.

[25]*Ibid.*, 74.

[26]*Ibid.*, 2.

[27]"The Hollow Corporation," *Business Week* (March 1986).

[28]*Ibid.*

[29]Gary L. Frazier, Robert E. Spekman, and Charles R. O'Neal, "Just-in-Time Exchange Relationships in Industrial Markets," *Journal of Marketing* 52 (October 1988): 52–67.

[30]James R. Freeland, "A Survey of Just-in-Time Pruchasing Practices in the U.S.," *Production and Inventory Management Control* 32 (Second Quarter 1991): 43–50.

[31]Charles R. O'Neal, "JIT Procurement and Relationship Marketing," *Industrial Marketing Management* 18 (February 1989): 55–63.

[32]Charles R. O'Neal, "The Buyer-Seller Linkage in a Just-in-Time Environment," *Journal of Purchasing and Materials Management* (Spring 1987): 7–13.

[33]Edward Allen Duplaya, "The JIT Purchaser and Non-JIT Supplier," *NAPM Insights* (October 1991): 8.

[34]Hall, Robert W. with APICS, *Zero Inventories* (Homewood, Ill.: Dow Jones-Irwin, 1983).

[35]Richard J. Schonberger, *Japanese Manufacturing Techniques—Nine Hidden Lessons in Simplicity* (New York: Free Press, 1983).

[36]Craig Waters, "Why Everybody's Talking About 'Just-in-Time'", *Inc.* (March 1984): 77–90. See also Doug Harper, "Zero Inventory Poses Questions for Distributors," *Industrial Distribution* (January 1985): 49; and Summar Aggarwal, "MRP, JIT, OPT, FMS?" *Harvard Business Review* (September-October 1985): 8–16.

[37]G. H. Manoochehri, "Improving Productivity with the Just-in-Time System," *Journal of Systems Management* (January 1985): 23–26.

[38]Lewis Schneider, "New Era in Transportation Strategy," *Harvard Business Review* (March-April 1985): 124.

[39]For a more detailed discussion of the JIT concept, see Chan K. Hahn, Peter A. Pinto, and Daniel J. Bragg, "Just-in-Time Production and Purchasing," *Journal of Purchasing and Materials Management* (Fall 1983): 2–10; and Richard J. Schonberger and Abdolhossein Ansari, "Just-in-Time Purchasing Can Improve Quality," *Journal of Purchasing and Materials Management* (Spring 1984): 2–7.

[40]Larry C. Guinipero and Charles R. O'Neal, "Obstacles to JIT Procurement," *Industrial Marketing Management* 17 (February 1988): 35–41.

[41]Larry C. Giunipero and Edward F. Keiser, "JIT Purchasing in a Non-Manufacturing Environment: A Case Study," *Journal of Purchasing and Materials Management* 23 (Winter 1987): 19–25.

[42]Heinritz, Farrell, and Smith, *Purchasing Principles and Applications*, 90.

[43]Joseph A. Bellizzi and Phillip McVey, "How Valid Is the Buy-Grid Model?" *Industrial Marketing Management* 12 (1983): 57–62.

[44]Patrick J. Robinson, Charles W. Faris, and Yoram Wind, *Industrial Buying and Creative Marketing*, Marketing Science Institute Series (Boston: Allyn and Bacon, 1967).

[45]Earl Naumann, Douglas J. Lincoln, and Robert D. McWilliams, "The Purchase of Components: Functional Areas of Influence," *Industrial Marketing Management* 13 (1984): 113–122.

[46]The Central General example is from Peter D. Bennett, *Marketing* (New York: McGraw-Hill, 1988): 138–139.

[47]*Ibid.*, 139.

[48]*Ibid.*

[49]*Legal Side of Purchasing* (Waterford, Conn.: Bureau of Business Practices, 1983), 1.

[50]*Ibid.*

3 Management of the Business Buying Function

Learning Objectives

After reading this chapter, you should be able to:

- Articulate the objectives of efficient business buying.
- Realize the role and significance of the buying center.
- Understand the relationship among quality, service, and price.
- Appreciate the importance of value analysis in business buying.
- Explain the relevance of the make-or-buy decision for the business firm.
- Distinguish among the tools and techniques used in handling the small order.
- Comprehend that there are distinct types of environmental forces that influence business buying decisions.
- Discuss purchasing's impact on company profits.

Chapter Outline

Learning Objectives

Objectives of Efficient Business Buying
- Objectives of Business Buyers
- Seven Rights of Business Buyers
- Purchasing Costs

The Buying Center

Quality in Business Buying and Selling
- Responsibilities of the Purchasing Department

Service in Business Buying and Selling
- Differentiation through Service
- Service as a Competitive Effort

Price in Business Buying and Selling
- Perceived Value

Value Analysis
- Development of Value Engineering
- Appropriate Tests Used

Make-or-Buy Analysis
- Ascertaining Profitability
- Reasons to Manufacture
- Participants in Make or Buy

Negotiation
- Analyzing Both Buyer and Seller Strengths

The Small-Order Problem
- The Centralized-Stores System
- The Petty-Cash System
- The Blanket-Order System
- The Electronic-Ordering System

Environmental Forces and Buying Decisions
- The Economic Environment
- The Physical Environment
- The Competitive Environment
- The Technological Environment
- The Legal-Political Environment
- The Ethical Environment

Purchasing's Impact upon Company Profits

Summary

Key Terms

Review Questions

Cases
- Case 3-1
- Case 3-2

Suggested Additional Readings

Endnotes

OBJECTIVES OF EFFICIENT BUSINESS BUYING

Objectives of Business Buyers

Business buyers have several distinct objectives in purchasing goods and services. In general, business buying objectives such as product and service availability, reliability of sellers, and consistency of quality, delivery, and price are important for all types of firms. However, different types of organizational buyers, such as manufacturers, wholesalers and retailers, government customers, and not-for-profit institutions, emphasize one or more of these objectives.

Throughout the years, much thought, attention, and research have been focused on American business organizations with the purpose of finding better ways, methods, and techniques of performing the tasks and developing the relationships that are so essential to the realization of the full potential of a dynamic, industrial world civilization. The materials acquisition-retention cycle in the overall purchasing process is undergoing rapid change as the business buying process has become a time-consuming and highly involved process. Business buying has evolved into a complex process of decision making and communication, which takes place over time, involves several organizational members, and includes relationships with other firms and institutions. No longer is business buying the simple act of placing an order with a vendor or a selling organization.

Seven Rights of Business Buyers

Most purchasing and materials management textbooks provide a list of *seven rights* that purchasing personnel would use in their standard statements as to their overall objectives in meeting organizational commitments. They would say that their primary objective is to purchase the *right materials* in the *right quantity*, for delivery at the *right time* and in the *right place*, from the *right source* with the *right service* and at the *right price*. Fulfilling this objective can be a difficult task for both the business buyer and the seller. This is because it is not efficient to buy at the right price if the purchased parts or materials are unsatisfactory from a quality or service standpoint, or if a late arrival creates a production-line shutdown. Furthermore, the right price might be a higher price than is normal for an emergency requirement, whereby the buyer cannot adhere to a normal delivery schedule. The more rational business buyer must attempt to balance out sometimes conflicting objectives and to make trade-offs to obtain the optimum mix of these seven rights. Conflicting objectives can cause major problems for the seller, especially with regard to delivery and service.

Purchasing Costs

Purchasing costs are the largest single element in the operation of many organizations. The magnitude of this job becomes apparent as managers learn of the importance of the cost of purchased goods and materials versus the sales dollar. In general, the ratio ranges between 40 percent and 60 percent of sales revenue (up to a reported 80 percent for Xerox copiers and Chrysler automobiles) and is generally the largest single component of expenditures in industry.[1] Thus, the decisions made by purchasing directly impact upon the costs and profitability of the firm. The purchasing function also expects to play a greater role in cost reduction projects of all types in the future.[2] Moreover, if the trend toward automation continues in industry at its present pace, it is conceivable that future expenditures for materials and equipment will represent an even larger portion of a company's sales income than is now the case.

THE BUYING CENTER

People within the business buying organization who are involved in the buying process are members of what is called a *buying center*. A key to success in business markets is understanding customer buying behavior. Such understanding is difficult to achieve, however, because the organizational buying process is often dynamic and complicated.[3] It is rare for one person in any particular organization to be solely responsible for the buying decision. Understanding the dynamics of interpersonal influence that drive the buying process may play a key role in the successful formation of business marketing strategies. In executing a strategy, if a seller does not identify and communicate with key influencers, the sale may be lost, despite technical superiority and competitive pricing. Yet, the identity of influencers is not always readily obvious, and the activities through which they exert influence are not well known.[4] Business vendors must determine who participates in an organizational purchase decision and what their influence is.[5] Usually several people are referred to as members of "the buying center," or the decision-making unit. The astute business marketer must determine the appropriate influences for a particular situation, a task that is not always quick and easy. Also, several people usually play the same role (several influencers in a purchase decision, for example), and one particular person may play two or more roles (decider and buyer, for example).

The size of a buying center varies with the complexity and importance of a purchase decision; and the composition of the buying group will usually change from one purchase to another, or even during various stages of the buying process. Both purchase situation and purchase phase are significantly related to buying center size.[6] Members of a buying center have various roles in the buying process, as shown in Exhibit 3-1.

EXHIBIT 3-1 **Roles of Buying Center Members in the Business Purchasing Process**

Role	Description
Users	Those who will use the product in question. Their influence on the purchasing decision can range from minimal to major. In some cases users begin the purchase process and even develop product specifications.
Gatekeepers	Those who keep a tight control on the flow of information to other members of the buying center. Can open the gate to members of the buying center for some salespeople, yet close it for others.
Influencers	Those who provide information to buying center members for evaluating alternative products or who set purchasing specifications. Normally, influencers operate within the buying center, such as quality control or research and development personnel. Yet, at other times influencers operate outside the buying center, such as architects who create very specific building requirements.
Deciders	Those who, in reality, make the buying decision, regardless of whether or not they hold the formal authority. A decider is often quite difficult to identify since deciders can be a company president, a purchasing director, or a research and development analyst.
Buyers	Those who are assigned the formal authority to select vendors and complete the purchasing transaction. Sometimes, the prerogative of the buyer is taken by other more powerful members of the buying center. Often a purchasing manager who carries out the clerical duties of the purchase order acts in the role of the buyer.

Business marketers have the critical task of determining who is involved and the specific role played by each buying center participant. On recognizing this, the marketers can tailor a sales presentation in terms of language, tone, and time to the appropriate role that the particular individual plays at an appropriate step in the business buying process. Marketers usually find that while most contacts are with purchasing department personnel, the buying center participants having the greatest influence are often not in the purchasing department at all. For example, Loctite Corporation, the manufacturer of Super-Glue and an industrial leader in adhesives and sealants, found that engineers were the most important buying influences in the products they were trying to market. As a result, Loctite focused its marketing efforts on production and maintenance engineers.[7] Table 3-1 illustrates some examples of typical buying influences and shows how they may affect buying decisions and marketing strategy. Note the implied influence of the production manager, the controller, the engineer, and the plant manager. These individuals will certainly affect the buying decision and are even regarded as "influencers." They may have the final say as to what is bought, especially if they are the "user." Also, the impact that the outcomes from one buying decision

TABLE 3-1 **Examples of Buying Influences and How They May Affect Business Purchasing Decisions and Marketing Strategy**

Buying Influence	Effects on Buying	Appropriate Marketing Strategy
Purchasing agent, buyer	Handles requisitions from the plant, maintains personal library of supplier's catalogs, does some discretionary purchasing, especially when delivery is critical. Usually honors sources recommended by key plant personnel.	See them regularly. Keep them informed if you see others in the plant. Keep them supplied with new product and price information. Offer them a benefit on every call. Allow them to pave the way to other buying influences in the plant.
Production manager, general foreman	Usually confined to specific production operations such as assembly, finishing. Can describe specific problems in detail.	Sell brand superiority, depth of your inventory, delivery, and your potential for contributing to productivity of production people and equipment. Leave catalog, put on general mailing list. Call only when you have real constructive offering.
Plant controller, head bookkeeper	With purchasing department, interested in terms of sale or systems contract.	Be fully prepared with terms stated simply. Come armed with benefits offered over and above those of others.
Director or vice president of engineering	Concerned with product or process improvements. Generally involved with future changes, seldom with immediate needs. Searches continually for new, improved products. Relies heavily on library of suppliers. Also relies heavily on technical aid from vendors. Strong influence on OEM and MRO product type and brand selection.	Responds favorably to outside help in the form of new, potentially useful data and technical counsel. Offer your complete catalog. Offer technical capabilities via your own experts. Personally introduce new, improved products regularly. Put on your general mailing list and keep supplied with your latest complete catalog.
Plant manager, general manager, vice president of operations, vice president of manufacturing	Key buying influence on larger plant expenditures. May direct vendors to key personnel and problem areas in the plants.	Receptive to constructive information. Often easier to reach than floor personnel. Contact periodically if possible with your management, to demonstrate your interest in serving, to sell your firm's capabilities, and to probe prospect's problems and plans. Keep informed on important product breakthroughs.

Source: "Finding the Real Buying Influence," *Industrial Distribution* 67 (June 1977), pp. 36, 37, 39.

have on subsequent decisions has been underemphasized.[8] Sellers should not overlook their importance in the buying decision process.

The buying center membership and the relative importance of different members vary from company to company. In engineering-dominated firms like Texas Instruments or General Dynamics, where ever-present technical innovation typically shortens the product life cycle, the buying center may consist almost entirely of engineers. In more marketing-oriented firms such as General Foods or IBM, marketing and engineering have almost equal authority. In a small manufacturing company, the buying center may consist of several individuals with very different backgrounds and demands. Members may consist of everyone from the CEO to a particular production worker, each having a say as to what is purchased in a particular situation. This complicates the task for business marketers, because many varied personalities and interests may have to be dealt with in a particular selling situation. Table 3-2 lists a number of different manufacturers involved in a variety of purchase situations and reveals who the true decision makers are.

CONCEPT QUESTIONS

1. What are the largest costs in the operations of many organizations?
2. What determines the size of the buying center?
3. What is the critical task for a marketer in regard to dealing with buying centers?

QUALITY IN BUSINESS BUYING AND SELLING

In the organizational or business buying environment, value is associated with suitability and overall cost, not price. The ideal quality level purchased is that which can be bought at the lowest total cost to fulfill the need or to satisfy the intended function for which the raw materials, parts, or subassemblies are being acquired. This distinction must be understood by the business seller, as the words *total cost* are being used here instead of the word *price*. Price implies spending a single dollar amount as opposed to the total costs associated with a particular purchase. Transportation cost, set-up cost, training, storage, and a variety of other potential incremental costs must be taken into account when buying quality. The potential seller's input regarding the quality required is often taken as valuable input (as perhaps it should be) by members of the buying center. Quality as a management issue cannot be viewed simply as another in a long line of fashionable management fads or quick fixes. The reality is that quality has become an important issue in the operation and strategies of many commercial organizations.[9]

TABLE 3-2 **Decision Makers in Selected Buying Centers**

Company	Capital Equipment	Decision Maker	Business Services	Decision Maker
Chemical manufacturer	Heat exchanger	Purchasing manager	Construction contract labor	Purchasing manager
Business safety products manufacturer	Automatic drilling machine	Engineer vice president of manufacturing	Plant janitorial service	Purchasing manager
Steel manufacturer	Coke oven	Purchasing manager	Maintenance repair contract	Buyer
Machine tooling company	Vertical boring mill	Vice president of operations	Fabricating work	Purchasing manager
Metal and wire manufacturer	Wrapping machine	Division manager	Machinery rigging for shipping	Traffic manager
Aerospace and automotive products manufacturer	Metalworking machine tool	Divisional purchasing manager	Technical consultant	Director of purchasing
Paper products manufacturer	Banding system	General manager	Vending machine service	Personnel manager
Petroleum products manufacturer	Gasoline storage tank	Buyer	Printing of advertising materials	Vice president of marketing
Mining equipment manufacturer	Executive office desk	Purchasing agent	Training for first-line supervisors	General manager
Engineering and construction company	Cooling vessel	Job supervisor	Tar sludge removal	Buyer Purchasing manager Divisional vice president
Home products manufacturer	Mixing machines	Buyer engineer	Drapery cleaning	Service manager
Building materials manufacturer	Pump	Engineer	Engineering services	Executive vice president

Source: Wesley Johnston and Thomas Bonoma, "The Buying Center: Structure and Interaction Patterns," *Journal of Marketing*, Summer 1981 (Chicago: American Marketing Association), pp. 150–151. Used with permission.

The final quality level purchased will depend to a large extent on the member of the buying center who has the final responsibility for the workability of the purchased component, installation, or service. Quality really has no meaning within the spectrum of business purchasing except as it is related to function and ultimate cost. If unnecessary quality is purchased, competitive pressure will force the unneeded quality out. Too much quality will lead to higher prices, which may ultimately cost the buying firm market share. Higher quality levels than what are actually needed increase cost unnecessarily. Only after the quality level that is needed is determined and agreed upon, should price be considered. Quality, therefore, is an important ingredient in price setting.[10]

Members of the buying center need to address the issue of quality regardless of where the quality specifications originate. Purchasing personnel must challenge what they perceive as being unnecessarily high quality levels. Buyers must work closely with external marketing personnel to help in their determination of what constitutes acceptable quality levels. For salespeople, quality has two linked facets: (1) It offers a way to examine the actual process of selling to determine what works and what does not work. (2) It can be a common language through which salespeople build stronger relationships with customers. Quality needs to become a total organizational response to building competitive advantage, and the sales force can help quality to focus on customer requirements.[11] Buyers have the right to question any requests for nonstandard, higher-priced, hard-to-get items or materials. A buyer must understand the basic concepts that underlie quality control. Without this knowledge, he or she cannot make informed determinations on quality issues.[12] Price is only one element of the total cost, as incremental costs must also be considered.

Responsibilities of the Purchasing Department

Whether or not the purchasing department has the responsibility of originating or coordinating the quality specifications, purchasing personnel are accountable for ensuring that proper quality specifications are part of the purchase contract. Within this framework, the purchasing department must accomplish the following:[13]

(1) Know what is wanted and pass this information on to the bidders and to the vendors. Buyers who demand more, get more.

(2) See that the seller performs according to the purchase quality specifications.

(3) Take the necessary steps to protect the buyer's company against financial loss resulting from materials or parts that do not meet the purchase specifications.

(4) Utilize suggestions from respected vendors in purchasing desirable product quality and reliability.

To accomplish the above tasks, the buyers, on occasion, will have to enlist the assistance of others, both inside and outside their respective companies, and to develop and make the purchase quality specifications workable. The final quality purchased is a measure of the degree to which the product meets the requirements of the purchaser, the distributor, and the ultimate consumer of the end product.

Let's take as an example Motorola, which is tackling a new challenge. It is taking the techniques used for increasing quality in manufacturing and ensuring quality to the supplier and extending these techniques to the way it buys corporate services. Motorola purchasing executives recently completed a quality symposium for travel suppliers—car rental and travel agencies, hotels and motels—in the first step toward an overhaul of travel buying and, eventually, the way the corporation buys other services. The seminar focused on issues that would create quality awareness. The idea stemmed from the trend in manufacturing to rationalize the supplier base, linking suppliers to manufacturers in cooperative partnerships for mutual benefit.[14]

SERVICE IN BUSINESS BUYING AND SELLING

The purchaser's desire for excellent service is a strong buying motive that can determine buying patterns. The term "service" is used here as an attribute, not as a product. (Services, as a product, will be discussed in detail in Chapter 13.) Service is measured by a vendor's ability to comply with promised delivery dates, specifications, and technical assistance. Service encompasses many tangible and intangible activities, such as an assurance of supply, technical help when needed, financial assistance, and inventory holding. Such service is required by business, government, and other institutions. A recent survey of purchasing managers revealed that buying services is considered a great deal more difficult than buying commodities.[15]

Differentiation through Service

The service-buying taxonomy, however, does not differentiate between purchased service per se and pre and postpurchase service, which is typically part of a product purchase. Service can and should be an important means of differentiation for the marketer. One study indicates that firms with a perceived service edge over their competitors can charge 10 percent more for their products.[16] Consequently, many sellers emphasize their service as much as their products. Often, a firm's only attraction to potential buyers is its service, because the product being purchased is felt by the buyer to be so standardized that it can be purchased from any number of companies. The marketer who provides such pre and postservice as technical assistance, reliable delivery, and a quick supply of replacement parts will have an edge over competing suppliers. Buyers who rely on the technical advice and assistance of marketers in solving their materials-use problems make it very difficult for competitors to disrupt such a relationship. The availability of replacement parts for machinery and equipment is extremely important, with speed being a vital component in the provision of this service. Sandia National Laboratories of Albuquerque, New Mexico, defines improved service level as "customers receiving frequent and timely deliveries of both stock and nonstock items, simplified ordering and receiving procedures, better product quality, immediate technical assistance, and quicker resolution of problems."[17]

Suppliers to organizational or business buyers must also place heavy emphasis on reliability of delivery. Purchasing directors, who normally receive the blame for late deliveries of materials purchased, will favor the source that always delivers as promised. Late delivery is by far buyers' biggest complaint about vendor performance. Fifty-seven percent of respondents in a 1987 poll by *Purchasing* magazine stated that delivery was their biggest gripe with vendors.[18] Respondents further reported that suppliers fail to notify them when a scheduled delivery will not be on time. Central Maintenance and Welding of Lithia, Florida, has found that the quality of service provided to the company has been deteriorating over the past three years. Reasons cited by purchasing executives have included problems in timely delivery, vendor quotes, inventory availability, long lead times, reduction in vendor work force, and ignored telephone calls.[19]

Also, marketing strategy must be adapted to variations in buyer perceptions of problems in selection, introduction, and performance. For example, a marketer of computers to buyers who have experienced major problems in the design of information processing systems and in training personnel to use the equipment should place heavy emphasis on offering technical service in system design and on providing training in the operation and maintenance of the equipment. At the same time, a manufacturer of dry-copying machines, which provide essentially no procedural problems in adoption and introduction to employees but which may provide major performance problems, would require a different strategy. For these machines, emphasis would be placed upon product reliability, the provision of technical servicing, and flexibility in adjusting to buyer needs. Therefore, the supplier will relate the product to a prospective application and reduce the problems that the customer is likely to encounter in adopting the product.

Service as a Competitive Effort

At times, the selling firm will even consider shifting its competitive effort to the area of service as opposed to price. This more subtle, indirect price competition is tantamount to direct competition. Prices, in effect, are reduced by the seller, who agrees to perform such additional service as holding the customer's inventory, extending the time of payments, or absorbing freight charges. The amount of service that a buying firm is able to obtain, and that a selling firm is able to provide, usually correlates directly with the skills and perceptions of the buying and selling personnel. The marketer with the strongest service capabilities will certainly be in a favorable position, all other things being equal. It must be recognized, however, that service can be easily copied, but excellent service cannot!

PRICE IN BUSINESS BUYING AND SELLING

Professional buying personnel seldom rely on a quoted purchase price in making buying decisions. They are concerned with the *total cost of the purchasing decision,* which takes into account a variety of factors, such as the amount of scrap or waste resulting from the use of the material, the cost of processing the material, the power consumed, the loss or damage liability, and a host of other variables that generate or minimize costs. For example, the price of a particular type of paint might be low but it may also be costly to apply. Additionally, the coal with low cost per ton might be high in volatile material, ash, or fusible elements and low in BTUs. Steel is cheaper than aluminum; yet, in many areas of the nation, particularly where rough terrain predominates, utility companies erect more aluminum high-voltage transmission towers than steel ones. The aluminum tower is not only cheaper to erect but, being impervious to most types of weather, is cheaper to maintain.

The buying center attempts to negotiate with preferred suppliers for better prices and terms before making the final selection. Innovative methods can be used to counter intense price competition. Consider the following example:[20] Lincoln Electric has instituted the "Guaranteed Cost Reduction Program" for its distributors. Under the program, whenever a customer requests a company to lower prices on Lincoln's equipment to match Lincoln's competitors, the company and the particular distributor guarantee that during the coming year they will find cost reductions in the customer's plant that meet or exceed the price difference between Lincoln's products and the competition's. Lincoln's sales representative and the distributor then get together and, after surveying the customer's operations, identify and help to implement possible cost reductions. If an independent audit at the end of the year does not reveal the promised cost reductions, Lincoln Electric and the distributor make good the difference, with Lincoln paying 70 percent and the distributor the rest.

Perceived Value

As noted earlier, purchasing personnel place a great deal of importance on the nonprice factors, such as the quality of the product relative to their specific needs and the availability of accompanying services, such as installation, repair, and maintenance services. Product quality and service availability come before price considerations, with quality and service levels determining price.[21] Potential supplier price quotations are not the simple matching process assumed in economic theory. Quoting a price generally results from a more complicated process, employing many factors that are often hidden from the marketer who does not always make a persistent investigative effort to uncover them. Marketers who investigate a variety of price-related issues before making price quotations are basing their prices on their respective product's *perceived value.*[22] These companies see the buyer's perception of value, not the seller's cost, as the key to pricing. They use the nonprice variables in the marketing mix to build up perceived value in the buyers' minds. Price is then set to capture the perceived value. Exhibit 3-2 describes how Caterpillar uses perceived value to set prices on its construction equipment. Only after the quality required to perform the function is determined does the buyer become concerned with price. The objective here is not to minimize the importance of price in the buying decision, but rather to call attention to the many other variables vital to the determination of the ultimate cost of the good or service purchased.

VALUE ANALYSIS

Value analysis, developed by General Electric in the late 1940s, is the task of studying a product and all of its components in order to determine ways of producing it at a lower cost, to improve quality, or with a material in greater or more stable supply. It is a creative task, analyzing the purpose or function an item is supposed to fulfill. The concept of value analysis can play an integral part in enhancing efficiency and profitability.[23] Value analysis, then, can be thought of as a scientifically organized method for reducing costs of manufactured items and for encouraging vendor cooperation in lowering costs of purchased items. Its ultimate purpose is to secure improved performance of components at less cost. It requires a team approach. It cannot be implemented by designers without input from production, purchasing, and marketing. It also requires active supplier participation.[24]

EXHIBIT 3-2 How Caterpillar Uses Perceived-Value Pricing

Caterpillar uses perceived value to set prices on its construction equipment. It might price a tractor at $24,000, although a similar competitor's tractor might be priced at $20,000. However, Caterpillar will get more sales than the competitor! When a prospective customer asks a Caterpillar dealer why he should pay $4,000 more for the Caterpillar tractor, the dealer answers:

$20,000	is the tractor's price.
$ 3,000	is the price premium for superior durability.
$ 2,000	is the price premium for superior reliability.
$ 2,000	is the price premium for superior service.
$ 1,000	is the price for longer warranty on parts.
$28,000	is the price to cover the value package.
$ 4,000	discount.
$24,000	final price.

The stunned customer learns that although he is being asked to pay a $4,000 premium for the Caterpillar tractor, he is in fact getting a $4,000 discount. He ends up choosing the Caterpillar tractor because he is convinced that the lifetime operating costs of the Caterpillar tractor will be lower.

Development of Value Engineering

Originally, value analysis was intended to apply primarily to parts already in production. It soon became obvious, however, that the study of a function could begin early in the design stages of a part or a product. Gradually, the scope of value analysis was expanded and refined to include preproduction functional analysis, which, in turn, became known as *value engineering*. Thus, "value analysis" and "value engineering" are considered to be interchangeable terms and are so used in this text.

A value-analysis program represents an effort to integrate the commercial skills of purchasing personnel with the technical skills of engineering and production personnel. Value analysis is appropriate when new technology develops, such as a new material, adhesive coating, or chemical. The result should be significant quality improvements, a new marketing appeal, reduced costs, or just keeping the product on par with competitive products.

Several years ago, Wang Laboratories set out to find and implement superior protective packaging that would also be cost- and labor-efficient. At the same time, Sealed Air Corporation was in the process of developing an innovative protective packaging system and sought a company to field-test the system in a high-volume packaging environment. Working in concert with Wang, Sealed Air was able to fine-tune its new system's performance based on feedback from Wang. The result was the automated Instapak Foam 'N Fill system. According to Phil Hashway, director of distribution for field operations at Wang, previous packaging methods just did not measure up. "Our goal was to come up with a better method of packaging, and Sealed Air came in and worked with us to help meet our packaging requirements. Productivity has increased 20 percent, and we have realized a 20 percent material cost savings because the automated system dispenses the Instapak chemicals in a premeasured amount."[25] This is a good example of vendor participation in a value-analysis effort.

Quality problems during production, or with the final product, can also lead to value analysis. Similarly, problems with the product in the field that result in customer dissatisfaction might give rise to complete product value analysis, rather than the analysis of only one particular part or component of the product.

Value analysis is also useful when the product reaches the latter part of the "market growth stage" or the early part of the "market maturity stage" of the "product life cycle." During either or both of these stages, design improvements in the basic product are often worthwhile, with value analysis being triggered by a cost squeeze experienced as a result of a flattening sales curve or of price competition.

Appropriate Tests Used

Value analysts apply a series of tests, indicated as questions to be asked, to a part, material, product, or service, to determine whether maximum value is being obtained for each dollar spent. These test questions are listed as part of Exhibit 3-3, which details the *value analysis approach* in a comparison of function to cost.

People resist change, and often a value-analysis effort will run head-on into the natural tendency of individuals to resist changes. Value analysis should be looked upon as an aid to the buyer in that it is a technique or tool that will allow the buyer to do a better job, to spend money more intelligently, and to be more creative. Marketing personnel, not only in the buyer's own organization but also those who work for present or potential suppliers, must become involved if value analysis is to be an orderly method of attacking problems that have already occurred, or that could occur in the future. Value analysis is not cost or price oriented; it is function oriented, with involved people trying to determine the best way of doing a job at the lowest possible cost. Sellers, due in large part to their

EXHIBIT 3-3 The Value-Analysis Approach: Comparison of Function to Cost

I. Select a relatively high-cost or high-volume purchased item to value analyze. This can be a part, material, or service. Select an item you suspect is costing more than it should.

II. Find out completely how the item is used and what is expected of it—its function.

III. Ask the following questions:

a. Does its use contribute value?
b. Is it cost-proportionate to usefulness?
c. Does it need all its features?
d. Is there anything better, at a more favorable purchase price, for the intended use?
e. Can the item be eliminated?
f. If the item is not standard, can a standard item be used?
g. If it is a standard item, does it completely fit your application, or is it a misfit?
h. Does the item have greater capacity than required?
i. Is there a similar item in inventory which could be used instead?
j. Can the weight be reduced?
k. Are closer tolerances specified than are necessary?
l. Is unnecessary machining performed on the item?
m. Are unnecessarily fine finishes specified?
n. Is commercial quality specified?
o. Can you make the item cheaper yourself?
p. If you are making it now, can you buy it for less?
q. Is the item properly classified for shipping purposes to obtain the lowest transportation rates?
r. Can cost of packaging be reduced?
s. Are you asking your suppliers for suggestions to reduce costs?
t. Do material, reasonable labor, overhead, and profit total its cost?
u. Will another dependable supplier provide it for less?
v. Is anyone buying it for less?

IV. Now:

a. Pursue those suggestions that appear practical.
b. Get samples of the proposed item(s).
c. Select the best possibilities and propose changes.

Source: Purchasing and Materials Management, 10th ed., by M. R Leenders and H. E. Fearon, 1993, pp. 57, 64, Homewood, IL: Richard D. Irwin, Inc.

exposure to other applications of their products (parts, materials, or services), are in a unique position to help the members of the business buying center obtain maximum value for each dollar spent. Value analysis is especially appropriate in straight- and modified-rebuy situations, when the business supplier is already familiar with what is presently being used and can offer suggestions for specification changes that will be to the advantage of both buyer and seller.

The business seller's knowledge includes that of materials, services, fabrication methods, and equipment. The salesperson should advise buyers on tolerances, finishes, or anything else that might affect the cost, as well as the feasibility of the design. The trained marketer should be an important part of the customer's value-analysis team, understanding the objectives of their programs and earning the customer's confidence, so that no facts about predicted quantities, function, end use, and the like will be withheld.

CONCEPT QUESTIONS

1. What is the ideal quality level to purchase?
2. How do business buyers measure service?
3. What is the primary difference between value analysis and value engineering?

MAKE-OR-BUY ANALYSIS

The decision of whether to manufacture a product in-house or to purchase it from the outside can have a significant impact on the long-term, as well as the day-to-day, operation of the firm. Deciding what should be made and what should be bought constitutes what is commonly referred to as the *make-or-buy analysis*.

The make-or-buy decision in an organization can originate in a variety of ways. Business salespeople may propose the alternative and then request permission to submit quotations on components that their companies are capable of producing. This decision can also result from situations of unsatisfactory vendor performance, such as an emergency created by delivery problems, poor product or component quality, or a seemingly unreasonable vendor price increase. The addition of a new product, a substantial modification of an existing one, or a value-analysis study of an existing product can suggest a make-or-buy feasibility study. Changes in sales volume and related variations in plant capacity can also prompt management to seek a make-or-buy investigation.

Ascertaining Profitability

When performing a make-or-buy analysis, buyers must be very careful, as some important points can be overlooked. All costs, such as delivery, direct labor, plant overhead, incremental purchasing cost, and opportunity cost of capital, must be considered; otherwise, the analysis will not be correct. Also, the make-or-buy decision may not be appropriate if there is a better alternative use of available resources. Salespersons, along with buying firm personnel, such as engineering and production supervisors, should supply the buyer with pertinent data that will contribute to a thorough analysis. Aggressive sellers should be especially aware of the value of their expertise in this area.

The make-or-buy decision will determine, to a large extent, the profitability of the organization; and, with this in mind, the activity must not be taken lightly by either the buying or the selling firm. In a new-product situation, the analysis would be undertaken during the decision phase. The postponement of this decision will, in all likelihood, require additional effort, time, and cost; so, the suggestion here is that there should be a formalized approach to the decision process. The buyer's objective would be to render the make-or-buy decision that maximizes the utilization of production, managerial, and financial capabilities. Too few business buyers take advantage of the vendor expertise available to them through their friends in marketing and sales; and it appears that buyers may be more creative in the future in applying their particular expertise to the business make-or-buy decision area. Such creativity could mean additional market share and the achievement of a long-lasting business relationship between seller and buyer.

Reasons to Manufacture

A company may undertake to manufacture, rather than purchase, for the following reasons: The item is required in large volume, is substantially of the same nature as the regular product, can be adapted to the existing production facilities, is capable of production by the company at a cost low enough to allow a savings over the price charged for the item by a supplier, and is not protected by patents so that sizeable royalties have to be paid. A company could choose to make a part even when it might cost more than buying it. This would apply to an issue such as ensuring a source of supply when faced with the existence of one or more unreliable suppliers. The decision to "make," rather than to "buy," is not uncommon and is frequently reported in the media.[26] Consider the following example: In 1980, the NCR Corporation announced that it would be spending nearly $200 million over four years to expand its internal capacity to develop and manufacture semiconductor parts, which are used as components in its computer systems and computer terminals. Previous to this time, the company was manufacturing 40 percent of its needs internally. The added internal capacity enabled the company to produce 60 percent of its annual requirements. This action significantly reduced the market for outside suppliers. NCR found it desirable from a performance and cost standpoint to enlarge its in-house capabilities. The firm also believed that greater in-house component capability would enable it to control quality, respond more quickly to its target markets, and protect its supply of components in times of production shortages.[27]

From this analysis of the problems involved in arriving at make-or-buy decisions, certain generalizations seem justifiable; although, as in all generalizations, exceptions must be made. Clearly, only in rare instances will either the make or buy argument be so conclusive as to dictate an obvious decision. Consequently, in most cases the solution will be a compromise based on judgment as to the course of action most conducive to the company's best interest. In a real sense, therefore, the correct answer to the question "What is preferable, make or buy?" is that "it all depends upon circumstances." Nevertheless, balancing all the arguments, the burden of proof in most situations seems to rest on those urging make, rather than buy.[28]

Participants in Make or Buy

Although firms have different organizational structures, those business functions usually involved in the make-or-buy decision include marketing, manufacturing, engineering, purchasing, and accounting. Figure 3-1 illustrates the decision-making process and the various functional groups involved. The marketing, manufacturing, engineering, and purchasing areas provide nonfinancial criteria, and the accounting area offers financial criteria for use in the make-or-buy decision. Because input for the make-or-buy decision comes from so many different sources within the firm, an interdisciplinary committee to implement the decision process is often advisable.

NEGOTIATION

Everyone, at one time or another, engages in some form of negotiation. The use of negotiation is almost a daily occurrence for those engaged in the organizational or business buying and selling process. It is no longer possible or sensible for executives to conduct negotiations totally by intuition and a few "traditional" guidelines. At a recent negotiations training session for its sales force, Smith-Kline Diagnostics of San Jose, California, made it a point to include their marketing people and key customer support people in the training. "Everybody has to be on board when sales negotiates an agreement with a customer," according to John Swotosh, marketing manager. "Negotiation is an attitude," says Douglas R. Holley, sales and technical manager of ICI Colors Group in Charlotte, North Carolina. "I want my salespeople to see negotiation as a process which can bring us closer together with our customers—not drive us apart."[29] In business negotiations, buyers and sellers come together to work out the terms of a purchase contract (for example, price, quantity, and delivery). While there has been an increased emphasis on problem solving, bargaining remains at the core of all negotiation interactions.[30]

Negotiation is a technique for the communication of ideas. Both buyers and sellers attempt to convince the other party to yield to their demands, with the

FIGURE 3-1 **Participants in the Make-or-Buy Decision**

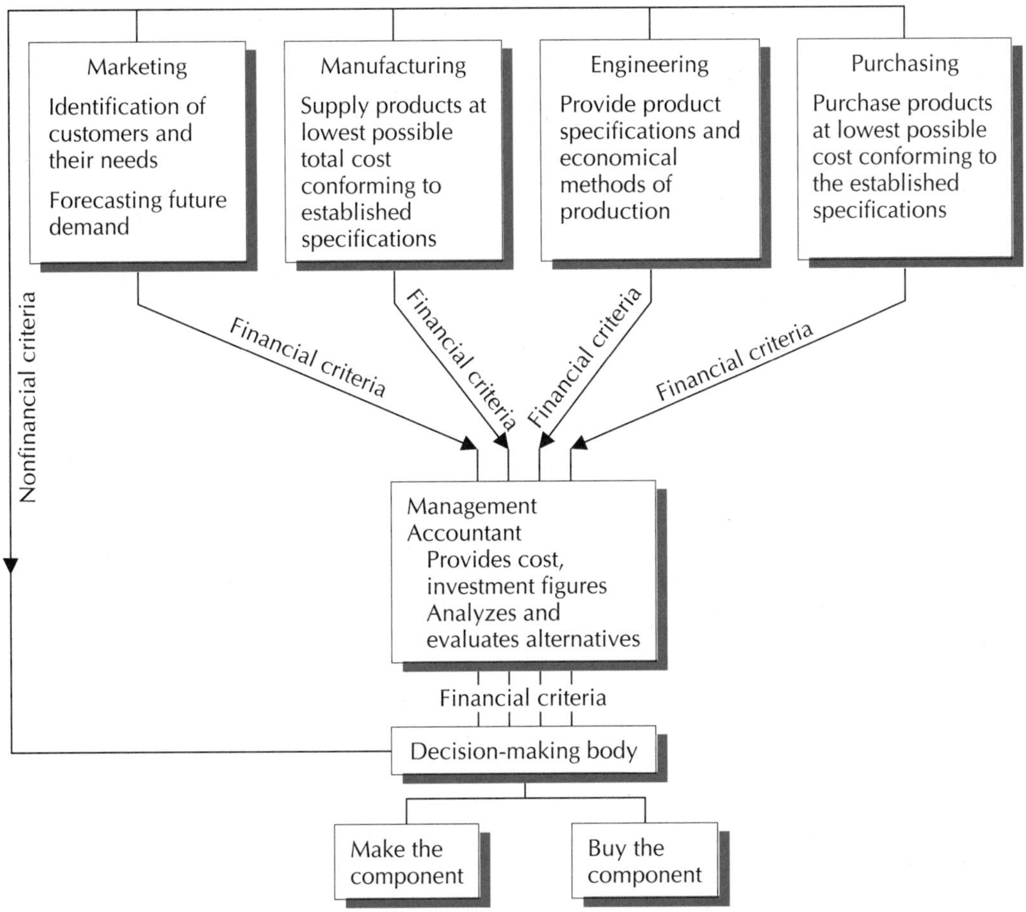

ultimate objective being to arrive at an agreement that will work to the benefit of both parties. Negotiation activities represent a structured process leading to an outcome.[31] Negotiation should be used in its broadest context, with quantity, delivery, payment terms, and service (among other things) being part of the purchase agreement that can and should be part of the bargaining process. The ideal negotiator, whether buyer or seller, should possess the complementary traits of courage, confidence (high self-esteem and self-acceptance), flexibility, humility, great patience, and charm (being likeable), an understanding of human nature and need-satisfaction; as well as the logical traits of high tolerance for ambiguity, strong cognitive complexity (abstract thinking), high intelligence, and realistic decision-making ability. Following the negotiating process, both sides must win something, and both sides must leave the session feeling good; otherwise, it was not a productive process. Figure 3-2 outlines the fundamentals of successful negotiation. It is interesting to note that communication is also a key element in successful negotiation.

Analyzing Both Buyer and Seller Strengths

One should never underestimate the strength of his or her adversary, for those buyers or sellers who attempt to enter a negotiation session unprepared will emerge as losers. Issues to consider in developing a sales negotiation strategy include who the buying influences are in the customer organization and what their interests, concerns, perceptions, and priorities of value are.[32] As was noted above, both sides must win something, and both must leave feeling good; otherwise, the negotiation was not a productive one. Helping suppliers to recognize that productive negotiations involve a great deal more than just face-to-face

FIGURE 3-2 **Fundamentals of Successful Negotiation**

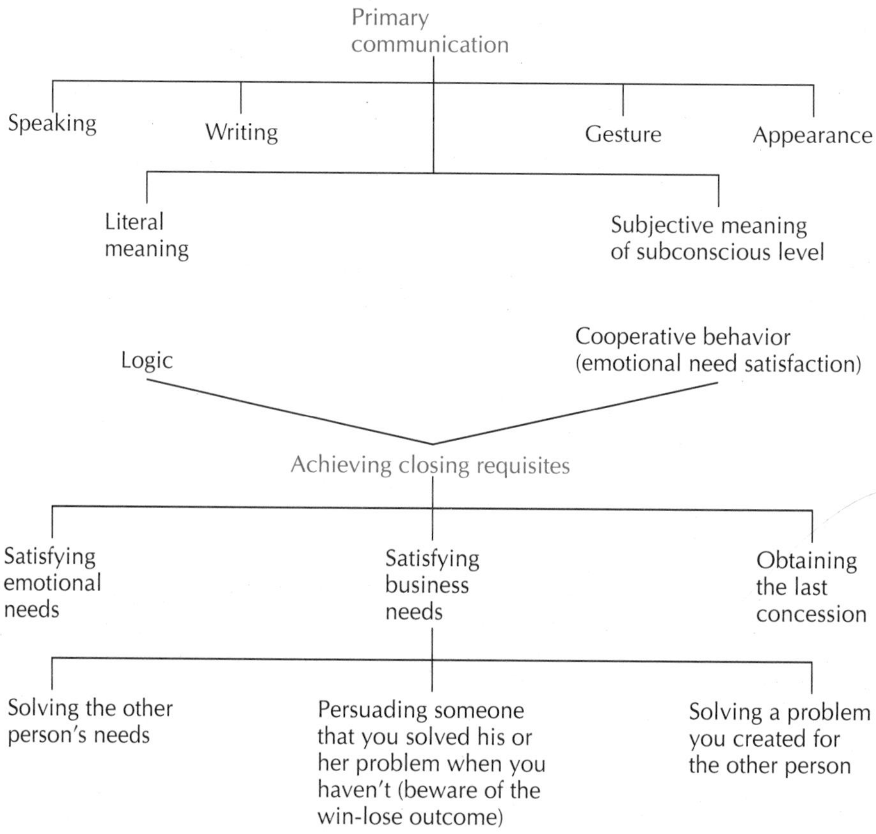

interaction with the purchaser is the ongoing challenge in developing competent sales professionals.[33]

Prior to a negotiation session, the buyer must learn as much as possible about the seller's position, and the seller should do the same in regard to the buyer. Both buyer and seller must attempt to analyze the other's primary negotiating objectives, along with their minimum and maximum positions on various objectives. Figure 3-3 presents a visualization of the position of the two parties from the buyer's standpoint. Note that both the buyer and the seller have maximum and minimum positions, indicating a willingness to give up certain things and an unwillingness to give up others. Note also that both have an objective and that the difference between the buyer's objective and the seller's is not very substantial. The object is to identify this area of difference and to work to reduce it to the point where both the buyer and the seller can agree to a contract.

THE SMALL-ORDER PROBLEM

Small orders are a continuing matter of concern in every organization (in both the buying and selling functions). Small orders are good examples of hidden costs that reduce profitability.[34] As a general rule, 70 percent of all requisitions only amount to approximately 10 percent of the total dollar volume purchased. One important consideration then becomes the cost of the system set up to handle small orders versus the cost of the items themselves. The lack of a small item may create a nuisance totally out of proportion to its dollar value—thus, assured

FIGURE 3-3 **A Buyer's Viewpoint of Both a Buyer's and a Seller's Negotiating Position**

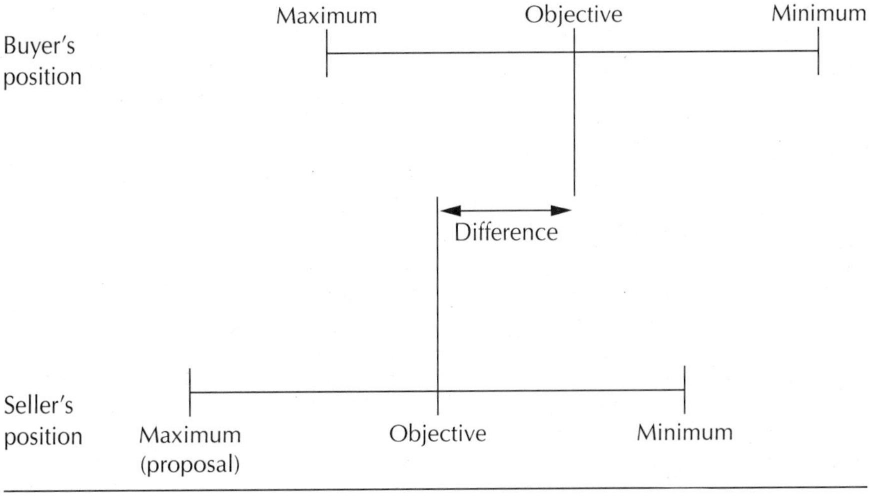

supply is the first objective to be met. Exhibit 3-4 describes a number of approaches that need to be used continuously to address the small-order question. Buyers and sellers must work closely together if these approaches are to work.

Because of anticipating the need for small purchases by the buyer, and the small profit or possible loss for the vendor in processing and shipping the order, specialized techniques have been designed to reduce the costs of buying and selling, while at the same time protecting the quality of the services rendered and received. The following techniques are suggested in handling small orders efficiently: a centralized-stores system, a petty cash system, a blanket-order system, and an electronic-ordering system.

The Centralized-Stores System

The centralized-stores technique consists simply of a designated, "centralized" (conveniently located) area set aside for supply items that are frequently ordered in small quantities, and that can be withdrawn on an as-needed basis. An *ABC analysis of inventory items* would indicate that the low-value "C" items would be prime candidates for inclusion in this system (nuts, bolts, lubricants, office supplies, and the like). A centralized-stores system makes sense especially when one considers that it costs approximately $200 to generate a typical purchase order (contract) today. One order, placed weekly, monthly, or quarterly, as opposed to several orders placed weekly, would save substantial dollars, while

EXHIBIT 3-4 Approaches in Addressing the Small-Order Problem

1. If the fault lies with the using department, perhaps persuasion can be employed to increase the number of standardized items requested.
2. Another possibility is for the purchasing department to hold small requisitions as received until a justifiable total, in dollars, has been accumulated.
3. A third method is to establish a requisition calendar, setting aside specific days for the requisitioning of specific supplies, so that all requests for a given item are received on the same day. As an aid to the storeskeeper, the calendar also may be so arranged that practically all the supplies secured from any specific type of vendor are requisitioned on the same day.
4. Still another method or procedure is to make use of the stockless buying or systems contracting concept.* This concept has been used most widely in the purchase of MRO (maintenance, repair, and operating supply) items.

*The technique of *stockless buying* or *systems contracting* (a term registered by the Carborundum Company) is relatively new and has been used most frequently in buying stationery and office supplies, repetitive items, maintenance and repair materials, and operating supplies (MRO). This latter class of purchases is characterized by many types of items of low value and needed immediately when any kind of a plant or equipment failure occurs. The technique is built around a blanket-type contract which is developed in great detail regarding approximate quantities to be used in specified time periods, prices, provisions for adjusting prices, procedures to be used in picking up requisitions daily and making delivery within 24 hours, simplified billing procedures, and a complete catalog of all items covered by the contract.

Source: Michael R. Leenders and Harold E. Fearon, *Purchasing and Materials Management* (10th ed.), Homewood, IL: Richard D. Irwin, Inc., 1993, pp. 51, 64.

at the same time freeing up both the buyer's and the seller's time for more important tasks. Creative buyers should consider such a system, and creative sellers who supply such items should also suggest such a system (desiring the buyer to use their products, of course).

The Petty Cash System

Assuming the $200 cost-per-purchase-order argument, forward-thinking buyers will consider the possibility of paying cash for supplies that can be bought locally, with the allowed dollar ceiling on an expenditure being quite arbitrary. Paying cash saves time and administrative expense on the part of both the buyer and the seller. The major drawback to such a system would be the possible inefficiency that might arise due to a lack of buying skills. However, this problem is more than compensated for by the savings realized by both the buyer and the seller in not having to generate a formal purchase order, with the resulting invoice generated by the supplier firm.

The Blanket-Order System

Considerable savings in time and paperwork can be made for both buyer and seller by consolidating monthly, quarterly, or yearly requirements of a particular purchased part, subassembly, or raw material into a single agreement; and by arranging for a single weekly, semiweekly, or monthly delivery against the agreement (*blanket order*). Both creative buyers and sellers will constantly seek to make their counterpart's job easier, and this approach is a natural move in that direction.

In addition to dollar savings in paperwork and time for both the buyer and the seller, the lumping of requirements into a single contract will usually enable the buyer to obtain better terms. The typical contract is written for one year, although both longer and shorter periods are used. The immediate advantage to the seller is an assurance of a certain workload, which might then allow the seller to plan capacity work-flow better and to make financial commitments accordingly. The immediate advantage to the buyer is the probability of a lower price for a larger, long-term contract, better delivery times, and an immediate release from routine buying tasks. As detailed in Exhibit 3-5, the blanket-order system offers a number of additional benefits to the user, ranging from lower ordering costs and less routine work, to ensuring a regular and timely flow of materials in times of shortages.

The Electronic-Ordering System

The pace of development in electronic systems is extremely rapid, and many buyers and sellers have a desktop keyboard and a visual display unit at their disposal. With this technology, the buyer can call up supplier records, showing

EXHIBIT 3-5 **Benefits of the Blanket-Order System of Handling Small Orders**

The blanket-order system offers six important benefits to the business or organizational buyer:

1. It requires fewer purchase orders and reduces clerical work in purchasing, accounting, and receiving.
2. It releases buyers from routine work, giving them more time to concentrate on major problems.
3. It permits volume pricing by consolidating and grouping requirements.
4. It sometimes ensures protection against price rises during the period of coverage.
5. It centralizes purchasing control.
6. The blanket-order system helps ensure a regular and timely flow of materials in times of shortages.

Source: Lamar Lee, Jr. and Donald W. Dobler, *Purchasing and Materials Management,* 5th Edition (New York: McGraw-Hill, 1991), p. 69.

each supplier's name, address, telephone number, list of salespeople, dates of recent sales visits, and transaction and performance records. Usually, these records would also indicate alternative supply sources, materials, and prices. Orders can be typed, changed, and eventually released for printing out. Open order files can be maintained, updated, and closed as needed, or as appropriate.

The uses and potential applications of electronic-ordering systems will explode in the future, as the potential for dollar savings and greater profit margins through a reduction in paperwork is both challenging and exciting. The typical purchasing department in both larger and smaller firms will be using electronic-ordering systems as the norm in the near future.

ENVIRONMENTAL FORCES AND BUYING DECISIONS

Marketing success depends upon developing a sound marketing mix (the controllable variables) adapted to the trends and developments in the *marketing environment* (the uncontrollable variables). The marketing environment presents a set of largely uncontrollable forces to which the company must adapt its marketing mix.

The purpose of *environmental analysis* is to identify and assess threats and opportunities as they are evolving in the marketplace. The company itself is part of the changing environment, since it develops and refines its basic competence in interaction with its customers' evolving needs. Virtually every aspect of the firm's marketing activities, and the competitive and customer response to them, will have some effect on the structure and functioning of the marketplace, especially in regard to the company's pricing policies, distribution strategies, and new-product marketing efforts.

Environmental analysis requires a continuous flow of information from a potentially limitless variety of sources. Any piece of information has value if it contributes to increased management awareness and understanding of the forces shaping the economy, the industry, and the market. The typical manager relies on a number of regular reports and publications for this type of information. From these information sources, he or she shapes a set of assumptions about the future that provides a basis for setting objectives and for the development of plans and programs. Among the most obvious sources of information are sales representatives, customers, distributors, trade associations, universities, government publications, the general business press, management associations, trade journals, professional publications, management consultants, and other managers within the firm.

Buyers and sellers must understand the environment within which they operate and must communicate with each other so that they can monitor, adapt to, and develop strategies to meet environmental changes that impact either or both the buying and selling organizations. Many firms are beginning to employ *environmental scanners* because of constant changes in their external environments. An environmental scanner is defined as a person who collects, studies, and analyzes data on the company's external environments. This person would monitor changes in the economic environment, the physical environment, the competitive environment, the technological environment, the legal-political environment, and the ethical environment.

The Economic Environment

The economic environment includes factors both at home and abroad, along with variables that determine the income and wealth-generating ability of the economy. Because of the derived nature of business demand, few business buyers and sellers are immune to its effects. The dangers of derived demand for business suppliers, when final consumers' demand for a product produced by these suppliers' customers begins to decline, must be understood and monitored. For example, Uniroyal, having the smallest sales volume of the five largest U.S. tire makers, was hit hard by the energy crisis of the early 1980s. The fact that people were driving less, resulting in less wear on their tires, combined with the introduction of the forty-thousand-mile radial tire caused Uniroyal's sales to decrease markedly. Top management decided to eliminate its weakest plants and to concentrate more on its more profitable specialty chemical businesses.[35]

The Physical Environment

Contained in the physical environment are not only the geographic characteristics or region of the country where the firm operates, but also the political stability of the country within the international environment and its location and transportation infrastructure. As transportation costs increase, business buyers will generally prefer suppliers whose mining, manufacturing, and storage facilities are nearby.[36]

The Competitive Environment

All other sellers who are competing for the patronage of the same business buyer are included in this environment. Many industrial firms find themselves in intensely competitive industries, where astute responses to competitive pressures are critical for such firms to maintain and/or improve their market positions. For example, in 1985, GTE's Sylvania Division built a computer database that can constantly monitor activities of fifty-one competitors. The Management Information of Competitor Strategies (MICS) supplements information from filings of the Securities and Exchange Commission and articles found in industry publications with assessments and reports made by GTE's field staff.[37] Additionally, some smaller firms remain viable in highly competitive markets by creating a unique product offering. For example, Steiger Tractor Company has netted sales well over $100 million by manufacturing a large articulated tractor. The articulated tractor differs from most farm tractors in that it has four-wheel traction for handling larger loads and bends in the middle for easier and smoother turning. Farmers can reduce their labor costs by as much as 33 percent per acre by using such a product.

Both domestic and global actions of competitors can greatly affect the firm's selection of target markets, product mix, distributors, and even the overall marketing strategy. For several years now, as productivity has been declining and labor costs have been rising, U.S. businesses have been losing market share to foreign rivals both at home and abroad.[38] For example, to compete in the world's largest automobile market, Mazda Motor Corporation has invested millions of dollars to modernize Ford's idled plant in Fort Rock, Michigan. Along with Toyota, Nissan, and Honda, Mazda (the fourth largest Japanese automobile maker) is now building compact cars in the United States.[39]

The Technological Environment

This particular environment consists of the application of science to develop new ways of doing various tasks. For instance, IBM, GTE, and Corning Glass are developing superconductors that will reduce the size of the quickest computers to no more than that of a shoebox and will enable trains to travel smoothly and comfortably at a speed of 300 miles per hour.[40] High technology, with the resulting *knowledge explosion*, has presented buyers and sellers with different sets of marketing problems and deserves special attention. Significant new developments in manufacturing technology have the potential for altering buyer-seller relationships. The increase in the number of high-tech marketing articles and entire issues offered by the more traditional business press, such as *Business Marketing*, the *Wall Street Journal*, the *New York Times*, to name but a few, serve to illustrate this point.

High technology represents a whole new arena for marketing theories, practices, and research. The requirement of a technical background for business sales and buying personnel has been especially noted in such areas as biotechnology, electronics, medical instrumentation, ceramics, and robotics. As is discussed in the box entitled "Business-to-Business Marketing in Action," buyers in the types of areas just cited must have the required technical training not only to understand the technologies of what they are buying, but also to talk the language of those with whom they are dealing. Researchers in one particular survey found that the typical educational background of a person selling robotics included an engineering degree. Some 77 percent of the executives in robotics who were interviewed indicated that an engineering degree was required for selection to their respective sales forces.[41] This focus on a technical background, rather than one in business or marketing (or a combination of the two), has potential implications for the buyer-seller relationship, which is of much concern to those in the business sector.

The Legal-Political Environment

Included in the legal-political environment are the rules and regulations that society has imposed on business firms and the political interest groups that affect the environment. Additionally, this environment would include international trade restrictions, government attitudes toward business and social activities, and government funding of selected programs.

Buyers and sellers in the business sector are regulated by agencies responsible for protecting businesses, consumers, and other interests of society from unrestrained business behavior. The dictates of agencies, such as the Food and Drug Administration, the Federal Trade Commission, the Environmental Protection Agency, and the Federal Communications Commission, must be adhered to by both buyers and sellers in the development of their products and overall marketing strategies.

Manufacturers must carefully consider product safety and ecological impact in the design of products and the location of plants, or face the same situation as Aerojet General. Aerojet General has, so far, spent more than $20 million in attempting to clean up its environmental pollution. TCE, a cancer-causing chemical used by Aerojet in the manufacture of rockets, was discovered in the groundwater underneath its California plant—a plant that is being called California's worst toxic-waste site.[42]

The Ethical Environment

Concern over ethical issues in marketing has intensified in recent years.[43] The norms or moral behavior that society imposes on business and marketers comprise the ethical environment. Ethics serve as part of a system for social control,

BUSINESS-TO BUSINESS MARKETING IN ACTION

TECH-TYPE BUYERS ARE NEEDED TO KEEP THE LID ON INFLATION

The only way to keep inflation under control for keeps is to assure that buyers understand the basic technologies of what they're buying. Otherwise, says Wayne C. Evans, they can't say "no" to opportunistic price hikes—and they can't help suppliers get "yes" answers on usable ideas presented to in-house technical people.

"That doesn't mean converting liberal arts or business graduates into engineers," says Evans, an industrial engineer who is director of purchasing for the Homelite division of Textron in Gastonia, N.C. "But they should be able to talk the language of those they're dealing with in design, manufacturing, quality, and vendor firms.

"They should be able to look at prints and relate them to the specifications," Evans continues. "It's especially important as far as tolerances are concerned, because new types of equipment are making it possible to achieve new tolerances—often at lower costs. As a bare minimum, buyers must be able to understand what is critical and what is less so."

Hit the books again.

Local schools and colleges often offer evening courses that will beef up buyers' technical know-how, Evans points out. He currently has three buyers taking what he calls "engineering-oriented" night courses at nearby institutions.

Moreover, this training is supplemented by in-house education. Every other Monday morning, the first hour of the work day is set aside for a group get-together of the 20-person purchasing staff. Evans himself leads some sessions, but he also schedules presentations by execs from design, manufacturing, quality control, etc.

"If nothing else, we go over systems and documentation," says Evans, "and at least every quarter we have critiques and exams."

Common language helps.

According to Evans, it's the "exchange of information" that's a vital part of purchasing's mission, and the department can truly live up to it only when buyers talk the common language of specifiers and suppliers.

"Every one of my buyers," he says, "is on either a new-product team, or a product-improvement team. The other team members come from design engineering and manufacturing engineering. The directors of the other deparments and I make the assignments from our staffs so that no team gets overloaded."

Under the team arrangement, the buyer's job is supplier communication, and vendors' technical contributions—especially early in the design process—go a long way toward cutting costs and saving time.

"We know we won't design ourselves into a corner," says Evans, "if the supplier who's going to make a part gets a chance to comment on the specs. Make-or-buy studies, also, are more accurate when buyers and everyone else on a team understand the manufacturing processes."

In addition, says Evans, the early involvement of suppliers, brought in by technically competent buyers, can trim literally "months" off new-product development times. This is especially important to a company such as Homelite, which has introduced 28 new products in the past year. "If you don't hit the 'window,' you miss the season."

Saying 'no' to inflation.

By the same token, he stresses, it takes a buyer who knows what he's talking about—in technical as well as economic terms—to deny unrealistic supplier demands for price increases.

"The inflationary pressures are already building," he says. "We're seeing it in some of the basic raw materials that are the drivers for fabricated goods: petroleum, resins, copper, and aluminum. For some producers, the very first sign of an upturn in business means it's time for a price increase."

As Evans sees it, the problem stems from too much emphasis on short-term bottom line results. Also alarming is the fact that the push for price hikes is in some cases accompanied by a fall-off in quality, as vendors seek to "ship everything they can sell."

The only way to keep all aspects of inflation down for the count, Evans concludes, is for buyers to stand fast against price increases and be equally tough about quality miscues. "Perhaps, in some cases, cooperative value analysis work with suppliers can lower their costs and enhance their reliability. But a technically minded buyer still has to be the catalyst for such cures," he says.

Source: Somerby Dowst, in *Purchasing*, September 10, 1988, p. 43.

a system that is important to buyers and salespeople, as well as their respective firms.[44] As key links between their organizations and their customers, business salespeople encounter situations that might lead to ethical conflict. The additional potential ethical problems within business marketing management will be studied in detail in Chapter 15.

PURCHASING'S IMPACT UPON COMPANY PROFIT

Purchasing plays an important role in regard to the impacts that occur from price increases or decreases for the goods and services procured. All other things being equal, a $1 savings in the purchase price results in a $1 profit increase. A cost increase by the same amount, on the other hand, harms the firm by $1 of decreased profit.[45]

The term "profit" applies to three key measures used to describe the periodic financial performance of a firm. The first is profit as a percentage of sales. This figure is a rough measure of how much is left over from sales revenue after all costs of the firm have been paid. It is the general measure of the profit-generating potential of sales and operating activities. The second measure is asset turnover. This is a measure of how effectively the assets in the firm are being utilized. It is found by dividing total assets into the sales revenue for the year. A high asset turnover is generally considered preferable to a low asset turnover. The third key measure is return on assets. This indicator is a measure of the profit-generating power of the firm based upon the assets necessary to produce the desired profit. This figure is related to the interest that people associate with savings account or money-market-fund earnings. Of course, a higher return figure is far more desirable than a lower one.[46]

The interaction of all the key company financial components to the overall profit is seen in Figure 3-4. A hypothetical company is shown with a revenue of $1.00 for the year. Purchases cost $.55; depreciation, $.15; and other costs of operation, $.25; for a total cost of $.95 for the year. Profit is $1.00 less the $.95, or $.05. Use of assets, cash, inventories, and other assets totals $.40. Sales are $1.00, which sets asset turnover rate at 2.5 times. Profit as a percentage of sales is .05

FIGURE 3-4 **Interaction of All Key Company Financial Components on Overall Profits**

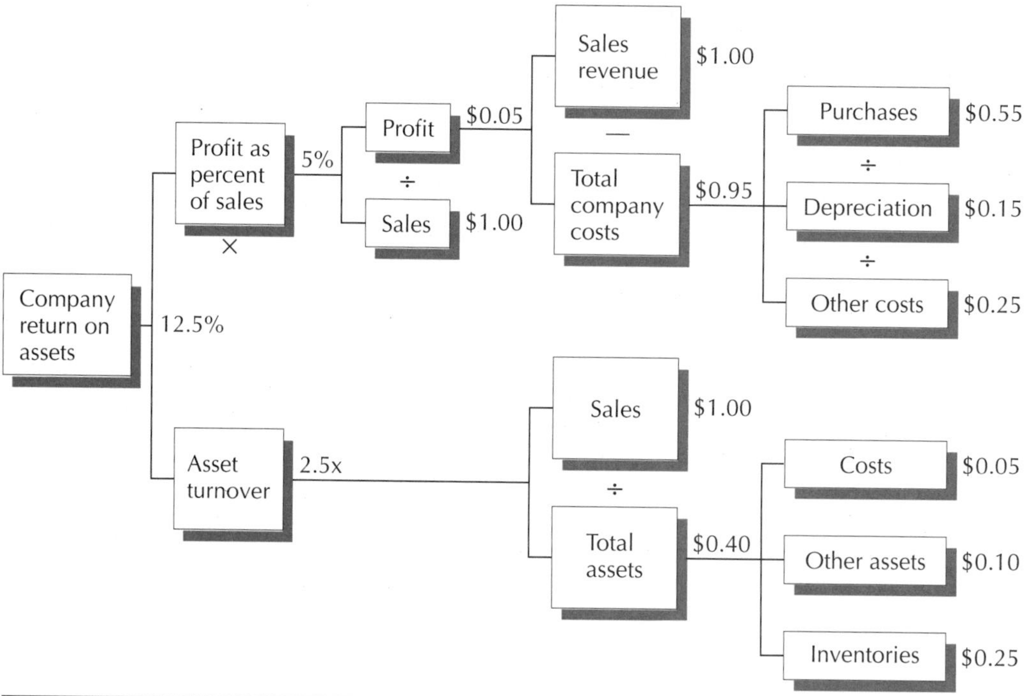

Source: Reprinted by permission from *Purchasing and Materials Management* by Joseph L. Cavinato, Copyright © 1984 by West Publishing Company. All rights reserved.

(or 5 percent), and the asset turnover rate of 2.5 times causes company return on assets to be 12.5%. This shows how a firm could have a low return on sales but a high turnover, resulting in a good overall return on assets. Another firm will have a very high return on sales but a low asset turnover, to result in a low return on assets. All three indicators are viewed separately, as well as in a combined manner.[47]

As can be easily calculated, a reduction in the purchase price by one cent reduces the cost of purchases from \$.55 to \$.54 and total company costs to \$.94. Profit is now \$.06, and profit as a percentage of sales has increased from 5 to 6 percent. Return on assets is now 15 percent (.06 × 2.5). Therefore, a reduction in purchase price has a direct positive impact upon profit and return on assets.

CONCEPT QUESTIONS

1. What should the buyer's objective be in the make-or-buy decision?
2. Why are some businesses now employing environmental scanners?
3. How do cost savings and cost increases affect overall company profits?

SUMMARY

1. Business buying has evolved into a complex process of decision making and communication, which takes place over time, involves several organizational members, and includes relationships with other firms and institutions. The primary objective of business buyers is to purchase the right materials in the right quantity, for delivery at the right time and in the right place, from the right source with the right service, and at the right price.
2. People within the business buying organization who are involved in the buying process are members of what is called the buying center. The critical task for the marketer is to be able to determine the specific role and the relative buying influence of each buying center participant. The buying center membership and relative importance of different members varies from company to company.
3. Creative purchasing people must understand and appreciate the relationship between quality, service, and price. They must work with people not only within their own firms but also with those sellers on the outside, to challenge quality, insist on the proper level of service, and look at price with a very critical eye. They must determine just what is a "proper" price in any given situation.
4. Value analysis is a scientifically organized method for reducing the costs of manufactured items and for encouraging vendor cooperation in lowering costs of purchased items. Its ultimate purpose is to secure improved performance of components at less cost.

5. The make-or-buy decision will determine to a large extent the profitability of the organization; and, with this factor in mind, the activity should not be taken lightly by either the buying or the selling firm. The buyer's objective should be to render the make-or-buy decision that will maximize the utilization of production, managerial, and financial capabilities.
6. All buyers face the so-called small-order problem. While this problem will probably never be entirely eliminated, there are tools and techniques available that will, at least, make this area somewhat more manageable. Creative buyers and sellers should recognize the opportunity involved here.
7. Business salespeople must recognize the existence of environmental forces that can have an impact upon the buying decision. Environmental scanners are being employed to collect and study data on economic, physical, competitive, technological, legal-political, and ethical environments which affect the firm's decision-making process. Education, intuition, and the seller's assistance can indeed help the buyer surmount some difficult obstacles as identified by the environmental scanning process.
8. Purchasing plays an important role in regard to the impacts that occur from price increases or decreases for the goods and services procured. All other things being equal, a $1 savings in purchase price results in a $1 profit increase, with a cost increase by the same amount harming the firm by $1 of decreased profit.

KEY TERMS

ABC analysis of inventory items
Blanket order
Buying center
Environmental analysis
Environmental scanners
Knowledge explosion
Make-or-buy analysis
Marketing environment
Negotiation
Perceived value
Total cost of the purchasing decision
Value analysis
Value analysis approach
Value engineering

REVIEW QUESTIONS

1. Why is business buying no longer the simple act of placing an order with a vendor or a selling organization?
2. What determines the size of a buying center? What is the critical task for business marketers regarding their dealings with buying centers?
3. Explain the role of quality in business buying and selling. In what ways can a firm's purchasing department take an active role in ensuring that proper quality specifications are part of the purchase contract?
4. Discuss the role of service in business buying and selling. Distinguish between pre and postsale service.

5. Discuss the role of price in business buying and selling. Distinguish between price and total cost.
6. Distinguish between value analysis and value engineering. Identify the appropriate questions that should be asked in any value-analysis study.
7. What business functions are usually involved in a make-or-buy analysis? Who generally participates in a company's make-or-buy analysis? Under what conditions might a company choose to make, rather than to buy, a particular product?
8. What are the problems involved for the seller in filling small orders for the business buyer? Discuss four systems by which small orders can be handled effectively and efficiently by business or organizational sellers.
9. What is the role of an environmental scanner in business marketing? Identify and briefly explain the significance of each of the six major external environments for the business marketer.
10. How is the purchasing function directly related to company profit? How do savings acquired by efficient and effective purchasing practices impact upon the company profit?

Cases

CASE 3-1 Northern Chemical Company

Marketing executives at Northern Chemical Company—headquartered in Minneapolis and a world leader in the manufacture and sale of chemicals, metals, plastics, pharmaceuticals, and consumer products—were wrestling with a new concept in building roofs on industrial and commercial buildings. Whatever marketing efforts they decided on would have to be consistent with the attitudes of a complex array of contractors, roofers, and architects.

In the past, Northern had manufactured only plastic insulation for roofing. This insulation was prefabricated into rectangular boardstock of two-by-four feet and of variable thicknesses necessary to meet the customers' desired insulating requirements. The product had not been very profitable for Northern.

THE BUYING PROCESS

On new construction or total roof replacement, the owners of the building play no essential role. They hire architects and give them certain guiding parameters—size, height, site, purpose, and operating conditions. The architect then develops the design and material specifications for the roof. Even subsequent management reviews rarely concern the roof itself unless there is a question of overall building shape or a necessity to reduce costs.

A third party, the general contractor, also has little knowledge regarding roofing and has little influence on design or materials. Such matters are turned over to the fourth party, the roofing subcontractor, whose workers actually build the roof. The subcontractor influences the architect directly and indirectly through feedback on the ease and success of the architect's plans and is the only party to influence the architect substantially.

Experimentation and innovation on roofing are not really in the architect's best interest. Experimentation is usually expensive, since worker unfamiliarity slows installation. Experimentation also requires a trust in manufacturers' products that architects do not have. Unfavorable past experiences with new products have resulted in a deep-seated mistrust of new products and the firms producing them. Architects question laboratory research results because some past results did not correctly identify product deficiencies or simulate the realities of application.

Subcontractors are even more resistant to change than architects. Their conservatism is based primarily on roofing labor conditions. New products often require extensive applicator retraining: and since retraining influences an applicator's productive time, it reduces a subcontractor's income. Furthermore, worker reeducation is an arduous task; roofing workers are not usually receptive to change. In addition, subcontractors also equate new products with increased callbacks. Some products have been introduced prematurely in the past, and unanticipated repairs and adjustments have been necessary. Finally, the manufacturer lacks field experience in application and, consequently, tends to underestimate application costs. If roofers rely on the manufacturer's projections, their profits may be reduced. Yet, roofers haven't had the experience to make their own estimates.

At the same time, few subcontractors have actually blocked introduction of new roofing products or designs, since they are rarely asked for advice during the writing of specifications. Most roofers bid for every job for which they can compete, and their strongest urge is to keep the work force busy even if it requires using new materials or design. Once the bid is won, only minor changes are permitted.

NORTHERN'S VIEW OF THE MARKET

In addition to the normal problems of entering a new market, Northern was considered a newcomer that did not understand the market. Architects and roofing contractors pointed to their plastic foam, a roofing product marketed many years before a need was established. Comments from architects and roofing contractors regarding Northern's sales force ranged from "unexceptional" to "technically incompetent in roofing."

On the positive side, nonresidential roofing was a large market, totalling $640 million in the United States alone. Northern also noted that firms competing for this market did not do so effectively. Manufacturers had a strong product orientation and failed to base their plans on market needs. Lack of marketing skill was demonstrated by their weak sales efforts and limited services. Finally, the roofing market was plagued with poor workmanship, poor quality of materials, and high liability. Fifteen percent of all roofs failed within five years.

Northern's new roofing concept was a patented system that modified the usual application of roofing materials. The system eliminated the major causes for the premature failures of built-up roofs. The new system was expected to perform much better than the conventional roof system, and the patent allows Northern to control the installation of the system. Even though Northern did not make any roofing materials other than insulation, the system allowed it to assure a good job because the insulation took most of the abuse in a properly installed roof.

MARKETING RESEARCH

Northern's marketing research yielded several conclusions about the typical roof installation procedures with which the new system would compete: (1) the workmanship of roofing crews was the worst of all the construction trades; (2) materials used in roofing had no product specifications at all and varied from job to job; (3) no special instructions or supervision had been provided to the roofers for the proper application of the plastic foam insulation; (4) owners and general contractors were apathetic—they wanted the roof on first and fast so all the other trades could work—and thus jobs were rushed and quality fell accordingly; (5) competition among the suppliers and the applicators was so intense that products were introduced with very little research and development. Quality was poor because the low prices wouldn't permit otherwise.

DISCUSSION QUESTIONS

1. Is this illustration of a business buying process more complex than most? Explain.
2. How can Northern help the decision makers realize that the firm has a quality product that they should seriously consider?
3. How would you attempt to introduce this product to the market?
4. Who makes the decision to buy the product?

Source: Cunningham and Cunningham, *Marketing: A Managerial Approach*, 1st Edition (Cincinnati, OH: South-Western Publishing Company) pp. 213–215.

CASE 3-2 Conner Peripherals

Conner Peripherals will exceed $1 billion in revenue after only four years of operations. This makes the company the fastest-growing manufacturer in the United States. It is a leading development company of hard disk drives for personal computers. It has continued to demonstrate U.S. superiority in the design and manufacturing of these devices. The company specializes in small, high-capacity, low-power-consuming hard disk drives. Without Conner Peripherals, the boom in notebook-sized computers probably would not have occurred.

Finis F. Conner, chief executive officer of Conner Peripherals, began his career in the computer industry working for Shugart Associates. Conner approached Al Shugart about developing mass storage devices for personal computers. These two formed Seagate Technology and pioneered a line of compact hard disk drives. Seagate's strategy was to mass-market low-cost hard drives for the personal computer market. Conner felt that more time and effort should be invested in developing new products. At odds with his partners, Conner left Seagate.

In December of 1985, Conner received a call from inventor John Squires. Squires had developed a 3.5-inch drive and needed capital to market it. Squires wanted Conner to back the operation with both capital and his name. The two formed a partnership, and Conner Peripherals was born. Conner approached Compaq Computer to help raise capital for the project. Compaq was so impressed with the product that it bought 49 percent interest in the firm and also the entire first-year's production. Compaq still owns 21 percent of the company and accounts for 25 percent of Conner's total sales volume.

The demand for Conner products parallels demand in the laptop computer market. Sales forecasters predict laptop sales will increase 45 percent a year for the next few years. Rapid growth in the market is making small, high-capacity hard drives an attractive market. Conner can expect strong competition from several other hard-drive manufacturing firms.

Conner is also gaining acceptance in the workstation market. Desktop workstation vendors have been hesitant in the past to purchase the new 3.5 technology. As reliability and performance of these drives have been clearly demonstrated, these companies have begun to purchase products from Conner and other manufacturers. Smaller, high-capacity drives mean the companies can reduce the overall size of the computer or workstation.

Conner's philosophy is to provide customers with what they want in terms of technological advantages. If it's low price customers are looking for, Conner turns them away. However, if small size or low-power consumption is important, then Conner Peripherals will work to develop a specific product to meet these needs. Conner's philosophy and marketing successes have led the firm to Fortune 500 status in only three years, a feat accomplished by only one other firm—Compaq.

DISCUSSION QUESTIONS

1. How does Conner Peripherals cater to the needs of business customers?
2. What buying situation do you feel best describes the hard-disk-drive market? Why?
3. How important is product quality for Conner Peripherals? How important is customer service?

Suggested Readings

Deagon, Brian. "Conner Seen Facing New Rivals." *Electronic News* (October 30, 1989); 16–17.
Kupfer, Andrew. "America's Fastest-Growing Company." *Fortune,* 13 August 1990, 48–54.
LaBianca, Giuseppe. "Smaller Drives Aim to Satisfy Needs of Workstation Market." *Electronic Business* (June 25, 1990): 91–93.

Source: C. Lamb, J. Hair, and C. McDaniel, *Principles of Marketing*, 1st Edition (Cincinnati, OH: South-Western Publishing Company, 1992) pp. 132–133.

Suggested Additional Readings

Clopton, Stephen W. "Microcomputer-Based Negotiation Training for Buyers." *Journal of Purchasing and Materials Management* 22 (Summer 1986): 16–23. **Advantages of, and guidelines for, microcomputer-based negotiation simulations.**

Dillon, Thomas F., and James A. Lorincz. "Buyers Holding Good Cards in Steel Negotiations/Steel Future Is Cast in Quality, Value, and Delivery." *Purchasing World* 30 (March 1986): 29–34. **Industry analysis and trends related to worldwide overcapacity, competition from imports, and joint ventures.**

______. "Staying Competitive Means Big Changes in Buyer/Service Center Relationships." *Purchasing World* 30 (October 1986): 77/M11–80/M14. **Discussion of service provided and associated costs in the steel industry.**

Fodor, George M. "Orchestrating a Pricing Strategy." *Industrial Distribution* 76 (August 1987): 30. **Product quality, delivery, and other added values generally assure success in business markets, but in an increasingly competitive marketplace, prices molded to buyer acceptance are a must.**

Graham, Jean M. "A Simple Idea Saves $8 Million a Year." *Purchasing* 112 (May 21, 1992): 47, 49. **A discussion of the advantages of bin stocking, single sourcing, supplier relations, and cost savings utilizing the case-study approach.**

Graham. John L. "The Problem-Solving Approach to Negotiations in Industrial Marketing." *Journal of Business Research* 14 (December 1986): 549–566. **Experiment with the problem-solving approach in negotiations, using causal modeling. Outcome criteria and assessment provided.**

Kapp, S. "Bearing Up against the Rising Sun." *Business Marketing* 72 (August 1987): 8. **Industrial distributors involved in selling bearings for transmission and power products are battling low-cost Japanese imports with high-profile customer service.**

Kyj, Myroslaw J., and Larissa S. Kyj. "Customer Service Competition in Business to Business and Industrial Markets: Myths and Realities." *Journal of Business and Industrial Marketing* 2 (Fall 1987): 45–53. **A review of the premise of customer service competition. The findings are integrated into a set of guidelines for the organization contemplating the use of customer service as a competitive tool.**

Leenders, Michael R., and David L. Blenkhorn. *Reverse Marketing*. New York: Free Press, 1988.

McWilliams, Robert D., Earl Naumann, and Stan Scott. "Determining Buying Center Size." *Industrial Marketing Management* 21 (February 1992): 43–49. **A microcontingency analysis of the purchasing process to include assessments and implications.**

Monczka, Robert M., Ernest L. Nickels, Jr., and Thomas J. Callahan. "Value of Supplier Information in the Decision Process." *International Journal of Purchasing and Materials Management* 28 (Spring 1992): 20–30. **Extension of earlier research into the value of various types of vendor information in the purchasing-decision process.**

Perdue, Barbara C., Ralph L. Day, and Ronald E. Michaels. "Negotiation Styles of Industrial Buyers." *Industrial Marketing Management* 15 (August 1986): 171–176. **Survey of business buyer-seller relationships using a typology of five styles of negotiating behavior.**

Rathbun, Craig, and Robert L. Janson. "Where Does the Time Go in Purchasing?" *Purchasing World* 29 (November 1985): 74–76. **Survey of how purchasing people spend their time, to include the negotiation process.**

Reck, Ross R. "Win-Win Negotiating: An Idea Whose Time Has Come." *NAPM Insights* 1 (February 1990): 11–12.

Williams, Alvin J., Steve Lacy, and William C. Smith. "Purchasing's Role in Value Analysis: Lessons from Creative Problem Solving." *International Journal of Purchasing and Materials Management* 28 (Spring 1992): 37–42. **Discussion and managerial implications of purchasing's role in the value-analysis process.**

ENDNOTES

[1]Cavinato, Joseph L. *Purchasing and Materials Management* (St. Paul, Minn.: West, 1984), 7.

[2]Lisa M. Ellram, "The Role of Purchasing in Cost Savings Analysis," *International Journal of Purchasing and Materials Management* 28 (Winter 1992): 26–33.

[3]Michele D. Bunn, "Taxonomy of Buying Decision Approaches," *Journal of Marketing* 57 (January 1993): 38–56.

[4]Julia M. Bristor, "Influence Strategies in Organizational Buying: The Importance of Connections to the Right People in the Right Places," *Journal of Business-to-Business Marketing* 1 (1993): 63–98.

[5]Daniel H. McQuiston, "Novelty, Complexity, and Importance as Causal Determinants of Industrial Buyer Behavior", *Journal of Marketing* 53 (April 1989): 66–79.

[6]Robert D. McWilliams, Earl Naumann, and Stan Scott, "Determining Buying Center Size," *Industrial Marketing Management* 21 (February 1992): 43–49.

[7]"Loctite: Home Is Where the Customers Are," *Business Week,* 13 April 1987, p. 63; and Bob Donath, "What Loctite Learned with Psychographic Insights," *Business Marketing* (July 1984): 100–101, 134.

[8]Donal W. Barclay, "Organizational Buying Outcomes and Their Effect on Subsequent Decisions," *European Journal of Marketing* (UK) (1992): 48–64.

[9]Neil A. Morgan and Nigel Piercy, "Market-Led Quality," *Industrial Marketing Management* 21 (May 1992): 111–118.

[10]For more discussion of this issue, see Tom Peters and Perry Pascarella, "Searching for Excellence: The Winners Deliver on Value," *Industry Week,* 16 April 1984, 61–62.

[11]Dick Schaaf, "Selling Quality," *Training* 29 (June 1992): 53–59.

[12]Richard B. Newman, "Insuring Quality: Purchasing's Role," *Journal of Purchasing and Materials Management* (Fall 1988): 4–21.

[13]Harold E. Fearon, Donald W. Dobler, and W. Killen, *The Purchasing Handbook*, 5th ed. (1992): 9-6 and 9-7.

[14]"Motorola Rates Its Service Suppliers," *Purchasing* 103 (November 5, 1987): 13.

[15]Caroline Reich, "A Tough Job Purchasing's Gotta Do," *Purchasing World* 33 (June 1989): 34–35.

[16]"King Customer," *Business Week,* 12 March 1990, 89–90.

[17]"Sandia Bucks Low-Bid Ritual," *Purchasing* 103 (September 24, 1987): 20.

[18]"Poor Delivery Performance Continues to Plague PMs," *Purchasing* 103 (November 5, 1987): 12.

[19]"Quality Is Up! Service Is Down!" *Purchasing* 102 (February 12, 1987): 21.

[20]See James Narus and James C. Anderson, "Turn Your Industrial Distributors into Partners," *Harvard Business Review* (March-April 1986): 66–71.

[21]See Peters and Pascarella, *Searching for Excellence*, pp. 61–62.

[22]"Picking the Perfect Perk," *Sales and Marketing Manager Canada* 32 (October 1991): 19–20.

[23]Alvin J. Williams, Steve Lacy, and William C. Smith, "Purchasing's Role in Value Analysis: Lessons from Creative Problem Solving," *International Journal of Purchasing and Materials Management* 28 (Spring 1992): 37–42.

[24]James Morgan, "If Cheap Products Are All You Get—You're Not Doing VA," *Purchasing* (June 16, 1988): 17.

[25]"Protective Packaging System Proves Itself in Field Test," in Value Analysis 1988—Special Report, *Purchasing* (June 16, 1988): 126B3–126B7.

[26]B. Charles Ames and James D. Hlavacek, *Managerial Marketing for Industrial Firms* (New York: Random House, 1984), 50.

[27]*Wall Street Journal,* 18 July 1980, 5.

[28]Michael R. Leenders and Harold E. Fearon, *Purchasing and Materials Management,* 10th ed. (Homewood, Ill.: Richard D. Irwin, 1993): 100–101.

[29]Robert E. Keller, "Preparing for Negotiations: The Sales Side," *NAPM Insights* (September 1992):. 16–17.

[30]Barbara C. Perdue, "The Aggressive Bargaining Tactics of Industrial Buyers," *Journal of Business and Industrial Marketing* 7 (Spring 1992): 45–52.

[31]Lloyd M. Rinehart and Thomas J. Page, Jr., "The Development and Test of a Model of Transaction Negotiation," *Journal of Marketing* 56 (October 1992): 18–32.

[32]Louis J. DeRose, "Define Value from Customer's Point of View," *Marketing News* 25 (March 4, 1991): 24.

[33]Keller, "Preparing for Negotiations," 16–17.

[34]Douglas M. Lambert, Mark L. Mennion, Jr., and John C. Taylor, "The Small Problem," *Management Decision* 28 (1990): 39–45.

[35]Mike Casey, "Tire Makers Survive Radial Changeover, Energy Crisis," *Houston Chronicle* (15 April 1984, 16.

[36]Niran Vyas and Arch G. Woodside, "An Inductive Model of Industrial Supplier Choice Processes," *Journal of Marketing* 48 (Winter 1984): 30–45.

[37]*Intelligence Update*, a newsletter published by Information Data Search, Cambridge, Mass.

[38]"Drastic New Strategies to Keep U.S. Multinationals Competitive," *Business Week,* 8 October 1984, 168–176.

[39]"Mazda to Build Compact Cars in U.S., Following Other Japanese Auto Firms," *Wall Street Journal,* 20 November 1984, 2.

[40]Anthony Ramirez, "Superconductors Get into Business," *Fortune,* 22 June 1987, 114–118.

[41]William L. Shanklin and John K. Ryans, Jr., *Essentials of Marketing High Technology* (New York: Lexington Books, 1984): 100.

[42]Bruce Ingersoll, "SEC Begins Inquiry of General Dynamics' Disclosure of Cost Overruns to Submarines," *Wall Street Journal*, 3 October 1984, 16.

[43]John Paul Fraedrich and O. C. Ferrell, "Cognitive Consistency of Marketing Managers in Ethical Situations," *Journal of the Academy of Marketing Science* 20 (Summer 1992): 245–252.

[44]I. Fredrick Tarwick, John E. Swan, Gail W. McGee, and David R. Rink, "Influence of Buyer Ethics and Salesperson Behavior on Intention to Choose a Supplier," *Journal of the Academy of Marketing Science* 19 (Winter 1991): 17–23.

[45]Cavinato, *Purchasing and Materials Management.*

[46]Victor H. Pooler and David J. Pooler, "Purchasing's Elusive Conceptual Home," *Journal of Purchasing and Materials Management* 17 (1981): 13.

[47]Cavinato, *Purchasing and Materials Management.*

Case Study

Trus Joist Corporation

Mr. Mike Kalish, salesperson for the Micro = Lam® Division of Trus Joist Corporation, had just received another moderately sized order for the product Micro = Lam laminated veneer lumber; however, the order held particular interest for him. The unique feature of the order was that the Micro = Lam was to be used as a truck trailer bedding material. This represented the second-largest order ever processed for that function.

Earlier in the fall of 1978, Mr. Kalish had spent some time in contacting prospective customers for truck trailer flooring in the Northwest and Midwest; however, the response from manufacturers had been disappointing. Despite this reception, smaller local builders of truck trailers were interested and placed several small orders for Micro = Lam laminated veneer lumber. The order Mr. Kalish had just received was from one of the midwestern companies he had contacted earlier, thus renewing his belief that the trailer manufacturing industry held great potential for Micro = Lam laminated veneer lumber as a flooring material.

COMPANY BACKGROUND

The Trus Joist Corporation, headquartered in Boise, Idaho, is a manufacturer of structural wood products, with plants located in the Pacific Northwest, Midwest, Southeast, and Southwest. Annual sales, which totalled over $78 million in 1978, were broken down into three major product categories: the Micro = Lam Division, contributing 7 percent of sales (the majority of Micro = Lam sales were internal); the Commercial Divisions, with 82 percent of sales; and the Residential Sales Program, with 11 percent of sales.

In the late 1950s Art Troutner and Harold Thomas developed a unique concept in joist design. They implemented a manufacturing process for the design, and then founded the Trus Joist Corporation. By 1978 the company employed over 1,000 people, of whom about 180 were sales personnel. The majority of salespeople were assigned to the regional Commercial Division sales offices; four outside salespeople were assigned to the Micro = Lam Division. The functions of selling and manufacturing were performed at each of the five geographically organized Commercial Divisions; therefore the salespeople concentrated on geographic selling. The Micro = Lam Division was more centralized in nature, conducting all nationwide sales and manufacturing activities from Eugene, Oregon.

EXHIBIT 1 **End of an All-Wood I-Beam (TJI)**

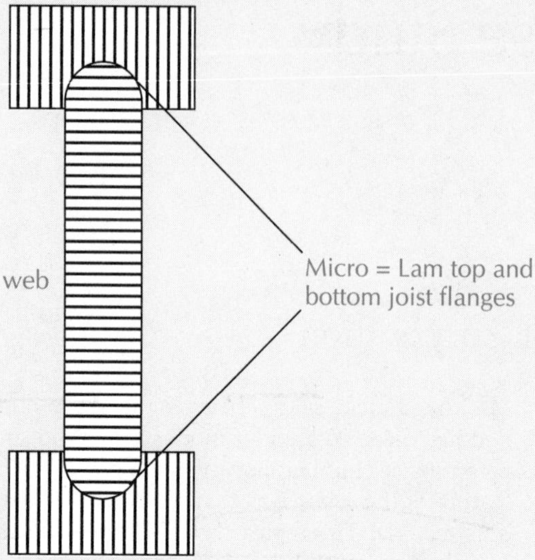

In 1971 Trus Joist first introduced and patented Micro = Lam laminated veneer lumber. The product is made of thin ⅒-inch- or ⅛-inch-thick veneer sheets of Douglas fir glued together by a waterproof phenol formaldehyde adhesive. Under exact and specified conditions the glued sheets are heated and pressed together. The Micro = Lam lumber, or billet,[1] is "extruded" from specially made equipment in 80-foot lengths and 24-foot widths. The billets can be cut to any customer-desired length or width within those limiting dimensions. The billets come in several thicknesses ranging from ¾ inch to 2½ inches; however, 1½ inches and 1¾ inches are the two sizes produced regularly in volume.

MARKETING MICRO = LAM

When Micro = Lam was first introduced, Trus Joist executives asked an independent research group to perform a study indicating possible industrial applications for the product. The first application for Micro = Lam was to replace the high-quality solid sawn lumber 2 × 4-inch trus chords[2] in its open-web joist designs and the solid sawn lumber flanges[3] on its wooden I-beam joist (TJI). Into the fall of 1978 this still represented the majority of Micro = Lam production. The findings of the research report suggested that Micro = Lam could be used as scaffold planking, mobile home trus chords, and housing components. These products accounted for about 25 percent of the Micro = Lam production. Mr. Kalish had also begun to develop new markets for Micro = Lam, including ladder rails and framing material for office partitions.

When marketing Micro = Lam to potential customers, Trus Joist emphasized the superior structural qualities of the product over conventional lumber. Micro = Lam did not possess the undesirable characteristics of warping, checking, and twisting; yet it did show greater bending strength and more structural stability. (One ad claimed, "Testing proves Micro = Lam to be approximately 30 percent stiffer than #1 dense select structural Douglas fir.") In some applications, Micro = Lam offered distinct price advantages over its competing wood alternatives, and this factor always proved to be a good selling point. Manufacturers were often concerned about the lead/delivery time involved in ordering Micro = Lam. Trus Joint promised to deliver within one to three weeks of an order, which was often a full two weeks to two months ahead of other wood manufacturers.

The industrial application report had also suggested using Micro = Lam as a decking material for truck trailers. This use became a reality when Sherman Brothers Trucking, a local trucking firm that frequently transported Micro = Lam, made a request for Micro = Lam to redeck some of its worn-out trailers. To increase the durability of the flooring surface, the manufacturing department of Trus Joist replaced the top two veneer sheets of Douglas fir with apitong. Apitong was a Southeast Asian wood known for its strength, durability, and high specific gravity. This foreign hardwood had been used in the United States for several years because of the diminishing supplies of domestic hardwoods. (See Exhibit 2.)

The pioneer advertisement for Micro = Lam as a trailer deck material had consisted of one ad in a national trade journal and had depicted the Micro = Lam cut so that the edges were used as the top surface. (See Exhibit 3.) The response from this ad had been dismal and had resulted in only one or two orders. The latest advertisement depicting Micro = Lam as it was currently being used (with apitong as the top veneer layers) had better results. This ad, sent to every major truck or trailer manufacturing journal as a news release on a new product, resulted in 30 to 50 inquiries, which turned into 10 to 15 orders. Approximately 15 decks were sold as a result of the promotion.

Everyone at Trus Joist believed that the current price on Micro = Lam was the absolute rock bottom price possible. In fact, most people believed that Micro = Lam was underpriced. The current price of Micro = Lam included a gross margin of 20 percent. The price of 1¼-inch-thick and 1½-inch-thick Micro = Lam was based on the costs of a

EXHIBIT 2 **Mechanical Properties of Wood Used for Trailer Decking**

Common Name of Species	Specific Gravity (percent moisture content)	Modulus of elasticity (million psi)	Compression Parallel to Grain and Fiber Strength Maximum Crush Strength (psi)
Apitong	0.59	2.35	8,540
Douglas fir	0.48	1.95	7,240
Alaska yellow cedar	0.42	1.59	6,640
White oak	0.68	1.78	7,440
Northern red oak	0.63	1.82	6,760
Micro = Lam*	0.55	2.20	8,200

*Micro = Lam using Douglas fir as the veneer faces of the lumber.

Source: Wood Handbook: Wood as an Engineering Material, USDA Handbook No. 72, rev. ed., 1974; U.S. Forest Products Laboratory.

EXHIBIT 3 **End View of Remanufactured Micro = Lam**

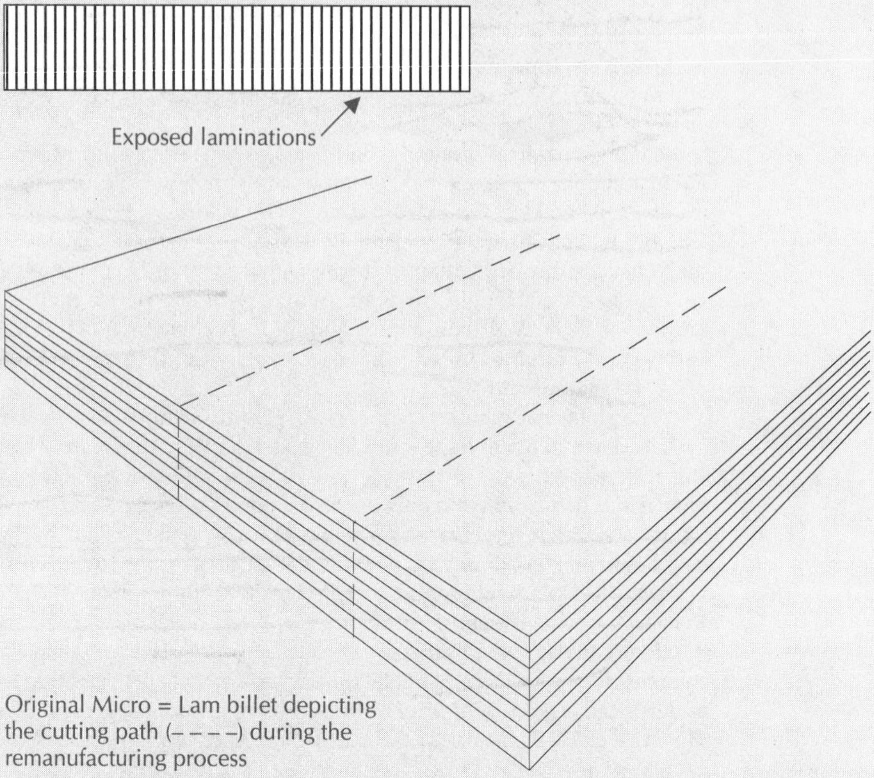

$1\frac{1}{2}$-inch billet. The total variable costs of a $1\frac{1}{2}$-inch material were multiplied by five-sixths to estimate the same costs of $1\frac{1}{4}$-inch material. There had recently been some discussion over the appropriateness of this ratio. Some of the marketing personnel believed that a more appropriate estimate of the variable costs for the $1\frac{1}{4}$-inch Micro = Lam would be the ratio of the number of veneers in a $1\frac{1}{4}$-inch billet to the number of veneers in a $1\frac{1}{2}$-inch billet, or $\frac{14}{16}$. At the present time, the costs of veneer represented 55 percent of the selling price. Glue cost was approximately 13 cents/square foot; fixed overhead represented 14 cents/square foot; and other variable costs amounted to approximately $12\frac{1}{2}$ cents/square foot. The total variable costs were divided by 0.80 to cover all selling and administrative expenses and to secure a profit.[4]

In 1977, truck trailer manufacturers ordered and used 46 million square feet for installation in new truck trailer construction. This figure was understated because redecking or replacement of worn-out floors of trailers had not been incorporated, and there was little organized information to determine what this potential could be. As of 1975, 236 truck trailer manufacturers produced \$646.7 million worth of trailers. (See Exhibit 4.)

EXHIBIT 4 **Truck Trailer Shipments and Dollar Value (by calendar year)**

	1975	1974	1973	1972	1971
Complete trailers and chassis	67,888	191,262	167,201	141,143	103,784
Value	$613,702,000	$1,198,520,000	$956,708,000	$795,500,000	$585,264,000
Containers	4,183*	10,108*	18,626	18,166	8,734
Value	$18,071,000	$27,343,000	$60,159,000	$51,527,000	$26,514,000
Container chassis	2,936	12,883	12,790	15,498	9,775
Value	$14,898,000	$42,076,000	$33,143,000	$39,028,000	$24,999,000
Total units	75,007	214,253	198,617	174,807	122,293
Value	$646,671,000	$1,267,939,000	$1,050,010,000	$886,055,000	$636,777,000

Author: Truck Trailer Manufacturers Association. Data for 1975 preliminary and subject to slight possible change.

*Containers not reported June-October 1974 and January-March 1975.

Source: Ward's Automotive Yearbook, 1978, p. 91

The problem Mr. Kalish saw with this aggregate data was that it was not broken down into the various segments of trailer builders. For example, not all of the 236 manufacturers produced trailers which used wooden floors. Among those not using wooden floors were tankers and logging trailers. Mr. Kalish believed that the real key to selling Micro = Lam in this industry would be to determine the segment of the trailer industry on which he should concentrate his selling efforts. Mr. Kalish also knew that he somehow had to determine trailer manufacturers' requirements for trailer decking. The Eugene-Portland, Oregon, area offered what he thought to be a good cross-section of the type of trailer manufacturers that might be interested in Micro = Lam. He had already contacted some of those firms about buying Micro = Lam.

GENERAL TRAILER COMPANY

Mr. Jim Walline had been the purchasing agent for General Trailer Company of Springfield, Oregon, for the past 2½ years. He stated, "The engineering department makes the decisions on what materials to buy. I place the orders after the requisition has been placed on my desk."

General Trailer Company was a manufacturer of several different types of trailers: low-boys, chip trailers, log trailers, and flatbeds. In 1977 General manufactured five flatbeds and redecked five flatbeds. General did most of its business with the local timber industry; however, it sold three flatbeds in 1977 to local firms in the steel industry.

The flatbeds General Trailer manufactured were 40 to 45 feet long and approximately 7 feet wide. Log trailers were approximately 20 to 25 feet long.

General Trailer manufactured trailers primarily for the West Coast market, although it had sold a few trailers to users in Alaska. On the West Coast, General's major competitors were Peerless, Fruehauf, and Trailmobile, all large-scale manufacturers of truck trailers. Even though General was comparatively small in size, it did not feel threatened, because "we build a top-quality trailer which is not mass-produced," as Mr. Walline put it.

General had been using apitong as a trailer decking material until customers complained of its weight and its expansion/contraction characteristics when exposed to weather. At that time, Mr. Schmidt, the general manager and head of the engineering department, made the decision to switch from apitong to laminated fir.

Laminated fir (consisting of solid sawn lumber strips glued together) was currently being used as the material for decking flatbeds, and Pacific Laminated Company of Vancouver, Washington, supplied all of General's fir decking, so General would only order material when a customer bought a new trailer or needed to have a trailer redecked. Mr. Walline was disappointed with the two- to three-week delivery time, since it often meant that much more time was needed before the customer's trailer was ready.

Laminated fir in 40-foot lengths, 11¾-inch widths, and 1¼-inch thicknesses was used by General. General paid approximately $2 to $3 per square foot for this decking.

Even though Pacific Laminated could provide customer-cut and edged pieces with no additional lead time, General preferred shiplapped fir in the previously noted dimensions, with the top two layers treated with a water proof coating.

The different types of trailers General manufactured required different decking materials. Low-boys required material 2¼-inch thick and General used 3 × 12-inch rough-cut fir lumber. Chip trailers required ⅝-inch-thick MDO (medium density overlay) plywood with a slick surface.

Mr. Walline said General had used Micro = Lam on one trailer; however, the customer had not been expecting it and was very displeased with the job.[5] Therefore, the current policy was to use only laminated fir for the local market unless a customer specifically ordered a different decking material. Trailers headed for Alaska were decked with laminated oak, supplied by a vendor other than Pacific Laminated.

Mr. Walline said that if he wanted to make a recommendation to change decking materials, he would need to know price advantages, lead times, moisture content, availability, and industry experience with the material.

SHERMAN BROTHERS TRUCKING

"We already use Micro = Lam on our trailers," was the response of Mr. Sherman, president of Mayflower Moving and Storage Company, when asked about the trailer decking material his company used. He went on to say, "In fact, we had hauled several shipments for Trus Joist when we initiated a call to them asking if they could make a decking material for us."

Mayflower Moving and Storage owned 60 trailers (flatbeds) which it used to haul heavy equipment and machinery. It had been in a dilemma for eight years about the types of material used to replace the original decks. Nothing seemed to be satisfactory. Solid apitong was tough, but it was too heavy and it did not weather very well. Plywood did not provide adequate weight distribution and had too many joints. Often the small wheels of the forklifts would punch a hole through the decks. Laminated fir was too expensive.

Mayflower Moving and Storage was currently redecking a trailer per week. It usually patched the decks until the whole bed fell apart; then the trailer would sit in the yard waiting for a major overhaul. By this time the trailers needed to have the crossbeams repaired and new bearings as well as a new deck.

Mr. Sherman went on to say, "The shop mechanic just loves Micro = Lam. This is because it used to take the mechanic and one other employee two days to redeck a trailer, and now it just takes the shop mechanic one day to do the same job." Advantages (over plywood and apitong) of the 2-foot × 40-foot Micro = Lam pieces were ease of installation, excellent weight distribution due to the reduced number of seams, and reduced total weight of the bed.

Mr. Sherman explained that Mayflower Moving and Storage usually purchased four or five decks at a time, and warehoused some of the materials until a trailer needed redecking.

Mr. Sherman thought the original decking on flatbeds was some type of hardwood, probably oak, which could last up to five years; however, similar decking material had not been found for a reasonable price. The plywood and fir decks used in the past 8 to 10 years had lasted anywhere from 1 to 2 years, and some had worn out in as little as six months. After using Micro = Lam for six months, Mr. Sherman expected the decking to last up to three to five years.

When asked about the type of flooring used in the company's moving vans, Mr. Sherman emphasized the top care that those floors received. "We sand, buff, and wax them just like a household floor; in fact, we take such good care of these floors they will occasionally outlast the trailer." The original floors in moving vans were made out of a laminated oak and had to be kept extremely smooth, allowing freight to slide freely. The local company purchased all of its moving vans through Mayflower Moving Vans. The only problem with floors in moving vans was that the jointed floors would occasionally buckle because of swelling.

The fact that Micro = Lam protruded ⅛ inch above the metal lip[6] which edged the flatbed trailers posed no problem for Sherman Brothers. "All we had to do was plane the edge at 40 degrees. In fact, the best fit will have the decking protrude a hair above the metal edge," Mr. Sherman said. Just prior to this, Mr. Sherman had recounted an experience which occurred with the first shipment of Micro = Lam. Because the deck was too thick, Mayflower Moving and Storage had about ⅛ inch planed from one side of the decking material. However, the company shaved off the apitong veneer, exposing the fir. Mr. Sherman said that he laughed about it now, but at the time he wasn't too pleased.

EXHIBIT 5 **Cross-Sectional End View of Trailer Decking (Tongue and groove)**

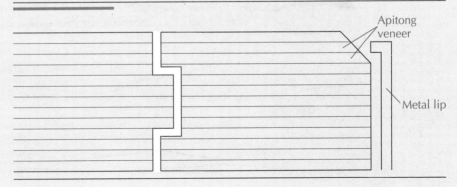

PEERLESS TRUCKING COMPANY

"Sure, I've heard of Micro = Lam. They [Trus Joist salespeople] have been in here . . . but we don't need that good a material." This was the response of Mel Rogers, head of Peerless's Purchasing Department, Tualatin, Oregon, when asked about the use of Micro = Lam as a truck decking material. Mr. Rogers, a 30-year veteran of the trailer manufacturing industry, seemed very skeptical of all laminated decking materials.

The primary products manufactured by Peerless (in Tualatin) required bedding materials very different from Micro = Lam. Chip trailers and railcar dumpers required metal beds to facilitate unloading. Low-boys required a heavy decking material (usually 2 × 12-inch or 3 × 12-inch rough planking) as Caterpillar tractors were frequently driven on them. Logging trailers had no beds.

Approximately 60 decks per year were required by Peerless in the manufacture of flatbeds and in redecking jobs. Micro = Lam could have been used in these applications, but fir planking was used exclusively, except for some special overseas jobs. Fir planking was available in full trailer lengths, requiring eight labor-hours to install on new equipment. Usually five or six decks were stocked at a time. The estimated life on a new deck was two to three years.

Fir planking was selected for decking applications on the basis of price and durability. Peerless purchased fir planking for $1,000 per MBF. Tradition supported fir planking in durability, as it was a well-known product.

Decking material thickness was critical, according to Mr. Rogers, as any deviation from the industry standard of 1⅜ inch required extensive retooling.

Any new decking materials for use in original equipment manufacture had to be approved by the Peerless engineering department. Alternative decking materials could have been used locally if specified by the customer.

Mr. Rogers was certainly going to be a hard person to sell on the use of Micro = Lam, Mr. Kalish felt. "Why use Micro = Lam when I can buy fir planking for less?" Rogers had said.

FRUEHAUF TRUCKING COMPANY

"I'd be very happy if someone would come up with a durable [trailer] deck at a reasonable price," was the response of Wayne Peterson when asked about Fruehauf's experience with decking materials. Mr. Peterson was service manager for Fruehauf's factory branch in Milwaukie, Oregon. Fruehauf Corporation, with its principal manufacturing facilities in Detroit, Michigan, was one of the nation's largest manufacturers of truck trailers.

The manufacturing facilities in Milwaukie produced 40-ton low-beds as well as assembled truck bodies manufactured in Detroit. The low-beds were subjected to heavy use, often with forklifts, which required a decking material of extreme strength and durability. Laminated decking materials then available were therefore excluded from this application.

The decking materials used in the truck bodies were specified by the sales department in Detroit, based on customer input. Generally, apitong or laminated oak was installed at the factory. Any new product to be used in original equipment manufacture had to be approved by Fruehauf's well-developed factory engineering department.

The Milwaukie operation also did about 15 redecking jobs per year. The decking material was specified by the customer on the basis of price and weathering characteristics. The materials used were laminated oak (11½ inches wide × 40 feet), apitong (7 inches × 1/38 inch—random lengths), Alaska yellow cedar (2 inches × 6 inches T&G), fir planking (2 inches × 6 inches T&G), and laminated fir (24 inches wide x 40 feet). Alaska yellow cedar was priced below all other decking materials, followed (in order) by fir planking, laminated fir, laminated oak, and apitong.

Fruehauf's suppliers of decking materials were as follows: laminated fir—Pacific Laminating, Vancouver, Washington; Alaska yellow cedar—Al Disdero Lumber Company, Portland, Oregon; and apitong—Builterials, Portland, Oregon. There were no specific suppliers for the other materials.

A minimum inventory of decking materials was kept on hand to allow for immediate repair needs only. Orders were placed for complete decks as needed.

A redecking job typically required 30 labor-hours per 7-foot × 40-foot trailer, including the removal of the old deck and installation of the new one. Decking materials that were available in full trailer lengths were preferred, as they greatly reduced installation time, improved weight distribution, and had fewer joints along which failure could occur.

The use of alternative products, such as composition flooring of wood and aluminum, was not under consideration.

Alaska yellow cedar and fir planking had the best weathering characteristics, while apitong and laminated oak weathered poorly. Oak and apitong did, however, have a hard, nonscratching surface that was desirable in enclosed use. When asked about the weathering characteristics of laminated flooring in general, Mr. Peterson responded, "It's all right for the dry states, but not around here."

COMPETITION

There were a large number of materials with which Micro = Lam competed in the trailer flooring market, ranging from fir plywood to aluminum floors. Trus Joist felt that the greatest obstacles to Micro = Lam's success would be from the old standard products like laminated fir and oak, which had a great deal of industry respect. For years oak had been the premier flooring material; recently, however, supplies had been short and delivery times long (two months in some cases), and prices were becoming prohibitive. (See Exhibit 6.)

Mr. Kalish had found that in the Northwest, Pacific Laminated Company was one of the major flooring suppliers to local manufacturers. Pacific Laminated produced a Douglas fir laminated product that was highly popular; however, like oak, it was relatively high priced. Despite the price, Pacific Laminated could cut the product to dimensions up to 2 feet wide and 40 feet long. Delivery time was excellent for its customers, even with special milling for shiplapped or tongue and groove edges and manufacturing to user thickness.

CONCLUSION

Although Mr. Kalish had had limited success marketing Micro = Lam to truck trailer manufacturers, he was concerned with the marketing program for his product. Several

EXHIBIT 6 **Decking Material Prices, November 1978**

Product	Price	Form
Alaska yellow cedar	\$650/MBF	2" × 6" T&G 15' lengths
Apitong	\$1.30–2/lineal foot*	1 3/8" × 7" random lengths
Fir planking	\$1/bd. ft.	2" × 6" T&G random lengths
Fir, laminated	\$2.50/sq. ft.	1 1/4" × 11 3/4" × 40'
Micro = Lam	\$1.30/sq. ft.	1 1/4" × 24" × 40'
	\$1.50/sq. ft.	1 1/2" × 24" × 40'
Oak, laminated	\$2.20/sq. ft.	1 3/8" × 1 1/2" × 40'

*Lineal foot = price per unit length of the product.

Sources: Al Disdero Lumber Company, Portland, Oregon; Builterials, Portland, Oregon

trailer manufacturers had raised important questions concerning the price and durability of Micro = Lam compared to alternative decking materials. He knew Micro = Lam had some strong attributes, yet he was hesitant to expand beyond the local market. Mr. Kalish was also wondering about the action he should eventually take in order to determine the additional information he would need to successfully introduce Micro = Lam nationally as a trailer decking material. One thought that crossed his mind was to define the company's marketing strategy for this product. Meanwhile, small orders continued to trickle in.

CASE STUDY ACTIVITY

Please advise Mr. Kalish of the Trus-Joist Corporation.

NOTES

This case is produced with the permission of its author, Dr. Stuart U. Rich, Professor of Marketing and Director, Forest Industries Management Center, College of Business Administration, University of Oregon, Eugene, Oregon.

[1]Micro = Lam is manufactured in units called billets, and the basic unit is one billet foot. The actual dimensions of a billet foot are 1 foot × 2 feet × 1 1/2 inches, and one billet is 80 feet × 24 feet × 1 1/2 feet.

[2]Trus chords are the top and bottom components in an open-web trus incorporating wood chords and tubular steel webs.

[3]Flanges are the top and bottom components in an all-wood I beam. Refer to Exhibit 1.

[4]All cost figures have been disguised.

[5]After purchasing Micro = Lam, General Trailer modified the material by ripping the billets into 1½-inch widths and them relaminating these strips back into 12-inch- or 24-inch-wide pieces of lumber. This remanufacturing added substantial costs. Also, the laminations were now directly exposed to the weather. Moisture could more easily seep into cracks or voids, causing swells and buckling. (See Exhibit 3.)

[6]Refer to Exhibit 5.

Part Three

Identifying the Customer

4 Business Marketing Research and Information Systems

Learning Objectives

After reading this chapter, you should be able to:

- Differentiate between business and consumer marketing research.
- Ascertain the major areas in which marketing research is used.
- Identify the similarities and differences between business marketing research and a business marketing information system (MIS).
- Discuss the steps involved in the business marketing research process.
- Recognize when it is appropriate to use either inside or outside marketing research specialists.
- Understand the differences between primary and secondary sources of research data and be aware of the disadvantages and drawbacks of each.
- Understand the reasons behind the often widely differing organizational designs and staffing needs of business research departments.
- Appreciate the role of marketing research in international business marketing.

Chapter Outline

Learning Objectives

Differences between Business and Consumer Marketing Research
- Focus of Business Marketing Research

Major Tasks of Business Marketing Research
- Market Potential
- Market-Share Analysis
- Market Characteristics
- Sales Analysis
- Forecasting
- Other Applications

Marketing Research versus a Marketing Information System
- Five Basic Elements of Future Marketing Information Systems
- Primary Uses of the Marketing Information System

The Business Marketing Research Process
- Planning the Research Design
- Preparation
- Field Operations
- Processing
- Tabulation, Analysis, and Interpretation
- Reporting

Using Outside or Inside Research Specialists—Make or Buy?

Developing Information Sources
- Secondary Data Sources
  - Internal secondary data sources
  - External secondary data sources
    - Governmental sources
    - Commercial sources
    - Professional publications
  - Other secondary data sources
  - Disadvantages and drawbacks of secondary data
- Primary Data Sources
  - Personal interviews
  - Telephone surveys
  - Mail surveys
  - Disadvantages and drawbacks of primary data

Organization of Business Marketing Research

Conducting International Marketing Research

Summary

Key Terms

Review Questions

Cases
- Case 4-1
- Case 4-2

Suggested Additional Readings

Endnotes

DIFFERENCES BETWEEN BUSINESS AND CONSUMER MARKETING RESEARCH

There are many differences between business and consumer marketing. However, is there a difference between business and consumer marketing research? This question can be answered by looking at the types of marketing research studies conducted and by comparing the types of research techniques used by consumer companies with those employed by business marketers. Table 4-1 presents a summary of such studies and comparisons.

An inspection of Table 4-1 will show that the widespread marketing research activities engaged in by consumer and business companies have some important commonalities, as well as some significant differences. Consumer-goods companies use marketing research in testing products, improving packaging, determining brand attributes and brand personality, improving the efficiency of advertising (both as to content and selected media), measuring the flow of sales, setting sales quotas both for products and for territories, and analyzing distribution costs. Business-goods manufacturers are less remote from their markets, and both their current and their potential customers are fewer and more easily identified than those for consumer products. Business markets are more sensitive to economic fluctuations, and the marketer has more opportunity to learn buyer preferences on a first-hand basis. When the channel of distribution is shorter, as is the case with most business products, communication becomes easier. For example, a machine tool producer or a specialty steel house has more direct customer contact than does a toothpaste manufacturer such as Procter and Gamble or Colgate-Palmolive.

Focus of Business Marketing Research

Businesses have realized that buyers, influencers, and end users can be researched just as consumers can. Marketing research has become a $10 billion market in the United States, as managers seek information to reduce the uncertainty of their decisions. But even in the economic boom years of the late 1980s, just $1 of every $10 spent to probe customers and market conditions was applied to business markets.[1] This phenomenon is rapidly changing, and business marketing research has pretty much caught up with consumer research. Business marketers now use most of the qualitative and quantitative techniques and procedures of consumer research, including computer-assisted telephone interviewing and multivariate analysis.[2] Business marketing research will focus less on product attributes than on such questions as to what is the potential in different areas and for different products; who makes buying decisions; who are members of the buying center; and which trade journals will provide the biggest return per advertising dollar spent.

TABLE 4-1 **Research Activities of 798 Companies**

Subject of Studies	**Percentage of Reporting Companies Doing Each Type of Research** *All Reporting Companies*	*Consumer-Product Companies*	*Business-to-Business-Product Companies*
1. Sales and market research			
Market potential measurement	93	97	97
Market characteristics	93	92	97
Market-share analysis	92	96	97
Sales analysis	89	96	97
Establishing sales quotas and territories	75	91	95
Distribution-channel studies	69	86	87
Sales-compensation studies	60	78	79
Test markets, sales audits	54	83	43
Promotional studies	52	73	32
2. Business economics and corporate research			
Business-trends analysis	86	79	97
Short-range forecasting	85	90	98
Long-range forecasting (over one year)	82	87	96
Pricing studies	81	88	93
Plant and warehouse location	71	76	84
Acquisition studies	69	81	47
3. Product research			
Competitive product studies	85	93	95
New product acceptance and potential	84	94	93
Testing existing products	75	95	84
Packaging research	60	83	65
4. Advertising research			
Ad-effectiveness studies	67	85	47
Media research	61	69	43
Copy research	49	76	37
Motivation research	48	67	26
5. Corporate responsibility research			
Legal constraints on advertising and promotion studies	51	64	60
Ecological-impact studies	33	40	52
Social values and policies	40	43	40
Consumers' right-to-know studies	26	32	21

Data reported by 798 companies to the American Marketing Association.

Source: Adapted from Dick W. Twedt, ed., *1978 Survey of Marketing Research* (Chicago: American Marketing Association, 1978), pp. 41, 43. Used with permission.

In the world of business marketing research, researchers are adopting techniques used by consumer marketers. One cause of this evolution is that U.S. firms have had to confront the determined marketing savvy of the Japanese, who have been rigorous with business research in their attempt to gain recognition among foreign customers. Other reasons include the trend toward increased levels of customer satisfaction and the European economic unification of 1992.[3]

Since business markets are generally more sensitive to economic fluctuations than are consumer markets, product-line forecasting is correspondingly more important. Business companies will use less advertising research than consumer companies because business-to-business companies rely more on the personal selling aspect of the promotional mix than do consumer firms. Business services of all kinds, such as business cleaning services or freight carriers, conduct research on customer wants and needs. A mortgage banker will consider establishing a research department because it might be easier to arrange financing when the borrower's activity has been formally and objectively analyzed. A truck-leasing agency, such as Ryder Truck, will consider conducting operating-cost research to demonstrate the value of its service to a prospective customer. Another way to compare business with consumer marketing research is to break down the various aspects of the research survey process. Table 4-2 compares the process of business versus consumer research, pointing out some of the more important differences between the two.

Surveys in business marketing often encounter different problems than those found when conducting consumer research; and, as such, the survey process is often very different. In Table 4-2, the student will note the special difficulties associated with respondent accessibility and cooperation on the business side. These are important differences, given the prevalence of the personal-interviewing technique.

MAJOR TASKS OF BUSINESS MARKETING RESEARCH

The extent to which business firms use marketing research is wide and varied. Below are the major areas where business marketing research is conducted.

Market Potential

Research must clarify the maximum total sales and profit potential of product-market opportunities. This type of clarification will help to direct the resources available for new-product introduction and product-deletion decisions.

Market-Share Analysis

Marketing research is assigned the task of determining the ratio of sales revenue of the firm to the total sales revenue of all firms in the industry, including the firm itself. The competitive environment is dynamic, making market-share

TABLE 4-2 **Consumer versus Business Marketing Research: What Are the Differences?**

	Consumer	Business to Business
Universe population	Large. Dependent on category under investigation but usually unlimited. 72.5 million U.S. households and 215 million persons.	Small. Fairly limited in total population and even more so if within a defined industry or SIC category.
Respondent accessibility	Fairly easy. Can interview at home, on the telephone, or use mail techniques.	Difficult. Usually only during working hours at plant, office, or on the road. Respondent is usually preoccupied with other priorities.
Respondent cooperation	Over the years has become more and more difficult, yet millions of consumers have never been interviewed.	A major concern. Due to the small population, the respondent is being over-researched. The purchaser and decision makers in the business firm are the buyers of a variety of products and services from office supplies to heavy equipment.
Sample size	Can usually be drawn as large as required for statistical confidence since the population is in the hundreds of millions.	Usually much smaller than consumer sample, yet the statistical confidence is equal due to the relationship of the sample to the total population.
Respondent definitions	Usually fairly simple. Those aware of a category or brand, users of a category or brand, demographic criteria, etc. The ultimate purchaser is also a user for most consumer products and services.	Somewhat more difficult. The user and the purchasing decision maker in most cases are not the same. Factory workers who use heavy equipment, secretaries who use office equipment, etc., are the users and, no doubt, best able to evaluate these products and services. However, they tend not to be the ultimate purchasers and in many cases do not have any influence on the decision-making process.
Interviewers	Can usually be easily trained. They are also consumers and tend to be somewhat familiar with the area under investigation for most categories.	Difficult to find good executive interviewers. At least a working knowledge of the product class or subject being surveyed is essential. Preferably more than just a working knowledge.
Study costs	Key dictators of cost are sample size and incidence. Lower-incidence-usage categories (for example, users of soft moist dog food, powdered breakfast beverages, etc.) or demographic or behavioral screening criteria (attend a movie at least once a month, over 65 years of age, and do not have direct deposit of social security payments, etc.) can up costs considerably.	Relative to consumer research, the critical elements resulting in significantly higher per-interview costs are: the lower incidence levels, the difficulties in locating the "right" respondent (that is, the purchase decision maker) and securing cooperation, time, and concentration of effort for the interview itself.

Source: Martin Katz, "Use Same Theory, Skills for Consumer, Industrial Marketing Research," *The Marketing News*, January 12, 1979 (Chicago: American Marketing Association), p. 16. Used with permission.

analysis a regular standard against which to compare the firm's current objectives and future performance. An expert system for market-share analysis has been developed. The prototype system, called SHANEX (Share Analysis Expert System) not only outputs numbers but also makes humanlike judgments based on those numbers in conjunction with additional information. This is an exciting development, and new systems will continue to come on-stream.[4]

Market Characteristics

Marketing research helps to identify opportunities and set objectives in the area of market characteristics as well. Much of what was studied in Chapters 2 and 3, in terms of buyer behavior, buying organizational changes, and so on, will be researched and reported on. How successful a firm has been in penetrating particular markets, and more important, why they have or have not been successful, are crucial pieces of data when setting objectives and a direction for the future.

Sales Analysis

Business marketing research is also a tool used in controlling marketing programs where actual sales records are compared with sales goals to identify strengths and weaknesses. Sales analysis, also called *microsales analysis*, traces sales revenues to their sources, such as specific products, sales territories, or customers. Common research breakdowns would include the following:

- Customer characteristics: reason for purchase, type of firm, and user versus middleman
- Product characteristics: model, size, and accessory equipment bought
- Geographic region: sales territory, city, state, and region
- Order size
- Price or discount class

This analysis is helpful to the business marketing manager in determining the direction of future efforts regarding product profitability, sales territory changes, product deletion decisions, and the like.

Forecasting

Both short-range and long-range forecasting are vital inputs to the marketing planning process. The amount a firm expects to sell during a specific time period under specific conditions and to specific segments affects both the controllable and uncontrollable factors that influence future business. Forecasts form the basis of all planning activity within the organization. The Conference Board has described the importance of sales forecasting in this manner:

> The sales forecast is an essential tool of management in any business. Those in charge—the hot dog vendor no less than the members of senior management at General Motors—require some means of gauging the probable direction and level of future sales. Lacking such predictions, there is no realistic starting point for setting the enterprise's course and safeguarding its profits.[5]

Forecasting is critical for cash flow estimates, plant expansions, projected employment levels, decisions regarding product-line changes, distribution-channel changes, and a host of other decision areas about which the firm must act upon regularly.

Other Applications

In addition to the above, the subjects to which business organizations apply their marketing research efforts have been studied and reported upon regularly by the American Marketing Association for over thirty years.[6] Additional data researched would include studies on sales quotas and territories, pricing, test-marketing audits, business trends, new-product acceptance, advertising research, and competitive differences. For instance, the box entitled "Business-to-Business Marketing in Action" describes how a construction company was able to use a marketing research study to position itself as "the contractor of choice" by asking its customers, architects, and designers questions about the worst features of its competitors. Marketing research can certainly be described as a widely diverse marketing function.

MARKETING RESEARCH VERSUS A MARKETING INFORMATION SYSTEM

Whereas marketing research is problem or project oriented, a *marketing information system (MIS)* uses procedures, hardware, and software to accumulate, interpret, and disseminate important data through reports to key marketing decision makers. A marketing information system can be defined as a system that scans and collects data from the environment, makes use of data from transactions and operations within the firm, and then filters, organizes, and selects data before presenting it as information to management.[7] It is imperative today that every firm manage and disseminate marketing information as effectively as possible. A marketing information system is a computerized model providing timely, accurate information to improve marketing decisions. It is a set of procedures and methods designed to generate, analyze, and distribute marketing decision-making information on a regular basis to key marketing executives involved in the decision-making process. A database marketing system has the ability to assemble massive amounts of marketing data and provide it in an almost infinite number of combinations, depending on what is needed.[8]

BUSINESS-TO-BUSINESS MARKETING IN ACTION

QUIZ CUSTOMERS FOR CLUES ABOUT COMPETITION

John Grubb wanted to distinguish his San Francisco construction company, Clearwood Building Inc., from a host of competitors. So, in early 1983, he and his brother Robert started talking to Clearwood's customers: the architects and designers who hired their services.

What, the brothers asked their customers, were the worst features of Clearwood's competitors? The answer: Bad manners, workers who tracked dirt across carpets, and beat-up construction trucks, which high-class clients objected to having parked in their driveways.

Those seemingly small points were the signal for a repositioning. The brothers decided to make Clearwood the contractor of choice among the Bay Area's upper crust. The company bought a new truck and kept it spotless. Its estimators donned jackets and ties. And its work crews, now impeccably polite, began rolling protective runners over carpets before they set foot in clients' homes. In less than two years, Clearwood's annual revenue jumped to $1 million from $200,000.

Keeping an eye on the competition, of course, is a vital part of running any business. But the way it is done is changing, particularly for small businesses. Increasingly, business owners are strengthening their ties to customers in the hope of gaining insights about competitors that they can turn to their advantage. "It's the difference between acquaintance and commitment," Robert Grubb says of the stronger links being forged.

The strategy of drawing closer to customers is a lesson some businesses are learning from Japan. There, tight bonds between suppliers and manufacturers have produced flexibility, cost savings, and quality levels that translate into export advantages. But the approach is also spreading because the notion of strategic planning, long practiced by big U.S. companies, is percolating down to smaller concerns. Owners are taking a longer-term view of their companies and a more disciplined approach to analyzing the players in their markets.

Robert Grubb, for example, was studying strategic planning at a business school when he began mapping competitive moves for Clearwood Building. He has since become president of DTM Products Inc., a Boulder, Col., plastic injection-molding concern, where he is using a similar approach. "We are looking at the competition by focusing on the customer," he says.

In DTM's case, the current concern is foreign competition. One major customer, for instance, recently told the company that an Italian competitor had delivered a "beautiful" sample mold.

"We said, 'Look, we are committed to you guys as a team member," Mr. Grubb says. "Rather than being defensive, we say, "That's great. What do you think the advantages are?' Through that kind of questioning, we can find out what they *can't* get overseas. We start realizing what we need to focus on in order to be their suppliers two, four, six, ten years from now."

Source: Reprinted by permission of *The Wall Street Journal*, © March 3, 1986, p. 17, Dow Jones & Company, Inc.

An important point to remember about the MIS is that it gathers important information from the disciplines of finance, production control, accounting (and others) and translates this information into useful form. Some information, such as certain data on competition or a particular market, may not exist within the firm. Often, the sales force will play a key role in gathering market data via sales-control systems such as call reports, quotes submitted, lost-order reports, and the like. Information about a company's environment and customers collected by the sales force is an important component of a marketing information system.[9] Some of this data may be available in published sources (secondary data) but may be difficult to find in accurate relevant form. Other data necessary to make a decision may not exist at all; primary data must be generated and may be obtained only after expending much time and effort, along with many dollars. In short, marketing information gathering is time-consuming and may be difficult, with the business firm spending much time and money on the effort. The MIS is designed to perform even more comprehensively by additionally gathering, analyzing, processing, and distributing marketing information gathered from marketing research. In most firms, marketing research departments have been created so that data not currently in existence can be obtained, although marketing research represents only one source of information for a marketing information system.

Figure 4-1 illustrates the marketing-information interface with the marketing decision-making process. Notice that the data—which would be in the form of facts, figures, and numbers—is fed to data organization, data analysis, and report generation. Key marketing executives now have the necessary information to make decisions concerning market share, entry into new markets, product adaptations, and the like. This information increases the likelihood of making good decisions.

Five Basic Elements of Future Marketing Information Systems

The MIS of the 1990s will emphasize the need for the system to be user-friendly and will have five basic elements:

(1) *Data bank*—a collection of libraries of information. In marketing, these include sales by type of outlet and geographic area, as well as customer data reported to the sales force resulting from sales calls.

(2) *Models*—ideas or hypotheses about the relationship between the factors that a marketing manager controls and the results sought.

(3) *Links*—a means of tying the data bank to other models.

(4) *Optimization*—a goal of improving the marketing decision maker's measure of success—whether it is increasing sales and profits or reducing expenses.

(5) *Systems interrogation*—a means of communicating with the entire system so that the manager can ask questions and get answers quickly (a good

FIGURE 4-1 **Schematic View of a Marketing Information System**

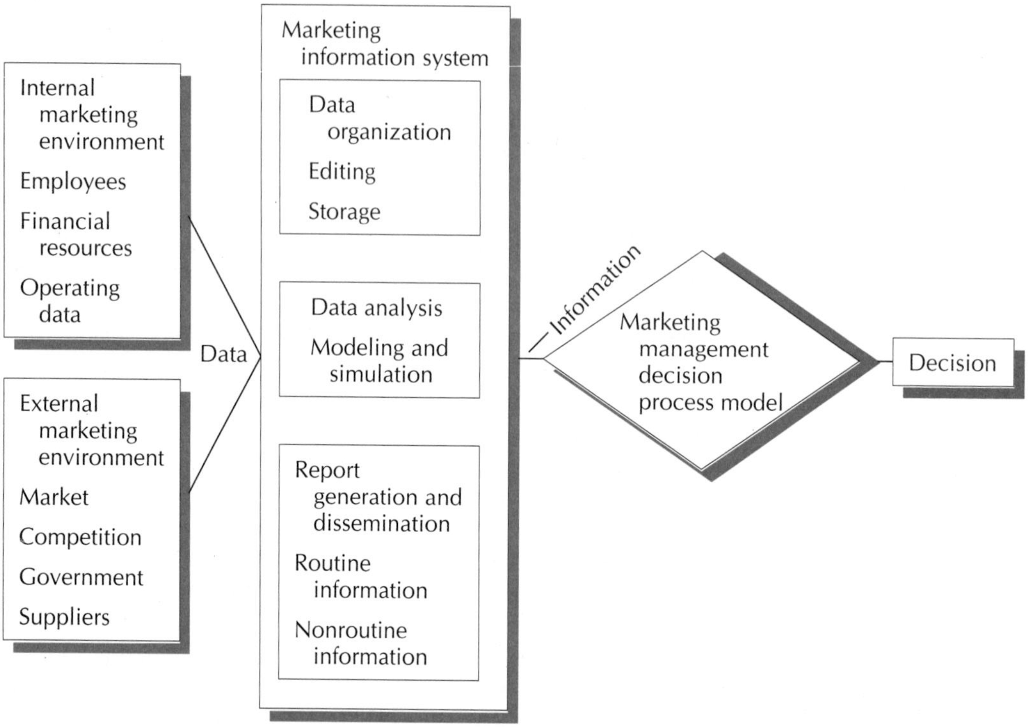

argument for direct access to the system through a terminal or personal computer on the manager's desk).

Primary Uses of a Marketing Information System

The 1990s and beyond will show that the MIS will serve as a nerve center, providing instantaneous information and monitoring the marketplace continuously so that management can adjust activities as conditions change.

Some marketing executives think that their organizations are too small to use an MIS; they feel that their marketing research department will provide adequate research data for effective decision making. However, as noted earlier, marketing research itself is typically focused on a specific problem or project; its investigations have a definite beginning, middle, and end. A marketing information system is much wider in scope. Figure 4-2 shows the various information inputs that serve as components of a typical firm's MIS. Information sources are broad and varied, and although all primary and secondary data are not included in the diagram, a brief review of Figure 4-2 will give the reader an overview and a better understanding of the depth and importance of a good MIS. (Primary data are

FIGURE 4-2 **Sources of Input to a Marketing Information System**

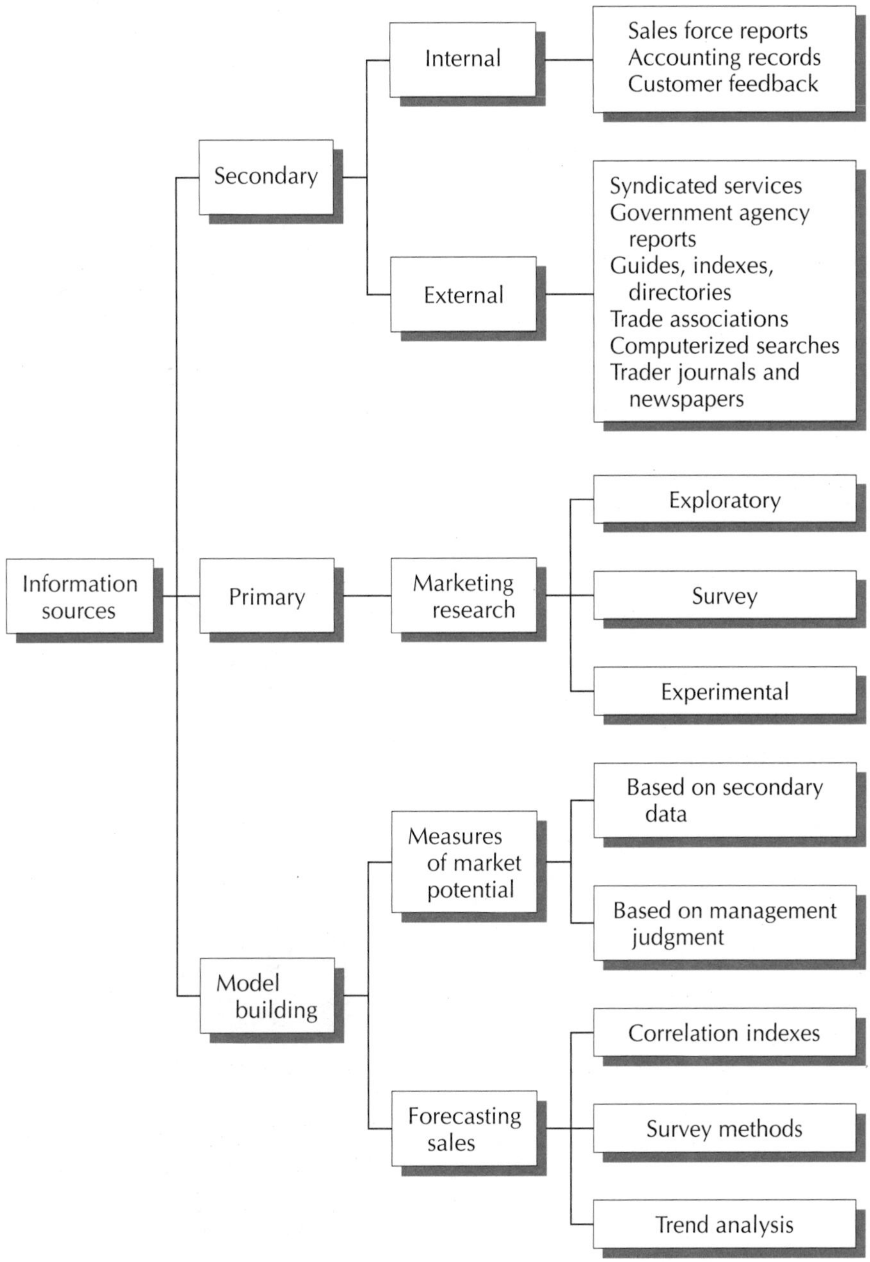

organized and collected for a specific problem, have not been collected previously, and must be generated by original research. Secondary data already exists.)

Finally, an effective MIS will enable the business marketing manager to make more effective decisions in overall marketing strategy. Making business marketing decisions without input from the marketplace is dangerous, considering the degree of competition encountered by most U.S. business firms. An MIS is intended to provide information about customer problems and dissatisfactions, potential intermediary problems, competitive acts, and other external and internal factors before crisis situations arise. A properly formulated MIS can be preventative as well as curative for problems or potential problems commonly faced by the practicing business marketing manager. Figure 4-3 illustrates the use of a marketing information system.

CONCEPT QUESTIONS

1. What is the major focus of business marketing research?
2. What is the role of sales analysis in business marketing research?
3. How does an MIS serve as a nerve center for the business firm?

FIGURE 4-3 **A Marketing Information System with an Example of Its Use**

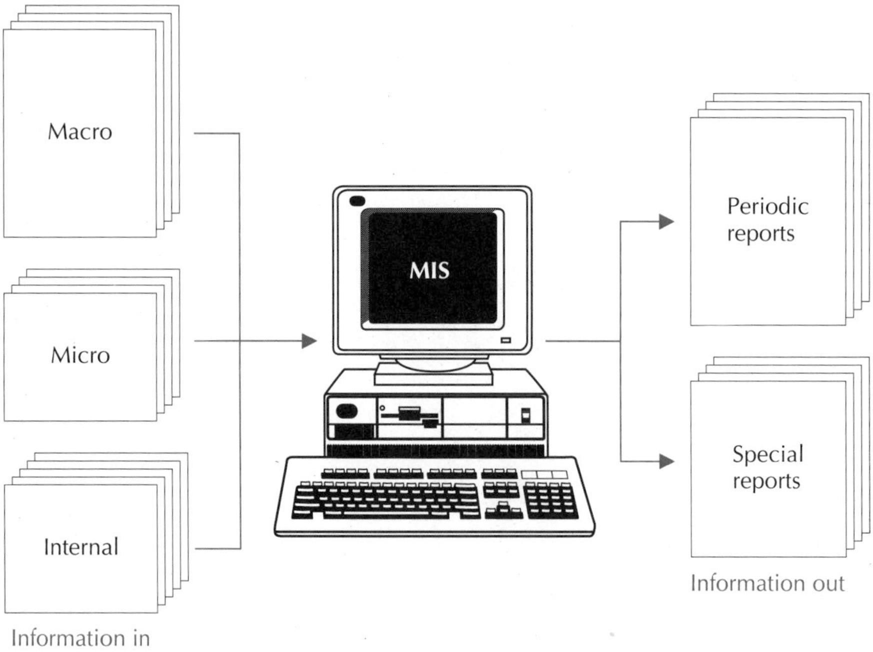

THE BUSINESS MARKETING RESEARCH PROCESS

Marketing research is undertaken to gather reliable marketing information to facilitate planning and control. Marketing research must be viewed as a process of primary phases and steps. Exhibit 4-1 shows the six primary phases and the fourteen principal steps needed to take a marketing research project from initiation to completion. Each step is important, so each will be examined in detail.

Planning the Research Design

Planning the research design has often been called the most important phase of a research project as many, if not all, of the qualitative and quantitative aspects of the study are conveyed by the chosen design. Step 1, problem recognition and definition, is critical, because if the research problem is not properly defined, the information produced by the research process is unlikely to have any value. Problem recognition and definition is the most critical stage in the marketing research process.[10] *Problem recognition and definition* involves specifying the types of information needed to solve a problem, while the design process culminates with a written project proposal that conveys the essence of a study to management. The typical proposal will contain a clear explanation of the study's objectives and value; it will also include statements of the research method to be used, what is to be measured, how the data will be analyzed, and the projected cost, with a schedule of when various aspects of the project will be completed.

EXHIBIT 4-1 **Primary Phases in the Course of a Research Project**

Planning the Research Design	Processing
1. Recognizing and defining problems	8. Coding and keypunching data
2. Research design and project proposal	9. Constructing the computer file
Preparation	**Tabulation, Analysis, and Interpretation**
3. Sampling plan	10. Generate tables
4. Data-collection and questionnaire-design considerations	11. Analysis
	12. Interpretation
Field Operations	**Reporting**
5. Scheduling interviews	13. Written report-oral presentation
6. Conducting interviews	14. Follow-up
7. Check-in, editing, and validation	

Preparation

If information to solve a problem cannot be found in internal or external published data, the researcher must then rely on primary data, which is collected from the field specifically for the study. This process may require taking a sample of the target population. Deciding on sample size requires that the sample size necessary to answer the research question with the required precision and confidence be calculated within a framework of time and cost restrictions. As an example, a marketing researcher needs data concerning the salability of a new feature on an automatic-packaging machine. Secondary data is not available, so the researcher must talk to potential users to determine whether or not the proposed new feature is indeed wanted or even needed by the target market. The sample size will be small, as a check of just a few potential users will provide enough information to make a decision. Questionnaire construction is a critical step here, as the respondent will be technically oriented, and the questions to be asked must be worded accordingly.

Field Operations

This activity involves meeting with the respondents and administering the questionnaire. The interviewer must ensure that all questionnaires are completed properly and that the number of completed interviews meets the research design specifications for cost and schedule. Ensuring the validity of the research findings requires checking whether the interviews were conducted according to the specifications of the research design. If this is not done, poorly worded questions will produce answers that may cause the firm to make a wrong decision as to the marketability of a new product or new product feature.

Processing

In this phase, the researcher codes and prepares the data for tabulation and analysis. *Coding* is the process by which numerical values or alphanumeric symbols are assigned to represent a specific response to a question. Either closed-ended or open-ended questions are generally used. With closed-ended questions, the respondent has a limited number of answer choices; answers to open-ended questions are not limited by the researcher beforehand. Respondents can say whatever they want and in their own words.

Tabulation, Analysis, and Interpretation

Having gathered the data, the researcher proceeds toward drawing conclusions by logical inference. *Tabulation* presents the data in tabular form, which allows the marketing researcher to communicate effectively with the business marketing executive. *Analysis* attempts to turn numbers into data, and then to turn data into attainable marketing information that can be well utilized by the marketing executive. *Interpretation* involves a clear statement of implications derived from the study's findings. These implications define the alternative courses of action consistent with the objectives and nature of the study. With the example previously mentioned, data is now available so that a recommendation and decision can be made as to the marketability of the new feature on the automatic-packaging machine.

Reporting

Although the technical research work has ended with the interpretation of the data into findings relevant to the problem, the researcher's work is not yet over. Much of the acceptance that the research results receive depends on the way in which they are presented. The report is often all the marketing executive sees of the project, and it is usually a source of great pride to the researcher.

The *reporting phase* of a research study typically involves a written report, an oral presentation, and a follow-up. All these should focus on the marketability of the new packaging-machine feature, while justifying the dollar outlay for the research study. The follow-up should try to measure the efficiency of the research project as a whole. This measurement would involve questionnaire analysis and respondent analysis, among other things. The aim is to improve the entire research process so that the decision-making process will be improved as well.

USING OUTSIDE OR INSIDE RESEARCH SPECIALISTS—MAKE OR BUY?

Who should conduct the marketing research studies needed? Should the business firm depend on internal "specialists," or should outside sources be employed? This decision is not too different from the make-or-buy analysis studied in Chapter 3.

It is not unusual for business firms to have marketing research studies (or portions of studies, such as the interviewing phase) conducted by outside organizations. Many organizations perform research activities on a contract or fee basis, including most advertising agencies, marketing research firms, management consulting firms, some universities, and trade associations. Seven factors are involved in the typical marketing research make-or-buy decision.[11]

(1) *Economic factors.* Can an outside firm provide the information more economically?

(2) *Expertise.* Is the necessary expertise available internally?

(3) *Special equipment.* Does the study require special equipment not currently available in the firm?

(4) *Political considerations.* Does the study involve deeply controversial issues within the organization? Studies designed to help resolve bitter internal disputes, or that might reflect unfavorably on some segment of the organization, should generally be conducted by an outside organization.

(5) *Legal and promotional considerations.* Will the results of the study be used in a legal proceeding, or as part of a promotional campaign? In either case, the presumption (which is not necessarily correct) that an outside firm is more objective suggests that one be used.

(6) *Administrative facets.* Are current workloads and time pressures preventing the completion of needed research? If so, outside firms can be employed to handle temporary overloads.

(7) *Confidentiality requirements.* Is it absolutely essential that the research be kept secret? As the need for confidentiality increases, the desirability of using an outside agency decreases.

DEVELOPING INFORMATION SOURCES

Information sources available to the marketing researcher can be classified broadly as either primary or secondary. As noted earlier, *primary data* are organized and collected for a specific problem, have not been collected previously, and must be generated by original research. *Secondary data* already exist. They are historical data previously gathered by people either inside or outside the firm to meet their needs. If those needs are similar to those of the researcher, there is no reason to collect primary data. Secondary data are usually cheaper and quicker to collect than are primary data, but industrial marketing researchers must always consider their relevance, accuracy, credibility, and timeliness.

Secondary Data Sources

Internal secondary data sources. Inside sources include marketing plans, company reports, and marketing information system (MIS) reports. Firms produce, assemble, distribute, and store enormous amounts of internal literature and statistics. Such reports can range from a simple, informational type of memorandum, to a several-hundred-page report describing some future direction that the firm will likely take. In reality, personnel in the accounting and sales departments are generally the most prolific producers of internal secondary data.

External secondary data sources. More general, more diverse, and simply "more" secondary data exist in sources outside the decision maker's firm. Sources of external secondary data include governmental, commercial, professional, and other sources. External secondary data can be subcategorized as information purchased from a vendor, free information, or information purchased at a nominal charge from a library. Many tools and services are available to library patrons to access secondary information.[12]

Governmental sources.[13] Federal and state government provides so much useful literature and statistics that it collectively accounts for more secondary data than any other source. Governmental agencies publish a number of census studies and other documents that are used extensively by marketing researchers. Examples include the following: *Census of Agriculture, Census of Business, Census of Manufactures, Census of Service Industries, Census of Transportation, Census of Wholesale Trade, Census of Population,* and the *Standard Industrial Classification Code.* Business-oriented census data, such as the development of the *Standard Industrial Classification (SIC) System,* has greatly enhanced the ability of the marketing researcher to conduct marketing research and to gather marketing intelligence. The *Standard Industrial Classification* code, published by the Office of Management and Budget and distributed through the U.S. Government Printing Office, uses a system that divides the nation's economic activities into broad industrial divisions—two-digit major groups, three-digit industry subgroups, and four-digit detailed industries. For example:

Division	Manufacturing	SIC Code
Major Group	Good and kindred products	20
Industry Subgroup	Canned and preserved fruits and vegetables	203
Detailed Industry	Frozen fruits, fruit juices, and vegetables	2037

Beyond four-digit detailed industries, the researcher can find data on five-digit product classes (for example, 20371 stands for frozen fruits, juices, and ades). The researcher can also find data on seven-digit products (20371-71 stands for frozen orange juice, concentrated).

The Standard Industrial Classification System is a numerical system set up by the federal government to classify the total economy into different segments. It was developed in the mid-1930s with the purpose of making it both easier and quicker for those collecting secondary data from the government to find information about their specific areas of interest. It was also intended to standardize government reporting of statistical data. SIC codes are used most appropriately by business researchers when they define industries.[14] The system categorizes business activities into several broad divisions and then subdivides them into major groups, subgroups, and detailed four-digit subgroups, as illustrated above. The SIC number assigned is based on the product produced or operation performed by each establishment. Firms with similar products, or those engaged in comparable production activities, are grouped together. The SIC manual is periodically updated to improve on the Code, although updates are infrequently made. The last three major updates occurred in 1957, 1972, and 1987. Although two firms may have different seven-digit codes for a specific industry, both would use the same four-digit code as a base; thereby providing a uniform system that can be easily used as a tool for research.

In order to make the Code workable, all economic activity within the United States is first divided into eleven separate categories. One of the eleven is an open category set up for nonclassifiable establishments. The major areas of activity are considered "divisions," with each of the eleven groups being given a unique alphabetical letter ranging from A to K to represent the division. Within each division, two-digit codes are given to break the industry down into "major groups." The number of two-digit groups depends on the size of the division that is being broken down. Within each two-digit code, the major groups are again divided into lower-level subgroups by adding a third code number. This three-digit level classifies "industry groups." Finally, the last digit is generated by dividing the three-digit codes down, with the resulting four-digit code relating to "specific industries." The system provides researchers with a structure that looks like an inverted funnel. By using this inverted-funnel structure in the research process, a researcher will start with the most general level of information and work down to the most specific level. This provides a quick and logical manner in which to secure data.

Expanded versions of the SIC Code follow the same system, the only difference being that additional sublevels have been established to an even more specific level. This same pattern is repeated to produce six- and seven-digit codes. The major reasons to collect data with the use of the SIC Code are (1) to collect information on a specific target market to be reached; (2) to research the competition within a specific market; and (3) to obtain information on a specific market and compare that information over time in order to note market trends within a specific industry.

Advantages of the SIC Code. Using the SIC Code has many advantages, the greatest of which is that the system itself is uniformly set up. Therefore, if researchers were looking to find data on companies within a regional area, they could cross-reference the location with the specific code for the industry of interest. By doing so, they could easily find similar information from all secondary data journals searched. The benefits can be found in the Code's uniformity, because it greatly reduces the amount of work needed to be done by the researcher. In the above-stated scenario, the researcher would need only to look at a limited amount of reference materials, thereby eliminating information and not having to worry about overlooking a prospect. The next major advantage can be found in its ease of use. With the inverted funnel structure illustrated earlier, a researcher can easily and quickly channel an area of interest down to a specific industry. Without the SIC Code, one must search for the specific industry first, which can be difficult, especially when an industry has more than one product, or when its products go by more than one technical name. Additionally, without the SIC Code, a researcher may spend much time in trying to find information, rather than in collecting and analyzing it. Because the SIC Code is easy to use, information can be gathered quickly, thereby providing a major advantage to those wishing to use it.

Limitations of the SIC Code. Although the SIC Code has many advantages, it is not without limitations. One of its first limitations relates to the data itself:

> Because the total output of a multiproduct establishment must be assigned to a single 4-digit industry (an unavoidable consequence of this type of system), the shipment's total for that industry will be somewhat overstated.[15]

Another limitation relates to the Code's method of identification of an industry when a company produces many products. The SIC Code lists industries under their major product produced, with the result being that many firms within that market may be omitted. A third limitation is the "nondisclosure rule," which

> bars the Census Bureau from publishing data that may disclose the operations of an individual employer. In other words, a large establishment that dominates a county's statistical listing cannot by law be listed, since the data for the county would constitute a virtual profile of this company's business operations. Because the largest establishments in a county are often affected by this rule, their shipments/receipts totals would be excluded from the Census Bureau's industry totals, leading to an understatement at the local level.[16]

This occurrence can be especially dangerous for researchers trying to compile industry trends.

A fourth limitation relates to the Code's current revision. Although the latest SIC manual has been improved greatly, many secondary data sources are not updated and will not be for several years. Because of this fact, researchers must put up with the faults of the old Code until the new revisions are used. A fifth limitation also relates to the topic of revisions. As times change, revisions will be needed, especially in highly technical industries that are entering new fields on a regular basis. Because the system is not updated on a regular basis, great amounts of information will be left out of the Code until the next revision is made.

Steps involved in using the SIC Code. It is now useful to explain how to use the SIC Code to target a specific market and to acquire information on it. The first step is to define the market that must be reached. Once a specific industry has been selected, the researcher should obtain a copy of the 1972 version of the SIC manual. After it has been searched, the updated 1987 version should be used for the collection of data, but only from those secondary data sources that have been updated to the 1987 version. Until all sources are on the 1987 version, it would be easier to start with the 1972 version of the SIC manual.

The next step is for the researcher to open the SIC manual to its table of contents, where the manual lists each of the divisions and the major groups within each division. Each of the major groups has a corresponding two-digit SIC Code, and it is here that the research actually begins. The researcher should then choose the division that is closest to the industry being researched. This industry may not be included as a specific division, so the open category must be looked at if this situation arises. Once the division has been selected, the researcher needs to choose from the many major groups. The one that comes closest to the industry being studied should be selected. If more than one area can be selected, the researcher ought to make a note of the other choices. This may occur when researching closely related topics, especially as one gets closer to a specific topic. If the search does not come close to the industry that is being sought, the researcher needs to go back to the other selections and work through the system again. Once the specific industry has been selected, research using the SIC manual is over. The researcher should record all the codes used to get to the specific industry and then put away the SIC manual. It must be noted that the specific industry selected may not be the one that is being searched; it may be the closest one to it. When looking at secondary data journals, the exact industry to be studied might be found through the use of an expanded version of the SIC Code. A limitation to these expanded versions of the Code is that not all are uniform. So, a code developed by one census may not give the same exact industry in another, but it will always be accurate to the four-digit code.

With the SIC codes at hand, all that is left for the researcher is to access the secondary data. There are many books, journals, and censuses that provide the secondary data on specific industries. Some may include only a two- or three-digit SIC code, but their potential usefulness should not be underestimated. For example, a regional census for a state may only need to list two-digit codes to provide more than enough information on a specific industry. Others use expanded versions of the SIC Code. Here, it will be necessary to find extended code numbers. The process is the same as looking up the four-digit code in the SIC manual; one just works from the broadest topic to the most specific. Once a source to search has been found, (for example, *Dun's Census of American Business* or *Predicasts Basebook*), all that remains to be done is to look up the SIC code, given the number of digits to be used, and record the data for analysis. Although this process is relatively easy, collecting the information can be tedious and can take a substantial amount of time.

In summary, the SIC Code provides an organized way to catalogue statistical data. Because it is a uniform system, its use can save great amounts of time. Although the SIC Code is successful in achieving the objectives it was created to meet, it still has major limitations, which were addressed above. One limitation, which predominantly came up in the 1987 modifications, was that the Code did not include enough industry classifications. Currently, many individuals still hold the opinion that the SIC Code is not as effective as it should be and that additional changes must be made.

> Recent surveys conducted by the Direct Marketing Association indicate that among mailers who use the SIC for list selection, only one in three find it an effective system.[17]

Currently, a new coding structure is being worked on, which will be called the SIC+2+2 enhancement. Under this new system, two more digits will be added to the government's four-digit codes. With the added levels, it will be possible to obtain SIC codes for almost any given industry through the use of the eight-digit system. However, the current system must be used until that time; and even though the Code has some limitations, it remains one of the best tools to use when conducting basic business marketing research today.

Additional governmental sources. Other relevant government publications would include the following: *Business Conditions Digest, Construction Review, Federal Home Loan Bank Board Journal, Federal Reserve Bulletin, Monthly Labor Review, Survey of Current Business, Weekly Business Statistics,* and *U.S. Industrial Outlook.*

Commercial sources. Several publications are distributed by the private sector and include the following: *Funk and Scott Index of Corporations and Industries, Annual Survey of U.S. Business Plans for New Plants and Equipment, Sales and Marketing Management, Survey of Industrial and Commercial Buying Power, Survey of Buying Power,* and *Thomas Register of American Manufacturers.*

Professional publications. Professional associations exist in many fields of business, service, and technology, and most are interested in securing and disseminating information between and among people having common, work-related interests. *Academic publications* cut across industries and provide for the exchange of ideas between marketing people, usually with an intellectual orientation. Some, like *Marketing News*, resemble newspapers and report current marketing events and issues. Others, such as the *Journal of Marketing, Journal of Marketing Research, Journal of the Academy of Marketing Science,* and the *Journal of Business and Industrial Marketing,* contain greater detail and are of greater interest. Other forms of academic publications would be the "proceedings" of professional meetings, research reports, monographs, and working papers. Exhibits 4-2 and 4-3 will assist the student in locating relevant secondary data in academic publications and in government documents, respectively. *Trade publications* focus on a particular industry and exchange both ideas and statistics between decision makers, usually with a pragmatic orientation. Most trade publications contain articles describing trends in their industry, case histories of successful firms, procedures to improve a firm's performance, and industry statistics. Most are listed in *Business Publication Rates and Data*, a publication of Standard Rate and Data Service, Incorporated. Each of the more than three hundred trade publications listed contain the publication's address and the advertising costs, circulation, and other useful data associated with it.

Other secondary data sources. The reader should be aware of sources of standardized market research information other than data supplied by government, professional, and commercial service publications. Such database sources are shown in Table 4-3. For example, public utilities will supply information on the number of new customer hookups and related data. Database sources such as *Directory of On-Line Databases* (Santa Monica, California, Cuadra Associates), *Information Industry Marketplace* (New York, R. R. Bowker), and *Encyclopedia of Information Systems*

EXHIBIT 4-2 **A Search Process for Secondary Data in Academic Publications**

1. Start your search by examining current marketing texts. Consult both introductory texts and advanced texts as well as texts on component parts of marketing business products; marketing management; marketing research and product price; distribution; and promotion strategy. Use tables of contents and indexes in these books to locate the topic. Depending on the level of the text and its scholarship, you will find varying levels of topic treatment. In the more rigorous texts you will find footnotes and suggested readings that lead to more detailed sources.
2. Pursue these footnoted and other referenced sources. Read them but also use them to search for work published later and earlier. If the source is a journal, check later and earlier annual indexes usually found as part of the last issue of each journal's annual volume. If the source is a proceedings, check later and earlier editions by scanning their tables of contents and indexes. While reading, be alert for other references to other related work.
3. Be especially alert for literature review articles and annotated bibliographies referenced in the preceding sources. Both of these identify and describe (and often evaluate) past research on the topic.
4. Refer to other published guides to academic publications, three of which are described here: one is the "Marketing Abstracts" section found in each issue of the *Journal of Marketing.* This section summarizes marketing literature in over 200 journals, trade magazines, university monographs, government reports, and business persons' speeches. Entries appear in numerous classes under seven main headings; they report details on the articles' original publication, summarize the article, and often comment on its significance. The second is a separate publication, *The Marketing Information Guide.* This periodical reviews over 100 marketing-related books, journals, pamphlets, and government reports every other month. Entries summarize the articles, appear in numerous classes under three main headings, and show original sources, including addresses and reprint prices. Finally, try the *Business Periodicals Index.* This monthly publication indexes nearly 300 business journals and trade magazines. It does not summarize indexed articles.
5. Obtain and review publications brochures of the American Marketing Association and Marketing Science Institute. Both of these list and describe special publications on many marketing topics.

Source: Walter Gross, "Research and Other Applications of the Marketing Abstracts," *Journal of Marketing,* 42, April 1978 (Chicago: American Marketing Association), pp. 32–37. Used with permission.

and Services (Detroit, Gale Research Company) are useful because they are periodically updated. In addition, the researcher will wish to consult an information specialist who works with on-line services in a library or corporate information center. Here, a specific database is accessed through a contract with an intermediary (referred to as on-line vendors), rather than directly from the database producer. The advantages of accessing a database through an on-line base are as follows:[18]

(1) One contract with the vendor can usually provide access to many different databases.

(2) Because there is only one contract, billing for the use of various databases is simplified with one periodic invoice.

(3) Search protocol is generally standardized over all the databases on the vendor's system, thereby simplifying the research process itself.

(4) The availability of an on-line database index may assist the researcher in pinpointing the individual databases most appropriate for a specific search.

EXHIBIT 4-3 A Search Process for Secondary Data Published by the Federal Government

1. If you have absolutely no idea about where to find data, start with the most recent edition of the *Statistical Abstract of the United States.* This annual publication summarizes social, political, and economic statistics for the nation and states in each of its more than thirty sections. You may find the data you seek in one or more of the nearly two thousand tables contained in these sections. If not, you will find *references at the foot of each table* leading to more complete and less aggregate sources. Pursue them.
2. If you know that data belong to a particular census, by all means start instead with those publications. Look for more current data in appropriate interim report series. . . .
3. If you have found nothing so far, check appropriate *subject bibliographies* issued by the Superintendent of Documents. Over 270 are currently available, free—individually treating such subjects as marketing research, the *Census of Population* educational statistics, how to sell to government agencies, patents and trademarks, prices and the cost of living, retirement, statistical publications, and women, for example. All refer to thousands of reports, articles, and statistical sources of potential interest to marketing researchers.
4. If you still have found nothing, begin the somewhat tedious task of searching through cumulative issues of the *Monthly Catalog to U.S. Government Publications.* This monthly publication indexes by author, by title, and by subject, everything the U.S. government disseminates to the public.

   Searching a privately published work, the *Index to U.S. Government Periodicals,* completes this step. This monthly publication indexes articles in over 160 federal government periodicals. . . . Entries identify subject, author, title, periodical, and *Monthly Catalog* entry number to allow retrieval.

   Step 4 is mandatory to locate government literature as distinct from government statistics.
5. If you meet little success so far, contact the appropriate government unit directly. Most offer help quite willingly; the Bureau of the Census even employs data "ombudsmen" and publishes a list of "Telephone Contacts for Data Users" as services for information seekers.

Source: Walter Gross, "Research and Other Applications of the Marketing Abstracts," *Journal of Marketing,* 42, April 1978 (Chicago: American Marketing Association), pp. 32–37. Used with permission.

While there are hundreds of on-line vendors, a few of the larger ones are listed below:

- Bibliographic Retrieval Service (BRS)
- Compuserve
- Dialog Information Service
- Dow Jones News Retrieval
- Mead Data General
- News Net
- System Development Corporation (SDC Search Service)
- Telmar Media Systems
- Vu/Text Information Services

These on-line vendors provide access to over two hundred databases in a variety of disciplines including science and technology, along with business and economics. Some provide electronic access to the full text of hundreds of business

TABLE 4-3 **Database Sources of Secondary Data**

Database	Description	Producer
Disclosure database	Contains business and financial information on more than 11,000 publicly owned companies in the United States that trade their securities on the New York Stock Exchange, American Stock Exchange, NASDAQ, or other exchanges.	Disclosure, Inc.
ECS Database	Contains information on more than 50,000 companies in the shipping industry worldwide.	ECS Marine
TRADSTAT	Contains published government import/export information on more than 65,000 products worldwide.	World Trade Statistic Database
Consumer Report	Contains the complete text of the major articles and product recalls published in the 11 regular monthly issues of *Consumer Reports,* a product-test and consumer advisory publication.	Consumer Union of United States, Inc.
Doane Marketing Research	Offers a variety of syndicated multiclient studies covering the sale, distribution, purchasing and usage of important agribusiness products and services.	Doane Marketing Research, Inc.
MARK	Provides references to market analysis of all branches of business	Marketing Journal

Source: Selections from *Encyclopedia of Information Systems and Services: 1993,* 13th ed., Edited by Amy Lucas and Annette Novallo, Copyright © 1971, 1974, by Anthony T. Kruzas, © 1978, 1981, 1982, 1985, 1987, 1988, 1993 by Gale Research Company. Reprinted by permission of the publisher.

databases, newsletters, company annual reports, and investment firm reports. New information technologies such as these will continue to revolutionize the acquisition of secondary-source market information, with access to these sources becoming a necessity in the world of business marketing research.

Disadvantages and drawbacks of secondary data. Secondary data were developed for purposes other than the particular study under consideration; thus, such data must be scrutinized for applicability and accuracy. Quotations or excerpts from secondary data are often misleading, and when taken out of context, a portion of secondary data can have different relationships and different interpretations. The very nature of secondary data makes it imperative that they be evaluated carefully before any use is made of them. The series of steps that a marketing researcher can use in evaluating the helpfulness of secondary data are presented in Figure 4-4. The researcher must also answer the questions below.

How recent are the data? Obsolescence is often a factor to be considered in the use of secondary data. Some secondary data are collected periodically; hence, the latest available data may already be obsolete.

FIGURE 4-4 **Evaluating Secondary Data**

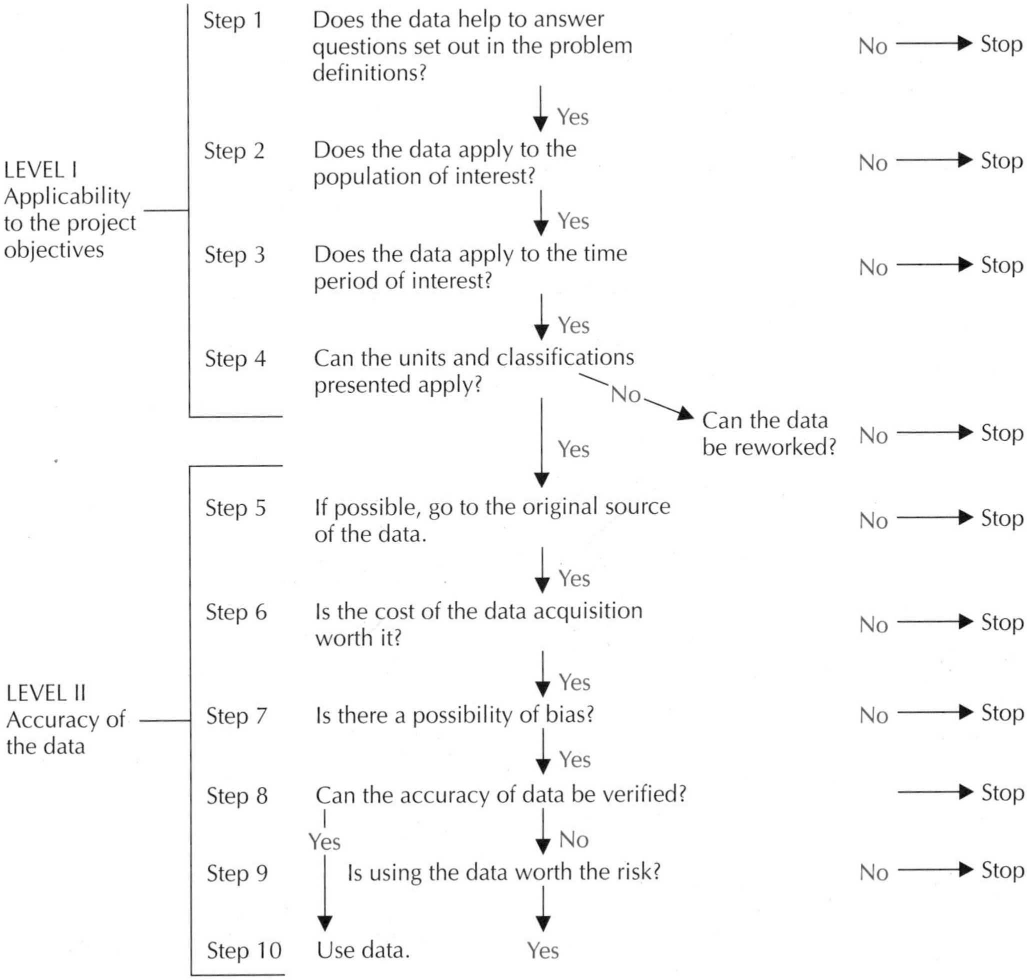

Is the coverage of data adequate for present purposes? This question relates not only to geographic coverage, but also to the type of products or establishments included in the data. For example, in studying the composition of an industry as reported by a trade association, it is important to determine whether the data cover all members of an industry, or are restricted to members of the association. The question of coverage becomes especially important in studying production data for individual products. In past Censuses of Manufacturers, plants were generally classified according to principal products. As a result, products that were produced widely, but as by-products of other goods, received relatively little mention. This was the case with a product such as nails, a by-product of some iron and steel plants.

In a sample survey, was an adequate sample decision used? This is especially important in the case of a mail survey where most of the sample members may not have replied, and bias in the data may have been substantial.

Might the data have been biased because of the nature of the sponsor or the objectives of the original study? This danger may arise when trade associations conduct attitudinal or profit studies. Association members may be reluctant to provide confidential data. Alternatively, if the association in a questionnaire indicated that a study had certain objectives, such as to show how poor a dealer's profit margins were, the results are likely to bear out the objectives. Here, it is advisable for the marketing researcher to seek a copy not only of the original questionnaire, but also of the cover letter.

Primary Data Sources

Although business marketing researchers must rely heavily on secondary data sources, research objectives may dictate that primary data must be collected. Primary data should only be generated after secondary data research sources have been exhausted, as there is always the problem of the availability and accessibility of respondents due to travel requirements, having appointment schedules, and the like. The most common method of obtaining primary data for the business market is through the use of surveys. The three survey methods commonly used with business respondents are (1) the personal interview, (2) the telephone survey, and (3) the mail survey. Table 4-4 compares these three survey methods as to cost, time, information quality, information quantity, the nonresponse problem, and interviewer bias.

Personal interviews. In the personal interview, the interviewer is in the presence of, or face-to-face with, the respondent. This allows maximum versatility of questioning methods (structured or unstructured, disguised or nondisguised) and a variety of question types. Interviews attempt to uncover content and intensity of feelings and motivations beyond the rationalized overt responses to structured questions. Because tape recordings are frequently used, interviews take a long time to complete, transcribe, and read, and must be analyzed by an experienced practitioner who knows both the technique and the business product category under study.

Telephone surveys. A telephone survey is the most convenient means of reaching respondents, while not being as flexible and versatile as the personal interview. Drawbacks of the telephone medium relate particularly to the lack of anything visual. Distance is not a serious obstacle, nor is cost, with the use of WATS lines.

TABLE 4-4 **Comparing Business Survey Methods**

Criteria	Personal Interview	Telephone	Mail
Cost	Highest per respondent	Second highest per respondent	Least per respondent
Time	Most	Least	Moderate
Information quality	In-depth, complex information	Complex information with prior contact	Somewhat complex information
Information quantity	Much	Little to respondent interest	Moderate according and the effort required
Nonresponse problem	Limited due to face-to-face contact	Hard to ensure contact with proper respondent	Hard to control
Interviewer bias	Difficult to identify and control	Difficult to identify and control	Controllable through rigorous pretesting

Mail Surveys. There is no interviewer in a mail survey to explain the purpose of the study, to induce cooperation, to ask the questions, to record the answers, and in general to cope with any problem that comes up. This is the main difference between mail and the other two methods, putting a great deal of importance on the construction of the questionnaire and any transmittal letters that may accompany it. Mail cannot be used to conduct an unstructured study where an interviewer is relied upon to improvise the questioning as the interview progresses. Once a mail survey is put in the mail, the business researcher can only let it run its course. If research results must be obtained quickly, mail is not the data collection method to use. However, mail is cheaper per completed interview as cost is confined to mailing lists, forms, and postage. Also, more confidential information may be divulged.

Disadvantages and drawbacks of primary data. Collecting primary data can be, and usually is, expensive. While versatility is a plus, speed and cost, along with an unwillingness (or inability) of the respondent to provide information, can be disadvantages. Mail and telephone surveys lack flexibility, and the use of unstructured questionnaires and questions is difficult. The accuracy of information obtained can be questioned; and sequence bias, where the respondent can change an answer after seeing a later question, will occasionally present a problem. In answering open-ended questions, respondents will tend to be more brief and more general in mail surveys than in personal or telephone interviews. Complex questions with rating scales or other procedures that can be confusing tend to draw more "no answers" in mail surveys. Finally, despite the improving returns being reported on mail surveys, many such studies still have large proportions of nonrespondents.

CONCEPT QUESTIONS

1. How does an MIS serve as a nerve center for the business firm?
2. Why has planning the research design been referred to as the most important phase of the marketing research project?
3. Of what value is the Standard Industrial Classification (SIC) System?

ORGANIZATION OF BUSINESS MARKETING RESEARCH

The organization and staffing of marketing research departments vary greatly, depending largely on the size and organizational structure of the individual company. These variations are the result of many factors, including the assignment of certain research activities to other departments, the type of products and markets involved, the relationship between the business firm and its advertising agency regarding who does what research, the extent of new product development, the personalities and attitudes of top operating executives, and the maintenance of a research library. Thus, it is impossible to state categorically how the ideal research department should be staffed.

Generally speaking, large business research organizations take a variety of organizational forms, with three types being the most common:

(1) Research organization set up by area of applications. Examples would be units established by product line, by business segment, or by geographic area.

(2) Research organization set up by function performed. Examples would be sales analyses, advertising research, or product research.

(3) Research organization set up by research technique or research approach. Examples would be mathematical and/or statistical analysis, field interviewing, or questionnaire design.

Many large firms would combine two or more of these research organization structures.

Some business-to-business firms will do some or all of their own research, whereas others depend heavily on outside sources (the make-or-buy decision, as studied earlier). Some firms have only a single marketing research department responsible for all research projects. Others have decentralized research activities, with decision making spread among several people at different levels or operating units. Whether centralized or decentralized, large or small, the business marketing research function will depend on the relative importance of that function within the firm and on the scale and complexity of the research activities to be undertaken. Again, there is no optimum method of organization for marketing research. The best organization will depend on the firm's needs and on the way it has organized the marketing function and other functions of the firm. Market research organizations will continue to play an important role in measuring and monitoring levels of customer satisfaction, since many companies see customer satisfaction as a way of differentiating themselves.[19]

CONDUCTING INTERNATIONAL MARKETING RESEARCH

Accurate, effective decision making is often dependent on the quality of information provided. Marketing research plays an essential role in providing accurate and useful information; but the job becomes somewhat more difficult when the researcher must deal with the problem of conducting marketing research overseas.

Foreign politics, or the politics of the host country, can range from being very friendly to being very hostile and even dangerous. The host country may view inputs negatively, even if the industrial product is needed to advance or modernize a local industry. (An adverse contribution to the balance of payments would be a reason for such a viewpoint.) For example, IBM ran into political opposition when, in planning to build a computer plant in Mexico, the company received objections from the Mexican government about IBM's policy of having 100 percent ownership of all off-shore facilities. Potential domestic politics (that is, criticism) must also be researched before an overseas venture is begun. Some labor and political organizations may accuse the firm of exporting both capital and jobs. Often, foreign investment is based on moral principle. The citizens of several countries prohibited investment in South Africa for years because of that country's past policy of apartheid. Knowledge of this public attitude would be critical information for the domestic marketing researcher, considering the tremendous investment the firm might have to make in such an effort.

The political risks involved in a foreign expansion must be researched. The threat of confiscation, expropriation, and domestication all apply to any potential future acts by a host government. Potential social unrest and the analysis of the political climate must be considered. These types of problems may help to explain why twelve U.S. firms decided to leave El Salvador during the 1980s.

Awareness and reputation (image) research studies, which measure the effectiveness of a firm's overall policies and communications, must be conducted.

This would include research on advertising, promotion, and public relations. In the mid-1980s, Westinghouse International authorized competitive image studies of competitive manufacturers of electrical equipment and components in five high-priority foreign markets in an effort to strengthen the overall position of its own international operations. Because the competitive image studies were conducted throughout the world (Europe, the Middle East, and South America), the services of a large international research firm (supplier) were required to ensure consistent and reliable data from country to country and to maintain the anonymity of the client.

In summation, a systematic attempt must be made to ascertain both opportunities and potential pitfalls when considering overseas expansion or export. The international marketer must face a complex and difficult political environment, but it can be made somewhat easier if prior marketing research is conducted.

CONCEPT QUESTIONS

1. How does a firm select the appropriate research organization structure?
2. How can the international marketing researcher's environment be made less complex and less difficult?

SUMMARY

1. A number of major differences exist between consumer research and business research. Business marketers are closer to their markets than are consumer marketers, and they can ascertain buyer preferences more easily. Business marketing research focuses on buying decisions and the buying center, whereas consumer research emphasizes product attributes and buyer motivation.
2. The extent to which business firms use marketing research studies is wide and varied. The major areas where marketing research is conducted usually fall within one or more of the following areas: market potential, market-share analysis, market characteristics, sales analysis, and forecasting.
3. Whereas marketing research is problem oriented or project oriented, a marketing information system combines procedures, hardware, and software; and then accumulates, interprets, and disseminates marketing information as effectively as possible.
4. Marketing research is undertaken to gather reliable marketing information to facilitate planning and control. Marketing research should be viewed as a process of primary phases and steps to include planning the research design; preparation; field operations; processing; tabulation, analysis, and interpretation; and reporting.

5. It is not unusual for business firms to utilize outside firms on a fee or contract basis to do either some or all of their marketing research. The decision to use either inside or outside marketing specialists is somewhat similar to the business make-or-buy decision.
6. Information sources available to the business researcher are of two types: primary or secondary data. Secondary data sources include both internal and external data. Internal secondary data include marketing plans, company reports, and marketing information system (MIS) reports. External secondary data involve government documents, commercial sources, professional publications, and a variety of other sources. There are a number of disadvantages and drawbacks to secondary data that the business researcher must consider. Primary data sources include personal interviews, telephone surveys, and mail surveys. The business researcher must be aware of the disadvantages and drawbacks to the use of primary data.
7. The organization and staffing of marketing research departments vary greatly, depending largely on the size and organizational structure of the individual company. These variations are the result of many factors, including the assignment of certain research activities to other departments, the type of products and markets involved, the relationship between the business firm and its advertising agency regarding who does what research, the extent of new product development, the personalities and attitudes of top operating executives, and the maintenance of a research library.
8. A systematic attempt must be made to ascertain both opportunities and potential pitfalls when considering overseas expansion or export. The international marketer's political environment is complex and difficult but can be made easier if prior marketing research is conducted.

KEY TERMS

Academic publications
Analysis
Coding
Data bank
Interpretation
Links
Marketing information system (MIS)
Microsales analysis
Models
Optimization
Primary data
Problem recognition and definition
Reporting phase
Secondary data
Standard Industrial Classification (SIC) System
Systems interrogation
Tabulation
Trade publications

REVIEW QUESTIONS

1. Define marketing research. Point out the major differences between business and consumer marketing research.
2. Identify and elaborate upon the five major tasks of business marketing research.

3. Distinguish between marketing research and a marketing information system. What are the basic components of a marketing information system, and how is a marketing information system used?
4. What is the general purpose of marketing research? Identify and briefly discuss the six phases involved in the course of a research project.
5. Distinguish between primary and secondary data, and between internal and external secondary data. Identify three primary types of external secondary data. Identify the steps involved in using the SIC Code. How can computer technology assist the researcher in locating relevant external secondary data?
6. Distinguish between personal interviews, telephone surveys, and mail surveys as methods of collecting primary data. Discuss some of the major disadvantages of both primary and secondary data sources.
7. What are the fundamental reasons for the sometimes wide variations among the organizational structures of research departments within business companies? Discuss the three most common organizational forms for the business marketing research function.
8. Give an example of how foreign investment can be based on moral principle. What is included in awareness and reputation (image) research?

Cases

CASE 4-1 Arlington Chamber of Commerce

The Arlington Chamber of Commerce has been serving businesses and individuals in Arlington, Texas, for the past forty-five years. Established to focus on economic development activities, the Arlington Chamber tries to bring employment opportunities to the city. The chamber also focuses on enhancing and diversifying the tax base in Arlington. Additional taxes and continued diversification of the businesses help fuel the growth of Arlington, Texas.

Arlington, Texas, is one of the fastest-growing cities in the United States. In the 1980s, Arlington ranked as the second fastest-growing city among cities with populations in excess of 150,000. This rapid growth makes Arlington an attractive city for business activities. Rapid growth usually means that there is a large resource of both skilled and unskilled labor available for companies. The chamber is always looking for ways to provide a progressive business environment for new and existing businesses. The chamber currently has seventeen hundred members.

A recent survey conducted by the Arlington Chamber of Commerce indicates that 80 percent of the companies that responded to the survey are locally owned and operated. Of the 6,795 companies sent the questionnaire, 635 responded. The chamber's goals for this survey were to collect information about the business climate in Arlington and to help plan the future direction of the chamber.

Some of the results of the survey indicate the following:

- 27.1 percent of the businesses are owned by women and minorities.
- More than 40 percent of the respondents have gone into business since 1983.
- Over 80 percent of the respondents employ twenty-five or fewer employees.
- 11 percent of the respondents export products/services outside the United States.
- 38 percent of the city's manufacturers are exporters.
- 14 percent rate Arlington as an excellent business climate;
- 58 percent rate it as good.

The chamber is excited about the results, claiming Arlington is a "hotbed" for entrepreneurs. There is some concern that these companies are not more active in exporting products. The chamber plans to provide more information to help encourage greater exports from Arlington businesses. There is also some concern that the minority- and women-owned businesses are merely figurehead companies vying for minority contracts.

DISCUSSION QUESTIONS

1. How much credibility would you place in the results of this survey? Why?
2. What is the nonresponse problem? How would you address the nonresponse problem?
3. Based on the results of this survey, would you move to Arlington, Texas, to start a new business? What additional information would you want? Where would you go to find this information?

Suggested Reading

Chapman, Lou. "Survey Reveals Arlington as Entrepreneurial Hotbed." *Fort Worth Star Telegram,* 21 November 1990, sec. 4: 1–2.

Source: C. Lamb, J. Hair, and C. McDaniel, *Principles of Marketing,* 1st Edition (Cincinnati, OH: South-Western Publishing Company, 1992) pp. 206–220.

CASE 4-2 International Marketing Research: An Entirely Different Animal

The most universal survey sampling problem in foreign countries is the language barrier. In India, for example, fourteen official languages are spoken in different parts of the country, while most business and government affairs are conducted in English. Similarly, in Switzerland, German is spoken in some areas and French in others. In the Republic of Congo, the official language is French, but only a small part of the population speaks this language fluently. Unfortunately, translating a questionnaire from one language to another is far from easy. For example, translating "out of sight, out of mind" from English to Danish became "invisible things are insane."

To overcome the language barrier, a questionnaire may first be written in English, and then a native speaker fluent in English can translate it into the local language(s). A third person should translate it back to English. This second translated version can then be compared with the original English version.

International marketing research can provide crucial decision-making information for international marketers. However, the U.S. business marketer must pay close attention to differences in such areas as language, culture, customs, and values.

DISCUSSION QUESTIONS

1. Can you think of some other barriers that an international researcher might encounter?
2. Would data interpretation be any different between international and domestic research?
3. Should a research firm always use local businesspeople for interviews?

Suggested Additional Readings

Alwin, Duane F., and John A. Krosnick. "The Measurement of Values in Surveys: A Comparison of Ratings and Rankings." *Public Opinion Quarterly* 49 (Winter 1985): 535–552. **A literature review, theoretical discussion, and empirical study of ratings and rankings of values in survey research.**

Bartran, Peter. "The Communication of Results: The Neglected Art in Marketing Research." *Marketing Intelligence and Planning* (UK), 3, No. 1 (1985): 3–13. **Guidelines for simplification and clarification in the presentation of research data.**

Churchill, Gilbert A. "Better Measurement Practices Are Critical to Better Understanding of Sales Management Issues." *Journal of Personal Selling and Sales Management* 12 (Spring 1992): 73–80. **A discussion of the nature and importance of measurement in dealing with sales management issues.**

Crispell, Diane. "Your Marketing Consultant." *American Demographics* 8 (September 1986): 64–65. **Marketing research-oriented software review, emphasizing a combination software/data package.**

Goldstein, Frederick A. "A Practical Guide to Gathering USA Market Information and the Current Status of Marketing Research in the U.S." *Journal of the Market Research Society* (UK), 27 (October 1985): 243–259. **Discussion of the most effective means of gathering market information in the United States, and a look at current trends in marketing research in the United States.**

Goyder, John. "Face-to-Face Interviews and Mailed Questionnaires: The Net Difference in Response Rate." *Public Opinion Quarterly* 49 (Summer 1985): 234–252. **A review of response rates between face-to-face interviews and mailed questionnaires in both the United States and abroad.**

Grabowski, Daniel P. "Building an Effective Competitive Intelligence System." *Journal of Business and Industrial Marketing* 2 (Winter 1987): 39–44. **There seems to be little need to establish an active competitive intelligence function as an integral part of a corporation's existing operations structure. An intelligence system can be organized utilizing existing resources, and an example of how such information can be used to predict a competitor's actions is presented.**

Gross, Irwin. "Critical Uses of Research in Business Marketing." *Industrial Marketing Management* 14 (August 1985): 165–170. **Discussion of the trends in marketing research for business marketing, and a look at the academic and professional activities of the Marketing Science Institute.**

Hague, Paul. "Market Research 1976–1986—Swings and Roundabouts." *Industrial Marketing Digest* (UK), 11 (First Quarter 1986): 85–91. **Current trends in business research, to include a shifting away from outside consultants.**

Jain, C. L. "Three Common Mistakes Made in Setting Up a Forecasting System." *Journal of Business Forecasting* 11 (Summer 1992): 2, 22. **A discussion of the common problems found in forecasting systems after they are put into place.**

Jobber, David "Improving Response Rates in Industrial Mail Surveys." *Industrial Marketing Management* 15 (August 1986): 183–195. **A review of prior notification, incentives, stamps, and various other techniques.**

______. "Questionnaire Factors and Mail Survey Response Rates." *European Research* (Netherlands), 13 (July 1985): 124–129. **Review of guidelines related to questionnaire construction for the improvement of responses to mail surveys.**

Kallis, M. Jeffery, and Joseph J. Giglierano. "Improving Mail Response Rates with Express Mail." *Industrial Marketing Management* 21 (February 1992): 1–4. **A study of the costs and the effectiveness of using express mail service to achieve greater response rates to mail surveys.**

Lidington, Simon. "Market Research—The Emotional Side of the Corporate Buyer." *Industrial Marketing Digest* (UK), 11 (First Quarter 1986): 147–154. **A discussion of psychographically segmented market segments and business buying decisions as they are affected by emotional considerations.**

Mock, Gail S.. and Dwight E. Thomas, "The Volume Forecasting Process: Linking Customers with Factories." *Journal of Business Forecasting* 11 (Spring 1992): 3–4. **A study involving the effects on volume forecasting of efforts to link customers with the factories from which they make purchases.**

Moorman, Christine, Rohit Deshpande, and Gerald Zaltman. "Factors Affecting Trust in Marketing Research Relationships." *Journal of Marketing* 57 (January 1993): 81–101. **Describes a comprehensive theory of trust in marketing research relationships.**

Narus, James, and Tor Guimaraes. "Computer Usage in Distributor Marketing." *Industrial Marketing Management* 16 (February 1987): 43–54. **A study of decision-making uses of results of mail surveys and personal interviews by business distributors.**

Piercy, Nigel. "The Corporate Environment Marketing Management: An Information-Structure-Power Theory." *Marketing Intelligence and Planning* (UK), 3, no. 1 (1985): 23–40. **A theoretical discussion of a new model in marketing that deals with organizational influences in decision making and information processing theory.**

Welch, Joe L. "Researching Marketing Problems and Opportunities with Focus Groups." *Industrial Marketing Management* 14 (November 1985): 245–253. **Guidelines for, and applications of, the use of focus groups in business marketing research.**

ENDNOTES

[1]Valerie Kijewski, Bob Donath, and David T. Wilson, *Business Marketing Magazine: Views from the Trenches* (Boston: Kent Publishing, 1993), 90.

[2]Donald A. Kunstler, "Sophisticated Consumer Research Tools Refine Business Marketing Analysis," *Business Marketing* 26 (August 1991): 32–34.

[3]Steve Weinstein, "Business Research: Evolving as Companies Adapt to a Changing Marketplace," *Marketing News* 23 (July 31, 1989): 1–2.

[4]Paul Alpar, "Knowledge-Based Modeling of Marketing Managers' Problem Solving Behavior," *International Journal of Research in Marketing* (Netherlands), 8 (April 1991): 5–11.

[5]David L. Hurwood, Elliott S. Grossman, and Earl L. Bailey, *Sales Forecasting* (New York: The Conference Board, 1988): 1.

[6]These studies are conducted at five-year intervals by the American Marketing Association, Chicago, Illinois.

[7]R. A. Proctor, "Marketing Information Systems," *Management Decisions* 29 (1991):. 55–60.

[8]"Just What Is a Database Anyway?" *Agency Sales Magazine* 22 (September 1992): 15–17.

[9]Stephen J. Grove, Mary C. LaForge, Patricia A. Knowles, and Louis H. Stone, "Improving Sales Call Reporting for Better Management Decisions," *Journal of Business and Industrial Marketing* 7 (Spring 1992): 53–60.

[10]Randall G. Chapman, "Problem-Definition in Marketing Research Studies," *Journal of Consumer Marketing* 6 (Spring 1989): 51–59.

[11]L. Adler and C. S. Mayer, *Managing the Marketing Research Function* (Chicago: American Marketing Association, 1977), 56–70.

[12]Vaughan C. Judd and Betty J. Tims, "Small Business Planning: Have You Looked in the Library?" *Business* 39 (July-September 1989): 3–15.

[13]This section is from James E. Nelson, *The Practice of Marketing Research* (Boston: Kent Publishing, 1982), 73–78.

[14]Marydee Ojala, "SIC Codes Revisited: Dun's Goes Marching Two by Two," *Outline* 13 (November 1989): 84–89.

[15]Richard Kern, "1987 Survey of Industrial and Commercial Buying Power- - - Indianapolis: A Profile of Industrial Change (Part 1)," *Sales and Marketing Management* (April 27, 1987): 36, 10–32.

[16]*Ibid.*

[17]Jerry Reisberg, "An Expanded SIC Code: Let's Do It Ourselves!" *Direct Marketing* (October 1987): 148–156.

[18]William R. Dillon, Thomas J. Madden, and Neil H. Firtle, *Marketing Research in a Marketing Environment,* 2d ed. (St. Louis, Mo.: Times Mirror, 1990), 119–120.

[19]Brian Oliver, "A Most Satisfying Form of Research," *Journal of Marketing Research* (April 30, 1992): 24–27.

5 Market Segmentation, Positioning, and Demand Projection

Learning Objectives

After reading this chapter, you should be able to:

- Appreciate the difficulty involved in successfully segmenting businessmarkets.
- Distinguish among undifferentiated marketing, differentiated marketing, and concentrated marketing.
- Differentiate between the micro/macro and the nested approach to business market segmentation.
- Understand how to evaluate potential market segments.
- Discuss six approaches by which a firm can position its products.
- Recall the purpose, problems, and general methods of sales forecasting.

Chapter Outline

Learning Objectives

Segmentation, Positioning, and Demand Estimation: An Overview

General Market Segmentation Strategy
- The Nature of Business Market Segmentation

Strategies for Business Market Segmentation
- Undifferentiated Marketing Strategy
- Differentiated Marketing Strategy
- Concentrated Marketing Strategy

Approaches to Market Segmentation
- Macro/Micro Segmentation
- The Nested Approach to Market Segmentation
  - An application of the nested approach
- Other Approaches to Business Market Segmentation

Segmenting Business Markets
- Type of Economic Activity
- Size of Organization
- Geographic Location
- Product Usage
- Structure of the Procurement Function

International Segmentation

Evaluating Potential Market Segments
- Market Profitability Analysis
- Market Competitive Analysis

Product Positioning Strategy
- Perceptual Mapping
- Positioning Business Products
  - Positioning by technology
  - Positioning by price
  - Positioning by quality
  - Positioning by image
  - Positioning by distribution
  - Positioning by service

Business Demand Projection
- Strategic Importance of Forecasting in Decision Making
- Definition of Some Basic Terminology
  - Market factor
  - Market index
  - Market potential
  - Sales potential
  - Market share
  - Market demand
  - Market forecast
  - Sales forecast
- Common Forecasting Problems
  - Forecasting mystique
  - Forecasting accuracy
  - Forecasting inconsistency
  - Forecasting accountability
  - Forecasting implementation

Selecting Forecasting Methods
General Approaches to Forecasting
Qualitative Approaches to Forecasting
Jury of executive opinion
Sales force composite
Survey of buyer intentions
Delphi method
Quantitative Approaches to Forecasting
Time-series techniques
Trend fitting
Moving average
Exponential smoothing
Adaptive control
Box-Jenkins
Causal techniques
Regression
Econometrics
Leading indicators
Diffusion index
Input-output analysis
Life-cycle analysis

Summary

Key Terms

Review Questions

Cases
Case 5-1
Case 5-2

Suggested Additional Readings

Endnotes

SEGMENTATION, POSITIONING, AND DEMAND ESTIMATION: AN OVERVIEW

Segmenting business markets is a difficult job, much more difficult than segmenting consumer markets. To be successful, the business marketer must be able to identify, analyze, and evaluate potentially attractive market segments; target the segments to be served; and then develop and communicate a positioning strategy that will differentiate the firm's offerings from others. This is no easy task indeed! Today, sophisticated segmentation is a critical marketing skill, but many practitioners are confused about how to integrate segmentation and planning.[1] Business customers are widely dispersed, yet geographically concentrated in certain areas of the United States. These customers differ greatly in many ways, making it difficult to discern which strategies are important and which are less important in developing marketing strategy in general, and in particular, in developing strategy for segmentation, positioning, and demand estimation.

GENERAL MARKET SEGMENTATION STRATEGY

Few business marketers or academicians have written extensively in regard to business segmentation strategy. Thus, some concepts from psychology and sociology, which most consumer marketers have found useful in their segmentation strategies, have received only limited application in business segmentation strategy and planning. In fact, business market segmentation can assist firms in several areas:

- *Analysis of the market.* Better understanding of the total marketplace, including how and why customers buy.
- *Selection of key markets.* Rational choice of market segments that best fit the company's capabilities.
- *Management of marketing.* The development of strategies, policies, and programs to meet the needs of different market segments profitably and to give the company a distinct competitive advantage.[2]

Business-to-business firms have different needs and wants, have different structures within the procurement function, are of different sizes, engage in different types of economic activities, and are in different geographic locations. *Business market segmentation* is the act of dividing a market into distinct groups of buyers with similar requirements. It is the foundation of the marketing strategy process and the driver of allocating resources. All other facets of strategy follow the selection of the targeted segments.[3]

The Nature of Business Market Segmentation

Figure 5-1 shows how the process of segmenting a market and selecting specific segments as targets is the link between various organizational buyers' needs and the organization's marketing actions. Market segmentation is only a means to an end: in an economist's terms, it relates supply (the organization's actions) to demand (customer needs). A basic test of the usefulness of the segmentation process is whether it leads to tangible marketing actions.[4] In business marketing, segmentation is achieved generally by forming user segments (identified by SIC code), customer-size segments, geographic segments (defined by boundaries between countries or by regional differences within them), product segments (based on technological differences, production economics, or product use), and the makeup of the organizational buying center. The primary task for the business marketer is to choose a variable or variables that so divide the market that prospects in a particular segment have similar responsiveness to some aspect of the marketing strategy. Once segments have been identified, the decision must be made as to which should be selected and pursued. Choices for selected

FIGURE 5-1 **Market Segmentation Links Market Needs to an Organization's Marketing Actions**

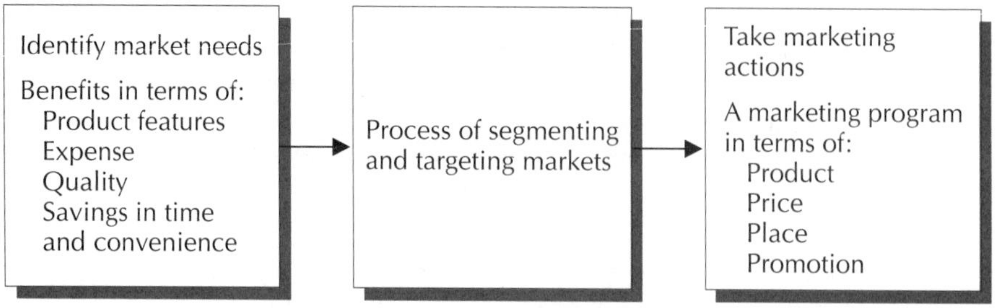

segments should be ones in which the maximum differential in competitive strategy can be developed, and ones capable of being isolated so that a competitive advantage can be preserved.[5]

The choice of identifying, analyzing, and pursuing wanted segments is not a straightforward task. Business marketers must weigh their strengths and weaknesses as compared with the competition. It also requires analytical marketing research to uncover specific market segments in which the identified strengths can be significant and in which the identified weaknesses can be overcome.

STRATEGIES FOR BUSINESS MARKET SEGMENTATION

Business marketing managers must determine what strategy will be used for different market segments. Three alternative market-selection strategies are available regarding segment similarities and differences: undifferentiated strategy, differentiated strategy, and concentrated strategy.[6]

Undifferentiated Marketing Strategy

An *undifferentiated marketing strategy* uses the concept of "market aggregation," wherein the total market is treated as if it were but one homogeneous market segment. Marketing management creates a single marketing mix to serve potential customers within this market. Therefore, only one distribution framework, one promotional program, and one pricing strategy are needed. This approach focuses on what is common in the needs of buyers, rather than on what is different. An example would be a business cleaning or business waste removal firm. The price per hour or per pickup would be the same for all potential users of the service, and the same promotional package would be aimed at buyers in several different industries. Undifferentiated marketing is defended on the grounds of cost economies, with the narrow product line keeping down production, inventory, and transportation costs. This particular strategy also lowers the cost of marketing research and product management. An undifferentiated marketing strategy might be adopted by firms that offer a homogeneous, staple product, such as gasoline or industrial lubricants, where product usage varies little by customer type.

Undifferentiated marketing strategy will expose the business firm to competitive attack by those firms that do differentiate. Although this strategyis reasonable where homogeneity exists, the situation is relatively infrequent in reality.

Differentiated Marketing Strategy

A differentiated marketing strategy is the strategy by which one firm attempts to distinguish its product from competitive products offered to the same aggregate market. An example of a firm using a differentiated marketing strategy would be IBM, which offers many hardware and software variations to different segments in the computer market. By differentiating its product or product line, the firm identifies several potential target markets. Each of these target markets may be attractive in demand, but they may differ substantially in other important aspects (such as size, product application, and technical expertise). With this strategy, the firm hopes to engage in nonprice competition and thus avoid, or at least minimize, the threat of severe price competition. Differentiated marketing strategy is justified when each segment is distinct; when there is very little cross-elasticity of demand; and when the potential size of each segment is large enough to provide a satisfactory return.

Although it can usually be shown that total sales may be increased with the marketing of a more diversified product line, such activity increases the cost of doing business. The following costs are likely to be higher when the firm elects to pursue a differentiated marketing strategy:[7]

(1) *Product modification costs.* Modifying a product or product line to serve different segment requirements usually involves additional research and development, engineering, and/or special tooling costs.

(2) *Production costs.* The longer the production set-up time for each product, and the smaller the sales volume of each product, the more expensive it becomes. If each product is sold in large volume, however, the higher costs of set-up time can be quite small per unit. However, innovative technology, including reduction of set-up time, flexible automation, and computer-integrated manufacturing has offset some of these additional production costs when pursuing a differentiated marketing strategy.

(3) *Administrative costs.* When a differentiated strategy is used, the firm must develop separate marketing plans for different segments. Such a

requirement usually means additional effort in marketing research, forecasting, sales analysis, promotion planning, and channel management strategy.

(4) *Inventory costs.* Managing inventories under a differentiated strategy is generally more costly than managing an inventory of only one product. Each product or product line must be carried at a level that reflects basic demand and must include a safety factor to cover unexpected variations in demand. The sum of the safety stocks for several products will exceed the safety stock required for one product.

(5) *Promotion costs.* Differentiated marketing strategy involves trying to reach different market segments with different variations of the promotional mix. Each segment may require separate creative advertising planning, sales strategy, etc.

Concentrated Marketing Strategy

Concentrated marketing strategy is practiced when the firm selects one or a relatively few segments on which to focus all its marketing effort. Through concentrated marketing, the firm achieves a strong market position in the segment because of its greater knowledge of the segment's needs and the special reputation it builds. Furthermore, the firm enjoys many operating economies through specialization in its production, distribution, and promotion functions. Such operating economies can help the firm to earn a high return on its investment.[8]

Concentrated marketing is, however, not without risk. A particular market segment's demand can turn downward, or a competitor may decide to enter the same segment. A good example of this situation can be found in the defense industry. General Dynamics has one primary customer—the United States government, whose Electric Boat Division, located in Connecticut and Rhode Island, builds submarines for the U.S. Navy. As defense spending is being curtailed in this area, the effect is being felt by many thousands of the firm's employees. Also, the addition of the Newport News, Virginia, facility as a competitor for both the "fast-attack" and Trident submarine programs has added the competitive element. For these reasons, some business-to-business firms decide to operate in more than one segment.

Figure 5-2 summarizes the key differences between undifferentiated marketing, differentiated marketing, and concentrated marketing.

APPROACHES TO MARKET SEGMENTATION

Fundamental means of segmenting business markets include macro/micro segmentation, the nested approach to segmentation, segmentation for maturing markets, and segmentation by purchase responsibilities of individuals within organizations. Each of these is discussed below.

FIGURE 5-2 **Three Alternative Market Selection Strategies**

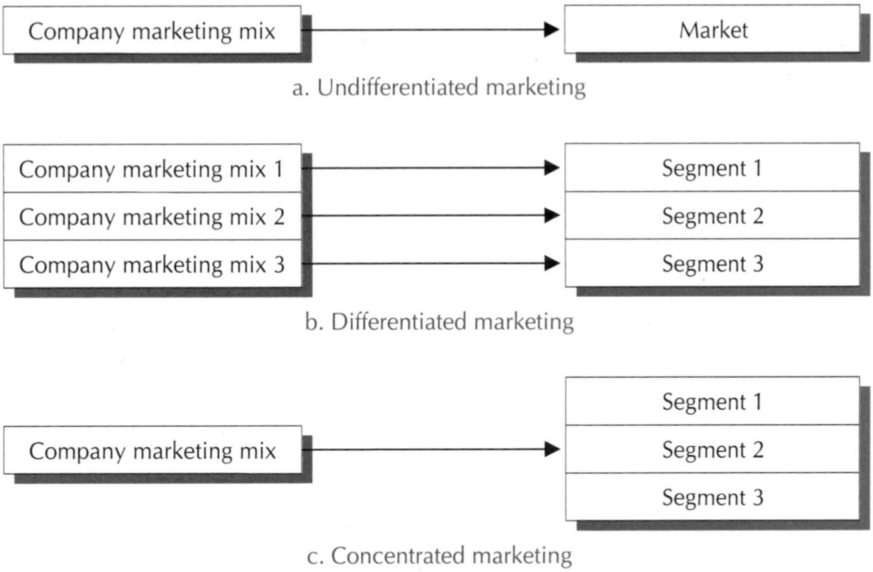

Macro/Micro Segmentation

"Macro segmentation" involves dividing the market into subgroups based on overall characteristics of the prospect organization (usage rates, SIC category, and so on). "Micro segmentation," on the other hand, pertains to characteristics of the decision-making process and the buying structure within the prospect organization (buying center authority, attitudes toward vendors, and so on). The business marketer would identify subgroups that share common macro or micro characteristics and then select target segments from among these subgroups.[9]

The Nested Approach to Market Segmentation

Thomas Bonoma and Benson Shapiro have developed a more detailed approach to business market segmentation which they refer to as a *nested approach.*[10] Their premise is that the distinction between macro segments and micro segments (as noted above) leaves out a number of potentially valuable segmentation variables. The nested approach stresses segmentation according to the amount of investigation required to identify and evaluate different criteria. Layers are arranged so as to begin with organization demographics as the area easiest to assess. Then come increasingly complex criteria, including company variables, situational factors, and personal characteristics, as diagrammed in Figure 5-3. The method integrates and builds on previous schemes for segmenting business markets and offers an approach that enables not only the simple grouping of customers and prospects

FIGURE 5-3 **Major Potential Bases for Segmentation (Nesting)**

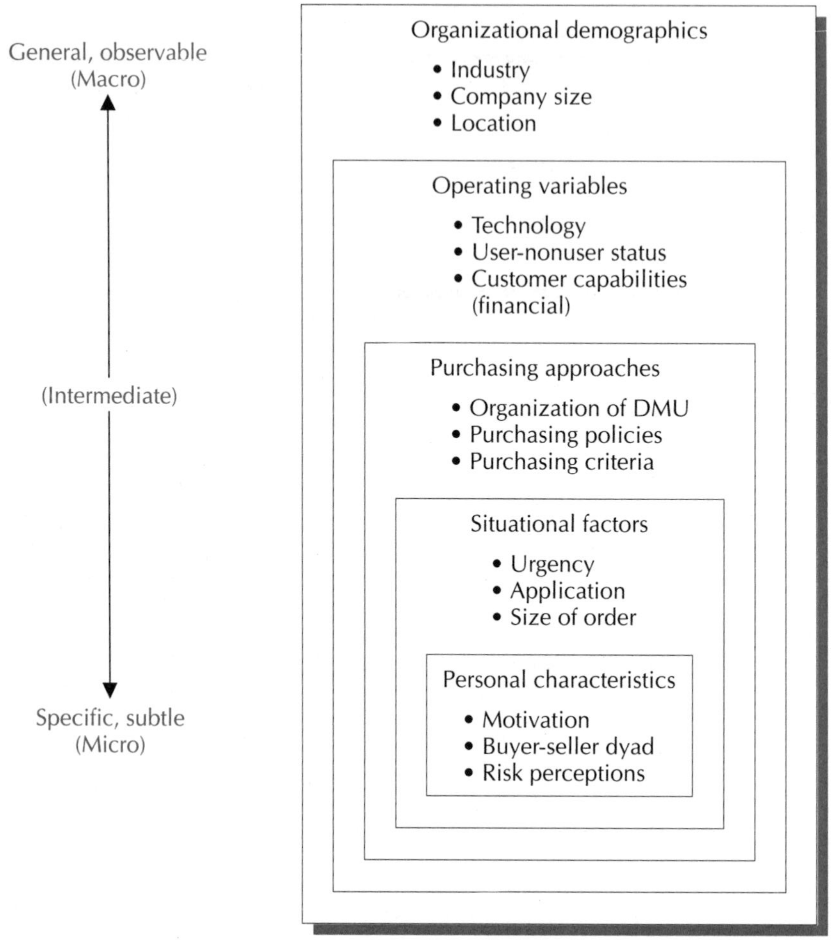

Source: Thomas V. Bonoma and Benson P. Shapiro, *Segmenting the Industrial Market,* Lexington, MA: Lexington Books, D. C. Heath and Company, 1983. Used with permission.

but also a more complex grouping of purchase situations, events, and personalities. The approach assumes a hierarchial structure that moves from broad, general bases to very specific bases. As illustrated in Figure 5-3, macro bases are in the outermost squares, micro characteristics in the innermost squares. (More specific customer characteristics are nested inside the broader organizational basis.)

An application of the nested approach. An example can be used to facilitate the understanding of this approach. Assume that a business-to-business firm is selling copiers and initially wishes to segment the potential market on broad organizational characteristics, such as company size, SIC category, or general location. The firm may decide to concentrate only on companies with several hundred or more employees, or companies engaged in manufacturing, or companies located in the northeastern United States. However, rather than stop here and focus on all companies that meet the desired criteria, the firm further segments the potential market on operating variables, such as whether the companies have a centralized copy center, buy or lease present equipment, or use copy equipment. If the firm focuses only on those prospects that have a centralized copy center, it might go one step further and target only those prospects that emphasize low price as a purchasing criterion, and so on. The marketer can move through all five phases of the nesting model if more specialization is needed, or can stop at any point. After several attempts at working completely through the nesting process, most firms will discover which segmentation criteria are likely to yield the greatest benefits.

Another word of caution is in order. The outer-nest criteria are generally inadequate when used by themselves in all but the simplest markets, because they ignore many significant buying differences among customers. Overemphasis on the inner-nest factors, however, can be too expensive and time-consuming for smaller markets. Shapiro and Bonoma suggest achieving a sense of balance between the simplicity and low costs of the outer nests and the richness and expense of the inner ones by making the choices explicit and the process clear and disciplined.

Other Approaches to Business Market Segmentation

Rangan, Moriarty, and Swartz have developed a buying-behavior-based framework[11] suitable for microsegmenting customers in mature business markets. They claim that in mature markets, segmenting customers on size, industry, or product benefits alone is rarely sufficient. Customer behavior in terms of tradeoffs between price and service is an important additional criterion. These authors feel that the nested approach (and others) do not capture the underlying dynamics of a maturing market. They advance the theory that considerable value can be gained by attempting to move toward buying-behavior-based segmentation.

Thomas[12] writes that managing business markets in today's complex, rapidly changing global environment requires approaches to market segmentation that lead to competitive advantage. His approach explores the use of purchase responsibilities among individuals within organizations as a basis for segmenting business markets. Knowledge that a firm's market may be segmented by purchase responsibilities may lead to more effective deployment of marketing resources. The use of purchase responsibilities to classify organizations represents an attempt to reduce some of the complexity involved in understanding the concept of the buying center. Different kinds of organizations may give rise to different kinds of buying centers, at least insofar as purchase responsibilities within the buying center are concerned.

CONCEPT QUESTIONS

1. What two conditions are necessary for a particular segment to be of interest to a business marketer?
2. What is the fundamental difference between a macro segmentation strategy and a micro segmentation strategy?
3. What is the basic premise of the nested approach to market segmentation?

SEGMENTING BUSINESS MARKETS

Many of the variables generally used by the marketer to segment the consumer market can also be used by the business marketer to segment the organizational market (for example, user status, degree of customer loyalty, and customer attitude toward the product). To expand upon the discussion of business market segmentation above, some of the categories of variables for segmenting organizational markets are identified in Figure 5-4 and are discussed in the following sections.

Type of Economic Activity

The Standard Industrial Classification (SIC) System discussed in Chapter 4, is a useful starting place to segment business-to-business firms according to primary economic activity. In addition to SIC data (several other sources of secondary data, also discussed in Chapter 4) will identify prospects for the business marketer's products or services.

Size of Organization

Segmentation on the basis of size, using variables such as volume of shipments, number of employees, market share enjoyed, and so on, may be a useful technique for business market segmentation. However, a note of caution is in order. Segmentation based on size alone is rather risky, as the prospect may or may not be a viable target. Just because an organization is large does not necessarily mean that it will be a large or heavy user of the product. However, segmentation on the basis of size is quite useful as a segmentation tool for the business marketer.

Geographic Location

Segmentation on the basis of location can also be used in segmenting organizational markets, as some industries such as textile manufacturing and furniture manufacturing are concentrated geographically.

FIGURE 5-4 **Examples of Segmentation Variables for Organizational Markets**

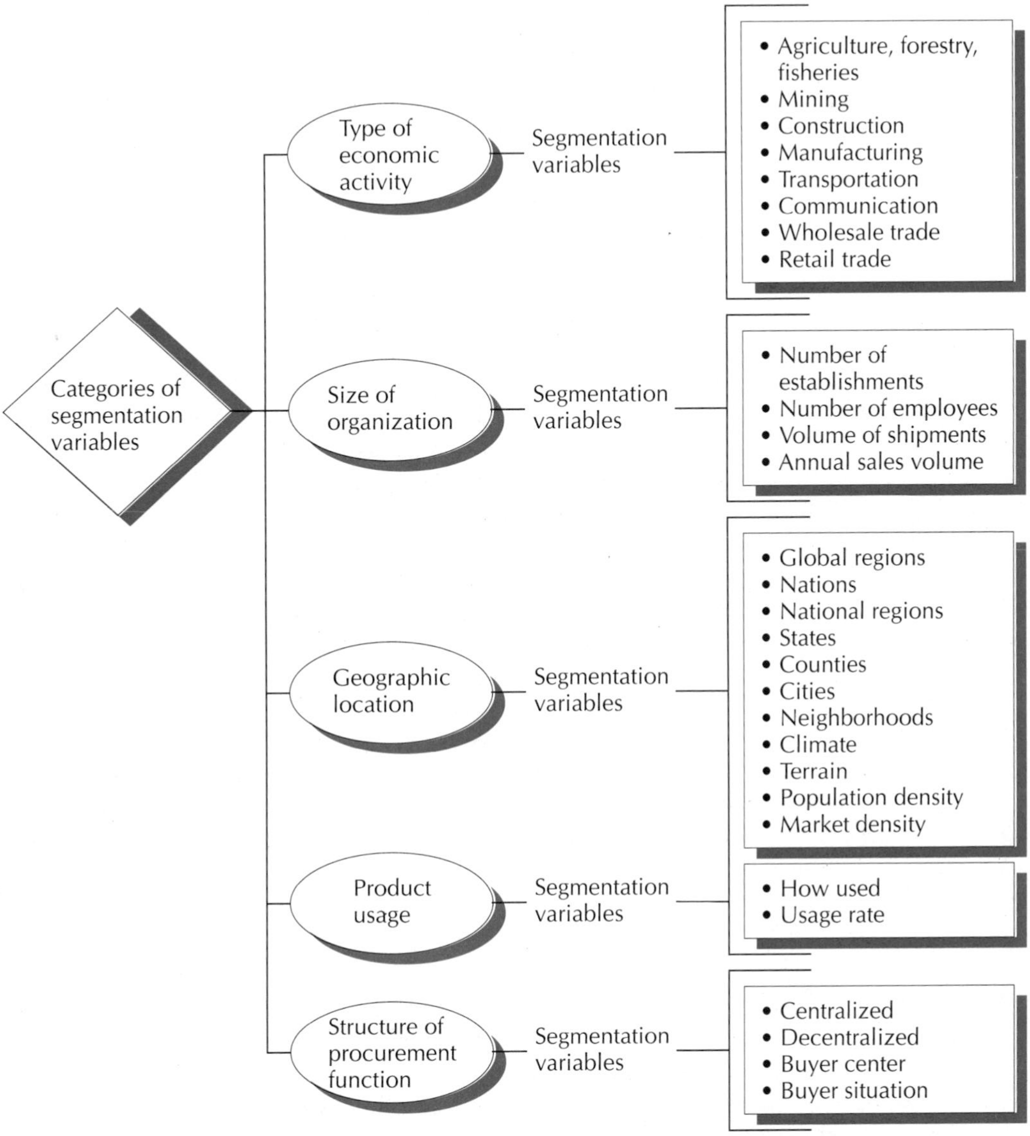

Source: Reprinted by permission of publisher, from *Segmenting the Industrial Market* by Thomas V. Bonoma and Benson P. Shapiro (Lexington, Ma.: Lexington Books, D. C. Heath and Company, Copyright © 1983, D. C. Heath and Company).

Product Usage

Many products are used in a number of different ways, making it possible to segment a market on the basis of product application. The manufacturer of a component such as an industrial fastener may attempt to market to industries incorporating the product into machine tools, precision instruments, office equipment, and missile systems. Additionally, segmentation is possible by usage rate (light, moderate, and heavy use).

Structure of the Procurement Function

Market segmentation strategy can also be affected by the manner in which the buying organization is structured. The buying behavior of the firm that centralizes the buying function will be quite different than one that uses decentralization. In a centralized situation, the members of the buying center will be in a stronger position to buy in larger quantities and to make quicker buying decisions; and they will be attractive targets to many potential competitors. When the buying decision is decentralized, the potential order size will be smaller, the number of potential competitors will be limited geographically, and a final decision on the price and quality aspects of the decision (especially in a modified-rebuy or new-task situation) may need final authorization from a centralized authority. Also, large buying organizations will respond to the seller's marketing mix and marketing stimuli differently than will smaller firms. The composition of the buying center can also present considerable demographic and psychographic differences among members of the center that will have to be considered by the business marketing manager. Finally, segmentation across buyclasses (as presented in Chapter 2) will impact segmentation strategy. As noted, the effort necessary to appeal to buying center members in new-task situations is very different from that needed to appeal to buyers in a straight-rebuy situation.

INTERNATIONAL SEGMENTATION

Macroeconomic forces, which are aggregated into four categories, are shaping international business and marketing strategies. The four categories are (1) regional integration and the emergence of the triad power (Europe, Japan, and the United States); (2) technology advances, especially the adoption of information technologies in business operations; (3) the emergence of an ideology-free world and the role of the market economy policy; and (4) a borderless economy as a consequence of global sourcing and global competition.[13]

The World Bank lists 126 countries. When a business firm decides to expand into foreign markets, it must evaluate all possible markets to identify the country or group of countries presenting the greatest opportunities. Initially, the firm may opt to enter one or a few countries, eventually broadening that base as the firm brings other countries within its fold. Research on international investment decisions has shown that the most critical factors affecting market segmentation are market size and growth, political conditions, competition, and market similarity.[14] The business-to-business firm must systematically evaluate all of these factors both initially and on a regular basis to be sure that company assets are directed toward the countries with the best opportunities. This screening process enables the firm to evaluate information about these factors regularly, thus becoming the basis for the development of international market strategy.

Successful competitive strategies during the 1990s will necessarily emphasize the development of approaches to pro-position or reposition marketing strategies with regard to shifting macroeconomic conditions.[15] Generally speaking, international market segmentation provides additional opportunities over and above domestic business. Massey-Ferguson decided long ago to focus on sales outside North America rather than to compete with firms such as John Deere, International Harvester, and Ford for the farm-equipment market. It took the company many years, but it now derives about 70 percent of its sales outside North America. As long ago as 1975, Massey-Ferguson's return was more than the combined return for both Deere and International Harvester.[16] The entire industry sustained losses in the 1980s, but Massey-Ferguson still fared better than its competitors.

For a product or service to be successful in any market, it must satisfy the customer's needs. American business marketers should understand that they must change, or at least slightly adapt, their marketing strategies when selling abroad. For companies that have committed seriously to international needs via market segmentation, performance can be quite encouraging. DuPont has done well in Japan (a market misunderstood by many) by recognizing the importance of market segmentation. The company, for example, maintains thirteen laboratories in Japan to work closely with specific customers to tailor particular products to meet particular customer needs.

EVALUATING POTENTIAL MARKET SEGMENTS

Market segmentation reveals the potential market opportunity faced by firms and what would appear to be the most attractive markets the business firm can serve. Before target markets can be chosen, the marketing manager has to decide which segments and how many segments will provide the best return, given limited resources. The relationship between business marketing strategy and financial performance must be examined, as it would seem appropriate to select those market segments that appear to be "profitable" and to disregard those segments that seem to be less profitable. Chosen segments must be able to be served at a reasonable cost to the firm, thus providing the necessary or required return on investment. Additionally, a "competitive analysis" should be undertaken to assess both the strengths and weaknesses of competitors within a segment and to identify further areas of opportunity for the firm. A competitive analysis and a profitability analysis will now be examined briefly as potential tools in the overall evaluation of potential segments.

Market Profitability Analysis

A market segment might have desirable size and growth characteristics and still not be attractive from a profitability point of view. (Many marketers would cite government defense procurement as an example of this phenomenon.) Michael Porter has identified five forces that determine the intrinsic long-run attractiveness of a whole market, or any segment within it.[17] His five-force model is shown in Figure 5-5. The model shows that the firm must assess the impact on long-run profitability of five groups: industry competitors, potential entrants, substitutes, buyers, and suppliers. The collective strength of these five competitive forces determines the ability of firms in an industry to earn, on average, rates of return on investment in excess of the cost of capital. The strength of these five forces varies from industry to industry and can change as an industry evolves. The strength of each of the competitive forces is a function of industry structure, or the underlying economic and technical characteristics of an industry. The five-forces framework does not eliminate the need for creativity in finding new segments in which to compete within an industry. Instead, it directs managers' creative energies toward those aspects of industry structure that are most important to long-run profitability; thereby raising the odds of discovering a desirable strategic innovation and the particular segment within which to market it. Further, even if the segment fits the firm's objectives, the firm must consider whether it possesses the skills and resources to succeed in that segment. The firm should avoid market segments where it cannot produce some form of superior value, resulting in predetermined profitability objectives.

Market Competitive Analysis

Demand and profitability are not the only key variables in a marketing plan; the number and types of competitors must also be analyzed. Competition both within and between segments is stronger today than ever before, partly because of the increasing strength of both domestic and foreign markets. The strategic approach that is most likely to succeed is a comprehensive one that starts with market segment preferences, and considers competitors' capabilities and costs, and the way in which competitive offerings are perceived.[18] Foreign competitors are strong and important factors to consider in the markets for machinery, steel, and chemicals, to name only a few. In response to market changes and unprecedented global competition, executives are drastically altering their business and marketing strategies to improve competitive advantage. Strategic actions may include downsizing, repositioning, market niching, altering the business portfolio, and strategic alliances between companies.[19] Competition cannot be avoided, and the actions of competitors cannot be controlled. Thus, profit potential depends to some degree on a careful analysis of the strengths and weaknesses

FIGURE 5-5 **Elements of Industry Structure**

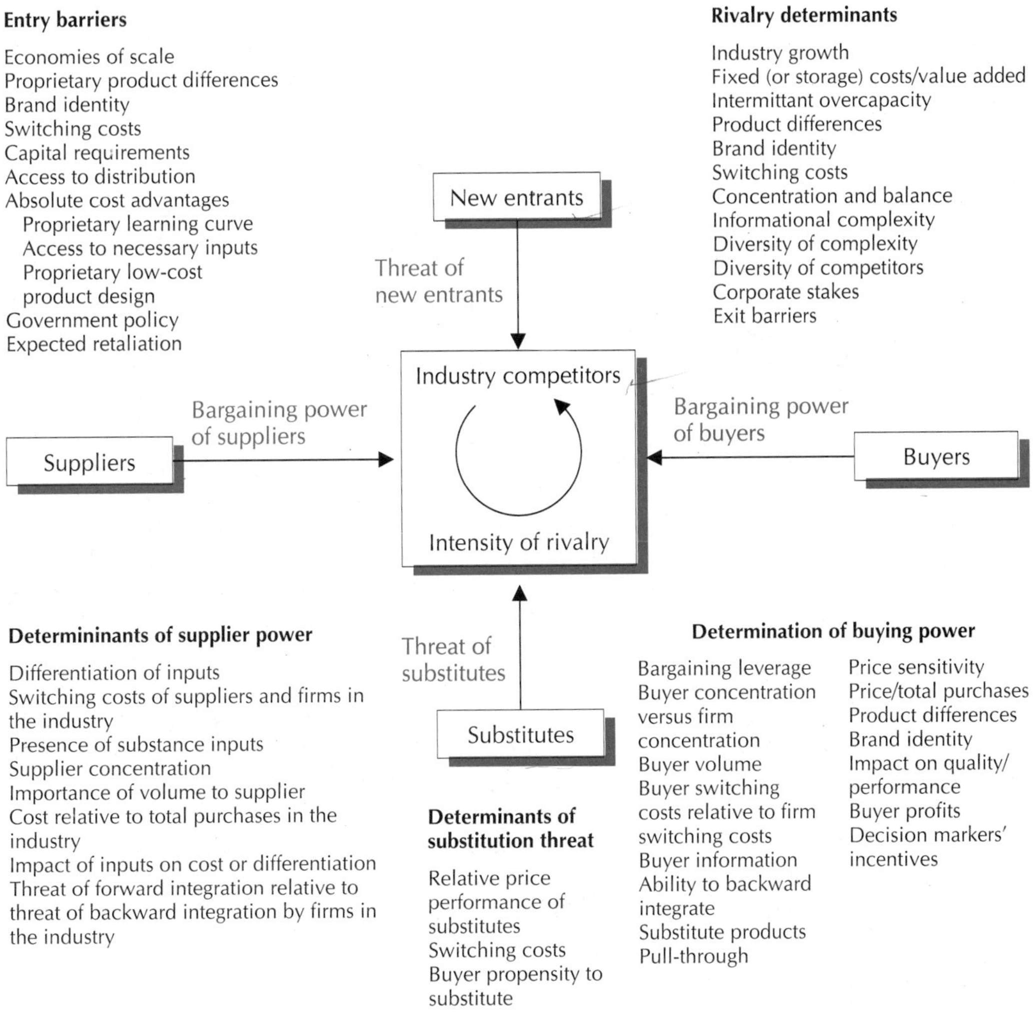

Source: Michael E. Porter, *Competitive Advantage: Creating and Sustaining Superior Performance.* (New York: Free Press, 1985), pp. 4–8, 234–36. Used with permission.

of existing or potential competitors. In evaluating market segments, the marketing manager should ask: "Who are the target competitors? What are the target competitors' strategic weaknesses? What are the design vulnerabilities of the target competitors?"[20]

The traditional view of competition can be expanded by reexamining Figure 5-5 and by recognizing again the five competitive forces that determine performance within a segment:

(1) Rivalry among existing firms

(2) Threat of new entrants

(3) Threat of substitute products

(4) Bargaining power of suppliers

(5) Bargaining power of buyers

The first force recognizes that an industry's performance is greatly affected by interfirm competition, and the second force points out that an industry will be stimulated by the entrance of a new competitor, regardless of any attempts by established competitors to erect barriers to entry. The third force suggests that the availability and suitability of substitute products, which indicate an elastic product demand, can pose a threat to existing products in the industry; and the fourth shows that business firms in a particular industry can be influenced by the potential power of suppliers. The fifth and final force acknowledges the potential bargaining power of buyers relative to suppliers within an industry. A major consequence of this view of competition is that the competitive arena may be altered over time due to the impact of the five forces upon the industry. For example, in the case of diamonds, all five forces are at low or negligible levels of intensity because of DeBeer's global control of diamond distribution. In contrast, where low barriers of entry exist, the number of firms tends to increase, leading to greater rivalry between competitors. Strategies of individual firms can also influence the five forces.[21]

In formulating strategy, the existing and potential competitors' strengths in the areas of research and development, finance, technical service, sales-force development, advertising, distribution, and organizational design must be studied before the firm makes a commitment to enter a particular segment. Companies need to practice "wrap-around" marketing, which encompasses both getting and retaining customers.[22] "Competitors are in business to defend or take market share from rival firms, and their ability to do so varies with their individual strengths and weaknesses."[23]

CONCEPT QUESTIONS

1. How can the structure of the procurement function affect market segmentation strategy?
2. What is necessary for a product or service to be successful in any market?
3. What is the role of a competitive analysis?

PRODUCT POSITIONING STRATEGY

Once potential markets have been identified, analyzed, and properly segmented (if appropriate), business marketers must carve a position or "niche" for their respective products in the minds of prospective customers. According to Sheth, competitive structures are created by product and market differentiation.[24] *Product position* is the way the product is defined by customers on important attributes, or the place the product occupies in customers' minds relative to competing products. Positioning applies to more than just products and services. A company's distribution channels, technologies, and techniques all occupy positions in customers' minds. Particularly in regard to technical and business marketing, it is critical to position not only your products, but also your company, your distribution channel, and frequently your technologies. Even if you are selling the product of the century, most customers will hesitate to buy it if they do not accept your company or your sales and support staff.[25] When National Cash Register (NCR) dubbed itself the "computer company" in a major advertising campaign, the promotional effort failed because people thought of NCR only as a manufacturer and marketer of cash registers. IBM could more easily have used this advertising copy, but did not need to since the general public already identified with them in this regard.

This term, "positioning," refers to the placing of a product in that part of the market where it will have a favorable reception compared to competing products. "Positioning" means different things to different people. To some, it might mean the segmentation decision, while to others it might address the "image" question. To still others, it might mean selecting which product features to emphasize. As a matter of strategy, a product should be matched with the segment of the market where it is most likely to succeed. The product should be so positioned as to stand apart from competitive products, reflecting the firm's unique combination of marketing variables that differentiate the product from competitive offerings. The box entitled "Business-to-Business Marketing in Action" describes how Inmac, a large California-based mail-order supplier of computer accessories to the organizational market, uniquely uses its popular, plain-talking catalogue and finely honed direct-mail techniques to deliver the company's message of dependable quality and service.

Perceptual Mapping

A technique for examining a product's position, relative to strengths and weaknesses of the product and compared to competitors, is called *perceptual mapping*. Perceptual mapping attempts to uncover how buyers evaluate a set of competing products by identifying the relative dimensions or features of each one.

BUSINESS-TO-BUSINESS MARKETING IN ACTION

INMAC'S CREATIVE APPROACH TO POSITIONING

Inmac is a large, California-based supplier of computer accessories to the business-to-business market. It launched an ambitious effort in 1987 to attract and hold large-colume customers to bolster its 10 percent share of the highly fragmented computer aftermarket. Largely thanks to Inmac's popular, plain-talking catalog—it plays up product benefits in simple, nontechnical language—the mail-orfer company got its foot in more than a few doors during 1987. Observes catalog consultant Dick Hodgson, president of Sargeant House of Westtown, Pennsylvania, "Inmac forgets that they are in the computer field, and treats the catalog as if they are selling to someone who doesn't know anything about computers." CEO and founder Kenneth Eldred relied primarily on direct mail to deliver the firm's message of dependable quality and service. "We started the company with apad and pencil in one hand, and a copy of David Ogilvy's *Confessions of an Advertising Man* in the other," Eldred says.

The company's corporate image seems to be a natural by-product of what they do. Boasts Eldred, "We really count on our catalog for tthe better part of our image." Splashed with color and irreverent humor, the catalog has won several design awards and is believed to be the key reason why solicited customers respond with enthusiasm. Experts say its ability to translate complex product data into pointed customer benefits has helped Inmac tap into a broad cross-section of potential customers. Instead of getting bogged down in detailing the advantages of an accessory for printers, for instance, catalog copy asks the provoking question, "Does your printer sound like a machine gun?"

Thos with questions can call a toll-free hotline for information on how to make their new computer accessories work the right way. "They don't have blinders on when it comes to people," says Hodgson. "They're a direct-marketing business, run like a marketing-oriented business."

With 60 employees working full-time at three separate research facilities to design new products—90 percent of the products sold carry the Inmac label—Inmac hopes to continue as the most comprehensive computer aftermarket source in the business. The company also shoots for newly designed products comprising 20 percent of total annual sales.

Source: "Eldred's Afterlife," *Marketing & Media Decisions* 23, no. 3 (March 1988), pp. 85–88. Used with permission.

As is evident in Figure 5-6, this map has opposite levels of one dimension on the ends of the X and Y axes, such as "strong-to-weak" customer-service programs on the end of the X axis, and "excellent-to-low" product durability on the ends of the Y axis. Perceptual mapping can be accomplished by using statistical tools, with the most popular being multidimensional scaling (MDS). Business buyers rate sellers' products or services on specified attributes, thereby evaluating the firm's position relative to the competition.

FIGURE 5-6 **Two-Dimensional Perceptual Map of Vendor Attributes of Copier Suppliers**

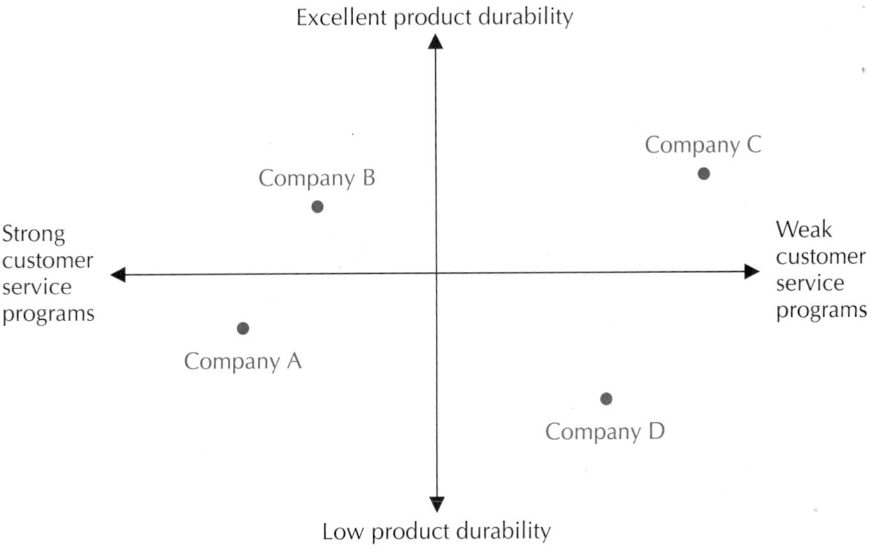

The perceptual map presented in Figure 5-6 illustrates the positions of four manufacturers of copiers. Product durability and customer service are the most important attributes in this market; business marketers within this industry try to position their respective products favorably on those attributes in relation to the competition. Organizational customers interviewed clearly perceive Company A as having a better service program than any of the competitors. However, Company A's product-durability level is not rated highly. Company C, on the other hand, is perceived as having the best product durability, but its product service is rated poorly. Company B has the strongest combined performance on both attributes. Company D is perceived by the buyers as having low product durability and a weak customer-service program. With such data, sellers are at least in a position to attempt to control their own destinies with regard to positioning strategy in relation to the competition.

Positioning Business Products

Positioning business products is often more difficult and subtle than positioning consumer goods. Positioning represents the place that a business product occupies in a particular market and is determined by researching the organizational buyer's perceptions and preferences for a product in relation to the competition. While advertising is the primary tool used to position products and services in the consumer market, personal selling, advertising, and trade shows are used in organizational markets. To evaluate the position of individual products or product lines relative to the competition requires not only extensive knowledge of the competitor's offerings but also access to the various members of the buying center. Few business firms recognize what their actual position is, nor do they understand how their customers perceive their position. Lack of top management support and managerial ignorance of the concept of positioning are generally responsible for this lack of awareness. Consequently, few business organizations purposely employ positioning strategy.

The gulf between the theory and practice of product positioning can be wide. In technical and business marketing, it is critical to position the company and its products, its distribution channels, and often its technologies. A position statement should be worded in terms of customer benefits, should define the value proposition, and should be very simple and easy to understand. Among other things, the positioning process involves: (1) recognizing business strategy; (2) comparing the product strategy with the business strategy; (3) understanding what target customers care about; (4) understanding competitors' positions; and (5) testing the proposed positioning.[26]

An initial step in understanding the opportunity of positioning alternatives is to study some of the ways in which a product-positioning strategy can be conceived and implemented. As shown in Figure 5-7, six possible approaches emphasized by the marketing strategist include positioning by technology, price, quality, image, distribution and service. Each of these will be discussed in turn. Several additional positioning strategies can be used in select situations, depending upon the particular industry (or segment), the competitive structure, the marketing expertise, and so on.

FIGURE 5-7 **Approaches to Positioning Strategy**

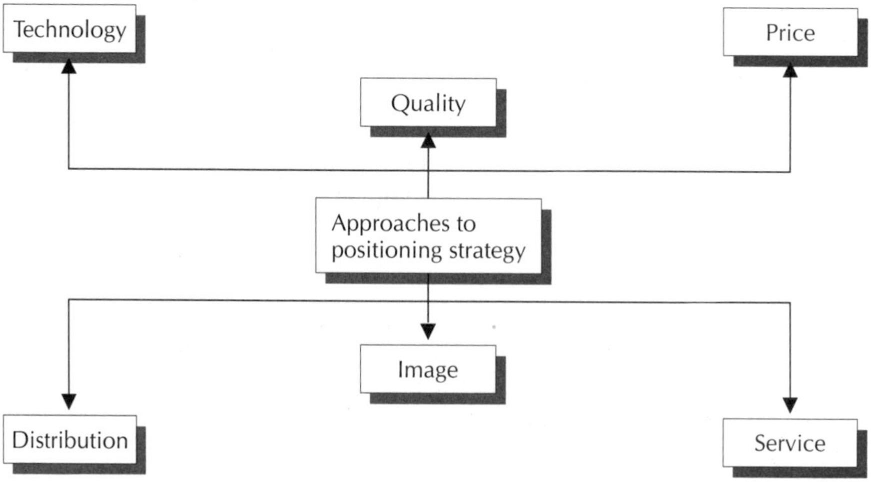

Positioning by technology. The high-technology business marketer must ascertain which industries or buying groups can use the firm's products and then array the industries in an ordered fashion. A high-tech firm should be able to determine which industries offer the greatest potential; which firms in these industries would benefit most from its products or processes; and which markets, in rank order, it will attempt to exploit. Often, there is a multitude of possible applications for any technology the firm could employ. Positioning by technology also highlights the time problems that are experienced by a high-tech business marketer. The nature of many high-technology products or processes suggests that the business marketer can be described as having each of the following:[27]

- A limited product/process life cycle.
- A limited lead time before competition responds with an equal or greater breakthrough or improvement.
- A desire to control the portions of its new technology that it introduces during any single time period, or to any single target market.

Rapid change puts tremendous pressure on the marketer and emphasizes the selection and the establishment of priorities for target markets.

Positioning by price. Astute business marketers know what their respective firms' total costs are (fixed, variable, and incremental) and will set prices accordingly. They will avoid cross-subsidizing product lines or underestimating overhead. By achieving the lowest delivered-cost position relative to competition (including freight charges and installation expense), the firm can build a strong position, in that the lowest costs generally provide the highest margins. Higher margins, in turn, present additional opportunities for future cost, price, or promotional battles with the competition. Time and again, it has been noted that higher market share and experience lead to lower cost. Thus, a new product should be priced to improve experience and market share. The combination of enhanced market share and experience gives a company such a cost advantage that it cannot profitably be overcome by any competitor of normal performance.[28]

Price is an important way of establishing product position. In setting prices, business owners must consider whether their goods or services are price elastic or inelastic.[29] *Price positioning* will require the development of large economies of scale in purchasing, manufacturing, selling, and distribution, using cumulative experience and increases in efficiency and volume to keep costs down. A number of firms have used the lowest delivered price as a key positioning strategy, not only to gain market share but also to combat challenges to their market leadership.[30] Texas Instruments (TI) used this form of leverage as the leader in new solid-state technology in the early 1970s to bring calculator production costs progressively lower. Lower costs provided opportunities to decrease price, which, in turn, opened up successively larger-volume market segments. This phenomenon increased demand

and again forced costs down. TI's success with the experience curve strategy to achieve the lowest delivered cost position was such that, by 1977, TI had gained market leadership in the personal calculator market—a position it held until the mid-1980s by maintaining its cost-leadership strategy.[31]

Positioning by quality. Although organizational buyers resist paying for unnecessary high quality, they generally will not compromise quality for a lower price. In recent years, the relationship between price and quality has been questioned by those who claim that improvements in product quality need not increase product costs.[32] For example, Charles M. Pigott, chairman and CEO at Paccar of Bellevue, Washington, is focused on two fundamental business objectives: profitability and customer service. Moreover, he sees the two goals as intrinsically linked. In thirty years, Paccar's net sales have grown from $142 million to nearly $2.2 billion. More impressive, the company has never had a net annual loss. For Paccar, the secret to success lies not only in its determination to control costs, reduce debt, and boost productivity, but also in its commitment to keeping customers satisfied through a continuous series of product-quality improvements. The Paccar Integrated Quality System (PIQS)—a company wide total-quality and training program that involves all employees regardless of job level and aims for zero defects in production—is a cornerstone of the process. Paccar is currently spending over $90 million to build a new, highly modernized Kenworth truck plant in Renton, Washington. This new factory will improve manufacturing efficiencies and expand truck-production capacity.[33] This type of thinking has liberated product quality, making it a separate strategic variable that the firm can use in its positioning strategy. Earlier explanations explaining the relationship between profitability and sales volume focused on the experience curve and the relationship between volume and cost. The works of Phillips, Chang, and Buzzell have shifted the focus to product quality.[34] This study found that product quality had a positive impact on performance measures, such as market share, profit, and return on investment. It was observed that high market share means high volume, which leads to lower per-unit product costs. Given this phenomenon, high quality can lead to lower costs through a favorable influence on market position. Some firms will have the delicate task of retaining the image of low price while simultaneously trying to upgrade their quality image. In this situation, the firm runs the risk that the quality message will obscure the basic "low price," "value" position. *Quality positioning* is a difficult, but frequently a highly lucrative, positioning strategy to employ.

Positioning by image. *Image positioning* stresses the importance of creating an exclusive image for a product by establishing a distinctive quality perception of the product's category that will place it in a class above all other products in the category. It should also be noted that image positioning is vulnerable to more specific product-oriented concepts by the competition. Coca-Cola Company, with 1992 sales of $13 billion, leads rival PepsiCo Incorporated in the global soft-drink market. Coke Classic brand leads Pepsi only slightly, and trails in supermarkets. Marketers say Pepsi's advertising is more vibrant and youthful, and it really is capturing the new generation.[35]

In some cases, a successful company image in one market may be a handicap in another. IBM, for example, had built a blue-chip name in the world of office equipment, but in the mass market it was perceived as cold and efficient. To launch its first mass-market product, the "Personal Computer" (PC), to small business concerns as well as to final consumers, IBM knew it had to "humanize" its image. The company decided to use Charlie Chaplin's "Little Tramp" in its advertising campaign to make the company and the product seem less threatening. The strategy worked. By combining its traditional aggressive marketing with low-cost production and a new, friendly image, IBM, in two years time, rocketed to number one in sales in the personal computer industry.[36]

Positioning by distribution. Many business-to-business firms think of distribution as a dilemma, or possibly as an unpleasant problem. Management's difficulties with distribution can often be traced to the fact that it has not made up its mind whether distribution should be part of the sales organization, the manufacturing organization, or the executive group. Too often, distribution is the neglected side of marketing. In contrast, some companies have outstripped their competition with imaginative strategies for getting products to their customers, and other marketing executives can learn from such creativity. The Federal Express system is so innovative and formidable that it might be considered a model even beyond the small-package delivery industry. Federal Express has successfully positioned itself in the package delivery business by promising customers delivery within a specific number of hours. If it fails, the customer receives a full refund. American Hospital Supply has gained the edge over its competition by linking up to hospitals and clinics with a sophisticated system of data processing, while Steelcase has set a standard for delivering complex office furniture installations, complete and on time.[37] There are still many opportunities available in which a business firm can employ *distribution positioning* and gain a competitive edge through efficient distribution.

Positioning by service. Positioning by service describes an attribute provided by the business marketer to assist the ongoing activities of the business buyer. This category can include technical assistance, repair services, information, delivery, parts availability, and financing, as well as advisory services such as tax or legal counsel. It can also include adding services to the present offering, or providing a higher level of quality of present services offered. A good example of service positioning is provided by Federal Express. Finding that its once unique overnight-package-delivery system had been emulated by numerous competitors, Federal Express executives rethought and redefined service as "all actions and reactions that customers perceive they have purchased." They proceeded to develop a sophisticated, centralized customer-service function to handle information provision, order taking, tracing, and problem solving. Federal Express executives believe that they can provide a higher level of service than the competition, and they also note that it would be extremely expensive for competitors to install the equipment and systems needed to duplicate their approach.[38] *Service positioning* is an important means of differentiation for the business marketer, and management's ability to use service positioning effectively to place a product in the market correctly could be a major determinant of company profit.

When a firm or provider establishes and maintains a distinctive place for itself and its offerings in the market, it is said to be successfully positioned. The economic war of recession and restructuring has created many casualties and has led to fundamental change and a new marketing environment. As a result, marketers must become professional team players, involved in areas such as logistics and cost reduction. They must also retain a clear sense of goals, product positioning, and business positioning.[39] In the increasingly competitive business-products sector, effective positioning is one of marketing's most critical tasks.[40] While the concept of positioning strategy is not new, its application in the business sector has multiplied with the proliferation of products, many with similar characteristics. All this activity has given credibility to the theory of positioning. The identification of an exclusive niche in the market, or the creation of a unique perception of the product or service that satisfies an unfulfilled customer need, can serve to distinguish the product or service from competitive offerings.

Finally, how does the firm get started on a positioning strategy? To help with this thinking process, six questions (simple to ask but difficult to answer) should be asked.[41] Specific questions that the firm should attempt to answer include the following:

(1) *What position does the firm presently own?* Determining what position the firm already holds in the mind of the prospect allows the marketer to tie the product service or concept to what is already there.

(2) *What position does the firm want to own?* This question involves the business marketing manager's assessment of what is the best position to hold from a long-term point of view. "Head-on positioning" should be avoided by all but the strongest of firms.

(3) *Whom must the firm outgun?* Generally, the marketing manager will attempt to avoid the competitor's strengths while exploiting obvious weaknesses. The marketer will try to select a position that no one else has a firm grip on, or "owns."

(4) *Does the firm have enough resources?* A big obstacle to successful positioning is attempting to establish a position with limited resources to commit to the effort. It generally requires substantial resources to establish a position, and even more resources to maintain it.

(5) *Can the firm stick it out?* The business marketing environment changes regularly and rapidly, so it is important for the marketer to develop a long-range point of view, determine the positioning strategy desired, and then stick to it. Indeed, a strong argument can be made that the firm should not change its basic positioning strategy unless forced to by elements in either the internal or external environment. Only tactics or short-term maneuvers that are intended to implement long-term strategy should change. Once a firm's position is lost, it may be difficult or even impossible to get it back again.

(6) *Does the firm match its marketing mix with its stated market position?* In determining a positioning strategy, the marketing manager must be able to match the elements of the marketing mix creatively with the stated position. Does the firm's advertising campaign, for example, match the firm's overall positioning strategy?

A business-to-business firm must have a good idea of the basic segments of the market that it can satisfy with its product or product line. Some business marketing practitioners would argue that some of the above-mentioned positioning strategies should be used, and that others will serve no useful purpose. Many of these arguments would depend on the firm's position within the industry. Is the firm a leader or a follower, an innovator or laggard? The main point is that product positioning studies are useful for giving the marketing manager a clearer idea of customer perceptions of market offerings.

BUSINESS DEMAND PROJECTION

When business marketers have successfully carved out a position for each product in all their product lines, they are then ready to forecast potential sales volume (that is, to estimate demand) for each product. There are both qualitative and quantitative methods of sales forecasting available for use, depending on the nature and the reliability of the data desired. Before discussing each of these methods, there should be a preliminary discussion of the strategic importance of forecasting, some commonly used forecasting terminology, and some of the typical problems found in the forecasting function.

Strategic Importance of Forecasting in Decision Making

With increasing complexity, competition, and change in the business environment, organizations need more reliable performance forecasts to be able to maintain favorable marketing position.[42] Few would deny that forecasting is one of the most important activities undertaken by the business-products firm, or that there are few other activities that are as shrouded in mystery and as misunderstood. *Forecasting* is used in the analysis, measurement, and improvement of current marketing strategy and in the identification and/or development of new products and new markets. Forecasting promotes and facilitates the proper functioning of the many aspects of the firm's activities (production, marketing, finance, research and development, purchasing, and so on). Accurate sales forecasting helps the marketing manager plan strategies and tactics and compile a marketing plan to achieve realistic profit targets or other objectives in the short, medium, and long run. It further assists the marketer in integrating a firm's mission, operating plans, and objectives with opportunities in existing and/or potential markets or market segments. H. O. Crafford, president of Crafford Tool and Die Corporation in Worcester, Massachusetts, insists on a revised sales forecast on a monthly basis. Crafford adds, "How can I plan, hire, train, buy materials, allocate vacation times, and/or do any number of things if I don't know what is going to happen over the next several weeks and months. Without an accurate, current sales forecast, I am flying blind, and I absolutely refuse to do that."[43] In short, accurate sales forecasting is an absolute "must" in the business market sector.

Definition of Some Basic Terminology

Before forecasting methods can be discussed, several terms will be defined, as there is a tendency to use these terms rather loosely.

Market factor. A market factor is something that exists in a particular market or segment that can be measured quantitatively and that is somehow related to the eventual market demand for a particular business product or service. As an example, the number of copiers three years old and older is, or may be, a market factor underlying the demand for replacement copiers. A market factor is something that affects the number of replacement copiers that can be either sold or leased in the immediate or short-term future.

Market index. A market index is simply a market factor that is expressed as a percentage, relative to a base figure. To illustrate, one market factor might be the number of firms owning the copier model X. In 1988, the market index for this factor was 155 (relative to 1986 equals 100). A market index might also consist of several market factors, such as the number of model X copiers five years old and older, where they are located based on geographic segmentation, types of substitutes available, and so on.

Market potential. The market potential for a product is the maximum possible sales of the product or product line by all firms in a particular market or market segment, within a given environment over a period of time. Market potential basically sets the upper limit for industry sales and serves as important data in helping the marketing executive in evaluating which opportunities should be pursued, based on interest, income, and segment size. Market potential in the copier industry can refer to total expected sales of copier model X within an entire market, or for only a segment of that market over a period of one year.

Sales potential. Sales potential refers to the maximum amount that the firm expects to receive in relation to the competition. It is an "ideal." For example, the marketer of copiers may speak of the number of units expected to be sold for copier model X on the West Coast over the next fiscal year.

Market share. Market share refers to the actual measurement of sales, by percentage, in relation to total industry sales. For example, the marketer would claim that the firm captured (or will capture) 20 percent of the market during the firm's 1990 fiscal year.

Market demand. Market demand would refer to the absolute amount of product that would be bought or leased by a particular customer segment within a very defined geographical area during a particular time period and using a specific marketing program. For example, the business marketer might refer to the sales potential of copier model X that would be bought or leased by health care facilities within three southwestern states during the first quarter of 1990, using a special, one-time-only sales promotion.

Market forecast. A market forecast refers to the expected sales of a particular product or product line within a given environment or specific environment over a specific time period by all marketers in the particular industry. For example, the marketer would define expected shipments of all copiers competing with copier model X by all marketers of copier machinery within territory C during the first quarter of 1990. The assumption is made that all will utilize a fairly uniform promotional technique.

Sales forecast. Sales forecasting refers to anticipating the amount that business buyers are likely to purchase of a specific product or product line within a specific market or market segment over a given time period and under a given set of conditions. To generate an accurate sales forecast, marketing strategy must be decided upon in advance. For example, the business marketer would estimate how many model X copiers will be sold or leased in the midwestern territory within the first quarter of 1990, using a preplanned promotional and pricing strategy.

Common Forecasting Problems

Before general sales forecasting techniques are discussed, an overview of the basic problems encountered by business marketers in dealing with these techniques will be presented.[44]

Forecasting mystique. Many business marketers, uninitiated and untrained in forecasting techniques, are apprehensive about forecasting methods for three primary reasons: (1) forecasting techniques range from simple to complex; (2) from qualitative to quantitative; and (3) from traditional to very nontraditional. Keeping current with these techniques in light of daily pressures is difficult.

Forecasting accuracy. Business marketers tend to be "optimistic doers," and their forecasts are often unrealistically high overall and lack accuracy of detail.

Forecasting inconsistency. The continual subjective modifications made by both forecasters and other decision makers tend to cloud forecasting data, which, in turn, impacts results. Modifications to a submitted forecast might range from adjusting or throwing out data because of unusual variations within the market or individual market segment, to adjusting the forecast because of a known bias by one of the participants in the forecasting process. While these modifications will usually make the ending forecast more accurate, the motive for these changes is often difficult to understand and explain.

Forecasting accountability. In some situations, the decision maker who develops a forecast does not have to live with a forecast decision that greatly impacts the line organization. Forecasting and the line organization become two different functions—one area being responsible for developing the forecast, the other area being responsible for achieving the forecast.

Forecasting implementation. Forecasts are the best estimates of sales in a given period. However, the distinction between forecasts and sales quotas, targets, and goals is not always made; thereby increasing the likelihood of misunderstanding and consternation between those people responsible for making the forecast and those responsible for carrying it out.

SELECTING FORECASTING METHODS

General Approaches to Forecasting

Preparing a sales forecast is intrinsic to the management function. Some business marketers make a forecast on a short-term basis (from one to six months); others prepare them on an intermediate-term basis (from six months up to two years); and still others prepare them on a long-term basis (over two years) in combination with one or the other above. There is, however, a measure of commonality here; business marketers prepare sales forecasts on a routine basis because the performance of the marketing manager is determined and measured (to a certain degree at least) by the accuracy of the forecasts made.

Two very subjective, very basic categories of sales forecasting methodology, based on management judgment in estimating potential, are the top-down method and the bottom-up method (also called the "build-up method".) With the *top-down method*, management begins by developing an aggregate measure of potential that is then disaggregated. Sales potential is first estimated, sales quotas are developed, and then a sales forecast is constructed. The initial estimate includes an analysis of economic and specific industry variables that might influence the sale of the firm's products, including indicators like GNP, capital expenditures, price indices, and others. A model or mathematical equation is often created to link economic and industry variables to individual company sales; it serves as a starting point in the forecasting process. An area of concern, and one that inhibits the expanded use of this general approach, is the assumed correlation of economic variables and quantity demanded, along with the assumption that this observable relationship will continue. However, it is a macro approach, is initiated by top management decision makers, and is appropriate in many situations.

The *bottom-up method* of forecasting originates with the sales force. This process estimates the number of potential buyers by adding the individual estimates by product line, geographic area, or customer group. Potential is estimated at the field level, and these estimates are then tallied to obtain total sales predicted. The logic behind this approach is that salespeople have a better feel for customer product requirements, customer inventory requirements, and conditions within specific sales districts or territories. An area of concern with this approach is that since sales forecasts eventually will lead to the establishment of sales quotas in most firms, the salesperson may underestimate the sales potential of a territory; or, if they are optimists, may tend to overestimate the sales potential. Perhaps the combination of both the top-down and the bottom-up approaches is best in most situations.

Qualitative Approaches to Forecasting

Qualitative approaches to forecasting employ managerial judgment to determine future expectations; they are often used when data are scarce (perhaps there is no relevant history, say, with a new product) or when good information is virtually nonexistent. These techniques rely primarily on qualitative or judgmental information, with the objective being to bring together in a logical, unbiased, and systematic way all information and judgments that relate to the factors being evaluated. Techniques for qualitative analyses include (1) jury of executive opinion (sometimes called executive panels); (2) sales-force composite (sometimes called sales-force estimates); (3) survey of buyer intentions (sometimes called market survey of user expectations), and (4) the Delphi method.

Jury of executive opinion. The jury of executive opinion consists of combining and averaging the outlooks of top executives from internal disciplines such as finance, production, marketing, and purchasing. It can be an effective method, especially when the top executive personnel are knowledgeable about situations that might influence sales and are open-minded and realistic concerning the future. A major criticism of this approach would be comments about ivory-tower thinking, referring the very real possibility that executive personnel are not in tune with some of the realities faced by field sales personnel.

Sales-force composite. Among business-to-business firms, the most often used technique or approach to sales forecasting is the sales-force composite. This approach combines each salesperson's estimate of future sales in a particular territory into a total company sales forecast. This total forecast is analyzed, adjusted, and perhaps compared with forecasts from other sources, and adjusted upward or downward if deemed necessary by high-level marketing management. Advantages associated with this method include the assignment of forecasting to those who will be held responsible for results, the utilization of specialized knowledge of people in the field, and the greater reliability and accuracy usually obtained. Disadvantages include using people who are not trained in forecasting and who may not view the function as an important part of their job; estimates that are either too optimistic or too pessimistic (as mentioned earlier in the discussion of the bottom-up approach); and the lack of potential salesperson perspective for future planning, which may result in forecasts based on present, rather than future, conditions.

Survey of buyer intentions. A survey of buyer intentions anticipates what buyers are likely to do under a given set of conditions and suggests that, at the least, major organizational buyers should be surveyed. In the business-products sector, various agencies carry out intention surveys regarding plant, equipment, and materials purchases, with the two best-known surveys being conducted by the U.S. Department of Commerce and the McGraw-Hill Book Company. Most of the estimates, surprisingly enough, have been within 10 percent of the actual outcomes. Advantages include giving the marketer a continual feel for the market and its needs, keeping the marketer abreast of competition, and the possibility that, as a side benefit, the approach will indicate where additional advertising, promotion, and personal selling pressure may be needed. Disadvantages of this approach would include the likelihood that many buyers may not know, or may be unwilling to reveal, their buying intentions; users may be too numerous, too hard, or too expensive to locate; and if indirect channels of distribution are used, distributors and representatives may not be willing to take on the extra work of tracing and questioning customers or potential customers on future buying intentions.

Delphi Method. The Delphi method is a group forecasting method that is a modified version of the "expert-opinion approach." It is accomplished by questioning experts individually and then providing them with anonymous feedback from others in the group until there is a convergence of the estimates or opinions of the total group. (This approach was developed during the late 1940s by the Rand Corporation.) Any set of information available to some experts is passed on to each of the other experts, enabling them to have access to all the information pertinent to the forecasting function. All questioning is handled impersonally by a coordinator, which virtually eliminates committee activity. This reduces the influence of certain psychological factors, such as specious persuasion, unwillingness to abandon publicly expressed opinions, and the "bandwagon effect" of majority opinions.[45] A coordinator analyzes the forecasts submitted, sends an averaged forecast back to participants, and asks each expert to submit another forecast. This process continues until a near-consensus is reached. Advantages of this approach would include accuracy, as results will tend to be better than other methods that neither employ the same level of detail, nor give the necessary attention to obtaining unbiased estimates. It is also an attractive approach when the budget for sales forecasting is limited, and when the risk or consequences of serious error in forecasting is low. Disadvantages of using this approach include the length of time needed to develop the consensus sales forecast, the tendency toward the use of "guesswork," and the possibility of infringing too much on valuable executive time. At International Business Machines Corporation, this technique is used to estimate if a market is ready for certain new equipment. IBM's own experts, chosen for their diverse backgrounds and knowledge of the market, get together in some isolated spot so that they can concentrate without interruption. Their anonymous estimates are quickly totaled by computer, a process that is repeated until consensus is reached.[46] Table 5-1 summarizes the qualitative forecasting techniques consider in this chapter.

Quantitative Approaches to Forecasting

Quantitative approaches to forecasting tend to be of a statistical/mathematical nature and can be divided into two broad categories: time-series techniques and causal techniques. *Time-series techniques* focus on historical data; *causal methods* rely on the relationship among various factors, both past and present, within the marketing environment. Five different time-series techniques will be introduced here. They include (1) trend fitting; (2) moving average; (3) exponential smoothing; (4) adaptive control; and (5) Box-Jenkins. Six different causal techniques will be introduced: (1) regression; (2) econometrics; (3) leading indicators; (4) diffusion index; (5) input-output analysis; and (6) life-cycle analysis.

Time-series techniques

Trend fitting. Trend fitting is a popular technique in which the forecaster fits a trend line to a series of deseasonalized sales data. Once the line is established, the forecaster simply extends it farther to project sales for the future. To put it another way, the analyst estimates the trend from past data and adds this figure to current sales to obtain a forecast. Trend fitting is very accurate for short-term forecasting and is usually reproduced in quantitative or graph form.

Moving average. With the moving-average method of forecasting, the forecaster computes the average volume achieved in several recent periods and uses it as a prediction of sales in the next period. The approach assumes that the future will be an average of past achievements, with the earliest period being dropped and the latest being added. Forecasters usually employ moving averages

TABLE 5-1 **Summary of Qualitative Forecasting Techniques**

Technique	Approach	Major Advantages	Major Disadvantages	Potential Application
Jury of executive opinion	Combines and acerages the opinions of top executives.	Limited budget. Executives are usually experienced and have a feel for customer needs.	Possibility of ivory-tower thinking. Use of valuable executive time. Lack of the use of a standard procedure.	New-product forecaasts. Medium- to long-range forecasts.
Sales-force composite	Combines salespeople's estimates of future sales.	Assignment of forecasting to those who will be responsible for results. Utilization of the knowledge of people in the field. Good reliability and accuracy.	Salespeople not usually trained in forecasting techniques. Salespeople may view the function as unimportant. Possibility of estimates either too optimistic or too pessimistic. Lack of planning ability.	Short- to intermediate-range forecasts. Effective when intimate knowledge of customers' plans are necessary, as in the case of probable buying plans on large proposals or bids.
Survey of Buyer intentions	Anticipates what buyers are likely to do under a given set of conditions.	Provides a continual feel for the market. Keeps abreast of the competition. Indicates where additional advertising, promotion, and selling pressure may be needed.	Buyer may not know or may be unwilling to reveal intentions. Users may be too numerous, too hard, or too expensive to locate. Channel intermediaries may be unwilling to participate.	With a well-defined or limited market. When intermediaries play an important role in the buy-sell exchange.
The Delphi method	Group forecasting method using feed-back from others ununtil a near-consensus is reached.	Accuracy. Limited budget for forecasting. Used when risk and consequence of serious error is low.	Length of time required. Tendency toward the use of guesswork. Use of valuable executive time.	Intermediate- to long-term forecasting. New-product forecasts. To indicate future technological events that might affect a market.

in conjunction with other methods, as it is good for short-term forecasting only. The data generated are in quantitative form, which is very explicit.

Exponential smoothing. Essentially, exponential smoothing is a moving-average technique with past forecast errors being adjusted by a weighted moving average of past sales by periods. The average is modified or weighted in proportion to the error in forecasting the previous period's sales. The new forecast is basically equal to the old one, plus some proportion of the past forecasting error. The more recent the observation, the heavier the weight assigned. This method is effective when the more recent period's sales are better predictors of the next period's sales than are those of earlier periods. Data generated are quantitative, definitive, and easily applied to forecast situations. Exponential smoothing will normally provide a highly accurate, short-term forecast.

Adaptive control. Adaptive control is similar to exponential smoothing, the difference being that optimum weights that will reduce the statistical error are derived from historical data. These weights are then used to forecast future demand. With each forecasting period, actual sales data are used to recalculate the optimal weights. Forecasts are more sensitive to historical data than the moving average and exponential smoothing techniques. This method is good for short- to intermediate-term forecasting. Output is explicit and is shown in either quantitative or graph form.

Box-Jenkins. Box-Jenkins is the most comprehensive time-series analysis/projection technique and enables the computer to select the statistical model of the time series that gives the best fit. The forecaster fits a time series with a mathematical model, which is optimal in the sense that it has smaller errors or variability than any other model fitted to the data. It is a very accurate but costly and time-consuming computational procedure. However, the data is quantitative and easily applicable to forecasting problems.

Causal techniques

Regression. Regression models are the most widely used causal models for forecasting. They attempt to relate sales predictions to elements of the system. Accuracy is excellent for short-term forecasting; cost of use is reasonable; and the technique is not overly complex. Output is in quantitative form and is quite explicit.

Econometrics. Econometrics is the application of regression analysis to business and economic problems. The model is a system of interdependent regression equations that describe an area of economic or profit activity and provide good forecasting accuracy for short-, intermediate-, and long-term time periods. Data derived is in quantitative form and is quite explicit.

Leading indicators. A leading indicator is a time series of an economic activity whose movement in a given direction precedes the movement of some other time series in the same direction. If the company has products with a dependent relationship on a variable whose changes precede changes in the firm's sales, profitable use can be made of this indicator. Accuracy for leading indicators is fairly good for short-term forecasting, but it is questionable for intermediate- and long-term forecasting. Output is produced in quantitative form and is very explicit.

Diffusion index. A diffusion index is the percentage of a group of economic indicators that are going up or down. A succession of low index numbers over a number of months in an expansionary period should precede an economic downturn. Short-term forecasting accuracy is only fairly accurate at best, and costs can be high. Output is in quantitative form and is very explicit.

Input-output analysis. Input-output analysis is concerned with the interindustry or interdepartmental flow of goods or services in the economy, or in a company and its markets. This method is not appropriate for short-term forecasting, is costly, and is time-consuming. The output is quantitative.

Life-cycle analysis. Life-cycle analysis consists of an analysis and the forecast of new-product growth rates based on S-shaped curves. Central to the analysis is the phase of product acceptance by various groups such as innovators, early adapters, early majority, late majority, and laggards. A growth curve is estimated and is reviewed as sales data are corrected. Forecasts are made by reading future points along the S-curve.

TABLE 5-2 **Summary of Time-Series Forecasting Techniques**

Technique	Approach	Major Advantages	Major Disadvantages	Potential Application
Trend fitting	Estimates the trend from past data and extends it to project future sales.	Low cost. Excellent short-term accuracy. Easy to use. Quick.	Many observations required for accuracy. Not effective in identifying turning points.	Good technique for products in the maturity phase of the product life cycle.
Moving average	Computed with the average progressing forward in time, as the earliest period is dropped and the latest is added.	Low cost. Short-term accuracy. Easy to use. Quick.	Will not forecast turning point. Not accurate for long-term forecasting.	Often used for inventory control for standard or low-volume items.
Exponential smooting	A moving-average technique with recent data being given more weight.	Low cost. Easy to use. Quick.	Will not forecast turning points. Not accurate for long-term forecasting.	Best used to forecast a highly stable sales series, similar to the application presented with the moving-average technique.
Adaptive control	Similar to smoothing with the addition of optimum weights that reduce statistical error.	More sensitive to historical data than previous methods. Short-term accuracy.	Costly. More time-consuming than methods mentioned above.	Excellent for forecasting sales demand on a monthly basis.
Box-Jenkins	A mathematical technique whereby the computer selects the statistical model of the time series that gives the best fit.	Short-term accuracy. Easy to use.	Costly. Time-consuming. Not accurate with long-term forecasting.	Best used in production and inventory control of large-volume items and forecasts of cash balances.

Tables 5-2 and 5-3 summarize the quantitative forecasting techniques considered in this chapter.

TABLE 5-3 **Summary of Causal Forecasting Techniques**

Technique	Approach	Major Advantages	Major Disadvantages	Potential Application
Regression	Relates sales predictions to elements of the internal and external environment.	Low cost. Short-term accuracy. Easy to use.	Data generated are only as good as the data from which derived. Lacks accuracy for long-term forecasting.	Prediction of overall market demand for a generic product type.
Econometric	An application of regression analysis. A system of interdependent regression equations that describe an area of economic or profit activity.	Good for short-, intermediate-, and long-term forecasting.	Costly. Time-consuming.	Used in the prediction of overall market for a generic product type.
Leading indicator	A time series of an economic activity whose movement in a given direction precedes the movement of some other time series in the same direction.	Will identify turning points. Will forecast overall business conditions.	Accuracy is questionable. Limited application. Costly. Time-consuming.	Forecasting changes in overall business conditions.
Diffusion index	The percentage of a group of economic indicators that are going up or down.	Will identify turning points. Fair to good short-term forecasting accuracy.	Costly. Time-consuming. Poor long-term forecasting accuracy.	Used for forecasting sales of overall product classes.
Input-Output analysis	Concerned with interindustry and interdepartmental flow of goods or services.	Will identify turning points. Good for intermediate- and long-range forecasting.	Costly. Time-consuming. Poor short-term forecasting accuracy.	Forecasting sales of business products and services over long periods of time.
Life-cycle analysis	Phases of product acceptance are analyzed.	Good for forecasting new-product sales. Good for intermediate forecasting.	Limited accuracy. Will not identify turning points. Costly. Time-consuming.	Forecasting of new product sales.

CONCEPT QUESTIONS

1. What is product positioning?
2. What does perceptual mapping attempt to uncover?
3. What is the general role of forecasting, or demand estimation?

SUMMARY

1. Segmenting business markets is a difficult job. To be successful, the marketer must be able to identify, analyze, and evaluate potentially attractive business segments; target the segments to be served; and then develop and communicate a positioning strategy that will differentiate the firm's offerings from others. Business market segmentation is the practice of dividing up a market into distinct groups that have common needs and that will respond similarly to a specific set of marketing actions.
2. Business marketing managers must determine what strategy will be used for different market segments. By adopting a strategy of undifferentiated marketing, the organization treats its total market as a single entity. Differentiated marketing is the strategy by which a firm attempts to distinguish its product from competitive brands offered to the same aggregate market. Through concentrated marketing, the firm achieves a strong market position in the segment because of its greater knowledge of the segment's needs and the special reputation it builds.
3. Macro segmentation involves dividing the market into subgroups based on overall characteristics of the prospect organization; micro segmentation pertains to characteristics of the decision-making process and the buying structure within the prospect organization. The nested approach stresses segmentation according to the amount of investigation required to identify and evaluate different criteria. This method integrates and builds on previous schemes for segmenting business markets; it offers an approach that enables not only the simple grouping of customers and prospects, but also more complex grouping of purchase situations, events, and personalities. Other approaches to market segmentation include a buying-behavior–based model for microsegmenting customers in mature business markets, and a model that segments according to purchase responsibilities among individuals within organizations.
4. Many of the variables generally used to segment the consumer market can be used by the business marketer to segment the organizational market. Five primary ways of segmenting business markets include type of economic activity, size of organization, geographic location, product usage, and structure of the procurement function.
5. When a firm decides to expand into foreign markets, it must evaluate all possible markets to identify the country or group of countries presenting the greatest opportunities. The business products' firm must systematically evaluate

market size and growth, political conditions, competition, and market similarity of each country on a regular basis, to be sure that company assets are directed toward the countries with the best opportunities.

6. Before target markets can be chosen, the business marketing manager must decide how many segments and which segments will provide the best return, given limited resources. A "competitive analysis" should be undertaken to assess both the strengths and weaknesses of competitors within a segment so as to identify further the areas of opportunity for the firm. Porter's five-force model shows that the firm must appraise the impact upon the long-run profitability of five groups: industry competitors, potential entrants, substitutes, buyers, and suppliers. In formulating strategy, the existing and potential competitors' strengths in the areas of research and development, finance, technical service, sales-force development, advertising, distribution, and organizational design must be studied.
7. Positioning refers to the placing of a product in that part of the market where it will have a favorable reception compared to competing products. Six approaches in positioning strategy include positioning by technology, price, quality, image, distribution, and service.
8. With increasing complexity, competition, and change in the business environment, organizations need more reliable performance forecasts to be able to maintain a favorable marketing position. Forecasting, or demand estimation, is used in the analysis, measurement, and improvement of current marketing strategy and in the identification and/or development of new products and new markets. Common forecasting problems faced by business products' marketing managers include forecasting mystique, forecasting accuracy, forecasting inconsistency, forecasting accountability, and forecasting implementation.
9. There are two major techniques for forecasting business demand. Qualitative approaches to forecasting employ managerial judgment to determine future expectations and are often used when data are scarce, or good information is virtually nonexistent. Quantitative approaches to forecasting tend to be of a statistical/mathematical nature and can be divided into time-series and causal techniques. Time-series techniques focus on historical data, while causal methods rely on the relationship among various factors, both past and present, within the marketing environment.

KEY TERMS

Bottom-up method
Business market segmentation
Causal methods
Concentrated marketing strategy
Differentiated marketing strategy
Distribution positioning
Forecasting
Image positioning
Nested approach
Perceptual mapping
Price positioning
Product position
Quality positioning
Service positioning
Time-series techniques
Top-down method
Undifferentiated marketing strategy

REVIEW QUESTIONS

1. In what kinds of areas can business market segmentation assist business-to-business firms? How is segmentation achieved in business marketing? What are three criteria in selecting business market segments?
2. Distinguish among undifferentiated marketing, differentiated marketing, and concentrated marketing as business market segmentation strategies.
3. Compare macro segmentation with micro segmentation. What is the nested approach to business market segmentation? What is its major premise? Why are outer-nest criteria generally inadequate when used alone to segment markets? How can mature business markets be segmented? What is the value of using purchase responsibilities among individuals within organizations as a method of segmenting business markets?
4. Identify five ways in which business markets can be segmented. Can you think of any additional ways in which a market might be segmented?
5. What is the first thing a business-to-business firm should do when considering expansion into foreign markets? What are the four critical factors affecting market segmentation in international markets?
6. What is the role of a competitive analysis in business market segmentation? Distinguish between a market profitability analysis, and a market competitive analysis as preconditions to selecting market segments.
7. What is meant by product position? Why is perceptual mapping used? Identify six ways by which a company could position a business product. What six questions should a firm ask in getting started with a positioning strategy?
8. When is forecasting used? What is the value of accurate sales forecasting?
9. Identify each of the following terms: market factor; market index, market potential, sales potential, market demand, market forecast, and sales forecast.
10. Discuss five common problems encountered by business marketing managers in sales forecasting.
11. Distinguish between the top-down and the bottom-up methods of sales forecasting. Discuss four qualitative methods of sales forecasting.
12. Differentiate between time-series techniques and causal methods of quantitative sales forecasting. Identify and explain five types of time-series techniques and six examples of causal methods.

Cases

CASE 5-1 AST Research, Inc.

A small U.S. computer marketer plans to turn the tables on NEC Corporation by cloning the giant Tokyo company's most popular computer and selling it to computer-hungry Japanese at lower prices. AST Research, recently introduced a computer that mimics NEC's PC-9801, a machine that has captured more than half of national Japan's personal-computer market, the world's second largest market after the United States.

The company's move is radical, and risky, because it centers on a product that is made purely for the Japanese market and so won't be sold in the U.S. While many Japanese companies take that tactic—NEC and others market personal computers in the United States that they don't sell at home—no foreign company has directly assaulted NEC's near monopoly of the Japanese market. NEC's machines have become de facto standards in Japan's booming business-computer market, much as IBM's personal computer is a de facto standard in the United States.

The AST machine could also become a test of how open the Japanese market really is for competitive U.S. products. Japanese trade officials often complain that U.S. companies, including computer makers, don't make products that match the buying patterns of Japanese shoppers. Among U.S. computer manufacturers, only IBM has managed to garner even a fraction of the Japanese personal-computer market. Apple Computer, which sells a Japanese-language version of its Macintosh computer, has only a minuscule share. NEC software won't run on either Apple or IBM machines.

DISCUSSION QUESTIONS

1. What bases are AST using for segmenting the computer market?
2. Do you think that AST's targeting strategy will be successful? Is it ethical?
3. What barriers do you think will be most difficult for AST to overcome?

Source: C. Lamb, J. Hair, and C. McDaniel, *Principles of Marketing*, 1st Edition (Cincinnati, OH: South-Western Publishing Company, 1992) p. 200.

CASE 5-2 The Gallo Wine Company

Companies like E&J Gallo Winery reportedly make millions of dollars each year from the sale of cheap wines, such as Thunderbird and Night Train, in skid-row districts. The alcohol content of these cheap wines is between 18 and 21 percent, about twice that of ordinary table wines.

Community and church groups have been critical of Gallo, Canandauga, Mogen David, and other makers of cheap, high-alcohol-content wines for profiting from winos.

Gallo has announced plans to discontinue selling these brands in grocery stores, bars, and other outlets in skid-row areas across the United States. A Gallo spokesman said that the ban on cheap wine sales in skid rows will probably affect every major metropolitan area in the United States.

Community groups have expressed pleasure with the wine maker's decision but doubt that the plan will have much impact. Some skid-row retailers are expected to purchase the wines on the black market or from retailers outside skid-row districts. Skid rows also typically rely on a network of entrepreneurial bootleggers who sell cheap wines to winos at higher than retail prices when liquor stores are closed late at night and on Sundays.

Even Gallo doesn't think its program will significantly dent alcoholism on skid row. "History shows that if alcoholics are deprived of one source of alcohol, they will simply find another, regardless of the cost," the Gallo spokesman said.

DISCUSSION QUESTIONS

1. Do you think that Gallo deliberately targeted skid-row alcoholics with brands such as Thunderbird and Night Train?
2. What effect do you think Gallo's new program will have on the sales of Thunderbird and Night Train?
3. Is Gallo demonstrating that it is a good community citizen by discontinuing sales of cheap wines in skid-row areas such as San Francisco's Tenderloin district?
4. Why not stop producing the products altogether?
5. What advice would you offer to the management of E&J Gallo Winery?

Source: C. Lamb, J. Hair, and C. McDaniel, *Principles of Marketing*, 1st Edition (Cincinnati, OH: South-Western Publishing Company, 1992) p. 150.

Suggested Additional Readings

Bowers, William P., and Stephen B. Jarrell. "Accuracy Analysis of Census Forecasts." *Journal of Business Forecasting* 11 (Summer 1992): 9–13. **A statistical study of the real accuracy of consensus-based forecasts.**

de Kluyver, Cornelius, and David B. Whitlark. "Benefit Segmentation for Industrial Products." *Industrial Marketing Management* 15 (November 1986): 273¥286. **Detailed example and guidelines for practical segmentation.**

Hlavecek, James D., and B. Charles Ames. "*Journal of Business Strategy* 7 (Fall 1986): 39–50. **Discussion of and guidelines for identifying and selecting industrial segments.**

Hlavecek, James D., and N. Mohan Reddy. "Identifying and Qualifying Industrial Market Segments." *European Journal of Marketing* (UK), 20, no. 2 (1986): 8–21. **Presentation of a three-stage model for segmenting by industrial-product application.**

______. "Identifying and Qualifying Industrial Market Segments." *Marketing Intelligence and Planning* (UK), 3, no. 1 (1985): 41–56. **Discussion of market segmentation guidelines using a product application.**

Jain, C. L. "Three Common Mistakes Made in Setting Up a Forecasting System." *Journal of Business Forecasting* 11 (Summer 1992): 2, 22. **The uncovering of typical mistakes made in establishing forecasting systems that aim for 100 percent accuracy. A separate model is utilized for each product.**

Jain, Subhash C. "An Integrated Approach to Competitive Analysis." "New Determinants of Competitive Strategy in Industrial Markets." In *A Strategic Approach to Business Marketing*, edited by Robert E. Spekman and David T. Wilson, 9–14. Proceedings Series. Chicago: American Marketing Association, 19854.

Lauer, Joachim, and Terrence O'Brien. "Sales Forecasting Using Cyclical Analysis." *Journal of Business and Industrial Marketing* 3 (Winter 1988): 25–32. **Presentation of a forecasting method involving construction and interpretation of the business cycle.**

Lefkowitz, Sanford H. "Measuring Forecast Productivity." *Journal of Business Forecasting* 11 (Summer 1992): 7–8. **A study of the advantages of, and the money saved (or made) with, sales forecasting techniques.**

Michman, Ronald D. "Linking Futuristics with Marketing Planning, Forecasting, and Strategy." *Journal of Business and Industrial Marketing* 2 (Spring 1987): 61–68. **Association of the science or art of anticipating and planning for the future with marketing planning and forecasting.**

Mitchell, Vincent-Wayne. "Using Delphi to Forecast in New-Technology Industries." *Marketing Intelligence and Planning* (UK), 10, no. 2 (1992): 4–9. **A study of the advantages, problems, and guidelines in using the Delphi method in forecasting in new technology industries.**

Novak, Thomas P., Jan de Leeuw, and Bruce MacEnvy. "Richness Curves for Evaluating Market Segmentation." *Journal of Marketing Research* 29 (May 1992):. 254–267. **The use of the concept of "richness curves" in measuring the effectiveness of market segmentation approaches.**

Plank, Richard E. "A Critical Review of Industrial Market Segmentation." *Industrial Marketing Management* 14 (May 1985): 79–91. **A literature review, current status, and outlook for industrial market segmentation.**

Robles, Fernando, and Ravi Sarathy. "Segmenting the Commuter Aircraft Market With Cluster Analysis." *Industrial Marketing Management* 15 (February 1986): 1–12. **Survey of business travel and cargo in regional airlines.**

Sheth, Jagdish N. "New Determinants of Competition Structures in Industrial Markets." In *A Strategic Approach to Business Marketing*, edited by Robert E. Spekman and David T. Wilson, 1–8. Proceedings Series. Chicago: American Marketing Association, 1985.

Shostack, G. Lynn. "Service Positioning through Structural Change." *Journal of Marketing* 51 (January 1987): 34–43. **Within service systems, a structural process design can be used to engineer services on a more scientific, rational basis.**

Smith, Paul. "The Who, What, Why of Industrial Segmentation (Part 2)." *Industrial Marketing Digest* (UK), 10 (Second Quarter 1985): 122–127. **Guidelines for different types of market segmentation.**

Stryker, Charles W. "Data, Decisions, and Development/1985 U.S. Totals/1985 State and County Totals/Guide to Using S&MM's Survey of Industrial and Commercial Buying Power." *Sales and Marketing Management* 136 (April 28, 1986): 6–7, 48–108. **Annual survey of the purchasing power of many industries.**

Wheeler, David R., and Charles J. Shelley. "Toward More Realistic Forecasts for High-Technology Products." *Journal of Business and Industrial Marketing* 2 (Summer 1987): 55–64. **Examination of the problem of over-optimistic forecasting in the high-technology arena to include reasons for this bias and suggestions as to how to make such forecasts more realistic.**

ENDNOTES

[1]Philip Kotler, "From Mass Marketing to Mass Customization," *Planning Review* (September/October 1989): 10–13, 47.

[2]Benson P. Shapiro and Thomas V. Bonoma, "How to Segment Industrial Markets," *Harvard Business Review* 62 (May-June 1984): 104–110.

[3]Thomas S. Robertson and Howard Barick, "A Successful Approach to Segmenting Industrial Markets," *Planning Review* 20 (November/December 1992): 4–11.

[4]Eric N. Berkowitz, Roger A. Kerin, and William Rudelius, *Marketing*, 3d ed. (Times Mirror/Mosby College Publishing, 1991): 191–192.

[5]Subhash C. Jain, *Marketing Planning and Strategy* 4th ed. (Cincinnati, Ohio: South-Western Publishing, 1992), 121–123. For an advanced overview, see B. F. Shapiro and T. V. Bonoma, "How To Segment Industrial Markets," *Harvard Business Review* (May-June 1984): 104–110.

[6]See Philip Kotler, *Marketing Management: Analysis, Planning, Implementation, and Control*, 7th ed. (Englewood Cliffs, N.J.: Prentice Hall, 1991), 281–285.

[7]*Ibid.*, 283.

[8]*Ibid.*, 281.

[9]For especially helpful discussions of market segmentation in industrial settings, see Arch G. Woodside and Elizabeth J. Wilson, "Large-Scale Application of Industrial Market Segmentation," in *A Strategic Approach to Business Marketing*, ed. Robert E. Spekman and David T. Wilson, (Chicago: American Marketing Association, 1985), 40–42; Thomas V. Bonoma and Benson P. Shapiro, *Segmenting the Industrial Market* (Lexington, Mass: Lexington Books, 1983); Peter Doyle and John Saunders, "Market Segmentation and Positioning for Specialized Industrial Markets," *Journal of Marketing* 49 (Spring 1985): 24–32; Jay L. Laughlin and Charles R. Taylor, "An Approach to Industrial Market Segmentation," *Industrial Marketing Management* 20 (Spring 1991): 127–136.

[10]Bonoma and Shapiro, *Segmenting the Industrial Market*, 104.

[11]V. Kasturi Rangan, Rowland T. Moriarty, and Gordon S. Swartz, "Segmenting Customers in Mature Industrial Markets," *Journal of Marketing* 56 (October 1992): 72–82.

[12]Robert J. Thomas, "Industrial Market Segmentation on Buying Center Purchase Responsibilities," *Journal of the Academy of Marketing Science* 17 (1989): 243–252.

[13]Jagdish N. Sheth, "Emerging Marketing Strategies in a Changing Macroeconomic Environment: A Commentary," *International Marketing Review* 9, no. 1 (1992): 57–63.

[14]William H. Davidson, "Market Similarity and Market Selection: Implications for International Market Strategy," *Journal of Business Research* 11 (December 1983): 439–456.

[15]Sandra M. Huszagh, Fredrick W. Huszagh, and Gwen F. Hanks, "Macroeconomic Conditions and International Marketing Management," *International Marketing Review* 9, no. 1 (1992): 6–18.

[16]"Massey-Ferguson's Success Story," *Business Week*, February 1976, 40.

[17]Michael E. Porter, *Competitive Advantage: Creating and Sustaining Superior Performance* (New York: The Free Press, 1985), 4–8, 234–236.

[18]Gary A. Getz and Frederick D. Sturdivant, "The Nuts and Bolts of Formulating Differentiation Strategy," *Planning Review* 17 (September/October 1989): 4–9.

[19]David W. Cravens, and Shannon H. Shipp, "Market-Driven Strategies for Competitive Advantage," *Business Horizons* (January/February 1991): 53–61.

[20]Ian C. MacMillan and Patricia E. Jones, "Designing Organizations to Compete," *Journal of Business Strategy* 5 (Spring 1984): 11–26.

[21]David W. Cravens, "Strategic Forces Affecting Marketing Strategy," *Business Horizons* (September-October 1986): 77–86.

[22]Philip Kotler, "Marketing's New Paradigm: What's Really Happening Out There," *Planning Review* (Special Edition) 20 (September/October 1992): 50–52.

[23]MacMillan and Jones, *Designing Organizations to Compete*, 11. Also see Michael E. Porter, "New Global Strategies for Competitive Advantage," *Planning Review* (May/June 1990): 4–14.

[24]Jagdish N. Sheth, "New Determinants of Competitive Structures in Industrial Markets," in *A Strategic Approach to Business Marketing*, ed. Robert E. Spekman and David T. Wilson, Proceedings Series (Chicago: American Marketing Association, 1985), 1–8.

[25]George P. Dovel, "Stake It Out: Positioning Success, Step By Step," *Business Marketing* 75 (July 1990): 43–51.

[26]*Ibid.*

[27]William L. Shanklin and John K. Ryans, Jr., *Essentials of Marketing High Technology*, Third Edition (Lexington, Mass.: Lexington Books, 1987), 148.

[28]Jain, *Marketing Planning and Strategy*, 461–462.

[29]"Positioning, Pricing and Promotion: Three Keys to Successful Marketing," *Profit-Building Strategies for Business Owners* 23, no. 1 (January 1993): 20–23.

[30]Barrie G. James, *Business Wargames* (New York: Abacus Press, 1985), 77–78.

[31]*Ibid.*, 78.

[32]David J. Curry and Peter C. Riesy, "Price and Price/Quality Relationships: A Longitudinal Analysis," *Journal of Marketing* 52 (January 1988): 36–51.

[33]Thomas W. Duncan, "Paccar's Customer Focus Drives Quality, Profits," *Fleet Owner* 87 (September 1992): 4, 78.

[34]Lynn W. Phillips, Doe R. Chang, and Robert D. Buzzell, "Product Quality, Cost Position, and Business Performance: A Test of Some Key Hypotheses," *Journal of Marketing* 47 (Spring 1983): 26–43. Also see David J. Curry, "Measuring Price and Quality Competition," *Journal of Marketing* 49 (Spring 1985): 106–117.

[35]Laura Zinn, "For Coke's Peter Sealey, Hollywood Is It," *Business Week* (March 15, 1993): 84–85.

[36]"Softening a Starchy Image," *Time*, 11 July 1983, 54.

[37]Louis W. Stern and Frederick D. Sturdivant, "Customer-Driven Distribution Systems," *Harvard Business Review* (July-August 1987): 34–37, 40–41. Also see Elizabeth J. Wilson and Arch G. Woodside, "Marketing New Products with Distributors," *Industrial Marketing Management* 32 (February 1992): 15–21.

[38]Christopher H. Lovelock, *Managing Services: Marketing, Operations, and Human Resources*, 2d ed. (Englewood Cliffs, N.J.: Prentice Hall, 1992), 263–264.

[39]Kenneth G. Hardy, "Tough new Marketing realities," *Business Quarterly* 57, no. 3 (Spring 1993): 77–82.

[40]G. Lynn Shostack, "Service Positioning Through Structural Change," *Journal of Marketing* 51 (January 1987): 34–43.

[41]Al Ries and Jack Trout, *Positioning: The Battle for Your Mind* (New York: McGraw-Hill, 1989), 219–226.

[42]Joachim Lauer and Terrence O'Brien, "Sales Forecasting Using Cyclical Analysis," *Journal of Business and Industrial Marketing* 3 (Winter 1988): 25.

[43]Based on a personal interview with H. O. Crafford on September 7, 1993, in Worcester, Massachusetts.

[44]This section is from George C. Michael, *Sales Forecasting*, Monograph Series no. 10 (Chicago: American Marketing Association, 1979), 1–4.

[45]John C. Chambers, Satinder K. Mullick, and Donald D. Smith, *An Executive's Guide to Forecasting* (New York: John Wiley and Sons, 1983), 44.

[46]Harry R. White, *Sales Forecasting: Timesaving and Profit-Making Strategies That Work*, Sales Executives' Club of New York (New York: Scott, Foresman, 1984), 31–33.

Case Study

Tuttle Corporation

Tuttle Corporation was a large manufacturer of detergents, soaps, waxes, and other cleaning products with sales of over $225 million per year. It operated manufacturing plants in two cities. The extensive line of twenty-four products was sold for use in business and in the home. Tuttle Corporation distributed to wholesalers and direct to chain-store organizations and large industrial users. Its sales force was organized geographically into four regions and each region was organized into seven or eight districts. The company advertised nationally on a large scale and utilized a small amount of cooperative advertising at the local level.

Perry McClain, marketing vice president of Tuttle Corporation, was pondering the need for a marketing information system[1] in the company. He had been highly displeased at times because of a lack of information. McClain could fully understand that information was not available to him on esoteric topics, but he could not understand or accept that information was not available to him on some topics that seemed highly relevant to his work and responsibility. Neither could he understand or accept the fact that information on some topics that came to him and was helpful in his work did not show up on a dependably recurring basis. For example, some data on transportation costs of deliveries to small accounts in January reached his desk in late February. He did not see such data again until a mid-April report that covered the month of March.

McClain was also concerned that the scope and amount of detail in the data appeared to be inconsistent in many reports that crossed his desk. For example, a report on lost accounts came to him regularly about three weeks after the close of every quarter; i.e., about April 20, July 20, October 20, and January 20. However, the composition of the report and the level of detail were so different from one quarter to another that he could mot make intelligent comparisons. The frequency and timeliness of the report were rather good, but the content left something to be desired. This problem seemed to be related to the basic commitment of the record-keeping people to the level of disaggregation in company data.

Concluding that the sales manager would know more about the need for a marketing information system than anyone else in Tuttle Corporation, McClain called in Ivan Ramsey for a conference. Ramsey seemed quite surprised at the vice president's interest and volunteered little in the interview, but he indicated that a marketing information system was certainly a good thing and a good goal to work toward. The two men agreed to meet again to discuss this subject sometime in the future at a time convenient to both.

Nothing happened regarding the marketing information system over the next six weeks. At that point McClain called in the director of marketing research, Charles Milano, to discuss a marketing information system. Milano seemed mildly surprised by the topic but enthusiastically endorsed the idea. Milano suggested that they meet again in thirty days. A day and time were then agreed on and Milano stated that he would prepare a draft of what the system should look like. McClain told Milano that he was looking for a system to supply him with "a sustained flow of pertinent information." McClain said further that he was tired of the "brush fire" approach to the gathering and reporting of information that had prevailed during the almost two years he had been with the company. (McClain, age forty-eight, came in as marketing vice president after extensive experience with several other companies.)

Milano presented his draft proposal at the time agreed on. This proposal is reproduced in Exhibit 1.

CAST STUDY ACTIVITY

Advise Perry McClain of Tuttle Corporation.

EXHIBIT 1 **Proposed Marketing Information System**

1. Internal Records Component

Subject	*Frequency of Report*	*Type of Data and Their Breakdown*
Dollar sales	Monthly	(a) current; (b) cumulative for year; and (c) as percentage of forecasted figure for (a) and for (b) by product by customer by type of customer by geographical territory by branch office making the sale by salesman
Gross margin on sales	Monthly	Same types and breakdowns as for dollar sales
Salesmen's expenses	Every two months if more than 2 ½% off the projected	(a) Dollar amount; and (b) as percentage of his sales by salesman by geographical territory
New customers	Quarterly	Forecasts of new customers' demand by customer by product by salesman
Delinquent accounts	Monthly	Dollar amount; length of delinquency by customer by salesman

2. Marketing Intelligence Component

Subject	*Frequency of Report*	*Type of Data and Their Breakdown*
Inventory of finished goods	Fifteenth and last day of the month	Physical units by product by location by product and location
Complaints from dealers, business users, and ultimate consumers	Quarterly	Twenty percent random sample of complaints by complainant
Monitoring by Tuttle sales force of competitors' displays, apparent personal selling tactics, prices, etc.	Quarterly	
Monitoring of competitors' introduction of new or redesigned products	Immediately	
Buying a monitoring of competitors' national and regional advertising from marketing research agencies	Monthly	
Monitoring of changes in policies and practices of pertinent government agencies	Quarterly; if warranted, immediately	
Buying research reports on consumption, brand preference, and stock levels from marketing research agencies that operate national panels of consumers and/or stores	Quarterly or every two months	
Buying a forecast of the U.S. economy from a consulting business economist	Every six months	

3. Marketing Research Component

Gathering, evaluating, interpreting, and reporting information on the basis of specific research projects having to do with (a) solving particular problems; (b) general planning; (c) determining strategy; and (d) determining tactics. A detailed report is submitted to the vice president at the end of each project.

Example 1. The current test market for Experimental Product 2.31 in Syracuse, New York, Akron, Ohio, Sacramento, California, and Charlotte, North Carolina.

Example 2. Study on perceived price-quality relationships of cleaning products.

Example 3. Image study of Tuttle Corporation's lavender-scented air freshener.

Source: Reprinted with permission of Macmillan College Publishing Company from *Cases In Marketing: Orientation, Analysis and Problems,* 2nd Edition, by Thomas V. Greer. Copyright © 1979 by Thomas V. Greer.

Part Four

Making and Moving the Goods

6 Product Development, Management, and Strategy

Learning Objectives

After reading this chapter, you should be able to:

- Recognize the two major approaches to new-product development.
- Describe four methods of organizing the new product development process.
- Relate how experience and learning curves can determine what happens to a product as it matures.
- Explain what forces impact upon a firm's decision to expand, contract, or maintain its product mix.
- Understand how quickly prospects will adopt a new product and to what extent they will replace the old one.
- Discuss strategic alternatives for each of the strategic business units in a company's product portfolio.
- Describe three options for product elimination.

Chapter Outline

Learning Objectives

Product Strategy in Business Marketing

Effective Product Management and Strategy

Business New-Product Development

- Types of New-Product Approaches
  - Technology push
  - Market pull
- The New-Product Development Process
  - Strategy development
  - Idea and concept generation
  - Screening and evaluation
  - Business analysis
  - Product development
  - Product testing
  - Product commercialization and introduction

Organization of the New-Product Effort

- Product Manager
- New-Product Committee
- New-Product Department
- New-Product Venture Team

The Product Life-Cycle Analysis

- An Application of the Product Life-Cycle Model
- Business Life Cycles and Experience Curves
  - Introduction
  - Market growth
  - Market maturity
  - Sales decline

Determinants of the Product Mix

- Technology
- Competition
- Changes in Levels of Business Activity
- Operating Capacity
- Market Factors

The Business Product Adoption-Diffusion Process

- Stages in the Adoption Process
  - Awareness
  - Interest
  - Evaluation
  - Trial
  - Adoption
- Factors Influencing the Rate of Adoption-Diffusion

Business Product Portfolio Classification, Analysis, and Strategy

- What Is the Product Portfolio?
- Diagnosing the Product Portfolio
- Product Portfolio Strategies

Business Product Deletion Strategy

- Harvesting
- Line Simplification
- Total-Line Divestment

International Product Strategy

Summary

Key Terms

Review Questions

Cases

Case 6-1

Case 6-2

Suggested Additional Readings

Endnotes

PRODUCT STRATEGY IN BUSINESS MARKETING

Product development, management, strategy, and deletion are important parts of the business marketing process, with the major concerns being both to measure and predict success and to execute proper strategy over the life of the business product. Success is more likely if the business organization can develop a unique or superior product or service, has knowledge of the market, and has a well-managed marketing effort.

Effective Product Management and Strategy

Effective product management and strategy are more important today than ever as the business-to-business sector positions itself to counter offshore competitors that have impacted the domestic market for several years and show no sign of abatement. In business marketing, it is critical to position products, the company, its distribution channels, and often the technologies. The market should be segmented and the targets chosen. The product or service is then developed that will give the company legitimate claims to the position it wants to occupy.[1] New-product development, a greater marketing orientation, more sophisticated marketing research, improved new-product introduction efforts, better attention to service marketing, a closer linkage with customers, and an increased global marketing effort—all are keys to meeting this challenge. New-product development success is the principal component through which the business-to-business firm can align its resources with the market environment to achieve organizational objectives. Figure 6-1 shows that new products have significantly contributed to profits in every industry listed.[2] At the same time, it must be recognized that approximately two-thirds of all commercialized new products fail in the marketplace for a variety of reasons. This situation is not likely to change.

FIGURE 6-1 **Contribution of New Products to Profit by Industry**

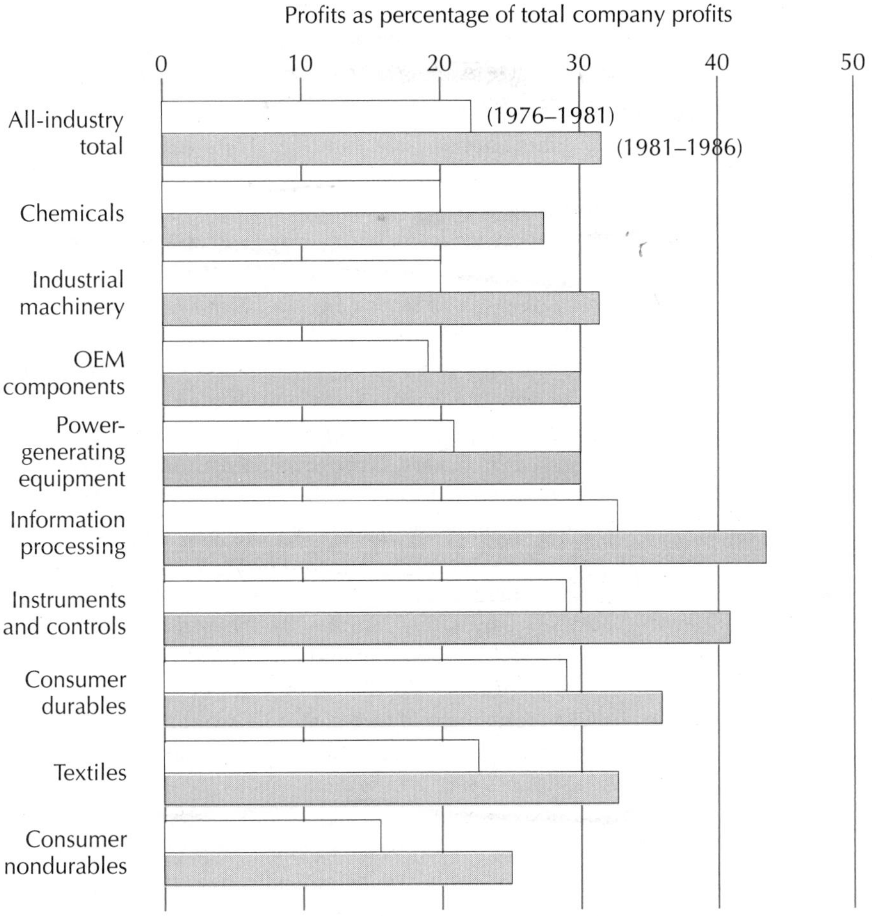

Source: Booz, Allen, & Hamilton Inc. Used with permission.

BUSINESS NEW-PRODUCT DEVELOPMENT

Innovation is the fuel of corporate longevity. Without continuous innovation, organizations sputter and die. In the opinion of many, the United States is losing its innovative prowess. However, there are some U.S. corporations that are still among the world's best. Caterpillar, 3M, Hewlett-Packard, Merck, Intel, and Johnson and Johnson have the ability to churn out new products at a dizzying pace. So the skill is not dead.[3]

In many business-to-business firms, the design of new products and services (especially scientific and technical products) is the sole responsibility of people within the engineering discipline. However, much marketing literature argues that business marketing managers should play a major role in the design (development) of new products through the guidelines that marketing research can provide as to customer wants and needs. It appears that the important role of business marketers in the design and development of new products and services is finally being recognized. A major concern of sales and marketing managers has to be new-product development.[4]

Two important trends are facing managers in the 1990s. First, worldwide enterprises are creating new technology at an increasing rate. In some segments of industry, technology is changing how business is conducted and the nature of competition. It is also changing product development and introduction processes by shortening the time firms have to bring new products to market.[5] New innovative products for the business marketplace are no longer speculative occurrences waiting to happen as a result of an engineering team's brilliant and instantly accepted discovery. New-product introduction in today's technology-driven business sector is loaded with risk, yet it is something that must occur if a firm is to remain viable.[6] Some of the past reluctance to use marketing personnel for new-product development is justified, given the lack of research training and the questionable quality of many industrial marketing research projects in the past. Many "quantitative" studies were based on approaches not necessarily appropriate for the identification and quantification of the wants or needs of the organizational customers. At the other extreme, "qualitative" market research studies provide some insight into customer wants and needs, but there has been some understandable and justifiable reluctance to use the resulting recommendations as guidelines for specific decisions.

Developments in mathematical psychology have introduced other tools such as the conjoint analytical approach, which among other tools makes it possible to obtain rigorous quantitative insights into customer needs and wants and their relative importance. These approaches have provided designers with valuable guidelines for the design of new products and services.

Types of New-Product Approaches

Most new-product development efforts follow, and can be classified as belonging to, one of two approaches: the technology-push process or the market-pull process.

Technology push. When the perceived value of a particular technology is great, *technology push* usually results. Once the product or process has been developed, the marketing function becomes important. The marketer has some form of technology and a vague notion of possible applications, and usually not much more. Most telecom products and services start with a technology-push phase.

A growing number of customers buy for reasons of availability, novelty, and price, even if the benefits are not fully defined.[7] Most of the truly great inventions of the period 1830 to 1915 fall into this category (for example, the steam turbine, triode, telephone). With a great invention, it is difficult to estimate the ultimate size of the market. Who, at the outset, could have estimated the market for computers or xerography? In fact, Sperry Univac is purported to have initially estimated that the size of the total computer market by the year 2000 would be one thousand or two thousand machines.[8] This type of product, in effect, follows "Say's Law" in economics: "Supply creates demand." This kind of success inspires all technology-push efforts, whether warranted or not.

Market pull. *Market pull* is primarily the result of marketing research methodologies of interviewing potential users about their needs and then developing solutions to those perceived market needs. This method carries the least business risk because there is less of a chance that the developed product cannot be sold. This approach is considered more difficult to manage than technology push because it requires more input and coordination from both the internal and external environments. Exhibit 6-1 shows a comparison of these two approaches. Note that the only differences between the two approaches are in the first and second steps. The market-pull approach identifies customer values and then creatively identifies solutions and approaches; the technology-push approach identifies technology and then creatively identifies possible customers/applications.

There are more similarities between these two processes than differences; and the point that should be made, whether the new-product development process is technology push or market pull, is that it is a process. The key to success lies in pursuing each step of the process thoroughly, professionally, and objectively.

The New-Product Development Process

New-product success has long been valued as an essential factor in maintaining the economic health of a business unit and as a critical means for improving business performance. Five basic attributes are found to be of exceptional

EXHIBIT 6-1 **A Comparison of Two New Product Approaches**

Traditional Customer-Driven Process	Technology-Driven Process
1. Identify customer values.	1. Identify technology.
2. Creatively identify solutions and approaches.	2. Creatively identify possible customers and applications.
3. Do homework.	3. Do homework.
4. Validate with market research.	4. Validate with market research.
5. Test.	5. Test.
6. Launch.	6. Launch.

importance in new-product success: 1) an open-minded and supportive and professional management; 2) good market knowledge and strategy; 3) a unique and superior product; 4) good communication and coordination; and 5) proficiency in technological activities.[9] As noted earlier in this chapter, approximately two-thirds of all commercialized new products fail. The new-product development process involves all aspects and functions of management, which need to be brought together to guarantee success.[10] From a marketer's vantage point, it must be realized that purchasing personnel can have a pivotal role in conceptualizing, structuring, and implementing the business new-product development process. The cross-functional orientation of purchasing employees enhances their capacity to serve as facilitators and conduits of information useful in product development.[11] This discussion will explore seven stages in the new-product development process. These stages include strategy development, idea generation, screening and evaluation, business analysis, product development, product testing, and product commercialization (product introduction).[12]

Strategy development. The successful implementation of strategy development requires cooperation among different groups, such as finance, research and development, corporate staff, and marketing. This situation makes product strategies difficult to develop and implement.[13] The point can be illustrated with reference to what was said about the Chrysler Corporation in the 1970s—that the engineering department in the company had such dominance that all other considerations were subordinated. As a 1975 *Fortune* article noted:

> Engineering considerations...dictate what kinds of cars the company makes. In the late fifties, when the auto makers were developing their first compacts, Chrysler's management wanted to build a rear-engine compact to compete with GM's Corvair. "Our engineers were not willing to go into the weight distribution that it would entail. There was no way this management could have even ordered the engineering department to do a rear-engine car." A decade later, as Ford and GM were preparing subcompacts, Chrysler's engineers concluded they could not design one that would both be competitive in styling and meet their standards for interior comfort.[14]

According to this article, too much engineering emphasis in arriving at strategic decisions was one of the major reasons for the Chrysler Corporation's poor showing in the turbulent 1970s. A fairly recent and much quoted survey of company practice with regard to new-product development found that over three-quarters of all firms have a specific new-product development strategy guiding their new-product development process.[15]

Idea and concept generation. The idea-generation stage will involve the search for product ideas or concepts that meet company objectives. These new ideas will usually come from the customer, although the sales department's distributors, suppliers, and other employees play an important role in this effort.

One very interesting way for a firm to get new-product ideas is by copying its competition. Exhibit 6-2 describes how Ford Motor Company conducts "autopsies" on competitors' products in a search for new-product ideas. However, this can be risky, as patent infringement lawsuits can badly tarnish a firm's image.

Many marketing analysts suggest that an open perspective is essential for generating new ideas. For example, a 3M employee came up with the idea for note paper that could be stuck to telephones, desks, paper, and walls by a small adhesive strip on the back. The employee thought of the idea because his place mark kept falling out of his hymn book during choir practice. Today, annual sales of Post-it-notes are around $40 million.[16] Top managers at Lockheed Corporation also encourage entrepreneurship among their staffs. They open their doors to new ideas for products and processes from all workers and give individuals and groups seed money to nurture those ideas. These entrepreneurs (or "intrapreneurs," to use another catchphrase) are given timetables to prove their ideas have merit. They are not penalized for failure, but rather are encouraged to learn from their mistakes and to try again.[17] It is advisable that the collection system for new-product ideas be a well-defined process for communicating the ideas from various sources to a collection point within the firm.

Screening and evaluation. The next step involves an analysis to determine which ideas submitted are pertinent and therefore merit a more detailed study as to potential feasibility and market acceptance. A sophisticated screening system

EXHIBIT 6-2 Conducting Autopsies: Sources for New-Product Ideas

What does it mean to be a "destruction engineer"? To find out, take a look at Robert Cameron of Ford Motor Company.

New ideas don't mean sending lots of dollars into research and development. As a matter of fact, they might even come from copying competitors. Cameron purchases new competing models from local dealers and spends two weeks disassembling each one. Along with his pool of mechanics, he takes an automobile apart and catalogs and inspects each of its thirty thousand parts.

When he discovers a product innovation, such as Nissan Stanza's wheel base, Cameron sends it through a battery of tests. In the case of the Stanza wheel base, he found that even a vise could not bend it out of shape. As a result, he sent the idea to the Ford management team, and they decided to adopt it for use in their own cars.

Ford Motor Company is well known for advertising that it has better ideas. But where do these new ideas come from? A new method for rolling up windows by GM, and a one-unit alternator and regulator by Toyota are good examples. Disassembling automobiles has also helped Ford's engineers to uncover competitors' mistakes, which would then not be repeated by Ford.

Although this type of activity might seem unethical and unfair, similar practices are also employed by GM and Chrysler. In a concern for patent infringement, the major auto makers frequently trade rights to certain improvements. Ford, for instance, swapped its innovative two-way tailgate to GM for the right to several of GM's patents.

Source: Kevin Totus, "Auto Makers Look for Ideas in Rivals' Cars," *Wall Street Journal* (July 20, 1982), p. 29. Reprinted by permission of *Wall Street Journal*,

can focus the energies of a company on creating and developing products that will have a greater likelihood of success.[18] For its internal screening and evaluation in its search for new products, Medtronic, a high-technology medical firm, has developed the "weighted point system" shown in Table 6-1, which establishes screening criteria and assigns weights to each one used to evaluate new-product ideas. The seventeen specific factors in the figure are grouped into six categories commonly cited as reasons for new-product failures. Medtronic believes that a score of at least 120 is needed on the "hurdle" in the point system to find a winning new product.[19]

The nature of this part of the analysis can be indicated by a series of questions meant to be informative but not exhaustive:

(1) Do we have or can we develop access to the necessary raw materials?
(2) Is the project of a scope that is feasible within our existing financial capability?
(3) Is there some synergy within our existing product line?
(4) Is it likely that our present customers represent a potential market, or must we develop entirely new markets?
(5) Could the product be marketed through our existing sales force and distributor organization?
(6) Does the idea appear to be within the capability of our product-development organization?
(7) What impact would the successful development of this product have on our existing products, markets, and marketing organization?
(8) Would the new product be capable of manufacture within our existing production facilities and with our existing skills?[20]

Negative answers to several such questions, or the recognition that significant new financial, managerial, marketing, production, or supplier resources would be required, would reduce the attractiveness of the idea.

Business analysis. The business analysis step, along with the remaining steps in the process, is the expansion of the idea or the concept through creative analysis into a "go" or "no-go" recommendation. Return-on-investment criteria are examined along with competition and the potential for profitable market entry. A more specific list of considerations during the business analysis stage would include demand projections, cost projections, competition, required investment, and profitability. Business marketers sometimes use break-even analysis, discounted cash flow, the Bayesian decision model, and simulation models to assess the likely profitability of promising new-product ideas.

Product development. The product development stage involves taking the product from an idea generated during a "brainstorming" session to a state of

TABLE 6-1 **A Weighted-Point System Used by Medtronic to Try to Spot a Winning New Medical Product**

General factor	Specific factor	Scale	Total points
Size of target market	Incidence of malady	Undefinable (0) — 10,000s (5) — 1,000,000s (10) ✓ — (15) — 100,000,000s (20)	12
	Product usage	One per many patients (0) — One per patient (5) ✓	5
	Cost-effective for health care system	No (0) — (5) — ✓ — Yes (10)	7
	Application of product	Other (0) ✓ — Spine (5) — Brain (10) — Brain-heart (15) — Heart (20)	3
Significant point of difference	Treatment evaluation	Similar to existing approaches (0) — Better than existing approaches (5) — Clearly superior to existing approaches (10) ✓	10
	Clearness of function	Questioned or uncertain (0) — (5) — ✓ — Direct cause and effect (10)	8
Product quality	Restore natural physiology	(0) — Partial ✓ (5) — (10) — (15) — Total (20)	6
	Restore viability	(0) — (5) — Partial (10) — ✓ (15) — Full (20)	13
	Characteristic of product	Capital equipment (0) — External → Permanently worn (10) — Implantable → Totally implanted (20) ✓	20
	Mode of operation	(0) — Chemical (5) ✓ — Mechanical (10) — Electrical-mechanical (15) — Electrical (20)	7
	Product development team	Physician only (0) — Engineer only (5) ✓ — Physician and engineer — Physician with engineering training (10)	6
Access to market	Physician users know Medtronic name?	No (0) — Some (50%) (5) — Yes (all) (10) ✓	10
	Inventor's ability, willingness to be champion	Not well known / Not willing to promote (0) — (5) — ✓ (10) — (15) — Well-known / Willing to promote (20)	8
Timing	Technologies in place	No (0) — Partially (5) — ✓ — Yes (10)	6
	Entrepreneur in place	No (0) — ✓ — Partially (5) — Totally (10)	4
	Social acceptance	Negative (0) — (5) — ✓ — Positive (10)	8
Miscellaneous	Gut feel about success	(0) — Uncertain (5) — Good chance (10) ✓ — Positive (15) — Highly positive (20)	12
Total			145

Source: Ed Bakken and Medtronics, Inc. Used with permission.

readiness for product and market testing. Activities during this particular stage are more difficult and time-consuming than would be expected. Something that looks great on paper can fail miserably when scientists, engineers, and production technicians try to create the physical product. Many new-product ideas are either abandoned or sent back for more study at this point in the development process. Exhibit 6-3 discusses the activities involved in the development of a new agricultural product, giving an indication of the time involved and the difficulties encountered during this phase of the process.

Product testing. Commercial experiments necessary to verify earlier business judgments are conducted during the product-testing stage. Testing takes place both in the laboratory and in the field, and involves both pilot production testing as well as presentation to the market for an indication of acceptance or rejection. Following satisfactory results in market testing, many companies will commercialize the product by listing it in the catalogue and turning it over to the sales force. More and more companies are now turning to market testing to indicate such things as the product's performance under actual operating conditions, the key buying influences, how different influences react to alternative price and sales approaches, the market potential, and the best market segments. Some market-test methods commonly used by business marketers in the new-product development process would include product-use tests, trade shows, distributor and dealer display rooms, and test marketing. While some product testing is necessary to some degree, there is a real risk of tipping the firm's hand to the competition during field testing.

EXHIBIT 6-3 Developing and Using a New Farm Product

Canadian wheat farmers in both Saskatchewan and Alberta have long used the practice of "fallowing," which is the process of leaving fields free of crops in alternating years. The use of fallowing allows the dry Canadian soil of the regions to accumulate extra moisture during the alternate years; and, therefore, crop yields are usually greater. Yet, fallowing also permits the growth of weeds, which serve to rob the fields of much of this stored moisture. Farmers typically use mechanical cultivation to eradicate the weeds, causing yet another depletion of moisture.

To solve this problem, Elanco Products, a division of Eli Lilly Canada, Inc., created a new product called HERITAGE Wheat Production System. This system uses herbicides to assist the farmer in improving crop yields over each two-year cycle, and use of the system also tends to aid moisture conservation, reduce soil erosion, reduce cultivation, and increase wheat yields.

Elanco understands that the adoption process is an immediate outgrowth of the new-product development process. During the days of the HERITAGE system's product introduction, Elanco solicited growers who would experiment with HERITAGE on their fields. They hoped that these "bell cow" growers would model the benefits of HERITAGE to their fellow-growers.

Dick Greschuk, a "bell cow" who farms four thousand acres, stated: "I like technology. I'll use anything that helps save money and works for me."

Source: Jeff Lieb, "Product Repositioning in the Face of Tradition: How Elanco Created a New Herbicide Market Niche," *Business Marketing* (November 1984), pp. 64–68. Used by permission.

Product commercialization and introduction. The final stage of development includes launching the new product through full-scale production and sales and committing the company's reputation and resources to the product's success.

The new-product development process is complex, difficult, interdisciplinary, challenging, and expensive. However, it is also a vital process necessary to sustain the profitable growth of the firm. A primary purpose of this process is to eliminate new-product ideas that do not seem feasible before extensive resources are expended on a potential product failure. New-product ideas within the new-product development process follow a characteristic decay curve, with a progressive elimination of product ideas during each stage of the process. Figure 6-2 gives an indication of this product idea elimination as it moves through the stages of the new product development process.

FIGURE 6-2 **Mortality Rate of New Products by Stage of Development**

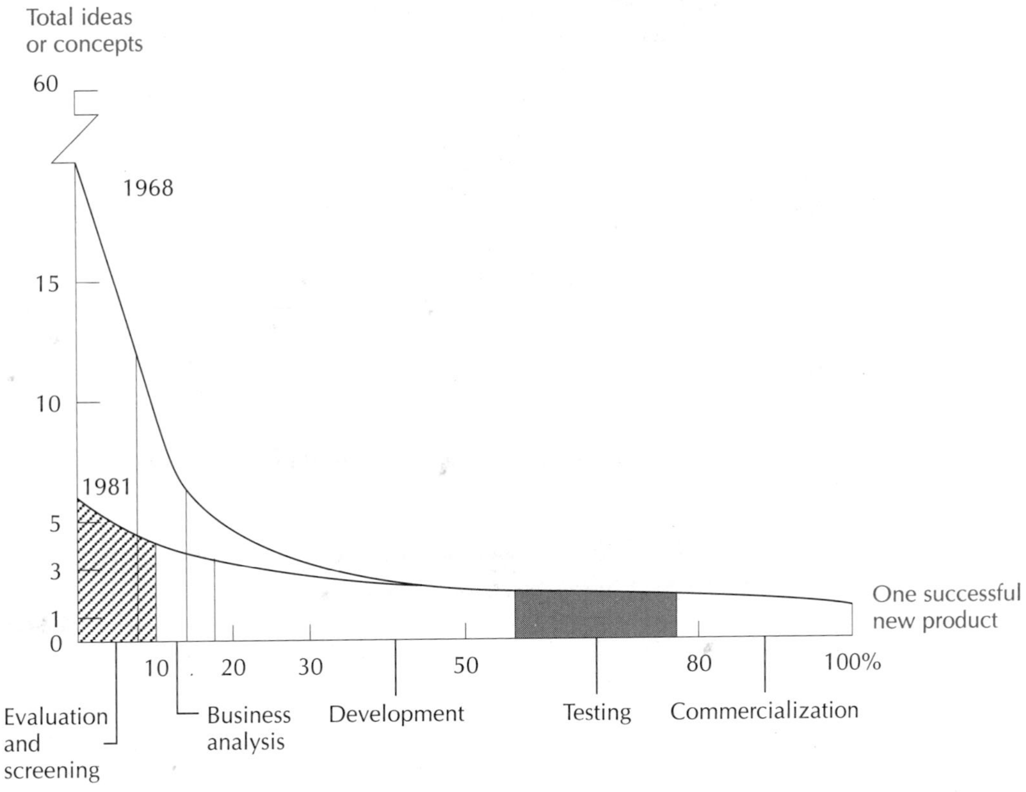

Source: Booz, Allen & Hamilton, Inc., 1982. Used with permission.

ORGANIZATION OF THE NEW-PRODUCT EFFORT

New-product development, evaluation, and management must follow good management practice if effectiveness, efficiency, and a reasonable likelihood of success are to be achieved. In most business-to-business firms, the new-product development effort involves a complex structure of line and staff relationships, with several departments involved in the development of new-product ideas. The problem of fusing these groups together in a manner that will bring their efforts to maximum productivity for the new product, and without destroying their effectiveness in producing and marketing mature existing products, is one of the most difficult problems that management faces. However, if profits from new products are to be realized, this is a problem that must be solved. Better communication is required to turn yesterday's new product development process away from being merely a series of functional steps. U.S. companies must make a special effort to extend participation in the new-product process to include all departments (including sales), as well as customers, end users, suppliers, production-equipment makers, and long-range planners.[21] As discussed below, there are a number of options or alternatives available to management.

Product Manager

Product managers are in charge of planning, organizing, implementing, and controlling new-product development; they also manage the product as it travels through its life cycle. Effective product-line management is greatly enhanced by the type of integrated new-product development provided by product managers. The *product management approach* requires the product manager to move the new product from the "idea generation stage" to the "product introduction stage," complete with service, technical assistance, and performance feedback. Union Carbide, Bell Helicopter, Texas Instruments, Uniroyal, and General Dynamics have all subscribed to the product management concept.

The product manager is a tactician who orchestrates the new-product effort, very much as are the advertising manager, the sales manager, the distribution manager, the sales promotion manager, and the marketing research manager. Product managers in the business market are often considered to be the equivalent of brand managers in the consumer market. Table 6-2 shows one view of the duties and responsibilities of business product managers. Notice the wide variety of tasks for which product managers are responsible, and the technical nature of some of the tasks most commonly performed by product managers.

New-Product Committee

The *new-product committee approach* involves a top management committee, consisting of representatives from marketing, production, accounting, engineering, and other areas, who review new-product proposals. Though not involved in the actual

TABLE 6-2 **Duties and Responsibilities of Product Managers in the Business Market**

Duty/Responsibility	Percent of Respondents Having This Duty or Responsibility
Oversees product(s) progress	91
Decides the nature of or initiates changes in ongoing products	70
Initiates product reengineering	67
Determines product deletion	65
Determines product phaseout	65
Determines markets to enter or depart	64
Initiates and controls new product conceptualization	64
Responsible for product profitability	62
Develops and presents product's budget requests	61
Initiates price changes	58
Preserves promotional strategy	57
Initiates market research analysis	57
Sets pricing strategy	55
Develops sales goals and objectives	55
Attends product committee meetings	52
Develops product control criteria	45
Has chief responsibility and decides which new products are added	42
Determines product's channel of distribution	39
Chairs product committee	36
Decides the type of promotional mix	35
Controls package changes	25

Note: Responses exceed 100 percent due to multiple answers.

Source: Reprinted by permission of the publisher from "Industrial Product Managers' Authority and Responsibility," Robert W. Eckels and Timothy J. Novotney, *Industrial Marketing Management,* 13 (1984) p. 73. © 1984 by Elsevier Science Inc.

development process, the committee is charged with evaluating these proposals. This approach allows for a minimum of organizational disruption. However, a disadvantage to this form of organizational structure is the possibility that demands of departmental priorities would supersede those of the committee. Committee participation is generally considered a part-time activity, secondary to the major needs of a particular department within the firm. Most firms must feel that the advantages outweigh the disadvantages because the new-product committee is the most common form of organizational structure for managing new products.[22]

New-Product Department

The *new-product department approach* creates a specific department to generate and evaluate new-product ideas, to direct and coordinate development work, and to implement field testing and precommercialization of the new product. This arrangement allows for a maximum effort in new-product development, but at the expense of major overhead costs incurred at the outset. The department head typically has substantial authority and relatively easy access to top management. One particular research study revealed that of 2,000 large firms in several industries 869 had formed new-product departments.[23]

New-Product Venture Team

The *new-product venture team approach* involves forming a task force representing various departments and giving responsibility for new-product implementation to a full-time staff. This task force is brought together and charged with the responsibility of bringing a specific product to the market, or a specific new business into being. This approach consolidates the communication between technical, marketing, and internal resource experts, which results in a sharing of information, an appreciation of other perspectives, and more rapid decision making. Marketing's role is to coordinate, integrate, and lead the process to implementation.[24] The venture team is normally dissolved once a new product is established in the market. Signode Industries creates independent venture teams in which half the members have a technical background and half are drawn from marketing and sales. The company, which was founded in 1916 and went private in recent years in a leveraged buyout, is a $750 million producer of steel and plastic strapping systems and business products. How do its teams work? After two weeks of listening to outside experts talk about trends and possible opportunities, a team spends about six months searching for unmet or unperceived market needs. Its only preconceived direction is that the company's strategic strengths should be emphasized. The full-time task of the team members, performed away from the company itself, is to generate new-product ideas. They are challenged to be creative and are reminded to encourage one another in the solicitation of new-product ideas. They search widely for information and ideas, with sensitivity to research and development (R&D), but using a market-driven, customer-oriented approach. They narrow their list of ideas from a few hundred to two or three at a later stage, and eventually they carry a product to market.[25]

CONCEPT QUESTIONS

1. What is the principal component through which a business-to-business firm can meet its organizational objectives?
2. What does the new product development process involve in most business-to-business companies?

THE PRODUCT LIFE-CYCLE ANALYSIS

Regardless of the type of product organization chosen by the firm, the management of new products throughout their useful lives is of paramount importance. The product life-cycle model, along with the importance of new-product development, has been utilized frequently in the marketing literature to show how sales of a product vary over time and how every product eventually leads to obsolescence. Where life cycles were once measured in years, today they more often are measured in months. For example, the average effective life span for commercial electronics is only two years. At 3M, products less than five years old account for 25 percent of sales.[26] Figure 6-3 points out that sales grow sharply during the market-growth stage but begin to flatten out during the market maturity stage. Sales reach their peak during the saturation stage and dramatically fall off during the decline stage. This information has been used to suggest effective marketing strategies over a product's projected life span. While the shapes of the sales volume and profit-margin curves will vary from product to product, the basic shapes and the relationship between the two curves are as illustrated in Figure 6-3. Note that profit peaks during the growth stage, whereas sales top out during the saturation stage.

It is quite important that management recognize what part of the life cycle a product is in at any given time. The competitive environment and the resultant marketing strategies will ordinarily differ depending upon the stage of the product life cycle involved.[27] Some strategic elements to consider would be

FIGURE 6-3 **How Sales and Profits of a Business Product Vary Over Time**

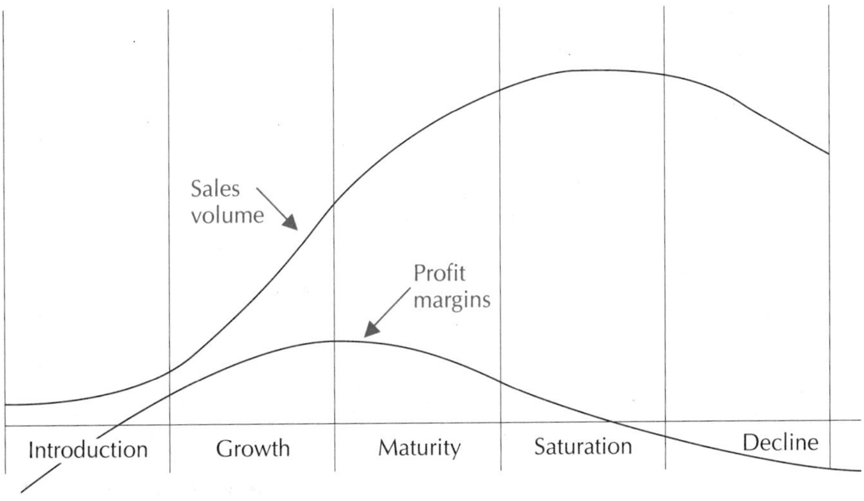

competitive action, return on investment, distribution decisions, and advertising strategy and emphasis.

An Application of the Product Life-Cycle Model

Technological advances can move products more quickly through their life cycles, often necessitating a product-deletion decision. Product life cycles for IBM's mainframe computers seem to be getting shorter; it introduced two computers in six years, and then four more in the following four years. On a price-performance basis, IBM's 4381 computer is about forty times better than the 360 it introduced in 1964, and Hewlett-Packard's model 41 CX calculator is over one hundred times better than its model 35 introduced in 1972.

A particular life-cycle period may be quite short, as it is in the electronics field where new-product development and introduction are daily events; or it may be quite long (a decade or more), as it has been for some products such as milling machines, standard fasteners, and industrial gears. However, sooner or later, all industrial products yield to new technology, being made obsolete by new technology that either reduces costs or improves performance characteristics.

Sandia National Laboratories in New Mexico has developed a novel supercomputer that relies on a controversial technology called "massively parallel processing." The theory behind the system is elegantly simple. Conventional computers require only one number-crunching processor; for most jobs, such as word processing and spreadsheets, that is enough. However, the problems tackled by supercomputers require billions of computations, and scientists have tried to improve performance by hooking tens or hundreds of processors together. With all the processors working simultaneously, the parallel computer solves the problem faster than its single predecessors. As a test, the Sandia team took three sample problems and smashed the speed limit each time. One example was calculating the stresses inside a building beam supported only at one end. The problem would have taken a powerful minicomputer twenty years to solve; the new machine finished in a week.[28]

Business Life Cycles and Experience Curves

Learning curve analysis, linked with the product life cycle, is another base for developing industrial product strategy.[29] This concept is based on the discovery that costs (measured in constant dollars) decline (usually from 10 to 30 percent) by a predictable and constant percentage each time "accumulated" production experience (volume) is doubled. This doctrine holds that causation runs from share building to cost advantage.[30] The curve illustrated in Figure 6-4 is an 85 percent *experience curve*. With every doubling of experience, costs per unit drop to 85 percent of their original level—a 15 percent reduction in costs for every doubling of cumulative production. Different products and industries experience different "learning" rates. The experience curve phenomenon has been supported

FIGURE 6-4 **An 85 Percent Learning Curve Requiring 1.0 Direct Labor Hour to Manufacture the First Unit (K = 1)**

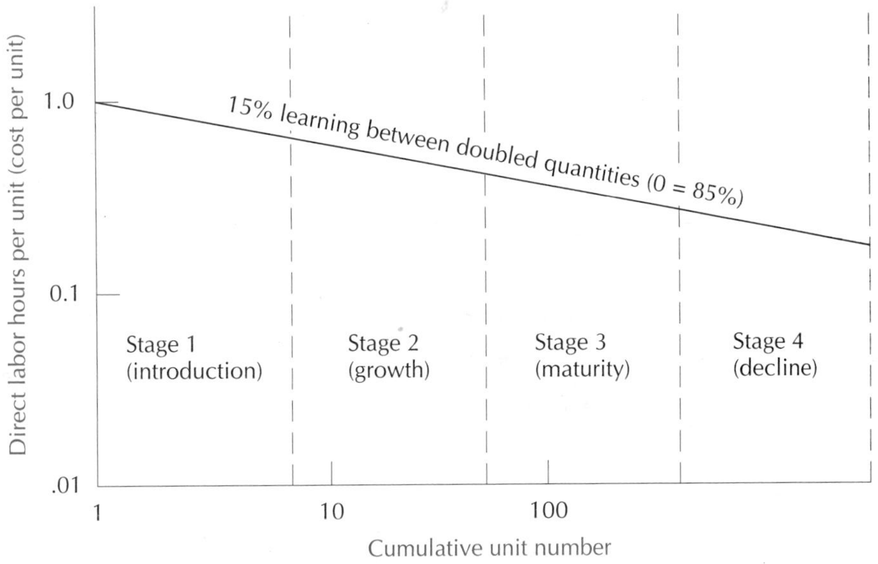

Source: George S. Day and David B. Montgomery, "Diagnosing the Experience Curve," *Journal of Marketing,* 47, Spring 1983 (Chicago: American Marketing Association), pp. 44–58. Used with permission.

in studies of numerous industries, including chemical, steel, paper, and electronics. The concept is especially relevant in high-technology markets such as semiconductors and computer memories.[31]

The learning curve phenomenon was discovered in the 1920s in the aircraft industry and was subsequently reported in 1936.[32] Simply stated, the rate of learning is such that as the quantity of units manufactured doubles, the number of direct labor hours it takes to produce an individual unit decreases at a uniform rate.

In a related concept, the term "economies of scale" (often confused with the experience curve) refers to the production efficiency attained as increased units are produced. It is a fixed-cost phenomenon, as seldom does an increase in production require an equivalent increase in capital investment, size of the sales forces, or overhead costs. In a stable environment, the firm will realize economies of scale by producing a uniform product, with perceivable demand, thereby guaranteeing efficiencies and higher profit levels. Learning, per se, helps the firm not only to increase profit levels, but also to lower the break-even quantity. The result is a reduction in fixed costs, because these are being spread over many additional units.

The task at hand is to explore what happens to a product as it proceeds from one stage of the product life cycle to the next. The model relationships discussed next examine how the learning curve can help to clarify the product life cycle.

Introduction. Product introduction, the initial phase of the learning curve, represents the highest-cost stage. Initial costs are high but drop rapidly with additional units produced. This phenomenon is vividly demonstrated for three different learning curves in Table 6-3. Given an 85 percent learning curve, if the cost to make the first unit is $10.00, the cost to make the thousandth unit will be only $1.98.

This phase of the learning curve is labeled Stage 1 in order for it to coincide with the introductory stage of the product life cycle shown in Figure 6-4. Sales are lowest here as the innovative firm tries to drive its costs down, as shown by the slope of the learning curve. As cost and price decrease, the product appeals to more users, resulting in increased sales.

Market growth. In the market growth stage of the product life cycle, rapid growth occurs, accompanied by dramatic cost decreases, as shown in Table 6-3. During this stage, the innovative firm should be utilizing cost decreases, as described by the learning curve, to its advantage in keeping costs below those of the competition. If the firm manages to succeed in this effort, it can also expand its market share, use price as a competitive weapon, and still generate an adequate profit margin.

Market maturity. During this particular stage, cumulative volume has reached the point where costs are about as low as they are going to get. (The data in Table 6-3 demonstrate this point.) For example, if a firm is riding an 80

TABLE 6-3 **Cost of a Specific Unit for Three Different Learning Curves All Having a First-Unit Cost of $10**

Cumulative Number of Units Made	90% Learning Curve	85% Learning Curve	80% Learning Curve
1	$10.00	$10.00	$10.00
2	9.00	8.50	8.00
3	8.46	7.73	7.02
4	8.10	7.22	6.40
8	7.29	6.14	5.12
16	6.56	5.22	4.10
32	5.90	4.44	3.28
64	5.31	3.77	2.62
1,000	3.50	1.98	1.08
10,000	2.47	1.15	.52
100,000	1.74	.67	.24
1,000,000	1.22	.39	.12
10,000,000	.86	.23	.06
20,000,000	.78	.19	.04

Source: George S. Day and David B. Montgomery, "Diagnosing the Experience Curve," *Journal of Marketing*, 47, Spring 1983 (Chicago: American Marketing Association), pp. 44–58. Used with permission.

percent learning curve and has built up a cumulative volume of ten million units, an increase in volume to twenty million units would only drop its cost by two cents (that is, for a first-unit cost of $10). Because further significant cost decreases are difficult to achieve, market penetration into new user segments is very slow. What the learning curve adds to the understanding of the maturity stage of the life cycle is that lower costs are associated with market penetration, which means increased sales. In Stage 3 of the learning curve (see Figure 6-4), cost reductions are progressively harder to achieve; thus, maturity occurs.

Sales decline. The sales decline stage is associated with Stage 4 in Figure 6-4. As the market becomes saturated, sales drop off. As this happens, it becomes impossible to achieve large enough increases in cumulative production to lower costs significantly in an attempt to stimulate sales. Marginal producers then drop out of the market.

Other learning curve variations, and their hypothesized effect on the product life cycle, have been explored in depth.[33] One theory contends that more frequent use of the learning curve will lead to enlightened marketing strategies and policies by fostering closer cooperation between the production and marketing functions within business-to-business firms. The experience curve can create the tendency to formulate marketing policies in a vacuum because it deals with price and not costs. Hence, the use of the learning curve in the marketing strategy selection process should help circumvent this apparent tendency.

DETERMINANTS OF THE PRODUCT MIX

The act of planning implies a course of action that has been thought through in advance so as to result in a consistent pattern of decisions regarding profits, market share, sales, and cash flow. This planning identifies the fundamental determinants of the product mix of a firm, including product-line depth and product-mix width, which would include the total number of items and lines offered by the business-to-business firm. The difficulties faced by management in formulating a sound product mix will become evident. In a historical context, recent trends in market dynamics and in technology development have increased the frequency of decisions concerning product-mix changes.[34] Management's role consists of adjusting to these forces as skillfully as possible, in light of the resources of the enterprise, and of guiding the business-to-business firm along product paths that lead to future growth and profits. The determinants discussed here are limited to those of a basic nature, and no effort has been made to treat in detail the various specific reasons or motivations underlying product action.

Technology

In times of rapid technological and market change, successful firms will be the leaders not only in adopting new technology but also in introducing new technology for competitive reasons. New technology provides the means for effective product innovation. The box entitled "Business-to-Business Marketing in Action" explains that Apple Computer has recently introduced a new generation of software that for the first time allows users who have never programmed a computer to create "stacks" of "interactive information." The release of this product has prompted Apple's competitors to accelerate testing of their own competitive models.

New-product development can be inspired by technological change as well as by customer need. However, product development should not lead to companies' emphasizing either a technological focus or a customer focus. The emphasis should be placed on achieving the proper coordination between the two areas.[35] Technical excellence is not a sufficient basis for success in product innovation. Innovation requires a mix of activities as the new technology is reshaped. (Capital, facilities, and perhaps new personnel are needed.) The electronics industry is a prime example of a field where myriad inventions have led to dynamic changes in products.

Technological shifts in product use and application require the maintenance of continuous contact with customers. Customer activities must be observed and monitored in order to determine the variations and changes in customer needs and wants that might suggest technological shifts in product use and application. These are the vital signs of impending product change. They signal opportunity for product variations or improvements and for new products altogether. The Muffco case is an interesting example of technological shift and resultant change in product requirements.

> Muffco is a manufacturer of mufflers and air cleaners for heavy-duty trucks and construction and mining equipment. Muffco's business is divided into two components by type of distribution: direct to original equipment manufacturers (OEMs) and distributor sales to the aftermarket.

BUSINESS-TO-BUSINESS MARKETING IN ACTION

YES, BUT WHAT DOES IT DO?

A guide to a new software generation

On his lecture tours, Bill Atkinson, father of the much-touted HyperCard program, likes to ask how many people have used his new computer software. Then he asks: "How many of you know what it *is*?" At a recent meeting in New York, more than 400 hands were raised in answer to the first question. When the second was asked, all but a few dropped—and the crowd roared with laughter. And how does Atkinson describe his baby? Is a "software Erector set" any help?

HyperCard is only the first in a new generation of software that defies the familiar categories of word processor, spreadsheet or database—and is giving the marketing folks fits. Another program, Agenda, had been termed "A spreadsheet for words" a third, Ize, is called a "textbase." All blend qualities of traditional programs to help users master mountains of information—and strip away the rigid rules that limit the flexibility of older programs. "The next great wave of applications is going to be these information systems," says Mitch Kapor, whose Lotus 1-2-3 helped kick off the personal-computing revolution. Esther Dyson, whose Release 1.0 newsletter covers the computer industry, says, "It's stupendous stuff."

But what do the programs *do*? Atkinson's HyperCard allows users who have never programmed a computer to create "stacks" of "interactive information." With a "stack" about fishing, a reader could instantly get facts on a particular species—or even cause an image of a carp to pop up on the screen. Though Apple Computer released HyperCard only in August, Macintosh owners have already used it to create thousands of "stacks"—many of which are being sold or swapped to other HyperCard users.

Like science fiction: Test versions of two other as-yet-unreleased programs help people find needles in the information haystack. Lotus's Agenda acts like a personal secretary, making sense of the notes you scribble to yourself. The user can ask to see only items about "Bill," or "beetles." If Bill collects beetles, Agenda can link the topics. It even "intuits" some links automatically; it recognizes that "next Friday" and "December 18" are the same and will consult both in compiling a to-do list. The Royal Bank of Canada uses Agenda to sort through news-agency stories. Some trial and error is involved. Hoping to gather stories on foreign political problems, bank employee George Goodwin had Agenda gather wire copy containing the word "stability." He got stories about gold and oil prices, but none about political stability.

Ize, from the Madison, Wisc.–based Persoft, offers another way to take arms against a sea of data. It builds ingeniously detailed indexes. Attorney Leland Hutchinson in Chicago uses Ize to help associates pinpoint thousands of paragraphs from contracts giving them a guide for their own work. Personal-computer consultant Roy Freborg says the program reminds him of computers in science fiction, which figure out what you mean when you ask them a simple question. He recalls seeing it for the first time and thinking, "Yes! This is what you should be able to do with a computer!"

The history of software is littered with good ideas that never caught on, and the success of these products will be tallied at the cash register. Apple gives HyperCard away with each new Macintosh—perhaps to get around having to explain it. Lotus, however, will charge a hefty $400 for Agenda, and Persoft plans to charge $445 for Ize.

As good as the new programs may be, they may offer only a hint of what's to come. Kapor, who began the work on Agenda before leaving Lotus, is now putting together an even more extensive program for the Macintosh. Every new category of software defied description at first, from spreadsheets to desktop publishing. Analyst Dyson predicts that the more information people have to assimilate, the more easily they will adapt to these information managers. Atkinson would agree. More and more, he says excitedly, his audiences are responding to his "what is it" question. "I'm getting a bunch of people raising their hands and shouting, 'A software Erector set!'" At least *they* understand it!

> Muffco's customer service department has been under considerable stress for several years. Business has been at a high level, but internal departments have not kept pace with demand. In an attempt to create order out of chaos, the customer service manager has isolated different activities and initiated reports that illustrate trends in various vital signs of the business:
>
> - Orders-received and order-aging reports
> - Time-required-for-shipment and back-order sales
> - Reports of complaints or compliments received by letter or telephone
> - Technical-information-request report
>
> In analyzing these reports, the customer service manager discovered two distinctive characteristics in the complaints about products and requests for technical information: first, that a new category of complaints began to develop regarding the contribution of air filters and mufflers to energy inefficiency; and second, that the number of requests for technical information about air filters and mufflers to improve energy efficiency had increased substantially.
>
> He reviewed these data with the engineering department manager and found that both developments preceded, by approximately six to twelve months, negotiations with OEM customers for products having performance characteristics that would improve the energy efficiency of their engines.[36]

This illustration does not conclusively prove that vital signs such as complaints and information inquiries are precursors of technological shifts and changes, but the thesis certainly seems logical. Muffco's management accepts this idea and now periodically reviews complaint and technical-information-request reports as part of its routine search for information and ideas that suggest the need for product changes and additions.

The automotive and homebuilding industries have experienced extensive energy-related change in their products. In both industries, dramatic technological shifts have resulted from product use and application requirements imposed by energy-conscious consumers, architects, homebuilders, and government agencies.

Blue-collar workers, technicians, engineers, scientists, supervisors, and managers are all constantly searching for ways to cut costs and to improve efficiency, effectiveness, productivity, and timeliness. (See the section on "value analysis" in Chapter 3.) This never-ending search by millions of people results in changes in product uses and applications—technological shifts that alter or abort life cycles, often causing new products to come into being.

Business marketing managers must continuously monitor the customer environment and search for evidence suggesting technological shifts. The marketplace yields these vital signs to the astute business marketer.[37]

Competition

A second important determinant of an industrial firm's product mix is the changes in product offerings of the competition. A change in a competitor's product mix could represent a major challenge to the company; and if that change is truly a significant improvement, such as a technological breakthrough, it may prove disastrous unless it can be matched or surpassed within a reasonable length of time.

Over the past several years, American companies have experienced dramatic changes in their domestic competitive environment. Small specialized competitors have exited or been swallowed up by larger multiindustry companies, often resulting in stronger, financially solvent, but more unpredictable competition. Foreign and multinational competitors have taken aim at the more profitable U.S. markets, which are easier to penetrate and pivotal to worldwide success, while building and maintaining barriers to entry by the U.S. companies themselves.[38] This competitive change has not been limited merely to new configurations of traditional competitors; it has also included a considerable number of new companies and complete substitution by new types of products.

Changes in Levels of Business Activity

Most business-to-business firms must deal with changes in business activity due to the presence of business cycles and seasonal variations. Many such firms expand their total product offering by adding product lines having different seasonal patterns to offset those of their present lines. Thereby, they are able to smooth out their production level and sales volume throughout the year. In somewhat similar fashion, some business firms add product lines that are less sensitive to business-cycle variations than are their existing lines.

Operating Capacity

A business-to-business firm will often expand its product mix if it discovers underutilized capacity in any part of its business. The underutilized capacity might be in any number of functional areas, such as production, sales, or research. For example, when new equipment is bought, there may be a period in which it is not totally utilized in satisfying existing demand, and there is pressure on management to find new products to keep such equipment busy. Similarly, when a marketing organization is set up to serve a particular market for a single product line, it often becomes apparent that the sales force could handle other lines as well; and pressure is generated to find new products that can also be sold profitably to that market.

Market Factors

Several market factors impact the business-to-business selling firm's product mix. A change in the business buyer's product mix, due to competitive action or technological innovation, could present an opportunity for the sale of additional quantities of various products, or an opportunity to capitalize on additional business. Additionally, the migration of industry into an area economically served by the business producer could help to offset losses from outward migration. Such activity, along with an increase or decrease in production capabilities, can lead to changes in the business product mix.

CONCEPT QUESTIONS

1. What does the new-product development process involve in most business-to-business companies?
2. What is the fundamental marketing value of product life-cycle analysis?
3. What is the role of competition in determining a business-to-business firm's product mix?

THE BUSINESS PRODUCT ADOPTION-DIFFUSION PROCESS

Business marketers are assigned the responsibility of not only assessing new-product success or failure time estimates but also of evaluating the substitution factor for a proposed new product. If a company decides to expand its product mix, business marketers must assess how quickly prospects will adopt a new product and to what extent they will replace the old.

The *adoption process* is the decision-making activity of the buying firm through which the new product or innovation is accepted. The diffusion of the new product, innovation, or service is the process by which the product or service is accepted by an industry over time. There are many similarities between the consumer in the consumer adoption process and the members of the business buying center, as both groups go through a basic five-step process in deciding whether or not to adopt something new.

Stages in the Adoption Process

Awareness. The buyer first learns of the new product or service but lacks much information about it. Awareness might come about by being exposed to sales promotion, having talked with other buyers, or by casual conversation with another member of the buying center.

Interest. The buyer seeks out additional information about the product or service by requesting either additional data from the potential seller, or perhaps by requesting that a member of the potential supplier's sales team make a sales call.

Evaluation. Here, the buyer (or another member of the buying center) considers, or makes a mental evaluation of, whether the new product or service would be useful. Consideration might be given to a value-analysis project, or quite possibly to a make-or-buy situation.

Trial. In this stage, adoption of the innovation takes place on a limited basis, as the buyer who makes a trial purchase carefully evaluates the "correctness" of the decision. If the new product or service is very expensive, radically new, or quite complex, the prospect might perceive the risk of a trial purchase to be greater than its benefits. Less expensive and less complex products might be distributed as free samples, with the goal being to induce prospects to try the new offering by reducing perceived risk.

Adoption. If the trial purchase worked as expected, then the decision is made to make regular use of the product. If the trial did not work as expected, then the product or service is rejected, at least for the time being.

As can be seen, the adoption process is a series of stages that a member of the buying center (or an individual, in the case of consumer goods) goes through in deciding whether to buy and make regular use of a new product or service. The *diffusion process* represents the spread of a new product, innovation, or service throughout an industry over time. The newness of an idea, manifested in uncertainty in the minds of potential adopters, gives the diffusion process its unique character.[39] The speed with which the industrial diffusion process takes place varies among industries, being very fast in the electronics industry, and possibly quite slow in the domestic steel industry. It has been suggested that the diffusion process is affected by such factors as word of mouth.[40] As in the adoption process, there are many similarities between the consumer group proceeding through the diffusion process and the members of the business buying center (representing a particular industry) proceeding as a group through the diffusion process over time. In the diffusion process, a few firms adopt at first (innovators), and then the number of adopters increases rapidly (early adopters and early majority) as the value of the product innovation or service becomes apparent. The rate finally diminishes as fewer potential buyers (late majority and laggards) remain in the nonadopter category. By the time laggards adopt something new, it may already have been discarded by the innovator group in favor of a newer idea or technology.

Factors Influencing the Rate of Adoption-Diffusion

The development and acceptance of new products, and the time spent in the introductory stage, vary greatly among different business-to-business firms. Some products diffuse very slowly into a particular market, while others may almost bypass this stage. Perceived advantage and perceived risk would play a part, along with common barriers to adoption, such as marriage to an existing facility, or incompatibility with existing products. Products that require major changes in manufacturing processes, or those that require a large outlay of capital, tend to diffuse slowly.

Another factor is technological uncertainty. Will the technology function as expected when placed into volume production? How about the perceived likelihood of technological obsolescence? What about the unpredictable quality of a new product or innovation, or other emerging technologies that can provide similar advantages? These and other factors force some potential customers to take a wait-and-see attitude before committing to a new-product adoption.

BUSINESS PRODUCT PORTFOLIO CLASSIFICATION, ANALYSIS, AND STRATEGY

Today, the underlying principle guiding new-product development combines external market needs with internal functional strength. This combination allows companies to develop a new-product portfolio that satisfies corporate strategic objectives.[41] Portfolio classification models are often used. They are intended to give a visual display of the present and prospective positions of business products according to the business attractiveness of the market and the ability to compete within the market.[42] The business marketer must regularly review the product portfolio, developing strategic alternatives for each of the company's current products, businesses, and new business possibilities. The concept of the product portfolio stresses the importance of viewing products not individually but as parts of a total system. This perspective allows for management's regular review of strategic alternatives and for corresponding resource allocation decisions.

What Is the Product Portfolio?

A product portfolio is the firm's offering of products or divisions, each of which can be identified as a *strategic business unit* (SBU); and most of which operate as a separate profit center that has its own management, its own set of identifiable markets and competitors, and its own marketing strategies. The industrial firm's product portfolio typically consists of related businesses and/or products grouped into SBUs that are homogeneous enough to control most factors affecting their performance. Resources are allocated to SBUs in proportion to their contribution to the corporate objectives of growth and profitability. The challenge of the 1990s will be to identify the SBUs in the firm's product portfolio that will enhance the overall corporate mission, while withdrawing support for those that will not.

The basic concept of the product portfolio was first put forth by the founder of the Boston Consulting Group, Bruce Henderson, in a booklet published on the subject in 1970.[43] Henderson looked at a firm's products or divisions as a mix of businesses that strategically interact and influence one another, principally in terms of their use of resources and their development of these resources against opportunities in a competitive marketplace. He described and evaluated products and divisions in terms of three dimensions:

(1) The attractiveness of the market, especially in light of the SBU's stage in the product life cycle.
(2) The business-to-business firm's position in the market in terms of market share.
(3) The firm's acknowledged or perceived strengths and weaknesses, relative to competitors.

One of the earliest and most widely implemented approaches is the cash quadrant or share/growth matrix developed by the Boston Consulting Group.[44]

Diagnosing the Product Portfolio

As shown in Figure 6-5, strategic business units can be classified into four categories. Businesses in each category exhibit different financial characteristics and offer different strategic choices. The four types of SBUs specified by the growth-rate matrix include "stars," "cash cows," "question marks," and "dogs."

FIGURE 6-5 **Matrix Quadrants of Four Categories of Strategic Business Units**

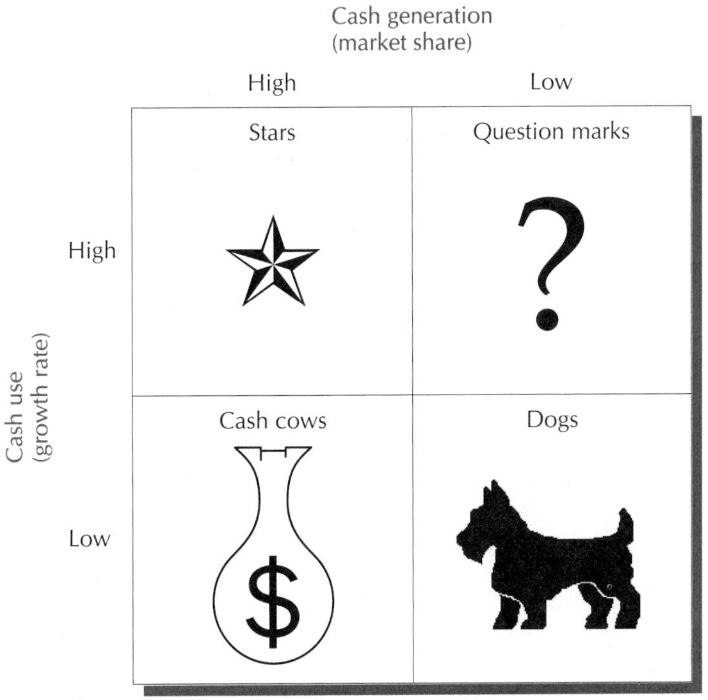

Source: The Boston Consulting Group, Inc., 1973, "The Experience Curve—Reviewed IV. The Growth Share Matrix or the Product Portfolio." All rights reserved. Printed with permission.

If market share and growth behave as expected, then this portfolio matrix tells a compelling cash-flow story with important investment and strategy implications. However, this is only one approach to portfolio analysis, and it is rather limited.

Product Portfolio Strategies

In a typical business-to-business company, there are products scattered in all four quadrants of the portfolio matrix. An appropriate strategy for products in each cell is given briefly in Table 6-4. First, a primary goal of an industrial company should be to secure a position with cash cows but also to guard against the frequent temptation to reinvest in them excessively. The cash generated from cash cows can be used to support those stars that are not self-sustaining. Surplus cash might be used to finance selected question marks toward a dominant market position. Question marks that cannot be funded might be divested. A dog could be restored to a position of viability by shrewdly segmenting the market; that is, by rationalizing and specializing the business into a small niche that the product concerned can dominate. If such is not feasible, the firm will consider harvesting the SBU by cutting off all investment in the business, with consideration given to liquidation of the unit when and if the opportunity develops.

TABLE 6-4 **Characteristics and Strategy Implications of Products in the Strategy Quadrants**

Quadrant	Investment Characteristics	Earning Characteristics	Cash-Flow Characteristics	Strategy Implication
Stars	Continual expenditures for capacity expansion Pipeline filling with cash	Low to high	Negative cash flow (net cash user)	Continue to increase market share, if necessary, at the expense of short-term earnings
Cash cows	Capacity maintenance expenditures	High	Positive cash flow (net cash contributor)	Maintain share and cost leadership until further investment becomes marginal
Question marks	Heavy initial capacity expenditures High R & D costs	Negative to low	Negative cash flow (net cash user)	Assess chances of dominating segment; if good, go after share; if bad, redefine business or withdraw
Dogs	Gradually deplete capacity	High to low	Positive cash flow (net cash contributor)	Plan an orderly withdrawal so as to maximize cash flow

Source: Reproduced from Subhash C. Jain, *Marketing Planning and Strategy* (3rd ed.) 1990, p. 482, with the permission of South-Western Publishing Company, Dallas.

Figure 6-6 shows the consequences of correct and incorrect strategic moves. For example, if a star is not appropriately funded, it could become a question mark, and finally a dog (disaster sequence). On the other hand, if a question mark is given adequate support, it can become a star, and ultimately a cash cow (success sequence).[45]

The product portfolio concept provides the business marketer with a useful synthesis of the analysis and judgments necessary as an SBU moves through the product life cycle and presents the marketer with a provocative source of strategy alternatives. The business marketer must remember that strategy consists of

FIGURE 6-6 **Product Portfolio Matrix: Strategic Consequences**

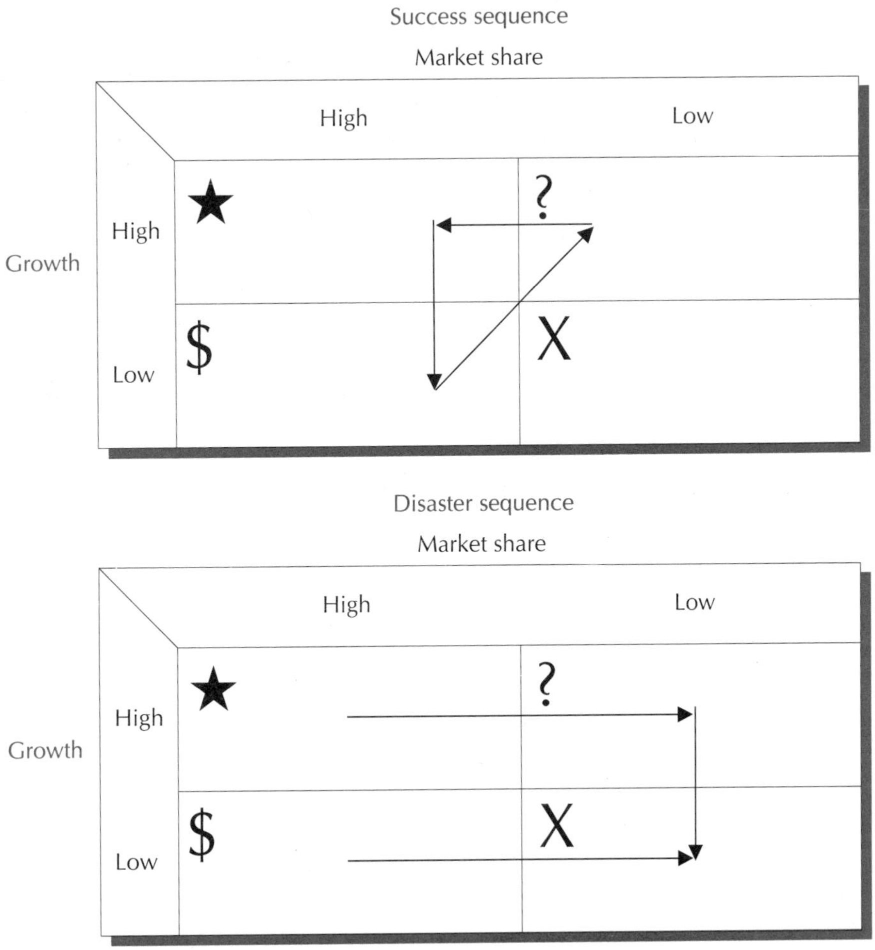

Source: The Boston Consulting Group, Inc., 1970, "The Product Portfolio."

doing the right things—deciding *what* must be done; tactics consist of doing things correctly—deciding *how* to do them. Marketing planners must plot the projected positions of each SBU under both present and alternative strategies, thus enabling them to decide what objectives each SBU should have, the strategies and tactics to use in achieving those objectives, and what resources to assign each strategic business unit.

BUSINESS PRODUCT DELETION STRATEGY

Any discussion of product development, management, and strategy, would not be complete without a brief review of a very difficult business marketing decision: when to drop a product, product line, or division. Once product performance deviations from established norms are identified and analyzed, management often discovers that weak product performance is seldom the result of one single factor. Factors often include poor sales performance, poor profit performance, and decline in market potential, among other reasons.[46] Rather, it generally results from a variety of factors that are frequently interrelated. Table 6-5 shows a range of reasons cited by respondents as the cause of unsatisfactory product performance. Note that noncompetitive price, production problems (such as inferior technology), and uneconomic batches of the product were the reasons most often cited for unsatisfactory product performance.

The idea that some products entering the decline stage of the product life cycle must be eliminated reflects the strategic thinking that every SBU plays an important part in making the product portfolio viable. When the SBU becomes

TABLE 6-5 **Statements Explaining the Unsatisfactory Performance of Specific Products Studied**

Statement	No. of Companies Citing
Uncompetitive price	7
Production problems (e.g., inferior technology, hard to assemble)	6
Not mass product, uneconomic batches	6
Too costly to produce and market	5
High costs to manufacture	5
Overengineered	4
Competitors dominated the market	4
Customer requirements not as expected	2
Low selling price	2

Source: Reprinted by permission of the publisher from "Revitalizing Weak Industrial Products," by George J. Avionitis, *Industrial Marketing Management* 14 (1985), pp. 93–105.

a drain on the financial and managerial resources of an organization, management has three alternatives in the strategy for product elimination: harvesting, line simplification, and total-line divestment.[47]

Harvesting

Harvesting strategy is applied to a product or business whose sales volume and/or market share are slowly declining. An effort is made to cut the costs associated with the SBU to help improve the cash flow. Harvesting leads to a slow decline in sales; and when the business ceases to provide positive cash flow, it is divested. The implementation of harvesting strategy would require, where appropriate, reducing maintenance of facilities; cutting advertising and research budgets; curtailing the number and scope of channel intermediaries used; eliminating small-order customers; and reducing service levels in terms of delivery time, sales assistance, and so on. DuPont followed the harvesting strategy in the case of its rayon business, and BASF Wyandotte applied harvesting to soda ash.[48]

Line Simplification

Line simplification strategy refers to a situation where a product line is trimmed to a manageable size by pruning the number and variety of products and services being offered. It is hoped that the simplification effort will help to restore the health of the line. This endeavor can lead to a variety of benefits, such as potential cost savings from longer production runs; reduced inventories; and a more forceful concentration of marketing, research and development, and other efforts behind a shorter list of products.

The decision to drop an SBU from the product line is a difficult one to make; despite the emotional aspects of this decision, the need for objectivity in this matter cannot be overemphasized. According to a classic article dealing with the elimination of weak product items and product lines:

> Putting products to death—or letting them die—is a drab business, and often engenders much of the sadness of a parting with old and tried friends... Too often management thinks of this as something that should be done, but which can be put off until tomorrow...This is why a definite procedure for deletion of products should be set up, and why the authority and responsibility for the various activities involved should be clearly and definitely assigned.[49]

Total-Line Divestment

Divestment strategy is a situation of reverse acquisition and is also a key dimension of marketing strategy. Divestment decisions are principally economic or psychological in nature; they may allow the firm to restore a balanced product portfolio. If the firm has too many high-growth businesses, its resources might be inadequate to fund such growth. If the firm has too many low-growth businesses, it will frequently generate more cash than is required for investment purposes and will build up redundant equity. For the firm to grow evenly over time, while showing regular earnings increments, a portfolio of both fast- and slow-growing businesses is necessary. Divestment can help to achieve this type of balance.

The use of this strategy is reflected in Allied Signal's selling off of its marine systems defense operation in 1988 because of flat defense spending, tepid earnings, and intensifying competition. Also, the Eaton Corporation has recently put its defense electronics business up for sale.[50]

When the decision is finally made to harvest, simplify, or divest a strategic business unit, a well-planned procedure is essential to the success of such an initiative. This move will likely cause some disruption and create concern among some distributors and customers, in addition to the uncertainty and anxiety experienced by members of the sales force, as well as by other employees. Steps should be taken to ensure minimal disruption among both internal and external constituencies.

INTERNATIONAL PRODUCT STRATEGY

In breaking into a foreign market, product success calls for a sound framework that relates the firm's goals to its resources.[51] A country in the early stages of industrialization does not necessarily have an adequate pool of trained technicians, so a product must be considered in relation to the environment within which it will be used. Equipment that requires a high degree of technical skill to operate, maintain, or repair can be inadequate in a country that lacks a pool of technically skilled labor. An example of this is reflected in a statement reportedly made by a manufacturer of agricultural equipment, commenting on the lack of cooperation of Thailand farmers in combining their plots into larger farms. The U.S. company wants to sell combines for harvesting rice and corn if the farmers could be persuaded to plant similar crops adjacent to each other. However, as the executive commented, "Until the farmers agree to cooperate, there are not going to be opportunities in Thailand to sell the large grain combines that we and other major companies manufacture." As competition increases on the international level, U.S. companies must become more marketing oriented to survive.

The life cycles of products also tend to vary in different markets. This could produce a longer overall product life cycle, because a product in a mature stage of its domestic life cycle may be perceived as new in a foreign market and thus be in the introductory stage of the product life cycle there. Yesterday's product in the United States may be today's product in another part of the world. Additionally, used capital equipment, or that which new technology makes obsolete, might be sold overseas.

CONCEPT QUESTIONS

1. How is the diffusion process related to the adoption process?
2. What is the basic value of product-portfolio analysis to the business marketer?
3. What types of activities are involved in implementing business product deletion strategy?

SUMMARY

1. Product development, management, and strategy are important parts of the business marketing process, with the major concerns being both to measure and predict success and to execute proper strategy over the life of the business product.
2. Business marketers are now beginning to replace engineers as having the most important role in the development of new-product ideas. Technology push and market pull are the two major approaches to new-product development. Technology push results when the driving force of a new product's development is the perceived potential of the technology itself; market pull is primarily the result of marketing research methodologies of interviewing prospective users about their needs, then developing solutions to those perceived needs. The new-product development process includes seven stages: strategy development, idea and concept generation, screening and evaluation, business analysis, product development, product testing, and product commercialization and introduction.
3. New-product development, evaluation, and management must follow good management practice if effectiveness, efficiency, and a reasonable likelihood of success are to be achieved. The major options available to the business marketer in organizing the new-product development process include a product manager system, a new-product committee, a new-product department, and a new-product venture team.
4. The information derived from product life-cycle analysis is generally used to suggest appropriate marketing strategies over a particular product's life span. Experience and learning curves can be used in conjunction with product life-cycle analysis to determine more specifically what is happening to a product as it moves from one stage in its life cycle to the next. Stages in the product life cycle include product introduction, market growth, market maturity, and sales decline.
5. Technology, competition, changes in the level of business activity, and the utilization of plant capacity can all have a marked impact on a firm's decision to expand, contract, or maintain the current product mix. The effective business marketer must understand each of these market forces in order to make appropriate decisions with regard to possible product-mix changes.
6. Business marketers have the responsibility of deciding how quickly prospects will adopt a new product and to what extent they will replace the old one. To

perform such a task, marketers frequently use both the adoption process and the diffusion process. The adoption process is the decision-making activity of the buying firm through which the new product or innovation is accepted; it includes the stages of awareness, interest, evaluation, trial, and adoption or rejection of the product. The diffusion process shows how a product is accepted by an industry over time.

7. The business-to-business firm should regularly review its product portfolio, developing strategic alternatives for each of the company's current products, businesses, and new business possibilities. The Boston Consulting Group categorizes each product or business division in a company according to four types of strategic business units (SBUs), to include stars, cash cows, question marks, and dogs. Strategies have been formulated for use with each of these four categories into which SBUs can be placed.
8. When to drop a product, product line, or company division is a very difficult task for the business marketer. Common product-elimination options include harvesting, line simplification, and total-line divestment.
9. In breaking into a foreign market, product success calls for a sound framework that relates the firm's goals to its resources. The life cycles of products tend to vary in different markets. This could produce a longer overall product life cycle, as a product in the maturity stage of the domestic life cycle may be perceived as new and thus be in the introductory stage of the product life cycle in a foreign market.

KEY TERMS

Adoption process
Diffusion process
Divestment strategy
Experience curve
Harvesting strategy
Learning curve analysis
Line simplification strategy
Market pull
New-product committee approach
New-product department approach
New-product venture team approach
Product management approach
Strategic business unit
Technology push

REVIEW QUESTIONS

1. Why are effective product management and strategy so important today? What are the major concerns of product management and strategy?
2. Why was there a reluctance in the past to give marketing personnel a major role in the design and development of new products? Discuss three major styles in organizing the new-product development process. Identify two approaches to new-product development. Describe each of the seven stages in the new-product development process.

3. Identify and discuss four major options that business marketers have in organizing the new product development process. Which option is most commonly utilized by business-to-business firms?
4. What is the fundamental value of product life-cycle analysis? How are learning curve analysis and experience curves used in product life-cycle analysis? Identify and describe each of the four stages involved in the product life cycle.
5. How do technology, competition, changes in the level of business activity, and the utilization of plant capacity impact upon possible changes in a business-to-business firm's product mix?
6. What is meant by the adoption process and the diffusion process? How can they be utilized together? Identify and describe the stages in the adoption process. What factors influence the rate of adoption? Diffusion?
7. Define product portfolio analysis. According to the Boston Consulting Group approach to product management, what is a strategic business unit? Identify four categories into which each strategic business unit within a business-to-business firm can be placed and indicate appropriate strategies for use with each of the four categories.
8. What are some common reasons for product failure? Indicate and explain three strategic approaches for the elimination of weak products.
9. What is necessary to product success when breaking into a foreign market? How can the life cycles of products vary between domestic and international markets?

Cases

CASE 6-1 Cincinnati Milacron

What started out as a chat over a cup of coffee soon led to Cincinnati Milacron's best-selling machine. Bruce Kozak, a regional sales manager, bumped into Harol Faig, a product manager, one Sunday in 1990. Kozak complained to Faig that the Japanese were swamping the market for plastics machinery. Milacron had been relatively blind to the Japanese invasion. Plastics machinery sales had been increasing each year but at a rate below that of total market increases. Milacron was losing market share even though sales were increasing.

Faig and Kozak began listing specifications that a machine would have to have to beat the Japanese. Within a month, Faig called Kozak and invited him to join a venture team. The machine had been dubbed the Hafakozaki. Faig and Kozak hand-picked a team to develop the new product.

Breaking down organizational walls, they selected members from marketing, engineering, and manufacturing. The initial time to develop the product, one year, was reduced to nine months. "If a woman can make a baby in nine months, so can we," Faig told his group. The project was renamed Project 270. The 270 days (nine months) were counted, and plans were made for President Daniel Meyer and Vice President David Noffsinger to flip the switch on that day.

The team started by visiting various customers of plastics machinery to find out what these people look for in a product. These visits revealed that price and lead time were two critical elements involved in the purchasing decision. Milacron had always assumed that the technical features of a product and the ability to customize a product were the most important features. The target objective became to reduce the cost of the product by 40 percent and to make the product "world-class," which meant standardizing it on the metric system as opposed to the U.S. measurement system. Milacron had always used the U.S. system.

The members of the group moved their offices closer together. Meetings were held each Monday so that everyone would be kept up-to-date on the developments. Instead of waiting until the weekly meeting to make decisions (which could cause delays), team members were encouraged to make decisions on the spot and then to report back on Mondays. Accounting information, usually kept secret from production and marketing people, was made available to the group. By reducing the number of parts, using cast parts instead of machine parts, and standardizing things such as screw sizes, the group was able to reduce the cost of the machine by 40 percent.

The prototype of the Vista, as the new machine was later named, was introduced on December 7, 1991—Pearl Harbor Day. In the first full year of production, the Vista sold 2.5 times as many machines as its predecessor had.

DISCUSSION QUESTIONS

1. Do you think Cincinnati Milacron would have been able to introduce a product like Vista without using a venture group? Why or why not?
2. Explain why you think a company like Cincinnati Milacron ends up with over three hundred different sizes of bolts used in manufacturing their machines.
3. Do you think the company will be successful in competing with the Japanese? Explain your answer.

Suggested Reading

Nulty, Peter. "The Soul of an Old Machine." *Fortune*, 21 May 1990, 67–72.

Source: C. Lamb, J. Hair, and C. McDaniel, *Principles of Marketing*, 1st Edition (Cincinnati, OH: South-Western Publishing Company, 1992) pp. 277–278.

CASE 6-2 Abbott Laboratories

According to *Business Week*, when Marcia Ryles, a pension fund consultant in Los Angeles, gave birth to her first child in November of 1989, her hospital gave her a survival kit before she left for home. With the blanket and toy bear came a large tin of Abbot Laboratories' powdered Similac, the leading infant formula. When her son Alex did not take to breast-feeding, Ryles turned to Similac. She didn't try other brands. Says Ryles, "I just didn't want to risk upsetting him by switching formulas."[52] This is a concern of most new mothers—a concern that Abbott and its competitors capitalize on.

Business Week also adds: "Abbott and its main rivals in infant formula, Bristol-Myers' Squibb Company and American Home Products Corporation, thrive on such customer loyalty. To be the first to reach new mothers with their product, Abbott, Bristol, and AHP court doctors relentlessly and give hospital nurses free formula. And since Abbott and others don't spend millions of dollars on consumer advertising, margins in this $1.6 billion business run up to 25 percent"[53] The market is highly competitive. As *Business Week* explains, Abbott and its rivals do many things to get doctors to use their formulas.

"Formula makers also offer periodic conferences to update doctors on infant nutrition. Dr. Lawrence M. Gartner, chairperson of the Pediatrics Department at University of Chicago Hospitals, says that, like other participants, he has all his expenses paid by Abbott when he attends Abbott-sponsored conferences. Abbott gives the University of Chicago free formula, as well as baby bottles, which Gartner estimates saves the hospital $100,000 a year. Bristol also donates its formula Enfamil to mothers who don't know which formula to use. 'What we give away has a direct influence on what mothers buy,' says Gartner. 'The ethics of this are troubling.'"[54]

DISCUSSION QUESTIONS

1. Is it ethical for infant formula manufacturers to give hospital nurses free formula? Is it ethical for the hospitals to accept the formula?
2. Are full-expenses-paid conferences for doctors ethical?
3. Should hospitals give formulas to mothers who don't know which formula to use?
4. What specific restrictions, if any, should be placed on the sampling of infant formula to hospital nurseries and mothers?

Source: C. Lamb, J. Hair, and C. McDaniel, *Principles of Marketing*, 1st Edition (Cincinnati, OH: South-Western Publishing Company, 1992) p. 234.

Suggested Additional Readings

Barczak, Gloria, and David Wileman. "Successful New Product Team Leaders." *Industrial Marketing Management* 21 (February 1992): 61–68. **A study of the autonomy, goals, and successes of new-product team leaders.**

Burt, David N., and William R. Soukup. "Purchasing's Role in New Product Development." *Harvard Business Review* 63 (September/October 1985): 90–97. **Discussion of purchasing's role in new-product development to include suggested methods of integration.**

Cardozo, Richard N., and Jerry Wind. "Risk Return Approach to Product Portfolio Strategy." *Long-Range Planning* (UK), 18 (April 1985): 77–85. **Managerial model and suggested guidelines for product-line decisions.**

Child, Robert W. "New Products—Making A Good Thing Better." *Canadian Business Review* (Canada), 12 (Summer 1985): 31–34. **Case study of various types of new-product strategies used by Dow Chemical of Canada.**

Choffray, Jean-Marie, and Gary L. Lilien. "A Decision-Support System for Evaluating Sales Prospects and Launch Strategies for New Products." *Industrial Marketing Management* 15 (February 1986): 75–85. **French case study of industrial product development and diffusion.**

Cooper, Robert G. "Industrial Firm's New Product Strategies." *Journal of Business Research* 13 (April 1985): 107–121. **Empirical study of the dimensions of new-product strategy in 122 Canadian firms.**

______, "Overall Corporate Strategies for New Product Programs." *Industrial Marketing Management* 14 (August 1985): 179–193. **Empirical study of five types of innovation strategy in industrial product development.**

Cooper, Robert G., and Elko J. Kleinschmidt. "An Investigation into the New Product Process." *Journal of Product Innovation Management* 3 (June 1986): 71–85. **Study of thirteen tasks involved with 252 new-product case histories at 123 business product manufacturers.**

Crowe, Thomas J., and Jose Pablo Nuno. "Deciding Manufacturing Priorities: Flexibility, Cost, Quality, and Service." *Long-Range Planning* (UK), 24 (December 1991): 89–95. **A discussion of strategic planning issues in setting manufacturing priorities.**

de Brentani, Ulrike. "Do Firms Need a Custom-Designed New-Product Screening Model?" *Journal of Product Innovation Management* 3 (June 1986): 108–119. **Comparison of four major product evaluation models, noting that similarities far outweigh the differences among them.**

Drozdenko, Ronald, and Sidney Weinstein. "From Experience: The Role of Objective in Vivo Testing in the Product Development Process." *Journal of Product Innovation Management* 3 (June 1986): 120–126. **Three case studies involving the quantifying of product testing and potential product advantages.**

Englewood, Christopher. "New Product Development for Service Companies." *Journal of Product Innovation Management* 3 (December 1986): 264–275. **Survey and applications of product introduction techniques.**

Espey, James. "A Multinational Approach to New Product Development." *European Journal of Marketing* (UK), 19, no. 3 (1985): 5–18. **Case study of a new-product development team in the liquor industry.**

Friedman, Hershey H., and Joshua Krauz. "A Portfolio Theory Approach to Solve the Product-Elimination Problem." *Mid-Atlantic Journal of Business* 24 (Summer 1986): 43–48. **Discussion of financial factors related to weak products, and guidelines for candidates for product deletion.**

Gagliano, Caren Calish. "How to Mine and Refine New Product Ideas." *Business Marketing* 70 (November 1985): 102–112. **Case study of an approach to new-product planned growth in the Netherlands.**

Gupta, Ashok K., S. P. Raj, and David Wilemon. "A Model for Studying R&D-Marketing Interface in the Product Innovation Process." *Journal of Marketing* 50 (April 1986): 7–17. **Discussion of a conceptual model of organizational structure and climate.**

Kleizen, Hendrikus G., George Beaton, and Russell Abratt. "Pharmaceutical Product Management in 1990: Will There Be Any Changes?" *European Journal of Marketing* (UK), 19, no. 7 (1985): 5–10. **Forecasting the future of product management in the South African pharmaceutical market.**

Mercer, J. A. T. "Product Life Cycles of the Windsurfer Market" *European Journal of Marketing* (UK), 19, no. 4 (1985): 13–22. **Case study of a successful test of the PLC concept in the United Kingdom.**

Milson, Murray R., S. P. Raj, and David Wilemon. "A Survey of Major Approaches for Accelerating New Product Development." *Journal of Product Innovation Management* 9 (March 1992): 53–69. **A discussion of how to eliminate unnecessary steps and delays in the development of new products.**

Moore, William L. "New Product Development Practices of Industrial Marketers." *Journal of Product Innovation Management* 4 (March 1987): 6–20. **A survey of the processes, problems, and strategic planning processes of industrial marketers engaged in new-product development.**

More, Roger A. "Developer/Adopter Relationships in New Industrial Product Situations." *Journal of Business Research* 14 (December 1986): 501–517. **Examples, problems, interorganizational framework, and implications for management regarding developer/adopter relationships arising from new-business-product situations.**

Paul, Ronald N. "Improving the New Product Development Process—Making New Technology Push Work." *Journal of Business Marketing* 2 (Fall 1987): 59–62. **Discussion of the legitimacy of technology push in developing new products.**

Polhill, Frederick. "New Product Development: Is the 3M Approach Inimitable?" *Industrial Marketing Digest* (UK), 10 (Fourth Quarter 1985): 13–24. **Case study of product teams and entrepreneurship.**

Ronkainen, Ilkka. "Using Decision-Systems Analysis to Formalize Product Development Processes." *Journal of Business Research* 13 (February 1985): 97–106. **Guidelines for minimizing risk in evaluating new-product ideas.**

Sykes, Hollister B. "Lessons from a New Ventures Program." *Harvard Business Review* 64 (May/June 1986): 69–74. **Case study of internal ventures, looking at determinants of success with a single-product focus in an entrepreneurial environment.**

Yoon, Eunsang, and Gary L. Lilien. "New Industrial Product Performance: The Effects of Market Characteristics and Strategy." *Journal of Product Innovation Management* 2 (September 1985): 134–144. **Presentation of a conceptual model for original and reformulated new products, with guidelines for new-product managers.**

ENDNOTES

[1]George P. Dovel, "Stake It Out: Positioning Success, Step by Step," *Business Marketing* 75 (July 1990): 43–51.

[2]Booz, Allen, and Hamilton, Inc., *New Products Management for the 1980s* (New York: Booz, Allen, and Hamilton, 1982), 7.

[3]Michel Robert, "Opportunity Search: What's That Knocking at the Door?" *Journal of Business and Industrial Marketing* 8 (1993): 24–39.

[4]Bob Donath, "The Customer as Consultant", *Sales and Marketing Management* 144 (September, 1992): 84–90.

[5]Nils-Erik Aaby, and Richard Discenya, "Strategic Marketing and New Product Development," *Journal of Business and Industrial Marketing* 8 (1993): 61–69.

[6]Frank G. Bingham, Jr. and Charles J. Quigley, Jr., "Venture Team Application to New Product Development," *The Journal of Business and Industrial Marketing* 4 (Winter/Spring 1989): 49–59.

[7]Alan Stewart, "ISDN Development and the CPE Marketplace," *Communication News* 28 (January 1991): 20–31.

[8]Eugene F. Finkin, "Developing and Managing New Products," in *Marketing Management Readings, From Theory to Practice*, 3d ed., ed. Benson P. Shapiro, Robert J. Dolan, and John A. Quelch (Homewood, Ill.: Richard D. Irwin, 1985), 263–275.

[9]Ian Barclay, "The New Product Development Process: Past Evidence and Future Practical Application", *R&D Management* 22 (July 1992): 255–263.

[10]Ian Barclay and Mark Benson, "New Product Development: Organization and Current Practice," *Leadership and Organization Development Journal* (UK), 11 (1990): 13–23.

[11]Alvin J. Williams and William C. Smith, "Involving Purchasing in Product Development," *Industrial Marketing Management* 19 (November 1990): 315–319.

[12]Booz, Allen and Hamilton, Inc., can be credited as the authors of this particular scheme in its report entitled *Management of New Products* (1968). Also, see the updated version, *New Products Management for the 1980s* (New York: Booz, Allen, and Hamilton, 1982), 7.

[13]Subhash C. Jain, *Marketing Planning and Strategy* 3rd ed. (Cincinnati, Ohio: South-Western Publishing, 1990), 424.

[14]Peter Vanderwicken, "What's Really Wrong at Chrysler," *Fortune,* May 1975, 176.

[15]Booz, Allen and Hamilton, Inc., *New Products Management.*

[16]Lawrence Ingrassia, "By Improving Scratch Paper, 3M Gets New-Product Winner," *Wall Street Journal* 31 March 1983, 31.

[17]Patrice Apodaca, "Flatter Organizations, Challenge Executives," *Investor's Daily* 17 October, 1988, 1, 34.

[18]Thomas D. Kuczmarski, "Screening Potential New Products," *Planning Review* 20 (July/August 1992): 24–31, 48.

[19]Eric N. Berkowitz, Roger A. Kerin, and William Rudelius, *Marketing* (St. Louis, Mo.: Times Mirror/Mosby College Publishing, 1986), 238–239.

[20]*Ibid.*, 123.

[21]George Gruenwald, "New Products: America's Not Out of the Game Yet", *Marketing News* 24 (May 14, 1990): 20.

[22]Robert Hisrich and Michael P. Peters, *Marketing Decisions for New and Mature Products: Planning, Development, and Control* (Columbus, Ohio: Charles E. Merrill Publishing, 1984), 29.

[23]Booz, Allen, and Hamilton, Inc., *New Products Management*, 20.

[24]Bingham and Quigley, *Venture Team Application*, 49–59.

[25]Robert O. Null, "The Team Approach to Business Expansion" (presentation to the Chicago Chapter of the Product Development and Management Association, February 26, 1986).

[26]Stanley F. Slater, "Competing in High-Velocity Markets," *Industrial Marketing Management* (November 1993): 255–263.

[27]For a discussion of strategies for reviving declining products and also some ideas for reintroducing abandoned products, see William Layer, Mushtag Luqmani, and Zahir Quareshi, "Product Rejuvenation Strategies," *Business Horizons* (November/December 1984): 21–28; and Mark N. Vamos, "New Life for Madison Avenue's Old-Time Stars," *Business Week* 1 April 1985, 94.

[28]"Faster than a Speeding Chip: A Novel Supercomputer," *Newsweek* 28 March 1988, 63.

[29]This section is from Louis E. Yelle, "Industrial Life Cycles and Learning Curves: Interaction of Marketing and Production," in *Readings in Industrial Marketing*, Manoj K. Agarival, Philip C. Burger, and David A. Reid (Englewood Cliffs, N.J.: Prentice-Hall, 1986), 104–111. Also, see George S. Day and David B. Montgomery, "Diagnosing the Experience Curve," *Journal of Marketing* 47

(Spring 1983: 44–58; and Hans B. Thorelli and Stephen C. Burnett, "The Nature of Product Life Cycles for Industrial Goods Businesses," *Journal of Marketing* 45 (Fall 1981): 97–108.

[30]William W. Alberts, "The Experience Curve Doctrine Reconsidered", *Journal of Marketing* 53 (July 1989): 36–49.

[31]Day and Montgomery, "Diagnosing the Experience Curve," 44–58.

[32]T. P. Wright, "Factors Affecting the Cost of Airplanes," *Journal of Aeronautical Sciences* 3 (February 1936), pp. 122-128.

[33]Yelle, *Industrial Life Cycles*, 311–318.

[34]Giovanni Azzone and Umberto Bertele, "Idle Capacity and Timeliness in Mix Change Decisions," *Engineering Costs and Production Economics* (Netherlands), 18 (January 1990): 269–274.

[35]Roland W. Schmitt, "Successful Corporate R&D," *Harvard Business Review* 63 (May/June 1985): 124–128.

[36]Dick Berry, *Industrial Marketing for Results* (Boston: Addison-Wesley, 1981), 42–43.

[37]*Ibid.*, 42–43.

[38]William E. Rothschild, "Competitive Analysis: The Missing Link in Strategy," in *Marketing Management Readings, From Theory to Practice,* 3d ed., ed. Benson P. Shapiro, Robert J. Dolan, and John A. Quelch (Homewood, Ill.:Richard D. Irwin, 1985), 235–247.

[39]Sid L. Huff and Jennifer McNaughton, "Diffusion of an Information Technology Innovation," *Business Quarterly* 56 (Summer 1991): 25–30.

[40]Fareena Sultan, John Farley, and Donald R. Lehmann, "A Meta-Analysis of Applications of Diffusion Models," *Journal of Marketing Research* 27 (February 1990): 70–77.

[41]Kuczmarski, "Screening Potential New Products."

[42]R.A. Proctor and P. J. Kitchen, "Strategic Planning: An Overview of Product Portfolio Models," *Marketing Intelligence and Planning* 8 (1990): 4–10.

[43]Boston Consulting Group, "The Product Portfolio," *Perspectives on Experience* (1970).

[44]See Bruce D. Henderson, *Henderson on Corporate Strategy* (Cambridge, Mass.: Abt Associates, 1979).

[45]Jain, *Marketing Planning and Strategy*, 295.

[46]S. J. Hart, "Product Deletion and the Effects of Strategy," *European Journal of Marketing* (UK), 23 (1989): 6–17.

[47]A portion of this discussion is based on Jain, *Marketing Planning and Strategy*, 75.

[48]K. R. Harrigan and Michael Porter, "End-Game Strategies for Declining Industries," *Harvard Business Review* (July/August, 1983): 118.

[49]Ralph S. Anderson, "The Death and Burial of Sick Products," *Journal of Marketing* 28 (April 1964): 1–7.

[50]"Shakeout Hangs over the Defense Industry as Spending Flattens and Arms Trade Slows," *Investor's Daily* 21 October 1988, 1, 32.

[51]This section is from Philip R. Cateora, *International Marketing,* 6th ed. (Homewood, Ill.: Richard D. Irwin, 1987), 387–402.

[52]"The Furor over Formula Is Coming to a Boil," *Business Week* April 1990, 52–53.

[53]*Ibid.*

[54]*Ibid.*

7 Business Price Planning and Strategy

Learning Objectives

After reading this chapter, you should be able to:

- Explain the pricing methods and strategies most commonly utilized by business price setters.
- Discuss the concept of price elasticity and the role of cost-benefit analysis in demand determination.
- Relate the changes that take place in the pricing element of the marketing mix throughout the various phases of the product life cycle.
- Describe conditions under which a price-leadership strategy would be used.
- Comprehend the importance and operation of competitive bidding in setting business prices in appropriate markets.
- Communicate the value of leasing as an alternative to purchasing in a business market.
- Distinguish among the various types of price adjustments commonly given in business purchasing transactions.
- Appreciate the nature of the pricing function in international business markets.

Chapter Outline

Learning Objectives

Business Pricing: An Overview

Major Factors Influencing Price Strategy

- Competition
- Cost
- Demand
- Pricing Objectives
  - Generate profit
  - Achieve return on investment
  - Maintain or increase market share
- Impact on Other Products
- Legal Considerations
  - Price fixing
  - Exchanging price information
  - Predatory pricing

Pricing Methods

- Marginal Pricing
- Economic Value to the Customer (EVC)
- Break-Even Analysis
  - Calculating a break-even point
- Target Return-on-Investment Pricing

Demand Assessment and Strategy

- Price Elasticity of Demand
- Cost-Benefit Analysis

Pricing across the Product Life Cycle (Life-Cycle Costing)

- Introduction Phase: New-Product Pricing Strategies
  - Price skimming
  - Market-penetration pricing
- Growth Phase
- Maturity Phase
- Decline Phase

Price-Leadership Strategy

Competitive Bidding in the Business Market

- Closed versus Open Bidding
- A Probabilistic Bidding Model

Leasing in the Business Market

- Advantages of Leasing for the Buyer
  - No down payment
  - Avoids risks of owners
  - Tax benefits
- Advantages of Leasing for the Seller
  - Increased sales
  - Ongoing business relationship with the lessee
  - Residual value retained
- Types of Lease Arrangements
- Types of business leases
  - Operating lease
  - Direct-financing lease

Pricing Policies in Business Pricing Strategy
- Trade Discounts
- Quantity Discounts
- Cash Discounts
- Geographical Price Adjustments

International Marketing Pricing Policy

Summary

Key Terms

Review Questions

Cases
- Case 7-1
- Case 7-2

Suggested Additional Readings

Endnotes

BUSINESS PRICING: AN OVERVIEW

Price planning is not a precise science, and considering the importance attached to the task, it is not an easy job. Because there are so many variables to consider, pricing decisions are often made by guesswork, intuition, or reliance on such methods as traditional markup percentages. A large number of both internal and external variables should be systematically studied if effective price strategy is to take place. Some writers have concluded that many managers are relatively naive when it comes to the price variable and that unsophisticated pricing methods prevail because of a lack of knowledge and understanding.[1] Like other components of marketing strategy, price planning and strategy involves intelligent input concerning environmental as well as operational conditions. Gaining an understanding of what customers would be willing to pay for existing or potential product offerings remains a challenging task for business marketers.[2]

Before marketers can determine how to make pricing work for them, they have to know what it is specifically that they want pricing to do for their business. Do they want to increase sales or market share, maximize cash flow or profit, deter competition from entering the company's niche, establish an image or position, or perhaps some combination of these objectives? Answers to these questions must be forthcoming before an intelligent job of price planning and strategy can be done.[3] Decision making for pricing is one of the oldest marketing topics, drawing significantly on the economics literature, which certainly predates most marketing pricing analyses. Other disciplines, including psychology and sociology, have also contributed to the development of strategic pricing material.[4]

MAJOR FACTORS INFLUENCING PRICE STRATEGY

As is shown in Figure 7-1, important factors that influence price strategy include competition, cost, demand, pricing objectives, the impact of price on other products, and legal considerations. Each of these is discussed below.

Competition

In most highly competitive markets, the use of certain strategic and tactical pricing practices is a key factor in determining profitability.[5] There are two kinds of competitive factors that influence price. One factor is the competitive effect on demand for the marketer's product. This includes competition from directly comparable products—Apple Computer against IBM, Moore Business Forms against Uarco Incorporated, and UPS against Federal Express. There is competition from substitute products—plastic against steel and synthetic against natural substances (synthetic versus crude rubber, for example). The other competitive factor is the reaction of competitors to any price move the business marketer might make. If the marketer raises the price, will the competition hold its price level and hope to pick up customers? If the price is lowered, will the competition ignore the change, move in aggressively, and possibly retaliate with a lower price?

Cost

Fixed and variable costs are of major concern to the business marketer charged with establishing price levels. If a manufacturer is a low-cost producer relative to competition, the firm will earn additional profits by maintaining prices at competitive levels. The additional dollars generated can be used to promote the product aggressively, hoping to increase the overall visibility of the business. On the other hand, if the costs are high in relation to the competition, the manufacturer

FIGURE 7-1 **Major Factors Influencing Price Strategy**

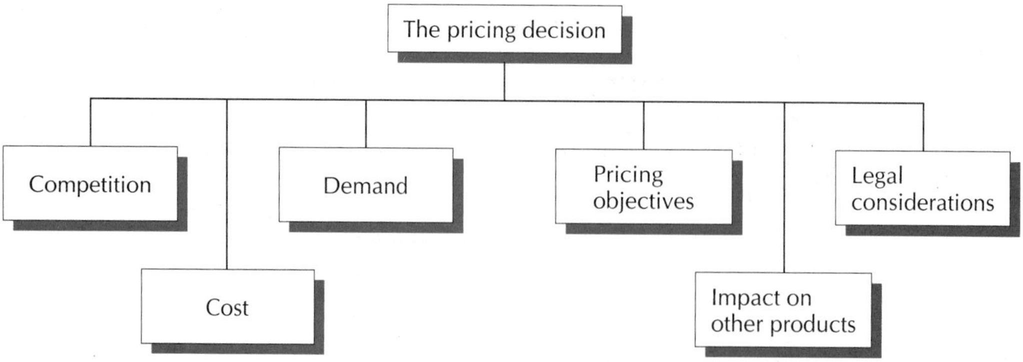

may be in no position to reduce prices, since such action can lead to a price war that it will probably lose. Various elements of cost must be differently related in setting prices, with the analysis demonstrating how computations of full cost, incremental cost, and conversion can vary and how these costs affect product-line prices.

Demand

Demand is based on a variety of considerations, of which price is just one. Some of these considerations are as follows:[6]

(1) Ability of customers to buy
(2) Willingness of customers to buy
(3) Benefits that the product provides to customers
(4) Prices of substitute products
(5) Potential market for the product (unfulfilled demand or saturated market)
(6) Nature of nonprice competition
(7) Segments in the market
(8) Customer behavior in general

All these factors (and more, such as psychological aspects) are interdependent, and it is not easy to estimate their relationship to each other precisely. However, they do point out that contemporary business buyers are highly sophisticated and that these buyers consider a wide variety of factors in deciding exactly what products to buy.

Pricing Objectives

An important step in pricing strategy is to determine goals and objectives prior to setting price points or levels. The principal pricing objectives of most business-to-business firms are the following.

General profit. Profit is probably the most often stated company objective. A profit-maximization goal is likely to be far more beneficial to the firm if practiced over the long run. If short-run profit is the goal, there is the tendency to cut cost, sometimes to the detriment of quality and customer service. A firm entering a new geographic market, or introducing a new product or product line, may be well advised to set low prices initially, so as to build a large customer base. In this case, the goal would be to optimize profits over the long run, focusing attention on the demand curve.

Achieve return on investment. Products may be priced to achieve a certain percentage return on investment. This criterion is typically selected as a goal by firms that are leaders in their industry—firms such as General Motors and Alcoa. With this approach, an organization prices its products to achieve a specific rate of return on investment. Alcoa, DuPont, General Electric, General Motors, Johns-Manville, and U.S. Steel price many products to yield a target return. This objective makes it simpler to measure and control the performance of separate divisions, departments, and products. The trend of using a target return as a pricing objective has brought the following results:

- Increased awareness and concern for the relationships among investments, capital, and profits in planning and budgeting
- The use of simple, explicit standards in measuring the returns of divisions, departments, and product groups
- The use of cost-plus pricing to ensure that target returns will be achieved

It must be noted, however, that this approach is not appropriate for all firms.

Maintain or increase market share. Maintenance of, or changes in, market share is a popular type of objective because market share is measurable and may be a better indicator of general financial corporate health than return on investment, especially when the total market is growing. Middlemen prefer to handle rapidly moving products and will tend to drop those falling behind. Gaining market share because of a good reputation for quality and customer service will generally affect long-run profits favorably.

These objectives are not necessarily mutually exclusive, nor is this list by any means complete. Other objectives such as overhead absorption, demand regulation, the establishment of market leadership, image projection, line-extension differentiation, and cash generation may work toward achievement of the firm's overall marketing objectives. If maintaining or increasing market share is a strong objective, then pricing action will reflect this orientation.

Impact on Other Products

Often the purchase of one product increases the likelihood of the purchase, by the same customer, of another product or product line. One product may enhance the value or the effective use of the other product, in addition to the possibility that some buyers might encounter savings in time and effort by purchasing two or more products from the same source. If, for example, a business buyer is buying a particular grade of tool steel from a local distributor to do a particular job, that buyer would be inclined to buy other grades of tool steel from the same supplier as the need arose. There is a strong likelihood that the buyer would also buy needed cutting tools and lubricants from that supplier. These complementary products would in all likelihood be price elastic, as the supplier's inventory and delivery capabilities would more than offset a possible price advantage gained by the buyer by shopping around. This scenario may not hold true if the purchase involved a major new-buy situation, or when the quantity to be bought is large enough to make the price element a major buying determinant.

Legal Considerations

Business marketers should be prepared to justify price levels, along with quantity and trade discounts. As shown in Exhibit 7-1, under the *Robinson-Patman Act*, quantity discounts are legal if the resulting price differentials do not exceed the cost differentials in manufacturing, selling, and delivering the product to buyers who are in competition with each other. Furthermore, although the Act does not discuss trade discounts specifically, several court cases seem to uphold the legality of offering separate discounts to separate classes of buyers, as long as the discounts are offered in return for services rendered (that is, marketing functions performed). Business marketers should be aware of the possible legal problems that can arise in using certain types of discounts and allowances. Care is needed to avoid engaging in illegal price discrimination, along with such practices as price fixing, the exchange of price information among competitors, and predatory pricing.

Price fixing. Price fixing is illegal per se. Collusion, or the practice of several competitors setting a price, is a direct violation of the Sherman Antitrust Act. Such price fixing is illegal even if the fixed prices are fair. Price fixing is more likely to happen when the number of firms in a particular industry is small, and the product is relatively homogeneous (as in the case of oligopolies). When there are many firms, or when heterogeneous products are involved, competitors will find it difficult to agree on what the fixed price will be.

Exchanging price information. This activity is related to price fixing and occurs when competitors exchange information regarding prices, inventory levels, and the like. It becomes illegal when it leads to price agreements, however, as this is tantamount to price fixing.

EXHIBIT 7-1 **Robinson-Patman Act (1936)**

SECTION 2(a) Makes it illegal to discriminate in price among different buyers of commodities of like grade and quality when the effects result in a reduction in competition at the sellers' level, at the buyers' level, or at the buyers' customers' level. Different prices can be charged if they do not exceed differences in the costs of serving different customers. The power to establish maximum limits on quantity discounts granted to any customer or class of customers—regardless of differences in the costs of serving—is given to the FTC.

Section 2(b) Continues the Clayton Act's provision of "meeting competition in good faith."

Section 2(c) The granting of "dummy" brokerage allowances—given by a seller to a buyer or a brokerage firm owned by the buyer—is illegal.

Section 2(d) and (e) Supplementary services or allowances such as advertising allowances must be made to all purchasers on a proportionately equal basis.

Section 2(f) It is illegal for buyers knowingly to induce discriminatory prices from sellers.

Predatory pricing. This practice involves the cutting of prices (usually by a larger producer) to a point that is at or below cost for the purpose of eliminating competition. It is an attempt to monopolize the market, and in most cases, is considered illegal.

PRICING METHODS

Once a complete study has been made of all the variables that can have a major impact on pricing in business markets, marketing managers can turn their attention to the development of specific pricing methods likely to appeal to these markets. In business pricing, neither cost nor demand approaches can succeed without regard for the other. Generating enough revenue to cover costs is a function of having competitive cost structure as well as sufficient demand. In the long run, all costs must be covered; yet, unless there is sufficient demand for the goods, there will not be revenues to cover the costs. Several pricing methods will be examined.

Marginal Pricing

Marginal pricing, also known as *contribution pricing*, is a basic conceptual approach to setting prices, with the aim being to maximize profits by producing the number of units at which marginal cost is just less than, or equal to, marginal revenue. The product is sold at that price. If the amount of additional revenue the firm receives from selling one additional unit is more than this marginal cost of producing that unit, then a profit is made. If the marginal revenue attained by producing an additional unit is less than the marginal cost of producing it, the firm will lose money on that additional unit, and it should not be produced. Consider the case of Chainco, a manufacturer of tread chain for crawler tractor vehicles.

> Chainco's regular business is the manufacture of tread chain for OEMs that produce crawler tractors for construction, agricultural, and military markets. Chainco employs a full-absorption cost system, which means that sales volume, revenue, and costs of manufacture are preplanned, and that variable and fixed costs are allocated over a program period, usually one year. This accounting method allows Chainco to calculate standard costs and levels of profitability of all their products for the program period. This approach is typical of many business-to-business companies and is characterized by an annual forecasting and budgeting ritual, with updating of standard costs. Chainco limits its planned government business to 10 percent of total forecast. Government items are distinguished as such and have standard costs, including allocation of appropriate program and standby fixed costs. At midyear, Chainco received a bid invitation from the Department of the Interior for a considerable amount of crawler chain of a type similar to that manufactured for OEM customers. This was a one-time sale opportunity that would not require selling expense or the normal allocation of administrative expense and fixed costs. They decided to use a marginal-pricing approach and bid the proposal on the basis of out-of-pocket variable and fixed

costs, plus profit. Using this approach, Chainco was awarded the contract. The bid price was less than standard cost for the items.[7]

Was this transaction a sound business deal? Most executives would agree that it was. Marginal pricing is often used by contract bidders to gain unplanned business, or to utilize idle capacity. Figure 7-2 illustrates the factors involved in this approach. The overall objective of marginal pricing is to recover variable cost for marginal volume with add-on for profit and/or to recover from negative variance. The graph shows the difference between regular business—planned volume

FIGURE 7-2 **Marginal Pricing**

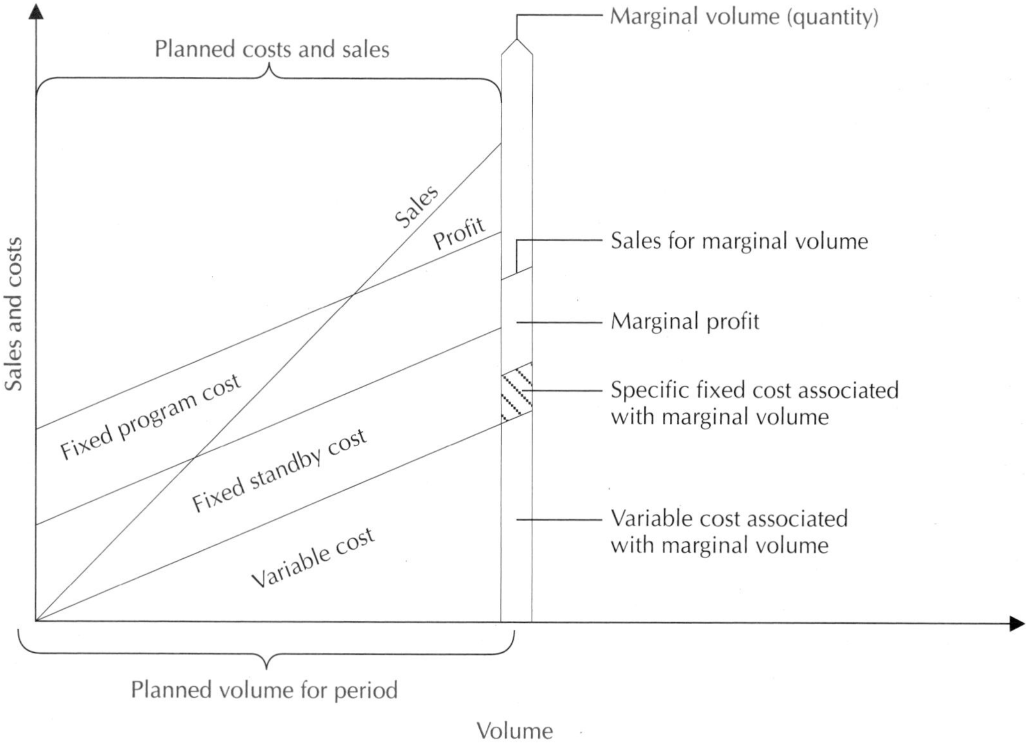

Pricing objective: Recover variable cost for marginal volume with add-on for profit and/or to recover from negative variance.

Pricing strategy: Depending on demand and capacity situation, price to gain volume to reduce idle capacity with profit add-on depending on specific situation.

Legend: Sales: Gross revenue from sale or profit
Profit: Gross profit above designated costs
Variable cost: Material, labor, variable overhead, and variable selling expense
Fixed standby cost: Planned operating cost under zero-volume condition
Fixed program cost: Planned cost for R&D, marketing, advertising, and improvement programs

for a period—and marginal business. In marginal pricing, adjusted fixed costs and marginal profit are substituted for conventional amounts.

Economic Value to the Customer

Many customers buy on price, which is visible and measurable. Some suppliers compete on the same basis for the same reasons. However, a strategic advantage based on the total value delivered to the customer is far less easily duplicated by competitors. As companies like 3M and Hewlett-Packard have shown, a value-based strategy can be a uniquely effective way over time to gain a commanding lead over the competition. Recognizing this fact, some firms use a relatively new method of analyzing their products' economic value to the customer (EVC).

This economic value is illustrated in Figure 7-3, when two products, X and Y, are compared. Because of favorable start-up and postpurchase costs, as well as an additional incremental value of $100 for product X, the buyer (customer) should be willing to pay twice as much for product X ($600) than for product Y. From the manufacturer's viewpoint, it costs $300 to produce product X. Therefore, any price in excess of $300 constitutes a profit. Since any price under $600 gives the buyer a better deal than what will be realized from buying product Y, the supplier of product X has a $300 competitive advantage. In addition, supplier X could price the product to the customer at $475, which would result in $175 in profit and a $125 advantage over product Y for the customer.[8]

FIGURE 7-3 **The Economic Value to the Customer (EVC) Concept**

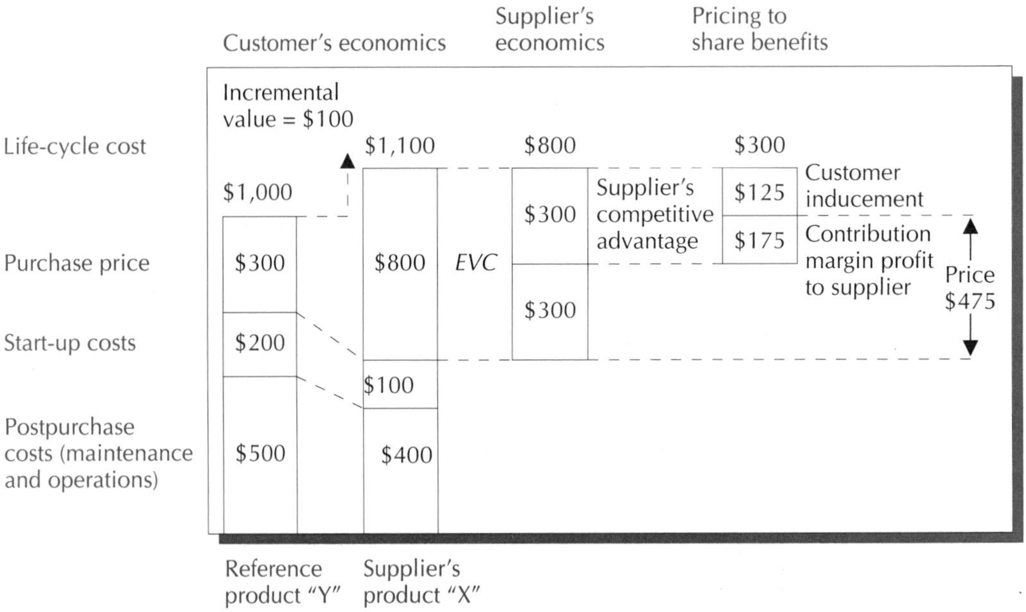

Adding value in this way can also mean making the product easier to use, making it more profitable, or giving it some other value advantage. Most professional buyers will pay a higher price when they perceive a greater value or benefit to them than what they would receive from buying a competitive product.

Break-even Analysis

Break-even analysis defines the point (break-even point) at which a firm's revenue will equal its total fixed and variable costs at a given price. Using various prices, a buyer can utilize the following formula to calculate the number of units that would have to be sold at each price to break even:

$$\text{Break-Even Point (BEP)} = \frac{\text{Fixed Cost}}{\text{Unit Price} - \text{Unit Variable Cost}}$$

Calculating a break-even point. Consider a company that manufactures a water sealer used to stop leaks in cement retainer walls. In 1990, the company sold 1,600,000 gallons of the sealer at a price of $3.00 per gallon with a variable production cost per gallon of $1.50. The fixed manufacturing costs were $1,550,000.

In 1991, more automated equipment will be used in production. This will increase the fixed manufacturing costs for the year to $1,785,000. The variable production cost per gallon has been estimated at $1.30 per gallon, and sales volume has a forecasted increase of 12.5 percent.

In 1990, the break-even point was 1,033,333 units, calculated as follows:

$$\frac{\$1{,}550{,}000}{\$1.50} = 1{,}033{,}333 \text{ units}$$

In 1991, the break-even point will be 1,050,000 units, calculated as follows:

$$\frac{\$1{,}785{,}000}{\$1.70} = 1{,}050{,}000 \text{ units}$$

Break-even analysis is a tool used by the business marketer to determine the level of sales required to cover all relevant fixed and variable costs. This analysis indicates the impact that different pricing strategies will have on profit margins; it also identifies the minimum price below which losses will occur. Price should not be set without first determining what will happen to profits at various price levels.

Target Return-on-Investment Pricing

Some business-to-business firms set annual return-on-investment (ROI) targets such as an ROI of 20 percent. *Target return-on-investment pricing* is a method of setting prices to achieve such an investment goal; it is one of the most widely used methods of establishing price strategy. Price is determined by adding a desired rate of return-on-investment total costs. A break-even analysis is performed for expected production and sales levels, and a rate of return is added.

Assume that a small business owner sets a target ROI of 10 percent, double that achieved the previous year. The owner considers raising the average price of a business widget to $54 or $58—up from last year's average of $50. To do such a thing, the owner can improve product quality, which will increase cost but which will probably also affect the decreased revenue from the lower number of units that can be sold next year.

To handle this wide variety of scenarios, the use of computerized spreadsheets to project operating statements based on various assumptions is clearly in order. Table 7-1 shows a computerized spreadsheet that results from software programs such as VisiCalc and Lotus 1-2-3. The assumptions are shown at the top, and the projected results at the bottom. The results from a prior year's operating statement are shown in the column headed "Last Year," and the assumptions and spreadsheet results for four different sets of assumptions are shown in columns A, B, C, and D.

In choosing a price or another action using spreadsheet results, the owner must (1) study the results of the computer simulation projections; and (2) assess the realism of the assumptions underlying each set of projections. For example, the owner sees from the bottom row of Table 7-1 that all four spreadsheet simulations achieve the after-tax target ROI of 10 percent. Yet, after more thought, the owner judges that it would be more realistic to set an average price of $58 per unit, allow the unit variable cost to increase by 20 percent to account for increased quality, and settle for the same unit sales as the one thousand units sold last year. In this computerized spreadsheet approach to target ROI pricing, the owner selects simulation D and has a goal of 14 percent after-tax ROI.

DEMAND ASSESSMENT AND STRATEGY

Before deciding just what type of pricing method to use in a particular market, the marketer must have a clear understanding of the nature of the demand in that market. Demand refers to the amount of a good or service that a buyer or buyers are willing and able to purchase at a particular moment at each possible price. Demand is more than a desire to purchase; it is the ability to purchase as well.

Price Elasticity of Demand

At lower prices, one may assume that more is bought. But how much more? Similarly, at higher prices, less is bought. Yet, how much less is actually bought—much less or only a little less? To answer a question such as this one, a business marketer should make use of the concept of *price elasticity of demand*, which states

TABLE 7-1 **Results of a Computer Spreadsheet Sim[illegible] a Target Return On Investment**

Assumptions or Results	Financial Element	Last Year	[illegible]	[illegible]	[illegible]	[illegible]
Assumptions	Price per unit (P)	$50[illegible]	[illegible]	[illegible]	[illegible]	[illegible]
	Units sold (Q)	1,[illegible]	[illegible]	[illegible]	[illegible]	[illegible]
	Change in unit variable cost (UVC)	[illegible]	[illegible]	[illegible]	[illegible]	[illegible]
	Unit variable cost	$[illegible]	[illegible]	[illegible]	[illegible]	[illegible]
	Total expenses	$[illegible]	[illegible]	[illegible]	[illegible]	[illegible]
	Owner's salary	[illegible]	[illegible]	[illegible]	[illegible]	[illegible]
	Investment	$20,[illegible]	[illegible]	[illegible]	[illegible]	[illegible]
	State and federal taxes	50%	[illegible]	[illegible]	[illegible]	[illegible]
Spreadsheet simulation results	Net sales (P × Q)	$50,000	$64,800	[illegible]	[illegible]	[illegible]
	Less: COGS (Q × UVC)	$22,000	$29,040	$26,[illegible]	[illegible]	[illegible]
	Gross margin	$28,000	$35,760	$32,780	$34,[illegible]	[illegible]
	Less: total expenses	8,000	8,000	8,000	8,000	[illegible]
	Less: owner's salary	18,000	18,000	18,000	18,000	18,000
	Net profit before taxes	$ 2,000	$ 9,760	$ 6,780	$ 8,760	$ 5,600
	Less: taxes	1,000	4,880	3,390	4,380	2,800
	Net profit after taxes	$ 1,000	$ 4,880	$ 3,390	$ 4,380	$ 2,800
	Investment	$20,000	$20,000	$20,000	$20,000	$20,000
	Return on investment	5.0%	24.4%	17.0%	21.9%	14.0%

simply that demand is elastic if quantity is highly responsive to price, and inelastic if not. In other words, "elasticity" is the relative change in the dependent variable divided by the relative change in the independent variable. The dependent variable is quantity demanded; the independent variable is price. Price elasticity of demand (E) is expressed as follows:

$$E = \frac{(\text{Initial Quantity Demanded} - \text{New Quantity Demanded})/\text{Initial Quantity Demanded}}{(\text{Initial Price} - \text{New Price})/\text{Initial Price}}$$

Price elasticity of demand assumes three forms: elastic demand, inelastic demand, and unitary demand. *Elastic demand* exists when a small-percentage decrease in price produces a larger-percentage increase in quantity demanded. Price elasticity is greater than 1 with elastic demand. *Inelastic demand* exists when a small-percentage decrease in price produces a smaller-percentage increase in quantity demanded. With inelastic demand, price elasticity is less than 1. *Unitary demand elasticity* exists when the percentage change in price is identical to the percentage change in quantity demanded. In this instance, price elasticity is equal to 1.

asticity of demand is determined by a number of factors. First, the stitutes a product or service has, the more likely that product will be lastic." Plastic and steel may be a substitute for each other in particular ons, so one or the other can be said to be price elastic. Second, products services considered to be necessities are generally "price inelastic." For ex- mple, office supplies, in general, are price inelastic, whereas new office furniture is price elastic. However, although the office-supplies product category is price inelastic, the demand for a specific brand, such as BIC pens, may be highly elastic. Thus, product categories and individual brands within the category may have totally different elasticities of demand. Price elasticity is important to the business marketing manager because of its relationship to total revenue and price-setting strategies. For instance, with elastic demand, total revenue increases when price decreases but decreases when price increases. With inelastic demand, total revenue increases when price increases and decreases when price decreases. Finally, with unitary demand, total revenue is unaffected by a slight price change.[9]

Cost-Benefit Analysis

Cost-benefit analysis (not to be confused with value analysis as discussed in Chapter 3) is the technique of assigning a dollar value to the costs and benefits of a product or service, along with the customer's usage of the product or service. When used in determining demand, cost-benefit analysis is an analysis of benefits received and costs incurred by the customer in buying and using a business product or service. The comparison of costs and benefits can be used to gain the customer's perspective of the business product or service, thereby allowing the business marketer the opportunity to set prices more realistically. Some firms see the buyer's perception of value, not the seller's cost, as the key to pricing. They use the nonprice variables in the marketing mix to build up perceived value in the buyer's mind. Price is set to capture the perceived value. (See Exhibit 3-2 for an example of perceived-value pricing.)

If the business marketer charges more than the buyers' perceived benefits of what the product or service is worth, company sales will suffer. Other firms may underprice their product or service. In such a situation, the product or service will sell well, but less revenue is generated than would be the case if price were raised to the perceived-value level.

CONCEPT QUESTIONS

1. What is the basic purpose of the Robinson-Patman Act?
2. Why is marginal pricing used by contract bidders?
3. What is the meaning of cost-benefit analysis in demand determination?

PRICING ACROSS THE PRODUCT LIFE CYCLE (LIFE-CYCLE COSTING)

In addition to controllable internal factors, external factors must be considered in developing prices for new products, along with changes in both environments, which may require a review of the prices of products already on the market. If a large, dominant firm in the industry raises or lowers prices, other firms in the industry will be forced to examine their prices, as the product or product line moves through the stages of the product life cycle. The nature of the demand for the product or service in question is one of the most important considerations in the pricing decision, and the business price maker must determine the precise relationship between changes in price and demand. In order to make the best decisions concerning price policy and specific pricing problems, the marketer should endeavor to learn as much as possible about the character of demand and how demand might be affected by adjustments in price in both the short and the long run, as the product moves through the product life cycle.

Introduction Phase: New-Product Pricing Strategies

A new product usually enjoys its greatest degree of differentiation during the introductory stage of the product life cycle (PLC), with demand being more inelastic at this stage than at any other stage of the PLC. However, the substantial investment that the firm must recover forces the price setter to decide just how fast it will be necessary to recover that investment. Whether an investment will be recovered quickly, or over the product life span, depends on such factors as the nature of the product, the projected product life, the nature of potential competition, and the financial strength of the firm. Two opposite pricing strategies for introducing a new product are *market skimming*, setting a relatively high price that will encourage competitive entry; and *market penetration*, setting a price at or near the point it will reach eventually after competition develops. With market penetration, the firm tries to gain a large volume of initial sales even though profit per unit may be low.

Price skimming. With price skimming, the introductory price is set relatively high, thereby attracting buyers at the top of the product's demand curve. This permits the recovery of research and development costs more quickly as the firm attempts to "skim" the market. DuPont is often cited as a prime user of a price-skimming practice. On a new discovery such as cellophane and nylon, the firm determined the highest price it could charge given the benefits of the new product over other products customers might buy. DuPont set prices that made it just worthwhile enough for some segments of the market to adopt the new material. After the initial sales slacked off, the firm lowered the price to draw in the next, price-sensitive, layer of customers. In this way, DuPont skimmed a maximum amount of revenue from the various segments of the market. As is demonstrated in Figure 7-4, a skimming strategy assumes that layers of customers can be peeled off the demand curve.

A price-skimming maneuver is not without potential problems, however. The high initial price tends to attract competition, as other firms see that the product is selling well at a relatively high price. Consequently, competitors tend to introduce rival versions. By the time the business marketer is ready to peel off the next layer of customers, rival offerings may well already be on the market. Therefore, a skimming strategy will be more effective when the product has a strong patent position, or when there are other barriers to market entry, such as extremely complex technology, or very high capital requirements.

Market-penetration pricing. Despite the many advantages, a skimming-price policy is not appropriate for all new-product introductions. High prices may maximize profits during the early part of the introductory phase of the PLC, but they also may prevent sales to many of the buyers upon whom the firm relies. The penetration pricing strategy uses low price as an entering wedge. Such an approach is likely to be desirable under any of the following conditions: (1) when sales volume of the product is very sensitive to price, even in the early stages of introduction; (2) when it is possible to achieve substantial economies in unit cost of manufacturing and distributing the product by operating at large volume; (3) when a product faces threats of strong potential competition very soon after introduction; and (4) when there is no "elite" market—that is, no class of buyers willing to pay a higher price to obtain the newest and the best.[10]

FIGURE 7-4 **Price Skimming**

If the original skimming price is within the expected price range 1, the marketer will peel off customers along the A portion of the demand curve. If the price is lowered within expected price range 2, the marketer will peel off the second layer of customers along the B portion of the demand curve.

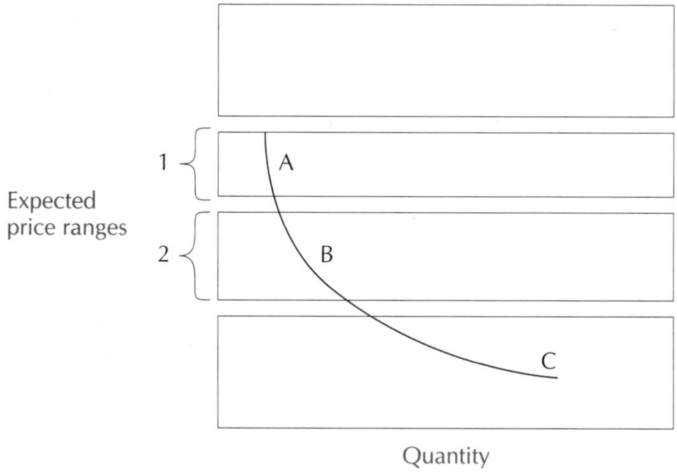

While a penetration pricing policy car
uct life cycle, this strategy should at least
marketed at all. Texas Instruments is a p
ing. This firm historically has set a price a
the market, experiences falling costs thro
curve concept, and cuts its price further a
the cumulative production volume of a
producing that product will decline at a p
experience in producing the product. Cos
tive, and operations in general become m

In contrast to DuPont's skimming str
tion pricing for some products. Dow pric
stresses low-margin, commodity produc

Growth Phase

A product in the growth phase of the PLC is generally faced with severe competitive pressures, with business buyers looking at price as being more important in the buying decision. The benefits of economies of scale, and the effects of the experience curve referred to earlier, might allow the firm to lower price as a competitive strategy. Competition is aggressive, as this is a period of rapid market acceptance and increasing profits. Profits tend to peak toward the end of the market-growth phase, and the producer faces a trade-off between high market share and high current profit.

Maturity Phase

To price appropriately in this phase, the business marketer needs to know when the product is approaching maturity. The marketer may find it desirable to reduce prices as soon as symptoms of deterioration appear. Some of these symptoms are as follows:[12]

(1) Weakening in brand preference. This may be evidenced by a higher cross-elasticity of demand among leading products, the leading brand being able to continue demanding as much price premium as it initially did, without losing any position.

(2) Narrowing physical variation among products. This occurs as the best designs are developed and standardized.

(3) Market saturation. The ratio of replacement sales to new-equipment sales serves as an indicator of the competitive degeneration of products.

(4) The stabilization of production methods. This is indicated by the slow rate of technological advance and high average age of equipment.

Decline Phase

This phase of the PLC presents the business price setter with a number of opportunities. Cost control becomes increasingly important as demand drops, possibly allowing the marketer to leave the price alone while maintaining short-term profit objectives as the product dies a natural death. In the absence of tight cost control, the strategy may be to raise price, taking advantage of the segments with inelastic demand. A final pricing strategy could be to use the product as a "loss leader." Pricing the product at cost, or even under cost—much the same as is done in consumer retail pricing strategy—might well help sell complementary products in the line.

PRICE-LEADERSHIP STRATEGY

In pricing a firm's products over their respective life cycles, business marketing managers in a leadership position must decide if and how they will pursue their task as a market leader. *Price-leadership strategy* prevails in oligopolistic situations; it is the practice by which one or a very few firms initiate price changes, with most or all the other firms in the industry following suit. When price leadership prevails in an industry, price competition does not exist. The burden of making critical pricing decisions is placed on the leading firm; others simply follow the leader.

Price leadership is found most often in industries whose products are similar, even standardized, and therefore considered by customers to be good substitutes for each other. In such industries, a firm would lose market share if it charged a higher price than its competitors. Price leadership is a way of coordinating prices without colluding. This practice is at once a sign of so much competition in an industry that all firms involved have to sell at about the same price in order to stay in business; or of so little competition that firms are able to coordinate their prices as they would under a collusive agreement. Usually the leader is the firm with the largest market share, such as U.S. Steel or IBM, or the firm that makes the first upward move. Implicit in the very fact of leadership is a willingness to live and let live. Price wars are rare, as price deviation is quickly disciplined.

Successful price leaders are characterized by the following description:[13]

(1) Large share of the industry's production capacity.

(2) Large market share.

(3) Commitment to a particular product class or grade.

(4) New, cost-efficient plants.

(5) Strong distribution system, perhaps including captive wholesale outlets.

(6) Good customer relations, such as technical assistance for business buyers, programs directed at end users, and special attention to important customers during shortage periods.

(7) An effective market-information system that provides analysis of the realities of supply and demand.
(8) Sensitivity to the price and profit needs of the rest of the industry.
(9) A sense of timing to know when price changes should be made.
(10) Sound management organization for pricing.
(11) Effective product-line financial controls, which are needed to make sound price leadership decisions.
(12) Attention to legal issues.

Price leadership requires certain things of leaders. The presence of a specific and consistent pricing strategy, the use of controlled power, and the recognition of the rights of followers to their respective market positions will sustain a leadership position. The threat of independent pricing action is always there, ready to break out if the leader fails to make the right decisions. The leader must be aware that if the wrong decisions are made, followers will, in all likelihood, destroy that position of leadership.

COMPETITIVE BIDDING IN THE BUSINESS MARKET

Buyers for business market leaders and followers alike engage in competitive bidding. *Competitive bidding* is a process whereby a business buyer will request price bids from interested suppliers on a proposed purchase or contract. This is an invitation to negotiate for the best combination of quality, service, and price. This process is used not only for custom-engineered products but also for standard manufactured products, components, and services. The buyer sends inquiries or "requests for quotations" (RFQ) to firms able to produce in conformity with requested requirements. The marketer must make the decision on whether or not to bid on a specific supply requirement or job, because the bidding process requires that quotes be received in final form by a certain deadline. Firms that bid for work must deal with the risks and uncertainties connected with such bidding. An individual firm's pricing objectives and perception of the factors influencing the pricing decision will to a great extent determine or dictate the policy to adopt on bid pricing.[14]

Competitive bids from several different firms for basically identical items will vary, even when internal cost structures might be essentially the same for all competitors. The market-price level is therefore not a specific value for a given item, but rather is a wide display of prices with fairly well-defined limits for each industry. Also important in deciding whether or not to bid is excess capacity and alternative opportunities to utilize this capacity. Related to this is the extent to which competitive bidders have excess capacity and, therefore, would be expected to bid low. For the business marketer, this could mean substantial opportunity along with substantial potential pitfalls. As explained in the box entitled "Business-to-Business Marketing in Action," conjoint analysis is an analytical tool that enables marketers to understand the bidding process better, particularly the reasons as to why some bids are rejected.

Closed versus Open Bidding

Government units (federal and local) and most public institutions are required to buy products and services on the competitive bidding system. In such a situation, the contemplated purchase is advertised in advance, giving the potential business supplier the opportunity to consider submitting a bid. Many of these bids are made public; thus, price competition is stressed. A price setter often is required to submit a performance bond along with the bid to assure that quality and service will not suffer due to the emphasis on price. Such a requirement may discourage some marketers from competing in this arena.

Competitive bidding can take the form of "closed bidding," which consists of sealed bids, all of which are opened, reviewed, and evaluated at the same time. Again, price is stressed, with the lowest bid usually winning the contract. Although the lowest bidder is not guaranteed the contract, this bidder will normally win the business if the bid is for standard products or services, or if the product is to be made to exact buyer specifications. Competitive bidding can also take the form of "open bidding," which is more informal, allows for negotiation, and is often used when there is much flexibility with regard to buyer specifications. Complex technical requirements would utilize an open bidding process, as would the purchase of products where specific requirements are hard to define precisely. Assume the buying firm needs tooling or machinery to accomplish a production task but does not know exactly what configuration the tooling or machinery should be. The buyer can show the seller what needs to be done, giving the seller great latitude in solving the problem. The buyer is, in effect, asking the seller to solve a problem. The seller would submit an "open" bid or "idea" and possibly discuss and modify it with members of the buying center; negotiate price, delivery, terms, and so on; and receive the contract. This open bidding process is quite common in high-tech industries.

Whether or not to bid, as mentioned earlier, can present the marketer with a dilemma. A number of criteria in determining whether or not to bid on a job are included in the following questions:[15]

(1) Is the dollar value of the job large enough to warrant the expense involved in making the bid?

(2) Are the product or service specifications ("specs") precise enough so that the cost of production can be accurately estimated?

(3) Will the acceptance of the bid adversely affect production and the ability to serve other customers?

BUSINESS-TO-BUSINESS MARKETING IN ACTION

CONJOINT ANALYSIS CAN EXPLAIN WHY SOME BUSINESS BIDS ARE REJECTED

Conjoint analysis can help business marketers understand the criteria prospective clients use when choosing suppliers. Selection criteria can be an especially perplexing issue when requests for proposals are solicited. After the winning bid is selected, the other bidders may find it difficult to understand why their bids were rejected.

The best way to gain that knowledge is through conjoint analysis. It yields answers superior to those developed through structured and unstructured postbidding interviews with clients, in which attempts to rationalize selecting the winning bid may cloud the postbid analysis conducted by marketing researchers.

By contrast, conjoint analysis is largely nonverbal. Respondents choose from "packages" of attributes and features, so it best replicates the bidding process.

Complex trade-offs are the "meat" of conjoint analysis. Any conjoint procedure has respondents evaluate various packages or sets of attributes. Once these attributes are combined, the number of possible variations can be in the hundreds. Therefore, a computer program is used before data gathering begins to reduce the packages systematically, so there is a need to present all possible alternatives. Based on its use to reduce the number of combinations, each respondent will typically evaluate sixteen to thirty-six combinations.

After ranking the choices, the buyer's judgments are "decomposed" into separate utility charts which graphically depict the results.

In any business bidding case, options are built from as few as five to as many as twenty factors involved in bidding. Each factor will then have two to four (sometimes more) "levels" or choices.

An orthogonal array creates the packages to be ranked. The array allows the number of packages shown to be minimized. After all the respondents make their choices, the data then are analyzed through a second computer program. If desired, the results can be organized for specific clusters—by "price-sensitive" compared to "service-sensitive" segments, for example. Conjoint analysis techniques can be applied in just about any industry.

Source: Gabriel M. Gelb, "Conjoint Analysis Helps Explain the Bid Process," *Marketing News,* 22, March 14, 1988 (Chicago: American Marketing Association), pp. 1, 31. Used with permission.

(4) How much time is available to prepare a bid?

(5) What is the likelihood of winning the bid considering the presence and strength of other bidders?

A Probabilistic Bidding Model

Once the marketing manager has determined that a potentially profitable bidding opportunity is present, a bidding strategy must be developed. A *probabilistic bidding model* is a mathematical technique used to determine prices in a bidding situation; it assumes that competitors will behave in the future as they have in the past. This bidding model provides an objective procedure for evaluating potential profits of different pricing alternatives by drawing on past data and by making assumptions as to how competitors will behave in a bidding situation.

All probabilistic bidding models focus on three criteria: (1) the size of the bid, (2) the profit expected if the bid wins, and (3) the probability that the submitted bid will win. The optimum bid is the one that will return the highest profit to the firm; it can be expressed with the following formula:[16]

$$E(x) = P(x)Z(x)$$

where: x = Dollar amount of the bid
Z(x) = Profit if the bid is accepted
P(x) = Probability of the bid being accepted at this price
E(x) = Expected profit at this price

The most difficult part of using this formula is estimating the probability of a given bid being the lowest one submitted. This factor is P(x), shown above,

TABLE 7-2 **Relationship of Zephyr's Bids to Anderson's Estimated Direct Cost**

Project	Zephyr's Bids	Anderson's Estimated Direct Costs	Percent
1	19,800	15,000	132
2	88,400	65,000	136
3	62,800	40,000	157
4	33,750	25,000	133
5	72,500	50,000	145
6	11,100	10,000	111
7	64,860	47,000	138
8	12,080	8,000	151
9	53,760	32,000	168
10	99,400	70,000	142
11	29,700	22,000	135
12	60,900	42,000	145
13	39,900	30,000	133
14	29,800	20,000	149
15	23,250	15,000	155
16	34,440	21,000	164
17	47,520	36,000	132
18	43,200	30,000	144
19	41,160	28,000	147
20	73,750	59,000	125

Source: W. J. Morse, "Probabilistic Bidding Models: A Synthesis," *Business Horizons,* April 1975, Table 1, p. 68. Used with permission.

and success will depend to a large degree on the marketer's ability and experience in competitive bidding. A relatively high bid price, with the resulting large expected profit, will have a low probability of being accepted in a competitive situation. A low bid would probably show the opposite—a high probability of being accepted but projecting little or no profit. The purpose of a probabilistic bidding model is to find the bid with the optimum combination of profit and probability of acceptance.

In the equation noted above, the expected profit equals the probability of winning with a bid of X, multiplied by the profit associated with that bid. To demonstrate the basic model, use is made of two hypothetical competitors. The Anderson Company is considering bidding on a project against one known competitor, the Zephyr Company. Because the contract will be awarded to the lowest bidder, Anderson wishes to determine the probability that its bid will be lower than Zephyr's bid. The first step is to obtain information on previous relationships between Anderson's estimated direct costs and Zephyr's bids on similar projects. These data are shown in Table 7-2. The second step is to analyze the data in Table 7-2 to determine the probability that Zephyr will submit a bid higher than any given percent of Anderson's estimated direct costs. The result of this analysis is presented in Table 7-3 and Figure 7-5.

If Anderson submits a bid of 140 percent of estimated direct costs, as Table 7-3 and Figure 7-5 indicate, there is a 55 percent probability that such a bid will be lower than Zephyr's bid. If Anderson submits a bid of 110 percent of estimated direct costs, its bid will probably be lower than Zephyr's. Because the

TABLE 7-3 **Probability of Underbidding One Known Competitor**

Bid as a Percent of Estimated Direct Cost	Number of Higher Bids	Percent Higher (Probability of Underbidding)
110	20	100
115	19	95
120	19	95
125	19	95
130	18	90
135	15	75
140	11	55
145	9	45
150	6	30
155	4	20
160	2	10
165	1	5
170	0	0

Source: W. J. Morse, "Probabilistic Bidding Models: A Synthesis," *Business Horizons,* April 1975, Table 2, p. 69. Used with permission.

FIGURE 7-5 **Probability of Underbidding One Known Competitor**

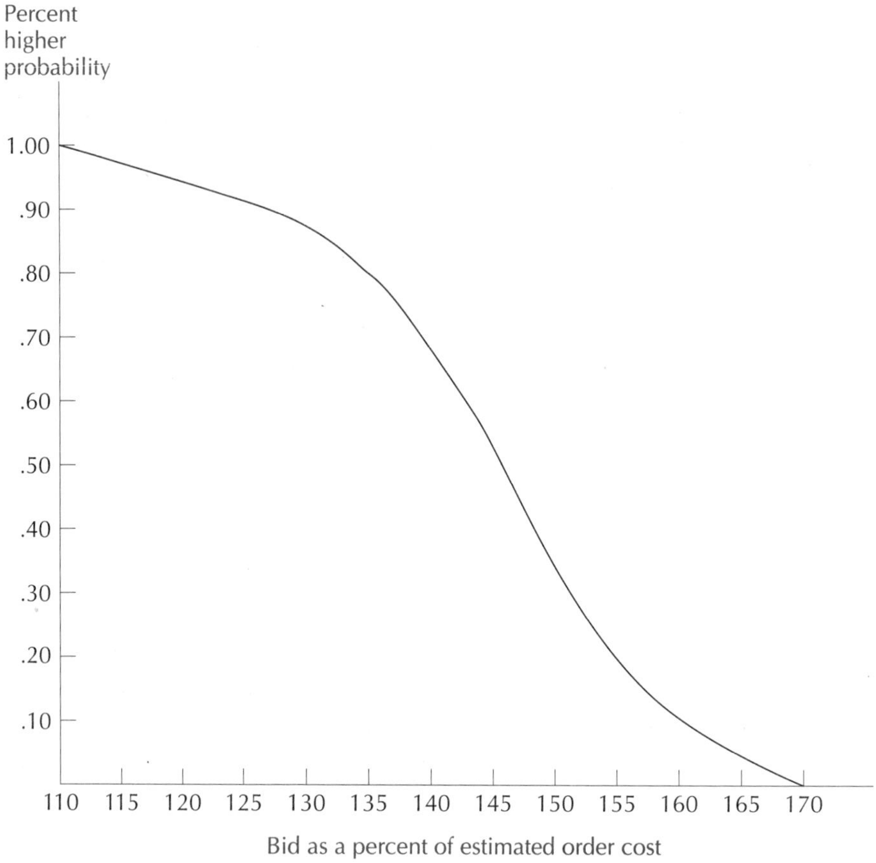

Source: W. J. Morse, "Probabilistic Bidding Models: A Synthesis," *Business Horizons,* April 1975, Figure 1, p. 70. Used with permission.

probabilistic bidding model considers only direct costs, the expected contribution margin of a bid must be determined. This computation is done by multiplying the difference between the bid price and the estimated direct costs by the probability that the bid will be accepted. To determine the optimum bid, the contribution margin, or contribution margin percent, on each bid under consideration must be multiplied by the probability that the bid will be lower than that of a competitor.[17] A bidder usually has several known or unknown competitors, and the model can be extended for these situations.

Models, such as the one presented above, are only one tool available to the business marketer; like other quantitative techniques, models usually cannot replace the professional judgment of the price setter. Other factors, some quantifiable and others nonquantifiable, must also be taken into consideration.

CONCEPT QUESTIONS

1. What is a price-leadership strategy?
2. How is price leadership sustained?
3. What is the purpose of a probabilistic bidding model?

LEASING IN THE BUSINESS MARKET

In addition to the choice of whether or not to engage in competitive bidding, business buyers must also decide in appropriate situations whether to buy or to lease an asset. In such situations, many business customers choose to lease rather than to purchase. For the astute business marketer, leasing can provide a very viable alternative to selling capital equipment. In FASB Statement no. 13, as amended and interpreted through May 1980 (latest change), a "lease" is defined "as an agreement conveying the right to use property, plant or equipment, usually for a stated period of time".[18] A lease involves a lessee and a lessor, with the "lessee" being the party who acquires the right to use the property, plant, or equipment; and the "lessor" being the party relinquishing the right in return for some form of consideration.

In the business market, leasing strategy is employed by most capital goods and equipment manufacturers, including those that market production machinery, postage meters, packaging equipment, textile equipment, copiers, and the like. As an example, in its 1988 financial statements, Farmland Industries reported leased assets including "railroad cars, automobiles...three fertilizer manufacturing facilities, electronic data processing equipment, and other manufacturing facilities." Indeed, almost any asset that can be acquired through purchase can be obtained through lease. Of the 600 companies recently surveyed, 542 companies, or approximately 90 percent, reported some form of lease arrangement.[19]

Leasing also lends itself to a "bundling pricing strategy." Bundling, also called "iceberg pricing," refers to the inclusion of an extra margin (for support services) in the price over and above the price of the product as such. This type of pricing strategy has been popular with companies that lease rather than sell their products. IBM once followed a bundling strategy, whereby it charged one fee for hardware, services, software, and consulting.[20] Failing to consider bundling as a strategic marketing variable may unnecessarily reduce the performance of the firm. The rationale behind product bundling is that it increases the firm's performance in creating a competitive advantage through increasing economics in providing the bundle, increasing product differentiation, increasing customer value, and/or raising entry barriers.[21]

Advantages of Leasing for the Buyer

From both the buyer's and seller's points of view, there are several advantages of leasing over purchasing. The following advantages pertain to the buyer.

No down payment. Lease agreements are frequently structured so that 100 percent of the value of the equipment is financed through the lease, making this an attractive alternative to a company that does not have sufficient cash for a down payment, or that wishes to use available capital for other operating or investing purposes. Because cash flow is critical to the survival and growth of a business, its management is very important.

Avoids risks of ownership. There are many risks of ownership including casualty loss, obsolescence, changing economic conditions, and physical deterioration. The lessee may terminate the lease (usually with a predetermined penalty) and thus avoid assuming the risk of these events. This flexibility is especially important to the buyer in a business where innovation and technological change make the future usefulness of a piece of equipment or facility highly uncertain. A good example of this condition in recent years has been the electronics industry with its rapid change in areas such as computer technology, robotics, and telecommunications.

Tax benefits. Many tax provisions grant benefits to owners of property. For example, prior to the 1986 Tax Reform Act, tax laws provided for investment tax credits that allowed owners of equipment a direct credit against income taxes payable either in the current period or in future periods through carryover provisions. If a lessor sells the asset, the benefits go with the property; but lease agreements can specify who gets the benefits. This flexibility makes it possible for the tax credits to be a significant element in lease negotiations. Further, by deducting lease payments, the lessee can write off the full cost of the asset. The tax deduction can be accelerated, since this is often spread over the period of the lease rather than the actual economic life of the equipment.

Advantages of Leasing for the Seller

Increased sales. By offering potential customers the option of leasing products, the marketer can significantly increase sales volume. Leasing can be a vehicle to attract customers who otherwise might find a product unaffordable. Market growth can be boosted since many more customers can afford to lease products than can afford to buy them.

Ongoing business relationship with the lessee. In leasing situations, the lessor and lessee maintain contact over a period of time, so that long-term business relationships will be promulgated through leasing.

Residual value retained. In many lease arrangements, title to the asset does not pass to the lessee. The lessor benefits from economic conditions that can result in a significant residual value at the end of the lease term. The lessor may lease the asset to another lessee or sell the property and realize an immediate gain. A lessor may also realize a profit from unexpected increases in residual values.

Types of Lease Arrangements

There are three basic ways of leasing equipment in the business sector. First, the business firm can lease directly to the customer, financing the lease arrangements itself. In essence, the seller acts as a financial institution would, operating on the basis of monthly or quarterly payments—much like repaying a debt to a financial institution. Second, several large firms have established leasing subsidiaries to provide this service to the business customer (John Deere and General Electric, for example). Third, lease transactions are arranged for customers through a lending institution involved in leasing to the business market. Examples of companies using such a practice include General Finance Corporation, U.S. Leasing, and C.I.T. Financial. This is called a "direct-financing lease" and involves a lessor who is primarily engaged in financial activities, such as a bank or finance company.

Types of Business Leases

The two types of leases from the lessor's standpoint are operating leases and direct-financing leases.

Operating lease. An *operating lease* is usually short term and cancellable. The lessor gives up the physical possession of the asset, but the transfer is considered temporary in nature. As such, the lessor continues to carry the leased asset as an owned asset on the balance sheet, and the revenue from the lease is reported as it is earned. Depreciation of the leased asset is matched against the revenue. Generally, the lessor provides maintenance and service, and the lease will not contain a purchase option. Under an operating lease, the lessor retains substantially all the risks and benefits of ownership.

Direct-financing lease. A *direct-financing lease* is noncancellable, usually long term, and fully amortized over the period of the contract. The sum of the lease payments exceeds the price paid for the asset by the lessor. The lessee is responsible for operating expenses, is usually given the option of purchasing the asset, and often, a portion of the lease payments will be applied toward the purchase of the asset.

PRICING POLICIES IN BUSINESS PRICING STRATEGY

Another important decision faced by business-to-business firms is the marketing manager's choice of what pricing policies to follow. The prices charged by the marketer are influenced by the different types of customers, the characteristics of the channel system, and the different geographic regions served. Initially, the business price setter must be concerned with "net price," which is the list price minus allowances for trade-ins and other cost-significant concessions made by the buyer, such as volume purchases and order pick-up versus delivery. The establishment of a list price provides the base from which discounts can be subtracted. Discounts come in many forms, with trade, quantity, and cash discounts being the most prevalent. In theory, discounts are simply cost savings realized by the manufacturer and passed on to intermediaries.

Trade Discounts

A *trade discount* is a deduction from the list price offered to an intermediary in return for services performed. Generally speaking, the more services performed by the intermediary, the higher the trade discount. These services would include inventory holding, the providing of customer credit, technical support for the manufacturer, and missionary sales work. A note of caution, however, is in order here. As business price setters contemplate trade-discount strategy, they should give considerable thought to the Robinson-Patman Act. As pointed out in Exhibit 7-1, this piece of legislation takes a dim view of price discrimination practices, such as giving a different discount schedule to basically the same types of customers. Discounts must be nondiscriminatory, and while the Robinson-Patman Act is difficult to police and enforce, the price setter should at least be aware of possible ramifications if charged with a violation of this act.

Quantity Discounts

A *quantity discount* is a deduction in the list price that a manufacturer gives either to channel intermediaries or to OEM users for buying in large amounts. Cost savings can be found in inventory storage, transportation cost per unit, sales calls, follow-up service, and order processing. The two primary types of quantity discounts available are "noncumulative discounts," which are discounts taken on each and every order made: and "cumulative discounts," which are given on a series of orders over a particular period of time. Quantity discounts are considered to be legal as long as business sellers can demonstrate that their costs are reduced by selling in large volume. In the case of cumulative quantity discounts, savings are harder to prove, in that the granting of such discounts does not necessarily result in reduced storage or order-processing costs. Manufacturers, with judicial support, may claim that they legally provide cumulative quantity discounts to meet similar competitive offerings.

Cash Discounts

A *cash discount* is a price reduction strategy to encourage buyers to pay their bills promptly, with a discount of 2/10, net 30 being common. (Payment is due within thirty days, but the buyer can deduct 2 percent from the total invoice amount for payment within ten days). This strategy typically improves the seller's liquidity and reduces credit-collection costs and bad debts. Again, as listed in Exhibit 7-1, the seller must be aware of the provisions of the Robinson-Patman Act, which stipulate that the same terms must be offered to all buyers, large and small alike.

Geographical Price Adjustments

Shipping costs heavily impact the ultimate cost of business products to the buyer, with prices being adjusted upward or downward, depending on who pays the transportation bill (the buyer or the seller). Transportation fees are an especially important factor when pricing large bulky products, such as business machinery and equipment that must travel a long distance. This part of the ultimate cost of the business product is usually settled through a negotiated agreement between the buyer and the seller. Several alternative price strategies are available to sellers, as the rate structure of transportation in the United States is highly complex, with class and commodity rates, local and joint rates, contract and transit rates, and so on. There are separate rate tariffs (or price lists) for various geographic regions; and shipments are classified into a number of groupings called "classes" for rate-quotation purposes. Given the complexity of the rate structure, the determination of the applicable (or lowest) rate for a shipment between two points is sometimes difficult and has become an important function of traffic management. Traffic management personnel must have knowledge of transportation tariffs, classifications, and rate structures.

INTERNATIONAL MARKETING PRICING POLICY

While pricing is one of the most neglected factors that influence international business success, it is a prime area to be considered before a product is sent to market.[22] Business price setters are becoming just as concerned about pricing in world markets as they have been in domestic markets. The pricing decision is at the core of every international business plan and impacts directly on the critical components of a company's marketing plan.[23] In Europe's business climate, the mere hint of an economic upturn would trigger price hikes of 5 percent or even

10 percent to increase corporate bottom lines. However, today's European market, swamped with goods after trade barriers dropped, is doing exactly the opposite. Price cuts are the norm. It would appear that many companies will be forced to overhaul pricing strategies and protect markets through mergers. For instance, in the computer industry, the trend of IBM PC clones and low-cost distribution has spread to the European markets.[24]

World trade is becoming increasingly important to the health of our economy and to the growth of U.S. companies. Every billion dollars in U.S. exports generates about twenty-five thousand jobs. Further, small firms represent the largest pool of potential exporters. A 1988 study shows that of ninety thousand companies that export, 25 percent are small businesses with fewer than one hundred employees.[25] Selling abroad requires time, personnel, planning, market research, attention to detail, hard work, and a focused attention on the role of pricing as a competitive tool. Differing tariffs, costs, attitudes, and methods of price quotation can often confuse the typical business marketing executive. Pricing activity will vary by company, by product, and by competitive conditions, among other things. Becoming a successful exporter depends upon the determination and commitment the entire company is willing to give to the endeavor.

Several additional factors impact international pricing policy. Pricing products in the international environment must be done with full consideration of cost considerations. The price of raw materials can fluctuate rapidly, and widely fluctuating exchange rates are an especially important consideration. Taxes and tariffs must be considered by the international trader, as these serve to discriminate against the importing of all foreign goods. Inflation must be considered, especially in countries experiencing rapid inflation or exchange variation. To effectively work this into final price is no easy task indeed. Channel length and infrastructures must also be considered, as channels are both longer and underdeveloped in many parts of the world. Long distribution channels (and transportation costs) add an additional burden to the job of effective, competitive price setting in international markets.

As a major part of the economic adjustment mechanism in the U.S. economy during the 1990s, firms must discover new markets, create new products, find new markets for old products, and find profitable new markets for new products. The same qualities that cause firms to succeed in domestic markets can be brought to bear on their ability to export profitability. However, to make this happen, business marketers must realize that pricing is one of the most complicated decision areas encountered by international marketers. Although an increasing number of U.S. firms look at the global market, very few understand the effect of currency fluctuations on the price competitiveness of the goods or services they export overseas. Companies should integrate foreign exchange at the very beginning of the planning process so that a fixed price can be a competitive price in the international market.[26] Pricing in this market will require detailed knowledge of costs and regulations (both present and anticipated), a keen sense of market strategy, and knowledge of exchange-rate fluctuations on a day-to-day basis.

CONCEPT QUESTIONS

1. What is a lease?
2. What are the major influences on the business price setter?

SUMMARY

1. Because there are so many variables to consider whose precise influence cannot be anticipated, pricing decisions are often made by guesswork, intuition, or reliance on such methods as traditional markup percentages. The major factors upon which the success of pricing strategy is based include competition, cost, demand, pricing objectives, impact on other products, and legal considerations. An important step in pricing strategy is to determine goals and objectives prior to setting price points or levels. The principal pricing objectives of most firms include profit generation, a satisfactory return on investment, and the maintenance or increase of market share. Often the purchase of one product increases the likelihood of the purchase of another product or product line by the same customer. Business marketers should be prepared to justify price levels, along with quantity and trade discounts.
2. Among the pricing methods and strategies commonly used by price setters are marginal pricing, break-even analysis, and target return-on-investment pricing. Marginal pricing is often used by contract bidders to gain unplanned business or to utilize idle capacity. A value-based strategy, such as the relatively new method of analyzing a product's economic value to a customer, can be a uniquely effective way to gain a commanding lead over the competition. Break-even analysis is undertaken to determine the point at which a firm's revenue will equal its total fixed and variable costs at a given price. Target return-on-investment pricing is a method of setting prices to achieve a particular percentage return on capital invested in the product in question.
3. Demand refers to the amount of a good or service that a buyer or buyers are willing and able to purchase at a particular moment at each possible price. Demand is elastic if quantity is highly responsive to price, and inelastic if it is not. Unitary demand elasticity exists when the percentage change in price is identical to the percentage change in quantity demanded. When attempting to determine demand, cost-benefit analysis is an analysis of benefits received and costs incurred by the customer in buying and using the business product or service.
4. A new product generally enjoys its greatest degree of differentiation during the introductory stage of the product life cycle. Pricing decisions at this stage of the product's life center either on price skimming or market-penetration pricing, depending on the nature of the market and the type of customer involved. There are specific price considerations that the marketer must ponder during each phase of the product life cycle with respect to profit, demand, and marketing strategy.

5. The price-leadership strategy prevails in oligopolistic situations; it is the practice by which one or a very few firms initiate price changes, with one or more of the other firms in the industry following suit. Price leadership is found most often in industries where products are similar, and even standardized; therefore, they are usually considered by customers to be good substitutes for each other.
6. Competitive bidding is a process whereby a business buyer will request price bids from interested suppliers on a proposed purchase or contract. Government agencies, and most public institutions, are required in most cases to use the competitive bidding system in buying products and services. Competitive bidding can take the form of either closed (sealed bid) bidding or open bidding. A probabilistic bidding model is a mathematical technique used to determine prices in a bidding structure; it assumes that competitors will behave in the future as they have in the past.
7. Many business customers choose to lease an asset rather than purchase it; and for the marketer, leasing can provide a very viable alternative to selling capital equipment. In the business market, leasing is employed by most capital goods and equipment manufacturers. There are several advantages of leasing over purchasing from both the buyer's and the seller's points of view. Two primary forms of business leases are the operating lease and the direct-financing lease.
8. The business marketer must be concerned with net price, which is the list price minus allowances for trade-ins and other cost-significant concessions offered by the seller. The establishment of a list price provides the base from which discounts can be subtracted. Discounts come in many forms, with trade, quantity, and cash discounts being the most prevalent. Geographical price adjustments are also frequently made to the list price.
9. World trade is growing increasingly important to the health of our economy and to the growth of U.S. companies. The pricing of products in the international environment must be done with full consideration of applicable costs, inflationary pressures, and channel length and infrastructure in each world market.

KEY TERMS

Break-even analysis
Cash discount
Competitive bidding
Cost-benefit analysis
Direct-financing lease
Elastic demand
Inelastic demand
Marginal (contribution) pricing
Market penetration
Market skimming
Operating lease
Price elasticity of demand
Price-leadership strategy
Probabilistic bidding model
Quantity discount
Robinson-Patman Act
Target return-on-investment pricing
Trade discount
Unitary demand elasticity

REVIEW QUESTIONS

1. Why is price planning not a precise science? Identify and describe the six major factors influencing pricing strategy. Discuss three common pricing objectives. What is meant by a complementary relationship?
2. Explain the pricing methods of (1) marginal pricing, (2) EVC, (3) break-even analysis, and (4) target return-on-investment pricing. What is the fundamental reason for using each of these methods?
3. What is price elasticity of demand? Distinguish among elastic, inelastic, and unitary demand. How can cost-benefit analysis be utilized in determining demand for business products?
4. Differentiate between price skimming and market-penetration pricing. Under what circumstances would you use each one? What are the primary price considerations in each phase of the product life cycle?
5. What is a price-leadership strategy? In what kinds of industries is such a pricing strategy commonly found? How does a business-to-business company maintain its price-leadership position?
6. What is the competitive bidding process, and what types of organizations typically use such a process? Identify five criteria that should be used by a firm considering whether or not to bid on a particular piece of business. What is the fundamental difference between an open bid and a closed bid?
7. What is a probabilistic bidding model? What kind of assumption does such a model make? On what three criteria do all probabilistic bidding models focus?
8. What is involved in a leasing agreement? What type of organization uses leasing transactions most frequently? Identify three advantages of leasing from a buyer's perspective and three from a seller's perspective. Distinguish between an operating lease and a direct-financing lease.
9. How is net price determined? Identify and discuss the three most prevalent types of price discounts. When are transportation fees an important pricing consideration?
10. Why is world trade becoming increasingly important to the health of our economy and to the growth of U.S. businesses? What are some important factors that business marketers should consider in setting prices for international markets?

Cases

CASE 7-1 American Excelsior

Imagine sending customers a package of Eco-Foam peanuts with nothing but a postcard inside. That's exactly what American Excelsior did. The catch? The peanuts used to pack the postcard were biodegradable. Customers were invited to test the biodegradability by putting a few pieces in a glass of water. Many customers had a good time performing chemistry experiments as they watched the new material dissolve.

American Excelsior is not a stranger to natural packaging. The company is the largest producer of excelsior, a cushioning medium composed of thin wood strips. Other companies have tried using popcorn and kraft paper for packaging material. The problem is that these materials do not meet the industrial-type requirements met by peanuts. Popcorn breaks into small pieces and clogs standard peanut dispensers. To switch to paper, companies must make a capital investment. Eco-Foam can be used in the normal peanut dispensers and does not suffer from the static cling that annoys users of the polystyrene peanut product.

Eco-Foam costs less than popcorn and paper, but it is more expensive than polystyrene. Polystyrene peanuts costs $.30 to $.60 per cubic foot. Eco-Foam costs $1 to $1.50 per cubic foot. American Excelsior is the exclusive licensee for the manufacturing and distribution of Eco-Foam peanuts in the United States. The current market for packing peanuts in the United States is 50 million to 60 million pounds per year. American Excelsior has about a 10 percent share of the market.

Moreover, Eco-Foam seems to address environmentalists' concerns by solving two complaints about the standard polystyrene loose-fill product. The traditional peanuts are manufactured with a chemical blowing agent, chlorofluorocarbon, which has been shown to be harmful to the Earth's ozone layer. Eco-Foam does not use chlorofluorocarbon. Eco-Foam is composed of 95 percent cornstarch and 5 percent polyvinyl alcohol. The manufacturing process is similar to that of many breakfast cereals—a process using heat and steam to form the pieces. This also makes the product biodegradable. In addition, the company recommends reusing the product. If that's not practical, Eco-Foam can be spread on the lawn and watered into the soil, since it's completely nontoxic. Customers have suggested that Eco-Foam could be used as a gravy thickener. However, the company does not recommend eating the product, although most of the employees of American Excelsior have tried it.

DISCUSSION QUESTIONS

1. How should American Excelsior price Eco-Foam peanuts? Do you think customers will pay more for environmentally sound packaging material? Give reasons to support your opinion.
2. Do you think American Excelsior should continue manufacturing polystyrene peanuts and just add Eco-Foam to the product line? Or should the company discontinue the polystyrene product? Give reasons to support your opinion.
3. Discuss a price policy that you would recommend to American Excelsior for its complete product line.

Suggested Reading

Streiffert, Kristi G. "Packaging Product Is Full of Potential." *Fort Worth Star Telegram* (November 26–December 2, 1990), Tarrant Business 9.

Source: C. Lamb, J. Hair, and C. McDaniel, *Principles of Marketing*, 1st Edition (Cincinnati, OH: South-Western Publishing Company, 1992) pp. 601–602.

CASE 7-2 Hudson Valley Tree Company

The Hudson Valley Tree Company sells a wide assortment of Christmas trees through the use of manufacturers' representatives. For a flat fee of 10 percent per tree, these representatives sell the trees to final consumers at various locations throughout particular target market areas. The trees sold include Douglas fir, Appalachian fir, Colorado spruce, and Vermont spruce. Hudson Valley Tree Company offers customers one unique advantage: No matter what kind of tree that customers select, they can keep it for more than one season. Hudson Valley sells plastic trees.

Most plastic trees range in price from $99 to $149. Between three million and four million trees were sold in 1992. That amount represents a mere fraction of the thirty-two million live trees sold each year. Manufacturers expect that number to change as acceptance for artificial trees increases. These new trees are much more realistic than those of just a few years ago. From a distance, fake trees can pass for real trees. Shorter needles and more numerous branches have replaced the old bottle-brush-style limbs. Nevertheless, the green steel trunks and lack of fresh pine aroma still give the artificial trees away. However, some ingenious manufacturers have designed imperfections into the plastic trees. Bare spots and extratall top branches can make a fake tree look more realistic. Customers can also shape the tree to their own specifications.

Representatives report that appearance and convenience are the main selling points that attract consumers to artificial trees. Owners can put the tree up in the first week of December and keep it up through New Year's Day without worrying about pine needles all over the floor or watering the tree stand. Since artificial trees are treated with flame-retardant materials, they are not a potential fire hazard. This is another advantage, especially for apartment dwellers. Many apartment landlords prohibit tenants from having live Christmas trees because they're flammable. For consumers with allergies, these trees are a blessing in disguise. Cost is another concern. For people who buy and use the tree for several years, the cost of the tree can be recouped in two or three years. In contrast, those consumers who go back to real trees after only one year pay an extravagant price. The environmental issue is a toss-up. The water and soil used by live trees could be used for other crops. However, the disposal of nonbiodegradable trees is a problem. Artificial trees don't last forever.

Marketers prefer to call artificial trees lifelike or convenience trees. The best-selling areas of the country for artificial trees are in the Northeast and the Midwest. California is the only place these trees haven't become popular. Unlike New England, California's climate and landscape do not match most people's image of a Christmas setting.

DISCUSSION QUESTIONS

1. Is the price for artificial trees elastic or inelastic? Give reasons to support your answer.
2. What type of pricing strategy would you recommend to Hudson Valley? Why?
3. How do you think Hudson Valley should deal with freight costs? What implications will this have with the manufacturer's representatives and in the marketplace?

Suggested Reading

Berry, John. "And You Never Need to Water It." *Adweek's Marketing Week*, 17 December 1990, 17.

Source: C. Lamb, J. Hair, and C. McDaniel, *Principles of Marketing*, 1st Edition (Cincinnati, OH: South-Western Publishing Company, 1992) pp. 602–603.

Suggested Additional Readings

Abratt, Russell, and Leyland F. Pitt. "Pricing Practices in Two Industries." *Industrial Marketing Management* 14 (November 1985): 301–306. **Survey of pricing models in the chemical and construction industries of South Africa.**

Dhebar, Anirudh, and Samuel S. Oren. "Dynamic Nonlinear Pricing in Networks with Interdependent Demand." *Operations Research* 34 (May/June 1986): 384–394. **Mathematical models for optimizing pricing decisions for a new product.**

Goetz, Joe F., Jr. "The Pricing Decision: A Service Industry's Experience." *Journal of Small Business Management* 23 (April 1985): 61–67. **Survey of pricing strategy, pricing objectives, competitive pricing, and cost-based prices in a service industry.**

Graham, Gord. "Push-Button Price Lists." *Canadian Business* (Canada), 59 (March 1986): 91–93. **Case study of cost and price computer applications in the Canadian appliance industry.**

Greenley, Gordon E. "The Contribution Method of Price Determination." *Quarterly Review of Marketing* (UK), 12 (Autumn 1986): 1–6. **A discussion of the contribution method of price determination, including an application of this pricing method.**

Krupp, James A. G. "ROI Analysis for Price Breaks." *Journal of Purchasing and Materials Management* 21 (Spring 1985): 23–25. **Discussion of trade-offs, quantity discounts, and inventory carrying costs.**

Lee, Hau L., and Meir J. Rosenblatt. "A Generalized Quantity Discount Pricing Model to Increase Suppliers' Profits." *Management Science* 32 (September 1986): 1177–1185. **Mathematical model dealing with the joint problem of ordering and offering price discounts.**

Meyerowitz, Steven A. "Tightening the Reins on Distributors' Prices." *Business Marketing* 71 (May 1986): 94–100. **Discussion of resale price maintenance, nonprice vertical restraints, and antitrust laws.**

Polastri, Riccardo P. "Estimating the Effects of Inflation on Prices: A Practical Approach." *Journal of Purchasing and Materials Management* 21 (Spring 1985): 9–16. **Example of forecasting techniques, historical pricing, and use of the correlation approach and a producer price index.**

Rao, Ram C., and Frank M. Bass. "Competition, Strategy, and Price Dynamics: A Theoretical and Empirical Investigation." *Journal of Marketing Research* 22 (August 1985): 283–296. **Price and market-share dynamics of new products, and an empirical analysis of the price paths of eight semiconductor parts.**

Sadrian, Amir A., and Yong S. Yoon. "Business Volume Discount: A New Perspective on Discount Pricing Strategy." *International Journal of Purchasing and Materials Management* 28 (Spring 1992): 43–46. **A discussion of the advantages of business volume discounts for buyers and suppliers.**

Shipley, David D. "Dimensions of Flexible Price Management." *Quarterly Review of Marketing* (UK), 11 (Spring 1986): 1–7. **Large survey dealing with the pricing policies and turbulent environment of manufacturing firms in the United Kingdom.**

Washburn, Stewart A. "Establishing Strategy and Determining Costs in the Pricing Decision." *Business Marketing* 70 (July 1985): 64–78. **Guidelines for and analysis of strategy selection and cost determination in the pricing decision.**

_____. "Understanding Competitive Price Changes." *Business Marketing* 70 (December 1985): 92–97. **Guidelines for price increases and price slashing.**

Wilcox, James B., Roy D. Howell, Paul Kuzdrall, and Robert Britney. "Price Quantity Discounts: Some Implications for Buyers and Sellers." *Journal of Marketing* 51 (July 1987): 60–70. **A taxonomy of price-quantity discounts and implications of price-quantity discounts for the ordering behavior of buyers and the formation of alternative channels of distribution.**

ENDNOTES

[1]Michael H. Morris and Corine van Erkom Schurink, "Pricing Behavior in Industrial Marketing: The Impact of Environmental Dynamics," *Journal of Business and Industrial Marketing* (December 1993): 28–43.

[2]James C. Anderson, Depak C. Jain, and Predeep K. Chintagunta, "Customer Value Assessment in Business Markets: A State-of-Practice Study," *Journal of Business-to-Business Marketing* 1 (1993): 3–29.

[3]Michael D. Mondello, "Naming Your Price," *Inc.*, July 1992, 80–83.

[4]Hugh M. Cannon and Fred W. Morgan, "A Strategic Pricing Framework," *Journal of Business and Industrial Marketing* (Summer/Fall 1991): 59–70.

[5]Elizabeth Bourdon, "Pricing Strategies in Highly Competitive Markets," *Management Decision* 30 (1992): 57–64.

[6]Subhash C. Jain, *Marketing Planning and Strategy*, 4th ed. (Cincinnati, Ohio: South-Western Publishing, 1992), 438.

[7]Subhash C. Jain, *Marketing Planning and Strategy* (Cincinnati, Ohio: South-Western Publishing, 1985): 716.

[8]John L. Forbes and Nitin T. Mehta, "Value-Based Strategies for Industrial Products," *Business Horizons* 24 (May/June 1981): 32–42.

[9]*Ibid.*

[10]Joel Dean, "Techniques for Pricing New Products and Services," in *Marketing Management Readings, From Theory to Practice*, 3rd ed., ed. Benson P. Shapiro, Robert J. Dolan, and John A. Quelch (Homewood, Ill.: Richard D. Irwin, 1985), 160–173.

[11]William Lazer and James D. Culley, *Marketing Management* (Boston: Houghton Mifflin, 1983), 566.

[12]Dean, "Techniques for Pricing," 170.

[13]Stuart U. Rich, "Price Leaders: Large, Strong, but Cautious About Conspiracy," *Marketing News* (June 25, 1982): 11.

[14]Akintoye Akintola and Martin Skitmore, "Pricing Approaches in the Construction Industry," *Industrial Marketing Management* (November 1992): 311–318.

[15]Adapted from Donald W. Dobler, W. L. Lee, and D. N. Burt, *Purchasing and Materials Management*, 5th ed. (New York: McGraw-Hill, 1990).

[16]The following discussion is based on W. J. Morse, "Probabilistic Bidding Models: A Synthesis," *Business Horizons* 18 (April 1975): 67–74.

[17]*Ibid.*, 69.

[18]"Accounting For Leases," FASB Statement, no. 13, as amended and interpreted through May 1980 (Stamford, Conn.: FASB, 1980),par. 1.

[19]Certified Public Accountants, *Accounting Trends and Techniques* (New York: American Institute of Certified Public Accountants, 1988), 188.

[20]Jain, *Marketing Planning and Strategy*, 459.

[21]Dorothy Paun, "When to Bundle or Unbundle Products," *Industrial Marketing Management* (February 1993): 29–34.

[22]Richard A. Lancioni, "Pricing for International Business Development," *Management Decisions* (1991): 39–41.

[23]Richard A. Lancioni and John L. Gattorna, "Strategic Value Pricing: Its Role in International Business," *International Journal of Physical Distribution and Logistics Management* (1992): 24–27.

[24]Bill Javetski, "Price War Is Raging in Europe," *Business Week*, 6 July 1992, 44–45.

[25]*The World Is Your Market* (U.S. Small Business Administration in cooperation with AT&T and UPS, 1990).

[26]Fred Cohen and Rhonda Price, "Competitive Pricing Strategies for Exporters," *Journal of European Business* (May/June 1991): 46–48.

8 Business Marketing Channel Participants

Learning Objectives

After reading this chapter, you should be able to:

- Recognize the functions of marketing channel members.
- Understand the nature of channel decisions.
- Appreciate the role and importance of direct channels.
- Comprehend the role and importance of various types of indirect channels.
- Discuss the nature of, and the contributing factors to, channel cooperation.
- Relate the reasons for channel conflict and the available remedies.
- Determine when to use intensive, selective, and exclusive distribution policies.
- Explain the nature of channel activities in international markets.

Chapter Outline

Learning Objectives

Functions of the Channel Intermediary

- Buying
- Selling
- Storage
- Transportation
- Sorting
- Financing
- Risk Taking
- Market Information

The Nature of Channel Decisions

Direct Channels

Sales-Volume Base

Indirect Channels

- The Business Products (Industrial) Distributor
  - Limitations to using business products distributors
  - Trends for business products distributors
- The Manufacturers' Representative (Agent)
  - Limitations to using manufacturers' representatives
  - Trends for manufacturers' representatives
  - Sales Agents and Brokers
  - Facilitating Agencies

Combining Direct and Indirect Channels

Channel Cooperation

- Methods of Channel Cooperation
  - Use of missionary salespeople
  - Involvement in the planning function of channel members
  - Promotional aid
  - Acting as a management consultant

Channel Conflict

- The Nature of Channel Conflict
- Conflict Management and Resolution
- A Legal Perspective on Channel Conflict
- Typical Problem Areas in the Manufacturer-Intermediary Relationship
  - Service and technical assistance
  - House accounts
  - Inventory levels
  - Marketing information and feedback
  - Training and support services
  - Second lines carried

Intensive, Selective, and Exclusive Distribution
Intensive Distribution
Selective Distribution
Exclusive Distribution

International Channel Decisions
Types of Indirect-Channel Intermediaries

Summary

Key Terms

Review Questions

Cases
Case 8-1
Case 8-2

Suggested Additional Readings

Endnotes

FUNCTIONS OF THE CHANNEL INTERMEDIARY

Business channel strategy must be an integral part of the firm's total operating system, meshing with production, finance, research, purchasing, and other functions of the business so as to make the maximum contribution to company objectives. Business marketing managers are learning that channels can create differential advantages, especially in instances in which competitors' products, prices, and promotional efforts are almost homogeneous.[1] The types of outlets available and the functions these outlets perform represent the structural elements of channel strategy.

Channel management is supposed to be a cooperative marketing strategy where manufacturers augment their direct sales channels with indirect channels of distribution to reach different segments more efficiently and effectively.[2] Also, manufacturers must occasionally modify their channels of distribution to keep their products available in broadening and maturing markets.[3] Effective channel management involves classifying the role of a product line within the corporation's product portfolio and managing the implications of interrelationships among product policy, product lines, and channel strategy.[4]

The current body of marketing literature recognizes the fundamental importance of distribution channel management and policies to manufacturers and distributors of business goods. From the earliest times to today's fast-paced and dynamic marketplace, geographically separated buyers and sellers have required the capability to move or to transfer goods and commodities physically. For the great majority of business products and services, a number of channel functions must be performed. Therefore, as shown in Figure 8-1, the marketing functions of buying, selling, storage, transportation, sorting, financing, risk taking, and market information must be carried out within the channel system. The types of organizations that perform these functions and tasks are an important channel management consideration. A brief explanation of these functions will create a framework from which the various channel alternatives available to the business marketer can be studied.

Buying

Some channel members buy products for resale to other intermediaries, to a final business user, or for their own use. Most act as a purchasing manager or a buyer, trying to determine how much of a particular product their customers will need over the next week, month, quarter, or other time period for which they must plan and buy. Buying in advance is most often a risky undertaking, as they are betting that their customers will indeed buy the material or parts on hand.

Selling

Intermediaries must be innovative in their use of the interpersonal skills of persuasion and problem solving as they close sales and develop strong business relationships. In most cases, the channel intermediary is picked because of the experience, knowledge, and expertise of the company in this area.

FIGURE 8-1 **Basic Channel Functions**

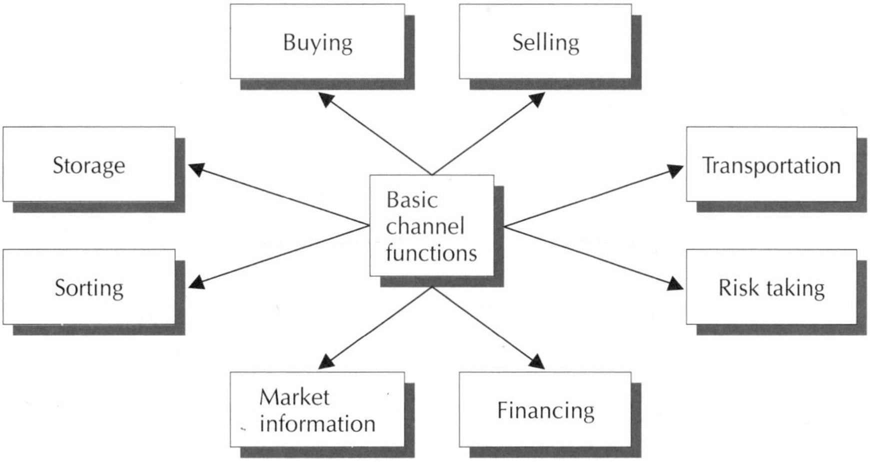

Storage

Effective inventory management requires a proper balance among buying, selling, and production. An inventory commitment is composed of stock to satisfy average or typical customer purchase requirements and to provide for a safety buffer to cover unexpected variations in demand and other types of customer buying emergencies. Stock must be in convenient locations to ensure timely delivery and must also be protected to prevent deterioration and loss.

Transportation

The business marketing manager is broadly concerned with managing the physical flow of the product through the intermediary and into the hands of the business user. (When title passes, the marketing manager of the business-to-business firm is no longer responsible for transport to the user; this function is assumed by the channel intermediary.) A vast array of transportation alternatives are available for intermediaries to use within their respective physical distribution systems, with the most common modes being rail, motor carrier, water, pipeline, and air. Each of these modes will be examined in detail in Chapter 9.

Sorting

Most intermediaries buy in large quantities and then break these shipments into smaller lots for resale to business users. The term *breaking of bulk* is commonly used to describe this function performed by intermediaries who take physical possession of the goods. This procedure allows the intermediaries to buy large quantities at reduced prices and to resell the goods at a price that will allow the intermediaries to make a profit.

Financing

If the intermediaries invest in inventory, sells and delivers the merchandise to the business user, and provides acceptable credit terms, then the intermediary is financing the exchange process. Most intermediaries who take title to and then resell merchandise allow the business user quite liberal terms in paying for the purchase. (Thirty days is standard, with sixty, ninety, and even one-hundred-and-twenty days not uncommon.) Most of these intermediaries operate small businesses and know their customers well. They offer extended terms quite often and tend to be lenient with credit. They are, in a sense, financing the purchase for their customers, much like a local department store or specialty shop would finance a final consumer's purchase of a new suit, with payment due (or at least partial payment due) in thirty days.

Risk Taking

Because of obsolescence and deterioration, risk is inherent in the ownership of inventory; this phenomenon is especially true today because of rapid advances in technology and the so-called knowledge explosion. Those intermediaries who buy in bulk and take title are betting that the merchandise will not become obsolete and will not deteriorate prior to its resale to the business user. The intermediaries in this situation must buy in large enough quantities to make the resale at a profit; at the same time, they must be careful not to buy in such large quantities that either obsolescence or deterioration could occur before resale to the business customer. The amount of risk involved generally depends upon the type of products being handled.

Market Information

Communication is a two-way function in the distribution channel, with messages relaying the need for exchange action and also serving to report progress toward desired end results. Channel communication is necessary and should be continuous as products are transferred and stored in anticipation of future transaction requirements. Information on assortment, quantity, location, and time becomes important and must be communicated between channel members if market opportunity is not to be lost. The accuracy of information concerning availability of merchandise, pricing conditions, product quality, and competitive conditions is important enough that it just might determine what type of channel intermediary will be used by the business marketer. The number of channel members who perform each of the identified marketing functions will influence the total operating expenses incurred, not only by the manufacturer, but also by a particular channel member. Each of the eight functions discussed earlier must be performed at least once in every channel, and some may be performed by several channel members.

Channel management and physical distribution management, as shown in Figure 8-2, fit under the distribution strategy variable of the marketing mix. The two components together comprise the distribution element of the marketing mix. Although channel management and distribution management are closely related, they are actually quite different; frequently, there is considerable confusion in regard to the distinction between them. Distribution management will be discussed in detail in Chapter 9. *Channel management* is a much broader and more basic component of the distribution strategy variable of the marketing mix than is physical distribution management. Channel management is concerned with the entire process of setting up and operating the organization responsible for meeting the firm's distribution objectives. *Physical distribution management*, on the other hand, is more narrowly focused on providing product availability at the appropriate times and places in the marketing channel. Quite often, channel management must be well underway before physical distribution strategy can even be considered.

FIGURE 8-2 **Strategic Variables in the Marketing Mix with the Distribution Variable Divided into Channel and Physical Distribution Components**

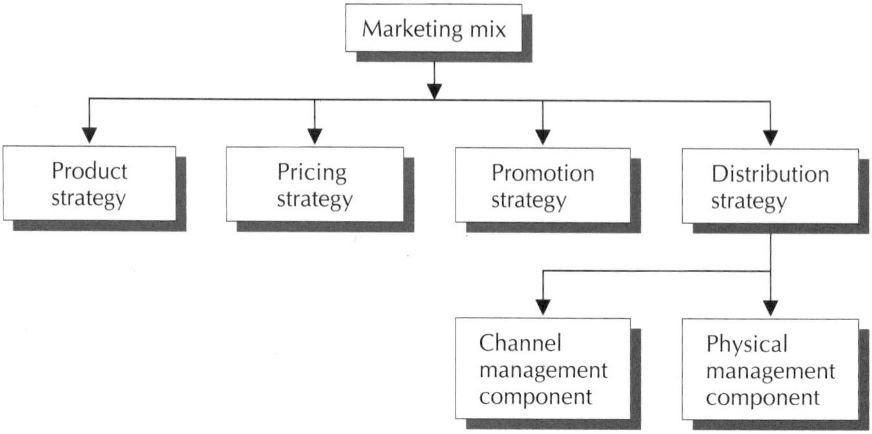

Source: Table, p. 9, from *Marketing Channels: A Management View,* Second Edition, by Bert Rosenbloom, copyright © 1983 by The Dryden Press, reproduced by permission of the publisher.

THE NATURE OF CHANNEL DECISIONS

The business marketing manager must regularly perform a critical reappraisal of the channels of distribution in use, with a careful eye on how well each channel member is carrying out the assigned functions. Business products users and intermediaries need a systematic framework for adjusting channel strategies in changing environments. This framework should recognize and balance the service needs of both producers and end users.[5] If the marketing manager changes the channel structure, a whole complex of marketing decisions is affected. Channel decisions are, by necessity, long-term arrangements. Channel management involves a semipermanent working relationship with either another function within the firm or the same relationship with an outside firm. To change or disrupt a long-term working relationship, while perhaps necessary, can become somewhat difficult and expensive.

Such amending should be done only for sound and serious reasons in that a bad decision will cause market share to suffer. The exercise of choice in channel selection should be done with utmost care. However, if change is later required, the business marketing manager must be in a position to execute that change, causing the firm as little disruption as possible. The marketing manager must have some alternative channels of distribution options available; thus, a discussion of both direct and indirect channels follows.

CONCEPT QUESTIONS

1. What is the basic difference in nature between channel management and distribution management?
2. What kind of time commitment is involved in channel contracts?

DIRECT CHANNELS

One alternative channel decision that the business marketing manager can make is the selection of a direct channel of distribution. *Direct channels* involve "direct selling" (that is, no external intermediary involved) to the industrial user, with or without the use of sales branches. A direct sale would include both generalists and specialists.[6] (Generalists sell the entire product line to all customers, whereas specialists concentrate on particular products, customers, or industries.) A *sales branch* is broadly defined as an off-site manufacturer's sales office, operating within a major market area, staffed with some technical personnel, and having the ability to ship most orders immediately from stock.

Sales-Volume Base

Whether the sales-volume base is sufficient to support a direct-selling program is a matter of judgment. The variables that will affect this judgment are absolute sales volume, the breadth and depth of the product line, the relative concentration or dispersion of potential customers, the size of the customers, and the amount of business that can be expected from each. If, at one extreme, the line of products that the manufacturer sells to any one market segment is narrow, and if potential customers are small and geographically dispersed, it is likely to be uneconomical to sell directly. At the other extreme, if the manufacturer's product line is broad, if customers are geographically concentrated, and if many buyers have the potential for purchasing in large quantities, it would be difficult to make a case for selling through independent distributors.

Usually, selling direct can be justified if any two of these three conditions are satisfied. Under such circumstances, the business marketer generally finds it less expensive to employ direct-sales representatives than to give a margin or a commission to an independent.

In sharp contrast to consumer goods, most manufactured business goods (as much as 60 to 70 percent) are sold directly to users. This trend will continue and become self-evident as business marketing observers analyze the reasons for direct sale. Rockwell International's Municipal and Utility Division markets water, gas, and parking meters to local municipalities and gas utilities through a direct-sales organization. The direct-sales approach is viable because the customers are large and well defined; the customers often insist upon direct sales; sales involve extensive negotiations with high-level utility management; and control of the selling job is necessary to ensure proper implementation of the total product package and to guarantee a quick response to market conditions. In fact, using a direct-sales force allowed the company to change its price schedule five times in six months and to negotiate all the important contracts required by those price changes.

INDIRECT CHANNELS

A second alternative channel decision that a business marketing manager can make would be the use of *indirect channels*. A 1989 study indicated that manufacturers are relying more on wholesalers and distributors than on their own direct-sales forces. Indirect channels are often considered to be a more cost-effective alternative.[7]

Indirect channels are warranted when the market is widely scattered, when many firms must be contacted, when small orders are common, and when goods are made for inventory rather than to fill specific orders. Once the manufacturer has determined that indirect channels are appropriate, the paramount question becomes, "Which type of indirect channel should be chosen?" As can be noted in Figure 8-3, business products distributors (often called industrial distributors),

FIGURE 8-3 **Alternative Choices of Indirect Channels**

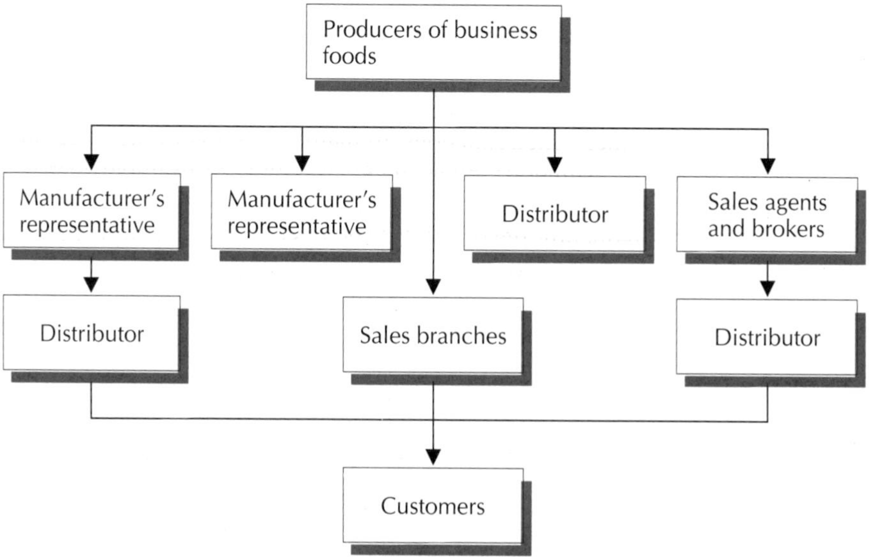

manufacturers' representatives (agents), and sales agents and brokers are possible choices, depending upon the nature of the industry involved and the distribution structure required.

The Business Products (Industrial) Distributor

Business products distributors are intermediaries who buy and take title to business products, who usually keep inventories of their products, and who sell and service these products. They are the most important single force in distribution channels, numbering approximately twelve thousand and accounting for approximately $50 billion in sales volume.[8] In one study, it was found that only 24 percent of all business marketing firms sell their products directly to end users exclusively; the remaining 76 percent use some type of intermediary, of which business products' distributors are the most prominent.[9] (See Table 8-1 for a more comprehensive profile of the business products distributor.) Business products distributors receive compensation for their services through a margin in the form of the difference between what they pay to the manufacturer and what they charge their customer. This is called a "trade discount." In addition to the traditional channel functions previously identified and explained, many distributors offer an interesting additional portfolio of services. The most frequently offered are stockless purchasing, literature updating, systems engineering, and guidance on such issues as pollution control.

The distributor is, first of all, a merchant intermediary, taking title to the goods for the purpose of resale. Operating generally as full-service wholesalers, distributors perform the same tasks that a manufacturer would have to provide in selling directly to the business user, very often at a lower final cost to customers. The distributor would undertake the performance of buying, selling, storing, transporting, sorting, financing, risk taking, and market information; a full-service channel member like this becomes expert in the provision of the above-mentioned functions. In many ways, distributors are similar to wholesalers in consumer channels. Ingersoll-Rand, for example, uses distributors to sell its line of pneumatic tools.

Frequently, the use of distributors lowers the final cost to customers. Because the distributor breaks bulk, provides inventory and delivery services, as well as appropriate personnel, the use of a distributor is often less expensive than using branch houses and company salespeople. In turn, the distributor's lower costs often are passed on to customers in terms of lower prices.

There are two major types of business products distributors: *general-line distributors*, handling a wide variety of business supplies and minor equipment, and selling to a broad spectrum of customers; and *limited-line distributors*, handling fewer, high-volume items such as steel, paper, or chemicals.[10] Such limited-line distributors are often called *jobbers*; although they take title, they do not necessarily carry the goods in inventory. In this situation, jobbers would have the

TABLE 8-1 **Profile of the Business Products Distributor**

Characteristics	General Line	Specialist
Median sales	$2,430,000	$2,239,750
Sales from stock	65.5%	60.0%
Number of invoices per year	13,000	7,500
Average invoice	$187	$299
Collections—median number of days outstanding	42	45
Year-end receivables value	$239,600	$268,000
Average monthly inventory values	$397,000	$309,000
Median inventory turnover on stock sales	3.5	4.0
Total number of employees	18.0	15.5
Number of outside salespersons	4	4
Number of inside salespersons	3	2
Square feet of warehouse space	15,000	10,000
Percent with 1 stocking location—no branches	67%	63%
Percent with 2 stocking locations—1 branch	13%	16%
Percent with 3 stocking locations—2 branches	8%	9%
Percent with 4 to 6 stocking locations—3 to 5 branches	8%	10%
Percent with 7 or more stocking locations—6 or more branches	4%	2%
Computerized operations	59.2%	55.1%
Percent of computerized users with own equipment	39%	93%
Percent of computerized users using outside services	11%	7%
Computer applications		
Accounts receivables	92.4%	90.1%
Sales analysis	89.4%	87.6%
Billing	88.6%	84.5%
Accounts payables	85.6%	73.9%
Customer analysis	73.8%	75.8%
Inventory records	78.8%	78.9%
Unit sales pricing	68.9%	57.8%
Purchasing	67.4%	54.7%
Sales order processing	65.2%	60.2%
Payroll	54.5%	45.3%
All others	61.4%	60.2%

Source: Reprinted from *Industrial Distribution*, July, 1984, Copyright © (1984) by Cahners Publishing Company, pp. 43–51.

manufacturers "drop-ship" the goods directly to their (the jobbers') customers. Limited-line distributors also include specialists who carry a line of particular goods, such as electrical wiring supplies, or who serve a particular industry, such as shoe manufacturers.

Limitations to using business distributors. After reading and thinking about the previous section, one could get the idea that signing on a distributor is a relatively easy task; and that once such a distributor has been obtained, the marketer has no additional distribution problems. Unfortunately, such is not the case, because for many manufacturers, the use of a distributor might not make sense. Exhibit 8-1 examines a number of problems involved in the use of distributors, ranging from overlapping territories to distributors' lack of appreciation for manufacturers' operational policies, procedures, and problems. Distributors are also often very difficult to control. They are generally independent business people; they do not particularly like to, and sometimes will not, take directions from others; and they usually carry or handle competing products. On many occasions, they will not emphasize the business marketing manager's products in particular. Additionally, the average distributor often does not possess the technical or service know-how to handle high-tech products. The box entitled "Business-to-Business Marketing in Action" describes how Japan's Epson Corporation, a leading manufacturer of computer printers, replaced all its distributors with others that the company believed would do a more effective job of selling the new computer product line to retail outlets.

Business products distributors also seek products that will ensure high inventory turnover and profit margins. Naturally, they will tend to stress lines that meet these criteria in their sales efforts.

Trends for business products distributors. In talking with a number of distributors, it seems that some of the major changes taking place within their ranks include the following: (1) More heavy (capital) equipment, such as large machinery,

EXHIBIT 8-1 **Problems with the Use of Business Products Distributors**

1. While the manufacturer might desire to retain larger customers as house accounts, the distributor wants access to these accounts.
2. The sophistication and managerial practices of many smaller distributors, operating "mom and pop" type of businesses, are often questioned.
3. Manufacturers desire to keep somewhat high industry levels in distributors' warehouses, whereas distributors wish to minimize such levels.
4. Distributors like to carry second lines in an effort to provide greater selection among competitive offerings for their customers; but manufacturers want distributors to feature their products, and not those of their competitors.
5. Distributors' networks often contain overlapping territories.
6. Distributors frequently demand many small and/or rush orders.
7. Distributors often do not seem sensitive to the operational policies, procedures, and problems of manufacturers.
8. Many distributors do not see manufacturers' promotional advice as relevant, and ignore manufacturers' sales representatives.

Source: Reprinted from *Industrial Distribution,* June 9, 1984, Copyright © (1984) by Cahners Publishing Company, p. 30.

BUSINESS-TO-BUSINESS MARKETING IN ACTION

CREATING A TEAM OF DISTRIBUTORS FOR EPSON PRODUCTS

Epson Corporation of Japan, a major manufacturer of computer printers, wanted to expand its product line by adding computers. Epson was not pleased with its existing distributors in that they could not effectively sell to new types of retail outlets. Jack Whalen, General Manager at Epson, secretly recruited a pool of new distributors to replace the current ones. He employed a recruiting company called Hergenrather and Company, and advised them as follows:

- Search for applicants who had two-step distribution experience (factory to distributor to dealer) in either brown goods (televisions, etc.) or white goods (refrigerators, etc.).
- The applicants would have to be CEO types who would be willing and able to set up their own distributorships.
- They would be offered $80,000 yearly salary plus bonus, and $375,000 to help them set up in business. Each would add $25,000 of his own money, and each would get equity in the business.
- They would handle only Epson products, but could stock the software of other companies. Each distributor would have a training manager and a fully equipped service center.

Hergenrather and Company found it difficult to locate motivated and qualified prospects. An advertisement placed in the *Wall Street Journal*, not revealing the company name, yielded close to seventeen hundred responses, mostly from unqualified job-seekers. The "Yellow Pages" were then utilized to secure names of current distributors. Hergenrather thereupon telephoned managers who were second-in-command. Interviews were arranged, from which a list of qualified prospects was identified. Whalen interviewed each of these prospects and chose what he considered were the best twelve. Hergenrather and Company was paid $250,000 for their efforts.

Terminating Epson's current distributors was the concluding stage in the process. This would be perhaps the most difficult step, at least from a tactical point of view, since the existing distributors had no knowledge of Hergenrather's activities. All current distributors were given a ninety-day notice of their replacement, regardless of the length of time which they had been in Epson's employ. Although most were shocked, they also had no contract in force. Whalen knew these existing distributors could not successfully handle Epson's extended product line and saw no other action as feasible in this situation.

Source: Arthur Bragg, "Undercover Recruiting: Epson America's Sly Distributor Switch," *Sales and Marketing Management* (March 11, 1985), pp. 45–49. Reprinted with permission of *Sales and Marketing Management.*

is being marketed through distributors. (2) Manufacturers are increasing their support of distributors to include sales aids, sales training, and other field-support services. (3) Distributors are becoming more sophisticated, as more and more college graduates and many quality engineers join their ranks. Available computer software has also contributed to the growing sophistication of distributors. (4) A trend toward specialization among distributors is more evident. Additionally, we are having a very difficult time converting our Cold War victory to expanded economic prosperity at home. Many distributors were major suppliers to defense-related industries and now realize that one of their most significant markets is at best downsized, and at worst, gone forever. New products and new markets must be found if all are to survive.[11] As distributors sell larger amounts of a particular product line, they tend to gain a great deal of expertise in that specific field. This phenomenon tends to feed on itself, as distributors expand that particular expertise to meet the additional demand created. This development of expertise seems to be a natural tendency as the distributor spends more and more time, money, and effort selling and promoting a certain line or type of product. (5) Manufacturers that use distributors are tending to depend more on them for a wide variety of marketing activities to include research, new-product development, and additional market coverage. Also, for many entrenched distributors, the use of "partnered" selling (partnership marketing) has been, and continues to be, a major competitive tool.[12] Table 8-2 discusses new directions in distributor operations. Among the more important new directions are the emergence of larger, more sophisticated

TABLE 8-2 **New Directions in Distributor Operations**

Changes in Distributor Operations	Impacts on the Manufacturer
Larger size	Larger, more sophisticated distributors are emerging.* A small number of well managed distributors can reduce a manufacturer's logistical costs and yield greater effectiveness of dollars spent on training and support. However, fewer uncommitted distributors would remain.
Distributor "supermarkets"	The distributor chain operation is an emerging force in American industry. This is a chain of regional or national outlets that are owned and/or managed by one corporation.** Chains may carry multiple brands rather than one exclusive name; can offer private labels in a number of brand categories; can use price discounting; and can offer wide and deep territories. A shift of power to the chain is a likely result.
Specialization	Concentrating efforts in restricted product lines is a trend that is also growing. Specialist distributors present buyers with efficient service, expert knowledge, and a multitude of brands in a narrow product line. These factors more closely tie end-user customers to the distributor from a manufacturer's point of view. A shift in control or market power to the specialist is again likely to occur. The business marketer might find the need to grant price concessions, heavy advertising, or direct sales controls to the end user in that the manufacturer's brand might be only one of many that the specialist handles.

Source: *Reprinted by permission of the publisher from Ronald D. Michman, "Trends Affecting Industrial Distributors," *Industrial Marketing Management*, 9 (July 1980), p. 214. Copyright 1980 by Elsevier Science Inc.; and **Jeremy Main, "The Chain Reaction That's Rocking Industrial Distribution," *Sales and Marketing Management*, 114 (February 28, 1976), pp. 41–45. Reprinted with permission of *Sales and Marketing Management*.

distributors; the rising popularity of distributor outlet chains; and the growing concentration of efforts in restricted product lines. It should be noted, however, that a survey conducted by *Industrial Distribution* in July of 1991 indicated that mergers in the industry have begun to wane. According to some industry experts, this hiatus is only temporary, and there will probably be more merger activity as the economy continues to recover.[13]

Despite the limitations mentioned earlier, the distributor's status as a full-service institution has brought this marketing intermediary recognition as an expert in the performance of many vital marketing functions. Generally speaking, distributors compare favorably with manufacturers' sales branches as far as costs of distribution are concerned; at the same time, they offer a more complete product line, provide possibly better market coverage, and aid in the development of small accounts. Table 8-3 summarizes the activities of some of the major firms that distribute business goods. Extensive market coverage, with the ability to sell in great volume, is evident.

The Manufacturers' Representative (Agent)

A *manufacturers' representative*, often called a manufacturers' agent, is a firm selling part of the output of one or more manufacturers whose products are related but noncompetitive. (See Exhibit 8-2 for a brief profile of a manufacturers' representative.) Manufacturers' representatives are getting more respect today from both distributors and manufacturers. They have made great strides in their attempt to gain acceptance.[14] Often, the shift to manufacturers' representatives (agents) by larger companies reflects the growing strength of the agency method of selling, the increased professionalism of the agents themselves, and the fact that using the reps is often more economical than any other way of selling.[15]

Manufacturers' representatives enter into a formal written agreement with each manufacturer covering price policy, territories, order-handling procedures, delivery service, warranties, and commission rates. They know each manufacturer's product line and use their wide contacts to sell the manufacturer's

EXHIBIT 8-2 **A Brief Profile of a Manufacturer's Representative**

Company	Central Southwest Bottling Company
Location	Claremore, Oklahoma
End-user market	Bottling industry
Estimated average commission	8 to 12 percent
Geographic market coverage	Oklahoma, Texas, Arkansas, Kansas, Louisiana, New Mexico, Colorado
Products handled	Plastic cases, decappers, empty-bottle inspectors, bottle filler replacement parts, conveyors, and case packers
Companies represented	Medium-sized and small bottle and bottling-parts manufacturers throughout the eight-state service area

TABLE 8-3 **Activities of Major Business Products Distributors**

Company	1974 Net Sales in Distribution	Estimated Number of Outlets	Area Served	Major Products
Associated Spring Corporation Bristol, Conn. *Distribution Group*	$73.7 million *36% of total company sales*	14 warehouses	United States and Canada	Automotive aftermarket, welding supplies, industrial maintenance supplies, industrial aerosols, special-purpose hardware, and fasteners
Bearings, Inc. Cleveland, Ohio *Bearings, Inc., Dixie Bearings, Bruening Bearings, Inc.*	$156.2 million	131 distribution centers	Essentially national; *25 states* excluding California	Bearings, industrial power transmission components, specialized seals, lubricants, bearing retaining devices, and tools
Curtis Knoll Corp. Cleveland, Ohio	$104.3 million *91% of total company sales*	15 warehouses *plus auto jobber outlets*	United States and *foreign markets*	Automotive aftermarket products and industrial maintenance products such as alloy plate and bar stock, tools, chemicals, cleaning insecticides, and paper
Ducommun, Inc. Los Angeles, Calif.	$210.3 million *97.2% of total company sales*	12 processing centers	United States for electronic; western and southwestern states for metal	Metals, tools and industrial suppliers, and electronic parts and components to industrial users
W. W. Grainger, Inc. Chicago, Illinois	$283.9 million *90% of total company sales*	134 branches	United States	Electric motors and accessories, fans, blowers, pumps, air compressors, hand and bench tools, arc welders, and materials-handling and storage equipment
Kaman Corp. Bloomfield, Conn. *Reliable Bearings & Supply; Western Bearings, Inc., BIT Co.*	$45.5 million *30.1% of total company sales*	51 outlets	11 western states, Hawaii, and British Columbia	Bearings, seals, hydraulic components, lubricants, rubber products, power transmission, and materials-handling equipment

products.[16] In contrast to a typical manufacturer's salesperson, a manufacturers' representative must have a broader-based knowledge of products in general.[17] Representatives comprise sales organizations that work independently and generally represent several different smaller companies within a particular industry or geographic area. Fred Holloway, manager of Yarway Corporation's Metering Pump Division of Blue Bell, Pennsylvania, values the twenty manufacturers' representatives that represent him, for a simple marketing reason. Says Holloway, "Manufacturers' representatives tend to be more knowledgeable about markets.

They have a closer relationship with the key buying influences in the processing industry markets we want to penetrate. Sales costs are not the prime factors for us." Holloway admits that if he had a direct-sales force, he would probably have stricter control over field selling; he also wishes that he did not have to compete for selling time with the other manufacturers whose products his reps also carry. "But our representatives give us the market coverage we believe we could not win otherwise," he says.[18]

However, not all firms using manufacturers' representatives are small. Manufacturers like National Semiconductor, ITT, Corning, Monsanto, Teledyne, and Mobil Oil are also included. National Semiconductor began using manufacturers' representatives in the early 1960s when the firm's sales were less than $50 million; the company continues this practice in the 1990s, even though it has become a billion-dollar manufacturer. Manufacturers' representatives generally do not take title to the goods they handle, nor do they provide an inventory function. They operate strictly on a commission basis and usually limit their sales efforts to a defined geographic area. Advantages of a manufacturer's using a manufacturers' representative include predictable selling expense; incurring little or no cost until sales are forthcoming; cost savings from manufacturers not having to utilize their own sales forces; and a greater intensity of territorial coverage in that the representative is able to make a profit in a smaller territory because of the multiple lines represented.

Limitations to using manufacturers' representatives. Again, one might think that it is an easy task for a manufacturer to acquire a representative and have distribution problems entirely eliminated. Fortunately, business marketing managers realize that such is not the case, because, for many manufacturers, the use of manufacturers' representatives or agents is not appropriate.

Representatives or agents often are difficult to control for the manufacturer. If the manufacturer's product line requires special care, representatives often are unwilling to provide such treatment. Additionally, only partial representation is secured because of the other manufacturers' lines carried by the representative. There is also the possibility of the representative severing the relationship, leaving the manufacturer with no distributive contact in the territory. Costs, too, could be greater than just the commission charged, since extra services demanded, such as the carrying of inventory, require additional compensation. Also, the representative generally prefers to concentrate on large customers and large orders; so, if the manufacturer has several small business customers in an area, these accounts can easily be slighted by very infrequent sales visits. Lack of available inventory also often creates a problem, as this type of intermediary is of little use when service or parts are needed quickly.

Trends for manufacturers' representatives. Many manufacturers' representatives entering the field today have an engineering background and are experts in the use of technical sales skills. They are selling mostly technical goods or services; they are representing fewer manufacturers; and they have expanded authority, making some of the marketing decisions usually made by the manufacturer. Typically, representatives have not stocked the goods they sell except for quickly needed replacement parts. However, there is a tendency toward "stocking reps," who provide at least a limited warehouse service. This practice will tend to increase costs, moving this type of institution a step closer to becoming a business products distributor. The majority of representatives are males, but more females are now beginning to enter the field. Commission rates are rising, with the current rate being about 10 percent.

Manufacturers' representatives can, in many cases, provide inexpensive coverage to more remote areas and to areas where demand cannot sustain a full-time company salesperson. Furthermore, this type of organization can serve to expand territories by the introduction of the respective manufacturers' product lines in their preliminary developmental stage. This activity might permit expansion and growth almost on a pay-as-you-go basis, via a commission on sales made.

Sales Agents and Brokers

Sales agents and *brokers*, like manufacturers' representatives, provide a sales effort, seldom carry inventory (unless on consignment), generally do not take title, and operate on a commission basis. The major difference between manufacturers' representatives and sales agents and brokers would be that sales agents and brokers may assume responsibility for more marketing functions, including promotional and pricing responsibilities. Additionally, sales agents and brokers tend to handle the entire output of several directly competitive manufacturers. Sales agents and brokers generally have no geographic restrictions on their territories and will provide market data and product-development guidance.

Sales agents and brokers may take over the entire selling function of the manufacturer. For example, Stake Fastener Company, a California-based producer of industrial fasteners, has an agent call on business users rather than employing its own sales force. Such a situation is especially appropriate where seasonal representation is desired; where marketing and sales skills are needed recurrently; where the major interests and skills of the manufacturer are in production; where a limited product line is offered; and where the market is widespread.

Brokers are most prevalent in the food industry. Their operation is typified by a seafood broker handling the pack from a salmon cannery. The cannery is in operation for possibly three months of the year. The canner employs a broker each year (the same one, if relationships are mutually satisfactory) to find buyers for the salmon pack. The broker provides information concerning market prices and conditions, and the canner then informs the broker of the desired price. The broker seeks potential buyers among chain stores, wholesalers, and others; and when the entire pack has been sold, the agent-principal relationship is discontinued until possibly the following year.[19]

Facilitating Agencies

Facilitating agencies facilitate the flow of goods from the manufacturer to either the channel intermediary or the final user. Facilitators would include advertising agencies; public relations firms; transportation and warehouse facilities; banks; and others that, although not actually in the channel, help the "flow" between buyers and sellers. Advertising agencies and public relations firms would provide the necessary business marketing communications, including catalogs and product literature, advertising, direct mail, trade shows, publicity, and public relations. Transportation and warehouse facilities, which when viewed as part of the logistics function, should maximize customer service and minimize distribution cost. Banks and other financial institutions serve as facilitating agencies when they provide the capital to purchase or lease business products. Some firms, such as General Motors, General Electric, and Westinghouse, directly provide the financing function themselves.

Facilitating functions assist the business marketer in supporting organizational operations and in performing the exchange function. Potential customers must be made aware of new product offerings, and must receive the product in the right quantity, at the right time, and in undamaged condition. Many of these same potential customers will require financing through unique leasing arrangements. The role of facilitating agencies should be clear.

COMBINING DIRECT AND INDIRECT CHANNELS

At this point in the discussion of business distribution strategy, the question again must be raised as to whether or not the business marketing manager should use direct channels, indirect channels, or a combination of the two. If indirect channels are selected, should the manufacturers' representative or agent be used, or should sales agents and brokers be employed? These, of course, are not easy questions for the marketing manager to answer. A wrong decision can easily impair market penetration and will lead to serious erosion in market share.

Planning and managing a mixed distribution system require business marketers to give special attention to the following four questions:

(1) What specific functions must the distribution system perform?

(2) Where in the system might these functions be carried out most economically?

(3) How do different customers buy, and which elements in the system can be most effective in meeting their needs?

(4) What legal constraints must be observed in relationships with independent resellers?

Direct selling to user-customers is preferred in more concentrated market areas having the sales potential to support fixed selling expenses. Independent distributors carrying multiple lines might then be the choice in thinner market areas where their broader product lines provide the base for operating profitably.

When a company's independent distributors and its own sales force operate in the same geographic area, the roles of each can differ in several ways. Each seeks to serve somewhat different kinds of customers, with the company sales representatives targeting accounts that want or need significant technical assistance and a direct relationship with its factory source; while distributors serve the customers for whom local sources of supply, credit, and highly personalized attention are important.

The roles of the direct-sales force and independent distributors are complementary in other ways as well. The direct-sales force often is utilized to perform "missionary selling" in an area and to develop sales volume that will ultimately go through distributors. Further, the company might assume certain distribution functions that it can perform more economically than individual distributors. For example, many companies maintain field stocks on which distributors may draw, thereby reducing the inventory levels that distributors must keep in their warehouses. Some manufacturers, such as Ford, General Motors, and International Harvester, keep computerized records of dealer inventories to enable dealers to draw on each other's stock to meet customers' orders quickly.

CONCEPT QUESTIONS

1. Under what circumstances should direct channels be used?
2. What is the primary role of facilitating agencies?
3. How can the roles of the direct-sales force and independent distributors be complementary?

CHANNEL COOPERATION

Whether direct, indirect, or both direct and indirect channels are used, how can business marketing managers design and operate the firm's distribution channels in order to foster enthusiastic *channel cooperation*? The essence of the marketing concept is customer orientation at all levels of distribution, with a particular emphasis on the idea of partnership to foster that orientation. The characteristics of the highly competitive markets of the 1990s has put a premium on the operation of harmonious manufacturer-dealer relationships.

The channel member's role must be thoroughly defined in the business-to-business firm's marketing strategy. By putting the principles of the marketing concept to work for them, the firm will attempt to inspire a feeling of mutual interest and trust with channel members that will help convince them that they are essential members of the marketing team. The fact that there is a mutuality of interest demands that business-to-business firms base their distribution programs on not only what they would like from channel members, but also on what channel members would like from them. To get maximum exposure for their lines from channel members, policies must be put in place that serve their channel members' best interests, and, therefore their own.

Methods of Channel Cooperation

How do suppliers project their organizations into their respective distribution channels? How do suppliers make the organization and the channel into one? One means of achieving such a goal is, again, for the supplier to foster a sense of "partnership" with their distributors. Once a distribution network has been chosen and the type and numbers of intermediaries needed has been determined, what is expected from channel members and what they can expect in return should be considered.[20] Armstrong World Industries of Lancaster, Pennsylvania, is a good example of a manufacturer that stresses the partnership concept in building a highly motivated team of channel members. In the firm's floor-covering division, for instance, all products are sold through independent wholesale distributors whom Armstrong views as partners in a quest to maintain a strong leadership position in the many types of floor coverings sold. Suppliers can also accomplish this difficult task by doing many things for their resellers that they typically do for their own organizations. Suppliers sell, advertise, plan, train, and promote for these firms. (A brief elaboration of these methods follows below.) The establishment of electronic information interchange linkages (among other tools) between channel members offers significant potential for the transformation of their relationship, with significant benefits for all participants.[21]

Use of missionary salespeople. *Missionary salespersons* aid the sales of channel members, as well as bolster the whole system's level of activity and selling effort. Training of resellers' salespeople and executives is an effective weapon of cooperation. The channels operate more efficiently when all are educated in the promotional techniques and uses of the products involved.

Involvement in the planning function of channel members. Such involvement is another powerful weapon of the supplier. Helping resellers to set quotas for their customers, studying the market potential for them, forecasting a member's sales volume, inventory planning and protection, and so on—all are aspects of planning assistance. For instance, American Hospital Supply helps its customers (hospitals) manage inventory and streamline order processing for hundreds of medical supplies.

Promotional aid. Aid in promotion through the provision of advertising materials (mats, displays, commercials, literature, direct-mail pieces), ideas, funds (cooperative advertising), sales contests, store layout, push money (PMs, or spiffs), signify another form of cooperation.

Acting as a management consultant. The large supplier can serve as a management consultant to channel members, dispensing advice in all areas of business, including accounting, personnel, planning, control, finance, buying, paper systems or office procedures, and site selection. Aid in financing would include extended credit terms, consignment selling, and loans.

By no means do these methods of coordination take a one-way route. All members of the channel, including supplier and reseller, see their own organizations meshing with the others and so provide coordinating weapons in accordance with their ability. Therefore, the manufacturer would undertake a marketing research project for the channel and also expect the resellers to keep records and vital information for the manufacturer's use. A supplier would also expect the channel members to service the product after the sale.

CHANNEL CONFLICT

When a business-to-business firm is not able to achieve cooperation among its various channel members, channel conflict arises. *Channel conflict* can be described as a situation in which one channel member perceives another channel member to be engaged in behavior that is preventing or impeding the other from achieving a set goal. It is, in essence, a state of frustration brought about by a restriction of role performance. The degree to which the behavior of one channel member could potentially destroy, thwart, or hinder the goal attainment of another is a function of goal incompatibility, domain dissension, and differences in perceptions of reality between them, as well as the extent of their interdependence. Most business marketing managers agree on the importance of channel control. In both business and consumer markets, manufacturers want control of distribution channels for better execution of their marketing strategies. Intermediaries have been assumed also to want control of the channel to avoid being bound by manufacturer-determined strategies.[22] The stage is set for conflict!

With respect to conflict versus cooperation in marketing channels, Gattorna has identified some critical factors underlying possible conflicts between channel members as follows:[23]

(1) Communications, structures, and decision-making processes.

(2) Manipulation of channel members by other members of the same channel.

(3) Introduction of new innovations (including new technology) that are resisted by barriers to change.

(4) Denial of legitimate claims for reallocation of power and functions.

(5) Differences between channel members in primary business philosophy.

(6) The exchange act itself, specifically in terms of reaching agreement on terms of trade.

These factors carry the seeds for conflict. Each channel member has a set of objectives and goals that are very often incompatible with those of other channel members. For example, large manufacturers tend to be growth oriented, whereas small- or medium-sized distributors are more interested in maintaining the status quo. The likelihood of conflict is high in such situations because, in their pursuit of policies that are congruent with "dynamic goals" (for example, increased market share and higher investment returns), the large manufacturers will likely adopt innovative programs that contradict the more static orientation of the small- or medium-sized manufacturers.

Ideally, the cooperation necessary to reduce conflict within a channel system should be present in whatever ways are needed to assist in doing the overall job better. Examples of typical channel conflict problems are detailed in Exhibit 8-3. The cooperation necessary to reduce such conflicts might be in the form of the simplification of procedures for ordering, pricing, or billing, or in a more involved area, such as securing promotional materials from the manufacturer's advertising program. Other areas of cooperation to reduce channel conflicts would appear in such diverse activities as market research, sales analysis, assistance in customer identification and determination of potential, product education, technical assistance, training programs, and delivery. Whatever type of cooperation is needed should be known and should be provided to the fullest extent possible. Again, when and if conflict exceeds a certain level, one of the parties will choose to pull out of the network.

EXHIBIT 8-3 **Examples of Channel Conflict Issues**

Issues Embodied in Conflict Incidents Occurring in the Manufacturer-Distributor Dyad

Manufacturer Complaints	*Distributor Complaints*
1. Lack of service by distributor's personnel	1. Product unavailability
2. Ineffective communication	2. Lag time in new-product development
3. Warranty administration	3. Ineffective communication for problem solving
4. Distributor cash-flow tightness	4. Product quality and defects
5. Documenting rebates and payments	5. Faulty sales forecasting
6. Loss and damages in delivery	6. Damages due to packing
7. Documenting advertising expenditures	7. Off-season financing burden
8. Weak market penetration by distributor	
9. Violation of sales policy	
10. Gaps in product line	

The Nature of Channel Conflict

Channel conflict most frequently takes the form of tension and disagreements between channel members. For example, from a wholesaler's perspective, manufacturers do not understand that the primary obligation of wholesalers is to serve their customers; and that serving the manufacturer is secondary. Manufacturers, on the other hand, feel that wholesalers too often pay them only lip service and often openly compete with them for business. Conflict management is not only essential, but it will also result in better performance of the channel system. A major source of conflict might be in the transactional process, since it is natural for the seller to desire a higher price than the buyer wants to pay; or for the buyer to want a lower price than the seller is willing to accept. The conflict in regard to price can be resolved through one party influencing the other party's position, or through both parties compromising on a price somewhere between the two extremes. Changes in other factors, such as the amount of service to be provided by the seller, may be necessary before the transaction can be completed. When conflicts are viewed in a rational perspective, firms will discover many more reasons for cooperation, rather than resorting to acts that contribute to conflict in the channel structure. The underlying reason for conflict is that two independent companies are involved, each of which has its own mission, objectives, and perspectives on how their business should be run. Compromise should not heighten conflict; it should reduce it. Negotiated solutions should be mutually satisfying to both parties, or the conflict has not been properly resolved.

Conflict Management and Resolution

For the business marketer, the problem of how to manage conflict must be resolved. The firm faced with a conflict situation with another channel member has several strategies available to manage the conflict. Some of these strategies would include waiting to see if the conflict issue and cause subside. This offers the firm the opportunity to monitor the conflict situation and to use the time to develop a well-thought-out plan of action to resolve the conflict. The use of various bargaining techniques that require compromise to solve the conflict is often helpful. Organizational changes often are necessary not only to reduce conflict, but also to serve as a warning system to identify stress in an early stage before it becomes a conflict. Possible organizational changes may include the appointment of a distributor "ombudsman," the appointment of an advisory board, and/or the short-term exchange of people between firms to develop more empathy in channel relationships. A reorganization of the entire channel system is also often considered. This strategy would include the deletion and the addition of specific members of a channel system, such as business products distributors or manufacturers' representatives (agents). As mentioned earlier in the chapter, this action can have serious ramifications, with a resulting loss of market share. Such action should be studied and carefully evaluated prior to implementation.

The shortening of product life cycles, especially in areas such as telecommunications, information processing, and other high-tech products, puts pressure on manufacturers for rapid market penetration. This causes conflict. Turbulent channel conflict must be managed and resolved, employing strategies that are collaborative rather than combative.[24]

A Legal Perspective on Channel Conflict

The very existence of different kinds of marketing institutions depends not only on their relative effectiveness in performing particular marketing functions, but also upon the methods and terms upon which they can buy and sell. Legislation that influences either the effectiveness with which marketing institutions compete, or the methods and terms employed by sellers, can be expected to have repercussions on the use of particular channels of distribution. With regard to most of the legal limitations referred to in this section of the chapter, one should note that the antitrust-enforcement agencies have been highly successful in terms of the number of court cases they have won when they have brought suit against alleged offenders. Furthermore, for a firm to defend itself adequately once charged with a violation, it generally must spend a large sum of money in preparing its case, given the complexity of the defenses available. The costs involved might, in fact, exceed the benefits of the company's winning the case. Business marketing managers might spare themselves considerable difficulties by devoting some of their energies to the avoidance of being in conflict with antitrust laws or with the edicts of the antitrust-enforcement agencies.

Major issues with potential legal ramifications would include exclusive dealing contracts, exclusive territorial arrangements, refusals to deal, and the like. The opportunities for channel conflict are limitless.

Typical Problem Areas in the Manufacturer-Intermediary Relationship

To avoid conflict while promoting effective channel strategy is difficult, and sometimes it seems impossible. A number of basic policy rules must be made and their enforcement carried out by the business marketing manager. These rules would involve such potential problem areas as service and technical assistance, house accounts, inventory levels, provision of marketing information, training and support services, and second product lines carried. A brief review of each of these potential problem areas follows.

Service and technical assistance. Service and technical assistance are big factors in the business market; out of necessity, they must extend into the channel of distribution. As an example, a business marketing manager can be forced to use a direct-channel strategy because of an inability to find intermediaries who want to provide service and technical assistance, or because of difficulty in finding an intermediary capable of providing such service. Or, the marketing manager could choose a particular intermediary, especially a business products distributor, on the basis of proven service facilities or personnel. In a similar vein, the marketing manager might be prohibited from using a manufacturers' representative because of the reluctance of many of these intermediaries to provide such service and technical assistance. If the product line requires significant service and/or technical assistance, the business marketing manager must be sure that the desired service is available and that it is equal to, or better than, the service offered by other manufacturers and middlemen competing for the same market.

House accounts. A *house account* can be loosely defined as "a customer with whom the manufacturer would rather deal directly (usually because of volume and/or service requirements), while turning the balance of the territory over to an intermediary." House accounts can be a touchy area, especially if the account is a very large or profitable one that the intermediary would desire to have as a customer. Here, in essence, the manufacturer tells the intermediary that all present and potential accounts within a defined geographical territory belong to the intermediary except... One would not have to stretch his or her imagination too far to realize that a loose, inconsistent policy regarding house accounts, in all likelihood, presents a potential legal problem area in the manufacturer-intermediary relationship.

Inventory levels. What should the policy be regarding how much inventory a stocking distributor will carry? Too little might result in lost sales due to stockouts, while too much might well jeopardize an intermediary's cash flow. Should the business marketing manager allow an intermediary to return obsolete or excess inventory? If such returns are allowed, should there be a "restocking" charge? The basic objective of the inventory function is to have products available to end users when they need them; so, the crucial problem is to determine the level of customer service desired or needed, and then to determine the balance between service on inventory availability and the costs associated with carrying the inventory. The higher the field inventory level, the higher the cost of invested dollars, potential obsolescence, and storage costs. This area is ripe for spawning manufacturer-intermediary conflict.

Marketing information and feedback. The business marketing manager must consider the information flow available between and among firms in the physical product-flow network. Will the marketing manager expect market feedback to assess trends in distribution patterns, to discern customer needs, to assess the effect of promotional campaigns, to obtain feedback as to company image, and to gauge competitive pressures? Some marketing managers expect market feedback from their channels of distribution and make this expectation a very specific channel objective. This operating procedure could well lead to channel members being selected on the basis of their willingness to provide such feedback. One might view such a managerial approach toward the collection of feedback as rather unrealistic in expecting a nonstocking intermediary (such as a manufacturers' representative, sales agent, or broker working strictly on a commission basis) to take time from the selling effort to search out market information, trends, and the competitive posture in a particular territory, region, or industry. However, can the marketing manager expect or even demand this service from the inventory-stocking industrial distributor? If a certain level of service is not forthcoming, might there be channel conflict brewing? This potential problem area must be discussed, settled, and agreed upon, prior to the execution of basic channel decisions.

Training and support services. Most intermediaries expect, even frequently demand, merchandising assistance from the manufacturer. Business marketing managers who want to stimulate and to hold intermediary interest must consider developing advertising and sales-promotion programs. Also, effective sales meetings and training programs must be considered as incentives for both sales and technical training. Factory training of intermediary sales personnel is indispensable. A substantial amount of knowledge can be acquired through programmed learning techniques at relatively low cost. Programmed learning exercises, combined with commercially available sales training packages, will enable most intermediary personnel to become thoroughly familiar with a supplier's product line. This kind of training is important because the sales personnel working for an intermediary tend to favor those manufacturers' product lines with which they are most knowledgeable and most comfortable.

What training and support-services policies should the business marketing manager adopt? What is affordable? Should the policies call for joint training programs with both the manufacturer and the intermediary sharing the cost? Will cooperative advertising be utilized, and will missionary sales work be required? Each of these areas can and often will lead to channel conflict if they are not effectively addressed early in the channel selection process. Reasonable and well-thought-out answers to these questions should enable the marketing manager to develop inventory policies that will be attractive to intermediaries.

Second lines carried. The stocking of competing lines of merchandise can also constitute a problem area in the manufacturer-intermediary relationship. Manufacturers tend to favor intermediaries who can afford them some measure of protection from competition; one way to gain this fragile security is to pick intermediaries who will limit the number of competing lines they carry. The business marketing manager is confronted with the task of persuading the channel member to do a job comparable with the manager's own direct-sales force, if such a force exists. To obtain this degree of control, the marketing manager will generally have to provide services and incentives, such that the intermediary will not want to, or have to, pick up competing lines.

Business marketing managers whose marketing and sales programs increase channel member profits, who treat distributors as customers when negotiating transactions, and who treat distributors as partners when in pursuit of specific customers will usually find that such intermediaries accept direction willingly.[25] Some firms recognize the "partnership concept" between manufacturers and intermediaries by preparing formal contracts to be signed by both parties. Columbus-McKinnon Corporation, a large firm, makes the following agreement with its distributors:

> The distributor will maintain an inventory that gives four turns based on last year's sales; will purchase at least $15,000 a year from the supplier; and will actively promote the sale of the supplier's products. The supplier (Columbus-McKinnon), in turn, extends the latest discount service and freight; contributes a specific amount to joint advertising; works a specified length of time with each distributor salesperson; and helps develop annual sales targets.[26]

Both company and distributors agree that a formal contract is the only effective way to operationalize the partnership idea and avoid potential misunderstandings.

INTENSIVE, SELECTIVE, AND EXCLUSIVE DISTRIBUTION

A business marketing manager can choose from one of three possible distribution alternatives in regard to the degree of market exposure a product item or a product line is to receive. Intensive, selective, or exclusive distribution can be used to reach the desired number of channel members within a specified geographic region. A marketer's decision in regard to the number of distributors to use is primarily based on the size of the market and the market share held by channel members. A brief examination of intensive, selective, and exclusive distribution follows.

Intensive Distribution

With *intensive distribution*, the marketing manager attempts to gain access to as many resellers, or to establish as many of the company's own reselling units, as possible within a particular geographic area. There are many cases where the type or expertise of the intermediary does not matter, but the maximum exposure does. For example, the Building Service and Cleaning Products Division of the 3M Corporation intensively distributes its Scotch-Brite surface-conditioning products through business distributors throughout the United States and Canada. This product line (abrasives) is used by a multitude of firms in several different industries, and various grades and sizes must be available for use on very short notice. If the business user cannot purchase that product immediately from a nearby source, a substitute will be used. On a standardized type of product with low unit cost, little sales effort might be required. Ready availability and immediate delivery become important. For instance, a manufacturer of nuts and bolts would desire widespread distribution of the product since the buying habits of the business user will be predicated on convenience of purchase. In this situation, the dominant factor is place utility, since brand insistence would typically be relatively weak. Generally, distribution saturation is attempted when the product price is relatively low and when buyers who frequently purchase the product are willing to accept a substitute. In this event, the marketing manager will often use multiple channels to saturate the market with the product. The channel policy of intensive distribution might cause the firm to use less than optimum channels from a single-channel profitability criterion; but intensive distribution can increase the firm's total profitability based on all its channels in the market area.[27]

Selective Distribution

With *selective distribution*, the business marketing manager distributes the product to a limited number of resellers in a particular geographic region. The business marketer is attempting to select only the better middlemen in utilizing a selective distribution policy. The marketing manager tries to preserve the company image while obtaining quality of representation, service, and adequate volume. Several screening criteria are utilized to locate the correct dealers. An accessory-equipment manufacturer will look for firms that are able to service its product properly. An electronics manufacturer would look for service ability and a quality dealer image. On the negative side, poor credit risks and chronic complainers are quickly removed from consideration.[28]

The goodwill of the intermediary is important, as well as the competency of the intermediary's sales force and the composition of the area as to potential customers. With a selective distribution arrangement, a better-than-average selling effort is expected; and adequate market coverage may be realized with more control and reduced costs than is the case with intensive distribution. Materials-handling equipment, electric motors, power transmission equipment, and tools typically fall into the category of straight- or modified-rebuy situations. The time spent in evaluating sources for these products is not great, yet the purchase is not always simple and repetitive. The buyer needs advice about applications, maintenance, and repair, and the buyer usually demands rapid product delivery, repair, and service. The manufacturer wants to be represented by a distributor who can satisfy these customer requirements.

Various reasons exist for choosing the selective method of distribution. The primary reasons are as follows:

(1) Distributors will generally give preferential treatment to the brand because of relatively limited competition.

(2) From a status standpoint, the intermediary will find it advantageous to distribute the product in the local industrial community.

(3) The intermediary will likely join in cooperative advertising campaigns, reducing costs to the manufacturer, while at the same time enlarging the promotional effort.

As was noted above, the more selective the distribution pattern, the greater the expected selling effort from the intermediary. Conversely, the more intensive the distribution pattern, the less the expected selling effort on the part of one reseller. A good rule of thumb seems to be that the more expensive the product, the lower the stockturn is; or the more important the repair service is, the greater should be the tendency for the business marketer to choose a highly selective distribution pattern.

Exclusive Distribution

When an *exclusive distribution* policy is used, the business marketing manager can exercise more control over pricing, promotion, credit, and other marketing functions by limiting the number of intermediaries handling his or her products in a particular geographic area. Where a strong selling effort is required, where service is a major factor, where full-inventory stocks are needed, where the capital investment is large, and where intermediary protection is important, an exclusive arrangement might be feasible. In these situations, the manufacturer will assure the intermediary that no sales will be made in a particular territory except through that specific intermediary. The manufacturer agrees to permit the intermediary to be the exclusive representative in a certain territory; and in return, the intermediary agrees to sell the manufacturer's products aggressively. Pettibone tower cranes and Skytrak extendable-boom forklifts are examples of business products sold by exclusive distribution.

The basic reasons for manufacturers to grant exclusive distribution agreements to intermediaries are as follows:

(1) To obtain market access if intermediaries believe that protection against intrabrand competition is needed; they would decline to handle the product without such a stipulation.

(2) As a motivational means to increase the distributor's sales efforts.

(3) To control the character and uniformity of resellers' operations.[29]

INTERNATIONAL CHANNEL DECISIONS

World trade is increasingly important to the health of our economy and to the growth of U.S. companies. Every one billion dollars in U.S. exports generates about twenty-five thousand jobs.[30] Exporting not only creates jobs but provides business-to-business firms with new growth, new markets, and hopefully, additional profits. Manufacturers introducing a business product to a foreign market face that same difficult decision: Should the product be marketed directly through a company sales force or a company distribution division, indirectly through independent intermediaries, or through a combination of the two? With so many U.S. manufacturers now marketing their products overseas, the motivation of channel partners needs to be addressed from an international perspective.[31] To an economist, this is a question of vertical integration, in which the choice is between primarily captive agents (direct) or primarily independent intermediaries (indirect).[32] As with domestic distribution, the former option generally affords the business-to-business firm more control than the latter.

When transcending national borders, business marketers face a host of constraints. People speak different languages, rules and regulations differ, and economic conditions and political stability can cause problems. However, for the first time in many years, U.S. companies are strategically positioned to profit from exporting their products and services to many nations. The U.S. and Foreign Commercial Service is a governmental international trade agency with a worldwide delivery system that will analyze a foreign market, conduct customized in-country studies of a firm's competition, and help business marketers choose the best channel of distribution overseas. (International trade specialists are based in 66 major U.S. cities and 126 locations abroad).[33] Trade specialists overseas do on-the-spot market research, including customized individual studies for qualified agents and/or distributors. They speak the host-country language; understand local customs, traditions, and trade regulations; and can be a particularly valuable resource when establishing overseas distribution outlets. The personalized search for qualified foreign representatives will identify up to six prospects who have examined product literature and have expressed interest in representing the firms.

Types of Indirect-Channel Intermediaries

With an indirect channel, the business marketer deals with one or more domestic middlemen, who in turn move and/or sell the product to foreign middlemen or final users.[34] These domestic middlemen are grouped under two broad categories: *domestic agents* (do not take title) and *domestic merchants* (take title but not necessarily possession). An agent represents the manufacturer, whereas a merchant (for example, a distributor) represents the manufacturer's product. The merchant has no power to contract on behalf of the manufacturer, but the agent can bind the manufacturer in authorized matters to contracts made on the manufacturer's behalf.

Agents can be further classified, with some representing the buyer and others representing the manufacturer. Those who work for the manufacturer include export brokers, manufacturer's export agents or sales representatives, export-management companies, cooperative exporters, and Webb-Pomerane associations.

Agents who look after the buyer's interests include purchasing (buying) agents/offices and country-controlled buying agents.

Finally, legal regulations, image, product characteristics, intermediaries' loyalty and conflict, and local customs are all additional factors that affect channel decisions. Business marketers must keep in mind that no matter how desirable the product might be to the foreign market, it must be made accessible to buyers. Much must be taken into account in designing and developing an international channel of distribution.

CONCEPT QUESTIONS

1. How does the marketing concept relate to channel cooperation?
2. What form does channel conflict normally take?
3. What does the practice of exporting goods and services provide for the U.S. economy?

SUMMARY

1. From earliest times, geographically separated buyers and sellers have required a capability to move or to transfer goods and commodities physically. The marketing functions of buying, selling, storage, transportation, sorting, financing, risk taking, and market information must be carried on within the channel system. Each channel function must be performed at least once in every channel, and some might be performed by several channel members.
2. Business marketers must decide whether to use direct or indirect channels. By their very nature, channel decisions are long term, so a careful consideration of channel needs and requirements is essential for the business marketing manager.
3. Direct channels involve direct selling to the business user, with or without the use of sales branches. In sharp contrast to consumer goods, most manufactured business goods are sold directly to users.
4. The use of indirect channels is warranted when the market is widely scattered, when many firms must be contacted, when small orders are common, and when goods are made for inventory rather than to fill specific orders. If the business marketer decides to use an indirect channel, he or she has a variety of options to include business products distributors; manufacturers' representatives (agents); sales agents or brokers; and facilitating agencies. There are, of course, both advantages and limitations to each of these options, and the business marketing manager must carefully weigh his or her requirements in light of what each of these intermediaries can offer.
5. Whether to use direct or indirect channels continues to be a question of utmost importance to the business marketer. Direct selling to user-customers might be

preferred in more concentrated market areas; whereas, independent distributors carrying multiple lines might be the choice in thinner market areas.

6. Channel cooperation, in essence, is the application of the marketing concept to the channel area in marketing. Business marketers must be aware of methods by which channel cooperation can be achieved.
7. The business marketing manager must constantly be vigilant in looking for evidence of present and potential conflict situations within the channel; he or she must be alert to ways in which such conflict can be reduced and/or avoided through greater efforts toward channel cooperation. In attempting to reduce channel conflict, the business marketer must be ever mindful of the legal issues involved in catering to the needs and desires of channel members.
8. Business marketers must decide the degree of market exposure which they desire for their products or product lines. The three primary choices include intensive, selective, and exclusive distribution; and the marketing manager must decide exactly which type of exposure offers the most appropriate benefits.
9. World trade is increasingly important to the health of our economy and to the growth of U.S. companies. Every one billion dollars in U.S. exports generates about twenty-five thousand jobs. Exporting not only creates jobs but provides business-to-business firms with new growth, new markets, and new profits. In transcending national borders, business marketers face a host of constraints, which include different languages, rules, regulations, and economic and political environments. Often, indirect channel intermediaries are utilized in international business marketing.

KEY TERMS

Breaking of bulk
Broker
Business products distributor
Channel conflict
Channel cooperation
Channel management
Direct channels
Domestic agent
Domestic merchant
Exclusive distribution
General-line distributor
House account
Indirect channels
Intensive distribution
Jobber
Limited-line distributor
Manufacturers' representative
Missionary salesperson
Physical distribution management
Sales agent
Sales branch
Selective distribution

REVIEW QUESTIONS

1. Identify and briefly discuss each of the eight functions of distribution channels.
2. What is a direct channel? Under what general conditions would direct channels be utilized?

3. What is an indirect channel? Under what general conditions would indirect channels be utilized?
4. Define business products distributor. What are the major limitations involved with the use of business products distributors? What major trends are currently associated with business products' distributors?
5. Identify manufacturers' representatives (agents). What are the major limitations involved with the use of manufacturers' representatives? Discuss the major trends currently related to the work of manufacturers' representatives.
6. How are sales agents and brokers used as intermediaries in indirect channels of distribution? What is the role of facilitating agencies in business marketing channels? What are some examples of business facilitating agencies?
7. How can business-to-business firms apply the marketing concept to their respective channel activities? What are some possible reasons for channel conflict? What are four common methods for securing cooperation in a business marketing channel? When can channel conflict benefit overall channel performance? Discuss several methods for reducing channel conflict and promoting greater channel cooperation.
8. Discuss six typical problem areas in the manufacturer-intermediary relationship.
9. Identify three levels of market exposure commonly used in business distribution. When would a physical distribution manager use each one?
10. What purposes does the exporting of business goods and services serve? What constraints are typically faced by business marketers as they cross national boundaries? Distinguish between two types of indirect channel intermediaries used in business international marketing.

Cases

CASE 8-1 Perrier Limited

Perrier-brand sparkling water had a 57 percent share of the designer water market in the United States in 1988. In February 1990, a problem in the company's filtration system caused the product to become contaminated with benzene. Benzene had been found to be a minor carcinogen. The company elected to make a full disclosure of the facts to the marketplace. Perrier accepted full responsibility and recalled $70 million worth of the product.

In April 1990, Perrier was about to begin shipping Perrier-brand sparkling water to the United States again. Kim Jeffrey, senior vice president of marketing, expected Perrier to be in 90 percent of the U.S. market within six weeks. For each new market entered, Perrier had scheduled a two-week media blitz to announce the reintroduction of the product. The campaign was called "We're Back." Perrier also scheduled sales promotion activities to coincide with the reintroduction of the drink. To tie in with the ad campaign, Perrier staffed cafes with workers wearing "We're Back" apparel to conduct sampling in its fifteen largest markets.

According to Perrier, the key to success of Perrier brand was going to be heavy reliance on distribution. Lost shelf space was going to have to be recaptured in the supermarkets. Perrier had never paid a retailer for shelf space for the product, a common industry practice, and did not intend to do so now. Space for the product was expected to come from "saved space." Jeffrey stated that retailers had saved space for the Perrier brand by stocking the lost space with other Perrier products.

Retailers' views on the shelf space issue were mixed. Some retailers felt that the high profit margin of the product (18 to 20 percent) would more than compensate for the shelf space needed. Other retailers claimed that Perrier would have to pay to get the shelf space back. Not only would Perrier have to pay for the shelf space, but it would have to spend a lot of money on advertising and sales promotion to convince many retailers to take the Perrier brand back.

Restauranteurs were expected to be another major stumbling block for Perrier. Perrier brand had about one-third of the total bar and restaurant market in 1989. To some restaurants, sparkling water is sparkling water and any brand will do. Some restaurants will take Perrier brand back and offer two brands of sparkling water to diners; others will not take Perrier brand back. In the end, it may be consumer demand that influences what brand of designer water restauranteurs offer. If enough requests for Perrier brand are made, restaurants will more than likely stock the brand.

Consumer research indicated that 85 percent of Perrier customers would buy the product again. Ninety percent of consumers felt that by admitting its mistake Perrier acted responsibly. These figures led Perrier management to believe that the company could recapture 85 percent of its sales by the end of 1991.

DISCUSSION QUESTIONS

1. Should Perrier have used a push or pull strategy to regain its market share? Why?
2. Many feel that the distribution channel contributes to the success or failure of the product. Is this true for Perrier?
3. Should Perrier have paid channel members to carry the brand? What potential problems would have arisen from this decision?

Source: C. Lamb, J. Hair, and C. McDaniel, *Principles of Marketing*, 1st Edition (Cincinnati, OH: South-Western Publishing Company, 1992) pp. 314–315.

CASE 8-2 Merisel, Incorporated

Micro America and Softsel merged in 1989 to become Merisel, one of the nation's largest distributors of computers and computer accessories. In a market where high product assortment and fast delivery can make the difference between making and losing the sale, being larger can be helpful. The high cost of maintaining inventory in several warehouses around the country has forced several of the larger distribution companies to explore mergers. By consolidating resources, Merisel has been able to reduce operating costs.

There is one area, however, in which being larger is not an advantage. Many of the high-end computer products are sold direct; that is, sold directly to the retailers without using a distributor. This means that in order to make a profit, distributors are forced to sell low-end merchandise. The problem comes in what to do with the DOA (dead on arrival), or defective, merchandise. The distributors are caught in the middle. The retailer wants immediate replacement, and most manufacturers will only repair, not replace, defective merchandise. Distributors take the loss.

Upon receipt of returned product from the retailer, the distributor sends a replacement product to the retail store. The distributor has to pay the freight for the second shipment. Then the defective product must be shipped to the manufacturer (another shipping expense). The manufacturer repairs the product and returns it to the distributor. Frequently, this product is missing the original packing material, original documentation, essential cables to connect the product to the computer, or some other item that may have been in the original box.

Unfortunately, the distributor now has a used product. This product cannot be sold as new and is therefore frequently sold at a below-cost price. Until the product is sold, it takes up valuable space in the warehouse. The problem with DOA merchandise is that it only affects the distributors; every other member of the channel is happy. Many companies will not accept product returns without all the original materials included in the original box. This requirement adds to the distributor's cost by necessitating a check of each and every product return for completeness.

In periods of slow sales, the problem of returns becomes even worse. John Thompson, senior vice president of operations for Merisel, was quoted as saying, "During a slow economy, people tend to return more product for one reason or another." Thompson views this as just a cost of doing business. "We see offering a lenient return policy a necessary service for our customers," he said.

DISCUSSION QUESTIONS

1. How should companies like Merisel handle dealer returns? Should this just be considered a cost of doing business?
2. Should manufacturers accept some of the cost for this returned merchandise? How about the retail stores?
3. Why do you think returns increase during slow business periods?
4. What types of channel conflict are present in the computer distribution channel? How should these conflicts be resolved?

Source: C. Lamb, J. Hair, and C. McDaniel, *Principles of Marketing*, 1st Edition (Cincinnati, OH: South-Western Publishing Company, 1992) p. 341.

Suggested Additional Readings

Bialaszewski, Dennis, and Michael Giallourakis. "Perceived Communication Skills and Resultant Trust Perceptions within the Channel of Distribution." *Journal of the Academy of Marketing Science* 13 (Winter/Spring 1985): 206–217. **Survey of distributors under the supervision of a single channel manager with implications for the trust relationship within a marketing channel.**

Butaney, Gul, and Lawrence H. Wortzell. "Distributor Power versus Manufacturer Power: The Customer Role." *Journal of Marketing* 52 (January 1988): 52–63. **Empirical study of how both customer market power and manufacturer market power have a role in determining distributor power.**

Carter, Joseph R. "Communicate with Your Vendors." *Journal of Purchasing and Materials Management* 22 (Winter 1986): 16–22. **Focus on exchange of information with an example of a systematically designed communication system.**

Constantin, James A., and Robert F. Lusch. "Discover the Resources in Your Marketing Channel." *Business*, 36 (July/August/September 1986): 19–26. **Discussion of channel management, marketing support systems, and interorganizational marketing relationships.**

Coughlan, Anne T. "Competition and Cooperation in Marketing Channel Choice: Theory and Application." *Marketing Science* 4 (Spring 1985): 110–129. **Empirical study of vertical marketing channels in the product-differentiated, duopolistic international semiconductor industry.**

Ferguson, Thomas E. "Customers' Diverse Needs Require Diverse Channels." *Business Marketing* 77 (March 1992): 64–66. **A discussion of the differing types of channels necessary to meet the distribution needs of diverse customers.**

Fine, Seymour H. "The Industrial Distributor Is Also Human," *Journal of Business and Industrial Marketing* 2 (Spring 1987): 55–60. **Study finding that producers of industrial goods are increasingly experiencing the need to develop stronger personal relationships with their distributors.**

Gaski, John F., and John R. Nevin. "The Differential Effects of Exercised and Unexercised Power Sources in a Marketing Channel." *Journal of Marketing Research* 22 (May 1985): 130–142. **Empirical study of the use of power and the presence of satisfaction and conflict within a marketing channel.**

Hague, Paul. "Sharpening the Distributor Network." *Industrial Marketing Digest* (UK), 11 (Fourth Quarter 1986): 145–150. **Evaluation of distribution networks with suggestions for improvement.**

Howell, Roy D., Robert R. Britney, Paul J. Kuzdrall, and James B. Wilcox. "Unauthorized Channels of Distribution: Gray Markets." *Industrial Marketing Management* 15 (November 1986): 257–263. **Theoretical discussion of alternative channels of distribution, including price-quality discounts, problems, and corrective strategies.**

Lele, Milind. "Matching Your Channels to Your Product's Life Cycle." *Business Marketing* 71 (December 1986): 60–69. **Discussion of the value added by the channel versus the low cost of the channel.**

Lucas, George H., Jr., and Larry G. Gresham. "Power, Conflict, Control, and the Application of Contingency Theory in Marketing Channels." *Journal of the Academy of Marketing Science* 13 (Summer 1985): 25–38. **Theoretical discussion of the behavioral dimensions of interorganizational channel relationships.**

Lusch, Robert F., and Robert H. Ross. "The Nature of Power in a Marketing Channel." *Journal of the Academy of Marketing Science* 13 (Summer 1985): 39–56. **Survey of the relationship between food brokers and food wholesalers.**

Magrath, Allan J., and Kenneth G. Hardy. "Manufacturer Services for Distributors." *Industrial Marketing Management* 21 (May 1992): 119–124. **A discussion and assessment of the affordability, uniqueness, simplicity, and profitability of manufacturer services offered to distributors.**

Michie, Donald A., and Stanley D. Sibley. "Channel Member Satisfaction: Controversy Resolved." *Journal of the Academy of Marketing Science* 13 (Winter/Spring 1985): 188–205. **Study of channel conflict and resolution in the industrial marketing channel.**

Miler, Richard Lee, William F. Lewis, and J. Paul Merenski. *Journal of the Academy of Marketing Science* 13 (Fall 1985): 1–17. **Theoretical discussion and model development of channel relations.**

Morgan, James P. "MRO Distribution—An Industry in Transition." *Purchasing* 112 (May 21, 1992): 50–57. **A study of MRO distribution with a look at the economic conditions, the problems, the inventory, and the working capital involved.**

Pilling, Bruce K., and Li Zhang. "Cooperative Exchange: Rewards and Risks." *International Journal of Purchasing and Materials Management* 28 (Spring 1992): 2–9. **A survey of firms that utilize cooperative exchange in channel relationships to include the types and dimensions of such relationships.**

Ransan, V. Kasturi, Andris A. Zoltners, and Robert J. Becker. "The Channel Intermediary Selection Decision: A Model and Application." *Management Science* 32 (September 1986): 1114–1122. **Decision framework and normative model of an intermediary network, to include an industrial marketing application.**

Reddy, N. Mohan, and Michael P. Marvin. "Developing a Manufacturer-Distributor Information Partnership." *Industrial Marketing Management* 15 (May 1986): 157–163. **Case study of support services and the sharing of information in the machinery industry.**

Shugan, Steven M. "Implicit Understandings in Channels of Distribution." *Management Science* 31 (April 1985): 435–460. **Model of learning, influence attempts, retail prices, and channel member profits in a channel of distribution.**

Skinner, Steven J., and Joseph P. Guiltinan. *Journal of Retailing* 61 (Winter 1985): 66–88. **Survey of manufacturers of farm supplies who are contractually affiliated with dealers.**

Sonnenberg, Frank K. "Partnering: Entering the Age of Competition." *Journal of Business Strategy* 13 (May/June 1992): 49–52. **A discussion of some of the problems encountered in utilizing partnerships in the distribution of goods.**

Sutton, Howard. "Marketing: Changing Channels." *Across the Board* 23 (January 1986): 12–13. **Trends in independent distribution, warehousing distribution, and telemarketing.**

Walker, Bruce J., Janet E. Keith, and Donald W. Jackson, Jr. "The Channels Manager: Now, Soon, or Never?" *Journal of the Academy of Marketing Science* 13 (Summer 1985): 82–96. **A job description and impediments to the implementation of the channel manager concept.**

Yovovich, B. G, "Partnering At Its Best." *Business Marketing* 77 (March 1992): 36-37. **A discussion of the beneficial effects of partnering between suppliers and customers involved in business marketing relationships.**

ENDNOTES

[1]Philip Maker, "Distribution: Key To Strategy," *Industrial Distribution* 71 (December 1981): 29.

[2]Frank V. Cespedes, and Raymond E. Corey, "Managing Multiple Channels," *Business Horizons* 33 (July/August 1990): 67–77.

[3]Kenneth G. Hardy, and Allan J. Magrath, "Planning for Better Channel Management," *Long-Range Planning* (UK), 21 (December 1988): 30–37.

[4]Frank V. Cespedes, "Channel Management in General Management," *California Management Review* 31 (Fall 1988): 98–120.

[5]Mini Hahn and Dae R. Chang, "An Extended Framework for Adjusting Channel Strategies in Industrial Markets," *Journal of Business and Industrial Marketing* 7 (Spring 1992): 31–43.

[6]Howard Sutton, *Rethinking the Company's Selling and Distribution Channels*, Report no. 885 (The Conference Board: 1986), 1.

[7]Allan J. Magrath, "High Cost of Direct Sales Spurs Strong Partnerships," *Marketing News* 23 (March 27, 1989): 10.

[8]"Profits Up Despite Lagging Sales," *Industrial Distribution* 77 (July 1987): 33.

[9]"Industry Markets Goods through Dual Channels," *Industrial Distribution* 75 (April 1985): 15.

[10]Victor P. Buell, *Handbook of Modern Marketing*, 2d ed. (New York: McGraw-Hill, 1986), 4–8.

[11]Steve Zurier, "If Not Defense, Then What?" *Industrial Distribution* 81 (June 15, 1992): 56–58.

[12]James P. Morgan, "MRO Distribution: An Industry in Transition," *Purchasing* 112 (May 21, 1992): 50–61.

[13]Jack Keough, "Merger Traffic Slows to a Crawl," *Industrial Distribution* 80 (August 1991): 10–16.

[14]Steve Zurier, "Finally Reps Get Some Respect," *Industrial Distribution* 80 (June 1991): 27–30.

[15]"Market Penetration and Longevity," *American Salesman* 26 (January 1991): 23–25.

[16]Philip Kotler, *Principles of Marketing*, 5th ed. (Englewood Cliffs, N.J.: Prentice-Hall, 1991), 410.

[17]Rex Fraley, "Being an Agent Means Being Professional," *Agency Sales Magazine* 21 (January 1991): 40–41.

[18]Thomas C. Reinhart and Donald R. Coleman, "Heyday for the Independent Rep," *Sales and Marketing Management* (November 1978): 51–54. Reprinted with permission from *Sales and Marketing Management* magazine, Copyright 1978.

[19]William J. Stanton and Charles Futrell, *Fundamentals of Marketing*, 8th ed. (New York: McGraw-Hill, 1987), 357.

[20]"Marketing Guide: Distribution," *Marketing* (November 7, 1991): 23-26.

[21]Ramon O'Calaghan, Patrick J. Kaufman, and Benn R. Konsynski, "Adoption Correlates and Share Effects of Electronic Data Interchange Systems in Marketing Channels," *Journal of Marketing* 56 (April 1992): 45–56.

[22]Gul Butaney and Lawrence H. Wortzel, "Distributor Power versus Manufacturer Power: The Customer Role," *Journal of Marketing* 52 (January 1988): 52–63.

[23]John Gattorna, "Channels of Distribution Conceptualizations: A State of the Art Review," *European Journal of Marketing*, 7 (1978): 470–512.

[24]Allan J. Magrath and Kenneth G. Hardy, "Avoiding the Pitfalls in Managing Distribution Channels," *Business Horizons* 30 (September/October 1987): 29–33.

[25]For a related discussion of manufacturers treating their intermediaries as partners, see Kotler, *Principles of Marketing*, 373–374.

[26]Duffy Marks, "Post Carborundum: Distributors Evaluate Their Vendor Relations," *Industrial Distribution* 7 (June 1983): 35.

[27]Ronald D. Michman and Stanley D. Sibley, *Marketing Channels and Strategies* (New York: Grid Publishing, 1980), 320.

[28]Carl McDaniel, Jr., and William R. Darden, *Marketing* (Boston: Allyn and Bacon, 1987), 413.

[29]Michman and Sibley, *Marketing Channles and Strategies*, 320.

[30]*Focus on the Facts: Opportunities in Exporting*, no. 7 of a Series (U.S. Small Business Administration in cooperation with AT&T).

[31]Bert Rosenbloom, "Motivating Your International Channel Partners," *Business Horizons* 33 (March/April 1990): 53–57.

[32]Erin Anderson and Anne T. Coughlan, "International Market Entry and Expansion via Independent or Integrated Channel of Distribution," *Journal of Marketing* 51 (January 1987): 71–82.

[33]For more information, see "It Makes Good Business Sense," U.S. Department of Commerce, International Trade Administration, U.S. and Foreign Commercial Service, Washington, D.C. 20230.

[34]This section is largely from Sak Onkvisit and John J. Shaw, *International Marketing: Analysis and Strategy* (New York: Merrill Publishing, 1989), 506–509.

9 Business Physical Distribution Management and Strategy

Learning Objectives

After reading this chapter, you should be able to:

- Discuss the importance of physical distribution (logistics) management.
- Comprehend the significance of deregulation policies.
- Appreciate the strategic role and importance of customer service.
- Differentiate between public and private warehouses.
- Understand the significance of inventory control in the distribution function.
- Explain what is involved in an order-processing cycle.
- Describe the importance of physical distribution in international markets.

Chapter Outline

Learning Objectives

Physical Distribution in the Business Market
- The Nature of Physical Distribution

Traffic Management: An Overview

Functions of Traffic Management
- Mode and Carrier Selection
  - Motor transport
  - Rail transport
  - Water transport
  - Pipeline transport
  - Air transport
  - Intermodal transport
- Routing
- Claims Processing
- Operation of Private Transportation

Deregulation

Customer Service
- Customer-Service Standards
- Examination of Cost Trade-Offs
- The Impact of Logistical Service on Channel Members

Warehousing
- Private or Public Warehouses?

Inventory Control
- Electronic Data Interchange
- The Just-in-Time Concept
- The E.O.Q. Model
  - Calculating the E.O.Q.

Order Processing
- The Order-Processing Cycle
- Shortening the Order-Processing Cycle
- Vendor Stocking

International Distribution

Conclusion

Summary

Key Terms

Review Questions

Cases
- Case 9-1
- Case 9-2

Suggested Additional Readings
Endnotes

PHYSICAL DISTRIBUTION IN THE BUSINESS MARKET

Regardless of which channel the business marketing manager selects, if the right product is not delivered to the right place, in the right quantity, by the right transportation mode, at the right price, and under the proper conditions, the buyer will be unhappy. Eventually, unhappy buyers will lead to reduced market share, and reduced market share will lead to a change in marketing management. To avoid this potential problem area, the marketing manager should do the following: (1) understand the importance of physical distribution in overall marketing strategy; (2) understand the role of logistics in physical distribution strategy; and (3) understand the importance of maintaining specific customer-service levels while still maintaining desired profit levels.

The Nature of Physical Distribution

Physical distribution has been defined as "adding value through the management of materials, inventory, warehousing, transportation, and customer service."[1] It has also been defined as "the process of planning, implementing, and controlling the efficient, effective flow and storage of goods, services, and related information from point of origin to point of consumption for the purpose of conforming to the customer's requirements."[2] Mr. George Gecowers of the Council of Logistics Management tells us that companies are replacing inventory with information. He explains this as a major movement of technology in the logistics and distribution functions. Firms are hesitant to stock the quantities that they have kept in previous years. Over 30 percent of the typical business-to-business firm's inventory (raw materials, component parts, and the like) has, in the past, been used as insurance against nondelivery or delays in delivery. Business firms cannot afford to do this today and rarely will do so. As evidence of this, we only need to look at the proliferation of such techniques as just-in-time, stockless purchasing, make-and-hold inventory agreements, and other such techniques.

Physical distribution has the potential to enhance the production, marketing, and profit performance of any company that produces a tangible product. The major roadblock to realizing this potential lies in the outdated perception that physical distribution is nothing more than a "semantic upgrading" of the industrial traffic function. As a result, physical distribution too often has been viewed in its narrow, historical context as the cost function that moves business raw materials and finished goods to meet manufacturing schedules. What far too few realize is that up to 20 percent of the cost of a product is the cost to move it!

Services, which provide benefits that are partially intangible, still must have supplies, raw materials, and inventory control systems. So even a service provider cannot totally avoid the physical distribution function. For example, the primary mission of a health care institution is to provide quality patient care. In order to provide the proper level of care, management must develop a good physical distribution system. The box entitled "Business-to-Business Marketing in Action" describes how physical distribution is a critical component in the major success of Rhode Island Hospital.

Physical distribution management is often referred to as "logistical management." Originating in the military, the word "logistics" refers to the design and management of all activities (basically transportation, inventory, and warehousing) necessary to make materials available for manufacturing and to make finished products available to customers as needed and in the condition required. Logistics thus embodies two primary product flows: (1) "physical supply," or those flows that provide raw materials, components, and supplies to the production process; and (2) "physical distribution management," or those flows that deliver the completed product to customers and channel intermediaries.[3]

One of the earliest attempts to define physical distribution was made in 1962 by Peter Drucker:

> Physical distribution is simply another way of saying the whole process of business. You can look at a business—particularly a manufacturing business—as a physical flow of materials. This flow is interrupted when we take the stuff and cut it or shape it, handle it, store it. These are turbulences which interrupt the flow...and materials may flow from the iron ore to the galvanized garbage can. But the flow runs through all functions and all stages, and this is the fundamental reason why it isn't being managed. It does not fit into the traditional structure of a functional organization.[4]

Although Peter Drucker's definition is dated, it is still a valid definition today. Additionally, the following definition has been developed by the National Council of Physical Distribution Management:

> Physical distribution is the term employed in manufacturing and commerce to describe the broad range of activities concerned with the efficient movement of finished products from the end of the production line to the consumer, and, in some cases, includes the movement of raw materials from the source of supply to the beginning of the production line. These activities include freight transportation, warehousing, materials handling, protective packaging, inventory control, plant and warehouse site selection, order processing, market forecasting, and customer service.[5]

Not all marketing managers would agree with any of these definitions. However, all would agree to the far-reaching effects of their respective physical distribution systems. Many may not even agree on what their physical distribution

BUSINESS-TO-BUSINESS MARKETING IN ACTION

PHYSICAL DISTRIBUTION AS THE ARTERY OF HOSPITAL SERVICE

The Rhode Island Hospital is a large New England hospital with 719 beds, a budget of over $168 million, and a staff of 5,000 persons. It provides the typical medical and surgical services of a hospital plus medical research projects and medical education programs. To support this level of activity, the hospital has an investment in inventories of over two million dollars and purchases over twenty-four million dollars' worth of materials per year (about 14 percent of total operating costs) with 25,000 to 30,000 purchase orders.

The physical distribution organization consists of six departments: Purchasing, General Stores and Inventory, Central Services, Laundry, Dietary, and Print Shop. They are integrated into the Materials Management Department, whose mission is to balance and coordinate the independent materials functions into a single work force in order to achieve high-quality service at the lowest cost. The focus of the department is on transportation and processing efficiency through the integration of functions and on the awareness of the total cost of supplying items to patients, including purchase, receiving, storage, and final disposal.

Purchasing is a key physical distribution activity in the hospital because purchasing expenditures account for roughly one eighth of operating costs. Purchases are made directly from suppliers, but this hospital and others are able to secure better prices on some items by collectively buying in volume through cooperatives such as the Hospital Association of Rhode Island. Advance buying is a common hospital purchasing practice. Although inventory storage costs increase, the benefits of buying before price increases can more than offset these added inventory costs. With the large number of purchase orders that are processed annually, the hospital computer controls its inventory levels system and types purchase orders automatically from the machine.

The General Stores and Inventory group is responsible for the receiving and storekeeping activities as well as delivery of the material to nursing stations. This group, under the Director of the Materials Management Department, is responsible for over 70 percent of the total inventory investments. Unique to the hospital setting is that departments outside the control of materials management maintain their own inventories. In this case, the Dietary Food and Pharmacy Departments carry and keep close control over stocks for their own purposes. Inventory levels are controlled by scientific procedures and computerized record keeping.

Central Services is a function that is unique to hospital physical distribution. In effect, it is the management of sterile goods inventories. Inventories in a hospital are of two types: sterile and nonsterile. The nonsterile stocks are managed by the General Stores and Inventory groups in much the same way as they are in a business firm. However, sterile goods must be handled more carefully to prevent contamination. The Central Services group, in addition to stock keeping, prepares "kits" of dressing and sterile materials for burn patients, operating rooms, nursing units, and other special purposes.

Source: Ronald H. Ballon, *Basic Business Logistics* (Englewood Cliffs, N.J.: Prentice-Hall, 1987), p. 51. Reprinted with permission.

system should do, or how it should perform. All would most likely admit that their company might present a unique marketing situation that could probably benefit from a creative application of physical distribution knowledge and experience.

TRAFFIC MANAGEMENT: AN OVERVIEW

Transportation is such a pervasive force that it is often taken for granted. Transportation costs have been a concern of business marketers for many years, but there has been more talk and theory development than action. However, the increased sophistication of computers, marketing information systems, and integrated channel networks has led to a greater appreciation of the potential profit contribution of those individuals holding the position of traffic (or physical distribution or logistics) manager. This person is responsible for coordinating and integrating all movement of materials, including transportation, internal movement (materials handling), and warehousing; the process of implementing a "total systems approach" is slowly being carried out. Transportation management, traffic management, logistics management, or physical distribution management (whichever title fits a particular situation) is not only a dominant aspect of the economy, it is also an outstanding career-choice area. As evidence of the increased importance that top management is placing on the distribution/logistics discipline, Mr. George Gecowers, executive director of the Council of Logistics Management, claims that the average annual income of the membership of his organization is between $40,000 and $50,000. Today's transportation manager enjoys a sharply elevated status from that of previous decades. Working with computers and electronic data interchange (EDI) systems, the manager is a highly skilled white-collar employee.[6]

FUNCTIONS OF TRAFFIC MANAGEMENT

The functions of traffic management are broad and vary in intensity with the type of industry, the type of product being shipped, and the size and number of shipments being transported. A brief discussion of mode selection, routing, claims processing, and the operation of private transportation follow.

Mode and Carrier Selection

The five basic transportation modes are road, rail, water, pipeline, and air.[7] Each plays an important role in the movement of business freight; specializes in certain commodities or geographical freight movement; and competes for a segment of the freight transportation industry. Table 9-1 explains that each mode also has some major advantages associated with it, related to such criteria as cost,

TABLE 9-1 **Major Advantages by Transportation Mode**

Mode	Major Advantages
Motor	Speed of delivery Diversity of equipment Great flexibility Frequency of movement Transfer of goods to other carriers Convenient both to shipper and receiver
Rail	Mass movement of goods Low unit cost of movement Dependability Long-haul moving Wide coverage to major markets and suppliers Many auxiliary services, such as switching and in-transit privileges Transfer of goods to other carriers Specialized equipment
Water	Very low unit cost of movement Movement of low-unit-value commodities Long-haul moving Mass movement of bulk commodities
Pipeline	Lowest unit cost of movement Mass movement of liquid or gas products Long-haul moving Large capacity Most dependable mode
Air	Frequent service to major markets Large capability (40,000 to 200,000 pounds in one aircraft) Overnight service within continental United States Most rapid speed of any carrier
Intermodal	Combines major advantages of two or more modes Cost savings Lower loss and damage claims due to containerization Extends service to more shippers and receivers Reduced handling and storage costs

speed, flexibility, distance traveled, and dependability. A brief profile of each of the major transportation modes available to business manufacturers follows.

Motor transport. The motor carrier (truck transport) is the primary mover of shipments up to about thirty tons. There are approximately thirty-five thousand motor carriers in the United States, in addition to independent trucking and private carriage operations owned by firms that transport their own products in company-owned vehicles. Truckers handle everything from heavy machinery to liquid petroleum, refrigerated products, agricultural commodities, motor vehicles, and building materials.

The strategic advantage of motor carriage is the complete door-to-door service provided. Trucks carry only about one-quarter of all ton-mile traffic, but about three-quarters of the total dollar value of merchandise transported. Trucks are faster than rail but are more expensive to use. The greatest disadvantage of motor carrier use is the carrier's susceptibility to interruptions by bad weather.

The motor carrier mode, probably more than all others, illustrates deregulation at its best and its worst. After several years of "semideregulation," more than one hundred major carriers have been forced into bankruptcy. All top ten carriers have had reduced profits over the last two years. Discounts are the buzzword today and can be had for the asking. Rate variances between carriers often fall into the range of 10 to 20 percent.

Rail transport. Rail transport competes for large shipment sizes, particularly bulk commodities, as distances increase over five hundred miles. A financially healthy rail system is essential to some agricultural and business producers if they are to remain competitive in markets across the country. Railroads dominate the other modes of transportation in terms of ton-miles carried, but they have lost higher-valued traffic to other modes. Approximately 37 percent of the freight hauled in the United States goes by rail. Among the advantages to rail shippers are more flexible rates and improved service through the use of more sophisticated equipment than was the case a decade ago. The railroad business overall should be better off as we move through the 1990s. Prices will stay relatively flat and buyers might actually get more for their money as some railroads achieve real customer-service enhancements.[8]

Water transport. With eighty-five hundred miles of navigable inland waterways available, the United States inland river system functions as a major cost-efficient and practical method of transporting many business products for firms seeking reduced transportation costs.

Reduced transportation cost is the biggest advantage to the inland river system. One gallon of diesel fuel will move one ton of commodity 59 miles by truck, 202 miles by rail, or 514 miles by barge tows. The fact that river barge service exists as a competitive transportation system influences the rail and truck industry to keep rates down. The trade-off in moving goods by water transport, naturally, is speed. While talk of air, rail, and truck transportation is in terms of hours or days, barge delivery time is discussed in terms of weeks.

The percentage of freight handled by water has remained fairly stable over the years (approximately 15 percent), and water transport is indispensable for overseas freight movement of all shipment sizes. Water transportation is available only to firms shipping certain commodities that have access to the river systems, the Great Lakes, or ocean ports.

Like surface carriers, shipowners are now having to seriously consider "asset utilization," a popular industry term that means "if it's too expensive to run a ship, then we won't run it." If ocean carriers are to assume greater market control, they are going to have to do it through enhanced service offerings. Several "top-tier" lines are now offering total logistics management, information systems, and "seamless" multimodal distribution.[9]

Pipeline transport. Pipeline transport provides low-cost transportation and is utilized primarily for oil-related and chemical-related liquids such as natural gas. However, a variety of products, from liquids to solids, such as coal (in the form of slurry, which is ground-up coal mixed with water to form sludge), can be transported via this mode. Probably the greatest advantage of pipelines, other than cost savings, is dependability. Routes are fixed, tend to be concentrated regionally, and are seldom affected by weather conditions. Speed is slow, but pipelines are second only to railroads in ton-miles carried domestically.

Air transport. Air transport offers rapid freight movement, with the air-freight buzzword being "time-sensitive." Although air freight is costly, its speed may create savings in lower inventory levels to offset the increased cost. Items that can be carried are limited by space constraints and have to be delivered and picked up at the destination. A wide variety of business products are shipped through this mode, such as electronic parts, small but specialized machinery, and replacement parts. Air transport is a volatile business. Factors such as shrinking capacity, booming fuel costs, rampant bankruptcies, and consolidation are all driving prices up.[10] U.S. air carriers generate freight revenues of over $9 billion annually.

Intermodal transport. The use of two or more transportation modes to move a product is called *intermodal transport*. A shipment of subassemblies destined for Japan might move through a combination of air, rail, water, and truck before reaching its final destination. "Birdybacking" (air and truck), "piggybacking" (rail and truck), and "fishybacking" (water and truck) are popular and economical intermodal forms of transport.

Routing

If the traffic manager has title to the goods (either inbound or outbound), then decisions concerning specific routes over which shipments are to move become the responsibility of that individual. A practice related to specifying routing instructions is the use of F.O.B. ("free on board") terms, which specify which party, the shipper or the receiver, controls carrier selection and routing of a given shipment. The term "F.O.B. origin" specifies that the receiver is responsible for all transportation charges, and "F.O.B. destination" indicates that the shipper is liable. Under F.O.B. origin, the freight receiver selects carriers and specifies routing. If management considers traffic control important, it will negotiate F.O.B. origin terms for inbound traffic, and F.O.B. destination terms for outbound traffic.[11]

Claims Processing

Freight claims are made against carriers for loss or damage to freight in transit, for unreasonable delay in the movement of freight, and for freight charges that have been improperly assessed. Because of the complexity of rate structures, many companies hire outside freight auditors to examine their freight bills at a commission rate of 50 percent of the amount of claims recovered. The physical distribution function within the business-to-business firm must present loss or damage claims to carriers as soon as possible after receipt of a shipment, as there is a time limit for filing a claim, in addition to the very real possibility of cases of divided responsibility for damage or shortage between the shipper and the carrier. The procedure of carriers in regard to over, short, and damaged freight vary to such an extent that the most logical practice for a traffic manager to follow seems to be one based upon past experience with the individual carrier.

Operation of Private Transportation

Many firms have instituted private carriage operations rather than using "for-hire" transportation. *Private transportation* (that is, the user and the carrier are one and the same) frequently offers potential savings in transportation costs, possibly better service because of the flexibility of routes and schedules, greater speed along with a reduction of loss and damages, and accessibility to transportation equipment when needed. Inadequate transportation service and uncertain delivery times may force the firm to use its own trucks. This investment may be significant (although leasing is common), but it may be necessary for service improvement.

CONCEPT QUESTIONS

1. What is physical distribution?
2. What is meant by logistical management?
3. What is intermodal transport?

DEREGULATION

With the movement toward deregulation, transportation carriers no longer could rely on federal agencies to set prices, which in turn stimulated price competition and has made it difficult for inefficient firms to survive. In the late 1970s, regulation had created so many absurd inefficiencies that lawmakers were driven to try competition. Deregulation allowed price cutting, permitted new entrants into trucking and let railroads merge, reorganize, and abandon unprofitable trackage.[12] Deregulation of the transportation industry has brought about a tremendous change in the competitive environment of that industry and has forced carriers to become more customer oriented. According to Jack Schang, Ryder/PIE's president, "Before deregulation, the successful companies were the efficient operators. Today that's not enough. Companies which remain operations-oriented and fail to focus on marketing will be further casualties."[13] The challenge for freight carriers is not only to keep their own costs in check but also to provide better service.[14] Before deregulation, trucking, rail, and air freight carriers were not permitted to compete on price, to guarantee delivery time, to vary routing, or to grant long-term, confidential-rate contracts. Without deliver-date guarantees, inventory management techniques such as JIT were impossible.

Benefits from deregulation have been widespread. Real bottom-line opportunities stemming from deregulation of the transportation industry have also become widespread.[15] Costs have fallen for all modes, with air freight costs down by 50 percent since 1980, and with business savings of $63 billion per year in reduced trucking costs and $5 billion in reduced rail costs. Robert Delaney, former vice president at Leaseway and now a consultant at the megathinktank Arthur D. Little in Cambridge, Massachusetts, has spent the past few years working up ways to quantify the savings from deregulation. Some of his findings are as follows:

- Before deregulation, a minimum of 30 percent of safety stock was required to offset transit time variance.
- Deregulation of transportation services has created a direct savings of $90 billion in logistics costs to U.S. businesses. This estimate is based on annual surveys of three hundred manufacturers, which indicate that the ratio of transportation expenditures to sales revenues has dropped by 21 percent since 1981.
- A reduction in manufacturing-cycle time, something the Japanese have been working on for years.
- Deregulation has spurred a great deal of efficiency. The frequent delivery of parts and components, direct to work stations in small lot sizes (which is routine today), requires the support of reliable transportation systems not available for most of the 1980s.
- Freight has become just like any other buy: A transportation procurement strategy must be developed that supports all other procurement strategies within the firm.[16]

Regulatory reform has spawned innovations that are being used to save time and money and to improve service, as has been previously noted. One such cooperative effort between purchasing and transportation that could not have been accomplished before deregulation has yielded excellent results for glass-products manufacturer Ball Corporation in Muncie, Indiana. The transportation of soda ash from the mine to the company's manufacturing destinations cost several thousand dollars per railcar prior to deregulation. The single railroad serving the mines would not negotiate its rates, because regulation effectively removed the threat of competition in this market. However, since deregulation, Ball's purchasing and transportation people have worked together with the supplier and a second railroad to produce more competition and lower costs. With the eased entry requirements resulting from the Motor Carrier Act, a trucking company began operations and agreed to carry the soda ash from the mines to a newly renovated transfer station two hundred miles away on the other railroad's line. From there, the railroad delivers the product to Ball's plants. This saves the firm $7 per ton, an annual saving of $126,000 at one site alone.[17] A closer correspondence between traditional purchasing concerns and traditional transportation or traffic management concerns has evolved. Many firms now view transportation as a "commodity" to be purchased in the market from alternative suppliers, much like any other commodity.[18]

As the pace of deregulation intensified in the 1980s, there were attempts to slow down, or even reverse the process (reregulation). In many cases, it has been firms within deregulated industries that have wanted to slow the process. However, from the beginning, a number of economists have been critical of the imposition of regulation on carriers; and studies of the effects of deregulation indicate that it has been highly successful. Transportation rates have decreased, service has improved, and shippers are pleased with the results. A significant gain from deregulation has been a substantial decline in the logistical costs of business.[19] Deregulation will prosper and expand; other industries, including banks, other financial-service institutions, and telecommunications, have been deregulated recently. More are sure to follow.

CUSTOMER SERVICE

Customer service as it relates to the physical distribution function consists of providing products at the time and location corresponding to the customer's needs. The starting point for any strategy is a thorough understanding of customer requirements. It is necessary to obtain data from customers regarding the importance of vendor attributes and the performance of major vendors on these attributes. A customer-service strategy can be established using the following methodology: (1) external audits, (2) internal audits, (3) evaluation of customer perceptions, and (4) identification of opportunities to gain differential advantage. When establishing customer service strategies, marketers need to identify the impact on corporate profitability of decisions affecting business segments such as products, channels, or customers.[20] The customer-service levels that might be provided range from very good to very poor. A 100-percent level of satisfaction would indicate that all customers are completely satisfied with product availability. The ideal solution to the problem of design of a physical distribution system is to develop minimum-cost systems for a range of acceptable levels of customer service; then, select the service level that makes the greatest contribution of sales less physical distribution costs. Customers would be 100 percent satisfied if a wide range of products were available at the right time and place in sufficient quantities to meet the needs and wants of all who are willing and able to buy. Of course, this condition rarely occurs, since the costs would be prohibitive. Yet, it is possible to achieve high levels of customer satisfaction with properly designed distribution systems.

Customer-Service Standards

Business-to-business firms operating effective logistics systems should develop a set of written customer-service standards. These serve as objectives and provide a benchmark against which results can be measured for control purposes. In developing these standards, the place to start is with the customers. What are their service needs? What do competitors offer them? Are the customers willing to pay a bit more for better service? After these questions are answered, realistic standards can be set and an ongoing measurement program established to monitor results. Typical standards relate to time, reliability, and loss or damage. The standards must be quantifiable and measurable, because during the control process, deviations from standards must be noted and investigated.

Company efforts to improve customer service cover a broad range of matters, some of which are far more dramatic in their impact than others. One effective means of service improvement is to identify the causes of customer-service complaints and then to institute changes to eliminate or minimize customer-service breakdowns. Exhibit 9-1 offers major categories, such as sales, traffic, warehousing, packaging, and inventory control, into which primary service complaints can be placed.

As part of business marketing strategy, the establishment of a customer-service policy is extremely important, because so many facets of customer service interface with other functions of the firm. A broad range of topics that affect customer service, such as credit rules, complaint procedures, minimum orders, order cycles, inventory returns, stockouts, and proposed deliveries, must be carefully examined. A helpful checklist as an evaluation tool in establishing customer-service policy is shown in Exhibit 9-2.

Examination of Cost Trade-Offs

Trade-off analysis can be defined as "the examination of the costs associated with each component of the physical distribution system for the purpose of

EXHIBIT 9-1 **Typical Customer-Service Complaints**

Traffic and transportation
Damaged merchandise
Carrier does not meet standard transit time
Merchandise delivered prior to date promised
Carrier fails to follow customer routing
Carrier does not comply with specific instructions
Errors present on the bill of lading
Condition or type of rolling equipment not satisfactory
Inventory control
Stockouts
Contaminated products received
Product identification errors
Poor merchandise shipped
Warehousing and packaging
Merchandise delivered late
Problem with containers in packaging plants
Special promotion merchandise not specified in delivery
Warehouse release form errors
Shipping incorrect types and quantities of merchandise
Papers not mailed promptly to headquarters
Field warehouse deliveries of damaged merchandise
Sales order service
Delayed shipments
Invoice errors
Sales coding errors
Brokerage errors
Special instructions ignored
No notification of late shipments
Name and address errors

Source: Charles A. Taff, *Management of Physical Distribution and Transportation,* 7th Ed. (Homewood, Ill.: Richard D. Irwin, 1984), p. 252. Used with permission.

ascertaining the combination of components that will yield the lowest possible cost for a particular level of customer service." The cost trade-offs in business product physical distribution must be examined to determine how and to what extent each component will be utilized in the physical distribution system. The interrelationships of various logistical system components are illustrated in

EXHIBIT 9-2 **Customer Service Policy Checklist**

Note: This checklist is intended only as a general guide to the formulation of customer service policy and makes no attempt to separate elements of external policy from those of internal policy. It also recognizes the overlap between terms of sale and customer service policy. Some elements of customer service policy may be influenced by legal requirements and/or trade customs, and, in that regard, should be interpreted by individual firms in the light of their own situation.

Credit Rules Affecting Customer Service

___ Must credit be established prior to acceptance of orders?
___ If open-account orders are acceptable, are there limits?
___ Are there credit limits for established accounts?
___ When will orders not be filled for credit reasons?
___ Is a responsible credit person readily accessible to customers?

Conditions Governing Acceptance of Orders

___ Are there any restrictions on method of receiving orders? (These might include requirements for placing orders through salespeople, brokers, etc., or a prohibition of telephone orders.)
___ Will the customer be required to order from a specific order-receiving location?
___ What information is required on the order?
___ What authority is required? (Formal purchase order, or restrictions on telephone or verbal orders.)
___ Are COD orders accepted?
___ Are there legal limitations? (This would include restrictions applicable to controlled subtances, export-import, licensing, or other credentials required by the purchaser.)
___ What is the policy when purchase orders conflict with terms of sale?

Materials in Short Supply

___ Is there a suitable allocation policy?
___ Is it legal?
___ Is there a single person in charge who is accessible to customers, customer service personnel, and salespeople at all times?

Materials in Short Supply

___ Has the mission of the customer service organization been fully defined?
___ Do the managers have the tools necessary to accomplish their tasks, including personnel, information systems, communications,etc.?
___ Do they have sufficient authority?
___ Are there formal selection and training policies for personnel?
___ Are customer service representatives to be assigned by account, or by product line?
___ Is there a policy whereby customer service managers spend a certain amount of time in the field contacting customers on location?

Source: Adapted from Warren Blanding, *Customer Service Newsletter* (Washington, D.C.: Marketing Publications); as found in Charles A. Taff, *Management of Physical Distribution and Transportation,* 7th ed. (Homewood, Ill.: Richard D. Irwin, 1984), p. 253. Used with permission.

Figure 9-1. The arrows indicate the trade-offs between activities that must be evaluated in (1) estimating customer-service levels; (2) developing purchasing policies; (3) selecting transportation policies; (4) making warehousing decisions; and (5) setting inventory levels.[21]

Analyzing the costs of alternative combinations of the components for a physical distribution system is essential to guiding the design of the system:

> Storing all finished goods inventory in a small number of distribution centers helps minimize warehousing costs, but leads to an increase in freight expense. Similarly, savings resulting from large-order purchases may be entirely offset by greater inventory carrying costs. In a nutshell, reductions in one set of costs

FIGURE 9-1 **Cost Trade-Offs Required in Marketing and Logistics**

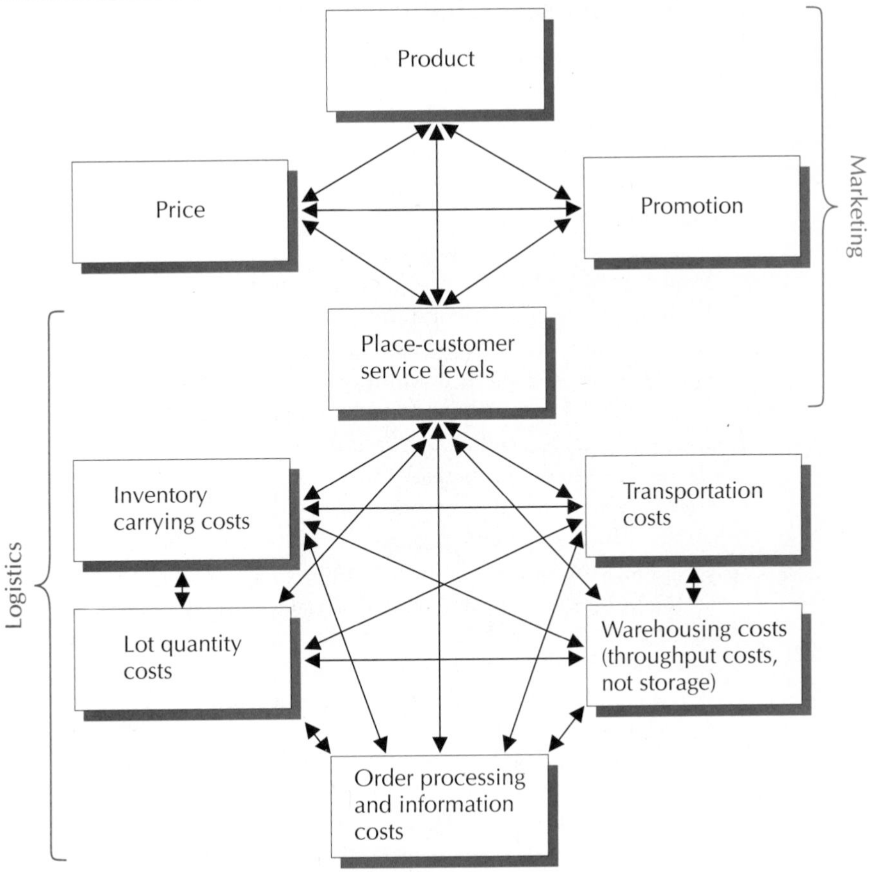

Marketing objective: Allocate resources to the marketing mix in such a manner as to maximize the long-run profitability of the firm.

Logistics objective: Minimize total costs given the customer service objective.

Where total costs equal: transportation costs + warehousing costs + order processing and information costs + lot quantity costs + inventory carrying costs.

Source: As shown in James R. Stock and Douglas M. Lambert, *Strategic Logistics Management,* 3d ed. (Homewood, Illinois: Richard D. Irwin, Inc., 1992), p. 42.

invariably increase the costs of other logistical components. Effective management and real cost savings can be accomplished only by viewing distribution as an integrated system and minimizing its total cost.[22]

Because some components of the physical distribution function are more important than others in a given firm, trade-off analysis must be directed to those components that make up the major portion of distribution costs.

The Impact of Logistical Service on Business Channel Members

In many firms, an effective customer-service strategy has not yet been attained. Failure to support markets in terms of service offered can be a costly practice; some firms are hesitant to offer different levels of service, out of fear they will violate provisions of the Robinson-Patman Act. This fear seems to stem from the fact that it is necessary for a firm to cost-justify its customer-service policies, and most of these companies do not have the needed cost information.[23] Demand is often thought of in terms of sales; yet, advertising, product, price, and customer service can also have a significant impact on demand. Customer service is often the physical distribution component that determines whether or not business customers will remain customers. Both order getting and order filling (physical distribution) are required for the long-range financial success of the firm.

Logistical service levels affect the relationship between the manufacturer and the customer, as well as the operations of channel members. Inefficient service to middlemen either increases their costs, by forcing them to carry higher inventory levels, or results in stockouts, leading to a loss of business. Poor logistical support in the channel negates the marketing effort of the firm by constricting potential sales and antagonizing middlemen. Both the length and the consistency of the order-cycle period (time from placement of orders to receipt of products) affect the level of distributor's inventories, which generally represent their highest asset investment and, according to Figure 9-2, one of the largest distribution expenses. Distributors will rarely remain loyal if poor logistical service is harmful to end users. Inventory control systems should be linked to manufacturers' information systems; and if intermediaries are to receive a sufficient level of logistical service, information systems must provide accurate sales forecasts. Alert business marketing managers must learn and be ever vigilant for the telltale symptoms of a poor physical distribution system.

WAREHOUSING

Decisions regarding the location of warehouse facilities offer tremendous opportunities for acquiring increased market share while generating cost savings. Unprecedented changes have occurred over the past several years in terms of foreign competition, transportation deregulation (as noted earlier), globalization of markets, the information explosion, and computerization. These trends have provided users of warehousing services with significant opportunities. For such users, computers, communication, and information technology can change the balance of power in the firm's channel of distribution and can be used to maximize the integration among warehousing, logistics, marketing, manufacturing, and other functional areas of the firm.

FIGURE 9-2 **Breakdown of Logistical Cost for Business Products**

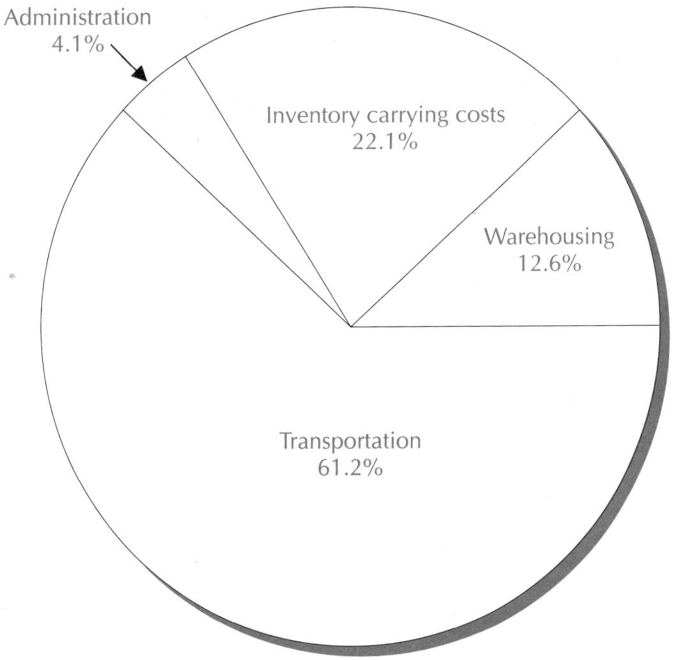

Transportation costs, warehousing costs, and inventory carrying costs account for the bulk of all physical distribution costs for a combination of consumer and business-to-business products. In the past decade, the share going to transportation costs has grown. (From the Council of Logistics Management, Annual Conference Proceedings, October 1986.) Used with permission.

Decisions on warehouse location affect delivery time to customers and the ability to meet customer-service expectations. As part of distribution strategy, marketing decisions on the number and location of warehouses are important in improving customer service and in supporting the inventory decisions of the firm. Warehousing is an important facilitating activity, with good warehouse location eliminating (or reducing) the need for costly air freight by keeping business products readily available in local markets.

The following example demonstrates the role of warehousing in physical distribution. W. W. Grainger manufactures and distributes its own motors, fans, blowers, and other products and parts; it distributes those of other producers as well. Sales in 1983 were over $860 million, an increase of nearly three times over sales of a decade earlier. One of Grainger's major strategic advantages is its distribution system—"having the right thing in the right place at the right time."[24] Grainger has 9,800 products and 2,400 parts that could present a distribution nightmare unless properly managed. Grainger's distribution is described as follows:

> All merchandise is gathered through 1.6 million square feet of warehouses near its Skokie, Illinois headquarters. (This hub was duplicated with a 1.4-million-square-foot building which opened in Kansas City in 1983.) There it is arranged into assortments shipped at least weekly, in full truckloads, to the stores. With less volume, Grainger would have to settle for half-filled trucks or less-frequent deliveries. The weekly deliveries, in turn, enable branches to satisfy buyers without holding huge inventories on their own.[25]

Private or Public Warehouses?

When space is owned or leased, such space is classified as a *private warehouse.* Private warehouses are primarily used when an organization's sales volume is relatively stable so that investment in a fixed facility is justified. Private warehouses might offer property appreciation or tax advantages through depreciation of the facility, in addition to giving the marketing manager total control over the warehouse operation as opposed to a public warehouse operation. Generally speaking, upper management does not regard owning a warehouse as a requirement for reducing company costs or enhancing profitable sales. With fast-response replenishment systems, flexible manufacturing, and other new approaches, throughput and inventory velocity are the keys to success.[26]

The alternative to owning or leasing storage space is the use of a *public warehouse.* These firms are operated by professional managers who provide warehouse services on a fee basis. Traditional public warehousing has been growing steadily over the past several years and is a major player in today's logistics sector. Most public operators are willing to supply virtually any type of service the customer wishes.[27]

Manufacturers offering a narrow product line to many market areas often find it economical to ship products to public warehouses instead of maintaining privately owned or leased warehouse facilities near production facilities. The use of a public warehouse is often the most economical way to serve marginal markets, or markets that the firm is beginning to develop but that do not yet justify an investment in a private facility. Providers of public warehousing must understand what creates value for their customers. Trends that will affect both shippers and public warehouse vendors include: (1) just one chance to produce a quality product and offer a quality service, (2) longer-term relationships, (3) an increased scope and level of logistics outsourcing; and (4) larger roles for importing and exporting.[28] Exhibit 9-3 identifies a number of the important factors influencing the choice of a public warehouse. Additionally, many public warehouses have begun to offer a variety of logistical services to their business clients beyond the physical handling and storage of materials and merchandise.

EXHIBIT 9-3 Factors Influencing the Choice of a Public Warehouse

The Warehousing Education and Research Council has published a paper by William R. Folz, senior vice-president of Tri-Valley Growers, which offers some advice on finding the right warehouse facility. The recommendations below are from his paper:

1. First, review the reasons for your requirement. Examine why you want to use a public facility.
2. Develop a list of warehouses you want to contact.
3. Contact each warehouse by telephone and set up a personal visit.
   a. *Housekeeping.* Develop a perception of what the facility looks like every day. Is there an ongoing plan for good sanitation?
   b. *Equipment.* Review equipment age, maintenance, number of makes, and equipment selection. A high percentage of old equipment may mean increased downtime and maintenance costs. A good maintenance program is a must. Keep in mind that the existence of a high number of makes may indicate a lack of purchasing strategy. Also, note whether the kind of equipment you require is readily available.
   c. *Operations control.* Study the procedures that the warehouse uses to control costs and improve efficiency.
   d. *The facility.* The building should be well maintained and meet your needs in terms of sprinklers, rail siding, dock doors, etc.
   e. *Management clerical procedures.* Review administrative and clerical controls and procedures for inventory management, customer service, claims, shipment logs, etc.
   f. *Insurance.* Know your insurance needs and inquire about the operator's coverage.
   g. *Proximity to rail yard/major highways.* Study the facility's transportation access.
4. Obtain outside references. Talk to other users of a facility to ask their opinion of the services provided.
5. Ask about the warehouse's financial condition. If you are potentially a large customer, you can demand financial information, and the operator will probably provide it.

Source: "How to Choose a Public Warehouse," reprinted from *Distribution* magazine, September 1984, Radnor, PA. Used with permission.

For example, Distribution Centers, Inc. (DCI), which operates out of Columbus, Ohio, maintains warehouse facilities in a number of major markets. DCI will repackage products to meet the orders of end users, label the orders, and arrange local delivery for them. DCI can also link its computer with that of the manufacturer to facilitate order processing and inventory updating.[29] More than fifteen thousand public warehouses operate in the United States today.[30]

CONCEPT QUESTIONS

1. What changes has deregulation brought about in the transportation industry?
2. Why is the establishment of a customer-service policy so important?
3. What effect do decisions on warehouse location have on customer service?

INVENTORY CONTROL

Business firms recognize that too high an inventory level causes high carrying costs and potential obsolescence. (Carrying costs arise when stocks of goods for sale are held. They consist of the opportunity cost of the investment tied up in inventory and the costs associated with storage, such as space rental and insurance.) For example, in the early 1980s in the earth-moving and farm equipment industries, John Deere and Company had an average of 59 days' inventory, Caterpillar Tractor had 88 days', and Massey-Ferguson an amazing 110 days' inventory.[31] Conversely, too low an inventory can result in high restocking and production costs, as well as the risk of lost sales and customer goodwill. The level of inventories is related to such factors as the movement and storage of materials. The amount of inventory in storage, in transit, and in processing can be substantially altered through coordinated management of the production, physical distribution, and sales functions. Capital costs in inventory, transportation, and storage and the costs of inventory obsolescence are traded off in order to control total costs and maintain minimal inventory levels consistent with production needs.[32] It does not seem reasonable to expect a firm to be able to fill and ship every order from inventory.

Because of this inventory-cost trade-off, most business marketing managers seem to accept the *80/20 axiom*: 80 percent of the sales are generated by 20 percent of the product line. The major implication of the 80/20 axiom is that marketers must manage their inventory selectively, treating fast- and slow-moving items differently. If a company has half its inventory committed to products that provide only 20 percent of the unit-sales volume, significant gains can be made by reducing inventories of the slow sellers to the point where their turnover rate approximates that of the fast sellers.[33] Inventory represents a sizeable investment for most companies, so the goal of inventory management is to minimize both the investment and the fluctuation in inventories, while at the same time filling customers' orders promptly and accurately.

Electronic Data Interchange

A new age has been born—the *Electronic Data Interchange (EDI)* Information Age. EDI is generally defined as computer-to-computer interchange of business documents.[34] EDI is designed to create an extremely customer-responsive environment, the quick response (QR), which is much like just-in-time (JIT) manufacturing. Its goal is to create a codependency (partnership) between sellers and buyers so the right product reaches the right place at the right time at the right price.[35] It provides the capability for a buyer to reorder merchandise as it is sold.

Electronic data interchange is a natural part of the evolution of automated systems, driven by such factors as JIT inventory management, the demand for fast and accurate deliveries, and the need to track more shipments through wider and more complex delivery pipelines. This technology streamlines the information flow by enabling buyers and sellers to exchange electronically such documents as invoices, purchase orders, freight bills, and bills of lading, along with other business documents. Documents move directly from computer to computer, saving time and reducing errors.

General Electric was one of the earliest proponents of EDI, recognizing the usefulness of the technology for a diversified, multinational organization with customers, suppliers, and operations across the world. It is GE's philosophy to use EDI as a critical instrument across the organization: to facilitate strategic supplier programs; to dramatically improve inventory management; to gain tighter control of funds in order to maintain a competitive advantage; and to improve customer service.[36] GE recognizes EDI as a viable management tool that will expand just as international business will expand dramatically during this decade.

Davis and Geck, a division of pharmaceuticals manufacturer American Cyanamid, relies on EDI for its purchase orders and invoices to improve efficiency with trading partners, says Larry Smenyak, director of customer service and distributor relations. The medical supply distributor replaced its existing order system with EDI a year ago and plans to explore EDI use for rebates and possibly for additional transaction sets. The company receives about 72 percent of customer purchase orders through EDI. "We can service more customers directly, achieve at least a 50 percent reduction in keypunching, and reduce head count," Smenyak says. According to Smenyak, an added bonus is the fact that the firm's customers are very pleased.[37]

Finally, "Cargo in transit is information in motion," says Steven J. Olson, The Harper Group's (San Francisco) vice president of information services and chief information officer. Logistics is a major component of a delivered product's price, and by the year 2000, more money will be spent on logistics information systems than on inventory carrying costs, according to Olson. EDI has enabled Harper to make changes in its human resources, refocusing staff to take on new types of jobs. "The company has doubled in revenue over the last three years, but our people are now spending more time servicing customers and less on internal management," Olson said.[38]

The EDI-based inventory-control system is attractive to both buyers and sellers from economic as well as other standpoints. The replenishment interval, as well as the lot sizes for the various buyers, can be modified easily, frequently, and inexpensively, as changing conditions warrant. This approach is consistent with and can be instrumental in moving toward just-in-time inventory management.

The Just-in-Time Concept

The *just-in-time (JIT) approach*, as introduced in Chapter 2, is a concept affecting inventory control, purchasing, and production scheduling. JIT principles are applied to multipoint distribution of product to customers. Every aspect of the process is analyzed to determine where there might be opportunities to minimize inventory levels and pipelines and maximize flexibility and throughput.[39] The basic idea of JIT is that carrying any inventory is "evil" because it uses up capital and covers up many problems, such as inefficiency, poor quality, erratic delivery, poor communications, and so on. (See Exhibit 9-4 for a brief discussion of how Chrysler has improved efficiency at its new Jefferson North assembly plant in Detroit, Michigan, and trimmed inventory levels sitting on the production floor by nearly $2 million.)

JIT inventory management makes sure that each person involved in the manufacturing process gets what is needed "just in time".[40] For instance, a Bendix plant recently adopted a JIT system and was able to convert ten thousand square feet of floor space from storage to manufacturing usage.[41] Black and Decker, IBM, Firestone, General Motors, Harley-Davidson, and many smaller firms are experiencing decreasing costs and higher quality with the system. General Motors claims to have saved $2 billion in one year with its use of the JIT system.[42] One-quarter of the respondents in a recent survey reported paying lower prices for inputs they purchased using JIT.[43]

To be effective in the firm's inventory-control function, just-in-time purchasing and production scheduling require very careful managerial monitoring. A high level of cooperation and coordination is called for between business suppliers and producers, and then between production and marketing people in the manufacturing firm.[44] Marketers must be prepared to change their methods when their customers are using the JIT system. JIT demands a willingness to meet specific customer requirements, including: (1) small lot sizes, (2) frequent deliveries, (3) exact quantities, (4) precise arrival time, and; (5) total delivered cost.[45] To implement the JIT concept in the United States, suppliers often have to maintain warehouses nearer to their customers (although the use of warehouses is generally inconsistent with the JIT concept). Public warehouses could be used to advantage here because of their flexibility and their proximity to many business parks and areas. However, as described in Exhibit 9-5, Micro Motion, a mass-flow instrumentation company and division of Emerson Electric Company, has developed an internal warehouse run by only one supplier in an effort to reduce physical distribution

EXHIBIT 9-4 Chrysler Puts JIT into High Gear

Compared to conventional automobile plants, there is very little inventory sitting on the 1.3-million-square-foot production floor at Chrylser's new Jefferson North assembly plant in Detroit, Michigan. According to Wayne Oeullette, production control manager, high-value parts, which account for 87% of the value of parts that go into a Grand Cherokee, arrive at the plant less than 6 hours before they are needed. These major parts come into the plant in sequence, explains Ouellette. The effects of in-sequence, just-in-time delivery is remarkable. Efficiency at Jefferson North has improved from one shift and less than 100 vehicles a day in January 1992 to 2 shifts and production of more than 700 finished vehicles 5 days a week in January 1993. As well as the system works, there is still room for improvement. For instance, materials delivery schedules were recently reworked, trimming inventory levels sitting on the production floor by nearly $2 million. Ouellette says that the system can probably be tightened up even more, and current inventories can be cut another 20% over time.

Source: Gary Forger, "Jeep Puts JIT in High Gear." *Modern Materials Handling*, 48 (January 1993), pp. 42-45. Used with permission.

costs and to provide more efficient service to customers. Because production schedules require timely supplies, shipments must arrive on time, or plants may have to be shut down. Different transportation modes have different degrees of reliability, so the choice of mode is very important. Exhibit 9-6 describes how General Motors uses both railroads and trucks in its JIT systems.[46]

EXHIBIT 9-5 Micro-Motion In-House Store Delivers Just in Time

Micro Motion is a mass flow instrumentation company and division of Emerson Electric Co. In 1988, Carol Brooks, purchasing manager, looked at the costs of buying 2,000 electronic parts from 50 suppliers and found it made more sense to set up an in-plant storehouse run by a single supplier. The company chose Schweber Electronics as its new supplier-partner. The in-house store involves components, including those purchased from other sources. Brooks reported that Micro has attained or exceeded all of its goals, including: (1) inventory reduction of $300,000, (2) fully 100% quality and 100% on-time delivery, and (3) an 88% reduction of purchase orders placed by Micro Motion. Maintaining profits in the 1990s, says Brooks, will mean abandoning the 'we-they' adversarial relationships with suppliers in favor of a 'win-win' partnership. Micro Motion offers Schweber first chance at new research and development proposals on new products.

Source: Julie F. Grasfield, "In-House Stores Deliver Just in Time," *Purchasing,* 109 (September 13, 1990), pp. 23–27.

EXHIBIT 9-6 Planning Rail and Truck Service for Just-in-Time Systems

Dependable restocking of supplies is a requisite in just-in-time (JIT) inventory systems to avoid production shutdowns, because these systems typically operate with minimal inventories of raw materials and parts. For a JIT system to be most effective, suppliers must be located close to the production plant. Then, the dependability of delivery will be improved.

General Motors (GM) felt that overnight delivery to its Lansing, Michigan, Oldsmobile assembly plant was essential to implement its JIT system. GM combines various parts in a shipment coming from Kalamazoo, Michigan, 118 miles from its Lansing plant. These parts are shipped and delivered the evening prior to the next day's production, allowing Oldsmobile producers to function with only a single day's inventory of such parts. GM needs, then, dependable, overnight delivery of these items at low costs. GM's answer was in Conrail's "Mini-Train," a small train making no stops between Kalamazoo and Lansing. The train left Kalamazoo at six in the evening, and had the parts available for use in Lansing by the next morning.

Problems with labor relations or bad weather can create real problems in meeting the tight delivery schedules necessary for a JIT system. For example, GM produces the Pontiac Fiero in Pontiac, Michigan, but buys plastic body panels for the Fiero from the Budd Company in Ohio, a distance of 131 miles. These panels are truck-delivered to Pontiac five times each day. When a February snowstorm covered Michigan, the panel deliveries were held up, slowing the Fiero assembly plant from its typical twenty-hour day to an eight-hour day.

Savings from the use of JIT systems can be major. GM estimates that it saved $1 billion in a two-year period by decreasing its average inventory by $30 billion.

Source: "Freight Transportation: A Revitalized Industry Emerges," Excerpted by permission of *Forbes* magazine (August 1, 1983) © Forbes Inc., 1993, pp. Ad 1–12; Jeremy Main, "The Trouble with Managing Japanese Style," *Fortune* (April 2, 1984), pp. 50–56. © 1984 Time Inc. All rights reserved. Mike Meyers, "Low Inventory Manufacturing Arrives Just-in-Time," *Minneapolis Star and Tribune* (March 11, 1984), p. 10.

Just-in-time strategies tend to be easier to implement in a repetitive manufacturing environment characterized by highly standardized products, a relatively stable demand, suppliers in close proximity, and a very cooperative work force. Marketing strategies often depend on whether the firm competes on the basis of cost leadership or product differentiation. If JIT is properly implemented, a company can integrate both the cost and differentiation strategies in making small, incremental product changes.

The new philosophy of buyer-seller linkage being adopted by JIT firms has significant implications for marketing management. The transition to single sourcing by original equipment manufacturers will require that suppliers develop highly differentiated offerings and become more proactive in marketing them.[47]

The E.O.Q. Model

Inventory-control analysts have developed a number of techniques to help the physical distribution manager effectively control inventory. The most basic of these techniques is the *economic order quantity* model (the *E.O.Q. model*). This particular technique emphasizes a cost trade-off between two costs involved with inventory: inventory handling costs, which increase with the addition of more inventory, and order costs, which decrease as the quantity ordered increases. As Figure 9-3 indicates, these two cost items are traded off to determine the optimal order quantity of each product. The E.O.Q. point in Figure 9-3 is the point at which total cost is minimized. By placing an order for this amount as needed, firms can minimize their inventory costs.[48] The E.O.Q. model has received widespread attention in the past two decades and is widely used in industry today.

Calculating the E.O.Q. The following formula is utilized to determine the E.O.Q.:

$$\text{E.O.Q} = \frac{2RS}{IC} \text{, where}$$

E.O.Q. = the economic order quantity (in units).
R = the annual rate of usage.
S = the cost of placing an order.
I = the annual inventory-carrying costs, expressed as a percentage.
C = the cost per unit of the item. The "unit" might consist of a single item or a prepackaged box, containing a dozen items, a gross, or even more.

In the formula, *R* is an estimate based upon the demand forecast for the item. *S* is calculated from the firm's cost records. *I* is also an estimate based upon the costs of such items as handling, insurance, interest, storage, depreciation, and

FIGURE 9-3 **Balancing Order Costs and Holding Costs for Inventory**

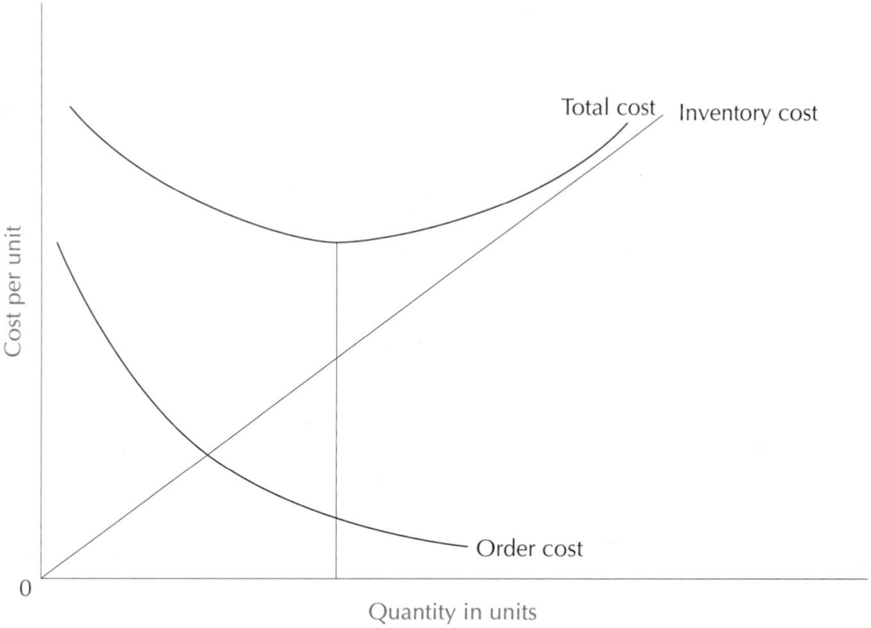

Source: "Balancing Order Costs and Holding Costs for Inventory," from *Marketing,* Third Edition, by David L. Kurtz and Louis E. Boone, Copyright © 1987 by The Dryden Press, a Division of Holt, Rinehart and Winston, Inc. Reprinted by permission of the publisher.

taxes. Since the cost of the item may vary over time, C is also likely to be an estimate. By inserting specific data into the formula, the E.O.Q. can be determined. Consider, for example, the following data:

$$R = 5{,}500 \text{ units}$$
$$S = 7.50$$
$$I = 10 \text{ percent}$$
$$C = \$12.90$$

$$\text{E.O.Q.} = \frac{(2)(5{,}500)(7.50)}{(12.90)(-10)}$$
$$= 252.9 \text{ units}$$

Since the E.O.Q. model involves a mathematical formula, the calculation often results in a fractional answer that must be rounded to the next whole number to determine the economic order quantity. Thus, the E.O.Q. in the above example would be rounded to 253 units.

ORDER PROCESSING

The establishment of an effective order-processing system is of major importance to the logistics efforts of business-to-business firms. Accurate and efficient processing of orders is one important measure of customer satisfaction; quick order turnaround time is increasingly becoming a competitive service offering for most firms. Shipping wrong orders, less than full orders, or damaged merchandise, as well as slowness and delays in processing orders, can result in a loss of considerable customer goodwill for organizations engaged in business marketing.

The Order-Processing Cycle

A customer's placing of an order is the starting point for any order-processing system. A company salesperson generally transmits the customer's order (via a computerized system) to the firm; and as the order enters the system, physical distribution managers must carefully watch both the flow of goods and the flow of information. The warehouse manager must then be notified to check inventory and assemble the order. In some cases, where current inventory is not sufficient to fill an order, back ordering must be done. While an order is being assembled, a variety of paperwork must be completed, such as a bill of lading, an invoice, notification to the customer that the order is being processed, and an indication of when the customer can expect receipt of the order. If the customer does not place regular orders, credit checking will also be required. A computerized order-processing system is all but mandatory today for all industrial distribution systems. Figure 9-4 provides a configuration of such an order-processing system. This type of information system provides very useful information to management in terms of customer analysis, product planning, and market behavior.

Shortening the Order-Processing Cycle

Business engineering studies of how sales orders are processed can serve to shorten the order-processing cycle. Some key questions to ask in this regard include the following: (1) What happens after the receipt of a customer purchase order? (2) How long does it take to check a customer's credit worthiness? (3) What procedures are utilized for inventory checking, and how much time is involved? (4) How quickly do production personnel learn of new-stock requirements? (5) Do sales managers have an accurate picture of current sales? General Electric operates a computer-oriented system that, upon the receipt of a customer's order, checks the customer's credit standing and whether or where the items are in stock. The computer then issues an order to ship, bills the customer, updates the inventory records, sends a production order for new stock, and relays the message back to the sales representative that the customer order is on its way, all in less than fifteen seconds.[49]

FIGURE 9-4 **Computer-Based Order-Processing System**

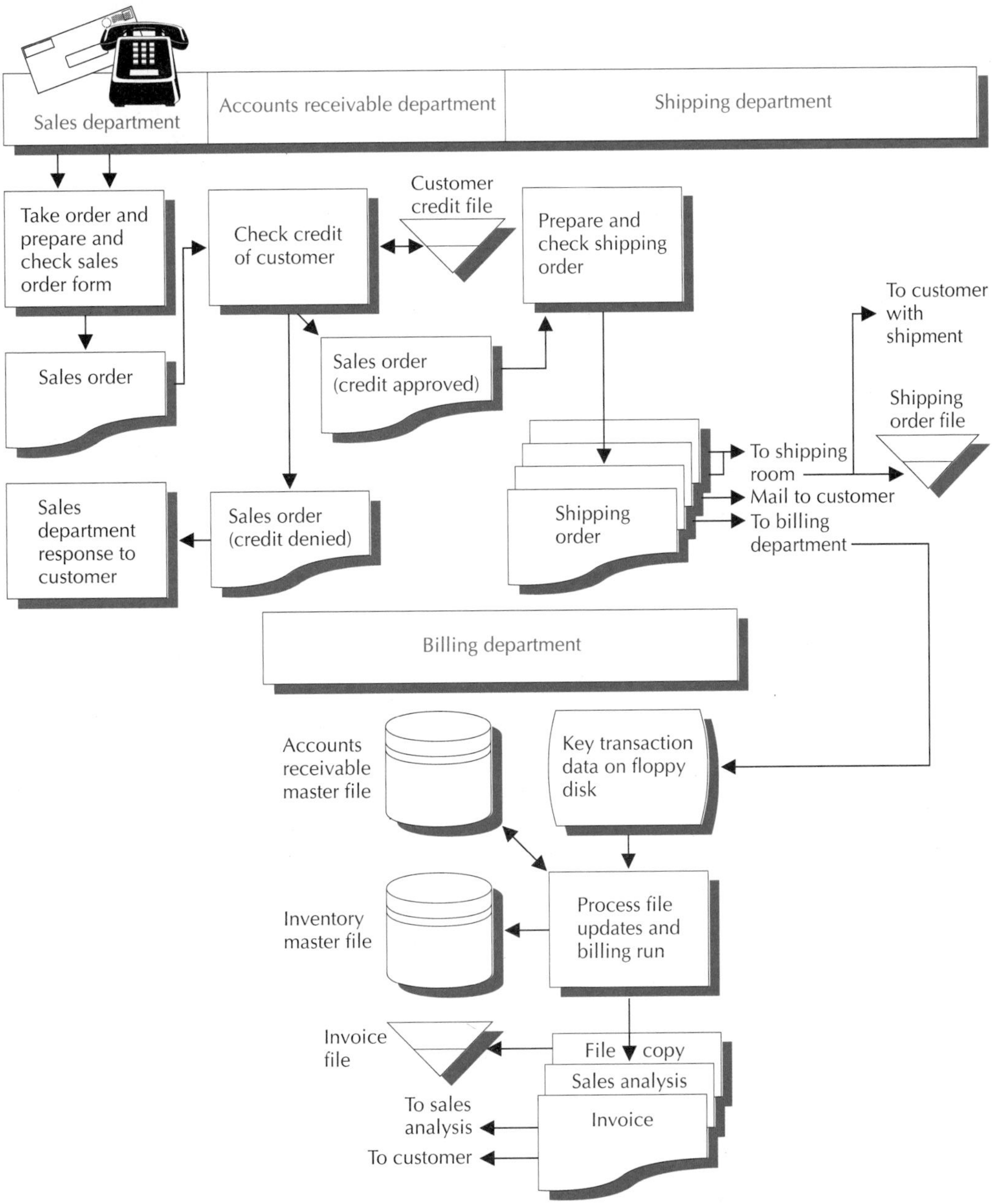

In addition to the physical movement of finished product to customers, information flow and accounting transactions must be managed: orders flow into sales and credit is checked; after approval, shipping orders instruct the warehouse to ship to the customer; finally, the billing department issues invoices for payment.

Source: Donald H. Sanders, *Computers Today* (3d ed.), p. 77, © 1988, McGraw-Hill Book Company. Reproduced with permission of McGraw-Hill.

Vendor Stocking

Vendor stocking is a practice in which the supplier maintains an inventory of frequently requested materials for business customers, thereby reducing their inventory carrying costs. This service provides major benefits both to suppliers and their customers. The Vallen Corporation, a distributor of business safety and health products, carries enough inventory on 250 items for Dow Chemical's Freeport, Texas, operation to satisfy 95 percent of Dow's requisitions immediately, with deliveries every two hours. If Dow needs a certain type of plastic container, the materials manager will transmit the order to Vallen's nearest branch office through the use of computer terminals. Such a capability removes Dow's need to shop by telephone, place rush orders, and maintain a stockroom.[50]

INTERNATIONAL DISTRIBUTION

International distribution costs can account for 25 to 35 percent of the sales volume of a product, a significant difference from the 8 to 10 percent for domestic shipments.[51] Furthermore, U.S. firms can become easily frustrated by the physical distribution problems overseas, including but not limited to, the enormous amount of paperwork involved. Delays, port congestion, inefficient materials-handling equipment, and poor road and rail networks also contribute to this frustration.

To move a business product between countries and within a country, there are three fundamental modes of transportation: air, water (ocean and inland), and land (rail and truck). To move goods between continents, ocean or air transportation is needed. When countries are connected by land (for example, North America), it is possible to use rail and highway to move merchandise from location to location, such as from the United States to Canada. In Europe, rail (train) is an important mode because of the contiguity of land areas and the availability of a modern and efficient train system.[52] The marketer must understand that there is no one ideal transportation mode. Each mode has its own special kinds of hazards.[53] Of course, moving merchandise across the ocean is a much more complex task than moving merchandise across the United States.

CONCEPT QUESTIONS

1. What does the E.O.Q. model of inventory control emphasize?
2. Why is the establishment of an effective order-processing system so important to the physical distribution function?

CONCLUSION

Physical distribution costs account for a substantial portion of a business-to-business firm's marketing expense. An ideal physical distribution system will minimize total costs while simultaneously providing timely traffic management, appropriate customer-service levels, convenient warehousing, carefully controlled inventory, efficient order processing, and effective channel design. A well-designed and well-operated physical distribution system can aid a business-to-business firm both in capturing and maintaining sizeable market share and in developing strong customer goodwill.

SUMMARY

1. Physical distribution has the potential to enhance the production, marketing, and profit performance of any company that produces a tangible product. Logistics, another term for physical distribution, embodies two primary product flows: physical supply and physical distribution management.
2. The functions of business traffic management are broad and vary in intensity with the type of industry, the type of product being shipped, and the size and number of shipments being transported. Primary functions of business traffic management include mode selection, routing, claims processing, and the operation of private transportation.
3. Deregulation of the transportation industry has brought about a tremendous change in the competitive environment of that industry and has forced carriers to become more customer oriented. Benefits from deregulation have included reduced logistics costs, greater efficiency, and shorter manufacturing-cycle time.
4. Customer-service standards serve as objectives and provide a benchmark against which results can be measured for control purposes. The establishment of a customer-service policy is extremely important because so many facets of customer service interface with other functions of the firm, such as credit rules, complaint procedures, minimum orders, order cycles, inventory returns, stockouts, and proposed deliveries.
5. Decisions regarding the location of warehouse facilities offer tremendous opportunities for acquiring increased market share and generating cost savings. Either private warehouses or public warehouses are used, depending upon the objectives of the firm involved.
6. Business-to-business firms realize that too high an inventory level causes high carrying costs and potential obsolescence; too low a level can result in high restocking and production costs, as well as the loss of both sales and customer goodwill. Electronic data interchange (EDI), economic order quantity, and just-in-time inventory control models are commonly used today in maintaining efficient inventory levels throughout the fiscal year.

7. Accurate and efficient processing of orders is an important measure of customer satisfaction, and quick turnaround time in processing orders is becoming a competitive service offered by many firms. Physical distribution managers are continually looking for ways to reduce the time involved in the order-processing cycle so as to reduce costs and to promote greater customer goodwill.
8. International distribution costs can account for 25 to 35 percent of the sales volume of a product. Furthermore, U.S. firms can become easily frustrated by the physical distribution problems overseas, including but not limited to, the enormous amount of paperwork involved. Air, water, and land are the three fundamental transportation modes in international markets; the international business marketer must understand that there is no one ideal transportation mode.

KEY TERMS

Air transport
Customer service
Economic order quantity model
80/20 axiom
Electronic data interchange (EDI)
Intermodal transport
Just-in-time (JIT) approach
Motor transport
Physical distribution
Pipeline transport
Private transportation
Private warehouse
Public warehouse
Rail transport
Trade-off analysis
Vendor stocking
Water transport

REVIEW QUESTIONS

1. Discuss three different viewpoints of physical distribution.
2. Identify five functions of business traffic management. Briefly discuss six methods of transportation available to business marketers. What are the basic advantages of using private transportation?
3. What are some of the changes that the deregulation of the transportation industry has brought about? What happened as a result of the intensified deregulation of American industry during the 1980s?
4. Explain what is meant by "customer service" in physical distribution management. How does a firm decide what level of customer service it should provide for its customers? Why is a company's establishment of a customer-service policy so important? How does cost trade-off analysis help to provide a minimum-cost physical distribution system?
5. What is the difference between a private and a public warehouse? How does the business marketing manager decide whether to use a private or public warehouse?
6. How is the 80/20 axiom related to inventory management? Describe how electronic data interchange (EDI), the E.O.Q. model, and the just-in-time concept of inventory management operate in business marketing.

7. What is involved in the order-processing cycle? What are the basic questions a physical distribution manager should ask in attempting to shorten the order-processing cycle? How does vendor stocking serve to reduce the time necessary to process an order?
8. What are some of the ways in which a business-to-business firm can become frustrated with physical distribution problems in overseas markets? What are the three forms of transportation commonly utilized in international business marketing?

Cases

CASE 9-1 Itel Distribution Systems

Itel Distribution Systems is part of the Itel Corporation family of third-party logistics services. Logistics involves the whole process of moving the product from the point of manufacturing to the ultimate consumer. "Third-party" means that companies like Itel do not take ownership rights to any of the products they move through the channel. No matter what the business, Itel Corporation can offer total distribution and warehousing solutions. Third-party warehousing is becoming increasingly popular with businesses today. As the cost of owning and operating warehouse facilities increases, businesses turn to companies like Itel Distribution Systems.

Itel offers its customers four key distribution services:

1. *Freight consolidation.* Itel services many companies. This enables shipments to be combined, thus reducing total shipping costs.
2. *Multimodal transportation.* Itel uses many different modes of transportation. This alleviates the need to contract with separate companies for different modes of transportation.
3. *Bulk transport and storage.* The company can provide bulk transport and storage of raw materials and deliver the product as needed.
4. *A comprehensive inventory system.* This includes bar-coding services, order processing, and packaging of shipments. In addition, an extensive computer system allows comprehensive access to information, including locating specific shipments.

The advantages for manufacturers in using third-party warehousing and distribution companies are twofold. First, the manufacturer has the ability to expand or contract its operations as changes in the market or sales level occur, without making major capital investments. Second, companies do not have to make any capital investment in warehouses or distribution vehicles. The capital can instead be used for production-capacity expansion or product improvements.

Using third-party companies is not without disadvantages. The major disadvantage is the loss of control. If a company turns over its warehousing and distribution functions, it loses control of the physical distribution process. The second disadvantage is that the company may be required to sign a long-term contract with the third-party distribution company, alleviating many of the advantages.

Itel Distribution Systems addresses the downside with its partnership focus. Itel is not a supplier of distribution services, but a partner in its customer's business. By taking total control of the customer's distribution needs, Itel gives companies the ability to focus on the specific needs of their business (concentrate on what they do best) and not worry about operating and managing the distribution facilities. For example, Itel leased railway track next to one of its customer's factories to provide shipping directly from the plant to one of Itel's warehouse facilities.

Itel now has a total of nine million square feet in thirty-nine distribution facilities. Through a series of expansions and contractions, Itel continues to grow. The company continues to focus on its customers' needs. To this end, Itel is organized regionally. By segmenting the United States into four distinct regions (West, Central, Northeast, and Southeast), Itel is able to offer some distinct advantages. Itel's strength lies in building personal relations between each region and its customers, not by applying the same formula in each region. Itel finds specific solutions to best meet the customers' needs. Itel wants its customers to have not only the support of a national company, but also the individual attention of a local company. Each region is supported by the company but is semiautonomous in its operation.

DISCUSSION QUESTIONS

1. What advantages and disadvantages come from Itel's decision to organize on a regional basis? What advantages and disadvantages could be gained in a national orientation?
2. Do you think Itel has done a good job in alleviating the disadvantages in using a third-party distribution company? Why or why not?
3. What advantages would Itel's customers have in using Itel? Would you recommend using a third-party distribution company?

Suggested Readings

Itel Distribution Systems company literature.

Source: C. Lamb, J. Hair, and C. McDaniel, *Principles of Marketing*, 1st Edition (Cincinnati, OH: South-Western Publishing Company, 1992) p. 414.

CASE 9-2 A-P-A Transport Corporation

In 1949, the Impatore brothers pooled their life savings and purchased two army surplus trucks to haul household goods in their area. This purchase started A-P-A Transport Corporation. From its humble beginnings, the company has enjoyed a steady growth. Today the company owns 779 trucks; 1,405 trailers; and 60 overseas containers.

A-P-A operates out of thirty-two terminals in the United States and Canada and services over thirty thousand communities. Employing nearly two thousand employees, A-P-A is the forty-second largest regular-route common carrier in the industry (based on gross revenue). Along with other trucking lines, A-P-A Transport is constantly looking for ways to reduce costs. Using heavier shipments is one way to reduce transit costs; however, most states have strict regulations regarding the maximum amount of weight a single truck can haul.

In conjunction with state and federal regulators, the trucking industry is looking into the merits of a new truck design. The new Turner truck design, named after former Federal Highway Administrator Frank Turner, uses more axles to distribute the weight. More axles on the truck and trailer combination means lower axle weights. This design provides two basic benefits. First, the annual wear and tear on the U.S. highway system could be reduced by $729 million. Second, heavier loads could be hauled by the new truck-trailer combinations; therefore, fewer trucks would be on the highway. As a result, distribution companies could expect to see a significant reduction in operating costs. Additional benefits would include lower insurance rates, lower fuel bills, and lower maintenance costs. Moreover, a recent Transportation Research Bureau (TRB) report suggests that the benefits to the U.S. economy could exceed $2 billion annually.

The Turner truck design is not without some disadvantages. The first concern in implementing this new design is the impact on the rail companies. If the trucking companies can increase the amount of weight per shipment, shipments on the railways will decline. The long-term impact on rail companies is not known. The second issue is the expense of improving some of the bridges in the nation that are not capable of supporting the additional weight of the new trucks. This is expected to cost $400 million. Finally, the trucking industry cannot expect local interest groups not to get involved in this issue. Many groups are currently lobbying the government to regulate the length and the width of truck-trailer combinations. Any proposed legislation affecting the trucking industry will be actively met by action from local interest groups.

Since all states are not likely to support the Turner truck design, adoption by trucking companies is expected to be slow at best. The TRB stopped short of wholeheartedly endorsing the proposal to recommend the adoption of the Turner truck design. The TRB did say that the proposal had merit and that the individual states should consider changing current size and weight regulations. However, a problem arises from the lack of coordination between states. If some states change the laws and other states don't, intrastate shipments using the new truck-trailer combinations may not be possible.

DISCUSSION QUESTIONS

1. What problems can A-P-A Transport Corporation expect to have in purchasing and using the Turner truck-trailers?
2. What advantages could A-P-A gain from federal legislation concerning the new truck-trailer design that state legislation would not have?
3. Should A-P-A be concerned with local interest groups? Why or why not?

Suggested Readings

"Profile: Motor Carrier Services." *Transportation and Distribution* (May 1990): 51.

Strah, Thomas M. "TRB Study Finds Benefits in Turner Truck Design." *Transport Topics* (October 8, 1990): 8.

Source: C. Lamb, J. Hair, and C. McDaniel, *Principles of Marketing*, 1st Edition (Cincinnati, OH: South-Western Publishing Company, 1992) p. 415.

Suggested Additional Readings

"Automated Warehousing—Opting for the Evolutionary Approach," *Retail and Distribution Management* (UK), 14 (July/August 1986): 49–53. **Trends in new technologies and automated storage-retrieval systems in the United Kingdom.**

Banerjic, Auitit and Snehamay Banerjic. "Coordinated, Orderless Inventory Replenishment for a Single Supplier and Multiple Buyers Through Electronic Data Interchange." *International Journal of Technology Management* 7, No. 4 (1992): 328–336.

Bertrand, Kate. "The Just-in-Time Mandate." *Business Marketing* 71 (November 1986): 44–55. **Trends and guidelines for sharing proprietary information, and a discussion of partnerships between vendors and customers and foreign competition.**

Bradley, Peter, "Intermodal Takes a Leap," *Purchasing* 112 (May 7, 1992): 61, 63. **Examples of cooperation and service improvements in intermodal transport.**

Buffa, Frank P. "Inbound Logistics: Analyzing Inbound Consolidation Opportunities." *International Journal of Physical Distribution and Materials Management* (UK), 16, No. 4 (1986): 3–32. **Discussion of and guidelines for materials handling and cost reduction.**

______. "Restocking Inventory in Groups: A Transport Inventory Case." *International Journal of Physical Distribution and Materials Management* (UK), 16, No. 3 (1986): 29–44. **Model comparison and test of an inventory theoretic cost model; four grouping methods are considered.**

Calantone, Roger J., and Michael H. Morris. "The Utilisation of Computer-Based Decision-Support Systems in Transportation." *International Journal of Physical Distribution and Materials Management* (UK), 15, No. 5 (1985): 5–18. **Survey of marketing and sales managers as to the use of computer-assisted decision making in the use of transportation.**

Christopher, Martin. "Implementing Logistics Strategy." *International Journal of Physical Distribution and Materials Management* (UK), 16, No. 1 (1986): 52–62. **Discussion of the total-systems concept of physical distribution and customer service.**

Compagno, Bud. "Manufacturers Profit from 'Quick Response.'" *Manufacturing Systems* 10 (June 1992): 36–41.

Dada, Maqbool. "A Two-Echelon Inventory System with Priority Shipments." *Management Science* 38 (August 1992): 1140–1153. **A discussion of the testing of a new inventory model to be used by companies with priority shipping needs.**

Dion, Paul A., Peter M. Banting, Sharon Pickard, and David L. Blenkhorn. "JIT Implementation: A Growth Opportunity for Purchasing." *International Journal of Purchasing and Materials Management* 28 (Fall 1992): 32–38. **A discussion of implementation of a JIT system of inventory control that includes the buyer's role and supplier relations.**

Dreyer, Jerome L. "The 1990s: The Decade of EDI Expansion." *Global Trade* (November 1990): 16–17.

Frazier, Robert M. ""Quick-Response Inventory Replenishment." *Retail Control* 54 (August 1986): 19–29. **Discussion of inventory management, problems, lead times, shorter buying cycles, and vendor relationships.**

Gagne, Margaret L., and Richard Discenza. "Accurate Product Costing in a JIT Environment." *International Journal of Purchasing and Materials Management* 28 (Fall 1992): 28–31. **A discussion of the advantages of and guidelines for activity-based costing in a JIT inventory system.**

Gattorna, John, and Abby Day. "Strategic Issues in Logistics." *International Journal of Physical Distribution and Materials Management* (UK): 3–42. **Discussion of trends and issues management in logistics planning.**

Graham, Jean M. "A Simple Idea Saves $8 Million a Year." *Purchasing* 112 (May 21, 1992): 47, 49. **A study of the cost savings in using techniques such as bin stocking and single sourcing.**

Haley, George T., and R. Krishnan. "It's Time for CALM: Computer-Aided Logistics Management." *International Journal of Physical Distribution and Materials Management* (UK), 15, No. 7 (1985): 19–32. **Discussion of trends in computer-based modeling in logistics management.**

Hinds, Ed. ""Linking Strategic Elements: Marketing and Distribution." *American Salesman* 31 (December 1986): 24–30. **Case study of just-in-time inventory control and quality control.**

Jenkins, Michael. "Gaining a Financial Foothold through Public Warehousing." *Journal of Business Strategy* 13 (May/June 1992): 53–57. **A discussion of the advantages, costs, and competitive advantage of third-party distribution.**

Jones, Thomas C., and Daniel W. Riley. "Using Inventory for Competitive Advantage through Supply Chain Management." *International Journal of Physical Distribution and Materials Management* (UK), 15, No. 5 (1985): 16–26. **Discussion and case studies of inventory management and the planning and control of an entire supply chain.**

LaLonde, Bernard J., and Raymond E. Mason. "Some Thoughts on Logistics Policy and Strategies: Management Challenges for the 1980s." *International Journal of Physical Distribution and Materials Management* (UK), 15, No. 5 (1985): 5–15. **Discussion of current trends in strategic logistics management, to include cost reduction, information systems, problem solving, and some new principles.**

Langley, C. John, Jr. "Information-Based Decision-Making in Logistics Management." *International Journal of Physical Distribution and Materials Management* (UK), 15, No. 7 (1985): 41–55. **Discussion involving information systems, quality control, resource planning, and the use of microcomputers in logistics management.**

Lele, Milind M. "Inventory Management: How to Control Your Critical Marketing Backfield." *Business Marketing* 71 (May 1986): 40–51. **Discussion of service-inventory-cost trade-offs, using a simulation approach with a computer-based model.**

"Materials Handling: A Big Life Ahead." *Purchasing World* 30 (September 1986): 67/M1–70/M4. **Trends in inventory control and production planning, in regard to automated storage-retrieval systems and robots.**

McDaniel, Steve, Joseph G. Ormsby, and Alicia B. Gresham. "The Effect of JIT on Distributors." *Industrial Marketing Management* 21 (May 1992): 145–149. **A discussion of the influence of a JIT inventory system on organizational buying behavior.**

McDonald, Mitchell E. "The Fast Track to Customer Service." *Traffic Management* 30 (April 1991): 54–56.

Mentzer, John T. "Determining Motor Carrier Backhaul Markets." *Industrial Marketing Management* 15 (August 1986): 237–243. **Discussions, examples of, and guidelines for information systems for determining motor-carrier backhaul markets.**

Newcombe, Tod. "Without Human Intervention." *Inform* 6 (November 1992): 32–35.

Peters, Melvyn. "Information Technology in Delivery Control." *International Journal of Physical Distribution and Materials Management* (UK), 16, No. 3 (1986): 45–56. **In-depth interviews with distribution managers in thirty United Kingdom companies, involving current usage of information technology in distribution firms.**

Sandler, Lester, and Thomas Tanel. "Toward Selective Inventory Control." *Purchasing World* 30 (April 1986): 52PW15–52PW21. **Discussion of stockouts, the Pareto Principle, demand categories, and strategic planning.**

Schary, Philip B. "A Strategic Problem in Logistics Control," *International Journal of Physical Distribution and Materials Management* (UK), 15, No. 5 (1985): 36–50. **Discussion of logistics control systems, involving the limitations of conventional cost accounting and the use of management information systems and data traces.**

Shapiro, Benson P., V. Kasturi Rangan, and John J. Sviokla. "Staple Yourself to an Order." *Harvard Business Review* 70 (July/August 1992): 113–122. **A discussion of the successes, problems, and management involvement with the order-processing cycle.**

Stenger, Alan J. "Just-in-Time: Make Sure You Know What You're Getting Into." *Purchasing World* 30 (March 1986): 64–67. **Discussion of the advantages, disadvantages, and inflexibility of just-in-time inventory control.**

Sterling, Jay U., and Douglas M. Lambert. "A Methodology for Assessing Logistics Operating Systems." *International Journal of Physical Distribution and Materials Management* (UK), 15, No. 16 (1985): 3–44. **Case study of a noncomputer-based assessment system with implications for the provision of more effective and efficient customer services.**

Tersine, Richard J., Marsha H. Nelson, and Susan J. Willer. "Enhancing Productivity with Automated Storage and Retrieval Systems." *Journal of Purchasing and Materials Management* 21 (Fall 1985): 19–24. **Discussion of increased productivity and efficiency in warehousing and materials management.**

Todd, Arthur W. "Buying Inbound Transportation: Part II." *Purchasing World* 30 (October 1986): 60–64. **Discussion of liability and accounting issues.**

"Ton-Miles to Go Before Any Real Hikes." *Purchasing World* 30 (April 1986): 39–40. **Survey results of a study of demand trends in the transportation industry, to include rates and transportation modes.**

van Amstel, M. J. Ploos "Physical Distribution and Product Characteristics." *International Journal of Physical Distribution and Materials Management* (UK), 16, No. 1 (1986): 5–13. **Investigation of linkages between physical distribution and product characteristics.**

Voorhees, Roy Dale, and John I. Coppett. "Marketing Logistics: Opportunities for the 1990s." *Journal of Business Strategy* 7 (Fall 1986): 33–38. **Discussion and trends in negotiated logistical services.**

ENDNOTES

[1]Victor P. Buell (ed.), *Handbook of Modern Marketing*, 2d ed. (New York: McGraw-Hill, 1986), 4–8.

[2]Definition provided by Mr. George Gecowers, executive director of the Council of Logistics Management, Fall 1993.

[3]For a comprehensive discussion of business logistics, see Ronald H. Ballon, *Business Logistics Management*, 3d ed. (Englewood Cliffs, N.J.: Prentice-Hall, 1991); Douglas M. Lambert and James R. Stock, *Strategic Physical Distribution Management*, 3d ed. (Homewood, Ill.: Richard D. Irwin, 1992); and Roy D. Shapiro and James L. Heskett, *Logistics Strategy* (St. Paul, Minn.: West Publishing, 1985).

[4]Peter F. Drucker, "The Economy's Dark Continent," *Fortune*, April 1962, 103.

[5]The National Council of Physical Distribution Management, Oak Brook, Ill., 1985.

[6]Michael White, "Transportation: The New Breed," *International Business* (October 1991): 46–49.

[7]This section is largely from Eric N. Berkowitz, Roger A. Kerin, and William Rudelius, *Marketing*, 3d ed. (Homewood, Ill.: Richard D. Irwin, 1991), Chapter 14.

[8]E. J. Muller, "Are Carriers Now In Control?" *Distribution* (February 1991): 25–30.

[9]*Ibid.*

[10]*Ibid.*

[11]Wayne Kenneth Talley, *Introduction to Transportation* (Dallas, Tex: South-Western Publishing, 1983), 93.

[12]Thomas G. Donlan, "Another Arkansas Hero: J. B. Hunt Took Hold of Deregulation's Opportunities," *Barrons*, 15 February 1993, 10.

[13]L. Minard, "Truckers and Shippers," *Forbes*, January 1984, 105.

[14]Peter Bradley, "Transportation Report 1992", *Purchasing* 113 (July 16, 1992): 54-63.

[15]Peter J. Walters, "The Purchasing Interface with Transportation," *Journal of Purchasing and Materials Management* (Winter 1988): 21-25.

[16]Peter Bradley, "Deregulation's Future: All Roads Lead to Lower Costs", *Purchasing* 105 (July 28, 1988): 54-81.

[17]Peter J. Walters, "The Transportation-Purchasing Interface," *Distribution* (January 1988): 56, 60.

[18]Edward A. Morash, "Using Transportation Intermediaries for Industrial Purchasing Decisions," *Journal of Business and Industrial Marketing* 2 (Fall 1987): 15-27.

[19]Thomas Gale Moore, "Unfinished Business in Motor Carrier Deregulation," *Regulation* 14 (Summer 1991): 49–57.

[20]David M. Lambert, "Developing a Customer-Focused Logistics Strategy," *International Journal of Physical Distribution and Logistics Management* 22 (1992): 12–19.

[21]Douglas M. Lambert and Howard M. Armitage, "Managing Distribution Costs for Better Profit Performance," *Business* (September/October 1980): 46.

[22]*Ibid.*, 47.

[23]See Douglas M. Lambert, *The Distribution Channels Decision* (New York: National Association of Accountants; and Hamilton, Ontario: Society of Management Accountants of Canada, 1978); Douglas M. Lambert and John T. Mentzer, "Is Integrated Physical Distribution Management a Reality?" *Journal of Business Logistics* 2, no. 1 (1980): 18–27; and Douglas M. Lambert and Howard M. Armitage, "Distribution Costs: The Challenge," *Management Accounting* (May 1979): 33–37, 45.

[24]William Baldwin, "Dollars from Doodads," *Forbes*, 11 October 1982, 56.

[25]*Ibid.*

[26]Joseph L. Cavinato, "Exercising Warehouse Management Options," *Distribution* (December 1990): 46–47.

[27]Lisa H. Harrington, "Public Warehousing: The Original Third Party," *Distribution* (February 1993): 46–52.

[28]Jay Gordon, "Warehousing: A Review for Management," *Distribution* (July 1992): 79, 369.

[29]Michael D. Hutt and Thomas W. Speh, "Realigning Industrial Marketing Channels," *Industrial Marketing Management* 12 (July 1983): 171–177.

[30]J. W. Farrell, "Computers Cut Distribution Network Down to Size," *Traffic Management* (February 1986): 64–67.

[31]Graham Sharman, "The Rediscovery of Logistics," *Harvard Business Review* (September/October 1984): 71–79. See also Roy Shapiro, "Get Leverage from Logistics," *Harvard Business Review* (May/June 1984): 119–126.

[32]Charles A. Taff, *Management of Physical Distribution and Transportation* 7th ed. (Homewood, Ill.: Richard D. Irwin, 1984), 18.

[33]James L. Heskett, "Logistics—Essential to Strategy," *Harvard Business Review* 56 (November/December 1977): 89.

[34]Mark A. Raney and Kenneth Walter, "Electronic Data Interchange: The Warehouse and Supplier Interface," *International Journal of Physical Distribution and Logistics Management* 22 (1992): 21–26.

[35]Daniel Biby, "Who Really Needs EDI?" *Industry Week*, 2 November 1992, 45–46.

[36]Robert A. Simmons, "EDI: The Competitive Advantage for the Future," *Global Trade* (November 1991): 12–14.

[37]Paul Jacobs, "EDI: Imaging Exploding," *Computerworld*, 20 January 1992, 80.

[38]Hal Glatzer, "EDI: The Information-Intensive Way to Move Cargo," *Computerworld*, 7 September 1992, 69, 73.

[39]James A. G. Krupp, "JIT in Distribution and Warehousing," *Production and Inventory Management Journal* 32 (Second Quarter 1991): 18–21.

[40]Craig Waters, "Why Everybody's Talking about 'Just-in-Time,'" *Inc.*, March 1984, 77–90. See also Doug Harper, "Zero Inventory Poses Questions for Distributors," *Industrial Distribution* (January 1985): 49; and Summer Aggarwal, "MRP, JIT, OPT, FMS?" *Harvard Business Review* (September/October 1985): 8–16.

[41]G.H. Manoochehri, "Improving Productivity with the Just-in-Time System," *Journal of Systems Management* (January 1985): 23-26.

[42]Lewis Schneider, "New Era in Transportation Strategy," *Harvard Business Review* (March/April 1985): 124.

[43]Paul A. Dion, David L. Blenkhorn, and Peter M. Benting, "Buyer Experiences with JIT: Some New Roles for Buyers," *Mid-Atlantic Journal of Business* 28 (June 1992): 112–123.

[44]For a more detailed discussion of the JIT concept, see Chan K. Hahn, Peter A. Pinto, and Daniel J. Bragg, "Just-in-Time Production and Purchasing," *Journal of Purchasing and Materials Management* (Fall 1983): 2–10; and Richard J. Schonberger and Abdolhossein Ansari, "Just-in-Time Purchasing Can Improve Quality," *Journal of Purchasing and Materials Management* (Spring 1984): 2–7.

[45]Charles R. O'Neal and Kate Bertrand, "Developing a Winning J.I.T. Marketing Strategy," *Small Business Reports* 16 (October 1991): 68–71.

[46]Berkowitz, Kerin, and Rudelius, *Marketing*, 395.

[47]Linda J. Morris and John S. Morris, "The Changing Manufacturing Environment: Implications for Marketing," *Journal of Business and Industrial Marketing* 7 (Spring 1992): 21–30.

[48]This section of the chapter is based on David L. Kurtz and Louis E. Boone, *Marketing* 3d ed. (New York: Dryden Press, 1987), 576–578.

[49]Philip Kotler, *Principles of Marketing*, 5th ed. (Englewood Cliffs, N.J.: Prentice-Hall, 1991), 376.

[50]William Baldwin, "Dollars from Doodads," 56.

[51]John F. Magee, William C. Copacino, and Donald B. Rosenfield, *Modern Logistics Management* (New York: John Wiley and Sons, 1985), 193.

[52]Sak Onkvisit and John J. Shaw, *International Marketing: Analysis and Strategy*, 2d ed. (New York: Merrill Publishing, 1993), 547.

[53]*Ports of the World: A Guide to Cargo Loss Control*, 13th ed. (CIGNA), 46–47.

Case Studies

McIlhenny Company—Producers of Tabasco Brand Products

McIlhenny Company, located on Avery Island in the Louisiana coastal marshes about seven miles south of the town of New Iberia, manufactured two products. One was very old and extremely well known around the world and the other was a much later addition. The first was Tabasco Brand Pepper Sauce, introduced in 1868, and the other was Tabasco Brand Bloody Mary Mix, introduced over 100 years later in 1972.

The key ingredient in the two products was the red pepper, known more technically as the *capsicum frutescens*. Ranging from three to four feet in height, this plant is a genus of the *Solanaceae* (nightshade) family. Its pungent flavored fruit is known as *tabasco pepper*, a varietal name. Cayenne pepper is a distinct variety not to be confused with *tabasco pepper*. Some species of this plant are bushy in appearance and are cultivated in tropical and subtropical regions. It is native only to the Western Hemisphere. Under its Central American and Mexican name, chili, the fruit was widely used in various sauces and to some extent as a flavoring in pickled foods.

The McIlhenny Company took great interest and pride in *capsicum*. The Indians of Central America and southern Mexico domesticated this plant around 2500 B.C. and used it widely as a seasoning for their diet of corn, squash, tomatoes, fish, and game. A friend of the founder of the present company brought back some of the seeds from Mexico following the Mexican-American War of 1848. By the late 1850s Edmund McIlhenny was growing *capsicum* plants in his vegetable garden on Avery Island. The company and the family worked for the next 120 years on improving the *capsicum* plant. Family members constantly involved themselves in selecting seed peppers for each new crop, and no outside pepper contaminated the strain in all those years. Botanists recognized the present plant as a distinct variety.

Until recently all the peppers used in the company's production had been grown on Avery Island, and 40 per cent of the peppers were still grown there. With the advent of federal and state unemployment compensation, food stamps, and many other welfare benefits, agricultural labor became increasingly difficult to obtain. Beginning in the early 1970s pepper crops brought to maturity could not be harvested because of lack of agricultural labor.

The company started raising peppers in Mexico, Guatemala, Honduras, Colombia, and Venezuela. The seeds for all foreign grown peppers were supplied by McIlhenny Company and no peppers were ever purchased on the open market. Some of the foreign peppers were propagated by contract under supervision of McIlhenny field people. In some instances the company leased land and raised the crop itself. The foreign grown peppers were shipped to Avery Island for curing and aging as soon as their condition permitted transportation.

After the picked peppers were ground up they were steeped in their own juices in large white oak reusable casks that were similar to whiskey barrels. A wooden cover with tiny holes drilled through it was placed on top of each cask. Next, a thick layer of salt from the company's Avery Island salt mine was spread over the cover. This salt seal allowed the actual vapors of fermentation to escape and at the same time prevented fresh air from ever entering the barrel. This mash had to be aged for three warm seasons of fermentation and strengthening. These seasons might be three summers or two summers and a warm spring. The company president personally inspected every single barrel for both smell and taste before releasing it for mixing with 100 grain vinegar and salt. Approximately 30 per cent mash was combined with 60 per cent vinegar and 10 per cent salt and the resulting mixture was stirred constantly for about a month. Then the remaining pieces of pepper seeds and skins were screened out of the sauce. The seeds and skins, called " chaff" after drying, were sold to unaffiliated organizations that steamed them to obtain oil of capsaicin, the stinging material in Ben-Gay balm, "red-hot" candies, and other products.

Tabasco brand pepper sauce was also made abroad. The first foreign production was in London, which was soon followed by production in Montreal, Mexico City, Caracas, and Madrid production operations were added later. However, the pepper mash used in these foreign operations was made on Avery Island and shipped abroad. All in all, approximately 55 million bottles were sold in 125 countries annually. Some foreign production was under licensing agreements and some was under partnership agreements. However, in every case it was required that samples of the finished sauce be submitted periodically to Avery Island for examination and approval. Foreign sales accounted for about 40 per cent of total sales and the percentage was rising.

McIlhenny Company distributed Tabasco Sauce and its newer product, Tabasco Brand Bloody Mary Mix, in the United States civilian market through food brokers. The personal selling effort was under the supervision of regional sales managers who were directed by a national sales manager. Military food brokers were used for the military segment of demand. The regular two-fluid-ounce container of Tabasco pepper sauce was supplemented by the development of a twelve-fluid-ounce size for restaurant chefs and a 128-fluid-ounce size for food manufacturers.

The company president, Walter Stauffer McIlhenny, thought that the company would aim toward further product diversification. He explained his thoughts in the following manner:

> We are constantly considering the addition of new products and have reviewed hundreds of suggestions. Obviously our prime purpose in adding a new product is to increase our profit. An important second consideration is that your account with your broker becomes more important with two or more items bringing greater revenues into his office. Accordingly the manufacturer is then in a position to command more effort from the brokers' retail force and their management team as well.

The advertising medium used for the pepper sauce was magazines, both consumer-type publications and those directed to restaurants and distributors. Among those selected in the latter category were *Food Service Marketing, Restaurant Business*, and *Institutions/Volume Feeding Management*. For the Bloody Mary mix the choice was basically the same, although a small amount of newspaper advertising was also done. For both products consumer magazines were emphasized. For sales purposes the planning unit was one dozen. The advertising allocation for pepper sauce was 40 cents per dozen, a figure that had not varied for the past twenty years. Of course, as physical sales volume had grown so had the total advertising budget.

The name Tabasco and the familiar diamond-shaped label were protected by a U.S. Patent Office trademark registration at an early date. Nevertheless, much litigation was required to combat firms that attempted copies or near copies of the famous name and marks. McIlhenny Company succeeded in confirming its exclusive rights to the name, the diamond label, and the color pattern of the packaging.

The "Bloody Mary" was one of the two or three most popular alcoholic mixed drinks in the United States. Apparently an American creation and still strongly identified with the United States abroad, it surfaced in the mid-1930s. The Bloody Mary was popular in its own right but also acquired a reputation within a few years as an antidote to hangovers. In the United States well over half of all vodka, the top selling distilled spirit, went into this type of beverage. Recipes for Bloody Marys varied, of course, as to stirring or shaking, serving with ice cubes or strained, ratios of ingredients, and the use of additives such as a sprig of mint or wedge of lime. What is more, product spin-offs had developed, including the Bloody Maria, made with tequila instead of vodka; the Danish Mary, made with aquavit instead of vodka; the Bull Shot, in which beef bouillon replaced tomato juice; and the Bloody Bull Shot, half tomato juice and half beef bouillon. However, virtually everyone included Tabasco Sauce and Worcestershire sauce with the spirits and juice or bouillon. Some people were purists and refused to use prepared mixes, but their numbers were apparently decreasing.

Over a period of years, Tabasco Brand Bloody Mary Mix achieved nationwide but somewhat spotty distribution. First a six-fluid-ounce can with an easy-open flip top was introduced, and later a twelve-fluid-ounce version in the same sort of can was brought out. Still later a thirty-fluid-ounce clear glass bottle with a screw-type lid was introduced. The most common price at retail for the first product was two for 69 cents, whereas for the second and third products the most common figures were 59 cents and $1.29, respectively. The ingredients were listed on the containers in the following order: concentrated tomato juice, water, fresh frozen concentrated lime juice, Worcestershire sauce, salt, and Tabasco pepper sauce.

McIlhenny Company had never experienced a product failure, but it had dropped two items many years before. In the early 1900s the firm operated a successful oyster canning plant. However, when the pressures of the Mississippi River at New Orleans began to pose a continuing threat to the city and the United States Army Corps of Engineers permanently diverted some of the water into the Atchafalaya Basin, the nearby oyster beds became muddy and could not survive. In addition, for a good many years McIlhenny packed green Tabasco peppers in vinegar under the label Island Pride peppers-in-vinegar. However, rising sales of the pepper sauce, which required ripened peppers, forced withdrawal of this item from the market.

Besides the pepper sauce and Bloody Mary mix, the McIlhenny family had other business interests. To be specific, they owned but leased the island salt mine to International Salt Company of Clarks Summit, Pennsylvania, which produced Sterling brand salt. Exxon Company produced oil on, and adjacent to, the island. Moreover, the family of Edward A. McIlhenny operated Jungle Gardens, a 200-acre area that was devoted to natural vegetation, botanical exhibits, and Bird City, a noted refuge.

McIlhenny Company, of course, continued to be owned by the descendants of Edmund McIlhenny and his wife Mary Eliza Avery McIlhenny, whose grandfather had first acquired the property.

FURTHER BACKGROUND ON THE MCILHENNY ORGANIZATION AND AVERY ISLAND

McIlhenny Company was started in 1868 by Edmund McIlhenny, a former New Orleans banker and grandfather of the present head of the enterprise, Walter S. McIlhenny. However, Edmund's father-in-law, Judge Daniel Dudley Avery of Baton Rouge, had acquired the island on which the business was located many years earlier. And Avery's father-in-law, John Craig Marsh, had acquired partial ownership in 1818. Since at the time of the case younger men of the family had also entered the management, six generations of the extended family had been involved in the island's economic activities. Known earlier by the names of E. McIlhenny and E. McIlhenny Sons, the organization was renamed McIlhenny Company in 1907.

Geologists do not consider Avery Island, once called Petite Anse (little handle), a real island. Yet it appears to be one, set as it is among a great expanse of marshes, swamps, and bayous about six miles from Vermillion Bay. Rising 152 feet above sea level, this island is really a column of solid salt about ten miles deep over which there is a cap of rich soil. Part of the island is covered with subtropical forest.

Indians produced salt on the island in early times. In the late 1700s John Hayes rediscovered the long abandoned brine springs and began producing salt. Because of a rise in demand occasioned by the need for salt in making munitions for the War of 1812, the salt works were expanded. However, after that war foreign competitors nearly put the salt operation out of business and the island's economy turned to the growing of sugar cane. Demand for salt again surged at the opening of the Civil War in 1861. John Marsh Avery, son of Daniel Dudley Avery, then re-established the island's salt industry, which quickly became the principal salt supplier to the Confederacy. In expanding the salt works Avery made the first discovery of rock salt on the North American continent. Admiral David Farragut of the Union Navy shelled the facility in 1862 in an unsuccessful attempt to halt company operations. In April 1863 a Union land force under General Banks attacked and totally destroyed the company's facilities. The family had to flee to San Antonio, Texas, for safety and to live with relatives. They could not return for over three years, during which time their rich plantation land and crops suffered badly from neglect.

The hardy pepper plants survived the years of neglect. With the salt business in ruins and food supplies monotonous in the post-Civil War period, gourmet Edmund McIlhenny had both the time and the inclination to experiment with recipes. He began experimenting with various ways of making a piquant yet pleasing pepper sauce. He refined the basic method for making the sauce, which was to crush the peppers, thus making a mash, then straining the mash, and adding salt and vinegar. The resulting aromatic mixture was then put into wooden barrels to age, so that the flavors and fragrances could steep and intermingle. McIlhenny let friends taste the concoction and found that they liked it. In 1868 he processed enough sauce for 350 bottles and sent the entire output as free samples to a selected group of wholesalers. In 1869 he received his first order for the sauce, which was assigned a wholesale price of $1 per bottle. Always highly conscious of spices and condiments, Europeans also accepted the new product. Like many other companies of the coastal South, McIlhenny was international in its outlook and opened an office in London in 1872.

Edmund McIlhenny died in 1890 and was succeeded by his son John Avery McIlhenny. Some members of the family were interested in the island's salt deposit. A firm called Chouteau and Price sank a shaft 90 feet deep in 1867 but abandoned operations in 1870. The American Salt Company and the family agreed on a lease in 1880 and the lessee began producing large quantities of salt, using the early shaft.

Transportation of the salt had always been a severe problem and promised to be so for the new product. Three alternatives were tried and all failed: a causeway running north toward New Iberia; an embankment and tramway to Bayou Petite Anse; and a canal to Vermillion Bay. In 1883 railway service from New Orleans to the West was inaugurated and in 1886 a branch was opened from New Iberia south to the island, thus solving the problem. By this time the New Iberia Salt Company had taken over the salt operations. In 1898 the family organized its own Avery Rock Salt Mining Company, which sank a new shaft, still in use, to a depth of 518 feet. The mining operation was put in the hand of Sidney Bradford, an engineer married to Edmund's daughter Marigold.

During the 1890s Avery Island became established as an important wildlife refuge. Edmund's second son, Edward (Ned) Avery McIlhenny, became a naturalist who made several scientific expeditions to the Arctic. Edward McIlhenny became alarmed that the snowy egret, a beautiful white heron native to the Louisiana swamps, was rapidly declining in number and faced extinction. This bird had been slaughtered by hunters who wanted a few special plumes for use in women's hats. After a long search Ned found eight egret chicks, which he took back to Avery Island and successfully raised. Counting on a trait found in some birds he released them in the late fall for their natural migration south across the Gulf of Mexico. In the spring, six of the birds returned to him to form the nucleus of the island's large bird colony called Bird City. Thereafter the company continued to show extraordinary interest in ecology and conservation.

In 1906 John McIlhenny was appointed a U.S. Civil Service commissioner and turned the firm over to his brother Ned, who served as president of the company for the next forty years. Ned wrote several books and many magazine articles on the topics of egrets, alligators, wild turkeys, and folk music. He personally banded 189,289 birds in order to accumulate data to study their migratory routes. Despite Ned's other interest, sales of Tabasco Sauce continued to rise during his long administration. He worked well with his brother Rufus, who took on some of the management burden in the later years.

Rufus died in 1940, at which time the company called in Walter Stauffer McIlhenny, the son of John McIlhenny and nephew of Ned, to participate in the management. However, World War II intervened and Walter McIlhenny, a Marine Corps reserve officer, went on active duty. Ned suffered a stroke and Walter succeeded him in 1949. Walter's interest in the corps continued and he rose in the Reserve to the rank of Brigadier General. He modernized the Tabasco production line with up-to-date filling and labeling equipment but retained the picturesque, atmospheric buildings. He selected a new advertising agency, hired the company's first national sales manager, and expanded company interest abroad.

Humble Oil brought in an oil well at the edge of the island in 1942, and in a few years there was an extensive field. Although oil was a severe potential threat to the island's ecology, the problem was solved in a variety of ways, such as by burying the pipelines, bypassing certain trees, and filling and sodding over pits.

APPENDIX TO McILHENNY COMPANY

Principal Competitors of Tabasco Brand Bloody Mary Mix

There were several noteworthy competitors of McIlhenny's new Bloody Mary mix. All of them were nonalcoholic, as was the McIlhenny entry. Selected information about the competitive products is now provided:

1. Holland House Bloody Mary Cocktail Mix, made by Holland House Brands Company, Ridgefield, New Jersey, a division of National Distillers. This organization had a line of drink mixes, which included Manhattan, Screwdriver, Side Car, Tom Collins, Whiskey Sour, Daiquiri, Pink Squirrel, and eighteen others, including a low-calorie version of the popular Whiskey Sour. A few of these products, including the Bloody Mary, were available in both liquid and instant dry mixes. However, the Screwdriver, Pink Squirrel, Love Bird, Grasshopper, Wallbanger, Tequila Sunrise, and Vodka (white) Sour were only available in an instant dry mix.

   This brand of Bloody Mary mix was offered in three variations. The first was Regular, which was designed and promoted to be a traditional Bloody Mary, whereas the second was Extra Tangy, "the traditional Bloody Mary with extra zesty flavor." The third was Smooth N' Spicy, "a unique flavor system consistent with contemporary taste preferences; a welcome change of pace from the traditional." These three mixes were promoted on the label as "skillful blends of choice ingredients backed by experience that dates back to 1887." The Traditional version from Holland House included tomato juice from tomato juice concentrate, lemon juice concentrate, natural flavors, salt, citric acid, monosodium glutamate, calcium carrageenan, hydrolyzed vegetable protein, iso-ascorbic acid, spice extractives, and less than 0.1 per cent each of sodium benzoate and sodium metabisulfite as preservatives. This brand was offered at a prevailing retail price of $1.09 in a twenty-four-fluid-ounce clear bottle with a screw-type lid. It was also offered in a six fluid ounce can at a prevailing price of 35 cents. Both the regular and extra tangy versions were available in such cans. At first the can had a solid top, but it was replaced by the easy-open flip top in 1978. Holland House Smooth N' Spicy was also available in a thirty-two-fluid ounce (one quart) clear glass bottle with a screw-type lid at a prevailing price of $1.30.
2. Snap-E-Tom, made by Heublein, Inc., Hartford, Connecticut. Heublein made several other mixes, such as the Hereford's Cows series. Snap-E-Tom had the following ingredients: water, tomato paste, green chilies, salt, onion, and citric acid. It was available as a single pack and a three-pack. The can had a solid top and contained six fluid ounces. The prevailing retail prices were 27 cents and 79 cents, respectively. Since Heublein had just introduced a bottled whiskey sour that contained the alcohol, many industry observers were watching to see if later there would be a bottled Bloody Mary that contained the vodka.

3. Libby's Bloody Mary Mix, made by Libby, McNeill, & Libby, Chicago. This product had the following ingredients: water, tomato paste, cider and distilled vinegar, salt, spices, dextrose, hydrolyzed vegetable protein, citric acid, onion powder, jalapeno peppers, soy sauce solids and dextrans, flavorings, sugar, monosodium glutamate, garlic powder, caramel color, and hydrogenated vegetable oils. It was offered only in a five-and-a-half-fluid-ounce can with an easy-open flip top, which was shipped and displayed as a six-pack. The prevailing price at retail was $1.25 per six-pack. Some retailers were willing to sell an individual can removed from the six-pack at a prevailing price of 21 cents.
4. Schweppes Bloody Mary Mixer, made by Schweppes U.S.A., Ltd., Stamford, Connecticut. This product had the following ingredients: concentrated tomato juice, water, Worcestershire sauce, lemon juice, vinegar, sucrose, citric acid, salt, red pepper, celery salt, black pepper, carrageenan. It was available in a twenty-five-fluid-ounce clear glass bottle with s screw-type lid at a prevailing price of 95 cents. This product was also offered in a four-fluid-ounce clear glass bottle in a three-pack at a prevailing retail price of $1.05. Some retailers were willing to break the three-pack and sell an individual bottle at 35 cents.
5. Mr and Mrs "T" Bloody Mary Mix, made by Mr. and Mrs. T. Products, a division of Taylor Food Products, Inc., El Segundo, California. This product had the following ingredients: water, tomato paste, concentrated tomato juice, vinegar, salt, sugar, invert sugar, dried onion, concentrated lemon juice, Worcestershire sauce, artificial flavor, spices, potassium sorbate and sodium benzoate as preservatives, and dry garlic. It was available as a single pack and consisted of a six-fluid-ounce can with an easy-open flip-type top. The prevailing price at retail was two for 65 cents. This brand was available also in a twenty-four-fluid-ounce size in a clear glass bottle with a screw-type lid at a prevailing retail price of 99 cents.
6. Heinz Bloody Mary Mix, made by H. J. Heinz Company, Pittsburgh, Pennsylvania. This product had the following ingredients: tomatoes, water, vinegar, corn sweetener, salt, concentrated lemon juice, hydrolyzed vegetable protein (with disodium inosinate, disodium quanylate), potassium sorbate as a preservative, molasses, spices, natural flavoring, anchovies, and onion powder. It was available in a thirty-two-fluid-ounce clear glass bottle with a screw-type lid. The prevailing price was $1.55.
7. Angostura Bloody Merry-Maker, made by A-W Brands, Inc., Carteret, New Jersey, a subsidiary of Iroquois Brands, Ltd., under license from Angostura, International, Ltd., Toronto, Canada. This product had the following ingredients: Worcestershire sauce, Angostura aromatic bitters, red pepper sauce, salt, celery flavoring, natural lemon flavor, and 0.1 per cent sodium benzoate as a preservative. It was available only in an eight-fluid-ounce clear glass bottle with a screw-type lid at a prevailing retail price of $1.59. This product was added in small amounts, usually three to five dashes, to vodka and plain tomato juice.
8. V-8 Spicy Hot Vegetable Juice Cocktail, made by Campbell's Soup Company, Camden, New Jersey. This product was being promoted both as an appetizer and as a mixer for alcoholic drinks. The ingredients were water, tomato

concentrate, concentrated juices of carrots, celery, beets, parsley, lettuce, watercress, and spinach, with salt, ascorbic acid (vitamin C), natural flavoring, and citric acid. It was available only in a six-fluid-ounce can with an easy-open flip top, and these cans were in a six-pack. The prevailing retail price was $1.09 per six-pack. Some retailers were willing to sell an individual can at a prevailing price of 19 cents.

9. Steero Bloody Mary Cocktail Mix, made by American Kitchen Products Company, Jersey City, New Jersey. This product had the following ingredients: tomato juice, water, lemon juice, Worcestershire sauce, salt, sugar, and spices. It was offered in an eight-fluid-ounce can with a solid top at a prevailing retail price of 39 cents. This company had just introduced a closely related product, Bullshot Cocktail Mix, which contained the following ingredients: water, tomato paste, monosodium glutamate, lemon juice, salt, citric acid, sugar, beef extract, caramel color, natural and artificial flavorings, spices, and Worcestershire sauce. This product was offered in an eight-fluid-ounce can with a solid top at a prevailing retail price of 43 cents.

In addition, three other brands should be acknowledged. Master's Mix Bloody Mary Mix, made by several companies under license from Professional Mixers, Inc., Sacramento, California, was available in a 25.6-fluid-ounce clear glass bottle with a screw-type lid. There was variation, but the prevailing retail price was about $1.39.

Schweppes's U.S.A., Ltd., was beginning to distribute Rose's Bloody Mary Mix under license from L. Rose and Company, Ltd. Both Schweppes and Rose were British organizations. Policies on package sizes and preferred prices were not completely settled yet. It appeared certain that Rose's would be in a twenty-four-fluid-ounce clear glass bottle with a screw-type lid and the retail price would be relatively high. Promotion as a prestige product was likely.

Sacramento Tomato Plus Vegetable Cocktail, made by Borden Inc., New York City, had recently moved from western to national distribution. It was made of the following ingredients: water, tomato paste, salt, dried chili pepper, ground celery seed, dehydrated onion, powdered onion, ascorbic acid (vitamin C), natural flavorings, and spices. Although this product was now being promoted as a self-contained beverage, observers considered it probable that the product would later be promoted as a mixer for vodka, gin, and aquavit. It was offered in a five-and-a-half-fluid-ounce can, and these were in a six-pack. The prevailing retail price was 99 cents. Some retailers were willing to sell an individual can removed from the pack at a prevailing retail price of 17 cents. This product was also available in a forty-six-fluid-ounce can with a solid top at a prevailing retail price of 81 cents.

CASE STUDY ACTIVITY

Advise the McIlhenny Company.

Source: Reprinted with permission of Macmillan College Publishing Company from *Cases In Marketing: Orientation, Analysis and Problems*, 2nd Edition, by Thomas V. Greer.

Crinshaw Company

Kenneth McMindle was manager of store number 220 in the Crinshaw Company, a large chain of department stores. Although this organization was the principal owner of a thriving insurance company, its main business was its several hundred stores. McMindle had been with the company for twenty-four years and had been adjudged an outstanding manager. He was quite loyal to Crinshaw's and had never worked for any other retailer. He had become an assistant store manager within three years, an accomplishment made by very few people in less than six years unless one worked in an extremely small store. By the time McMindle was in his early forties he had become a district manager over seventeen stores. He did well in that position for three years, but he had been very fond of merchandising and wanted to return to store management. In addition, he did not enjoy traveling, although his district did not cover a particularly large geographic area. McMindle was given his choice of nine stores that were either about to be opened or in which the manager was about to retire. This freedom of choice was a major compliment paid him by top management.

McMindle had chosen store 220, a new suburban store in a Midwestern metropolitan area of about 150,000 population. It was in the same district over which he had been manager. His replacement as district manager was Ralph Jungkind, an old friend who had operated a Crinshaw store in a city about forty-five miles away but in the same district. Planners in company headquarters intended this new store to carry the usual department store merchandise lines except for the full furniture line. Only patio and camping furniture was to be carried, and that was restricted to the late spring and summer seasons. The store was not intended to be large by department store industry standards, but was to be above average size for the Crinshaw Company. The average store in that chain did an annual volume of about $2,200,000, but this store was expected to do about $3,600,000.

Crinshaw was conservative and not given to flashy promotion. Its merchandise was medium quality and seldom included fads. Crinshaw enjoyed a reputation for ethical and dependable if not fashionable and exciting merchandising. The company's financial condition was sound and the stock was widely held.

The Crinshaw organization operated one other store (number 131) in the metropolitan area. It was located about seven miles away in a shopping center on the opposite edge of town and was essentially stable at about $2,050,000 net sales a year. It handled no hard lines except small appliances, but had been under no pressure from the headquarters people to change. Its manager, who was due to retire in ten months, had spent thirty-three years with the company. No replacement had been selected. It was possible that McMindle would be consulted for advice on making the replacement choice in that he knew this metropolitan area and its characteristics well. The store facilities occupied by store number 131 were in need of refurbishment, but it was not an urgent matter. The store had occupied that building for seventeen years and the lease had another two and a half years to run.

Crinshaw emphasized soft goods, and until about fifteen years ago restricted itself to such lines. The chain's net sales were still nearly 84 percent soft goods, but this percentage was declining every year. The hard lines earned satisfactory markups, and the company was eager to increase such sales. However, it required time to sharpen the company's buying expertise and to change the public's expectation that no hard lines would be found at Crinshaw's. In addition, the company had always shown extreme regard for the views of its local managers. On this factor, they were often the envy of managers in competing companies. Some Crinshaw store managers had resisted the addition of hard lines and delayed their introduction by two or three years, and some stores devoted a disproportionately small amount of floor space to the new hard lines. Some store managers protested (many with justification) that the amount of space in the building leased by the company could not accommodate a greater variety of goods without hurting the established lines. Most of these leases would run several more years. Furthermore, moving to another building could be disruptive of established patronage. In addition, some fixtures might not fit a new facility. The problem was compounded in that 7 percent of the stores that were located in structures the company owned.

The market researchers at the home office of Crinshaw in New York City had predicted $3,600,000 for store number 220, which was located in Wagonwheel Plaza, a shopping center developed by Hoadly Brothers of Chicago. Under McMindle's leadership the store did $3,803,000 its first year, $4,256,000 in the second year, and $5,003,000 in the third year, which had just ended. Net profits as a percentage of net sales were satisfactory. The sales per square foot were well above the average for the company and the department store industry. McMindle's personal sales forecasts, which he had not reported to New York, were $5,550,000 for the fourth year, $6,000,000 for the fifth year, and $6,175,000 for the sixth year.

Instead of a fixed lease payment annually, the owner of the store number 220 building had asked for 1.1 percent of net sales. Crinshaw's headquarters organization had agreed to this arrangement for a six-year contract, since they had tacitly assumed that a fixed monetary sum for six years would have cost them about 11 percent more the first year. Executives of Hoadly Brothers had known McMindle for several years and had had great confidence in the Wagonwheel Plaza location and in him. Hoadly Brothers was willing to gamble on the percentage instead of a riskless fixed payment. According to the contract, the cost to cancel the lease early was a flat $18,000.

The average Crinshaw store did 7 percent of its volume in major appliances (excluding stereo equipment), whereas the Wagonwheel Plaza store did 5 percent of its business in such appliances. For small appliances, the figures were 2 percent and 4 percent, respectively. The average figure for sporting goods was 2 percent, whereas the Wagonwheel Plaza store figure was 3 percent. The typical Crinshaw store did 3 percent of its volume in stereo equipment, records, and tapes.

Hugh Bock, senior buyer for stereo equipment, records, and tapes at the home office of Crinshaw, was perturbed by the number of stores doing little volume in his line. One such store was Wagonwheel Plaza, which confined itself to two models of stereo sets on the floor. It would order a unit like one of those two demonstrators if the customer wanted to buy. The salespeople in major appliances and small appliances took turns answering the inquiries customers made about the stereo equipment. The store handled no records or tapes. In the first year Wagonwheel Plaza sold four units at an aggregate of $1,110, in the second year five units for $1,455, and in the third year six units for $1,895. Bock noted and commented widely that store number 220 did 83 percent of its volume in soft goods this year and 84 percent the year before, and that as a new and "progressive" store it probably should be doing no more than 74 percent in soft goods. Stereo equipment, records, and tapes had been the largest movers in hard-line sales in about one-fifth of the Crinshaw stores.

Bock had the ear of all the top executives at headquarters. Two years before he had been hired away from a chain of hard-lines stores where he had been extremely successful as the stereo buying supervisor at headquarters. Although only thirty, Bock had already worked successfully for a stereo equipment manufacturer as well as for the chain mentioned previously.

McMindle had answered Bock without undue delay, and he advised the buyer that his opportunities with stereo equipment, records, and tapes were extremely limited because another shopping center just one mile away also had such a specialty store. The second plaza, Lyndale Center, had the stereo store, plus a hardware store, a shoe store, a cafeteria, a jewelry shop, a gift shop, a gas station, a coffee shop, and parking for 695 cars. In addition to Crinshaw's and the stereo shop in Wagonwheel Plaza, there were two women's and girl's apparel stores, two shoe shops, a gift shop, a fabric shop, a men's and boy's apparel store, a sporting-goods store, a bake shop, a gourmet food shop, a table-service restaurant, a hairdresser, a barber shop, a drugstore, a supermarket, a travel agency, and a parking lot for 500 cars. McMindle estimated that the Wagonwheel Plaza stereo shop had a volume of about $340,000 and the Lyndale Center stereo shop just under $400,000. Both carried a limited line of records and tapes, but they did not push them hard. For the whole metropolitan area he estimated the demand for stereo equipment at around $1,650,000, but he could not make an estimate for tapes and records. His estimates in the past had proved rather accurate. McMindle also knew that in the metropolitan area three department stores, one music store, one home appliance store, two furniture stores, and one other stereo specialty shop offered stereo equipment for sale, and that another department store had withdrawn from stereo equipment about six months before.

Bock retorted to McMindle's letter of explanation, "You have avoided full-line furniture, which about 20 percent of Crinshaw stores are handling. And you have virtually avoided stereo equipment. Two demonstrators are worth less than none at all. You make us look like Hicksville! Why don't you consider putting your management expertise to the making of a balanced variety of merchandise in your store? The two stereo shops should constitute a challenge for you, not an insuperable obstacle."

McMindle became provoked. In a letter to Bock, with a carbon copy to each vice-president and the district manager, McMindle challenged Bock to negotiate a contract with a stereo manufacturer such that McMindle could reduce the prevailing stereo set price in Crinshaw stores by about 10 or 11 percent and thus slightly underprice the two stereo shops nearby. "Then I will sell them as fast as you can have them shipped to me!" After a day of reflection McMindle was bothered by a fact that he knew very well. Expressed as a percent of cost, Crinshaw's had a markup of about 40 percent on stereo sets, but the two independent stereo shops nearby had a markup of about 50 percent.

Two days later McMindle received a telegram from Hugh Bock stating that in about twelve days sixty-five stereo sets (seven different models) would arrive at store number 220, and that the retail price would be 8 percent below the ordinary retail price. The sets would carry a markup of 25 percent of retail selling price, he said. More would follow when inventory levels were worked down. Instead of the manufacturer's brand name appearing on the merchandise, as it ordinarily did on stereo equipment sold at Crinshaw's, a Crinshaw house brand would appear. (About 50 percent of Crinshaw Company sales came through their own house brands. About the same figure applied in store number 220.) In getting this price, Bock advised, he had not sacrificed any functional quality in the product. Rather he had economized on the quality and workmanship of the wood, plastic, and chrome used in the composition of the cabinets and cabinet trim. McMindle realized that, under existing company policy, he could reject the shipment of stereo equipment when it arrived. In addition, he could cancel it immediately.

CASE STUDY ACTIVITY

Advise Kenneth McMindle, the manager of Crinshaw's store number 220.

Suggested Reading

Ballou, Ronald H. *Business Logistics Management*, 3d ed (Englewood Cliffs, N.J.: Prentice-Hall, 1991).

Lambert, Douglas M. and James R. Stock. *Strategic Physical Distribution Management*, 3d ed. (Homewood, Ill.: Richard D. Irwin, 1992).

Shapiro, Roy D. and James L. Heskett. *Logistics Strategy* (St. Paul, Minn.: West Publishing, 1985).

Part Five

Promoting and Selling the Goods

10 The Personal Selling Function in Business Marketing Strategy

Learning Objectives

After reading this chapter, you should be able to:

- Appreciate the scope and nature of the business salesperson's daily activities.
- Understand the nature of the cost of a business sale.
- Uncover a sales prospect's important buying needs.
- Identify different sales approaches for reaching the business buyer.
- Discuss important current trends in business personal selling.
- Describe the business selling process and its associated activities.
- Comprehend how to sell effectively in international business markets.

Chapter Outline

Learning Objectives

How Personal Selling Differs between Business and Consumer Markets

A Profile of Personal Selling
- Selling
- Cooperative Relationships with Channel Members
- Planning
- Decision Making
- The Management of Communication

The Cost of Personal Selling
- The Cost to Close a Business Sale

Understanding Buyer Behavior
- Understanding Buyer Needs
- Methods Used to Uncover Important Buyer Needs

The Selling Spectrum
- Approaches to the Business Sales Presentation
  - The formularized (AIDA) model
  - The buying-decisions model
  - The problem-solving model

Types of Sales Positions and Selling Styles in the Business Market

Some Contemporary Trends in Business Selling
- The Importance of Systems Selling
- The Importance of Telemarketing
- The Emergence of the Saleswoman
- The Usage of Terminals and Laptop Computers
- The Rapid Growth of Audio-Visual Aids

The Personal Selling Process: A Business Salesperson's Perspective
- Preliminary Activities
- Face-to-Face Activities
- Follow-Up Activities

International Business Selling

Summary

Key Terms

Review Questions

Cases
- Case 10-1
- Case 10-2

Suggested Additional Readings

Endnotes

HOW PERSONAL SELLING DIFFERS BETWEEN BUSINESS AND CONSUMER MARKETS

Personal selling involves persuasive deliberate contact between a buyer and a seller for the specific purpose of creating an exchange between them. Personal selling is widely utilized in the sales of both consumer and business goods. In the case of most consumer goods, such as shampoo, clothing, and automobiles, personal selling is used as a complement to other elements in the promotional mix, which also includes advertising, publicity, public relations, and sales promotion. On the other hand, personal selling is generally the primary or most fundamental means of selling business goods such as photocopiers, computer systems, and machine parts; and the other elements of the promotional mix are frequently employed to support or to augment the persuasiveness of the personal selling function.

So that we might understand why personal selling typically plays a more important role in selling to business buyers than to final consumers, Table 10-1 examines some important differences in the nature of the marketing mix between final consumers and business buyers. First, there are far greater numbers of final consumers than business buyers, and indirect methods of creating a sale are more frequently successful when greater numbers of buyers are available. Second, business buyers most often buy more technical and more sophisticated products and services than do final consumers, requiring more explanation and personal demonstration. Third, final consumers generally make smaller-volume purchases than do business buyers, who often have special product or service design needs and who like to negotiate price rather than adhere to the typical, one-price policy so common in final consumer purchasing. Fourth, final consumers are normally reached through longer, more indirect distribution channels; business buyers seem to be more effectively approached through shorter, more direct distribution channels, involving more frequent contact with salespeople. Fifth, final consumers tend to develop less personal relationships with the majority of salespeople with whom they come into contact, as opposed to business buyers, who frequently form both professional and personal relationships with business salespeople from whom they buy repeatedly over a period of years. Sixth, and last, sales teams are often used. The sales team is able to answer specific questions relating to engineering, financing, installation, production capabilities, services available, and other factors that the salesperson alone may be incapable of answering.

In short, final consumers often see salespeople merely as convenient sources of supply of particular and usually ordinary products and services. On the other hand, business buyers more typically view business salespeople not only as product and service experts from whom they can seek purchasing and inventory advice, but also as good friends and the critical link between the manufacturer and themselves.

TABLE 10-1 **Differences Between Business and Consumer Marketing**

Factors	Business-to-Business Customers	Final Consumers
Customer size	Relatively few customers	Many consumers
Products	Technical and sophisticated, requiring explanation through personal contact	Less sophisticated, relying on mass media for explanation
Purchase size	Large volume	Small volume
Price	Negotiated pricing	One-price policy
Distribution channels	Shorter, more direct	Longer, less direct
Promotion	Personal selling is emphasized with support from business mass promotion	Advertising is emphasized with support from personal selling
Relationships	Formation of both personal and professional relationships	Less personal and enduring relationships

A PROFILE OF PERSONAL SELLING

The professionalization of the sales force has come about as greater numbers of college-educated individuals (often with technical or business backgrounds) have moved into sales, as training programs have expanded (both sales and product or technical training) and training technology has improved, and as a response to increasing professionalization of the purchasing function.[1] For most business sellers, success involves several factors, including looking at marketing and selling as an integrated process. Several tips covering various aspects of the marketing process can help salespeople improve their sales skills. These would include:

- Understand how customers run their businesses
- Show how the product or service fits into the customer's business
- Segment the business market in order to tailor the product and marketing program to each group of customers
- Find ways to value-price to suit each segment
- Be certain the benefits being marketed remain clear, current, and important
- Understand how customers buy and fit the selling to their buying process
- Talk with everyone who has a role in the buying process
- Communicate to each member of the buying center the message that will address that person's chief concerns

- Make all actions and communications consistent with the predetermined level of quality, service, price, and performance
- Understand the competition's strengths and weaknesses[2]

How exactly do business salespeople spend their time during the course of a workday? In both the short term and the long term, systematic planning will yield a number of benefits.[3] The business salesperson's day is quite long, averaging over nine-and-a-half hours. In time spent on the job, less than 40 percent is taken up by actual face-to-face selling, while approximately one-third is used in traveling and waiting for interviews. These statistics, when combined with the approximate $235 to $300 cost per business sales call, paint a picture of a busy executive who must make every minute count when in a face-to-face selling situation with a business buyer. To gain a real understanding of the role of business salespeople, one must understand both the scope and the nature of their daily activities. The contemporary business salesperson faces more intense competition and a more well-informed and sophisticated prospect than ever before. The salesperson performs many types of activities, including selling, maintenance of distributor relationships, planning, decision making, and managing communications. Several of these activities will be examined briefly.

Selling

Selling includes both servicing established accounts and prospecting for new accounts. The business salesperson describes the product and offers reasons as to why it should be bought. Additionally, the salesperson is frequently called upon to provide consulting services. For example, salespeople are frequently asked to demonstrate how their products mesh with the product design and operational aspects of the customer's firm, since the products being sold will either become part of the customer's products or be used in producing them.

Cooperative Relationships with Channel Members

Business salespeople must also maintain cooperative relationships among various members of the distribution channels with whom they are involved, or face the consequences of channel conflict, which will often lead to problems involving delivery service, damaged or deteriorating goods, and misunderstandings about the specific role of each of the channel members. Salespeople sometimes find themselves helping customers, who have become personal friends over several years of professional association, with various managerial problems, ranging from inventory control to the recruitment, motivation, and retention of sales personnel. More so than ever before, a salesperson who basically calls on wholesalers is asked to assist customers in their selection of appropriate resellers.

Planning

In light of the intense competition involved in most types of business selling, salespeople are now spending a major portion of their time "planning" their activities. Effective planning on the part of salespeople involves the scheduling and routing of sales calls, determining the frequency of contact with established accounts, and assigning the proper amount of time to prospecting for new accounts. Also included are the evaluation of tapped and untapped sales potential within the total sales territory; providing assistance to the sales manager in budgeting and in sales forecasting for a particular sales territory over a specific period of time; and taking on the role of master strategist in the decision-making process of establishing goals, objectives, strategies, and techniques by which a certain territory can be fully and profitably reached.

Decision Making

Highly relevant to each of the sales activities discussed above is a fourth one, decision making. Salespeople must choose how to allocate their time in the most productive and efficient manner. Choices must be made in light of various constraints and opportunities; frequently, the more structured decisions are aided by the utilization of formal rules or models. For example, a company does not enjoy the same rate of net profit on every sale. In most firms, a large proportion of the orders, customers, territories, or products account for only a small share of the profit. This relationship between selling units and profits has been referred to as the 80/20 axiom (mentioned in Chapter 9), in that 80 percent of a firm's profits are accounted for by 20 percent of its selling units. When this axiom is applicable, salespeople will tend to devote the lion's share of their time to that most profitable 20 percent of the selling units.

A final aspect of decision making concerns the unstructured or unexpected demands placed upon business salespeople. Problems in production or shipping, changing customer needs, competitive movements, labor disputes, conflicting demands from multiple customers, and a whole host of other economic, political, or climatic factors require that the salesperson be able to make quick decisions with information that is both limited and imperfect.

The Management of Communication

Another type of activity performed by business salespeople is the management of communication. Research has indicated that salespeople typically spend more than 70 percent of their working hours in communication.[4] The salesperson plays an important communication role in the link between the customer and the manufacturer or distributor. A typical business salesperson generally has contact with the entire buying center in the customer's organization. As is shown in Exhibit 10-1, this buying center is comprised of purchasing agents,

EXHIBIT 10-1 **Who Participates in the Business Buying Process?**

Users	Users are the members of the organization who will use the product or service. In many cases, the users initiate the buying proposal and help define the product specifications.
Influencers	Influencers are persons who affect the buying decision. They often help define specifications and also provide information for evaluating alternatives. Technical personnel are particularly important as influencers.
Buyers	Buyers are persons with formal authority for selecting the supplier and arranging the terms of purchase. Buyers may help shape product specifications, but they play their major role in selecting vendors and in negotiating. In more complex purchases, the buyers might include high-level officers participating in the negotiations.
Deciders	Deciders are persons who have formal or informal power to approve or select the final suppliers. In routine buying, the buyers are often the deciders, or at least the approvers.
Gatekeepers	Gatekeepers are persons who control the flow of information to others. For example, purchasing agents often have authority to prevent salespersons from seeing users or deciders. Other gatekeepers include technical personnel and even personal secretaries.

materials managers, or groups of customers responsible for company purchases. To reach many of these decision makers, the salesperson must successfully penetrate the walls erected by the various company "gatekeepers," such as receptionists, secretaries, telephone operators, and even the higher layers of the buying center such as "deciders" and "influencers." During both presale and postsale activities, the salesperson must frequently deal with accountants, clerks, distribution personnel, and production managers. Within their own respective organizations, salespeople must deal with their immediate supervisor, advertising staff, accountants, marketing researchers, shippers, and a variety of other support personnel. Most business salespeople are also expected to be expert communicators in recruiting and training new salespeople; in responding to constant requests for information from new, established, and potential customers; and in efficiently generating the required paperwork necessary to process orders, to document expense reports, to file progress reports, and to keep customers informed of new and innovative products and trends within their company and industry.

Salespeople in many corporations rely on electronic mail systems as an integral part of the internal communication process. In small firms, the best strategy may be to hold regular meetings where proposed issues are discussed in an open forum.[5] The business salesperson, in summary, is required to impart a positive image of the company and its products and to convince others in an assertive manner to buy from the company. The typical salesperson, then, must be highly skilled in interpersonal communication.

THE COST OF PERSONAL SELLING

The cost of personal selling has risen 160 percent over the past decade, according to the Laboratory of Advertising Performance (LAP), a division of McGraw-Hill Research. Note that this is a conservative estimate because it does not include costs such as sales training and the hidden paycheck (for example, insurance and retirement benefits). Respondents in this LAP study included 836 vice presidents of sales and sales managers of business-to-business companies.[6] As we proceed through the 1990s, costs continue to rise. An advertisement in *Reader's Digest* costs less than a penny per reader, but the cost of an average business sales call is estimated to be between $235 and $300.[7] Table 10-2 provides the costs of sales forces as a percentage of total sales in more than twenty selected industries.

TABLE 10-2 **Sales Force Costs Across Twenty Selected Industries**

Industry Group	Sales Force Cost as a Percentage of Total Sales
Agriculture	4.7%
Amusement/recreation services	2.5
Apparel/other textile products	3.0
Business services	4.2
Chemicals	4.0
Communications	3.8
Construction	5.0
Electronic components	4.3
Electronics	4.2
Fabricated metal	3.8
Food products	1.7
Instruments	5.4
Insurance	4.0
Machinery	3.8
Manufacturing	3.0
Office equipment	2.8
Paper/allied products	4.8
Primary metal products	3.8
Printing/publishing	3.2
Rubber/plastics	3.0
Wholesale (consumer)	2.2
Wholesale (industrial)	3.2
Average	3.7%

Source: Dartnell Corporation, 26th Survey of Sales Force Compensation, 1990. As reported in "Compensation and Expenses," *Sales & Marketing Management* (June 17, 1991), p. 76. Reprinted with permission of *Sales & Marketing Management*.

Another useful way to comprehend the enormous cost of the personal selling function is to consider that it takes approximately $20,000 to train a salesperson effectively, and that there is an average annual turnover of three hundred thousand salespersons. A simple calculation will show that this training and the subsequent loss of salespeople cost the national business sector approximately $6 billion per year.[8]

The Cost to Close a Business Sale

Another approach one might take in looking at sales costs is to examine the cost to close a business sale. It costs an average of $1,114 to close a sale.[9] The $235 to $300 cost of a business sales call is estimated without consideration as to whether a sale was made or not. Since only about 6 percent of business sales are made via one sales call, 9 percent by two calls, and 33.5 percent by three calls, the cost to close a business sale is significantly higher than the figure quoted above. The McGraw-Hill Research Department researched 787 business marketing companies and ascertained that an average of 4.3 calls are needed to close a business sale. The cost to close a business sale has recently been found to be as much as $2,000 in some cases.[10] This study also found that total costs to close a sale varied by industry. For example, an average of 3.8 calls were necessary to close a sale in the lumber industry, and an average of 5.6 calls were typical in business services.[11] Because the cost of personal selling can vary so significantly depending on such factors as the type of product and industry, the size of the firm, and the degree of personal contact with prospects necessary to close a sale, business-to-business companies must constantly monitor and assess the best methods by which to distribute and sell their products and services.

CONCEPT QUESTIONS

1. How do business buyers typically view business salespeople?
2. How does one gain a real understanding of the role of a business salesperson?
3. Why is the cost to close a business sale higher than the average cost of a business sales call?

UNDERSTANDING BUYER BEHAVIOR

Business buyers use a decision-making process very similar to that used by final consumers. Both are interested in products and services that provide the type of benefits for which the buyer is searching. Any buyer is interested in what the product will do for the buyer. *Benefit selling* appeals to the customer's personal motives by answering the question, "What's in it for me?" Benefit selling is facilitated by the use of *benefit segmentation*, which divides the total business target market into individual groups according to the particular utilities or benefits expected from a specific product or service. For example, in the case of an industrial janitorial service, one group of companies may be looking for dependability and reliability, while another may be looking for the use of specific cleaning procedures. The business marketer who is able to use benefit selling to reach prospective customers is demonstrating a willingness to understand and meet the buying needs and objectives of those prospects.

Understanding Buyer Needs

Buying center members seek to buy for many reasons. Some of the more common reasons usually evolve from some aspect of the cost and quality of the product. Specific primary buying needs and motives include increasing profits, increasing sales, producing a quality product, improving the operation's efficiency to create cost reductions, helpfulness of the salesperson's service, payment, trade-in allowances, delivery, and buying a product at the lowest price. If salespeople hope to be successful, they must determine each prospect's important buying needs. They can then develop a sales presentation that emphasizes their respective product's features, advantages, and benefits and explains how their product can fulfill the prospect's needs.

A salesperson's initial task upon meeting the prospect (for the first time) is to differentiate between important buying needs and those of lesser or no importance. Figure 10-1 illustrates the concept that buyers have both important needs and other types of needs that are not primary reasons for buying a product. A business salesperson must determine the prospect's important needs and concentrate on emphasizing product benefits that will satisfy those needs. Benefits that would satisfy a prospect's unimportant needs should be deemphasized in the sales presentation. If, for example, buying center members say that price is important, but the salesperson determines that they can afford the product and are also interested in quality, then the salesperson must emphasize the quality of the product being sold.

People buy for reasons other than what the product will actually do or what it costs. Although customers usually buy the product to solve the rational need that the salesperson perceives to be important, they may also buy to satisfy an emotional need, which is not so easily recognized. It is important to understand this sales concept and to learn to determine the prospect's important buying needs. Some of the most common psychological buying needs would include fear, risk aversion, security, curiosity, a desire to succeed, and self-preservation.

FIGURE 10-1 **Seller Matches Buyers' Important Needs to Products' Benefits and Emphasizes This in Sales Presentation**

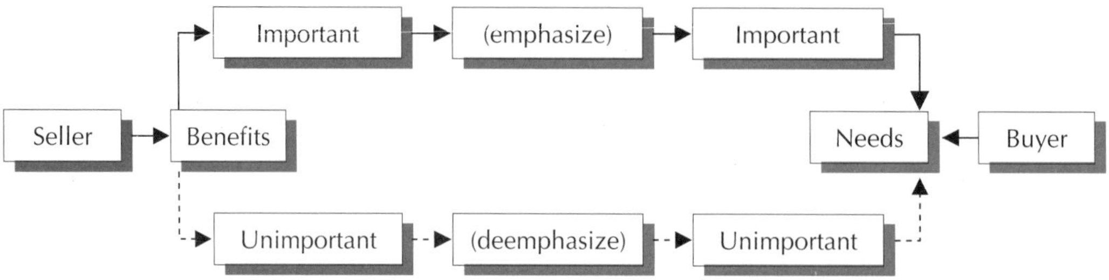

Methods Used to Uncover Important Buyer Needs

A business salesperson must determine which buying needs are most important to the customer. How can this be done? Several methods are frequently utilized to uncover important needs:

- *Ask questions.* Questions can often bring out needs that the prospect would not reveal, or does not know exist. The salesperson asks, "Is a faster, more feature-oriented copier important to you?" "Yes, it is," says the buyer. "If I could give you the quickest, most multifeatured copier currently on the market, would you be interested?" However, care must be exercised, as salespeople cannot play "twenty questions" with the prospect. There are only so many questions that can be asked before the prospect will begin to show signs of irritability.
- *Observe.* Look at the prospects and study their surroundings. Experienced salespeople can determine a great deal about people by observing such things as the way they dress, or where they live or work.
- *Listen.* Prospects may drop leading remarks like, "I would really like to have a more efficient payroll system than the one I am now using."
- *Talk to others.* Ask others about a prospect's needs. For example, ask an office manager's secretary about the manager's level of satisfaction with a personal computer.
- *Combination.* A skillful salesperson may talk to others, listen to a prospect, probe with questions, and make careful observations—all in an effort to uncover the prospect's needs.

Once a salesperson has ascertained a prospect's major buying need, he or she is ready to relate the customer's needs to his or her product's benefits. Business salespeople can effectively sell to the business buyer only after they have determined the prospect's buying needs and motivations and have identified the problems they are attempting to solve in purchasing a particular product or service. Basically, this is what selling is all about.

It is rarely an easy task for salespeople to learn a customer's needs and to demonstrate how their respective product or service directly benefits and fully speaks to such needs. Business buyers, and other members of the buying center, typically have a multitude of different needs; they may not clearly understand or see their unconscious needs or problems. The salesperson's challenge is to understand the behavioral style of each prospective buyer and convert customers' apparently unconscious needs into recognized and understood needs. Exhibit 10-2 offers several behavioral styles that prospective buyers typically exhibit when interacting with business salespeople.

Business buyers and sellers are engaged in a special and unique relationship. As the salesperson attempts to understand and to meet a prospect's needs, that same prospect is evaluating this particular supplier's capability and rating the salesperson according to the buyer's likes and dislikes. Exhibit 10-3 identifies the characteristics of both outstanding and least desirable salespersons, according to a select group of purchasing managers. Outstanding salespeople were thought to have such qualities as thoroughness and good follow-through, and the least desirable salespeople often used high-pressure selling tactics and talked too long about irrelevant matters. Only an understanding of the dynamic nature and interdependency of this buyer-seller relationship will enable the business salesperson to have a true understanding of buyer behavior.

EXHIBIT 10-2 Uncovering the Behavioral Styles of Buyers

What behavioral styles do buyers exhibit when interacting with salespeople? Buyers can be classified into the following categories:

- The *hard bargainer* obtains several price quotations or uses several sources of supply for the same item; salespeople may find it difficult to make a sale.
- The *sales job facilitator* is amenable to a salesperson's solicitations and even attempts to make the transaction go smoother.
- The *straight shooter* behaves with integrity and propriety; these buyers rarely use their buying power to obtain concessions.
- The *socializer* enjoys the personal interaction of the buyer-seller relationship.
- The *persuader* will attempt to market his or her own company to salespersons to stimulate a favorable impression of the buying firm.
- The *considerate buyer* displays compassion and concern for the salesperson; these buyers may be willing to accept substitute products.

A mutually beneficial exchange relationship results when the salesperson tailors selling strategy to a buyer's behavioral style.

Source: Alan J. Dubinsky and Thomas N. Ingram, "A Classification of Industrial Buyers: Implications for Sales Training." *Journal of Personal Selling and Sales Management* 1 (Fall-Winter 1981–82), pp. 46–51. Used with permission.

EXHIBIT 10-3 **Buyers Rate Salespersons: Likes and Dislikes**

A sample of three hundred purchasing managers was asked to identify the characteristics of both outstanding and least desirable salespersons:

The characteristics attributed to the outstanding salesperson were as follows:

- Thoroughness and follow-through
- Complete product knowledge
- Willingness to pursue the best interests of the buyer within the supplier firm
- Sound marketing knowledge and willingness to keep the buyer informed

Among the characteristics that can alienate buyers are as follows:

- Hard-selling, high-pressure tactics
- Talking too long about unrelated matters
- Exhibiting little interest in meeting the buyer's real needs.

Source: Reprinted by permission of the publisher from Larry C. Giunipero and Gary J. Zenz, "Impact of Purchasing Trends on Industrial Marketers," *Industrial Marketing Management* 11 (February 1982), pp. 17–23. Copyright 1982 by Elsevier Science Inc.

THE SELLING SPECTRUM

Approaches to the Business Sales Presentation

After the earlier steps in the sales process of prospecting and qualifying have been completed, several general approaches to the business sales presentation must be considered. Three major approaches are found in (1) the formularized model (AIDA), (2) the buying-decisions model, and (3) the problem-solving model. Figure 10-2 reveals the process used in the three models. Each furnishes an insight into the buying-selling process, but from a different point of view.[12]

The Formularized (AIDA) model. (AIDA is an acronym for Attention, Interest, Desire, and Action.) In the *formularized (AIDA) model*, the salesperson takes the prospect through the first three stages in order to evoke action (purchase) from the buyer. An inherent danger in this type of sales presentation is that the mental states of the salesperson and the prospect may not be at the same stage of the selling formula. For example, the salesperson might assume that the prospect is at the "interest" stage, when, in fact, the prospect may already be at the "desire" stage. In this type of situation, the salesperson may well lose the sale due to the prospect's impatience or inability to engage in spontaneous purchase action. However, the formularized model seems to be well suited for use by a relatively new salesperson who is too inexperienced to recognize the actual buying motives of individual prospects.

The buying-decisions model. The *buying-decisions model* assumes that the prospect will make a series of smaller, individual decisions before making the

FIGURE 10-2 **Three Approaches to the Buying-Selling Process**

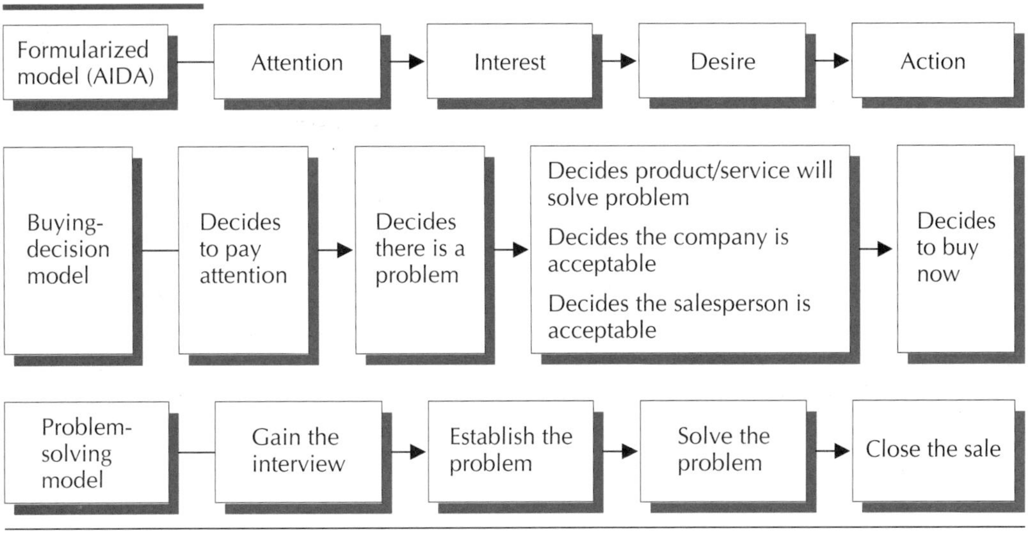

final decision either to accept or to reject the product. Therefore, the salesperson will tailor the presentation to achieve a number of decisions aimed at an ultimate decision to purchase the product or service in question. For instance, a photocopier salesperson would lead an office manager toward the final decision of investing in a new copying machine by having the manager decide such issues as how large a copier is needed, what features the copier must have, how much usage the copier is likely to receive, how clear the reproductions must be, and how much the office manager is prepared or willing to spend on a photocopier. Once the prospect has made these decisions, it is much easier for the salesperson to promote the features and benefits of the product in a way that will lead the potential buyer to a positive purchasing decision. Once again, a possible weakness in this model is that the salesperson and the prospect may be at different stages of decision making at any given point in time. The salesperson must carefully lead the prospect through each of the prepurchase decision stages in order to keep the model going in a positive direction. Only the successful closing of the sale can prevent the prospect from regressing to an earlier prepurchase decision stage.

The problem-solving model. The *problem-solving model* centers on the specific needs, motives, and objectives of the prospect. There must be an air of mutual trust and respect between the salesperson and the prospective customer; and, as such, the problem-solving model is quite similar to the need-satisfaction theory of personal selling. The salesperson must skillfully integrate product knowledge into the solution of the problem so as to exert *expert power* (the degree of perceived knowledge, information, and skill possessed by the power holder) over the prospect. Expert power exists when the power vested in a person by qualification or experience is acknowledged. It is a comparative form of power that must be granted by those over whom it will be exercised.[13] Expert power of the salesperson has been found to be a stronger determinant of perceived trust by the customer than has *referent power* (the degree of perceived attraction between the salesperson and the customer).[14] A prospect who can accord a salesperson expert power is much more likely to allow the closing of a sale because he or she generally feels more comfortable in accepting the judgment of the salesperson that the product or service will solve the prospect's purchasing need or problem. In this case, "what you know" seems to be, for once, more important than "whom you know." The problem-solving model seems to be a particularly useful sales model when "creative selling" (helping the customer buy) is needed.

Types of Sales Positions and Selling Styles in the Business Market

Reaching business markets effectively requires a great variety of types of salespeople and selling styles. The following represent the major types of salespeople typically employed to serve business markets: account representatives, detail salespeople, sales engineers, nontechnical business products sales representatives, and service salespeople. (Exhibit 10-4 offers a brief description of the activities of each of these types of salespeople.) Another way to look at the business selling function is to classify salespeople by the tasks that they per-

EXHIBIT 10-4 **Classification of Business Sales Personnel**

Account representatives	Salespeople who call on customers who are already established.
Detail salespeople	Salespeople who provide details relative to promotional activities. Such a salesperson might visit the offices of medical doctors and attempt to inform them of the specific possibilities of a new drug. These salespeople seldom get credit for a sale; instead, the credit usually goes to an intermediary.
Sales engineers	A title originally bestowed to increase esteem of those who held it is that of *sales engineer.* This title has come to signify that the salesperson has technical know-how relative to the construction and/or application of the product. Salespeople in such areas as heavy machinery, electronic parts and equipment, and raw materials often bear this title.
Nontechnical business products sales representatives	Individuals who sell nontechnical, tangible products, such as floor wax.
Service salespeople	Service salespeople are in the business of selling services; that is, intangibles. They may sell such things as management consulting and advertising. There is also the *missionary salesperson* classification, which is defined in this text.

form. Sales tasks are activities carried out by salespeople and can be classified into two broad categories: creative selling and service selling. *Creative selling* deals with arousing demand and influencing patronage; *service selling* assists the customer in bringing the sale to completion.[15] Service salespeople need to master the price/value relationship, if for no other reason than selling and reinforcing the sale are often essential parts of providing the services in question.[16]

A useful classification, as proposed in the classic article by H. Robert Dodge, might include four types of sales tasks: development, missionary, maintenance, and support.[17] Figure 10-3 arranges these tasks in a continuum, with examples of each type of sales task. *Sales development* refers to the creation of customers through methods such as motivating a customer to change suppliers, whereas *missionary sales* provide necessary personal selling assistance. *Maintenance selling* involves the continuation of present sales volume from existing customers, and *support sales* provide continuing service to the buyer and occasionally involve

FIGURE 10-3 **Continuum of Business Sales Tasks**

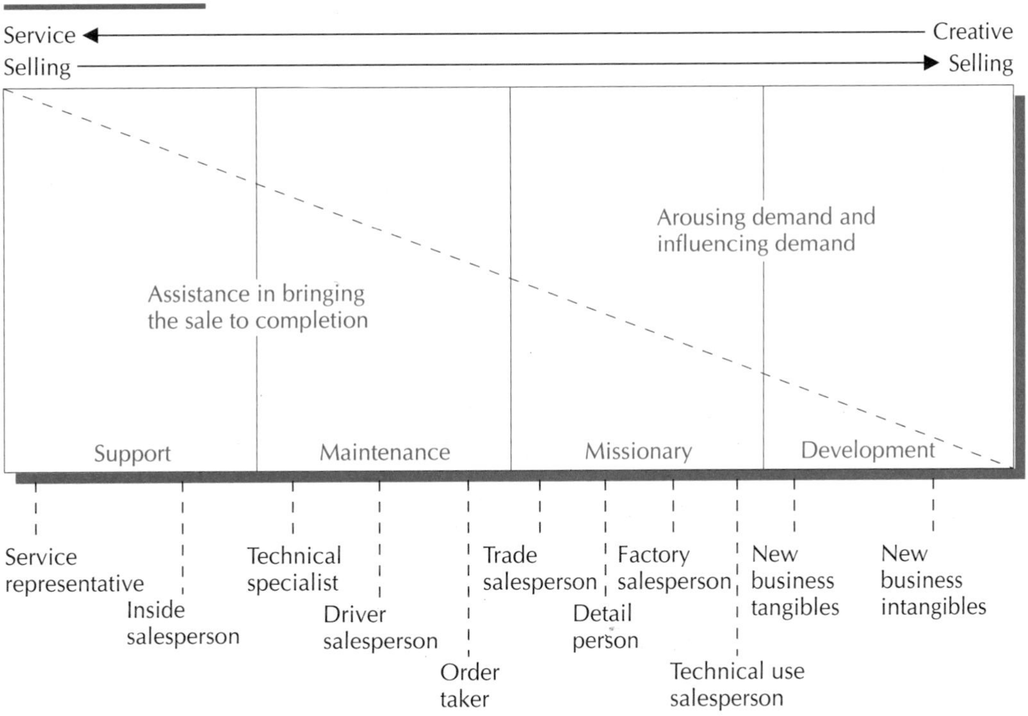

Source: H. Robert Dodge, "The Role of the Industrial Salesman," *Mid-South Quarterly Review,* January 1972, p. 13. Used with permission.

selling directly to the buyer by suggesting a replacement item rather than the repair of an older product. All these tasks are important, and each makes a significant contribution to the total marketing effort.[18]

Figure 10-4 provides a model of career paths in business selling, and Exhibit 10-5 briefly describes the activities of various levels of business sales job titles. The two career paths shown in Figure 10-4 seem quite similar, but in reality are quite different. The sales career path leads to a position that may or may not involve aspects of the sales manager's job, such as planning, direction, organization, and control over the activities of others. This is an important distinction, as the best salesperson does not always make the best sales manager. Different skills must be acquired before successful salespeople can make the necessary adjustments to being successful sales managers. This topic will be explored in detail in Chapter 11.

Among the major contemporary selling styles utilized in reaching business markets are consultative selling, negotiation, systems selling, telemarketing, and team selling. (See Exhibit 10-6 for a brief definition of each of these styles of business selling.) Due to their increasing popularity and usage by business marketers, more complete discussions of systems selling and telemarketing follow.

FIGURE 10-4 **Career Paths in Business Selling**

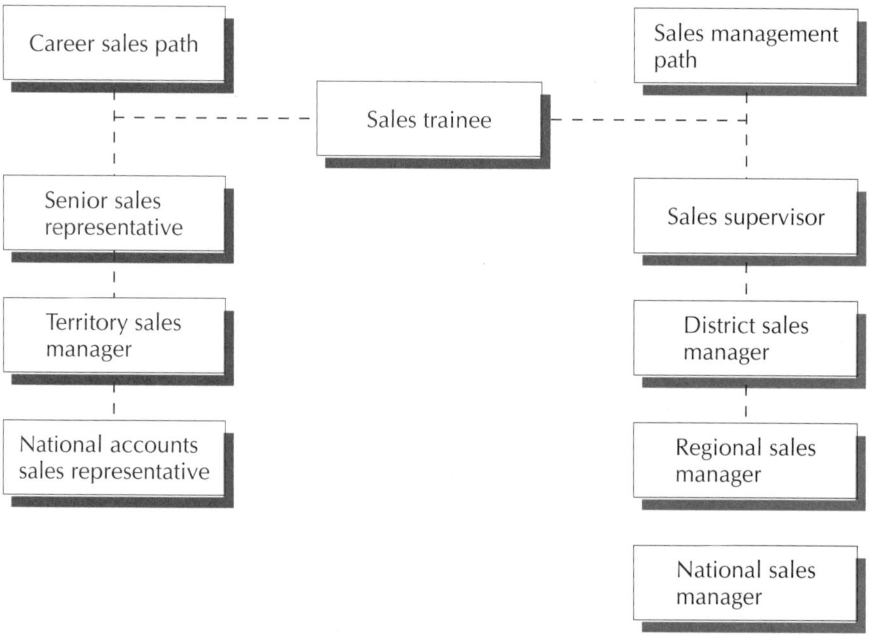

EXHIBIT 10-5 **Typical Business Sales Titles**

Top-Level Marketing Management

Marketing vice president. Typically, the top marketing executive in the company or division.

Sales vice president. Sometimes another title for marketing vice president, but sometimes the top sales executive who will report to either the president or the marketing vice president.

Top-Level Line Sales Management

National sales manager. The top sales executive responsible for all sales-force-related activities.

General sales manager. Another title for national sales manager.

Middle-Level Sales Management

National account sales manager. Usually responsible for a separate, high-quality sales force that calls on national accounts. Often the only person in the national account sales force and responsible for actual selling; but the accounts are so large that the position needs a relatively high-level manager.

Regional, divisional, or *zone sales manager.* These are titles for high-level field sales managers to whom other field sales managers report. Occasionally, the titles are used for first-level sales management jobs in which salespeople are managed.

Market sales manager. A sales manager responsible for salespeople calling on a specific group of accounts. Often this position has marketing responsibility in addition to sales management and perhaps sales responsibility. A company that specializes its sales force by market will have one market sales manager to head each separate sales force.

Product sales manager. The same as market sales manager except that the job is organized around a product line instead of a customer category. Product sales managers are usually more involved with product-oriented decisions than are market managers.

Lower-Level Sales Management

District or field sales manager. The first-line sales manager to whom the salespeople report.

Upper-Level Sales Positions

Account executive, key account salesperson, national account salesperson, and *major account salesperson.* These people are responsible for selling to major accounts.

Typical Sales Positions

Salesperson, field salesperson, territory manager, account representative, and *sales representative.* All are typical titles for the salesperson responsible for selling and servicing a variety of accounts.

Staff Sales Management

These positions are usually functionally oriented and include titles, such as *manager of sales training, sales analyst,* etc. The typical staff responsibilities include training, recruiting, and sales analysis. More general staff positions include the title *assistant to the national sales manager.* Assistant national sales managers may be either line or staff managers. Staff positions may occur at any level in the organization. Some companies with divisional sales forces, for example, have a job of *corporate vice president of sales* who has no line sales management responsibility. Other companies have *regional* or *area sales vice presidents* responsible for aiding salespeople from various divisions with major account sales. This is found, for example, in some weapons marketers where various product-oriented divisions call upon the same buying organization.

EXHIBIT 10-6 Common Business Selling Styles

- *Consultative selling* occurs when the salesperson assumes the role of a consultant, helping to improve the profitability of the client. The consultative salesperson, by becoming an expert on the client's business operations, providing analytical expertise, and solving problems, attempts to offer a level of value beyond competitors.
- *Negotiation* describes a selling style designed to maximize the benefits of a transaction for both buyer and seller. The goal is to form a saleperson-customer partnership with common objectives, mutually beneficial strategies, and a common defense against others outside the partnership.
- *Systems selling* has evolved to meet the rising sophistication and increased materials-management concerns of organizational buyers. The salesperson for a business-forms supplier might begin by defining a prospect's record and information needs, then prescribe a package of machines and forms, offer a recommended layout of facilities, establish a training program for employees, and design operating procedures and maintenance arrangements.
- *Team selling* occurs when the business-to-business seller assembles a team of personnel with functional expertise that matches the specialized knowledge of key buying influences within the customer firm. The mode of operation adopted by the selling team varies by selling situation. Occasionally, the entire sales team will take part in the presentation to the buying center, while in other cases, team members are contacted at various points in the selling process when the salesperson requires technical expertise.

SOME CONTEMPORARY TRENDS IN BUSINESS SELLING

The Importance of Systems Selling

Business salespeople have increasingly recognized that business buyers prefer to buy a whole solution to their purchasing problem and not make all the separate decisions involved. Consequently, many firms have adopted the practice of *systems selling* as a marketing tool. Systems selling has two components. First, the supplier sells a group of "interlocking products." For example, the supplier sells not only glue, but applicators and dryers as well. Second, the supplier sells a system of production, inventory control, distribution, and other services to meet the buyer's need for a smooth-running operation. Systems selling is a key business marketing strategy for winning and holding accounts.[19] Precision Industries of Omaha, Nebraska, was convinced that systems selling was the wave of the future and, as such, developed a package of products and services that would attract high-end customers. A major customer recognized that the company spent too much money on routine items and asked Precision to help it reduce its paperwork and in-house inventory costs, as well as help control shop-floor maintenance costs through improved product training.[20]

Systems selling is a key business marketing strategy in bidding to build large-scale business projects, such as dams, steel factories, irrigation systems, sanitation systems, pipelines, utilities, and even new towns. Companies such as Bechtel, Fluor, and other project engineering firms must compete on price, quality, reliability, and other attributes to win awards. The award often goes to the firm that best meets the customer's real needs. Consider the following:[21]

> The Indonesian government requested bids to build a cement factory near Jakarta. An American firm made a proposal which included choosing the site, designing the cement factory, hiring the construction crews, assembling the materials and equipment, and turning over the finished factory to the Indonesian government. A Japanese firm, in outlining its proposal, included all of these services plus hiring and training the workers to run the factory, exporting the cement through their trading companies, and using the cement to build some new office buildings in Jakarta. Although the Japanese proposal involved more money, its appeal was greater, and they won the contract. Clearly, the Japanese viewed the problem not as one of just building the cement factory (the narrow view of systems selling), but of running it in a way which would contribute to the country's economy. They saw themselves not as an engineering project firm, but as an economic development agency. They took the broadest view of the customer's needs. This is true systems selling.

It is likely that systems selling will continue to be popular in business markets as buyers increasingly appreciate the opportunity to find quick, convenient, and total solutions to their buying problems.

The Importance of Telemarketing

Telephone sales, or *telemarketing*, now plays integral cost-cutting and revenue-generating roles in many business-to-business corporations. By the late 1990s, it will be a widely used tool by most organizations in virtually every industry. Telemarketing's major impact today is in business applications, not only in soliciting and retaining business customers, but in managing and servicing accounts, taking orders, and conducting surveys among other marketing functions. Companies using the technique include IBM, Merrill Lynch, General Electric, and Allstate. (See Exhibit 10-7 for more descriptive examples of business firms currently using telemarketing as part of their promotional mix.) The rapid expansion of business telemarketing is most attributable to the ever increasing cost of making a sales call in person. Additionally, the typical sales representative will make an average of four to five sales calls per day, while a telecommunicator will make an average ten to fifteen phone contacts in one hour. Although the final sale will not always be closed on the telephone, telemarketing will screen prospects on whom the company can focus its sales and marketing efforts. Finally, in addition to cutting costs, the company's telephone-sales strategy gives it direct input from customers.[22]

At Fairfield, Connecticut–based General Electric Company, telemarketing permeates so many business operations that "determining senior management's role in setting telemarketing strategy is a question we are dealing with right now," according to Richard J. Huether, GE's manager of telemarketing development.[23] At GE, telemarketing is teamed up with direct mail, fliers, and other promotional approaches. Says Huether, "I hesitate to say that what we are doing is replacing salespeople. We, instead, are better utilizing the strengths of our sales organization. Many of our people are engineers, and taking orders isn't the best use of their

EXHIBIT 10-7 **Telemarketing—The Wave of the Future in Outside Selling?**

The job of outside selling—the kind where the salesperson goes to the customer, in contrast to inside (or across the counter) selling—is changing dramatically these days. Instead of the traditional in-person sales call, a growing number of sales representatives are using the telephone and/or the computer to talk with customers. In effect, outside selling—especially outside business selling—is going electronic.

The prime factor accounting for this change is the dramatic increase in the costs of keeping salespeople on the road. Some companies estimate that their travel expenses—transportation, hotel, and meals—are higher than their sales representative's compensation (salary, commission, and bonus).

Telephone selling, of course, has been used by many companies for decades. What is new today, however, is the innovative use of communication systems involving the telephone, television, and sometimes the computer, to aid a company's selling effort and other marketing activities. The term *telemarketing* has been coined to describe these marketing communication systems.

Raleigh Bicycles used telemarketing to reduce the amount of personal selling needed for contacting its dealers. In the first year, sales force travel costs were reduced by 50 percent, and sales in a single quarter were up by 34 percent. Avis uses computer-assisted telemarketing programs in its fleet-leasing operations to locate and qualify prospects, and to generate good leads for its salespeople. The program cuts sales force costs, substantially improves the sales force's available selling time, and reduces the time required to close a sale by one month. The B. F. Goodrich Chemical Group provides yet another example of the use of telemarketing to support field sales. Goodrich uses a "telemarketing center" for order-taking, customer service, and information dissemination purposes. When customers contact the company, a center specialist calls up the customer's account file on a computer screen, records the order, checks the inventory supply, and talks with production and shipping to schedule shipment when necessary. Field sales personnel are then provided current inventory data and estimated arrival times of customer orders. Field sales representatives can then schedule follow-up visits to high-volume order accounts, thus increasing both the number and the quality of personal and professional contacts between B. F. Goodrich and its best customers.

Some companies—Louisiana Oil and Tire Company, for example—have increased sales and reduced costs by taking their field salespeople away from their traveling jobs and bringing them into the

continued on next page

time."[24] Business-to-business firms spent $28 billion on telemarketing in 1986, so telemarketing will likely continue to be a big sales buzzword throughout the 1990s.[25]

The Emergence of the Saleswoman

Business sales was once considered to be exclusively a man's world. In 1972, women constituted only 4.7 percent of the nonretail sales force; by 1980 that proportion had increased to 10.6, and by 1989 it had nearly doubled the 1980 figure to reach 20.4 percent.[26] Many of the reasons why women were excluded from business selling for so many years were based on sexual stereotypes that included "tradition," women's "inability" to travel and to be away from home overnight, their presumed lack of technical knowledge, sexual exploitation, the priorities of marriage (either getting or staying married), and children. These last two factors were presumed to cause excessive absenteeism and turnover. Yet, during the last decade, business selling seems to have finally

EXHIBIT 10-7 **(continued)**

office. Industrial Fabricators of Jackson, Tennessee, has done the same. This company replaced its field sales force of 39 individuals with an in-house telemarketing department of 14 persons. With this change, sales of industrial-strength wiping cloths went up 25 percent, while selling costs decreased by 30 percent. In the office these representatives have been trained to sell by telephone. In effect, personal selling and order taking are being moved from the field to a well-trained inside sales force. The field selling in these firms is shifting to sales promotion work, such as instructing customers or providing technical advice and service.

In some companies, telemarketing is making the order-taking sales representative virtually obsolete. For instance, American Hospital Supply and some of its customers have a sophisticated mainframe computer capacity so that the buyer's computer can talk to American Hospital's computer. The buyer's computer can determine product availability and shipping dates; and, finally, can even place an order. No salespeople are involved, and there is a lot less paperwork. Ford, Chrysler, General Motors, and American Motors are jointly developing a system whereby a manufacturer and its large suppliers will communicate electronically. This system will eliminate many personal sales calls and a mountain of paperwork.

In Europe, firms in the automobile, chemical, steel, and shipbuilding industries are developing electronic communication systems involving manufacturers, suppliers, and even customers agents and shipping agents.

The examples cited above will save millions, and perhaps even billions, of dollars of personal selling expenses, and other communications expenses. Furthermore, these telemarketing processes are expected to increase the operating efficiency and time responsiveness of the participating industries.

Source: "Rebirth of a Salesman: Willy Loman Goes Electronic," *Basiness Week,* February 27, 1984, pp. 103–104; "Detroit Tries to Level a Mountain of Paperwork," *Business Week*, August 26, 1985, p. 94; John I. Coppett and Roy Vorhees. Reprinted by permission of the publisher from "Telemarketing: Supplement to Field Sales," *Industrial Marketing Management,* August 1985, pp. 213–16, copyright 1985 by Elsevier Science Inc.; Roy Dale Vorhees and John I. Coppett, Reprinted by permission of the publisher from "Telemarketing in Distribution Channels," *Industrial Marketing Management* 12 (1983), p. 106, copyright 1983 by Elsevier Science Inc.; "Industrial Newsletter," *Sales & Marketing Management* 131 (November 14, 1983), p. 32. Reprinted with permission of *Sales & Marketing Management.* Ed Zotti, "There's Madness in Their Methods," *Advertising Age,* November 28, 1983, pp. M54–M57; and Lawrence Strauss, *Electronic Marketing* (White Plains, N.Y.: Knowledge Industry Publications, 1983). Used with permission.

tapped this vital source of new sales power—women. Saleswomen are perceived by professional purchasing people as capable of meeting the same requirements and expectations as male salespeople.[27] Business sales may still be dominated by men, but a growing number of women are prepared to meet the challenge posed by this type of selling.[28]

Although much of the initial pressure to hire women for business sales positions came from the Equal Employment Opportunity Act and affirmative action guidelines, the success of women in these positions has led many companies toward the employment of increasing numbers of business saleswomen. Brown and Bigelow, a manufacturer of advertising specialty items, had no saleswomen until the mid-1980s. Today, 25 percent of its salespeople are women. At Xerox, women make up over 40 percent of the sales force.

More and more women are moving into business sales and assuming positions that were formerly strictly the domain of males. Contemporary business saleswomen are selling everything from high-tech computer systems and aluminum siding to steel, lumber, and machine parts. Priscilla Crafford, a senior sales representative with Planco Plastics in Providence, Rhode Island, recently sold 184 percent of her quota, placing her among the top five salespeople in the company and earning her an all-expenses-paid trip to Hawaii.

A 1978 study compared the responses of 169 business salesmen and 20 business saleswomen in similar jobs in regard to job satisfaction, job-related self-confidence, perceptions of the management control system, and career goals.[29] The findings in this study clearly revealed that business saleswomen do differ from their male counterparts in how they view their jobs. In contrast to the males in the study sample, the women expressed greater importance for independence in their work and for meeting different people; relatively low satisfaction in the areas of coworkers and supervision; lower self-confidence on many of the job-related measures used in the study, such as promotion possibilities and looking forward to a secure future; and a less-favorable view of their firm's management control system. The findings of this study suggested that business saleswomen are different from their male counterparts in similar jobs, and that sales managers should take those differences into consideration in their leadership style, management control systems, and training programs.

Another study in 1984 examined how purchasing managers rated business salesmen and saleswomen in a variety of job-related criteria.[30] Responses from the study sample indicated that men were rated higher on (1) knowledge of the companies being sold to, (2) product knowledge, (3) understanding of the buyer's problems, (4) provision of technical assistance, and (5) presentation of new ideas to buyers. Comparatively, women were rated higher on (1) being vigorous and having a lot of drive, (2) knowing how to listen, (3) preparing for sales presentations, (4) following through on deliveries, (5) personalizing the sales presentation, (6) willingness to expedite rush orders, and (7) not bypassing the purchasing people. A careful analysis of this study seems to indicate not only that business saleswomen are rated somewhat higher than their male counterparts in providing postsale services, attentiveness to detail, enthusiasm for their jobs, and a socially comfortable selling environment; but also that women are competent and effective in business field selling, and that most purchasing professionals do not harbor negative feelings in regard to their employment.

Finally, in a recent study, Kennedy and Lawton interviewed both men and women at a Fortune 100 company shortly after they were hired and again one year later. It was found that the level of job involvement was higher for women than for men, women reported less job satisfaction, fewer opportunities for fraternization, fewer role models, and lower perceived opportunities for influence in their environments than did men. It would appear from this study (and the others cited) that marketing organizations must resolve these problems. Marketing and sales management is challenged to address these issues as we move through the 1990s.[31]

The Usage of Terminals and Laptop Computers

Portable computer terminals—which include a keyboard, a flat display screen, a hard-copy printer, and an acoustical coupler—can be fitted into a regular-sized briefcase. These terminals are now widely utilized in business selling because they enable sales representatives to solve customer problems during the sales presentation; to communicate with their home or branch offices; to process invoices; and to check on delivery times, past sales records, current prices, and call schedules.[32]

The use of portable computers to solve customer problems is demonstrated in the following example. Valmont Industries, a manufacturer of irrigation systems, equips its dealer salespeople with portable computers for use when they call on farmers. Before the terminals were used, salespeople spent four or five hours with a hand calculator and a long formula to get a solution to the customer's irrigation problems. Now, the salesperson plugs the portable computer into a wall socket in the farmer's home, attaches a telephone to the terminal's acoustical coupler, and telephones Valmont's home office. The salesperson types in the information on the farmer's problem, and in about ten minutes, the central computer sends back a printed analysis of what equipment is needed and how much it will cost the farmer. Valmont's district offices can also be contacted in this same manner. Salespeople can also use the portable terminals to check their electronic mailboxes on a daily basis. Valmont leases the terminals on a monthly basis, resulting in savings of time, rather than of money.[33]

Permanent terminals are also widely used now in business selling. These terminals are hard-wired to central computers, usually at the home or district office. Salespeople can use them at various sales offices to plan sequences of sales calls and to identify customer needs and wants. The most highly desirable usage of permanent terminals would be for customers to install their own on-site terminals and connect them to the salesperson's mainframe computer system. In this way, the customer could order directly, and much paperwork and time would be saved for both buyer and seller.

General Electric's Sentry System has been designed to sell electrical supplies and equipment to business contractors and to commercial accounts. Using this system, General Electric agrees to stock specific items at prenegotiated prices. If customers wish to place an order, they first log in on a terminal. The computer then asks a series of questions, and the buyer itemizes the order. Next, the computer informs the buyer of the total value of the order and processes it for delivery on the next working day. The Sentry System has been designed for large-order and/or frequent-order customers. Customers must rent the terminals; consequently, the system is not very feasible for small accounts. When General Electric's salespeople call on Sentry System accounts, they are able to spend their time on introducing new products and solving customers' problems, rather than on writing up orders.[34]

Laptop computers generally weigh between six and eighteen pounds; and because they are now as fully functional as desktop machines and offer portability, they appear to be taking market share away from desktop computers. Zenith Data Systems' Z-183 combines a hard-disk drive with long battery life and a readable screen, while Grid's Gridlite Model 1032 uses a high-impact plastic case, weighs only nine pounds, and uses a simple 720K floppy-disk drive. In Canada, Bernie E. Beleskey has rigged his own office on wheels in a 1984 GMC van, complete with telephone, fax, and laptop computer. He racks up thirty-seven hundred miles per month as marketing director for Investment Center Financial Corporation, a seller of financial services. Beleskey likes his setup so much that he hopes to sell the same package to some of the 180 agents he supervises.[35] As we move through the 1990s, additional major advances in technology can be expected.

The Rapid Growth of Audio-Visual Aids

Over the last fifteen years, one of the fastest growing trends in the business selling field has been the stepped-up use of such audio-visual aids as filmstrips, movies, and videotape cassettes. Since people receive over 80 percent of their knowledge from their sense of sight, salespeople who use visual reinforcement as they talk are in a better position to communicate product benefits to prospects.[36] These devices have also assisted the business salesperson in making more selling points in less time. While filmstrips and movies have been long utilized in sales training programs, many more companies are now sending them to the field with the salesperson. Used primarily in the past for heavy equipment selling, audio-visuals have gained considerable appeal during the last few years because of their increased portability and simple design.

CONCEPT QUESTIONS

1. How can business salespeople uncover buyers' most important needs?
2. What is systems selling?

THE PERSONAL SELLING PROCESS: A BUSINESS SALESPERSON'S PERSPECTIVE

In order to get a real sense of the personal selling process in business markets, one must simplify the description and focus on the important elements. From the perspective of the business salesperson, a sequence listing of the most fundamental steps in personal selling can be generated. Of course, each firm in each different business selling situation would have its own set of unique steps. For instance, a Xerox photocopier salesperson roughly follows five steps: approach, survey, demonstration, proposal, and close.[37]

Preliminary Activities

The *preliminary activities* arm the business salesperson with the tools necessary to close a sale effectively, as well as the ability to create the type of sales situation most favorable to meeting actual customer needs and wants. The first task is to review customer accounts to ascertain which customers should be serviced next; in addition, the salesperson could determine which current customers could be placing larger orders of the same merchandise, or procuring other product items and product lines that the seller has to offer. Salespeople can also simultaneously identify new prospects while carefully scanning the sales territory. During these preliminary activities, sellers must also allocate sufficient time to the formal assessment of customer needs, resources, limitations, likely objections to sales points, and so on; in other words, business salespeople must attempt to monitor and to update their profile of each account on an individualized basis.[38] This type of activity also enables salespeople to tailor their sales presentations to meet the needs and wants of the prospect by turning each product feature into a critical customer benefit. Salespersons should then make sure that they are thoroughly familiar with their own respective product mixes, as well as with the respective product offerings of competitors. After satisfying these preliminary sales activities, sellers are then ready to generate a call schedule, make appointments, and design the form and content of the face-to-face activities involved in the selling process.

Face-to-Face Activities

Face-to-face activities consist of three primary steps: introduction, presentation, and close. In the "introduction stage," the salesperson attempts to capture the attention of his or her prospect; to create a positive selling atmosphere; and to build a comfortable professional, and perhaps personal, rapport with the prospect. (See the box entitled "Business-to-Business Marketing in Action" for a discussion of the use of humor in setting the mood for a business sales presentation.) Additionally, the salesperson must glean information about the customer's specific needs and wants in order to "set the stage" for the upcoming sales presentation.

The "presentation stage" focuses on actually "getting down to business." The salesperson tries to present his or her product or service in the most favorable light to individual members of the buying center; each product feature is associated with a customer benefit that will hopefully be of some importance to the prospect. Alert salespeople will constantly study their prospects, looking for both verbal and nonverbal cues as to how the presentation is progressing and how the prospects are receiving the information being disseminated. Certain cues from prospects such as yawns, frequent checking of watches, frowns, wrinkled fore-

BUSINESS-TO-BUSINESS MARKETING IN ACTION

HUMOR CAN BE YOUR BEST SALES TOOL: SALESPEOPLE SAY THE KEY IS KNOWING YOUR CUSTOMERS

For Rich Little, it's impersonations. For Mark Russell, satire. And for Robin Williams, insanity.

All of these entertainers have one thing in common. They know how to make people laugh. As a salesperson, you're never going to be expected to bring the house down on opening night. But you are expected to maintain relations with customers.

In their book, *The Magic of Thinking Big in Selling* John Doherty and Robert G. Hoehn say there's nothing like a well-placed joke to put you and your prospect at ease. The authors maintain that when you recognize a humorous situation and respond to it with a smile or a casual comment, prospects tend to relax and pay more attention to your sales presentation.

One of the real benefits of using humor, say the authors, is that it gives you total control of the selling situation. A lighthearted approach invites your customers to loosen up, listen, and ask questions. It creates a positive frame of mind that will ultimately put you in a better position to close sales.

Ed Weiss, a salesperson with Raritan Supply Company of Edison, New Jersey, agrees with the authors, saying that during his 35 years in sales, humor has been his most effective tool. "I'm not afraid to tell a joke, even when I first meet somebody," says Weiss. "It's not effective for me to go into a situation and pound on business. As far as I'm concerned, the guy who won't laugh at a joke has a problem—a problem that I'm not in a position to fix."

Tom Bullock, a sales manager at the Kaner Company in Los Angeles, maintains that any business day is a good time for a joke. "This is a tough business with people screaming about delivery schedules and under a lot of strain to get production moving. One of the best ways to reduce the tension is to use humor."

The key to using humor in business, says Roger Thibault of Valcourt Industrial Supply Company, Fall River, Massachusetts, is to know whom you're talking to. Says Thibault, "Be real careful when you use ethnic humor. If somebody is serious and doesn't have time for your antics, know when to back off."

However, Mario Mendoza, a salesperson at the Kalamazoo, Michigan, branch of GRS Industrial Supply Company, may have said it the best, "Nobody is going to buy a $100,000 machine if they don't feel comfortable with the person they are buying from. Humor is an extension of your personality, and that, in the end, is what we all sell."

Source: Steve Zurier, "Strictly for Salesmen," *Industrial Distribution* 77 (February 1988), p. 51. Used with permission.

heads, or raised eyebrows should never go unnoticed or ignored by salespersons. Such feedback generally serves as rather definitive evidence of the ineffectiveness of the sales presentation from the prospect's point of view.

Almost inevitably, the prospect will raise one or more objections to various selling points made by the salesperson. Frequently, these objections can be turned into actual reasons for buying the product or service;[39] but they can at times also mean that the product or service features and benefits outlined by the salesperson might be unclear to, or even disbelieved by, the prospect. In these latter cases, the salesperson may succeed or fail in closing the sale based on how well he or she has formerly thought out and practiced possible responses. Exhibit 10-7 outlines a four-step method by which the business salesperson can handle sales resistance. These four steps include establishing readiness, clarifying the objection,

EXHIBIT 10-7 **The Four-Step Method of Handling Sales Resistance**

Step 1—Establishing Readiness

Prospect	That price is far too high.
Salesperson	Everything seems to cost more today, doesn't it?
Prospect	You're sure right about that.
Salesperson	Your firm expects you to make profitable purchases?
Prospect	Yes, I do my best.
Salesperson	This means you have to analyze carefully the full value in any proposition, doesn't it?
Prospect	Yes, but I still say that your price is out of line.

Step 2—Clarifying the Objection

Salesperson	Might I ask what you consider a fair price based on your value analysis?
Prospect	Well, I don't have exact figures, but I'd say about 30 cents less a unit.
Salesperson	What unit value would you place on our guarantee of uniform quality from batch to batch?
Prospect	I don't know, but that doesn't amount to much. We test a sample out of each delivery ourselves.
Salesperson	That sounds like a good precaution if you are not certain of quality. What does that cost?
Prospect	I'd say about 5 cents prorated over the normal order.
Salesperson	From a cost standpoint, what is your optimum order quantity?
Prospect	About 1,000 units.
Salesperson	Would it increase your unit cost to order 4,000 at a time?
Prospect	There would be some more dollars tied up in inventory.

Step 3—Mentally Formulating the Order

Salesperson	(Our price breaks 30 cents a unit at 4,000 quantity. The buyer's estimate of testing cost is 5 cents. I can meet the price if I can get an order for 4,000 with delivery in modules of 1,000 as needed.)

Step 4—Questioning to Have the Prospect Answer the Objection

Salesperson	If you could eliminate the testing of incoming purchases, it would save you at least 5 cents a unit, wouldn't it?
Prospect	This is right, but we would need to be certain of quality if we did.
Salesperson	Would a guarantee covering replacement of goods plus any and all costs or damages through faulty quality be attractive?
Prospect	Yes.
Salesperson	Would you place an order if you could save 5 cents under your own unit value estimate?
Prospect	I sure would.
Salesperson	By ordering 4,000 units, you gain the advantage of our volume price, which is 30 cents less per unit than when purchases are in smaller quantities. We will guarantee quality as I have outlined above so you can save the 5 cent unit cost of testing.

mentally formulating the order, and using questioning to have the prospect answer the objection. During the entire sales presentation, and particularly during the time that objections to selling points are being raised, the salesperson must work diligently to get the prospect actively involved in the presentation, and genuinely interested in learning more about the product or service that the salesperson is attempting to sell. Some of the methods the salesperson can use to involve and to interest prospects include (1) stopping the presentation for a moment to inquire whether or not prospects have understood a particular product or service feature and the resulting benefit; (2) probing for likes and dislikes and for general customer preferences in regard to the product or service being sold; and (3) giving prospects an opportunity to handle the product, or to explain any questions or problems that they might be having with the selling points being offered by the salesperson. Generally speaking, during the presentation stage, the salesperson strives to convince prospects that it is in their best interests to purchase the particular product or service that the salesperson is offering.[40]

The ultimate and most critical step in the face-to-face interaction is the "closing." Of course, the purpose of any close is to ask the prospect for a formal commitment to purchase. Any number of closing techniques may be utilized in an effort to finalize the sale, including a restatement of product or service features and benefits, repeating successful responses to prospects' objections, and better arranging the terms of sale to suit the needs and desires of the prospect. Exhibit 10-8 describes some additional closing techniques commonly used in business selling. Whether salespeople are successful or not in actually obtaining the close, they should strive to conclude the sales interview on a highly positive note. This type of effort will typically lead to future opportunities for them and their prospects to meet again and perhaps to reach a sales agreement at a future time.

Follow-Up Activities

A most important point to mention at this time is that the business selling process does not end with the "close." Earlier in this chapter discussion we indicated that salespersons must attend to a wide variety of *follow-up activities* once the sale has been completed. Following up after the sale is really customer service, and good customer service is a powerful sales tool. The follow-up activity should be carefully planned. A timed follow-up program may lead to large secondary orders.[41] A truly successful sale requires that an order be completed and that all support arrangements (product design, order processing, credit approval, shipping, delivery, and the like.) be completed in a timely manner. After the sale, if the selling company is actively following the tenets of the marketing concept, customer satisfaction with both the product or service sold and the entire selling process must be evaluated, with changes made when and where appropriate and necessary. Salespeople should reflect upon the reasons as to why their sales presentations resulted in an exchange or a failure. If salespersons are unable to close the sale, they should carefully and thoughtfully examine those individual and collective factors that most likely accounted for the no-sale situation.

EXHIBIT 10-8 Closing Techniques Used in Business Selling

Closing is simply asking for an order. There are many ways to do this. The professional industrial salesperson knows several closing techniques from which to select one that fits the specific prospect and selling situation. Some effective closing techniques are described below.

The *alternate proposal close* offers the prospect a choice between details. "Do you prefer a truck or rail shipment?" "Will the standard drill suit your needs, or would you prefer to go with the superior model that you have been examining?" The philosophy of this close is to ask for a relatively minor decision.

The *assumptive close* assumes that the prospect will make a commitment. After receiving a positive buying signal and verifying this with a trial close, the salesperson proceeds to write up the order or complete a shipping form. Then the prospect is asked to "sign your name here so that I can process the shipment."

The *gift close* provides the prospect with an added inducement for taking immediate action. "If you sign the purchase order today, I'm sure we can have the order delivered to you next week."

The *action close* suggests that the sales representative take an action that will consummate the sale. "Let me arrange an appointment with your attorney to work out the details of the transaction."

The *one-more-yes close* is based on the principle that saying yes can become a habit. The salesperson restates the benefits of the product in a series of questions that will result in positive responses. The final question asks the prospect to complete the sale.

The *balance-sheet close* is an effective technique to use with procrastinators. The salesperson and the prospect list the reasons for acting now on one side, and the reasons for delaying action on the other. If the salesperson has built a persuasive case, the reasons for immediate action will outweigh the reasons for delaying. Then the salesperson can ask for the order.

The *direct close* is clear and simple. The salesperson asks for a decision. Many salespeople feel that this is the best approach, especially if there are strong positive buying signals. Frequently, the salesperson summarizes the major points that were made during the presentation prior to asking for the close.

Exhibit 10-9 details many of the worst mistakes that business salespeople can make in the planning and implementation of a sales call. Some, and perhaps many, changes might have to be made in each of the various stages of the selling process. Follow-up activities usually also involve the salesperson's maintaining strong and positive relationships with as many members of the buying center as possible. Again, this type of activity most often results in future opportunities for the salesperson to meet with numerous members of various buying centers, again in an effort to consummate previously lost sales. In conclusion, salespeople should constantly monitor both their internal and external environments to note changes in competitive activities, governmental regulations, the economic climate, customer preferences, market behavior, and other factors that could affect the selling effort. They should continually work to sharpen and refine their product knowledge, selling skills, and communications effectiveness.

EXHIBIT 10-9 **The Seven Deadly Sins of Business Selling**

When purchasing agents were asked as part of a survey to indicate the types of selling behavior that most typically accounted for lost sales opportunities, they listed the following "deadly sins":

1. *Lack of product knowledge.* Salespeople must know their own product lines as well as the buyer's, or nothing productive can take place.
2. *Time wasting.* Unannounced sales visits are a nuisance. When salespeople start droning on about golf or grandchildren, more time is wasted.
3. *Poor planning.* Even a routine sales call should be preceded by some homework—maybe to see if it's really necessary.
4. *Pushiness.* This includes prying to find out a competitor's prices, an overwhelming attitude, and "backdoor selling."
5. *Lack of dependability.* Failure to stand behind the product, to keep communications clear, and to keep promises.
6. *Unladylike or ungentlemanly conduct.* "Knocking" competitors, "boozing" at a business lunch, sloppy dress, and poor taste are not professional.
7. *Unlimited optimism.* Honesty is preferred to the hallmark of the "Good News Bearers" who will promise anything to get an order. Never promise more than you can deliver.

A few of the more vigorous comments from purchasing agents who were disenchanted with certain behavioral characteristics of business salespeople:

- "They seem to take it personally if they don't get the business, as though you owe them something for constantly calling on you."
- "I don't like it when they blast through the front door like know-it-alls, and put on an unsolicited dog-and-pony show that will guarantee cost saving out in limbo somewhere."
- "Many salespeople are willing to give you the delivery date you want, book the order, and then let you face the results of their short quote."
- "They try to sell you, rather than the product."
- "After the order is won, the honeymoon is over."
- "Beware of the humble pest who is too nice to insult, won't take a hint, won't listen to blunt advice, and is selling a product you neither use nor want to use; yet, won't go away."

INTERNATIONAL BUSINESS SELLING

International markets will present both special problems and tremendous opportunities for business salespeople as we move through the decade of the 1990s. In the United States, we carefully study both our customers and the culture to which they belong. Should we do any less for our customers and prospects in international markets? Examples of business selling mistakes made by U.S. salespeople abound. Accepting a Japanese executive's business card and casually placing it into a pocket or wallet would be considered rude by that individual. The Japanese believe that the name, written or spoken, is something close to sacred. Similarly, presuming that all the French executives sitting in a business meeting speak English, without first asking in French whether they do so, is a tactical blunder; because the French are extremely proud of their heritage and their language.[43]

International business salespeople must deal with differences in language and currency, political and legal uncertainties, different kinds of buying wants and needs (to include differences in purchasing needs arising from the physical characteristics of people in other countries), and dissimilarities in culture and national policies. "Knowing your customer" is just as important abroad as it is at home, whether selling computers in North Africa, equipment and installations in Western Europe, or raw materials in Asia. A leading U.S. manufacturer of small power tools wished to do business in South Korea and shipped a number of different tools to newly found customers in that country. To the frustration and dismay of this company's international sales force, although many potential shoppers expressed an interest in these tools, very few were ultimately sold. After conducting a marketing research study specifically designed to determine the reasons for this phenomenon, the American salespeople learned that South Koreans liked the tools and would have been willing to purchase them if they had been scaled down to fit the size of the average Korean male's hand.

U.S. salespeople must realize that they are the foreigners in other countries and should conduct themselves accordingly. They must recognize, appreciate, and be sensitive to the differences between how business is conducted in the United States and how it is conducted in each country in which they are working. Increased international selling by U.S. firms will force sales people to become familiar with foreign language, culture, and politics.[43]

CONCEPT QUESTIONS

1. What is the ultimate and most critical step in face-to-face sales interaction?
2. What is an example of a mistake that a U.S. business salesperson might make in a foreign market?

SUMMARY

1. Personal selling involves persuasive and deliberate contact between a buyer and a seller for the specific purpose of creating an exchange between them. Personal selling is the primary promotional tool utilized in business selling and is generally supported by the other elements, such as advertising, publicity, public relations, and sales promotion. In this manner, business selling differs greatly from consumer selling, which relies much more heavily on mass selling tools, and on advertising in particular.
2. Business selling can only be truly appreciated when both the scope and the nature of salespeople's daily activities are understood. Such activities typically include selling, maintenance of distributor relationships, planning, decision making, and managing communications.
3. The cost of a business sales call has been rising rapidly over the last decade, as has the cost of personal selling in general. Because the cost of personal selling can vary so significantly, depending on such factors as the type of product and industry, the size of the firm, and the degree of personal contact with prospects necessary to close a sale, business-to-business companies must constantly monitor and assess the best methods by which to distribute and sell their products and services.

4. Buyers in the business sector seek to buy for many reasons, including increasing profits and sales, producing a quality product, helpfulness of the salesperson's service, trade-in allowances, and so on. Once salespeople have identified the prospect's important buying needs, they can specifically tailor a sales presentation to that prospect; they can capitalize on the features, benefits, and advantages of their product or service that most directly match the prospect's buying needs, wants, and preferences.
5. Business salespeople can use different approaches in their sales presentation depending upon the type of customer or the selling situation involved. These approaches include the formularized, buying-decisions, and problem-solving models. Reaching business markets effectively also requires a great variety of types of salespeople and selling styles. A careful analysis of selling tasks can aid the salesperson in deciding what priorities to place on which selling activities to ensure a more successful sales effort.
6. Personal selling in business markets is constantly evolving and growing ever more complex. Among the most important contemporary trends in business selling are systems selling, telemarketing, the increasing presence of saleswomen, the sales assistance provided by both portable and permanent computer terminals, and the rapid growth of audio-visual aids as helpful tools during the sales presentation.
7. The business selling process can be examined in a variety of ways, but understanding it from the salesperson's viewpoint seems highly appropriate. The business selling process basically involves three main selling activities: preliminary activities, face-to-face activities, and follow-up activities. Each of these involves a multitude of tasks and plays an important role in the effective selling of business products and services. Business salespeople should constantly monitor both their internal and external environments, looking for important changes in the buyer-seller interactive process; and they should continually sharpen and refine their product knowledge, selling skills, and communications effectiveness.
8. International markets will present both special challenges and tremendous opportunities for business salespeople during the decade of the 1990s. International business salespeople must learn to deal effectively with international markets in terms of differences in language and currency, political agendas, laws, buying wants and needs, culture, and national policies. U.S. salespeople must know their international customers just as well as they know their domestic clients.

KEY TERMS

Benefit segmentation
Benefit selling
Buying-decisions model
Creative selling
Expert power
Face-to-face activities
Follow-up activities
Formularized (AIDA) model
Maintenance selling
Missionary sales
Preliminary activities
Problem-solving model
Referent power
Sales development
Service selling
Support sales
Systems selling
Telemarketing

REVIEW QUESTIONS

1. How does the use of personal selling differ in consumer markets and business markets? What is the primary promotional element utilized in selling to each of these markets?
2. Discuss the five primary activities that business salespeople typically perform on a daily basis. Why is decision making so intertwined with the other four activities?
3. What factors cause the cost of personal selling to vary so significantly?
4. Explain the importance of using benefit selling in reaching business buyers effectively. Discuss five methods by which a business salesperson can identify the important buying needs of his or her prospects.
5. Describe three major models commonly used in making business sales presentations. Under what circumstances would the use of each one seem most appropriate?
6. Define the four basic types of sales tasks: development, missionary, maintenance, and support. Discuss four major contemporary selling styles used in reaching business markets.
7. Define systems selling and explain its importance in selling to the business market. Why has telemarketing become such a major force for penetrating both new and established business markets?
8. Why were there so few saleswomen in business selling for so many years? Why are they increasing in such large numbers today? How are portable and permanent computer terminals currently being employed in business sales? What constitutes the ideal customer application of permanent computer terminals for business selling? What is the value of laptop computers?
9. Why have audio-visual aids gained such popularity as tools to use in making business sales presentations over the past decade? Which types of visual-aid equipment are used most frequently in business selling?
10. Distinguish among preliminary activities, face-to-face activities, and follow-up activities in the business selling process. How do business selling tasks differ among the introduction, presentation, and close stages of face-to-face selling activities? Why are follow-up activities an illustration of the use of the marketing concept in selling to business buyers?
11. What are the primary differences between conducting business in U.S. markets and transacting business in international markets? Why is it just as important for U.S. business salespeople to know their international customers as well as they know their domestic customers?

Cases

CASE 10-1 Clemson Meat Company

The Clemson Meat Company is a family-owned meat processing and packing company that sells high-quality perishable meat products directly to retail grocers and supermarkets. The company was started in the 1930s, and the main processing plant is located in a large western city. The company's sales volume, about $85 million a year, has been increasing about 10 to 12 percent a year, and management expects this growth rate to continue.

However, like most meat packers, Clemson operates on a narrow net-profit margin. In the previous year, Clemson incurred a small loss. The company has no control over the price of live hogs, its main raw material. Consequently, Mr. Peter Jauch, the vice president of sales, is looking for a way to cut sales operating expenses in the hope of contributing to profit.

THE MEAT MARKET

The Clemson products are divided into six categories. Each salesperson sells the full line. The six product groups and their share of the company's sales are as follows: fresh pork, 60 percent; wieners, 12 percent; bacon, 12 percent; ham, 6 percent; sausage, 6 percent; and lunch meats, 4 percent.

Since meat products are perishable, orders have to be filled very quickly. Clemson's small size makes it flexible enough to receive orders one day and ship them the next. Clemson sells in fourteen western states. The company sells to some thirty-five hundred accounts, but Mr. Jauch estimates that the potential in these states is about three times that number. Clemson sells primarily to retailers. Each salesperson handles six or seven large accounts. In the Colorado market, for example, two retail supermarket chains—King Soopers and Safeway—account for about 85 percent of Clemson's sales. In general, the retail accounts have been decreasing in number but increasing in average size. Consequently, Mr. Jauch believes that the company can continue its growth without adding more salespeople, at least for the next few years.

Clemson's major competitive advantages are its flexibility and its modern production facilities. For example, the company operates a hot dog machine that manufactures thirty thousand wieners per hour. The company's major limitation, as Mr. Jauch sees it, is that Clemson is too small to advertise as heavily as its major competitors.

THE SALES COMPENSATION PLAN

Clemson's twenty-two sales representatives have a thorough knowledge of meats and the meat industry. They are usually hired from competitive firms. They are paid with a combination salary and bonus plan. Salaries range from $2,000 to $3,000 per month. The bonus, a percentage of salary, is based on how much a sales representative exceeds his or her quota. Tonnage quotas in each of five categories of processed meats are assigned to each sales representative. These quotas are based on past sales, as adjusted for current economic conditions and market outlook. The quotas and bonuses are computed quarterly.

The bonus is a certain amount paid for each ton of meat sold in excess of quota. To encourage a balanced selling job of all products, management set limits for the bonuses in each category of processed meats. For example, the total bonus paid for selling hot dogs could not exceed 12 percent of salary. These limits in the other product categories are as follows: ham, 6 percent; sausage, 12 percent; lunch meat, 12 percent; and bacon, 10 percent. Thus, a sales rep's total bonus for all products was limited to 52 percent of his or her salary. Most other firms in the industry pay their sales forces a straight salary.

The salespeople are also provided with unlimited expense accounts but are required to submit itemized statements. Clemson allows its sales force to grant an allowance or discount of four cents per pound as a concession to customers in special situations.

IS A NEW COMPENSATION PLAN NEEDED?

Recently, it was brought to Mr. Jauch's attention that the sales of three reps were fluctuating by about five hundred thousand pounds from one three-month period to the next. This represented 10 to 12 percent of the average four to five million pounds of meat sold by each salesperson during a quarterly period. Apparently, in order to exceed their volume quotas, these individuals were convincing some of their customers that they needed more meat than was actually the case. The retail buyers would consequently be overstocked one period and would underbuy the next in order to balance things out. Fluctuations of this sort caused production inefficiencies, thus increasing costs.

Upon further investigation of past records, Mr. Jauch discovered that on virtually all their orders, these same three sales representatives were shaving 4 cents a pound from the list price, which should be allowed only as a special price concession. Thus, Clemson was not achieving its planned profit margins in these territories. Moreover, sales on low-margin products far exceeded sales of high-margin items. As a final point, Mr. Jauch felt that the travel and business expenses of these sales reps were much too high.

Each of the three sales representatives involved had been with Clemson for over ten years and were well established in his or her territory. Each handled a large number of accounts. These salespersons were very good—they knew meat and could sell it. They liked to write up big orders. They consistently won or came close to winning the annual sales contest for the greatest volume sold. They also had the highest earnings last year.

DISCUSSION QUESTIONS

1. Are the three sales representatives marketing oriented?
2. Should major changes be made in Clemson's compensation plan for its system? If so, what would you recommend?

Source: Cunningham and Cunningham, *Marketing: A Managerial Approach*, 1st Edition (Cincinnati, OH: South-Western Publishing Company, 1992) pp. 345–347.

CASE 10-2 The Saturn Division of General Motors Corporation

Originally, Saturn was intended to be a completely innovative car division for General Motors. GM was to invest $5 billion in completely automated manufacturing lines to build the Saturn. The price of the original subcompact models were expected to be in the $6,000 range. However, what first rolled off the Saturn assembly line was a compact. The car is available as a four-door sedan or a two-door coupe and sells for $10,000 to $12,000. Moreover, GM dropped the estimated production from 500,000 cars to 120,000 cars.

THE TARGET MARKET

Historically, General Motors has drawn distinct lines between its divisions. Cadillac was the high-end division, while Chevy was the low-end. Now GM has high-end Buicks competing with low-end Cadillacs. Oldsmobile is GM's experimental division, even though the most traditional Oldsmobile drivers are older women. Saturn is positioned to appeal to college-educated men and women, especially professionals. The four-door sedan will be aimed at a slightly older, more needs-driven audience. The two-door coupe will most likely appeal to a slightly younger crowd more concerned with styling.

Saturn is targeted to pull customers from the import car market. The initial models are to be pitted against the Honda Civic and the Toyota Corolla. GM wants 80 percent of Saturn buyers to be converts from import cars. Industry experts fear the division may actually pull buyers from other GM divisions such as Chevrolet/Geo and Pontiac. Thus, Saturn may add to GM's problems, not solve them. Jack Trout, president of Trout and Reis, says that a lack of product distinction poses a major problem for GM. The Saturn resembles so many other GM models that Saturn's price advantage may not be enough to sway customers from buying the established car models.

ADVERTISING

General Motors selected Hal Riney and Partners to develop the initial advertising campaign. One problem facing Riney is that the car his company has to pitch is not the car it thought it would be promoting. Some advertising executives offered the following recommendations to Riney:

> Saturn should be careful about wrapping itself in a country or company. Customers are buying a car; they're not buying patriotism. If it were that simple, there wouldn't be many Japanese cars on the road.
>
> —*Scott Gilbert, Executive Vice President, General Motors*
>
> The advertising has to turn around a negative perception of the quality and reliability of domestic cars. The theme should focus on Saturn as a new kind of American car.
>
> —*Chuck Valentine, Senior Vice President, General Motors*
>
> Riney should use a value position, like, at long last you don't have to spend an exorbitant amount of money for a terrific car. —*Jack Trout, President, Trout and Reis*
>
> The most important hurdle is to increase awareness. Its selling points are high value and high quality. Those tangible messages must come across.
>
> —*John Hammond, partner, J. D. Power and Associates*

The company is expected to pursue both a model-specific advertising campaign and a corporate campaign. The key issue concerning the corporate campaign will be to tie the Saturn division back to General Motors. All the employees at Saturn are proud to be associated with GM, but they are concerned with how the GM-Saturn connection is going to sit with the consumer.

CUSTOMER SATISFACTION

The Saturn division has elected to pursue a strategy of promoting customer satisfaction rather than waging a price war. While most car manufacturers tend to offer cash rebates to consumers as an enticement to buy now, Saturn will offer a thirty-day, money-back guarantee. This offer, similar to an offer made by Volkswagen, will allow Saturn purchasers to return the car within thirty days or 1,500 miles if they are not completely satisfied with their new car.

Saturns will also come with a three-year, 36,000-mile, bumper-to-bumper warranty. Owners will not be required to pay a deductible for warranty repairs. GM's customary warranty is three years, 50,000 miles, with a $100 deductible for repairs.

DISCUSSION QUESTIONS

1. What potential problems might GM have with dealers and salespeople selling the Saturn automobiles? What changes, if any, would you recommend to the company?
2. What do you think is more important to sell cars—advertising, sales promotion, or personal selling activities? Give reasons to support your opinion.

Suggested Readings

Serafin, Raymond. "GM's Saturn Enters Crucial Period." *Advertising Age*, 23 July 1990, 16.

White, Joseph B. "GM Puts Low Price on Saturn to Sell in Small-Car Field." *Wall Street Journal*, 5 October 1990, B1, B7.

Source: C. Lamb, J. Hair, and C. McDaniel, *Principles of Marketing*, 1st Edition (Cincinnati, OH: South-Western Publishing Company, 1992) pp. 529–531.

Suggested Additional Readings

Dunn, Dan T., Jr., and Claude A. Thomas. "Strategy for Systems Sellers: A Grid Approach." *Journal of Personal Selling and Sales Management* 6 (August 1986): 1–10. **Discussion of and guidelines for a problem-solution grid related to systems selling.**

Hafer, John, and Barbara A. McCuen. "Antecedents of Performance and Satisfaction in a Service Sales Force as Compared to an Industrial Sales Force." *Journal of Personal Selling and Sales Management* 5 (November 1985): 7–17. **Discussion of the conflicting results of two studies comparing performance of members of a service sales force and of a business sales force.**

Hite, Robert E., and Joseph A. Bellizzi. "Differences in the Importance of Selling Techniques between Consumer and Industrial Salespeople," *Journal of Personal Selling and Sales Management* 5 (November 1985): 19–30. **Comparative analysis of differences in the importance of selling techniques between consumer and business salespersons.**

Ingram, Thomas M., Charles H. Schwepker, Jr, and Don Hutson., "Why Salespeople Fail." *Industrial Marketing Management* 21 (August 1992): 225–230. **A discussion of the reasons why business salespeople fail to close sales.**

King, Bob. "Ploys and Counterploys in Sales Negotiation." *Industrial Marketing Digest* (UK), 10 (Third Quarter 1985): 101–105. **Guidelines for negotiation techniques between business salespeople and their customers.**

Macintosh, Gerrard, Kenneth A. Anglin, David M. Szmanski, and James W. Gentry. "Relationship Development in Selling: A Cognitive Analysis," *Journal of Personal Selling and Sales Management* 12 (Fall 1992): 23–34. **A discussion of sales prospecting and of building trust in both initial and follow-up sales calls.**

Merrett, Bernie. "Industrial Companies Talk to Clients but Seldom Listen." *Sales and Marketing Management in Canada* 26 (December 1985): 19–20. **Discussion of market surveys, market research, and problem identification.**

Moncrief, William C. "The Key Activities of Industrial Salespeople." *Industrial Marketing Management* 15 (November 1986): 309–317. **Survey of shared versus industry-specific sales activities.**

Mouritzen, Russell H. "Client Involvement Through Negotiation: A Key to Success." *American Salesman* 32 (May 1987): 16–18. **Guidelines for relationships and negotiation skills in personal selling.**

Pesmen, Sandra. "Fleet on the Street." *Business Marketing* 77 (May 1992): 20–21.

Rosenthal, Alan. "How to Improve Presentations." *Business Marketing* 77 (June 1992): 40–41. **Guidelines toward more successful business selling.**

Schurr, Paul H., Louis H. Stone, and Lee Ann Beller. "Effective Selling Approaches to Buyers' Objections." *Industrial Marketing Management* 14 (August 1985): 195–202. **Survey of business salespeople, price objections, indecision, and techniques for handling resistance.**

Shipley, David D., and Julia A. Kiley. "Industrial Salesforce Motivation and Herzberg's Dual Factor Theory: A UK Perspective." *Journal of Personal Selling and Sales Management* 6 (May 1986): 9–16. **Divergent findings in a survey of 114 business salespeople as to job satisfaction and dissatisfaction.**

Spekman, Robert E., and Wesley J. Johnston. "Relationship Management: Managing the Selling and Buyer Interface." *Journal of Business Research* 14 (December 1986): 519–531. **Discussion of competitive advantage, cross-functional interdependencies, and decision processes.**

Swan, John E., and Johanna Jones Nolan. "Gaining Customer Trust: A Conceptual Guide for the Salesperson." *Journal of Personal Selling and Sales Management* 5 (November 1985): 39–48. **Discussion of exchange relationships and a model of trust among business salespersons and their customers.**

Swan, John E., I. Frederick Trawick, and David W. Silva. "How Industrial Salespeople Gain Customer Trust." *Industrial Marketing Management* 14 (August 1985): 203–211. **Survey and model development of trust attributes, critical salesperson behaviors, and sales techniques.**

Taylor, Thayer C. "Laptops and the Sales Force: New Stars in the Sky." *Sales and Marketing Management* 138 (April 1987): 50–55. **Sales productivity applications for portable computers.**

Wagle, John S. "Using Humor in the Industrial Selling Process." *Industrial Marketing Management* 14 (November 1985): 221–226. **Guidelines for the use of humor in business sales presentations.**

ENDNOTES

[1]Linda Rochford and Thomas R. Wotruba, "New Product Development under Changing Economic Conditions: The Role of the Salesforce," *Journal of Business and Industrial Marketing* (December 1993): 4–12.

[2]Michael F. Hruby, "Tips for Industrial Marketers," *Sales and Marketing Management* 142 (May 1990): 68–76.

[3]John Lidstone, "Planning to Negotiate with Major Customers," *Marketing Intelligence and Planning Review* (UK), 8 (1990): 51–57.

[4]Donald W. Caudill and Denny L. White, "Twelve Rewards of Becoming a Powerful Listener," *Agency Sales Magazine* 21 (February 1991): 29–31.

[5]Philip Carpenter, "Bridging the Gap between Marketing and Sales," *Sales and Marketing Management* 144 (March 1992): 28–31.

[6]"Average Business-to-Business Sales Call Increases by 9.5%," *Marketing News* (September 12, 1988): 5.

[7]Gilbert A. Churchill, Neil M. Ford, and Orville C. Walker, Jr., *Sales Force Management*, 4th ed. (Homewood, Ill.: Richard D. Irwin, 1993), 119.

[8]Statistics provided courtesy of Professor George W. Wynn, School of Business, James Madison University, Harrisonburg, Virginia.

[9]Pat Friedlender, "When Is It Time to Get a New Booth?" *Business Marketing* (February 1993): 48.

[10]"Sales Tactics Take on a New Look as Corporations Rethink Strategy," *Wall Street Journal*, 28 April 1988, 1.

[11]Henry Bernstein, "How to Recruit Good Salesmen," *Industrial Marketing* 50 (October 1965): 70. Also, see John A. Byrne, "Motivating Willy Loman," *Forbes*, 30 January 1984, 91.

[12]James R. Young and Robert W. Mondy, *Personal Selling: Function, Theory, and Practice* (Hinsdale, Ill.: Dryden Press, 1978): 156–160.

[13]Peter Crutchley, "Power and Influence," *Credit Management* (August 1992): 28–29.

[14]Paul Busch and David T. Wilson, "An Experimental Analysis of a Salesman's Expert and Referent Bases of Social Power in the Buyer-Seller Dyad," *Journal of Marketing Research* 13 (February 1976): 3–11.

[15]Eugene M. Johnson, David L. Kurtz, and Eberhard E. Scheuing, *Sales Management: Concepts, Practices, and Cases* (New York: McGraw-Hill, 1986), 55.

[16]Paula C. Kringle, "Training Salespeople to Sell Service," *Training*, Sales Training Supplement (May 1989): 14–18.

[17]H. Robert Dodge, "The Role of the Industrial Salesman," *Mid-South Quarterly Review* (January 1972): 11–15.

[18]*Ibid.*, 13.

[19]Philip Kotler, *Marketing Management: Analysis, Planning, Implementation, and Control*, 6th ed. (Englewood Cliffs, N.J.: Prentice-Hall, 1988), 212. Also see Albert L. Page and Michael Siempliski, "Product Systems Marketing," *Industrial Marketing Management* 12 (1983): 89–99.

[20]Steve Zurier, "Precision Partnering," *Industrial Distribution* 81 (June 15, 1992): 61–62.

[21]*Ibid.*, 212.

[22]Stephanie Anderson Forest, "PC Slump? What PC Slump?" *Business Week*, Industrial Technology Edition, 1 July 1991, 66–67.

[23]Rick Burnham, "Telemarketing's Role Grows in Corporations," *Investor's Daily*, 13 October 1988, 1, 34.

[24]*Ibid.*

[25]Bob Donath, "The $100-Billion Marketing Mix," *Business Marketing* 71 (June 1986): 4.

[26]U.S. Department of Labor, *Employment and Earnings* (Washington, D.C.: Government Printing Office, 1972, 1980, 1989).

[27]Robert W. Cook and Robert J. Corey, "A Confirmatory Investigation of Industrial Buyer Image of the Saleswoman," *Journal of the Academy of Marketing Science* (Summer 1991): 199–207.

[28]Bill Kelley, "Selling in a Man's World," *Sales and Marketing Management* 143 (January 1991): 28–35.

[29]John E. Swan, Charles M. Futrell, and John T. Todd, "Same Job—Different Views: Women and Men in Industrial Sales," *Journal of Marketing* 42 (January 1978): 92–98; see also Paul Busch and Ronald Bush, "Women Contrasted to Men in the Industrial Salesforce: Job Satisfaction, Values, Role Clarity, Performance and Propensity to Leave," *Journal of Marketing Research* 15 (August 1978): 438–448.

[30]John E. Swan, David R. Rink, G. E. Kiser, and Warren G. Martin, "Industrial Buyer Image of the Saleswoman," *Journal of Marketing* 48 (Winter 1984): 114; see also "Women Often Better Reps, Miller Reports," *Industrial Marketing* (June 1977): 1.

[31]Ellen J. Kennedy and Leigh Lawton, "Men and Women in Industrial Sales: Satisfaction and Outcomes," *Industrial Marketing Management* 21 (February 1992): 5–14.

[32]Douglas J. Dalrymple, *Sales Management: Concepts and Cases*, 4th ed. (New York: John Wiley and Sons, 1991), 118.

[33]*Sales and Marketing Management* (March 14, 1983): 22–24.

[34]Thayer C. Taylor, "GE Posts a Sentry to Give Customers Better Service," *Sales and Marketing Management* (December 6, 1982): 46–48.

[35]*Business Week*, 10 October 1988, 104.

[36]*Exchange*, no. 17 (Stamford, Conn.: Xerox Learning Systems): 3.

[37]G. David Hughes and Charles H. Singler, *Strategic Sales Management* (Reading, Mass.: Addison-Wesley, 1983), 82.

[38]"The New Supersalesman: Wired for Success," *Business Week*, 6 January 1973, 45–49.

[39]Daniel K. Weadcock, "Your Troops Can Keep Control and Close the Sale—By Anticipating Objections," *Sales and Marketing Management* (March 17, 1980): 104.

[40]G. Ray Funkhouser, "A Practical Theory of Persuasion Based on Behavioral Science Approaches," *Journal of Personal Selling and Sales Management* (November 1984): 17–25.

[41]"Training Agency Salespeople: Follow-up before and after the Sale," *Agency Sales Magazine* 22 (May 1992): 54–57.

[42]"Helpful Hints and Faux Pas in International Sales," *Information World* (September 16, 1985): 30.

[43]"Partnership Selling: The Wave of the Future," *Marketing News* (December 19, 1988): 17.

11 Business Sales Management

Learning Objectives

After reading this chapter, you should be able to:

- Identify the changes that take place when a business salesperson is promoted to sales manager.
- Explain the common forms of sales-force organization.
- Understand the critical role of recruitment, selection, and training of the sales force in business sales management.
- Realize the great importance of effective direction and motivation of the business sales force.
- Appreciate the role of continuous monitoring and evaluation of sales performance.
- Relate how to build an effective sales force in a foreign country.

Chapter Outline

Learning Objectives

Business Sales Management: A Leadership Challenge

Selecting the Sales Manager

- Perspectives
- Goals
- Responsibilities
- Satisfaction
- Job Skill Requirements
- Relationships

Basic Types of Sales Organizations

- The Line Organization
- The Line and Staff Organization
- The Functional Organization
- The Centralized versus Decentralized Organization
- Organizing by Specialization
  - Geographic specialization
  - Sales activities
  - Product specialization
  - Customer specialization
  - Combination organizations

Staffing the Business Sales Force

- Determining Sales-Force Size
  - Turnover expected
- Recruitment and Selection
- Recruitment
  - Conduct a job analysis
  - Prepare a written job description
  - Develop sales job qualifications
  - Sources of sales recruits
- Selection

Training and Developing the Business Sales Force

- Purposes of Sales Training
- What the Training Program Should Cover
  - Company knowledge
  - Product knowledge
  - Selling techniques
  - Customer knowledge
  - Competitive knowledge
  - Time and territory management
- Who Should Do the Training?
  - Home office sales training
  - Field or local sales training
  - Private consulting organizations and professional trainers
- Evaluating Sales Training

Directing and Motivating the Business Sales Force

- Providing Leadership
- Sales Quotas
- Compensation

Sales-Force Analysis and Evaluation

- Why Analyze and Evaluate Salespeople?
- Who Should Analyze and Evaluate Salespeople?
- When Should Analysis and Evaluation Be Done?

Managing U.S. Salespeople in International Markets
Selection
Orientation and Training
Compensation

Summary

Key Terms

Review Questions

Cases
Case 11-1
Case 11-2

Suggested Additional Readings

Endnotes

BUSINESS SALES MANAGEMENT: A LEADERSHIP CHALLENGE

Few areas in the business sector are in more need of a systematic approach to problem solving than the sales management function. The first qualification for a sales manager is leadership. As Figure 11-1 indicates, the sales manager must not only attempt to allocate financial resources efficiently, but he or she must also attempt to allocate, maintain, direct, and control a large group of people who are often rather independent and who are not in daily contact with management. Effective sales management in the business sector is critical to the successful allocation of scarce resources in a free, competitive economy. As was noted in Chapter 10, personal selling involves deliberate and persuasive contact between buyer and seller. Sales management, on the other hand, involves a multitude of challenges. Sales management is multifaceted because managers must be people oriented. Management of the sales function has often been described as both an art and a science, requiring the sales manager to walk a tightrope between subjective creativity and objective detachment.

SELECTING THE SALES MANAGER

One of the primary reasons firms face difficulty in selecting a sales manager is that many changes accompany a promotion from subordinate to supervisor. Selling skills and management skills are different, and not all good salespeople make good sales managers. Yet, many firms still tend to promote individuals in this

FIGURE 11-1 **The Leadership Functions of Sales Managers**

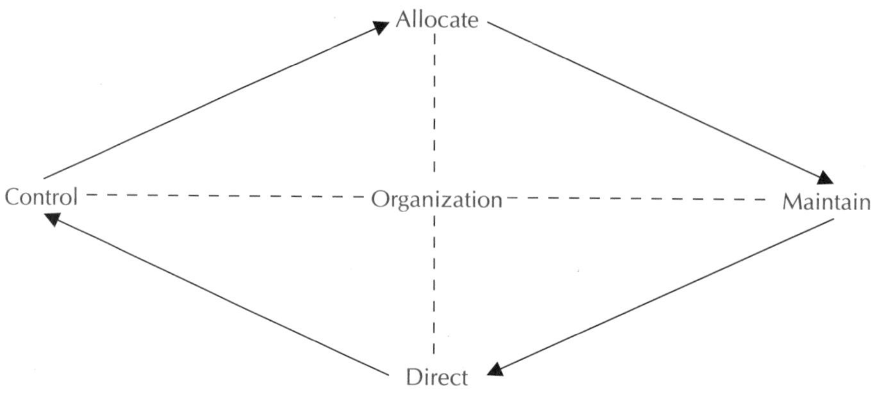

way. The qualities that make a good, effective sales manager are often significantly different from those that make an effective salesperson.[1] Selling and managing require nearly opposite skills.[2] Changes accompany this promotion, some of which are immediate and apparent; others are less obvious and tend to take an individual longer to adjust to. To be a successful sales manager, it is important to adopt different perspectives, goals, responsibilities, and satisfaction, as discussed below.[3]

Perspectives

Selling is doing, travelling, constantly testing your own individual abilities, and being in control of your own destiny. Successful sales managers, however, must delegate, coach, counsel, and keep the big picture in mind. Plans and decisions must be made that take into consideration the goals and well-being of the sales team and the organization as a whole.

Goals

The sales manager must be concerned with the total organization, whereas the salesperson's focus is on meeting personal goals. This is not to imply that the sales manager does not have personal goals, but only to highlight the fact that his or her personal goals must mesh with the personal goals of the individual salespeople in accomplishing overall organizational goals and objectives.

Responsibilities

Progressive business-to-business firms recognize that the sales management function is related to traditional marketing activities such as pricing, distribution, product development, information collection, and advertising, in addition to other business activities and disciplines. The contemporary business sales manager recognizes the necessity of making a sale at a profit, in addition to monitoring customer reactions to company products, service and policies, and the sales methods employed by the individual salespeople.

Satisfaction

The salesperson receives much satisfaction in making a sale, in many cases, after several months of hard work. The sales manager, however, receives satisfaction from seeing people succeed; especially if the sales manager indirectly contributed to that success through guidance, training, and perhaps prodding.

Job Skill Requirements

The sales manager must not only exhibit superior knowledge of products, policies, and selling techniques, but he or she must also become proficient at communicating, delegating, planning, managing time, directing, motivating, and training others—no easy task!

Relationships

New relationships must develop, as the sales manager not only must get things done through the sales force, but must also work with and through internal peers such as the manufacturing manager, the purchasing manager, the engineering manager, and the financial manager, to name just a few. For the sales manager to do an optimal job, top management support is important. Managerial performance criteria, such as profit accountability and decision-oriented reports from top management, can help significantly in enabling sales managers to increase the productivity and profitability of the sales force.

BASIC TYPES OF SALES ORGANIZATIONS

Just as important as selecting exactly the right type of sales manager is choosing the most appropriate type of sales organization plan. The business sales force can be organized in several ways, with the key to organizational design being logical consistency. Developing the structure is not easy; the final decision depends on the needs and objectives of the firm. Although there are many variations, the line organization, the line and staff organization, and the functional organization are the most common and most basic in the business sector. Each will be studied, followed by a discussion of modifications to these basic types—modifications based on the need to centralize or decentralize, or to organize by activity, product, customer, geographic territory, or some combination of these.[4]

The Line Organization

The *line organization* is the simplest design; it is often used by small business-to-business firms; and, as shown in Figure 11-2, it has a clear line of authority from the highest level of sales management down to the salesperson. In its simplest form, a line organization prescribes that the sales manager recruits, hires, trains, and supervises the salespeople, in addition to designing sales territories, forecasting sales levels, and carrying out other functions or special projects as assigned by top management. When the firm is small, this organizational structure is efficient, effective, and very flexible. However, as the firm grows, and as problems become more complex, the line organization tends to overburden the managers.

The Line and Staff Organization

When highly specialized skills are needed (advertising, marketing research, and the like), and when the volume of work becomes overwhelming for one person, *line and staff organization* emerges. The line function is primary, while the staff function is supportive in nature. Staff people provide the manager with specialized skills and report to the line position that they support. Sales analysts and training directors are directly supportive of field sales, so these people generally report directly to the general sales manager, as is demonstrated in Figure 11-3. A staff specialist can only recommend policy or action.

The Functional Organization

With *functional organization*, the staff specialist is given line authority to control a function. As an example, the training specialist would have authority over the business salespeople for all training. Each specialist is (hopefully) highly qualified, so out of this structure should come improved performance in each functional area. Figure 11-4 offers a diagram of the sales management activity organized by function.

FIGURE 11-2 **A Simple Line Organization**

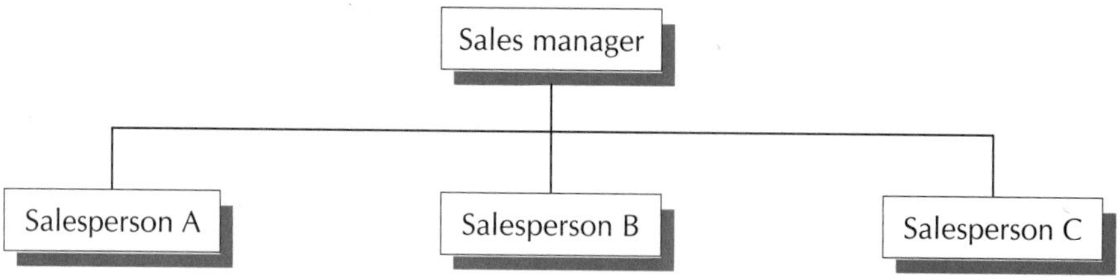

FIGURE 11-3 **A Line and Staff Organization**

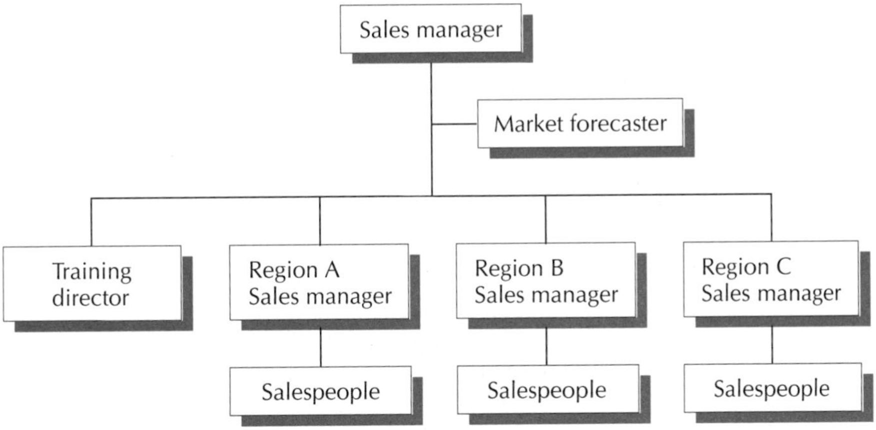

FIGURE 11-4 **A Functional Organization**

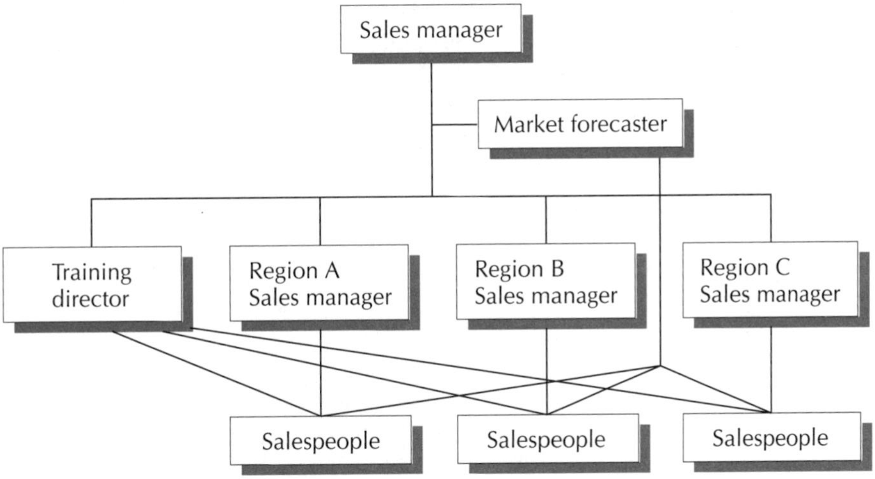

The Centralized versus Decentralized Organization

The *centralized versus decentralized organization* decision concerns the organizational location of the responsibility and authority for specific sales management tasks, such as planning, forecasting, budgeting, and recruiting. For example, RIBCO Industries, a business-to-business supply firm located in Providence, Rhode Island, allows the individual, company-owned sales branches to do most of the planning and recruitment at the local level; while sales forecasting and financial budgeting are performed at headquarters. Generally, some functions are centralized at company headquarters, while others are spread among branch or field offices. Some factors that influence the decision would be the following: cost, size of the sales force, geographic size of the market, the role of personal selling in the promotional mix, the need for decentralized inventories, and the need for service.[5]

Organizing by Specialization

In addition to the various types of sales-force organizations that have been analyzed, some firms find that additional efficiencies and economies may accrue through organization by (1) geographical specialization, (2) sales activities, (3) product specialization, (4) customer specialization, and (5) combination organizations. This form of organization is commonly referred to as *organization by specialization*.

Geographic specialization. *Geographic specialization* is the most common way to organize a business field sales force, with each territory treated virtually as a separate company or profit center. Note that three separate and distinct territories (Dallas, Chicago, and Omaha) have been established in the example of geographic organization shown in Figure 11-5. Some firms may have further breakdowns between the general sales manager and the salespeople by having branch, district, or field sales manager units. Advantages of this form of organization would include smaller territories whereby salespeople learn more about their customers and their needs; better cultivation of local markets; faster reaction time to external environmental changes; and usually, better service at less expense. Some disadvantages might include lack of the salesperson's knowledge of all business products within a line; too much time spent on business products and customers who are easier to sell; and, with the creation of multiple offices, a duplication of services and administrators.

Sales activities. A company can grow by selling additional products to present customers, or by searching for and selling to new customers for present products. Many business-to-business companies have found it useful to separate these two functions into separate sales groups, thus allowing the firm to place special emphasis on searching out and selling new accounts. The company may choose to divide the group when (1) there is significant difference in the skills needed, or (2) fast growth through acquiring new accounts is considered necessary.

Product specialization. Organization by business *product (product-line) specialization* is often reserved for large and diverse product lines where technical knowledge is important to maintain efficiency. General Electric and Westinghouse have used this structure effectively, as have IBM and Xerox. A company may have regional, district, and even area managers within each product or product-line sales force. A typical sales force organized in this manner appears in Figure 11-6. Notice that there are a product manager and salespeople for both Product A and

FIGURE 11-5 A Sales Force Organized on a Geographic Basis

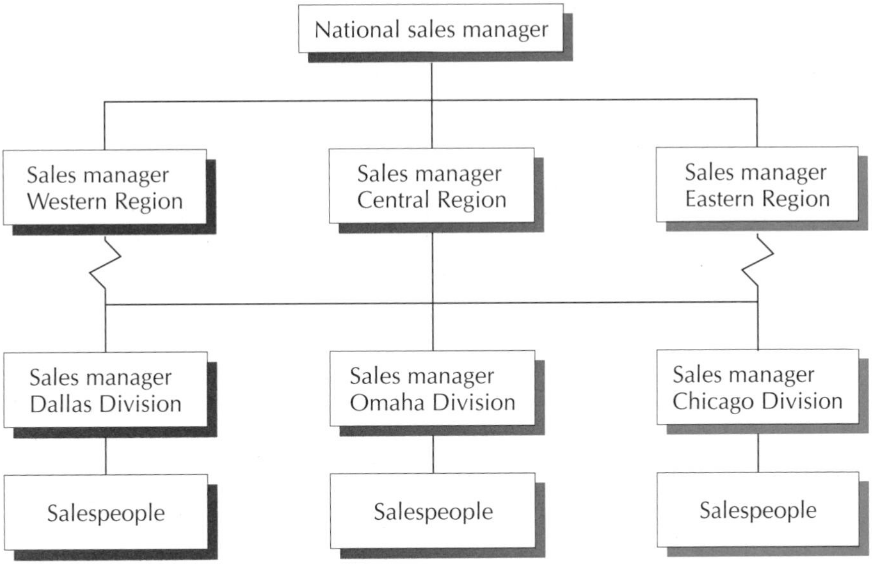

FIGURE 11-6 A Sales Force Organized on a Product Basis

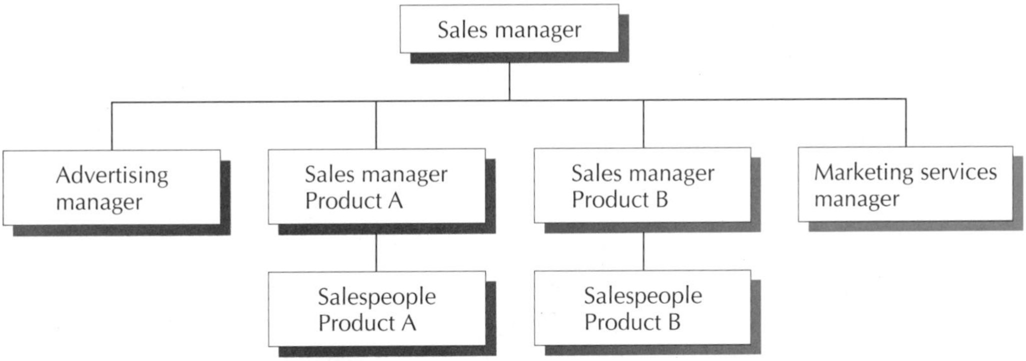

Product B, but that the advertising department and the marketing services department handle appropriate needs for both products. Product specialization allows salespeople and sales managers to concentrate their efforts on particular product lines or individual items. This allows a high degree of specialized attention, which will substantially increase the efficiency of each product or product-line sales force. It also allows for decentralization, whereby decisions can be made by those closest to the problems. On the downside, however, two or more salespeople may be calling on the same customer, which may not only upset the customer but might also cause an expensive duplication of sales effort, resulting from having more than one representative in the same geographic locality.

Customer specialization. With *customer specialization*, a salesperson sells an entire product line to selected buyers. This approach is consistent with the marketing concept, with the emphasis on customer satisfaction, as the salesperson is knowledgeable about the unique problems and needs of each group of customers. In addition, special attention is paid to major customers.[6] Greater feedback of new product ideas and new marketing methods may also accrue through the customer-oriented sales-force organization. The biggest disadvantage would be the potential for overlapping territories along with a concomitant increase in costs.

Combination organizations. Combinations of types of business sales organizations allow the company to choose the structure that best serves immediate objectives. Figure 11-7 illustrates a sales force organized by territories, products, and customers. Most firms develop some type of combination organization as they grow in size. General Foods, DuPont, and National Cash Register all use a combination sales organization.

CONCEPT QUESTIONS

1. Why are selling skills and management skills different?
2. What are the four basic methods of organizing a business sales force?

STAFFING THE BUSINESS SALES FORCE

After a company has decided upon the most appropriate manner in which to organize its sales function, it must turn its attention to the recruitment and selection of competent sales representatives. The sales manager may be very competent and refined in other skills, but he or she will be doomed to failure by hiring poorly qualified salespeople on whom training, compensation, and motivation techniques will have a negligible impact. If sales managers were given a choice of skills at which to become proficient, recruitment and selection would certainly have to be among the most popular choices.

Determining Sales-Force Size

A business-to-business firm must be as careful in buying the services of salespeople as it is in making the products that these people sell. The number of

FIGURE 11-7 **Sales Force Organized by Territories, Products, and Customers**

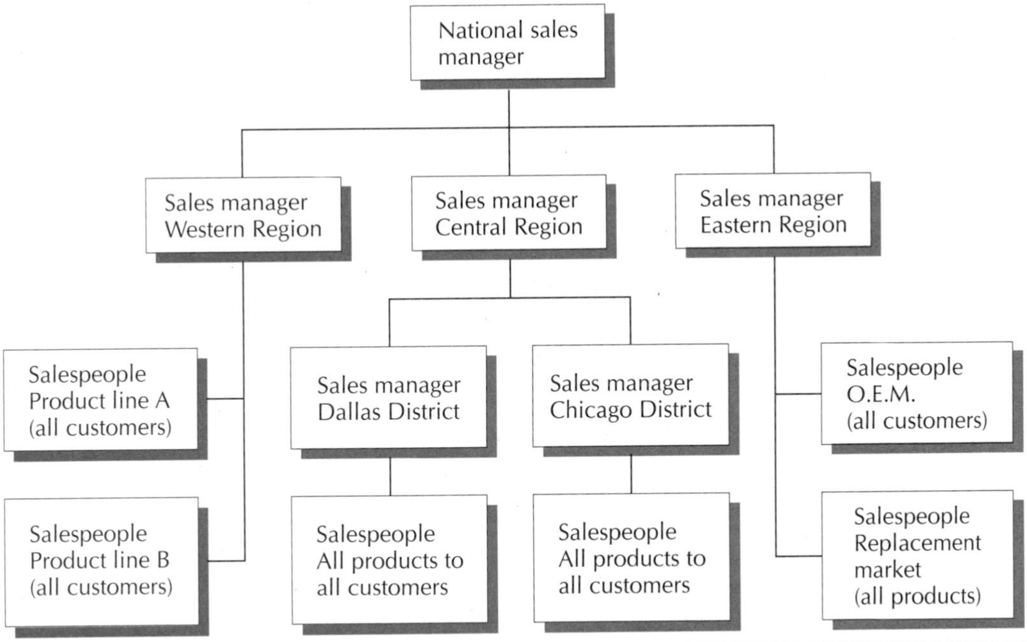

salespeople to hire depends primarily on two things: growth and turnover. Growth dictates the need for additional sales volume, while turnover creates a need for replacements. Turnover rates vary among industries: they range from a low of 5 percent for transportation equipment firms to a high of over 20 percent in business services sales forces.[7] Exceptionally high turnover levels may indicate problem areas with sales management. As noted earlier, management of the sales force is both an art and a science, with excessive turnover indicating potential problems in hiring, training, compensating, and motivating the sales force.

Turnover expected.[8] For many business-to-business firms, turnover is a persistent problem. The formula for sales-force turnover is as follows:

$$\text{Turnover} = \frac{\text{Number of salespeople hired during the period}}{\text{Average size of sales force during the period}}$$

Thus, a 50-percent turnover (which would be totally unacceptable in most business sales departments) would result if one hundred people were hired in a year, assuming the average size of the sales force was two hundred. A 50-percent turnover rate does not necessarily mean that half the sales force was replaced during a particular period of time; perhaps only fifty to seventy-five positions had to be filled, but some of these had to be replaced twice. Generally speaking, a firm can reduce the turnover rate by upgrading the job, screening more carefully, and tailoring supervision more closely to the requirements of the job. In addition to growth and turnover, other considerations involved in determining how many salespeople to hire are increases or decreases in the incidence of competitive activity, changes in products, and economic conditions.

Cundiff and Govoni identify three rational methods of approaching the problem of determining the optimal size of the sales force: the workload method, the sales-potential method, and the incremental method.[9] The "workload method," sometimes called the buildup method, categorizes accounts based on their sales and potential importance. The frequency and length of sales calls are determined for each category, with larger accounts (or those with large-volume potential) being called on often (every two weeks or perhaps once per month). Small accounts (or those with low-volume potential) may be called on every three months or longer. This method incorporates several factors in determining the number of sales personnel needed, including:[10]

- Number of accounts in the territory
- Number of sales to be made
- Frequency of sales calls on given customers
- Time intervals between sales calls
- Travel time around the territory
- Nonselling time

The number of accounts multiplied by the call frequency equals the total number of sales calls per year that must be made by the sales force. The necessary interview time is estimated by subtracting time devoted to nonselling activities (such as travel time) from total work time available. The necessary interview time is found by adding together the total time needed for each customer category. In the final step, the yearly interview time available to a sales representative is divided into the total number of hours of customer interview time the firm needs. The result is a fairly accurate estimate of the number of salespeople needed. This method, although simple and easy to use, does not recognize the fact that all customers do not have similar characteristics and requirements.[11]

In the "sales potential method," the yearly sales volume is divided by the volume each salesperson can be expected to sell. The resulting number is adjusted for turnover among sales-force personnel and territorial differences in travel time. A major drawback of this method is that sales volume depends on the number of salespeople selling for the firm.[12]

The "incremental method" of determining sales-force size is based on the assumption that an additional salesperson may be hired if profit contributions from sales made by that person exceed the costs of hiring that person. The major element to consider is total incremental or marginal cost relative to the incremental or marginal revenue of the territory. This method is theoretically attractive but impractical because of the difficulties encountered in estimating marginal sales directly produced by the added salesperson, in addition to the difficulty of estimating marginal costs and costs of production and distribution.[13]

Finally, other factors (including instinct) must also be considered when estimating the number of salespeople needed in the next year or two. Other internal and external conditions, including the level of economic activity and labor relations, may impact the decision heavily.

Recruitment and Selection

Once business sales managers have determined the size of the sales force, they must then become concerned with the *recruitment and selection process*. The task of "recruiting" is to find and attract qualified applicants for sales positions, while "selection" is a screening or sequential filtering process whereby candidates who do not meet the hiring criteria are not given further consideration.

Recruitment

The task of finding and attracting qualified applicants for sales positions is a difficult, time-consuming task, with improved sales recruiting being a major goal of most business sales managers. The cost of inefficient sales recruiting will not only drain company resources but will also cause an inordinate amount of time to be spent in this process. An important first step in the recruitment process is to analyze the job thoroughly and to prepare a list of qualifications needed for successful performance. Such a process tends to ensure that new recruits have a reasonably good chance of being successful in a particular sales situation. Three specific procedures should be followed at this point in the process: (1) conduct a job analysis; (2) prepare a written job description; and (3) develop sales job qualifications for selectees (*job specification*).

Conduct a job analysis. A *job analysis* refers to a careful and objective study and written summary of the business-to-business selling job in question. It includes a definition of roles or activities to be performed and the determination of the personal qualifications needed for the position. It is commonly used in the preparation of job descriptions, the writing of job specifications, recruitment and selection, performance evaluations, training and development, and compensation.

Prepare a written job description. As noted above, the job analysis is used, among other things, to develop a job description. A *job description* details the components of the sales job and the functions or activities salespeople must perform, such as prospecting, travelling, selling, and providing service assistance. The job description should be committed to paper; should be acceptable to salespeople and management; and should be specific, inclusive, short, and easy to read. In summary, it is a detailed statement of the job in terms of specific functions and activities. It is a profile of the sales job, showing the functions that must be performed, and how much time, effort, and attention should be placed on each function or activity of the job.

Develop sales job qualifications. The duties and responsibilities outlined in the job description should now be put into a set of qualifications that the job seeker should have in order to perform the sales job satisfactorily. The qualifications spell out critical characteristics needed; these would include decisiveness, energy and enthusiasm, maturity, assertiveness, sensitivity, and openness, among others. Some positions would require a high level of enthusiasm, while others might involve little supervision, possibly necessitating the hiring of a mature, experienced person.

Sources of sales recruits. Several sources of sales recruits are often used, with referrals coming from both outside the company through friends, customers, and suppliers, as well as from internal sources. The most frequently used sources are (1) company sources, (2) company salespeople, (3) educational institutions, (4) professional associations, (5) suppliers and customers, (6) employment agencies, and (7) advertisements. Each can be compared, once enough time has elapsed to determine which method gets the best recruit for the money spent.

Selection

Once the firm has accumulated a pool of candidates, the next step is to select and lure the best business salespeople for the job at hand. Figure 11-8 shows how hiring criteria for sales jobs are used to guide the process of selecting salespeople from a pool of available applicants. Too often, sales managers think of the managerial function of hiring as a one-way decision; whereas, it is really only effective when it involves decision making on the part of the applicant as well as management. Both parties have a financial stake in making the right decision. The company desires to select the type of salesperson who will succeed and remain with the organization, thereby eliminating, or at least minimizing, the considerable costs of training replacement personnel. The applicant is gambling a segment of his or her occupational lifetime in the hope of realizing an optimal return. Information retrieved from application forms, interviews, background checks, and tests is compared with a set of hiring criteria; those who best meet such standards receive the job offers; those who do not are rejected. Usually the process begins with a review of the application forms, then moves on to interviews and background checks, and concludes with some psychological and achievement tests.

While firms might vary in the time sequence of the steps outlined above, the selection interview inevitably becomes the final step in the employment decision. The sales manager must now resolve moot points, make judgments on

FIGURE 11-8 **A Model for Selecting Salespeople**

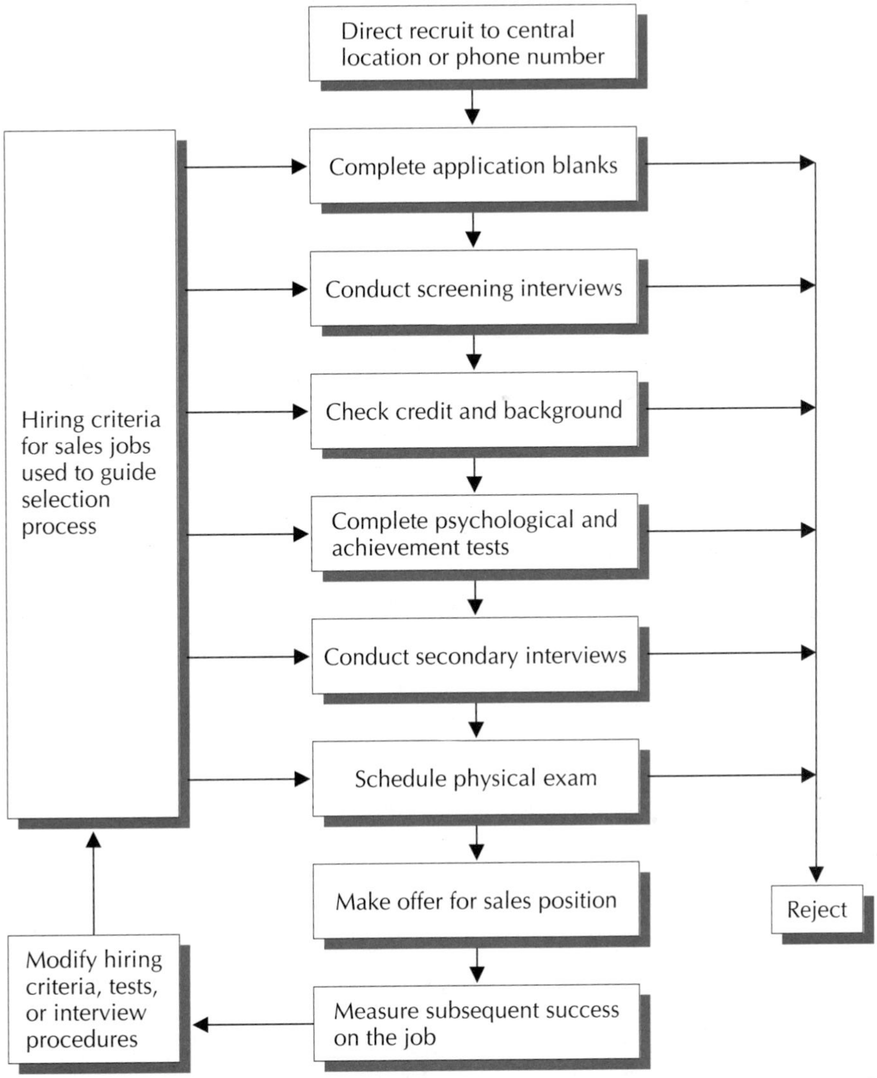

Source: Douglas J. Dalrymple and Leonard J. Parsons, *Marketing Management: Strategy and Cases* (4th ed.), p. 675, copyright © 1990 John Wiley & Sons, Inc. Reprinted by permission of John Wiley & Sons, Inc.

the capabilities and overall talents of the candidates, and decide whether or not a candidate will fit as a member of the sales team. At the same time, there are many legal and ethical restrictions on the uses of various traditional selection tools. Also, if applicants are rejected, they should feel that the rejection was in the best interests of both the company and themselves.

TRAINING AND DEVELOPING THE BUSINESS SALES FORCE

Now that sales representatives have been properly recruited and carefully selected, the sales manager (either directly or indirectly) has the responsibility of training and developing the sales force. Successful sales managers direct their training efforts with methods that enhance the productivity of the salespeople under their supervision.[14] Willie Loman, the tragic 1940s hero of Arthur Miller's *Death of a Salesman,* worked for a small family-owned business. In preparation for his selling position, he received only a calling card and a sample case; the rest was up to him. Willie represented the end of a somewhat romanticized era for salespeople, as today the business salesperson needs more than friends, a good shoe shine, and a pleasant style to obtain orders. *Sales training* is imperative and must be conducted on a continuous basis. Even the best, most experienced salesperson requires training on product knowledge, competition, and new selling techniques, along with the development of a host of other mandatory knowledge and skills. To be successful, salespeople need training in many different topical areas in addition to product knowledge, policies, and procedures.[15]

Purposes of Sales Training

Companies are primarily interested in training to increase sales, productivity, and profits. H. O. Crafford, president of Plantations Plastics, Riverside, Rhode Island, expressed this interest in the following way:

> I support training, retraining, and other development activities that will achieve results. I am interested in and will support activities that provide rewards to the employee, higher return to the stockholders, and enable continued growth of the business. In other words, I am interested in that which affects the bottom line. Although training cannot always be evaluated as readily as some other functions, better training is eventually reflected in on-the-job results.[16]

At Plantations Plastics, all sales trainees spend one week in basic orientation ("Boot Camp" as Mr. Crafford calls it) and two weeks in the factory actually working on the production line. After this initial training, the trainee spends one month in a specific sales territory, after which he or she spends two additional weeks at the plant. During this two-week period, the trainee works in order processing, customer service, and telemarketing.

Finally, the trainee is assigned to a specific territory, working under the close supervision of a territory sales manager. The trainee is encouraged to continue his or her education (technical and/or commercial skills at company expense) and is required to attend seminars at company headquarters held on a quarterly basis.

There are specific purposes of training other than improving general sales volume. These purposes tend to relate to the type of training being offered and include the following:

- To improve morale, thereby reducing absenteeism and turnover.
- To create and foster an information flow from headquarters or the field-sales office to the salesperson, and to encourage feedback from the salesperson.
- To improve knowledge of the product, the competition, and the customer; to improve time and territory management; and to improve selling techniques.
- To increase sales of a particular product, product line, or customer category.
- To encourage and develop future sales managers.

All training programs should be designed and conducted with specific purposes or goals in mind. In order to provide adequate training for all members of the business sales force, a comprehensive program needs to be established that will provide instruction in the skills and information needed by such a sales force. Training and retraining should never be done just to say that one has such a program, as such thinking might well be self-defeating, and the more senior members might reject it. Hire the right salespeople, train them well, retrain them when appropriate, and the sales management task will generally become somewhat easier. The objectives of many training programs reflect new selling strategies. For example, the major goal of DuPont's sales training is "to make would-be representatives aware of the importance of developing customer relationships."[17] DuPont's trainees focus heavily on learning everything possible about their customers' businesses.

What the Training Program Should Cover

The basic principle in relation to sales training priorities has been to direct the major part of training to those areas deemed necessary for the business salesperson to do an adequate selling job. However, as sales organizations become more complex, more computerized, and more international, this role of the sales manager in a training effort is compounded, and new priorities may have to be set. The sales manager must choose and rank priorities in deciding what information to impart, what skills to teach, and when to teach them. Although specific content will vary, an analysis of training needs usually reveals the necessity of training in a combination of the following general areas: (1) company knowledge, (2) product knowledge, (3) selling techniques, (4) customer knowledge, (5) competitive knowledge, and (6) time and territory management.

Company knowledge. A prospect will want to know if the firm will stand behind its product offerings, so salespeople without basic knowledge of their companies may give the impression of incompetence on the part of the entire organization. Facts about the firm's history, size, and reputation provide needed assurances, especially to the customer contemplating the purchase of expensive equipment that will require costly installation and servicing. Also, knowledge of the firm's history and capabilities can increase morale, confidence, and efficiency among the firm's sales representatives. Policy on allowable returns, advertising allowances, freight costs, payment terms, cancellation penalties, and minimum orders should be known and understood by the salesperson.

Product knowledge. Because of the importance of product knowledge in addition to the accelerating nature of technological change, most business sales managers provide ongoing or continuous product training to their respective sales forces. Product information stressed in company training programs tends to highlight special features, end uses, applications, and optional equipment. Also stressed would be advantages compared to competitive offerings. Product features must be turned into customer benefits, which means that the salesperson must have enough product knowledge to feel confident in presenting the goods or services.

Additionally, when a firm changes the organizational structure—say, from a sales organization built around products to a market-oriented organization—additional training for experienced sales representatives may be needed. Xerox Corporation has retrained four thousand of its sales representatives who sell the firm's entire product line. The firm changed to a market-oriented organizational structure; to implement this strategy, it spent close to $20 million annually on its sales training program.[18]

Selling techniques. To be successful, selling techniques must be based on how people buy; most sales managers believe that a logical, sequential series of steps exists that, if followed, will convert a prospect into a customer. The "selling process" is an adaptation by a salesperson to the decision process of business buyers; it is a starting point in understanding the use of numerous persuasive communications techniques. Business sales managers (or trainers) teach the use and application of several broad selling techniques involving selling benefits, using benefits, being organized, qualifying prospects, obtaining appointments, and employing proper presentation format, among others. Salespeople, both beginners and "old pros" alike, must be reminded that selling is a process that starts with prospecting, moves forward through several steps to the sale, and ends with follow-up and service.

Customer knowledge. Sales trainees are taught who the customers are, where they are, and how important they are. Experienced business salespeople need additional essential knowledge concerning changes in the segments in which they are selling and trends and changes that might be noted over time, which also need to be addressed. Sales by product or product line should be reviewed for each customer or customer class, noting trends that are up or down, and why such is the case. Each major customer or prospect is studied, with discussions centered on members of the buying center, buying policies and procedures, buyer attitudes, and strategies to be employed either to sell the prospect, or to expand sales to present customers. Market research findings are shared with salespeople, exploring test market results, product and competitive sales, and buyer behavior findings.

Competitive knowledge. New sales recruits must be introduced to different types of customers, their needs, their buying motives, and their buying habits. Sales management must provide information on competitors' products, policies, services, competitive advantages and disadvantages, warranties, and credit policies, among other things. "Know thy competition" is wise counsel to both recruits and seasoned sales professionals alike. Does the company's copier cost more than competitors', run faster, last longer? Will your company's automatic packaging machinery, while costing more initially, run longer and with less service or breakdowns than the competitor's machinery? Does your refuse removal company pick up daily, while the competition picks up once or twice a week? Questions such as these must be answered in any honest appraisal of the competition. Accurate knowledge allows the salesperson to approach prospects with the greatest needs for your product or service. Accurate competitive knowledge allows the business salesperson to feel more confident and to present product features and benefits more forcefully and more effectively. Knowledge increases the probability of success, while ignorance increases the probability of failure.[19]

Time and territory management. A *sales territory* represents a group of current and potential customers. In order to achieve optimum efficiency and effectiveness in servicing accounts within a specific territory, salespeople must plan and control activities carefully. An effective business sales manager and/or trainer knows that prime selling time is too precious to waste. The problem of effective time and territory management is particularly important for territorial salespeople, as the cost of a salesperson's time has been increasing steadily and rapidly over the past several years. It has been broadly estimated that the cost of a business sales call today exceeds $250, so selling effectiveness in the light of escalating selling costs has resulted in a focus on time and territory management as a top-priority training endeavor.

Who Should Do The Training?

Business sales training programs are normally conducted at a central companywide site by professional trainers, in the field by branch managers and sales personnel, and by private consulting organizations and professional trainers. In general, the training site, the relative sophistication of the facilities, and the professionalism of the trainers are determined by the particular training needs involved and by the size of the firm's sales training budget. One study indicates that about 63 percent of all company sales training programs are in-house, about

6 percent are outside only, and the remaining 31 percent involve both in-house and outside personnel.[20] The following sections will cover the three most widely used modes of sales training.

Home office sales training. Many large firms have a *sales training department* that acts as a sort of nerve center for all sales training activities undertaken by the company. Most of these centralized training facilities are designed to supplement the basic sales training done in the field by a field sales manager or branch manager, acting as a liaison between the home office and the field. Training policies and procedures for the entire sales organization emanate from this training unit, and the sales training director usually reports to either the national sales manager or the vice president of sales. (For example, Uarco, Incorporated, has its home office training facility located in Barrington, Illinois, and ADP has its facility in northern New Jersey.) These centralized training units concentrate on "professionalizing" the selling skills of sales representatives who have several months or even many years of experience, in addition to training field sales managers wishing and/or needing to update their training skills. These facilities have classrooms, closed-circuit television and videotapes, projection equipment, and nearby facilities for housing trainees during the course of the training period.

Many small companies cannot afford to hire staff trainers. This fact, along with the tendency of staff trainers to schedule far more training than is required, necessitates close supervision of trainees to minimize this potential problem.

Field or local sales training. *Field or local sales training* exposes the trainee to the real-world business sales environment, whereby the techniques learned in a formal training session can be tried, with additional necessary training being pinpointed and provided as necessary. A note of caution is in order here. Too many companies put new salespeople in out-of-the-way corners of field sales offices, providing little attention, supervision, and training, while expecting sales orientation and training to take place automatically through absorption of the sales office atmosphere. This mentality and "modus operandi" should be avoided, as trainees may feel disillusioned and may question their choice of employment. However, on the plus side of the ledger, field or local sales training moves the learning process closer to the customers. It introduces a measure of realism, as the recruit will observe top salespeople selling to customers similar to those they will encounter in their own, yet-to-be-determined territories.

Private consulting organizations and professional trainers. Many *private consulting firms* provide sales training services that are sold to business and industry and are conducted by professional trainers, most of whom have extensive experience in the areas they teach. Most private consultants who provide sales training services develop programs tailored to the client's products, personnel, and sales policies. These programs are given periodically, and the charge to the firm is normally negotiated on a per-student basis. Many outside suppliers exist, but perhaps the most popular are Learning International, Wilson Learning Corporation,

Forum Company, and Dale Carnegie. Learning International, for example, has worked with 80 percent of the Fortune 500 business-to-business corporations. Dale Carnegie conducts programs that are licensed through franchises. Many companies, such as DuPont, use more than one outside supplier.[21] In addition to consulting organizations, many business schools within institutions of higher learning provide sales training for businesses on a fee basis. Trainers are typically business school faculty members, and the price approximates that charged by private firms. Bryant College in Smithfield, Rhode Island, with its Center for Management Development, along with the Daniel Management Center at the University of South Carolina, the Center for Professional Development at Clemson University, and the Management Development Center at the University of Tulsa, among others, are recognized for their expertise in sales training, along with a host of other disciplines and specialty areas offered. Some institutions of higher learning provide training of this kind not only as a service to the business community, but also as a partial answer to financial exigency.

Evaluating Sales Training

The costs of sales training are substantial, with the sales training budgets of many large business-to-business companies involving hundreds of thousands of dollars or more. Whether or not this investment is paying off presents the problem of determining and, where possible, measuring the contributions made through sales training. A three-step evaluation process is suggested at this point:

(1) Set objectives (both overall and specific) for the company sales training program.
(2) Determine whether the objectives as set are being met, or have already been met.
(3) Try to measure the effect of training on profitability.

Some objectives cannot be measured, or at the very least, are difficult to measure; while other performance criteria can be measured without much difficulty. Some criteria that a firm might measure in order to demonstrate the effectiveness of a sales training program are listed in Exhibit 11-1. Although not all these criteria will be used by every company, many will be helpful in evaluating the effectiveness of a sales training program.

A training program is designed to take a salesperson from the present level of competence to some desired level of proficiency. If the program is successful, objectives will have been met, and the salesperson will be able to perform some new skills successfully. If performance is not up to expectations, then perhaps parts of the training program should be changed. Both these scenarios suggest that the sales executive must constantly review current training programs to see if they are still pertinent, relevant, and practical. If a particular training program has remained exactly the same over a long period of time, it is entirely possible

EXHIBIT 11-1 **Specific Criteria to Measure When Determining the Effectiveness of Sales Training**

Absenteeism	Number of calls
Average commission per sale	Number of lost customers
Average size of the sale	Percentage of objections overcome
Average time to "break even"	Product mix sold
Bad-debt ratio	Qualitative call improvement
Competitive investigations	Ratio of carload sales to total sales
Complaint letters	Referral rate
Compliment letters	Reduced cost of training
Developing new product demand	Reduced training time
Earnings of salespeople	Reduction in legal actions
Implementation of promotional programs	Sales-force turnover
Improvement in sales-rank position	Sales forecasting accuracy
Improvement of call quality	Sales/phone call ratio
Increased active selling time	Sales/travel ratio
Items per order	Sales volume
New customers per week/month	Volume increase for existing accounts
New/old customer ratio	Volume of returned merchandise

Source: C. Robert Patty, *Sales Manager's Handbook*, Reston Publishing Company, 1982, pp. 118–120. Used with permission.

that it no longer satisfies the needs of the marketplace, the company, and the salespeople. Frequent evaluation and reevaluation help to assure that training needs and development programs remain sensitive to the changing internal and external environment.

Learning International suggests measuring the effect of the training it provides by using a control group (which is not involved in the program) and an experimental group (which receives the training). The calculation of training benefits is as follows:

$$\text{TE} = \frac{\text{CES} - \text{CCS}}{100 + \text{CCS}}$$

where: TE = Training Effect
CES = Change in Environmental Training Group (%)
CCS = Change in Control Group (%)

For example, the training group in a specialty industrial chemicals firm increased its sales by 13.4 percent, while sales in the control group rose by only 6.4 percent. The training effect was then a 6.5 percent increase, measured as follows:

$$\text{TE} = \frac{13.4 - 6.4}{100 + 6.4} = \frac{7.0}{106.4} = 6.5\%$$

If the two groups were well matched at the start of the training "experiment," the result can be attributed to the training program. A disadvantage of this method is that it does not demonstrate how long the effects of the training will last.[22]

CONCEPT QUESTIONS

1. What is the best-known quantitative method for staffing the business sales force?
2. What are some common purposes of business sales training?

DIRECTING AND MOTIVATING THE BUSINESS SALES FORCE

At this point, it is generally assumed that the business sales manager has hired capable salespeople, has trained them well, has effectively organized the sales force, and has assigned these salespeople to territories that will optimize sales. Now the sales manager must effectively direct and motivate each salesperson to capitalize fully on his or her potential. Is the sales quota system fair? Is the compensation system important? Is it fair? All these factors and more will play an important part in a sales force's performance; and while it may sound simple in theory, in reality it is very difficult for sales managers to accomplish. This section of the chapter will attempt to present many of the interrelated factors that influence sales-force performance; it will also identify what can be done to achieve optimal performance from the members of the business sales force.

Providing Leadership

Leadership can be referred to as getting others to work willingly and enthusiastically to achieve the objectives of the organization. It is not just good management; it is also a matter of establishing values, sharing visions, creating enthusiasm, maintaining focus on a few clear objectives, and building a sales force that works as a team. The box entitled "Business-to-Business Marketing in Action" describes how Strong Tool Company of Cleveland, Ohio, has developed both its inside and outside sales staffs into an integrated team. Successful business sales managers vary greatly in style, from autocratic to laissez-faire leadership. Figure 11-9 indicates some of the trade-offs between the use of authority by the sales manager and the amount of freedom allowed the salesperson;

BUSINESS-TO-BUSINESS MARKETING IN ACTION

BUILDING A SALES STAFF INTO A TEAM

Your outside salespeople boast that they are the ones who bring in the business. On the other hand, the inside salespeople claim that without them, the accounts would never be maintained. Sound familiar?

Bill Gerhauser, operations manager at Strong Tool Company in Cleveland, Ohio, says his company tries to ease the tension between the two sales staffs by having the inside salespeople meet with their assigned outside counterparts at least once every business day.

Says Gerhauser, "Our goal is to open the lines of communication so each side understands the other's problems. The fact is that it's possible to be an inside salesperson and not understand the big picture. The problem we have is that instead of explaining how our customers operate, the outside salespeople often assume that the inside salespeople already have this knowledge."

To remedy this situation, Gerhauser notes that on a selective basis, Strong Tool's outside salespeople bring inside salespeople along with them on their sales calls. Gerhauser says it's hard to put a dollar value on the success of the program but maintains that the tactic works, particularly on the more complicated accounts.

"We make it clear to our outside salespeople that taking an inside salesperson along with them on an account is simply one option they can use in putting together a sales program," Gerhauser explains. "But for building rapport with an important customer, you can't beat it."

John Monoky, a sales consultant from Toledo, Ohio, says that while some distributors have opted for a strategy similar to Strong Tool's during the past few years, many still experience poor relations between the two sales departments. He claims that a large portion of this animosity stems from managers who narrowly view the inside sales function.

Notes Monoky, "Distributors ask their inside people to sell, but don't give them any exposure to what they are selling, or provide the necessary sales training. Then they hold up the prize of an outside sales job. Just because someone is an excellent inside salesperson doesn't mean they will succeed out in the field."

Monoky maintains that one way to build a sales staff that works well together is to take a hard look at the types of personalities that succeed in sales positions. For example, Monoky says that the best outside salespeople are good time managers, have excellent verbal skills, and are entrepreneurial in nature.

"These are the people who work best in an environment which permits a great deal of freedom," Monoky adds," the kind of individuals who enjoy dealing with people face to face."

Conversely, the profile of an inside salesperson is one who's detail oriented, works best in a structured environment, enjoys working over the telephone, and is managerial in nature.

"The classic personality for an inside salesperson is the kind of person who would love to spend their day playing with a personal computer," Monoky notes.

Source: Steve Zurier, "Build a Sales Staff that Works as a Team," *Industrial Distribution,* 77 (April 1988), p. 67. Used with permission.

FIGURE 11-9 **A Continuum of Leadership Styles for Sales Managers**

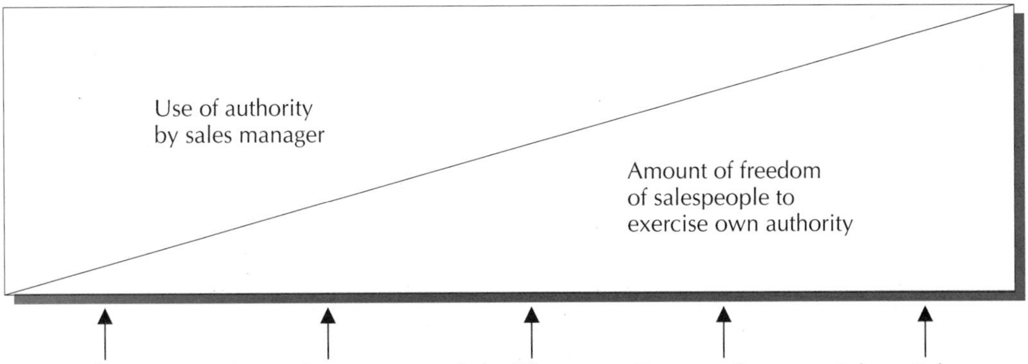

Autocratic
Sales manager makes all decisions. Rewards and punishes, depending on compliance.

Persuader
Sales manager makes all decisions, but recognizes they must often be sold to the sales force.

Consultive
Sales manager asks for ideas of salespeople but still makes final decisions.

Democratic
Sales manager serves as moderator of discussion and allows sales force to make decision.

Laissez-Faire
Sales manager exercises little control. Committed to implementing whatever decision is made.

Source: Harvard Business Review, "How to Choose a Leadership Pattern," by Robert Tannenbaum and Warren H. Schmidt (May/June 1973). Copyright 1973 by the President and Fellows of Harvard College: All rights reserved.

Exhibit 11-2 discusses some of the more important characteristics of both strong and weak leadership.

It should be noted that any one particular sales manager may use a variety of leadership styles, depending on whom they are dealing with. A particular sales manager may be autocratic but friendly with a new sales trainee; democratic with an experienced employee who has many good ideas; and laissez-faire with a trusted, long-term employee. Much research has been conducted in an ongoing effort to find out what makes a person an effective leader. There is no such thing as leadership traits that are effective in all situations, nor are there leadership styles that always work best. The style that should be used at a particular time depends on the sales manager, the salespeople, and both the internal and external macro and micro environments faced.

Sales Quotas

A *sales quota* is simply a goal; something that is set for a particular product line, division, or sales representative. It is a management tool that, if correctly used, should stimulate the sales effort in terms of physical units, dollars, or both. Quotas can be a powerful means of motivating salespeople if handled correctly. There are several different uses for quotas, including: (1) to provide

EXHIBIT 11-2 The Twelve Golden Rules and the Seven Deadly Sins of Leadership

1. *Set a good example.* Your subordinates will take their cue from you. If your work habits are good, theirs are likely to be too.
2. *Give your people a set of objectives and a sense of direction.* Good people seldom like to work aimlessly from day to day. They want to know not only what they're doing but why.
3. *Keep your people informed* of new developments at the company and how they'll affect them. Let people know where they stand with you. Let your close assistants in on your plans at an early stage. Let people know as early as possible of any changes that'll affect them. Let them know of changes that won't affect them but about which they may be worrying.
4. *Ask your people for advice.* Let them know that they have a say in your decisions whenever possible. Make them feel a problem is their problem, too. Encourage individual thinking.
5. *Let your people know that you support them.* There's no greater morale killer than a boss who resents a subordinate's ambition.
6. *Don't give orders.* Suggest, direct, and request.
7. *Emphasize skills, not rules.* Judge results, not methods. Give a person a job to do and let him or her do it. Let an employee improve his or her own job methods.
8. *Give credit where credit is due.* Appreciation for a job well done is the most appreciated of "fringe benefits."
9. *Praise in public.* This is where it'll do the most good.
10. *Criticize in private.*
11. *Criticize constructively.* Concentrate on correction, not blame. Allow a person to retain his or her dignity. Suggest specific steps to prevent recurrence of the mistake. Forgive and encourage desired results.
12. *Make it known that you welcome new ideas.* No idea is too small for a hearing or too wild for consideration. Make it easy for them to communicate their ideas to you. Follow through on their ideas.

The Seven Sins of Leadership

On the other hand, these items can cancel any constructive image you might try to establish.

1. *Trying to be liked rather than respected.* Don't accept favors from your subordinates. Don't do special favors trying to be liked. Don't try for popular decisions. Don't be soft about discipline. Have a sense of humor. Don't give up.
2. *Failing to ask subordinates for their advice and help.*
3. *Failing to develop a sense of responsibility in subordinates.* Allow freedom of expression. Give each person a chance to learn his or her superior's job. When you give responsibility, give authority too. Hold subordinates accountable for results.
4. *Emphasizing rules rather than skill.*
5. *Failing to keep criticism constructive.* When something goes wrong, do you do your best to get all the facts first? Do you control your temper? Do you praise before you criticize? Do you listen to the other side of the story?
6. *Not paying attention to employee gripes and complaints.* Make it easy for them to come to you. Get rid of red tape. Explain the grievance machinery. Help a person voice his or her complaint. Always grant a hearing. Practice patience. Ask a complainant what he or she wants you to do. Don't render a hasty or biased judgment. Get all the facts. Let the complainant know what your decision is. Double-check your results. Be concerned.
7. *Failing to keep people informed.*

Source: "To Become an Effective Executive, Develop Leadership and Other Skills," *Marketing News* (April 1984), p. 1. Used with permission.

incentive, (2) to provide a basis for compensation, and (3) to evaluate a salesperson's performance.

Quotas are based on company and sales objectives that are established during a particular planning process, with quotas being determined for virtually any result and time period relevant to a particular selling job. Quotas can be in the form of sales quotas, expense quotas, profit quotas, or activity quotas. Quotas must be established fairly, be within the reach of salespeople, be easy to understand and control, and be consistent with company revenue goals. Sales quotas are a quantitative tool that must be used to direct, control, motivate, and evaluate sales activities and salespeople. Sales quotas should uncover strengths and weaknesses in the selling structure, improve the compensation plan's effectiveness, control selling expenses, and enhance sales contents. Finally, many business sales and marketing managers advocate the joint setting of quotas between sales managers and salespersons. If the salesperson has no part in the establishment of the quota, there is less chance that the quota will be a meaningful motivator, as the quota may be judged as being too high or too low.

Compensation

Employees listen closely when the president of Electro-Scientific Industries in Portland, Oregon, reports sales and profits, with few in the audience not grasping the subtleties of before-tax and after-tax profits. This degree of awareness is not surprising, as the employees are paid 25 percent of the before-tax profits each quarter, with a fourth of that going straight into their pockets and the rest into retirement or stock ownership accounts. They are not alone. Raychem, Tektronix, Johnson Wax, Lowe's Companies, Hewlett-Packard, Goldman-Sachs, Marion Labs, Readers' Digest, and Quad/Graphics, among others, are paying out some portion of before-tax profits to all employees, either outright or into trusts.[23]

A sound, solid, equitable compensation plan is essential to successful management of the business sales force. However, there is some confusion and disagreement about the role of financial incentives as motivators. Some sales managers feel that salespeople are motivated strictly by financial rewards, while others feel that financial compensation is relatively unimportant as a true motivator of behavior. An accurate analysis probably lies somewhere in between these two extremes. In terms of payment plans, the trend seems to be away from straight-salary and straight-commission compensation plans. Today, most company sales compensation plans feature salary plus incentive in the form of a commission or a bonus, as Table 11-1 indicates.

Most discussions with sales executives would reveal a consensus that (1) compensation is the most important element in motivating a sales force; and (2) a properly designed and applied compensation package must be geared to both the needs of the company and the products and services the firm sells, while at the same time allowing the company to attract good business salespeople and keep them motivated to produce at increasing rates. Although compensation is clearly fundamental to the motivation of salespeople, the issue is far more complicated than simple payment rewards. The amount of satisfaction and the sense of personal achievement that individuals feel from performing tasks are also important for motivation. It is suggested that the motivation of sales team members can be achieved through the following additional factors:

(1) Task clarity.

(2) Recognition of achievement of short-term objectives with incentive pay (bonuses, stock options, and so on).

TABLE 11-1 **Alternative Sales Compensation and Incentive Plans, 1985**

Method	All Industries 1985	All Industries 1984	Consumer Products 1985	Business Products 1985	Other Commercial Industry 1985
Straight salary	17.4%	17.1%	9.3%	14.1%	30.4%
Draw against commission	6.5	6.8	7.5	6.0	7.0
Salary plus commission	30.7	29.0	22.4	35.8	23.4
Salary plus individual bonus	33.7	33.6	45.8	32.5	29.3
Salary plus group bonus	2.7	2.3	4.7	2.1	2.9
Salary plus commission plus individual or group bonus	9.0	11.2	10.3	9.5	7.0
Total	100.0%	100.0%	100.0%	100.0%	100.0%

Note: Some year-to-year differences reflect changes in the organizations reporting.

Source: "Alternative Sales Compensation and Incentive Plans, 1985," May 6, 1984, by the New York Times Company. Reprinted by permission.

(3) Recognition of achievement of long-term objectives with status-enhancing rewards (title, promotions, and the like).

(4) Job enrichment rewards (trips to professional conferences).

The motivational impact of the above factors relate to both monetary incentives and peer and public recognition of achievement. Thus, a more broad-based and relevant motivational effect is achieved.

SALES-FORCE ANALYSIS AND EVALUATION

All firms evaluate their salespeople—whether the firm is large or small; whether it is in consumer, business-to-business, government, or export sales; whether it sells goods or services; and whether it employs one or several thousand salespeople. The evaluation may be formal or informal, the form may be simple or complex, and its conclusions may be based on objective criteria or on executive opinion. Whatever its scope, sales-force analysis and evaluation takes place in all companies, because without it the supervision of salespeople is impossible.

Why Analyze and Evaluate Salespeople?

What does a sales manager expect to accomplish through sales-force analyses and evaluations? The following list suggests desired outcomes:

(1) To determine areas where each salesperson needs improvement.

(2) To assess the validity of the standards used.

(3) To spot people who are ready for promotion, salary raises, or assignment to new territories and responsibilities.

(4) To supply evidence on salespeople who should be disciplined or terminated.

(5) To check the effectiveness of the sales compensation plan, training, supervision, recruitment, territory assignments, and operating procedures.

An evaluation plan should be tailored to the specific company for which it is being used. In one company, sales calls made per day may be an important criterion of performance, while in another it may be the number of new accounts opened. Regardless of what specific tasks are being analyzed and evaluated, the overall evaluation program should be realistic, motivational, participatory, flexible, and specific. It is better to have no formal analysis and evaluation program than to have a poorly designed and administered one.

Who Should Analyze and Evaluate Salespeople?

Most business sales managers would agree that the salesperson's immediate superior should be the primary evaluator. Most evaluations would include constructive criticism as supplied by the immediate supervisor; they would also include recommendations for any raises and promotions. Some companies use an entire regional management group and a home office personnel specialist to evaluate salespeople, as shown in Figure 11-10. The specialist would ensure that approved evaluation procedures are followed and that each person being evaluated is treated fairly.

FIGURE 11-10 **Possible Management Input into Performance Evaluation of a Salesperson**

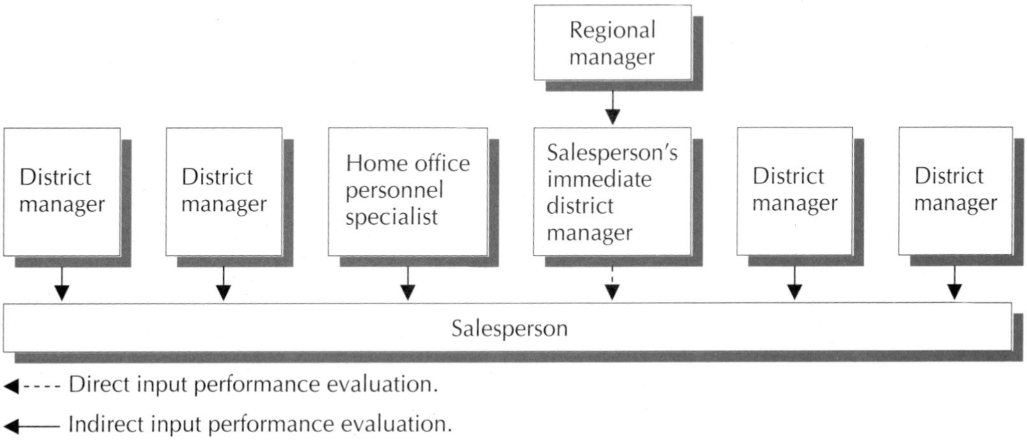

Source: Table, p. 699, from *Sales Management,* Second Edition, by Charles Futrell, Copyright © 1988 by The Dryden Press, A Division of Holt, Rinehart and Winston, Inc., Reprinted by permission of the publisher.

When Should Analysis and Evaluation Be Done?

Informal evaluation should be almost a daily occurrence, as mistakes made should be brought to the salesperson's attention as soon as possible. Other than for routine corrections, a formal evaluation program should be conducted on a regular basis. The primary determinants of the frequency of formal evaluation should be determined by the time required to evaluate and the activities involved in the evaluation cycle. As a general rule, a minimum of one formal evaluation should be completed yearly for each salesperson.

MANAGING U.S. SALESPEOPLE IN INTERNATIONAL MARKETS

To develop an effective sales organization in another country, the business sales manager must appreciate and understand the sales manager–salesperson roles and the expectations of salespeople in that country. Such relationships differ from one country to the next. The U.S. philosophy, which emphasizes individuals' theoretical control over their own destinies, is completely alien to other cultures. U.S. salespeople expect pay based on merit and promotion in accordance with performance compared to other salespeople in the same firm. In other nations, such as Japan, the sales manager–salesperson relationship may be much like a family relationship—the salesperson expects job security, seniority, and reward for loyalty.[24]

After formulating a policy for the management of a sales force in a foreign country, the business sales manager must implement this policy through the selection, orientation and training, compensation, and motivation of such salespeople.

Selection

Selection is crucial to the success of an overseas appointment. It is desirable to establish the selection criteria and to adapt the criteria carefully to ensure that the right person is chosen. Exhibit 11-3 lists considerations of selection. Potential candidates could be rated as either satisfactory or unsatisfactory according to each of the criteria listed. The salesperson showing the highest satisfactory ratings overall could be the final choice. Additionally, the candidate's spouse should be involved in the selection process right from the beginning. Many failures arise from the spouse's reluctant transfer in the first place, followed by an inability to adapt to the host country's conditions.

Further, before accepting the overseas assignment, candidates and their spouses should be given an opportunity to visit the country in question. Even a trip of a week or so can be helpful to them in arriving at a more comfortable decision.[25]

EXHIBIT 11-3 Interview Criteria for International Candidates

Motivation

- Investigate reasons and degree of interest in wanting to be considered.
- Determine desire to work abroad, verified by previous concerns such as personal travel, language training, reading, and association with foreign employees or students.
- Determine whether the candidate has a realistic understanding of what working and living abroad requires.
- Determine the basic attitudes of the spouse toward an overseas assignment.

Health

- Determine whether any medical problems of the candidate or family might be critical to the success of the assignment.
- Determine whether the candidate is in good physical and mental health, without any foreseeable change.

Language ability

- Determine potential for learning a new language.
- Determine any previous language(s) studied or oral ability (judge against language needed on the overseas assignment).
- Determine the ability of the spouse to meet the language requirements.

Family considerations

- How many moves has the family made in the past between different cities or parts of the United States?
- What problems were encountered?
- How recent was the last move?
- What is the spouse's goal in this move?
- What are the number of children and the ages of each?
- Has divorce or its potential, death of a family member, etc., weakened family solidarity?
- Will all the children move; why, why not?
- What is the location, health, and living arrangements of grandparents, and the number of trips normally made to their home each year?
- Are there any special adjustment problems that you would expect?
- How is each member of the family reacting to this possible move?
- Do special educational problems exist within the family?

Resourcefulness and initiative

- Is the candidate independent; can the candidate make and stand by decisions and judgments?
- Does the candidate have the intellectual capacity to deal with several dimensions simultaneously?
- Is the candidate able to reach objectives and produce results with whatever available personnel and facilities, regardless of the limitations and barriers that might arise?
- Can the candidate operate without a clear definition of responsibility and authority on a foreign assignment?
- Will the candidate be able to explain the aims and company philosophy to the local managers and workers?
- Does the candidate possess sufficient self-reliance, self-discipline, and self-confidence to overcome difficulties or handle complex problems?
- Can the candiate work without supervision?
- Can the candidate operate effectively in a foreign environment without normal communications and supporting services?

Adaptability

- Is the candidate sensitive to others, open to the opinions of others, cooperative, and able to compromise?
- What are the candidate's reactions to new situations, and efforts to understand and appreciate differences?
- Is the candidate culturally sensitive, aware, and able to relate across the culture?
- Does the candidate understand his or her own culturally derived values?
- How does the candidate react to criticism?
- What is the candidate's understanding of the U.S. government system?
- Will the candidate be able to make and develop contacts with peers in the foreign country?
- Does the candidate have patience when dealing with problems?
- Is the candidate resilient; can he or she bounce back after setbacks?

continued on next page

EXHIBIT 11-3 **Interview Criteria for International Candidates (continued)**

Career planning	Financial
• Does the candidate consider the assignment other than a temporary overseas trip? • Is the move consistent with the candidate's progression and that planned by the company? • Is the candidate's career planning realistic? • What is the candidate's basic attitude toward the company? • Is there any history or indication of personnel problems with this employee?	• Are there any current financial and/or legal considerations which might affect the assignment, e.g., house purchase, children and college expenses, car purchases? • Are financial considerations negative factors, i.e., will undue pressures be brought to bear on the employee or family as a result of the assignment?

Source: David M. Noer, *Multinational People Management*, Washington, DC: The Bureau of National Affairs, 1975, pp. 55–57. Used with permission.

Orientation and Training

Sales personnel selected for overseas assignments should be oriented to the new job and provided with appropriate training. Essentially, orientation should cover the terms and conditions of the assignment, language training, and cultural training.[26] The salesperson should be given a clear and concise overview of the company's overseas policies and procedures; its compensation program; information on housing, schools, and transportation in the host country; and information on moving arrangements. The salesperson should also receive basic language training since language is the key to a country's culture and permits understanding of both the fundamental and the subtle differences among the customs and values of various foreign markets. Squibb, IBM, Kodak, and NCR give special attention to the sales training function.

Finally, both academic and interpersonal cultural training should be given. Academic training involves the provision of books, films, slides, maps, and brochures about the country in question; interpersonal training includes making arrangements for the candidate and his or her family to visit the host country and to meet with those individuals living in the United States who are very familiar with the country of assignment.[27]

Compensation

Salespeople away from their home country cost the firm more because they must be paid additional compensation. This extra compensation covers three factors. First, it is a premium for climatic conditions in the host country, separation from friends and extended family, cultural shock, and subjection to situations of political instability and economic risk in conditions of unstable currencies. Second, it is an allowance for housing, children's schooling, return trips home on a periodic basis, income tax, and overall cost-of-living expenses. Third, there are certain prerequisites common in host countries for particular positions (like car and driver, servants, and club memberships). Here again, NCR and IBM (among others) are pioneers in the motivation and compensation of their overseas sales forces.

Considering the expenses involved in transferring nonnative salespersons to host countries, the company should make a careful study of the conditions of each country and undertake regular reviews of any changes. The overhead to keep watch on the changes in costs, taxation, facilities, and currency values is by no means negligible. Experts in the field are high priced, and their travel budgets are large. Nevertheless, the cost is a sound investment if, as a result of a reasonable compensation program, the salespeople have confidence in the home office's policy toward them. These necessary prerequisites secure their profitable contribution to the company's performance.[28]

In addition to the above criteria for a specific position, the typical candidate for an international sales assignment is married, has two school-aged children, is expected to stay overseas three years, and has the potential for promotion into higher management levels. These characteristics of the typical selectee are the basis of most of the difficulties associated with getting the best of the qualified to go overseas, keeping them there, and assimilating them on their return.[29] As U.S. companies become more global-minded, investment in recruiting and selecting management is expected to increase. More companies now believe that if they do not have managers with global skills, they will lose the competitive edge. Executives considering an overseas assignment should first (1) understand that the decision is a personal decision, (2) get advice from family, friends, and other expatriates, (3) conduct a personality profile, (4) make a preliminary trip to the assignment location, and (5) consider the personal feelings of each family member.[30]

CONCEPT QUESTIONS

1. What is the value of leadership in business sales management?
2. Why should the performance of a business sales force be routinely evaluated?
3. What is the difference between U.S. and Japanese salespeople in the way in which they perceive job motivation?

SUMMARY

1. The first qualification for a sales manager is leadership, as this person must attempt not only to allocate financial resources efficiently, but also to allocate, maintain, direct, and control a large group of people who are both independent and not in daily contact with management.
2. Some of the major changes that occur when a salesperson is promoted to sales manager include changes in perspectives, goals, responsibilities, sources of satisfaction, job skills requirements, and professional relationships.

3. Common forms of organization of the sales force include line organization, line and staff organization, functional organization, centralized versus decentralized organization, and organization by specialization. Organization by specialization can be along the lines of geographic specialization, sales activities, product specialization, customer organization, or some combination of these.
4. One of the most important of all the sales manager's tasks is the recruitment and selection of competent salespeople. The sales manager should first determine the size of the business sales force. Then, the task of recruitment includes conducting job analysis, preparing a written job description, developing job qualifications, and tapping various internal and external sources of sales recruits. Next, the right salespeople must be selected, which involves decision making on the part of the applicant as well as the sales manager.
5. Sales training must be continuous and should include instruction in product knowledge, competitive knowledge, new selling techniques, development of sales skills, and knowledge of time and territory management. Companies are interested in providing sales training for a variety of reasons, but primarily to increase sales volume, productivity, and profits. Sales training is generally provided by home office sales trainers, field or local sales training, and/or private consulting organizations and professional trainers. Because the costs of sales training are substantial, careful evaluation of the effort should be undertaken on a regular basis.
6. The sales manager must effectively direct and motivate each salesperson to capitalize on his or her potential. Sales managers must provide proper leadership, personal and professional support, and attractive compensation. Appropriate sales quotas should be set for each salesperson as part of an effective overall supervision and motivation function.
7. An evaluation program for the evaluation of business salespeople should be tailored to the specific company for which it is being used. The overall evaluation program should be realistic, motivational, participatory, flexible, and specific. Both formal and informal evaluations should be completed on a regular basis.
8. To develop an effective sales organization in a foreign country, the employer must understand the sales manager–salesperson roles and the expectations of salespeople in that country. Such relationships vary from country to country. After formulating a policy for the management of a sales force in a foreign country, the business sales manager must implement this policy through the selection, orientation and training, and compensation of such salespeople.

KEY TERMS

Centralized versus decentralized organization
Customer specialization
Field or local sales training
Functional organization
Geographic specialization
Job analysis
Job description
Job specification
Leadership

Line organization
Line and staff organization
Organization by specialization
Private consulting firms
Product (product-line) specialization
Recruitment and selection process
Sales quota
Sales territory
Sales training
Sales training department

REVIEW QUESTIONS

1. Identify and discuss six types of changes that can occur when a salesperson is promoted to sales manager.
2. Differentiate among the five major types of sales-force organizations. Identify five means by which a sales force can be organized by specialization.
3. Explain how the size of a sales force can be determined by the workload method, the sales-potential method, and the incremental method. How is sales-force turnover determined?
4. What are the roles of a job analysis, a job description, and a job specification in recruiting business salespeople? What are some common sources of sales recruits? Explain how the selection process for business salespeople is conducted.
5. Identify six fundamental purposes of sales training. Discuss six areas of instruction that should be included in any business sales training program.
6. Describe three types of sales training methods. What are the steps involved in the sales training evaluation process? What method for determining the effect of sales-force training does Learning International suggest?
7. How does a sales manager utilize leadership skills in directing and motivating the sales force? What are sales quotas, and how do business sales managers establish them? How is compensation related to the successful management of the business sales force? How often should a sales manager evaluate the sales performance of the individual members of the sales force?
8. How are recruitment and selection of business salespeople carried out by U.S. sales managers in international markets? What is involved in orientation and training programs in international markets? How do perceptions of job motivation differ between Japanese and U.S. salespeople?

Cases

CASE 11-1 Custom Wheel Lights, Incorporated

The 3M company dominates the reflector market. Reflectors have many uses; most commonly they are used on bicycles and other vehicles. That's where Custom Wheel Lights, Incorporated, may have the competitive edge. The company manufactures a reflective adhesive strip that can be attached to the rim of any wheel. In a recent "reflect-off" at American Airlines, Custom Wheel Lights beat 3M. Now all American Airlines ground vehicles have these new reflector strips.

The reflector strips replace the old circular red reflector. The Custom Wheel Lights' reflectors are ten times brighter than the traditional reflective strips. A few placed strategically on the inside of a wheel rim create the impression of a bright circular light at night. The technology used to produce the strips is unique. The core secret is "microprism technology." Tiny beads of aircraft aluminum are placed on a strip in exact-sequence spacing at a density of fifty-thousand per square inch. The effect, under light, resembles a pulsing strobe light.

The reflective quality is only part of the story. To be truly marketable, the strips had to be able to accept paint, be laminated, and be waterproof and wearproof. Moreover, the strips needed to peel easily from a paper-release liner, then stick to the desired surface permanently. Manufacturing a product with these capabilities was difficult. The company spent months searching through paint laboratories to find the right combination of paints and laminates to meet these specifications.

Custom Wheel Lights initially targeted bicycle shops with its product. One early problem was that the bicycle shop business is highly fragmented. Most bike shops are locally owned and operated and are not part of a large chain. This made the problem of selling to them even harder. Custom Wheel Lights encountered an even bigger dilemma. Bicycle shops didn't want to bother with the reflector strips. As far as these stores were concerned, reflectors were the bicycle manufacturer's responsibility.

The company then adjusted its strategy and began a courtship with Fisher-Price. Fisher-Price has emerged as a major player in the bicycle market. In obtaining Fisher-Price's business, Custom Wheel Lights had to redesign the product. It became imperative to design the reflector strips to the manufacturer's specification and not supply a generic reflector to the whole market.

The company's initial success has been tremendous. The company has been able to sell the product to a German company for the bicycles it manufactures. Custom Wheel Lights earned the distinction of Exporter of the Year for 1991 by the Dallas district of the U.S. Small Business Administration. The company is now exploring selling the reflectors to the manufacturers of truck wheels.

DISCUSSION QUESTIONS

1. What was wrong with Custom Wheel Lights' decision to sell its product to bicycle shops instead of manufacturers?
2. As the company grows, what type of sales structure would you recommend for the sales force? Give reasons to support your answer.
3. What potential problems may occur if Custom Wheel Lights adopts a straight-commission system? How would you compensate the sales force? Why?

Suggested Reading

Piller, Dan. "A Light in the Darkness." *Fort Worth Star Telegram* (February 11–17, 1990), Tarrant Business 11.

Source: C. Lamb, J. Hair, and C. McDaniel, *Principles of Marketing*, 1st Edition (Cincinnati, OH: South-Western Publishing Company, 1992) pp. 526–527.

CASE 11-2 Coke Gets Off Its Can in Europe

When the maker of the world's most popular product changes the way it does business, you at least have to take notice. When it makes this change in the market that it expects to be its most profitable in the 1990s, you ought to put down whatever you're doing and look more closely. You might learn something.

The company is Coca-Cola, the market is Europe, and the changes are far-reaching. Coke is breaking out of its narrow, old role as image marketer and supplier of ingredients to local independent bottlers. Now, Coca-Cola is buying into bottlers, replacing the managers with its own, and shaking up Europe's difficult, increasingly powerful retailers with scrappy, brash U.S. merchandising methods. Rather than letting local bottlers simply serve their own regions as in the past, the company is setting sales and marketing strategy companywide.

Coke has invested $385 million in bottling operations in Britain, France, Belgium, the Netherlands, and Germany. As a result, volume has been increasing over 10 percent annually, more than twice the U.S. rate. Europe's operating profits in 1989 were 29 percent of Coke's total. Says Coca-Cola president, Douglas Keough, "We think the 1990s is the decade of Europe."

The rationale for the strategy is clear. Sales management believes that the great ads can take Coca-Cola only so far, "The consumer," says Keough, "has got the message " The key to growth in Europe is better selling where the cola meets the customer. That means closer relationships with retailers, bolder merchandising, cheaper prices, and faster delivery.

DISCUSSION QUESTIONS

1. From the perspective of a sales manager, how would you describe Coca-Cola's old and new philosophies about business marketing in Europe?
2. What effects do you think Coca-Cola ownership of bottlers in Europe will have on Coca-Cola sales volume, market share, and profits?
3. What potential problems might Coca-Cola face by replacing European bottling company managers with American managers.

Source: C. Lamb, J. Hair, and C. McDaniel, *Principles of Marketing*, 1st Edition (Cincinnati, OH: South-Western Publishing Company, 1992) p. 110.

Suggested Additional Readings

Apasu, Yao. "The Importance of Value Structures in the Perception of Rewards by Industrial Salespersons." *Journal of the Academy of Marketing Science* 15 (Spring 1987): 1–10. **This study uses value structures to explain business salespersons' perception of rewards. Recruitment and selection of salespeople may also be based partly on values.**

Berry, Dick. "A Method to Portray and Analyze Sales Performance." *Industrial Marketing Management* 16 (May 1987): 131–144. **A study of ratio analysis, market changes, data series, and plot sequencing.**

Blumel, Robert T. "Pull Your Pay Stub and See How You're Faring." *Purchasing World* 30 (December 1986): 33–39. **Salary survey including statistical data, trends, and compensation criteria.**

Castleberry, Stephen B., and John F. Tanner, Jr. "The Manager-Salesperson Relationship: An Exploratory Examination of the Vertical-Dyad Linkage Model." *Journal of Personal Selling and Sales Management* 6 (November 1986): 29–37. **Implications for organizational behavior, management style, and leadership are offered.**

Cespedes, Frank V. "Sales Coordination: An Exploratory Study." *Journal of Personal Selling and Sales Management* 12 (Summer 1992): 13–29. **A discussion of how sales managers work with salespersons to achieve successful sales coordination.**

Chonko, Lawrence B. "Organizational Commitment in the Sales Force." *Journal of Personal Selling and Sales Management* 6 (November 1986): 19–27. **An examination of expectancy theory, motivation, and measurement of sales-force performance.**

Cook, Roy A., and Roy Herche. "Assessment Centers: An Untapped Resource for Global Salesforce Management." *Journal of Personal Selling and Sales Management* 12 (Summer 1992): 31–38. **A study of the use of assessment centers in the selection and development of business salespeople.**

Cron, William L., Alan J. Dubinsky, and Ronald E. Michaels. "The Influence of Career Stages on Components of Salesperson Motivation." *Journal of Marketing* 52 (January 1988): 78–92. **Researchers have found that career stage is related to salespeople's attitudes, work perceptions, and performance. This study addresses this area and provides implications for sales management practice and research.**

Dubinsky, Alan J., and Thomas N. Ingram. "From Selling to Sales Management: A Developmental Model." *Journal of Business and Industrial Marketing* 2 (Spring 1987): 27–36. **Presentation of a model that sales executives can use in developing potential sales managers. Valuable sales management skills are identified, and methods for providing skill development are offered.**

Erffmeyer, Robert C., K. Randall Russ, and Joseph F. Hair, Jr. "Traditional High-Tech Sales Training Methods." *Industrial Marketing Management* 21 (May 1992): 125–131. **A survey of the different high-technology sales methods utilized by business-to-business firms.**

Head, Robert G. "Restoring Balance to Sales Compensation." *Sales and Marketing Management* 144 (July 1992): 48–50, 52–53. **A study of job satisfaction related to type of financial incentives offered.**

Jenkins, Steven. "Key Account versus Field Sales: Resolving the Conflict." *Industrial Marketing Digest* (UK), 11 (Fourth Quarter 1986): 105–110. **Guidelines, standards, approaches, and techniques for account development.**

______. "Sales Management: How to Land a Key Account." *Industrial Marketing Digest* (UK), 12 (First Quarter 1987): 137–142. **The use of negotiations and sales techniques in planning, organizing, and implementing business sales.**

Jolson, Marvin A., and Lucette B. Comer. "Predicting the Effectiveness of Industrial Saleswomen." *Industrial Marketing Management* 21 (February 1992): 69–75. **A survey on the traits and performance variables related to success among women in business sales careers.**

Kelley, Bill. "From Salesperson to Manager: Transition and Travail." *Sales and Marketing Management* 144 (February 1992): 32–36. **A discussion of the training, problems, and guidelines for success involved in the transition between salesperson and sales management.**

———. "Keeping Salespeople on the Road." *Sales and Marketing Management* 138 (April 1987): 56–61. **Survey of operating and maintenance costs of automobile fleets in many companies.**

Kennedy, Ellen J., and Leigh Lawton. "Men and Women in Industrial Sales: Satisfaction and Outcomes." *Industrial Marketing Management* 21 (February 1992): 5–14. **Report of a research study on the variables that lead to satisfaction and other positive rewards from a career in business sales.**

Petrone, Joseph A. "The First Ninety Days." *Sales and Marketing Management* 144 (September 1992): 66–72. **A study of new sales managers and their new roles to include travelling with salespeople, setting standards, measuring results, completion of paperwork, and maintaining credibility.**

Sales and Marketing Management 138 (June 1987): 41–68. **Fourteen articles on America's best sales forces. Case studies of many companies in many industries.**

Smith, Daniel C., and John E. Prescott. "Couple Competitive Analysis to Sales Force Decisions." *Industrial Marketing Management* 16 (February 1987): 55–61. **Case study and discussion of performance measures based on predetermined criteria.**

Taylor, Thayer C. "Hewlett-Packard Gives Sales Reps Competitive Edge." *Sales and Marketing Management* 138 (February 1987): 36–41. **A company analysis of automation, use of portable computers in business sales, and sales-force productivity.**

Templeton, Jane. "Peer Prestige Puts Pow in Salespower." *Sales and Marketing Management* 138 (June 1987): 76–78. **Analysis of the use of employee rewards in motivating salespeople.**

Waldrop, Heidi. "The Rewards of Noncash Incentives." *Sales and Marketing Management* 138 (April 1987): 110–112. **Survey of executives as to the effectiveness of using noncash incentives to motivate the sales force and to stimulate increased productivity.**

ENDNOTES

[1]For another perspective, see Alan M. Schechter, "Thinking, Acting Like a Manager Is a Prime Requisite in Transition," *Marketing News* (September 27, 1985): 14.

[2]Jack Falvey, "The Making of a Manager," *Sales and Marketing Management* 141 (March 1989) 42–47, 83.

[3]Adapted from Charles Futrell, *Sales Management*, 3d ed. (New York: Dryden Press, 1991), 10–11.

[4]Adapted from C. Robert Patty, *Sales Manager's Handbook* (Reston Publishing, 1982), 285–300.

[5]For an interesting discussion of sales-force organizational structure, see Ram C. Ras and Ronald E. Turner, "Organization and Effectiveness of the Multiple-Product Sales Force," *Journal of Personal Selling and Sales Management* (May 1984): 24–30. Also see Jayashrel Mahajan and Asoo J. Vakharia, "A Multiobjective Approach and Empirical Application of Sales-Organization Design," *Decision Sciences* 21 (Summer 1990): 608–625.

[6]For further discussion, see John Barrett, "Why Major Accounts?" *Industrial Marketing Management* 15 (1986): 63–73. Also see Thayer C. Taylor, "Xerox's Sales Force Learns a New Game," *Sales and Marketing Management* (July 1985): 48–51. Also see Caroline Reich, "Big Spenders Get Big Wheel Treatment," *Purchasing World* 33 (November 1989): 25–27.

[7]"Business-to-Business Sales Force Turnover Rate Rises to 9.4%," *Laboratory of Advertising Performance*, Report #8054.1 (McGraw-Hill, 1986). Also see Lynn G. Coleman, "Sales Force Turnover Has Managers Wondering Why," *Marketing News* 23 (December 4, 1989): 6, 21.

[8]This discussion of turnover is from Robert F. Hartley, *Sales Management* (Columbus, Ohio.: Merrill Publishing, 1989), 213.

[9]Ronald R. Still, Edward W. Cundiff, and Norman A. P. Govoni, *Sales Management: Decisions, Strategies, and Cases*, 9th ed. (Englewood Cliffs, N.J.: Prentice-Hall, 1981), 63–68. Also see Richard F. Wendel and Walter Gorman, *Selling*, 5th ed. (New York: Random House Business Division, 1988), 576–577.

[10]Futrell, *Sales Management*, 289.

[11]*Ibid.*, 290.

[12]Wendel and Gorman, *Selling*, 576.

[13]Futrell, *Sales Management*, 291.

[14]David J. Good, "Coaching Practices in The Business-To-Business Environment," *Journal of Business and Industrial Marketing* 8 (1993): 53–60.

[15]"Study Reveals Sales-Training Needs of Business Marketers," *Marketing News* (March 13, 1989): 6. Also see Christopher J. Butler, "Hiring and Training: The Failure Factor," *Sales and Marketing Management* 144 (September 1992): 123–124.

[16]From a personal interview in 1993 with H. O. Crafford of Plantations Plastics, Riverside, Rhode Island.

[17]"DuPont Turns Scientists into Salespeople," *Sales and Marketing Management* (June 1987): 57.

[18]Taylor, "Xerox's Sales Force." See also Jennifer Reese, "Getting Hot Ideas from Customers," *Fortune*, 18 May 1992, 86–87.

[19]Robert J. Calvin, *Profitable Sales Management and Marketing for Growing Businesses* (New York: Van Nostrand and Reinhold, 1984), 24–26.

[20]Jack Gordon, "Where the Training Goes," *Training* (October 1986): 50.

[21]Thomas R. Wotruba and Edwin K. Simpson, *Sales Management* 2d ed. (Boston: PWS-Kent Publishing, 1992): 356. Also see Jeremy Main, "How to Sell by Listening," *Fortune*, 4 February 1985, 52–54.

[22]Wotruba and Simpson, *Sales Managment*, 363–364.

[23]T. C. Hayes, *New York Times*, 6 May 1984, F17.

[24]Edward W. Cundiff and Marge Tharp Hilger, *Marketing in the International Environment* 2d ed. (Englewood Cliffs, N.J.: Prentice-Hall, 1988), 337–338.

[25]Rosalie L. Tung, "Selection and Training of Personnel for Overseas Assignments," *Columbia World Journal of Business* (Spring 1981): 68–78. Also see Dawn Gunsch, "Preassignment Trips for Families Reduce Failed Overseas Assignments," *Personnel Journal*, 72 (February 1993): 16.

[26]See Burton W. Teague, *Selecting and Orienting Staff for Service Overseas* (New York: The Conference Board, no date given). See also Jefferey L. Blue and Ulric Haynes, Jr., "Preparation for the Overseas Assignment," *Business Horizons* (June 1977): 61–67. Also see Tamar Cavusgil, Ugur Yavas, and Sandy Bykowicz, "Preparing Executives for Overseas Assignments," *Managements Decisions* 30 (1992): 54–58.

[27]Subhash C. Jain, *International Marketing Management*, 3d ed. (Boston, Mass.: Kent Publishing, 1990), 582.

[28]*Ibid.*, 584–585.

[29]Herbert Huffen, "So You Still Want an Overseas Assignment," *Across the Board* (June 1985): 64.

[30]Daniel B. Richardson and Vincent Rullo, "Going Global: Are You Ready for an Overseas Assignment?" *Management Accounting* 73 (June 1992): 31–39.

12 Advertising and Sales Promotion Strategy in Business Markets

Learning Objectives

After reading this chapter, you should be able to:

- Appreciate the role of promotion in business marketing and how it differs from the role of consumer promotion.
- Identify the steps involved in creating a business promotion plan.
- Explain how objectives are set for a business promotion campaign.
- Differentiate among the various promotional tools available to the business promotion campaign manager.
- Recall two primary methods by which the effectiveness of business promotion campaigns can be measured.
- Relate the role of advertising, publicity, and sales promotion in the development of international business promotion campaigns.

Chapter Outline

Learning Objectives

An Overview of Business Promotion

Creating a Promotional Plan for Business Markets

Setting Objectives for a Promotional Plan

Developing The Promotional Budget
- Prioritizing the Promotional Expenditure

Determining and Implementing the Promotional Mix
- Business Advertising
  - The nature of business advertising
  - The goals of business advertising
  - Media selection
    - Print media
    - Broadcast media
    - Direct marketing
  - Business advertising content
  - Use of advertising agencies
- Business Publicity
  - Techniques to secure publicity
- Business Sales Promotion
  - Trade shows and exhibits
    - Deciding whether to participate
    - Selecting the show
    - Trade show objectives
    - Trade show budget
  - Contests, sweepstakes, and games
  - Advertising specialties

Measuring the Effectiveness of the Business Promotion Campaign
- Pretesting and Posttesting
- Responses to Business Advertising

Following Up and Modifying the Business Promotion Campaign When Necessary

Promotional Strategy for International Markets
- International Advertising
- International Publicity and Sales Promotion

Summary

Key Terms

Review Questions

Cases
- Case 12-1
- Case 12-2

Suggested Additional Readings

Endnotes

AN OVERVIEW OF BUSINESS PROMOTION

Advertising, publicity, and sales promotion are communication methods used by marketers to remind or persuade existing and potential customers that the product or service exists (as opposed to personal selling, which is verbal communication with a prospective customer). In the business market, advertising, publicity, and sales promotion pave the way for the sales call. In this chapter, and as shown in Figure 12-1, *business promotion* refers to the use of the promotional tools of advertising, publicity, and sales promotion as seller-generated efforts to gain information while delivering marketing messages to business markets. The cost per thousand (CPM) of such promotional methods is relatively inexpensive when compared to the cost of personal selling. Additionally, these methods reach many customers quickly and make widespread distribution possible. A well-targeted group of professional users is a solid database for business promotion.[1]

Business markets tend to be geographically concentrated with relatively few companies purchasing large amounts (the 80/20 axiom). Although only 10 percent of U.S. manufacturing firms employ more than one hundred workers, these firms supply approximately 80 percent of the value added by U.S. manufacturing. These relatively few large buyers represent a potentially lucrative market for business marketers. Due to the geographic concentration of these markets and the substantial purchasing volume of most firms, personal selling dominates the promotional mix. Consequently, the role of business promotion traditionally has been to support the personal selling function. Business promotion can and should aid sales representatives in introducing new products, product lines, and services to either established or potential customers.

Organizational buyers tend to be part of a much larger buying center or decision-making unit, tend to purchase in large quantities, and tend to base their

FIGURE 12-1 Business Promotion and the Flows of Information and Persuasion

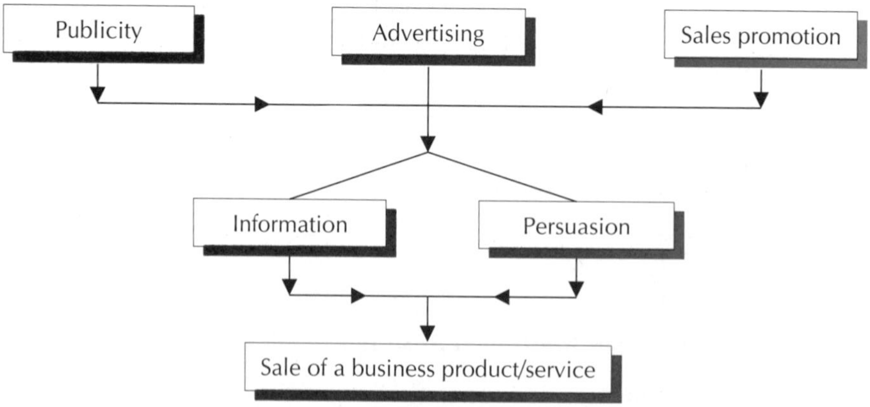

purchases on relatively exact specifications. Therefore, purchasing managers are considered by some to be less susceptible to promotional appeals that stress brand names. However, business buyers are nonetheless human and are often subject to the same appeals found effective in consumer advertising. In addition, not all business markets are concentrated, nor do all firms purchase in large volume. The cost of sending salespeople to many scattered business accounts can be prohibitive. Promotion must assume the "selling" function for small orders or low-margin products. Carle Instruments is one company that has experienced success using promotional techniques to sell business goods.

Carle Instruments markets products designed for business use and university research. Customers do not buy in large volume; consequently, sales efforts must be spread over many buyers. Carle found both its sales force and business products distributors to be ineffective, so it turned to print media and publicity. It uses an advertising agency to create high-quality, integrated promotional pieces. Inquiries are promptly and courteously answered by telephone or personal letter. As the only sales tool employed, promotion must both create the company's image and tout the benefits of its products. Carle is but one company of many that has found that good products and services can be effectively marketed without a sales force. Business buyers have responded favorably to direct-mail inquiries, keeping sales costs to a minimum. Many firms are shifting more of their personal selling budget to direct techniques to minimize selling costs, while making personal selling more effective.[2]

CREATING A PROMOTIONAL PLAN FOR BUSINESS MARKETS

Effective promotion often helps sales; ineffective promotion can waste millions of dollars and even seriously damage company image. Figure 12-2 demonstrates that creating a promotional plan for business markets involves five steps, which include the following: (1) setting objectives, (2) developing a promotional budget, (3) determining and implementing the promotional mix, (4) measuring the effectiveness of the promotional program, and (5) following up and modifying the promotional campaign, if necessary. This process results in a promotional campaign, which is a carefully planned sequence of promotions centered around a common theme and geared to specific objectives.

SETTING OBJECTIVES FOR A PROMOTIONAL PLAN

Promotional campaigns need specific, realistic objectives. The establishment of appropriate objectives should be the starting point for every such campaign. It is difficult, and probably imprudent, to plan a promotional program unless

FIGURE 12-2 **Steps in a Business Promotion Campaign**

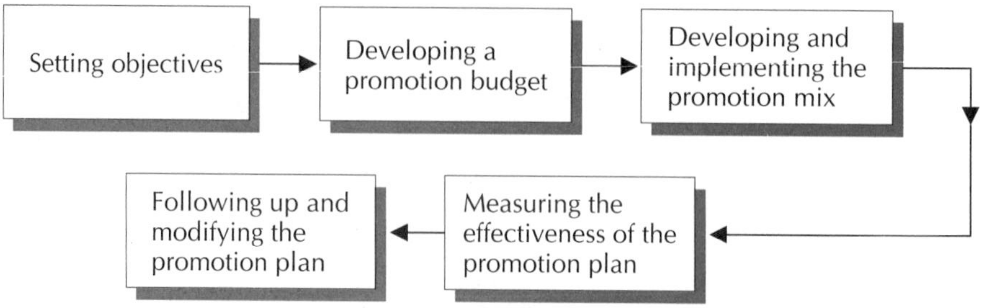

marketers first establish the objectives they are trying to attain. These promotional objectives tend to vary greatly. While it is difficult to quantify such objectives as "friendly image," baseline marketing research can provide initial measures to gauge almost any campaign. Whenever possible, it is preferable to express objectives in dollar amounts. (Objectives need to be "bottom line" in nature.) An objective to generate a certain number of sales leads often results in leads that do not produce sales or profits. For instance, the marketing objective of a promotional campaign may be to generate $3.5 million in sales with a 15 percent ROI (return on investment). Total sales volume and market share are widely utilized sales indices offered by firms such as A. C. Nielsen, Market Research Corporation of America, and Audits and Surveys, Incorporated. Market-share and sales-volume data assist a business marketing manager in determining whether or not a firm's objectives are being met.[3]

DEVELOPING THE PROMOTIONAL BUDGET

After the marketing manager has established promotional goals and has identified appropriate market segments, a solid, cost-effective promotional budget must be developed. This is not a simple nor an enviable task, as there are no concrete guidelines or guaranteed techniques to ensure maximum success. According to a recent budget survey, marketers are increasing their advertising and sales promotion outlays. Some are increasing their budgets because they feel a strong market presence is important in the event of a downturn in business. Most increase budgets in an attempt to increase market share or to move into new markets.[4]

Ideally, the budget needs to be set at a point where the last dollar spent on promotion equals profits from the sales produced by that dollar (that is, marginal utility). However, in reality, because of the enormity of associated problems, this marginal concept is all but impossible to apply.[5] Common techniques for setting budgets include affordable, competitive parity, percentage of sales, and objective and task.[6] As can be seen in Figure 12-3, many firms employ more than one method, although the objective-and-task and affordable methods are most commonly used by business-to-business organizations.

Prioritizing the Promotional Expenditure

Business promotion budgets have traditionally been spartan for reasons too numerous, diverse, and illogical to warrant further discussion. It is the marketer's job, however, to set the budget and to ensure the most return for every dollar spent. Economists tell us that the first dollar spent on promotion yields the greatest return, with a diminishing ratio of return from additional expenditures. However, this is only the case if the money is spent in an "optimal" fashion. Operationally, this requires a prioritization of all promotional efforts in terms of

FIGURE 12-3 **Common Techniques for Setting the Business Promotion Budget**

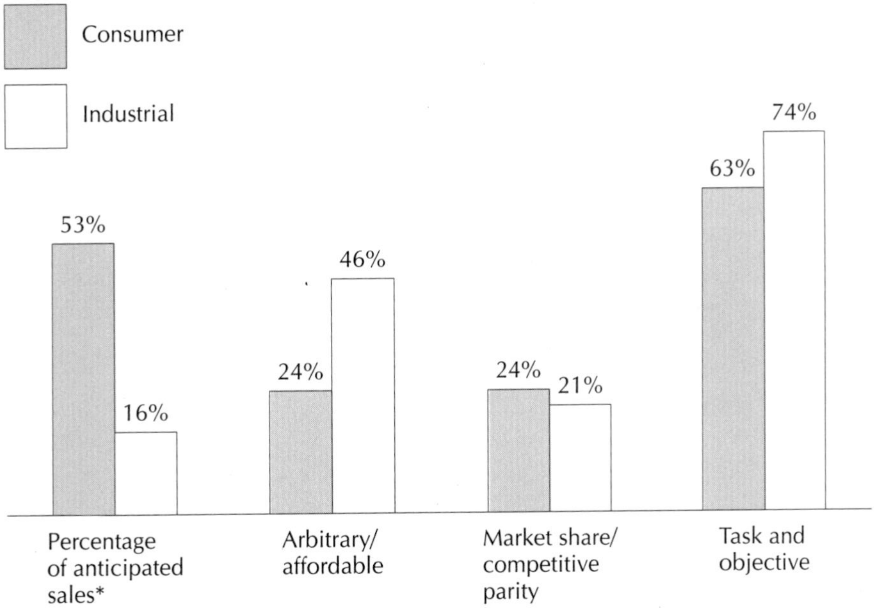

Percents add to more than 100 because of multiple responses.

*Also, 20 percent of the consumer goods firms and 23 percent of the industrial goods organizations use current or past years' sales.

Source: Vincent Blasko and Charles Patti, "The Advertising Budget Practices of Industrial Marketers," *Journal of Marketing,* Fall 1984, pp. 104–10. Used with permission.

their potential contribution to the firm. How to spend the promotional budget is a tougher and more crucial question than how much to spend. Examine the curve in Figure 12-4 and notice the flatness at the top of the curve. The greatest contribution to the firm is made with the initial dollars spent. A larger budget will often contribute little profit.

The first step in setting priorities with regard to the promotional dollar is to prioritize the target audience. Figure 12-5 identifies and ranks target audiences, linking the most effective means for reaching each audience. The astute marketing manager spends budgeted dollars by starting at the top of the pyramid and working down. Contrary to popular belief, advertising is a low-priority item in the promotional budget.

CONCEPT QUESTIONS

1. What are the three basic promotional methods used in marketing?
2. Why should appropriate objectives be the starting point for any business promotion campaign?
3. What is the ideal point at which the business promotion campaign should be set?

FIGURE 12-4 **The Contribution of Advertising Expenditures to Profit**

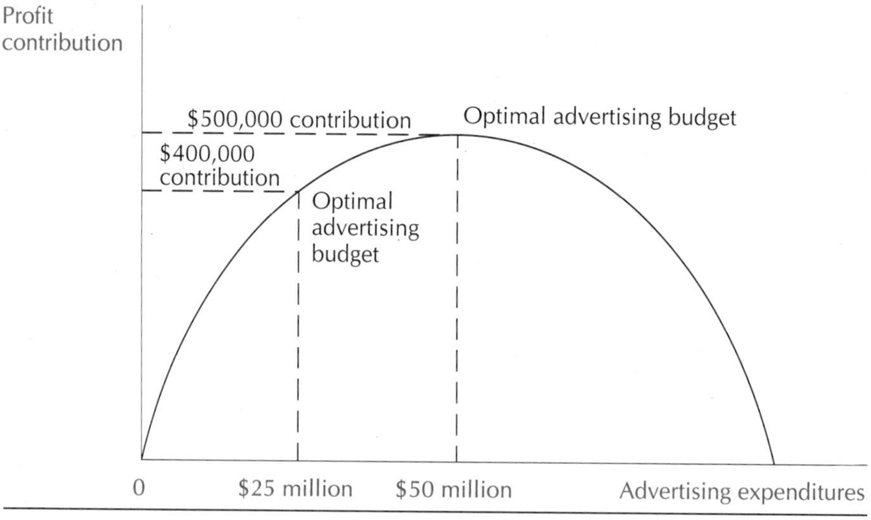

FIGURE 12-5 **Identifying Target Audiences and the Most Effective Ways to Reach Them**

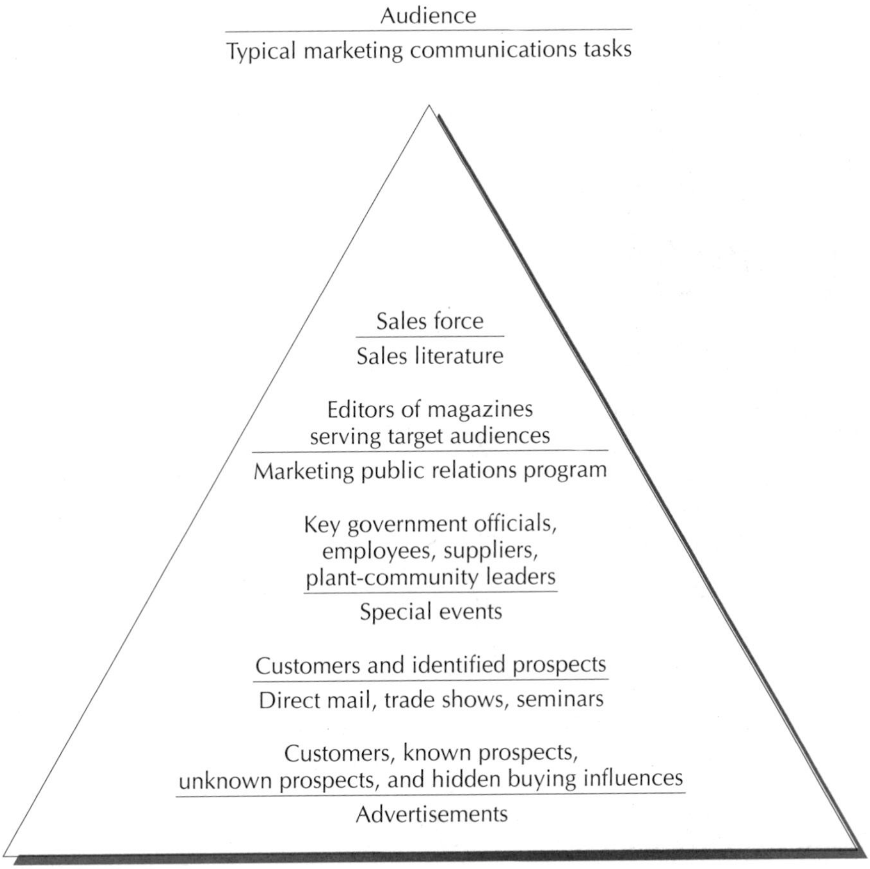

Note: How to read: moving downward, size of audience increases. The cost of communicating is more expensive, and ability to isolate influentials is more difficult.

Source: Robert F. Roth, *International Marketing Communication* (Lincolnwood, Ill.: Crain Books, 1982), p. 41. Used with permission.

DETERMINING AND IMPLEMENTING THE PROMOTIONAL MIX

Business Advertising

The nature of business advertising. As pointed out in Table 12-1, *business advertising* is considerably different from consumer advertising. Business

TABLE 12-1 **Differences between Business and Consumer Advertising**

Business Advertising	Consumer Advertising
Rational appeals	Emotional appeals
Views profit motive as a primary purchasing criterion	Recognizes personal gratification as a primary buying motive
Smaller part of the entire selling function	Larger part of the entire selling function
Utilizes smaller percentage of the sales dollar	Utilizes larger percentage of the sales dollar
Addresses a somewhat limited market	Speaks to a very large and diverse market
Places greater emphasis on direct mail	Places less emphasis on direct mail

advertising features product-oriented appeals and views the profit motive as a primary purchasing criterion. It assumes a relatively smaller part of the entire selling function than does personal selling and utilizes a smaller percentage of the sales dollar. It also addresses a somewhat limited market and places greater emphasis on direct mail. Conversely, consumer advertising emphasizes people-oriented appeals, recognizes personal gratification as a primary buying motive, shoulders a greater burden in the total selling effort, spends a larger share of the sales dollar, speaks to a very large and diverse market, and places less emphasis on direct mail.

The goals of business advertising. Business advertising campaigns should not necessarily be based on sales goals. Measuring their effectiveness begins with a set of specific objectives that are attainable, timely, and measurable. Common advertising objectives include: (1) building product awareness; (2) inducing trial and retrial of new market entries; (3) increasing market share; (4) stimulating short-term sales; (5) countering competitor's offerings; (6) buying space with distributors; (7) building line acceptance; (8) intensifying usage; (9) sustaining product preference; (10) aiding the sales staff by introducing buyers to product offerings; (11) reviving a brand that is in the decline stage of its product life cycle; and (12) confirming buyers' purchase decisions. Insufficient advertising forces a product offering to stay locked within a sealed environment, unable to sufficiently interact with the outside world.[7] Business advertising generally has one or more of four specific goals:[8]

(1) It is generally designed to make the advertiser favorably known to its current and potential customers.

(2) It often attempts to convey specific and technical information about the characteristics of a particular product or products manufactured by the advertiser.

(3) Either or both of these effects, when achieved, tend to ease the salesperson's job. The company that the salesperson represents becomes better known, and the products that the salesperson handles become more familiar to potential purchasers as a result of the advertising.

(4) Finally, due to improved sales performance as a result of advertising, it is usually assumed (or at least hoped) that business advertising will help to reduce overall selling costs.

Each of these objectives will now be discussed in more detail.[9]

Business advertising should increase customer or potential customer awareness and improve the advertiser's image in customers' minds. Unlike most consumer advertising situations, business prices are often negotiated. There might be considerable comparative shopping, which may result in competitive bidding. Structural and performance standards may be specified; often, several different specifications from different departments or divisions with differing needs must somehow be fulfilled. Finally, the personality and skill of sharply competitive salespeople often come into play.

What possible effect can business advertising have on this process of rationalizing objective and subjective purchasing standards and influences? Business advertising can have a significant beneficial effect just in making potential customers aware of potential suppliers and reinforcing satisfaction among existing customers. An enormous challenge to business advertising is to select an image that will attract the eyes of readers.[10] Theodore Levitt makes the point below:

> A company's reputation improves the chances of getting a favorable first hearing and an early adoption of the product. Thus, corporate advertising that can build upon the company's reputation (other factors also shape its reputation) will help the company's sales representatives.[11]

Business advertising should supply information about specific products and services of interest to customers. In addition to increasing an advertiser's visibility to potential customers, advertising should provide specific information about the products and/or services of the advertiser that purchasing managers need to know to appraise that advertiser's offerings properly. There are two important assumptions being made here. The first is that organizational buyers are looking for detailed information about the products and/or services they buy; the second is that advertisers know what information is relevant to their customers. As such, it is interesting to discover evidence that business advertisers in four product categories, studied by Gordon McAleer, do not understand the considerations that influence prospective purchasers in their respective product categories. McAleer studied the buying motivations of four kinds of purchasers: consulting engineers, electrical contractors, architects, and nonresidential building contractors. He then studied the purchasing motives imputed by advertisers to these groups. "The results were disconcerting," McAleer reported, "since the advertising managers did not seem to understand the major considerations which influence the purchase of their products. The finding would indicate that business advertising managers are performing their tasks less effectively than they should."[12]

Although the results of McAleer's study cannot be generalized to all areas of business advertising, the evidence indicates that knowledge of buying motives is no less important among business purchasers than among the consuming public. If advertisers do not know what is going on in the minds of their customers, they would be well advised to find out, so as to keep their advertising messages from being irrelevant and possibly ignored.

Business advertising should make the salesperson more productive. One of the fundamental justifications for advertising over the years has been the belief that it paves the salesperson's entry into both established and prospective customers' firms. According to a recent study by the Advertising Research Foundation and the Association of Business Publishers, increases in business advertising lead to greater sales and profits.[13] Although it might be difficult to prove in specific situations, there is growing support that positive interaction between advertising and sales efforts is real and substantial and that it is a major reason for investing in advertising. Exhibit 12-1 reflects the effects of advertising on the personal selling effort at IBM.

If business advertising improves sales performance, it must reduce selling costs. It is one thing to come to the general conclusion that advertising helps a salesperson's performance, and yet another to quantify just how much savings are generated by such a relationship. No one seems to know just how the advertising-salesperson relationship operates, or what the exact economics of the relationship are. However, the subject is important because it means that business advertisers must figure out for themselves the proper budget levels for their advertising and personal selling programs. Also, solid evidence of productivity and carefully reasoned program

EXHIBIT 12-1 **The Effects of Advertising on the Personal Selling Effort at IBM**

Sales Productivity Study
Advertising/Mail Generated Leads 1981

Average hours to close the order:

Electronic typewriters: without lead 4.4—with lead 1.2
Displaywriter: without lead 19.7—with lead 3.2
Series III: without lead 23.8—with lead 3.4
51XX: without lead 12.8*—with lead 9.5
S/34: without lead 37.5*—with lead 17.5

*Not including prospecting time

Source: Presentation handout by Robert H. Hutchings, manager of advertising and promotion, IBM.

plans are necessary for business advertising operations to avoid budget cuts.[14] Lilien, Silk, Choffray, and Rao make the point in the following statement:

> There is no indication about what the overall budget should be, or about what split between advertising and personal selling expenditures would be most efficient.[15]

Media selection. Business advertising is now viewed much like consumer advertising, and this fact has stimulated broader media selections. Business advertising is now run on prime-time specials, business cable television networks, and in consumer magazines.[16] When advertising is used, management must select the *media mix*. The media mix is some combination of the following types of advertising media: print media, broadcast media, and direct marketing. (Exhibit 12-2 shows the percent of growth in expenditures by U.S. advertisers from 1991 to 1992.)

Print media. Print media includes business publications, professional publications, general business publications, trade directories, and general consumer publications, such as *Time*, *Newsweek*, *Scientific American*, and *Golf Digest*. Business publications are of two basic types: horizontal and vertical. *Horizontal*

EXHIBIT 12-2 **Expenditures by U.S. Advertisers—Percent Growth from 1991 to 1992**

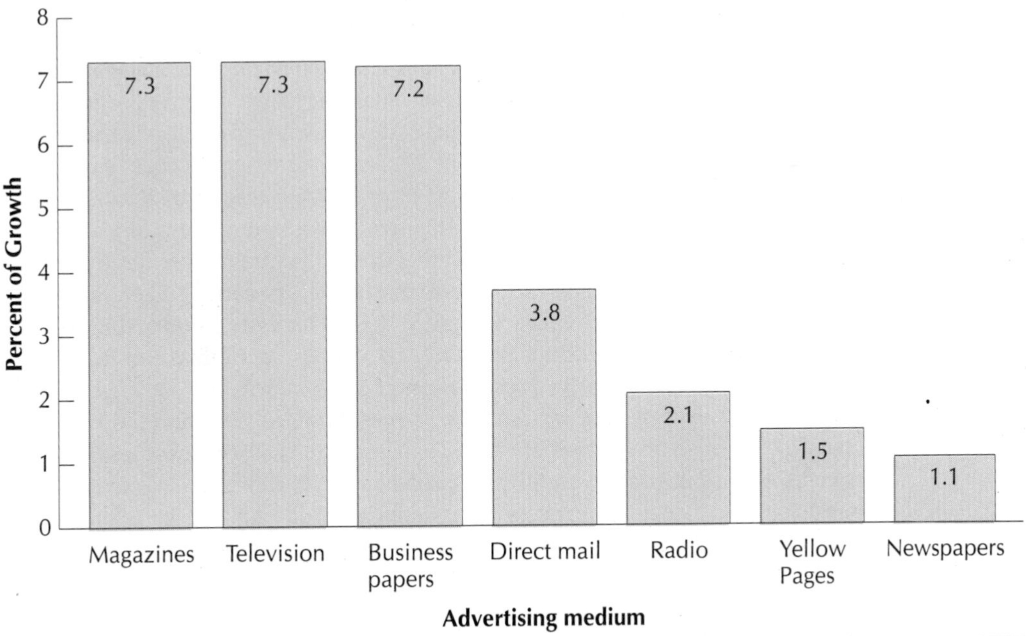

Source: Reprinted with permission from *Advertising Age*, May 10, 1993. Copyright Crain Communications Inc., 1993.

publications are intended for buyers who have similar functions in their companies, regardless of their specific industry, such as *Industrial Maintenance and Plant Operation* published for those maintaining and operating industrial plants of over fifty employees; and *Purchasing*, a news magazine for purchasing executives. *Vertical publications* are those discussing current issues and problems of a single industry, such as *Frozen Food Field*, edited for management personnel in the frozen food industry; and *Mechanical Contractor*, designed to meet the needs of the large heating, plumbing, piping, and air-conditioning contractor. Ganson Avery, manager of marketing and planning in automotive controls for Eaton Corporation in Carol Stream, Illinois, and president of the Chicago chapter of the Business/Professional Advertising Association, predicts that horizontal publications will fare better than vertical ones during the 1990s. He claims that advertisers in vertical publications can easily reach the same audience through more cost-efficient means, such as direct mail.[17]

Professional publications include research journals and trade and professional association journals, edited for physicians, dentists, architects, and other professionals (for example, *Architectural Digest*).[18] Their editorial range varies from reporting new technical developments to discussing how to run offices more efficiently and profitably. Much advertising is directed to professionals, since they are an important influence in recommending or specifying the products that their clients will need.

Industrial trade directories have long been used as an important promotion medium in business advertising. Most industries have their own directory and buyer's guide, with descriptions of products and product lines and lists of various firms marketing and selling the product lines. Trade directories are a highly effective way to get particular advertisers' names before their respective target audiences. Although there are numerous statewide and private trade directories, the best known and most popular is the *Thomas Register of American Manufacturers*, comprised of nineteen volumes and over 60,000 pages with 50,000 product headings and listings from 123,000 business-to-business companies. One of Thomas's largest customers is General Electric, which buys over three hundred sets per year for both its domestic and international concerns.[19] The greatest advantages of industrial trade directories are their selectivity in reporting on individual companies and product titles and their high credibility and acceptance rate by both large and small advertisers and buyers.

General business publications, such as *Fortune*, *Business Week*, and the *Wall Street Journal*, cut across a wide variety of industries; with their business and editorial content, these publications address a broad range of issues and concerns of interest to executives in all aspects of business and industry. About 60 percent of the space in general business publications is used for advertising.

Broadcast media. *Broadcast media*, generally thought to be only for consumer advertising, are receiving increasing attention from advertisers who serve highly geographically concentrated markets and who want to get around the intense business advertising competition in older, more traditional, and well-established business media. Both large and small firms have used radio advertising through the years. Standard Oil of New Jersey attempts to speak to a select audience of managerial decision makers, financial executives, and government officials through appropriate radio stations and time periods. Another veteran radio user is Timken Roller Bearing Company of Canton, Ohio, which runs fifteen radio spots a week during morning and evening drive times in the upper Midwest, to reach select audiences in cities where there is great involvement with the automotive industry. However, this medium is not appropriate for all business marketers, in that costs cannot be justified unless the product has multiple uses across many industries.

While print media forecasts call for virtually flat revenues during the 1990s, broadcast media is anticipating continued growth. As cable penetration and cable audiences continue to grow, advertisers are diverting more national television dollars to this medium, which has become more sophisticated in its marketing and is producing more original programming.[20] Television advertising by business-to-business firms has more recently become increasingly popular and more highly visible through the efforts of such giants as IBM, Hewlett-Packard, Xerox, and Federal Express. As the average cost of sales calls continues to increase, one supplier of food equipment began to advertise heavily on television, with classified advertisements in local newspapers; a twenty-four-hour, toll-free answering service; and direct mail as support media.[21] With the sales call now averaging over $250, this type of practice will increase.

As a final note, Beck offers us seven tips on how to ruin a business advertising effort: (1) Confuse the reader with an obtuse or unintelligible headline. (2) Run the ad only once, twice at most, so that prospects do not have any time to build interest. (3) Focus on a favorite topic, such as the business and how great it is. (4) Be sure not to distinguish the product or service from others. (5) Pretend the market already knows as much about the product as the company does. (6) Make the assumption that the prospect thinks exactly as the company does. (7) Ignore professional advertising advice.[22] Astute marketers will not let these things happen.

Direct marketing. Along with print and broadcast media, business marketers have turned to direct-marketing techniques for cost-effective lead generations to facilitate the sales of their products and services.[23] More companies are learning that direct marketing can help them market more cost-effectively.[24] Direct marketing in the business sector has experienced rapid sales growth in recent years. According to Arnold Fishman, total mail order sales alone for business products in 1989 amounted to some $50 billion. Of this total, supplies and services were the fastest-growing sectors, reaching some $14.5 billion.[25] This phenomenon indicates the widespread use and functional diversity of direct marketing in the business sector. *Direct marketing* includes direct mail, data sheets, business catalogues, and telemarketing.

Historically, over 80 percent of the manufacturers of business goods have used direct mail as part of their promotion effort. *Direct mail* is especially important where the market for a business product or service is concentrated, because direct-mail pieces can be specifically targeted to key individuals and can focus on the key buying motives of that individual. In cases where there is a limited number of potential customers, direct mail offers a relatively less expensive medium in which to maintain contact with them than does advertising in business or professional publications. Direct mail is direct marketing only when it elicits a response from the target audience. Otherwise, it is just another advertising medium among magazines, television, and radio. Responses can be either business reply mail or via telephone.

Some of the more common business uses of direct mail include rapid distribution for a new product, paving the way for a salesperson's call, an aid to convince distributors to handle a particular product, a means to build strong company image, testing the acceptance of new products, and following up a salesperson's call to emphasize selling points made during the oral presentation. Business services are also frequently promoted through the use of direct mail. Peat-Marwick, a "Big-Six" accounting firm with revenues in excess of $3 billion, uses direct mail in selling its services to the financial community. Its direct-mail campaigns are not offer driven, but are instead intended to create awareness and to convey an interest in providing up-to-date tax, auditing, and management services. According to Adrian Dessi, director of marketing services, "We know who we are. Consequently, our direct mail letters are `chocked-full' of valuable information that directly impacts the businesses of our clients and prospects."[26]

Direct mail is also a helpful promotional tool for the business marketer because it is not very difficult to compile lists of prospects from responses to trade and professional advertisements and from intracompany telemarketing operations. Mailing lists can also be acquired through industrial directories and mailing list houses, such as Dun and Bradstreet's Marketing Services Division and National Business Lists. Direct mail can also be disadvantageous if appropriate prospects are not clearly targeted and identified, or if direct-mail pieces are discarded as junk mail.

Data sheets are useful because sales representatives often have the answers to many of the highly sophisticated questions posed by technical buyers. Data sheets can be left with appropriate buyers who might make the purchasing decision when the sales representative is not present. Exhibit 12-3 offers some guidelines for advertisers in creating data sheets that sell.

Business catalogues are another segment of direct marketing. Today, catalogue copy that intermixes sales psychology with product descriptions is increasing so rapidly it is becoming more than a trend.[27] Catalogue marketers came out of the 1980s with a virtually identical approach to the marketplace.[28] Annual growth rates of 20 to 40 percent are not uncommon.[29] Catalogues are created and designed for highly segmented business buyers for comparison shopping, for acquiring information on new products or new product applications, and for determining current prices for particular items of interest. Catalogues make the distributor's job a bit easier, because it would be difficult for distributors to stock a manufacturer's

EXHIBIT 12-3 Creating Data Sheets That Sell

1. Include as much technical information as possible. Data sheets should answer all the customer's questions. When the information isn't there, the data sheet is worthless.
2. Good product data sheets explain and highlight technical features to show customers what benefits they will receive when they buy the product.
3. Use photographs. Nothing beats photographs for establishing what something looks like and how it works.
4. Use competitive data sheets to help customers make the comparisons between products.
5. Use 8 ½" × 11" pages so the data sheet doesn't get lost at the bottom of the file folder.
6. Know your reader. Make the content and technical depth of your data sheet compatible with the background and buying interests of your readers.
7. Know where in the buying process the data sheet fits in. Know the environment in which it will be used. Will there be advertising support, public relations, distributors, salespeople, catalogues, brochures, direct mail, and word of mouth?
8. Ask for customers' help in preparing the data sheet.
9. Use one writer for the entire project: the ads, the public relations, and the highly technical sheets.
10. Figure out how many people you would like to have read the data sheet: multiply the number by four to arrive at the number of sheets needed.

complete product mix. Historically, buyers have rarely used only a catalogue in deciding to make a purchase. However, the increasing ability to communicate economically over long distances, the growing concern over rising inventory costs, and the greater need today for marketers to serve many smaller and geographically diffuse customers are all good reasons why buying through catalogues is becoming more attractive and cost-effective.

A recent survey conducted by the Quick Corporation showed a marketing view of the business mail order industry. Among the findings of the study were the following: (1) business catalogues have increased 20 to 50 percent in recent years; (2) competition is getting fierce and margins are becoming slim; (3) there is an ever growing number of targeted mailings; (4) databases and compiled lists are being utilized more; and (5) businesses are becoming more comfortable with purchasing through the mail.[30]

More direct marketers are turning to telemarketing as a cost-efficient, productive addition to the mail. While telemarketing is more expensive than mailing on a cost-per-contact basis, the response rate is greater.[31] *Telemarketing* as a promotional tool (and a form of selling, as discussed in Chapter 10) greatly aids the business advertiser in making follow-up calls to check the receipt and effectiveness of various forms of printed and broadcast media, direct mail, data sheets, and catalogues. American firms spend more on telephone-based marketing than they do on any other medium. Such expenditures exceed $55 billion per year. Coordination between the telemarketing effort and other promotional tools is both important and necessary. Some marketers may not admit it, but they are using telemarketing. "Many companies think telemarketing is a dirty word," says Sandra Pernick, president of Direct Response Corporation, Des Plaines, Illinois, "but all businesses use some form of telemarketing whether they want to call it that or not." The number of structured telemarketing programs has increased

EXHIBIT 12-4 **A Well-Created Business Advertisement (page 1)**

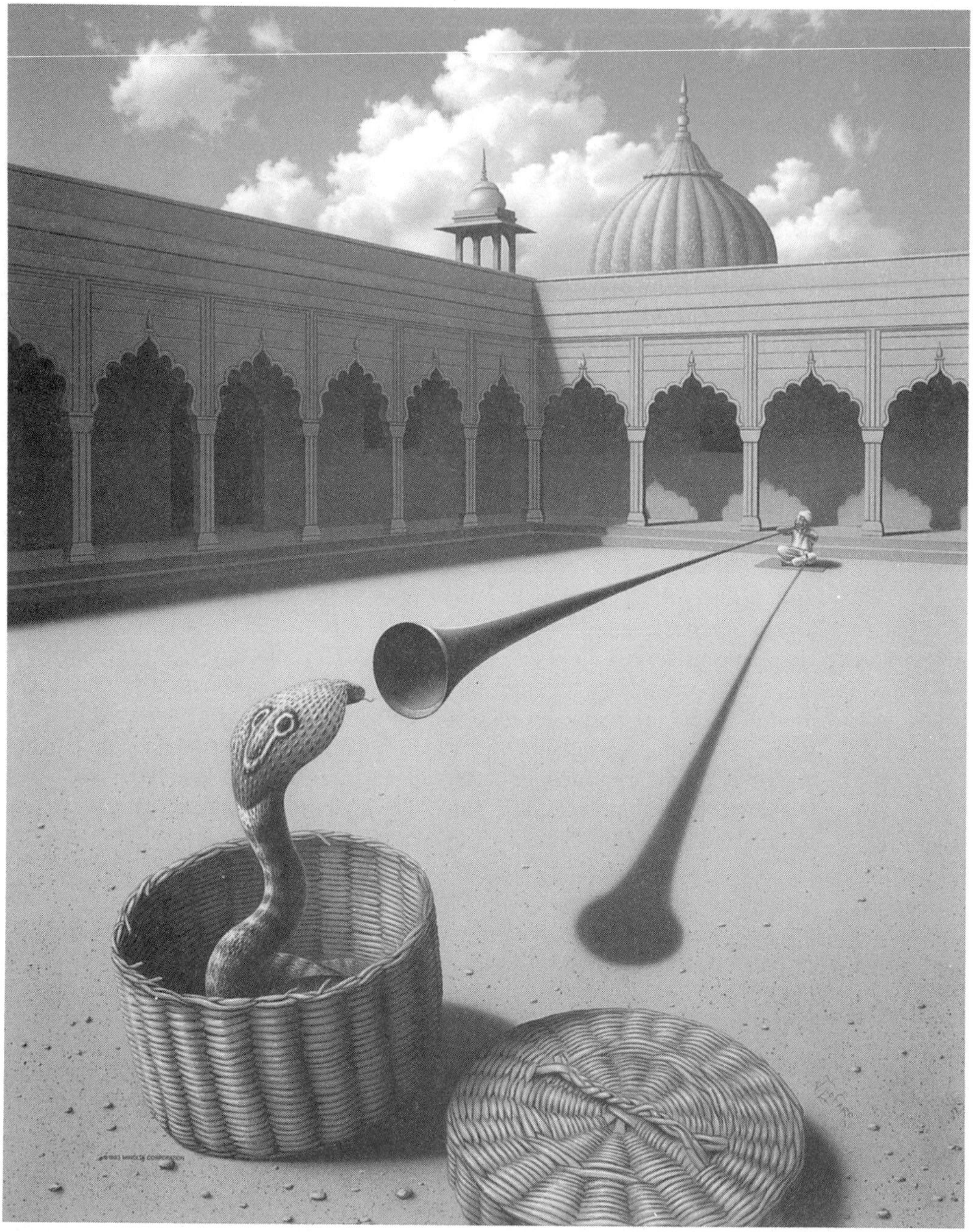

EXHIBIT 12-4 **A Well-Created Business Advertisement (page 2)**

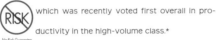

MAYBE THE BEST WAY TO HANDLE RISK IS TO AVOID IT ALTOGETHER.

That's why Minolta created the No-Risk Guarantee. It takes you out of harm's way by letting you decide whether you're happy with the copier's performance.

Even better, it covers our EP 9760 Pro Series Copier, which was recently voted first overall in productivity in the high-volume class.*

RISK
No-Risk Guarantee

Here's how it works: If you're not completely satisfied with our copier within the first three years of normal operation, we will replace it with an identical or comparably equipped model, free of charge. In other words, it works or it walks.

An award-winning copier combined with an ironclad guarantee? The only risk involved is passing this opportunity up. For more information, call 1-800-9-MINOLTA.

NO-RISK COPIERS
ONLY FROM THE MIND OF MINOLTA

MINOLTA

*Source: Thomas A. Minnelia, author of *The Copier Productivity Primer*
See an authorized Minolta copier dealer for complete details.

Source: Claritas Corporation, Alexandria, Virginia, in *Marketing News* (March 14, 1988), p. 9. Reprinted with permission.

dramatically among business marketers to the point that they have become almost routine. "No company should go without telemarketing, even if it's as simple as a customer service line," says Pernick.[32] Telemarketers often "man" telephone hotlines that enable customers to phone in for specific products, services, and price information. According to Joseph Misiura, president of Chicago's SMS Supply Company, "If you don't create an awareness of how effective a selling tool the telephone can be, you'll never improve. We just came to the realization that 90 percent of our communications are over the telephone and that our inside sales department could be doing a better job of selling."[33]

Telemarketing revenues multiplied sixteen times in the last decade and now account for 46 percent of all direct-marketing sales.[34] Companies are using telephone systems for promotion, order processing, sales support, and customer service. Telemarketing's potential would seem to be limited only by the imaginations of its users. Telemarketing is not a substitute or replacement for a regular sales force. It should complement and supplement other elements of the promotional mix, so that overall promotional efficiency can be improved. Telemarketing as a promotional tool will continue to expand.

Business advertising content. The effective business product or service advertisement will typically contain several elements. First, a short headline presents an interesting or intriguing idea of enough significance to readers to whom it is addressed that they will wish to pursue the idea further. An explanation or amplification of the headline then develops a limited number of specific appeals that are carefully designed to show the potential users that the product or service will be useful to them and will fill an actual need or want. The copy then describes the distinctive features of the product or service, offering evidence of the desirability and proof of claims made for it. Finally, the reader is urged to take some action; where feasible, specific courses of action are suggested.[35] Note that the headline, subheadline, and copy of the advertisement shown in Exhibit 12-4 illustrate these concepts.

Excellent photography and clear illustrations increase readership, while strengthening headlines or elaborating on them. Art, however, should not be used for its own sake. Generic images do not convey messages. It is better to use testimonials, case histories, and other copy-heavy advertisements than to be burdened with weak pictures. A study by Lebhar-Friedman Research and Information Services of New York City of 481 corporate decision makers found that frequently run colorful advertisements, such as the one shown in Exhibit 12-4, are the best for business advertising. Eight out of ten respondents said they are more favorably impressed and influenced by four-color than by black-and-white advertisements.[36]

Use of advertising agencies. *Advertising agencies* are specialist organizations equipped to provide a range of advertising services to their clients. They work on advertising strategy and campaigns, prepare copy and layouts, study markets, select media, and carry out the actual physical production of the advertisement to include its placement in selected media. During the past decade, the advertising management responsibility among small- to moderate-sized corporations has gradually been turned over to the well-integrated, total communications type of agency.[37]

Most media have historically allowed agencies 15 percent on the cost of the space or time purchased. In the marketing of consumer goods, this commission, plus markups on purchased services, usually represents the total income of the agency available to cover costs of operation and leave a profit. For many marketers of business goods, this method of payment does not result in an amount large enough to cover agency costs, and the contract with the agency includes an additional lump-sum payment proportionate to the services contemplated.

The advertising agency brings the client a wide breadth and depth of experience in marketing that can seldom be duplicated by the experience of a single company. It must also be able to provide the qualities of imagination and innovation in an unusual degree. In Cleveland-based Media II's study of one hundred business-to-business companies in northeastern Ohio with annual net sales of between $8 million and $100 million, creative marketing services, such as copywriting, art, and logotype creation, were found to be the most important factor in selecting an advertising agency. Creative services outweighed marketing services in importance by two to one.[38]

Contrary to these advantages, advertising agencies are not as universally used by business-to-business concerns as they are by consumer goods firms. Some firms believe that they can save money by avoiding an agency; they also may believe that they can do a better job themselves because of their greater understanding of their own business and customer base. Advertising agencies, on the other hand, believe that such companies do not know what they are talking about, save less money than they think, and sacrifice creative independence. A fuller discussion of this controversial topic is provided in the box entitled "Business-to-Business Marketing in Action." There is little question that the advertising agency has an important place in the marketing of business products. Although there are some types of activities it cannot perform as well as in-house departments, there are others it can do better or more economically. If an advertising agency is used, the challenge for marketers is to achieve an effective partnership between the company and the agency. Exhibit 12-5 discusses DuPont's partnership with six advertising agencies.

Business Publicity

Business publicity is defined as "stimulation of demand for a business product or service by planting commercially significant news about it in a print or broadcast medium without payment by the sponsor."[39] Publicity can be a powerful mass-promotion tool for the business advertiser. Publicity can serve to help build or add to a firm's prestige; to introduce a new product or service, a

BUSINESS-TO-BUSINESS MARKETING IN ACTION

IN-HOUSE ADVERTISING IS CAUSING AGENCY CONCERN

Rhode Island–based machine tool builder Brown and Sharpe's gradual weaning away from advertising agencies over the years—culminating recently with longtime agency Marquis/Bennett's decision to resign the account—may represent a trend.

Industrial companies think they can save money—and perhaps do the job better—on their own.

Agencies, on the other hand, assert that such companies don't know what they're talking about, that the companies don't save as much money as they think, and that the companies sacrifice creative independence.

"We've seen a bit of that happening lately, companies going in-house with their advertising," said Stauch-Vetromile principal Fred Stauch, who doesn't like what he sees.

Stauch had no problem reeling off a list of companies, besides Brown and Sharpe, that shun an "agency of record" in favor of doing their own adverstising or farming it out piecemeal:

L. G. Balfour Co., the Attleboro, Mass., jewelry manufacturer; Avanti Communications Corp., the Newport maker of high-speed digital communications equipment; Data Translation of Marlboro, Mass.; Augat's Alco Switch Division; Ispe of Mansfield, Mass.; and others.

The lure for Balfour is a "substantial cost reduction," said Jim Lutz, vice president of market development. "It's always tough to compare year to year, but I'd say we have 25 to 40 percent savings" over hiring an agency, he said.

Balfour spends more than $1 million a year on promotional acitivities—everything from overhead and salaries for its fifteen advertising-related employees (managers, artists, photographers, and support staff), to the creation of collateral materials and the placement of print advertising.

Lutz said about 95 percent of Balfour's promotional work is done in-house. He said agencies frequently make informal pitches for some of the company's work, "but we do relatively little media advertising, which in turn makes us less attractive to agencies."

Brown and Sharpe historically has had three advertising agencies—one each for its three divisions.

"It was hard to get any consistency," said Mark De Cellibus, director of corporate communications. "We needed to get some control over the situation. The net result is that we've been able to pull together something I'm proud of, and I think the ad managers (of the three divisions) are too."

The company spends about $1.2 million a year on advertising—again, that's everything from overhead to trade shows.

Bob Bennett, president of Marquis/Bennett, isn't so sure Brown and Sharpe is on the right track.

The company is using "an awful lot of freelancers," he said, so "they don't have a cohesive approach on a corporate level. Lots of people get a piece of Brown and Sharpe, and in my opinion that's not the way to do it."

Bennett said that in 1981 Brown and Sharpe made up 95 percent of his agency's business. He said the account billed between $500,000 and $1 million a year.

By early this year, when Marquis/Bennett decided to resign, the account billed about $290,000, and made up only 10 percent of the agency's business, he said. The agency claims billings of $4.1 million for last year, and projects $5.1 million this year.

Spencer Bennett Nowak has seen a similar erosion of business from one of its biggest clients—East Greenwich, R.I.–based Gulton Industries, a maker of thermal printers.

"When we first went to work with them ten years ago we did almost everything," said agency president Ed Nowak. "Today we just do media and ad creation." He said the account bills less than half the $500,000 a year it once did.

Stauch said he is convinced that such companies are making a mistake.

He said the biggest lure for the companies is reduced costs, "but I don't think anybody has really taken the time to do a cost analysis." Companies not only have to pay salaries and benefits, he said, but they have to buy equipment—desktop publishing systems, for example. "They're just not set up for it."

Stauch also said that the creative product "suffers tremendously" and "doesn't have the pizzazz of work done outside."

He said companies lose their creative objectivity because employees won't stand up to their boss.

"I know it because I've seen it," said Stauch, who has worked with John Hancock in Boston and Procter and Gamble.

De Cellibus's response is the recent National Machine Tool Builders Association awards show. "We just found out we won twelve awards there," he said. "It's a unique show in that the work is judged by the end user. I'd say going in-house has lent us good results."

Source: Jeffrey L. Hiday, "In-House Advertising Agency Causing Concern," *Providence Sunday Journal*, June 5, 1988, p. F–6. Used with permission.

product or service improvement, or a product or service application; to provide the salesperson with easier entry into the offices of current and prospective customers; and to increase the company's visibility and the desirability of its product mix.

Techniques to secure publicity. The public relations or advertising department is usually charged with the responsibility for developing favorable publicity that comes to the attention of not only consuming publics, but also the company's suppliers, distributors, employees, creditors, stockholders and investors, and the general public. As shown in Exhibit 12-6, four techniques for getting in the news are the press release, the exclusive feature, the press conference, and press kits. Additionally, publicity can be generated from five major areas: management activities, product promotions, sales activities, manufacturing and engineering, and personnel activities.[40] Management activities that are good sources for publicity include personnel changes and promotions; speeches and special appearances at banquets, graduations, and professional meetings; and stories about the company's history and future. The private lives and interesting

EXHIBIT 12-5 DuPont's Partnership with Six Advertising Agencies

With over six hundred products, Du Pont is the eighth largest industrial advertiser in the United States and works closely with six advertising agencies: BBDO, Rumrill-Hoyt, Sudler & Hennessey, Barnum Communications, Kelly Advertising, and N. W. Ayer, Inc. Harry E. Davis of Du Pont has said, "I hate to sound trite and talk about the old 'partnership' bit, but because of the way we do it, we and our agencies are really pulling the oars together."

Du Pont does not abide by the standard 15 percent commission structure for advertising agencies. Rather, it has a time-based fee compensation program that it negotiates annually with each agency. The compensation is determined by time rates and direct personnel costs, indirect agency cost allocations, profit margins, and an inflation adjustment. Other expenses such as production are billed at net cost.

Du Pont's cooperative attitude toward its agencies is also faciliated by a two-way performance auditing program. Du Pont annually rates each agency account group on a scale of 1 to 5 according to:

- Background knowledge of markets and products
- Administration of account
- Initiative in developing facts and ideas
- Responsiveness
- Cost consciousness
- Evaluation and recommendation of media
- Quality of art
- Understanding advertising fundamentals
- Quality of copy
- Quality and efficiency of production
- Budget control
- Maintenance of schedules and paperwork
- Attention to detail
- Maintenance of contact
- Use of ad research

To get the other side of the equation, agency people rate Du Pont's performance on:

- Background knowledge of markets and products
- Annual budget preparation
- Determination of marketing and advertising objectives
- Development of facts and ideas
- Stimulation and encouragement of agency personnel
- Constructiveness of criticism
- Scheduling of assignments
- Validity of media requests
- Responsiveness of requests
- Overall administration of work load
- Cost consciousness
- Budget control
- Clarity and completeness of instructions
- Attention to detail
- Maintenance of schedules and paperwork
- Use of ad research
- Maintenance of contact

The responses to both of these questionnaires are studied by senior management at the agencies and in Du Pont's marketing communications department. These senior managers then meet to determine which procedural changes need to be made or which personnel may need new assignments.

Source: Based on Bob Donath, "Managing the Partnership: How Du Pont Works with Its Six Advertising Agencies," *Business Marketing,* September 1983, pp. 70, 72, 74, 76. Used by permission.

activities of managerial personnel, to include hobbies and charitable and volunteer activities, show a different side to those who work for what are frequently perceived as "insensitive corporate giants."

Product promotions provide numerous sources of publicity. New-product announcements are perhaps the most common source. For instance, a new product could have three or four business uses, each with its own story; or the product may have a unique design or feature that warrants a special story. Sales activities are somewhat harder to publicize, but not altogether impossible. Sources for publicity here include national and regional sales conferences and trade shows, sales training programs, and recognition of key sales personnel. In this area, publicity can also be used as a means to raise and maintain the morale of the company's sales force.

EXHIBIT 12-6 **Four Techniques for Getting in the News**

Press Release. An announcement to the news media of significant changes in a firm or product or to introduce a new product. It is the most popular technique for obtaining publicity.

Exclusive Feature. An in-depth article or broadcast message about something of interest to a particular public. An exclusive feature could focus on a new concept, an industry trend, a special new technique, and so on. The feature usually does not focus solely on a company's products but will use them as examples to illustrate certain points. An exclusive feature usually requires extensive coordination between public relations personnel and editors or broadcast managers.

Press Conference. A meeting for the media sponsored by the firm. Press conferences can be overdone and used too often. They should be used to announce major news items such as the introduction of a new product or the appointment of a new president.

Press Kits. Sometimes used in connection with a press conference and may include press releases, pictures, tapes and films, product samples, and complimentary passes.

Publicity about manufacturing and engineering aspects of the product or company can serve to build confidence in the minds of customers. For instance, a better or unusual method of manufacturing or storing a product; technical employees recognized for their skills; and a flawless safety record are all useful and effective sources of publicity. Personnel activities with possibilities for publicity include winners of safety, waste-reduction, environmental, and cost-cutting awards; and employees' community involvement and leisure-time activities.

One of the real advantages of publicity is that the media time or space used is free of charge for the company, but it must be remembered that publicity can be negative, too. For example, McDonnell-Douglas Corporation experienced very negative publicity when its DC-10 aircraft resulted in air crashes and the loss of human life, as did Union Carbide with its chemical leak in Bhopal, India. Although publicity can work against a firm at a given point in time, its effects are usually short term; through time and positive promotional efforts, any damage can generally be reversed.

Business Sales Promotion

Business sales promotion was formerly considered by marketers as only a set of short-term inducements to create interest among salespeople, intermediaries, and customers. In many firms today, sales promotion ventures well beyond creating short-term value for various prospects. It has become the driving force that links personal selling, advertising, and publicity into a meaningful, integrated promotional program. Although there are many forms of sales promotion activities available, business marketers very commonly use trade shows and exhibits; contests, sweepstakes, and games; and advertising specialties.

Trade shows and exhibits. *Trade shows* have emerged as a significant component in companies' total marketing and selling strategies and budgets, as well as being places where information is exchanged and major buying demands are made within a given industry. Trade shows have been reported as the second largest component of the total advertising budget allocation in firms marketing business products. For example, COMDEX, the annual computer industry trade show in the United States, brings together over one thousand exhibitors at Chicago's McCormick Place each year and attracts more than 125,000 visitors from one hundred countries.[41] Trade shows have become a key way for big business to do even bigger business and a cost-effective way for smaller businesses to make their mark. Today, the trade show industry generates some $50 billion annually, with overall financial impact of shows continuing to grow, according to Trade Show Bureau research.

The gathering of an entire industry at one time in one place at a trade show is a most effective way to do business. Studies have shown that over half of the audience at a trade show is planning to buy and that 80 percent or more of the attendees are a buying influence for one or more of the types of products exhibited.[42] Trade shows are an ideal showcase, with exhibitors putting their best on display for the decision makers and buyers who will visit their booths. The large crowds of attendees often result in salespeople making more sales presentations per day at the typical show than they would normally make during an entire month in the field.[43] The rapid growth in interest in trade shows at the senior management level has influenced the number of professionals recruited to manage a company's trade show budgets, programs, and participation.[44]

In an increasingly competitive world, business marketers are required to define markets more closely, develop new tactics, strategize more comprehensively, and target selling more selectively. Trade shows are a medium to this end. Trade shows are gaining in popularity due to their high-touch nature. From 1979 to 1993, the number of expositions has more than doubled, as have the size of shows, the number of participating exhibitors, and the number of cities that have built new convention centers designed to capture a host-city share of the revenue generated by the better than forty-five million visitors who attend these annual events.[45] Trade shows produce quantifiable sales results if they are adequately researched and strategically organized for the (1) special dynamics of the trade show environment and (2) the special dynamics of interaction between exhibitor staff and the prospective buyers. Firms selling to a particular industry display and demonstrate their products for the purpose of promoting and selling these products. Other firms (suppliers), such as Kitzing Exhibits Marketing Service, evaluate the sales-producing potential of the firm's promotional resources with a trade show marketing agency. A well-done trade show exhibit can provide access to key decision makers, contact with prospects, and an opportunity to further service present customers. It also offers an opportunity to publicize a significant contribution to technology, or to demonstrate both new and old products. According to Thomas V. Bonoma, executives can gain more from trade shows by understanding the benefits offered and choosing the events accordingly. Also, for many firms, trade show expenditures are the major (or only) form of organized marketing communication activity other than efforts by the firm's sales force and/or distributors.[46]

Over forty-five million people attend over nine hundred trade shows every year. Furthermore, over ninety-one thousand firms display their merchandise and spend in excess of $7 billion annually in exhibits. The cost per potential customer is less than half that of a personal business sales call.[47] Business sales costs have risen constantly over the past decade, now amounting to between $250 and $300 per visit. Approximately four calls are needed to close the average sale, which pushes the total sales call into four figures per order. Recent figures indicate that closing a sale from a direct business sales call averages $1,114.[48]

Statistics show that trade shows are a very cost-effective way of generating sales. The Trade Show Bureau researched some studies done by Cahners Advertising Research and Exhibit Surveys Incorporated and found that the average cost of a sales call in 1989 was $259. In contrast, the average cost of reaching a trade show visitor was $142. Furthermore, it takes an average of 4.3 sales calls to close a typical sale, but only a letter or a phone call to close a qualified trade show lead.[49] The participating vendors expect several benefits, including generating new sales leads, maintaining customer contacts and goodwill, introducing new products, meeting new customers, and selling more to present customers. Benefits derived can be broadly grouped into selling and nonselling categories, with selling categories offering access to key decision makers and an expanded opportunity to service present customers. Nonselling aspects include the availability of intelligence about competitors and the chance to test new products.[50]

Trade show managers classify shows as either horizontal or vertical. Vertical shows promote products and services to a single industry or specific profession. An example of such a show would be the National Operating Room Nurses' Association Meetings and Exposition, which exhibits products designed for operating-room nurses. A horizontal show, on the other hand, promotes a type of product to a variety of industries; for example, the COMDEX show mentioned earlier that features computers, peripherals, and software for any and all industries.[51]

The days of all fun and little work at trade shows seems to have disappeared. Today, marketing-driven corporations are holding exhibit staffs and programs accountable for quotas, goals, and objectives. For example, more money is going into preshow preparation. A case in point was Ex-Cell-O Corporation's gearing up for the International Machine Tool Show. Before the show, the company launched an all-out campaign to get 300 VIPs to visit its exhibit and attend a special hospitality event on a cruise ship. Efforts included direct mail, tie-ins with trade advertisements and press events, and a one-on-one sales push in the field. The effort was considered a success when 275 VIPs attended Ex-Cell-O's live production demonstration and cruise.[52] Getting more bang for the trade show dollar is what it's all about. Tools used in the months before a trade show directly affect exposition success or failure. Preshow preparation includes exhibit booth setup; electrical, plumbing, and communications services; audio-visual equipment; and booth decorations and furniture. The exhibiting firm may also want to have a hospitality suite in the headquarters hotel to entertain valued customers, a preregistration procedure for potential and existing customers, and a postshow list of attendees.[53] See Figure 12-6 for an overview of how the typical trade show exhibit dollar is spent.

Deciding whether to participate. Trade Show Bureau data indicated that, on average, 47 percent of a typical trade show audience plays a role in the decision to buy from at least one major product category at the event, and 18 percent make the final decision. Further, 64 percent of all visitors travel more than two hundred miles to attend a trade show, with 29 percent of attendees being owners, partners, presidents, vice presidents, and general managers.[54] Although trade shows are costly, the question a company must answer in considering trade show participation is whether such an endeavor will be profitable. Trade show sales are often completed on the show floor or in a single follow-up call. (A study by Exhibit Surveys found that 78 percent of the attendees at the National Computer Conference had purchased a product within a year after the 1984 exhibition.)[56] Clearly, trade shows can help a firm establish accounts, develop awareness of its products or services, and help increase market penetration.

FIGURE 12-6 **How the Exhibit Dollar Is Spent—Allocation of Direct Exhibit Costs (1989–1991 Average)**

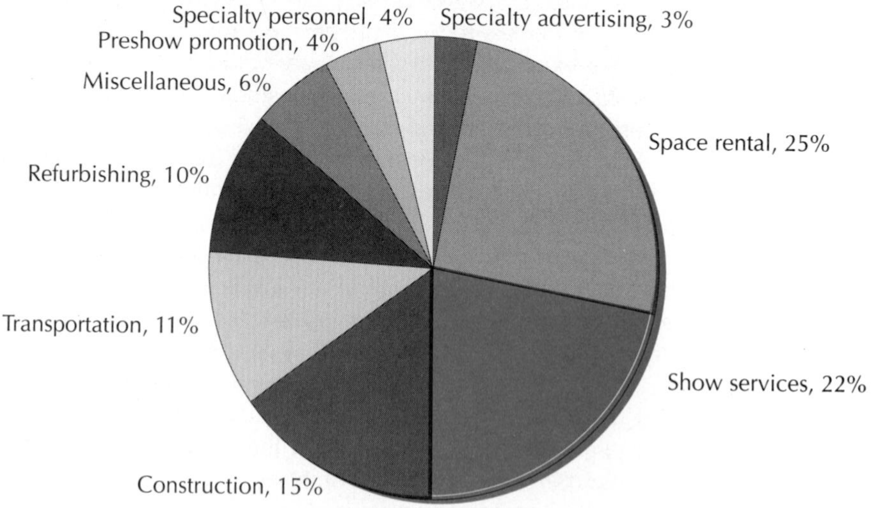

Source: Exhibit Surveys, Inc. for Trade Show Bureau, 1992. Trade Show Bureau, 1660 Lincoln Street, Suite 2080, Denver, CO 80264.

Selecting the show.[57] There are more than eight thousand trade shows in the United States each year, and entering all of them would be wasteful and quite expensive. The challenge is to select and enter those shows that will help to achieve the company's short-term and long-term strategic goals. Show sponsors can provide a list of the expected attendees along with a profile of their potential job titles and job responsibilities. Some additional criteria to consider when determining whether or not to participate include:

Location—The majority of trade show visitors live within five hundred miles of the host city. Therefore, evaluate the location to determine who is likely to attend.

Facilities/Services—Telephones and other needed communication equipment, along with adequate floor space, and electrical and water outlets must be available.

Restrictions—Does the show prohibit certain types of products or display signs, or limit the number of booth personnel?

Past Success—Does the particular trade show have a successful history?

Dates/Scheduling—Do the show's dates conflict with other industry events?

Trade show objectives. The setting of specific trade show objectives is important when making decisions as to what shows to participate in, whom to send, and how much to budget for the effort. Overall objectives might include introducing a new product, increasing market share, and building image. Once objectives have been decided, then specific goals for accomplishing each objective must be determined and defined. Specific goals may be to boost sales for a declining product or product line, identify potential customers, attract new channel intermediaries, conduct competitive intelligence, or conduct research regarding a potential technological innovation.

Trade show budget. Excluding booth personnel, the average cost to participate in a trade show in 1988 was over $35,000. The cost of an exhibit depends on furnishings required, services required, and hardware needed. A modest exhibit in a single booth space will cost at least $2,500 to $5,000; a multispace exhibit will cost $100,000 or more. How much to budget for this effort is a difficult decision to make. Payback is difficult to measure, and tangible results may not be known for months, or even years. Gary Lilien's ADVISOR studies provide the practitioner with some help with the difficult job of trade show budgeting. The level of spending on trade shows is likely to be higher if the product or product line is in the early stages of the product life cycle, if it is experiencing high sales volume, if the firm employs a strongly aggressive marketing plan, and if the product or product line has low customer concentration.[58] The marketing manager must weigh the total cost and time commitment against expected sales and image impact.

Contests, sweepstakes, and games. *Contests, sweepstakes, and games* are also used by many business marketers. These tools provide customers with a chance to win something—such as cash, trips, or goods—as a result of either luck or extra effort. A contest calls for customers to submit an entry—a jingle, an estimate, or a suggestion—to be examined by a panel of judges who will select the best entries. A sweepstakes calls for customers to submit their names in a drawing. A game presents customers with something every time they buy, which may or may not help them win a prize. A sales contest induces dealers or distributors to redouble their sales efforts over a specific time period, with prizes going to the top performers.[59]

Advertising specialties. An *advertising specialty* can be defined as "a useful item with a message on it," such as a pen, a calendar, or the ever popular back scratcher. Advertising specialties are items that bear the company name, logo, or advertising message and are given away to present and potential customers.[60] Marketers find advertising specialties to be one of the most effective means for reaching a target audience and holding its attention.[61] From an intensive study of the specialty advertising industry—which sampled specialty distributors, suppliers, and users, as well as media representatives, advertising agency personnel, and advertising educators—a number of conclusions were reached by the researchers:

(1) Too many advertisements running too close together in business media are creating an ever increasing opportunity for advertising-specialty programs to replace media advertising. Advertising-specialty products offer a strong alternative to an already overcrowded media situation.

(2) Businesses have increasingly realized that in mature markets, especially service businesses, relationships with clients must be established and maintained. Advertising specialties are well suited for both of these promotional objectives.

(3) Suppliers have, in recent years, offered the industry a supply of products that are technically superior and can be applied to advertising-specialty programs as promotional vehicles.

(4) Users and other relevant publics are gaining a better behavioral understanding of the advertising-specialty process. The learning reinforcement-based effects are the source of the most successful advertising-specialty programs.

(5) Marketers are only beginning to learn how to design more comprehensive marketing strategies, which include advertising-specialty items along with media and public relations efforts.[62]

Historically, business advertising specialties have been regarded as mere gimmickry and have not been taken very seriously as an effective sales promotional vehicle. However, this negative image is beginning to change, and the use of advertising specialties appears to be on the rise.

Advertising specialties offer great versatility when used in a planned campaign. Trade show exhibitors can specifically target their audience with an item the visitors will remember. For example, Harris Calorific, a value manufacturer, had an objective of generating traffic to its exhibit from a select group of 240 dealers attending the American Welding Society's Trade Show. Harris was convinced that if its salespeople could spend just a few minutes with each dealer, its dealer network could be greatly increased.

> Prior to the trade show, Harris Calorific mailed a vinyl executive desk folder to selected dealers. Each folder included an invitation for the dealers to stop at the Harris booth. However, the front of the folder was intentionally hot stamped with gold to indicate the place for a personalized nameplate that could be picked up at the booth. This was a tactic instrumental in ensuring exhibit traffic because recipients wanted to pick up their personalized nameplates which could be affixed to enhance the appearance of the folder. As a result, 63 percent of the targeted dealers visited the booth to pick up their nameplate, and Harris quadrupled the number of leads normally generated at the show. The 37 percent who didn't show up were later contacted by Harris representatives. Harris signed up twenty-five distributors.[63]

The use of prizes, coupled with advertising-specialty items, can also be effective. The United States Surgical Corporation (USSC) increased its turnout 36 percent in one year by offering nurses a chance to win a fur coat. A customized folder was mailed to seven thousand members of the Association of Operating Room Nurses. Over three thousand of these prospects registered for the trade show, and twenty-two hundred visited the USSC booth. The inside cover of the folder contained a scratch-off circle. Nurses had to remove the circle at the booth to be eligible for ten different prizes, including a color television set and a fur coat. Everyone who visited the display received a coffee mug imprinted with the company's logo.[64]

As these examples show, it is possible to gain an advantage over the competition with the creative use of specialty advertising.

CONCEPT QUESTIONS

1. What is the role of the advertising agency for a business-to-business firm?
2. Why is business sales promotion no longer considered to be only of short-term value to the marketer?
3. What is the primary benefit of contests, sweepstakes, and games to the business customer?

MEASURING THE EFFECTIVENESS OF THE BUSINESS PROMOTION CAMPAIGN

Two of the most commonly used methods of measuring the effectiveness of a promotion campaign are both pre- and posttesting and responses to advertisements.

Pretesting and Posttesting

Pretesting of promotional pieces measures, among other things, the subjects' awareness of the product or service at issue through a series of questions about it, or a number of situations to which respondents react, thereby indicating their current knowledge about the product or service. In posttesting, those who have been exposed to advertisements, publicity pieces, or sales promotion devices are questioned as to their aided recall, unaided recall, recognition, comprehension, believability, and brand awareness (where applicable) in regard to the promotion. If respondents have purchased a product or service as a result of the promotional piece or activity being studied, they will usually be asked to indicate satisfaction with, and frequency of usage of, the product or service.

Responses to Business Advertising

Traditionally, one of the most popular methods of measuring the effectiveness of business advertising has been through the response that the company received to print and broadcast advertisements and to direct marketing efforts. For print media, usually coupons or tear-away sheets are put on advertisements placed in various forms of business publications and direct marketing pieces. Advertisers generally assume that if a particular advertisement or direct marketing effort receives a large mail-in or phone-in response, it is an effective promotional piece. Likewise, if an advertisement using a broadcast medium receives a considerable number of inquiries, it is also felt to be successful.

Business marketers, often puzzled by the value of advertising, can now find answers to some long-asked questions. By fielding scaled-down versions of the pioneer controlled ad-weight study developed by the Advertising Research Foundation (ARF), marketers can learn:

- Whether they should advertise in the first place.
- If they do advertise, how much of it will be profitable.
- Whether advertising cuts will hurt or help profit.[65]

The $390,000 research project developed by the ARF and its research project partner, the Association of Business Publishers (ABP), offers a practical model for testing business print advertising. The ARF/ABP weight test measures how different amounts of advertising affect sales for several business products. By carefully segmenting markets, matching different levels of media coverage to each segment, and accurately tracking sales, researchers can devise a marginal cost model for their advertising. They can estimate how much profit an additional dollar of advertising will generate. The overall goal of this activity is to know when advertising levels reach the point of maximum profit.[66]

FOLLOWING UP AND MODIFYING THE BUSINESS PROMOTION CAMPAIGN WHEN NECESSARY

Basic management theory suggests that any process currently being used should be periodically reviewed and modified, if necessary. Certainly, such is the case with business promotion. In order for business marketing managers to evaluate the promotional campaign properly, they must return to the objectives that were initially established for the campaign. Were the objectives met? Were they exceeded? Did the campaign fall short of the objectives? If so, by how much?

If the campaign has not met the intended objectives, then each specific segment must be analyzed to determine which stage or stages require further analysis and modification. If the campaign has met or exceeded the stated objectives, it is generally helpful to identify the stage, or stages, in the campaign that were most or least successful in that regard. Even in a successful promotion campaign, some parts of the system might need rethinking, and perhaps some modification.

PROMOTIONAL STRATEGY FOR INTERNATIONAL MARKETS

International Advertising

The promotion of business goods and services is also an important part of the marketing mix for international markets.[67] As with domestic markets, the purposes of international business promotion are to inform, persuade, and remind customers in overseas markets of the availability of certain goods and services. The three primary components of international business promotion are also advertising, publicity, and sales promotion.

The problems of business and consumer marketers are often quite different, as has been pointed out several times in this text. This is especially true in regard to international advertising. Many international business advertisers find that only a large agency with offices or affiliates in many markets can do the job adequately. (Table 12-2 lists the ten largest American agencies in terms of worldwide billings.) Firms planning large campaigns must often deal with a large international agency. Overseas offices are usually staffed with multilingual, multinational personnel, allowing each country to be treated as a distinct market. Agency selection is a time-consuming and laborious job, but it is a critical step for the international advertiser and must be done thoroughly and professionally.

TABLE 12-2 **Top Ten Advertising Agencies by Worldwide Billings**

Rank	Agency	Worldwide Billings 1987*
1	Young & Rubicam	4,905.71
2	Saatchi & Saatchi Advertising	4,609.44
3	Backer Spielvogel Bates	4,068.70
4	BBDO Worldwide	3,664.50
5	Ogilvy & Mather Worldwide	3,663.80
6	McCann-Erickson Worldwide	3,418.50
7	J. Walter Thompson Co.	3,221.80
8	Lintas: Worldwide	2,787.20
9	DDB Needham Worldwide	2,581.55
10	D'Arcy Masius Benton & Bowles	2,494.28

*In millions of dollars.

Some guidelines to use in developing an international promotional program are the definition of advertising goals, preparation of a campaign plan, review and approval of the plan, copy development and testing, media planning, budget approval, campaign implementation, and measurement of advertising effectiveness. Not an easy job indeed! Many countries have more than one official language (Canada and Norway have two; Belgium, three; and Switzerland, four); people's attitudes and the way they think may be different; and the social, economic, technological, and political environments may be quite different than what the domestic business marketing manager is used to.

An important decision for international advertisers to make is whether the advertising campaign should be standardized worldwide or localized. Standardized advertising has advantages in that a successful campaign in one country is often effective in another as well. Also, standardized advertising is cost-efficient. On the other hand, localized advertising recognizes cultural differences among nations. In the final analysis, the choice between standard and local advertising should be based on such considerations as levels of education, experience and competence of personnel in either the foreign advertising agency or the affiliate of a domestic agency, degree of nationalism and rate of economic growth in the targeted country, customers of the country, attitudes toward authority, and independence of media from governmental control.

International Publicity and Sales Promotion

Publicity programs, which give the firm and its products broad exposure to customers and prospects, as well as third-party endorsement by the media, provide a cost-effective use of a limited promotion budget. Good publicity and good public relations mean adapting to the publics of individual countries. Although positive publicity and effective public relations will minimize a firm's problems in foreign markets, some problems will persist in spite of the best corporate diplomacy and media cooperation and support.

Sales promotion tools tend to stimulate new attitudes toward the product being promoted, as few can resist the lure of something for nothing. Just the feeling that something can be had for free creates a strong desire for the product among buyers, no matter from which country or region. The role of sales promotion in other countries does not vary from what it is in the United States. Yet, an appropriate sales promotion program for an overseas market should be geared to the local environment. Historically, sales promotion has been an American phenomenon. However, today sales promotion tools are increasingly being used to supplement advertising and personal selling throughout the free world.[68]

CONCEPT QUESTIONS

1. How do international business advertisers determine whether an advertising campaign should be standardized worldwide or should be localized?
2. What is necessary to have good international publicity and public relations?

SUMMARY

1. Promotion in business marketing refers to the use of the promotional tools of advertising, publicity, and sales promotion. Business promotional tools generally serve to strengthen the personal selling effort and can be very effective in paving the way for sales representatives, in introducing new products and product lines to both established and prospective customers, and in creating goodwill between the selling and purchasing firms.
2. Creating a promotional campaign involves the following five steps: setting objectives, developing the promotional budget, determining the promotional mix, measuring the effectiveness of the promotional plan, and making any necessary changes in the campaign.
3. There is a great need for specific, realistic objectives for any promotional campaign. The establishment of appropriate objectives should be the starting point for every promotional campaign. Whenever possible, it is preferable to state objectives in quantitative terms so that they can be more easily measured.
4. Ideally, the promotional budget should be set at a point where the last dollar spent on promotion equals profits from the sales produced by that dollar. This is only possible, however, if the money is spent in an optimal fashion. Therefore, there must be a prioritization of all promotional efforts in terms of their potential contribution to the firm.

5. A firm can use advertising, publicity, and sales promotion in its promotional mix. Business advertising has very specific goals and generally employs printed media, broadcast media, and direct marketing to deliver its message to selected target markets. The advertising agency provides the client with a wide breadth and depth of experience that can seldom be duplicated by a single firm; yet, a number of firms prefer to use their own in-house advertising departments. Business publicity can be generated from the five major areas of management activities, product promotions, sales activities, manufacturing and engineering, and personnel activities. Business sales promotion has become the driving force that links personal selling, advertising, and publicity into a meaningful, integrated promotional program; it includes trade shows and exhibits, contests, sweepstakes, games, and advertising specialties.
6. Two of the most commonly used methods of measuring the effectiveness of promotional campaigns are pretesting and posttesting and determining responses to print media advertisements. Pretesting and posttesting methods determine how much respondents knew about the product or service before the advertisement and how much they learned about it from the advertisement. If a business advertisement is successful, usually there will be strong mail or telephone response.
7. In order for marketing managers to determine the degree of success of promotional campaigns, they must first determine if the campaign met its initial objectives. If the objectives were not met, each stage of the campaign should be analyzed to see where the problems are. These parts of the campaign will generally need rethinking and probably some modification.
8. International business promotion also involves advertising, publicity, and sales promotion. International business advertisers must determine whether or not to standardize their advertising campaigns worldwide or according to local or nationalistic lines. International publicity must be carefully adapted to local publics, as should international sales promotion. Once considered only an American phenomenon, sales promotion is being increasingly used throughout the free world as a supplement to personal selling and advertising.

KEY TERMS

Advertising agencies
Advertising specialty
Broadcast media
Business advertising
Business catalogues
Business promotion
Business publicity
Business sales promotion
Contests, sweepstakes, and games
Data sheets
Direct mail
Direct marketing
General business publications
Horizontal publications
Industrial trade directories
Media mix
Professional publications
Telemarketing
Trade shows
Vertical publications

REVIEW QUESTIONS

1. What three promotional tools are commonly utilized in business promotion campaigns? When does promotion play a primary role in selling business products and services? Why is promotion usually only a support effort for personal selling activities in business marketing?
2. What are five stages in the development of a business promotion plan? What is a promotional campaign?
3. Why is it preferable to express the objectives of promotion in dollar amounts? How are market-share and sales-volume data useful to the business marketer?
4. Ideally, at what point should the promotion budget be set? Identify the four major methods by which business promotion budgets are determined.
5. Discuss four major goals of business advertising. How is business advertising different from consumer advertising?
6. Identify three primary media mix elements in business advertising. Discuss four types of print media, two types of broadcast media, and four types of direct marketing efforts.
7. What should the typical effective business advertisement contain? How can advertising agencies be of great value to the firm? Why are many firms reluctant to use advertising agencies? How do advertising agencies counter this reluctance?
8. What purposes does publicity have in the business-to-business firm? From what five major areas does the firm generally derive its publicity? How can business publicity be negative? Provide a recent example of this phenomenon.
9. How has the perception of sales promotion changed for the business-to-business firm from a decade ago to the present? Discuss three types of business sales promotion tools.
10. Discuss two of the most commonly used methods to evaluate the effectiveness of a promotional campaign. What is involved in following up and modifying (when necessary) a business promotion campaign? What advertising research questions does the ARF/ABP weight study model answer for the business marketer?
11. How does a business-to-business firm engaged in international operations decide whether or not to standardize a promotional campaign worldwide or according to national or regional norms of particular markets? What is necessary to have good publicity and public relations in international business markets? Why do you think the use of international business sales promotion has been increasing at such a rapid rate?

Cases

CASE 12-1 U.S. Companies Learn to Deal with the Japanese Media

Today, over sixty American companies are now listed on the Tokyo Stock Exchange, and many more want to sell their products and services to Japan. With more U.S. companies than ever now doing business with the Japanese, chances are increasing that public relations managers will soon need to work with the Japanese media.

Part of the difficulty in dealing with the Japanese press is the language barrier. Meaningful television and radio interviews with Americans are difficult because of the need for English-to-Japanese translations. Additionally, the public relations managers must also understand the complex Japanese culture. Unlike the United States, the print media in Japan are much more influential than the broadcast media. The country has a booming newspaper, magazine, and trade press industry. The market is so massive that approaching it effectively takes in-depth local knowledge and experience.

Foreigners build credibility with the Japanese media through face-to-face contact. Beyond the factual information foreign businesses offer, the media want the opportunity to ask questions. Therefore, the most productive means of media contact in Japan are press conferences and one-on-one interviews. These personal presentations are especially important because one of the key publicity techniques in the United States, the press release, is almost unheard of in Japan.

DISCUSSION QUESTIONS

1. What can American companies do to ease the transition into foreign public relations?
2. What is the most effective public relations approach in Japan? How does that differ from other countries?

Source: C. Lamb, J. Hair, and C. McDaniel, *Principles of Marketing*, 1st Edition (Cincinnati, OH: South-Western Publishing Company, 1992) p. 487.

CASE 12-2 Cause-Related Promotion

Everything looks like a billboard nowadays. Even charities lend their names to commercial advertising pitches. Companies call it "cause-related marketing." These companies will donate to charity, if they can borrow the charity's name and credibility to promote their products. Likewise, more charities are asking corporate America to sponsor their causes despite the danger that they may appear to be endorsing products.

Not-for-profit groups have long relied on the media to donate their nearly $3 billion a year in free public service ads. Now some charities are beginning to use paid messages—underwritten by major companies—because they want to reach specific audiences better. Either the groups produce the advertisement and give sponsors a credit line, or the corporations insert plugs for charities into their own ads. The American Cancer Society has recently eased its opposition to national corporate partnership and has begun courting big athletic shoemakers and sporting goods companies about a joint antismoking campaign aimed at minority youths. "Their markets and our markets are similar," says a Cancer Society official. The Boy Scouts of America are also looking to corporate backers such as American Airlines and Phillips Petroleum to increase stagnant membership.

Corporations also see potential benefits in sponsoring not-for-profit organizations. Upjohn and Ciba Consumer Pharmaceuticals recently sent thirteen million "mature" consumers cents-off coupons for pain-relief consumer products made by the two companies. The coupons carried the Arthritis Foundation's logo with Ciba's promise to donate 25 cents for every coupon received up to $50,000, while Upjohn offered 50 cents up to $100,000. The Arthritis Foundation's deal also included a mention on its annual telethon, use of the logo on grocery store ads, and energetic support for the whole promotion by members of the charity's local chapter.

Charities can't just ask for donations from corporations anymore. Instead, organizations like Easter Seals and the Arthritis Foundation have to bring corporations something that links up with their products and promotions to secure a donation or to acquire media time. Invariably, corporate sponsorship will grow because more not-for-profit groups are vying for public service ads, and advertisers increasingly preach corporate philanthropy. Unfortunately, it looks as if charities are now governed by the "I'll scratch your back if you scratch mine" law imposed on them by the big corporations they depend on for funds.

DISCUSSION QUESTIONS

1. Are these charities really endorsing the product in the promotion?
2. Should charities endorse products and/or services?
3. Was the product approved by the charity as a "safe" and effective product, as in the case of the aspirin coupon?

Source: C. Lamb, J. Hair, and C. McDaniel, *Principles of Marketing*, 1st Edition (Cincinnati, OH: South-Western Publishing Company, 1992) p. 431.

Suggested Additional Readings

Bencin, Richard L. "Telefocus: Telemarketing Gets Synergized." *Sales and Marketing Management* 144 (February 1992): 49–53. **A discussion of the expanded use of telemarketing in sales prospecting, direct-mail campaigns, and video brochures.**

Bly, Robert W. "The Twelve Most Common Direct Mail Mistakes . . . And How to Avoid Them." *Business Marketing* 72 (June 1987): 122–128. **Problems and guidelines in writing direct-mail pieces.**

Davids, Meryl. "How to Plan and Place Corporate Advertising in Print Media." *Public Relations Journal* 42 (December 1986): 29–30, 33. **Guidelines for media purchases and criteria for media selection.**

Dunn, William. "How To Sell the Story." *American Demographics* 14 (April 1992): 50–52. **A discussion of the effective use of publicity campaigns, press releases, and interviews in the promotion of products and services.**

Gordon, Howard L. "Advertising That Really Grabs Buyers." *Business Marketing* 72 (July 1987): 78–89. **Copy, emotions, and graphic arts in business advertising.**

Kelley, Bill. "Advertising on a Shoestring." *Sales and Marketing Management* 144 (July 1992): 92–93, 96. **Guidelines to aid small businesses in getting the most out of a minimal advertising budget.**

Li, Richard P. "The Hunt for Direct Marketing Success." *Direct Marketing* 49 (March 1987): 38–42. **A study of direct-mail campaigns, market segmentation, database management, and statistical modeling.**

Madden, Charles S., and Marjorie J. Caballero-Cooper. "Expectations of Users of Specialty Advertising." *Journal of Advertising Research* 32 (July/August 1992): 45–52. **A survey of firms to glean what results they are hoping for with the use of specialty advertising.**

Nadal, Miles S. "Sales Promotion Gives You the Competitive Edge." *Sales and Marketing Management in Canada* (Canada), 27 (October 1986): pp. 33–34. **Advantages, trends, and expenditures in the use of sales promotion for a competitive edge.**

Newhall, Jerry S. "The Care and Feeding of a Cash Cow." *Sales and Marketing Management* 144 (May 1992): 40–47. **A discussion on the effective use of promotion in marketing products with high market share in low-growth industries.**

O'Keefe, Philip. "Get Discovered with Directories." *Business Marketing* 72 (June 1987): 130–137. **Discussion of the value of business promotion through trade publications, trade directories, and reference services.**

Pfaff, Fred. "How Business Talks to Business: Like It Is." *Marketing and Media Decisions* 22 (May 1987): 83–97. **Study of expenditures and innovations in business advertising campaigns, and a discussion of trade publications.**

Piercy, Nigel. "The Politics of Setting an Advertising Budget" *International Journal of Advertising* (UK), 5, no. 4 (1986): 281–305. **Exploratory study of organizational structure and the power of the marketing department in setting the advertising budget.**

Schaefer, Wolfgang. "Readers Per Copy of Trade Publications." *European Research* (Netherlands), 14 (1986): 198–201. **Discussion of magazine-penetration measurements in the Federal Republic of Germany, to include a new measurement model.**

Seelig, Pat. "Advertising Specialties." *Incentive Marketing* 161 (May 1987): 104–108. **Study of many companies using giveaway items imprinted with the company name and coupled thematically with a mass-media advertising campaign.**

"Should Telemarketing Be Done In-House or through an Agency?" *Business Marketing* 77 (August 1992): 44–45. **Experts discuss the pros, cons, and successes of using telemarketing both in-house and through agencies.**

Stoeger, Keith A. "Three, Two, One, Contact!" *Direct Marketing* 50 (June 1987): 114–115. **Study and discussion of business advertising, telephone selling, customer relations, and customer services in business markets.**

Summerfield, Cy. "Business Press Advertising Can Reduce Sales Costs." *Sales and Marketing Management in Canada* (Canada), 27 (September 1986): 33–34. **Survey of 461 Canadian**

advertising executives about the effectiveness of business press advertising in reducing business sales costs.

Swayne, Linda E., and Thomas H. Stevenson. "Comparative Advertising in Horizontal Business Publications." *Industrial Marketing Management* 16 (February 1987): 71–76. **Study of the trends in three leading U.S. industries.**

West, Reg. "Sales Promotion: Cutting Risks," *Marketing* (UK), 29 (June 11, 1987): 39, 41. **Study of new technologies, projective techniques, promotional maps, and quantitative measurement in sales promotion.**

Williams, Terry Considine. "I Saw It on Radio—Will Direct Response Radio Return to the Golden Ad Days?" *Direct Marketing* 49 (October 1986): 50–56, 82. **Trends in, and advantages of, radio advertising, to include per-inquiry marketing.**

Young, Gary G. "Trade Show Practices: Time for Evaluation." In *Marketing in a Dynamic Environment*, edited by Michael H. Morris and Eugene E. Teeple, 1–11. The Atlantic Marketing Association, 2 (October 1986). **Nationwide survey of trade show practices involving the setting of objectives, show selection criteria, and performance of trade show effort.**

Zibrun, S. Michael. "Business-to-Business: A Value-Added Service to Build Opportunity." *The Journal of Business and Industrial Marketing* 2 (Winter 1987): 67–76. **Overview of telemarketing to add incremental business—its roots, structure, pitfalls, and potential.**

ENDNOTES

[1]Bruce Whitehall, "How Rentokil's 'Affinity Club' Captures Professionals—At Work or Play," *Industrial Marketing Digest* (UK), 14 (Third Quarter 1989): 73–82.

[2]William G. Nickels, *Marketing Communication and Promotion*, 3d ed. (Columbus, Ohio: Grid Publishing, 1984), 145.

[3]Carl McDaniel, Jr., and William R. Darden, *Marketing* (Boston: Allyn and Bacon, 1987), 568.

[4]Tom Eisenhart, "'89 Ad: Promotion Budgets Increase 10%," *Business Marketing* 74 (March 1989): 46–48.

[5]McDaniel and Darden, *Marketing*, 569.

[6]Philip Kotler, *Principles of Marketing*, 5th ed. (Englewood Cliffs, N.J.: Prentice-Hall, 1991), 430–437.

[7]Robert M. Cohen, "Advertising Effectiveness: First Know Your Objectives," *Sales and Marketing Management in Canada* 30 (October 1989): 10–12.

[8]This section is from William M. Weilbacher, *Advertising* (New York: Macmillan, 1979), 445–446.

[9]*Ibid.*, 446–448.

[10]"Making It Pretty When Your Product Is Nitty-Gritty," *Business Marketing*, 76 (April 1991): 55–57.

[11]Theodore Levitt, *Industrial Purchasing Behavior: A Study in Communication Effects* (Boston: Division of Research, Harvard Graduate School of Business, 1965).

[12]Gordon McAleer, "Do Industrial Advertisers Understand What Influences Their Market?" *Journal of Marketing* 38 (January 1974): 15.

[13]"Study: Increase Business Ads to Increase Sales," *Marketing News* 22 (March 14, 1988): 13.

[14]Bob Donath, "Busting Budget Bean Counters," *Marketing News* 26 (August 31, 1992): 9.

[15]Gary L. Lilien, Alvin J. Silk, Jean-Marie Choffray, and Murfidhar Rao, "Industrial Advertising Effects and Budgeting Practices," *Journal of Marketing* 40 (January 1976): 24.

[16]Rebecca Fannin, "The House That B-to-B Built," *Marketing and Media Decisions* 24 (May 1989): 56–64.

[17]Lynn G. Coleman, "The Crunch Has Come: War, Recession Change the Role of the Business-to-Business Marketer," *Marketing News* (March 4, 1991): 1, 16–17.

[18]Lee M. Cassidy, "Americans: A Print Media Profile," *Marketing Communications* 14 (February 1989) 26–27.

[19]"Thomas Register Ranks as King of Catalogues," *Advertising Age,* 7 March 1985, 54.

[20]Betsy Frank, "Trends: As Saatchi Sees It," *Marketing and Media Decisions* (August 1990): 29–30.

[21]Joseph Bohn, "Food Equipment Maker Tries Local Television," *Business Marketing* (April 1985): 106–112.

[22]Gordon Beck, "Seven Ways to Ruin Your Business-To-Business Advertising," *Business Marketing* 77 (February 1992): 56.

[23]This section is based on Frederick A. Russell, Frank H. Beach, and Richard H. Buskirk, *Selling: Principles and Practices* (New York: McGraw Hill, 1988). Contribution and further analysis by Bruce Buskirk.

[24]Karen J. Marchetti, "Take a Direct Route for Cost-Effective Marketing," *Marketing News* 25 (July 22, 1991): 14–15.

[25]Arnold Fishman, "1989 Mail Order Overview," *Direct Marketing* (September 1990): 41–44.

[26]Adrian F. Dessi, "Big-Business-to-Big-Business Direct Mail," *Direct Marketing* (April 1988): 58–60.

[27]Herschell Gordon Lewis, "Direct Marketing: Our Twin Brother," *Catalog Age* 7 (August 1990): 117–118.

[28]Stan Rapp, "New Challenge for Look-Alike Catalog Marketers," *Direct Marketing* 52 (April 1990): 73–75.

[29]J. Schmidt, "Starting Up a Business Catalogue," *Direct Marketing* 50 (July 1987): 74–75. See also Cyndee Miller, "Coming Decade Seen as Golden Era for Business-to-Business Mail Order," *Marketing News* 22 (March 14, 1988): 1–2.

[30]J. Miller, "The Shape of Business Cataloging," *Direct Marketing* 50 (August 1987): 100–104.

[31]Alicia Orr, "A Dynamic Duo: The Phone and the Mail," *Target Marketing* 14 (January 1991): 47–48.

[32]Sandra Pernick, "Business Marketers Shouldn't Be Ashamed of Telemarketing," *Marketing News* (March 13, 1989): 16.

[33]Steve Zurier, "Strictly for Sales," *Industrial Distribution* (September 1988): 65.

[34]Ernan Roman, "The Newest Member of the Media Mix," *Marketing Communications* (June 1987): 72–74; and "Telemarketing," *Marketing Communications* (June 1987): 75. See also Louis Weisberg, "Telemarketing: A Growing Art Form," *Advertising Age,* 27 June, 1987, S9–S10.

[35]Ralph S. Alexander, James S. Cross, and Ross M. Cunningham, *Industrial Marketing,* 2d ed. (Homewood, Ill.: Richard D. Irwin, 1961), 445.

[36]"Study Shows That Frequent Four-Color Ads Attract More Attention in Trade Press," *Marketing News* 22 (March 14, 1988): 13.

[37]George Black, "Business Marketing Agencies Must Offer Integrated Services," *Business Marketing* 76 (August 1991): 24–27.

[38]B. Kelley, "Surprising Times in Ohio," *Sales and Marketing Management* 138 (June 1987): 109.

[39]*Report of the Definitions Committee* (Chicago: American Marketing Association, 1960).

[40]This section is from Robert F. Lusch and Virginia N. Lusch, *Principles of Marketing* (Boston: Kent Publishing, 1987), 446–447.

[41]Jerome D. Williams, Srinath Gopalakrishna, and Jonathan M. Cox, "Trade Show Guidelines for Smaller Firms," *Industrial Marketing Management* (November 1993): 265–275.

[42]Trade Show Bureau, "Reach Your Prospects for Less at Trade Shows," Research Report No. SM20 (Denver, Colo.: Trade Show Bureau, 1991).

[43]Daniel C. Bello and Ritu Lohtia, "Improving Trade Show Effectiveness by Analyzing Attendees," *Industrial Marketing Management* (November 1993): 311–318.

[44]David A. Kaminer, "Trade Shows: How Big Business Does Bigger Business," *Business Marketing* 76 (November 1991): 2–4.

[45]"Expositions in Today's Marketing Mix," Trade Show Bureau Multi-Level Curricula (Denver, Colo.: Trade Show Bureau, 1993), 1.

[46]Thomas V. Bonoma, "Get More Out of Your Trade Shows," *Harvard Business Review* 61 (January/February 1983), 75. See also Roger A. Kerin and William L. Cron, "Assessing Trade Show Functions and Performance: An Exploratory Study," *Journal of Marketing* 51 (July 1987): 87–94.

[47]"How to Win at the Show," *Sales and Marketing Management* (February 4, 1985): 48–50.

[48]Pat Friedlander, "When Is It Time to Get a New Booth?" *Business Marketing* (February 1993): 48.

[49]Mark L. Goldberg, "Tricks of the Trade Show," *Small Business Reports* (September 1991): 17–20. (Published by Business Research and Communication, Monterey, CA).

[50]Bonoma, "Get More Out of Your Trade Shows."

[51]Valerie Kijewski, Eunsang Yoon, and Gary G. Young, "How Exhibitors Select Trade Shows," *Industrial Marketing Management* (November 1993): 287–298.

[52]McDaniel and Darden, *Marketing*, 557–558.

[53]David E. Tester, "'Tools of the Trade' Don't Belong in the Circular File," *Marketing News* (March 13, 1989): 21.

[54]"Trade Shows: A Major Sales and Marketing Tool," *Small Business Reports* (June 1988): 34–39. (Published by Business Research and Communication, Monterey, CA).

[55]Mark L. Goldberg, "Tricks of the Trade Show."

[56]"The Power of the Trade Show," *Business Marketing* 71 (May 1986): 37.

[57]This section is based largely on "Trade Shows: A Major Sales and Marketing Tool."

[58]Gary L. Lilien, "A Descriptive Model of the Trade-Show Budgeting Decision Process," *Industrial Marketing Management* 12 (February 1983): 29.

[59]Philip Kotler, *Marketing Management: Analysis, Planning, Implementation, and Control*, 6th ed. (Englewood Cliffs, N.J.: Prentice-Hall, 1988): 652.

[60]Thomas M. Maker, "Guided Tour of Grand Plans for '92 Marketing," *National Underwriter* (October 21, 1991): 33–47.

[61]Kevin Doyle, "Getting the Message Across," *Incentive Marketing* 166 (February 1992): 67–70.

[62]Charles S. Madden and Marjorie J. Caballero-Cooper, "Perceptions of the Specialty Advertising Industry: Implications for Business Marketers," *Journal of Business and Industrial Marketing* 2 (Fall 1987): 42.

[63]H. Ted Olson, "Trade Show Techniques," *Direct Marketing* (March 1989): 82–86.

[64]*Ibid.*, 82.

[65]Bob Donath, "How Should You Advertise?" *Business Marketing* (April 1988): 78, 82–86.

[66]*Ibid.*, 82–86.

[67]This section is largely from Courtland L. Bovee and William F. Arens, *Contemporary Advertising* 4th ed. (Homewood, Ill.: Richard D. Irwin, 1992).

[68]This section taken from Subhash C. Jain, *International Marketing Management*, 2d ed. (Boston, Mass.: Kent Publishing, 1987), 564–565, 593; and Vern Terpstra, *International Marketing*, 5th ed. (New York: Dryden Press, 1991), Chapter 12.

Case Studies

Northern New Jersey Manufacturing Company

Northern New Jersey Manufacturing Company was a producer of several kinds of industrial equipment listed in Exhibit 1. It developed from the efforts in the late 1940s of a gifted engineer and inventor, Sidney Hovey, who patented several of his ideas for variations on standard products. He founded and was active in the firm for over twenty-six years until his death.

Hovey had been very interested in the selling activity of his company and had a strong sense of professionalism that he used in personally selecting people for his sales force. He himself managed the sales force until it grew to a size of three men, at which time he secured the services of Herbert Staley as sales manager.

Before Staley's arrival and for several years thereafter, Hovey told the salesmen expressly the names of firms he wanted them to call on. The founder was acutely interested in the reputation of his young company. His concern with reputation included product characteristics as promised, delivery on time (critical to customers for these goods), and ethical, highly reserved business conduct by the salesmen. However, this concern for reputation was not restricted to these factors. Hovey also wanted to have as his customers those who enjoyed the finest reputations themselves. For example, he told his salesmen never to solicit the orders of a small firm then known by the name of Reihnan and Loykas, for he considered the owners to be social climbers

EXHIBIT 1 **Northern New Jersey Manufacturing Company Sales by Product, Selected Months**

Product	September	July	September Last Year	September Two Years Before
Dryers	$21,000	$34,500	$35,000	$32,200
Sprayers	7,700	7,500	8,000	7,800
Planers	4,100	4,300	4,000	3,900
Power saws	3,200	3,000	3,000	3,100
Drills	4,200	4,100	4,000	3,900
Sanders	9,500	7,300	7,200	7,000
Metal buffers	7,500	4,900	5,000	4,800

without proper backgrounds. In addition, he did not like an advertisement of theirs he once saw in a weekly business newspaper. He also instructed his salesmen not to call on Heather Glow, Inc., because it had been turned down for a loan at the bank that Hovey used. This was despite the fact that Heather Glow found credit at another bank.

Not all the instructions were negative, however. Hovey had the salesmen, all of whom were engineers, visit Camden Mills, Stone and Kruger, and South Coast Metals time after time even though all three were committed to other sellers and other product designs. He wanted Northern New Jersey Manufacturing Company to be a name that such firms knew and respected. He also cultivated several large national companies, such as Combustion Engineering, American Machine and Foundry, Kaiser Industries, Westinghouse, and Melpar.

After Hovey's death, Staley continued these policies for the better part of a year. At that point James Watts, the new president hired in from the outside, had a long talk with the sales manager and explained that he felt some changes were desirable. The firm should try to maximize sales and abandon all the "notions and pretensions," as he termed them. The salesmen should be put on a combination salary plus commission. The two other executives in the company, the finance man and the production man, spoke up with thorough endorsements of such changes. The existing policy was straight salary.

With some misgivings, Staley devised a new compensation structure for his four salesmen. Under this plan he estimated that a salesman would earn about 80 per cent of his compensation through salary and about 20 per cent through commissions. The plan was announced on August 1 and the men were told it would go into effect in thirty days. Sales in August slumped about 17 per cent from the same month one year earlier and about 14 per cent from the same month two years earlier.

After one month of use, the sales manager conducted a preliminary inquiry into the results of the new compensation policy. The results appeared to be that the easier to sell items were moving adequately, and the one item that was rather difficult to sell (the dryer) was moving very poorly. Exhibit 1 gives the comparisons of September to the last month under the old policy (July) and to September one year before. Staley presented his analysis to Watts but cautioned him about premature inferences from these data. The sales manager said that he would repeat his comparisons after another month. In the meanwhile, the president told the sales manager to urge the salesmen to solicit orders for dryers.

At the beginning of November, Staley anxiously studied the results for October, as presented in Exhibit 2. He had taken a preliminary look at some fragmentary data about October 16 but he knew that those data were undependable. In addition, the company had usually experienced a mild upswing in the fall season.

Staley was in his office reflecting on the figures in Exhibits 1 and 2 when Douglas Guglielmi, the production manager, and Richard Acker, the finance and accounting manager, both walked in. After several minutes of friendly conversation about sports and the weather, Guglielmi said that he and Staley jointly had a problem. To be specific, the mix of sales was apparently changing radically, which was upsetting his production schedule, company general plans, and deliveries. Richard Acker then added what Staley already knew, that the dryers had been earning the highest unit margin, while the sanders and metal buffers had been earning the lowest unit margin. Total profits were beginning to go down.

EXHIBIT 2 **Northern New Jersey Manufacturing Company Sales by Product, Selected Months**

Product	October	October Last Year	October Two Years Before
Dryers	$23,000	$36,000	$35,400
Sprayers	7,900	8,400	8,200
Planers	4,300	4,200	4,000
Power saws	3,300	3,200	3,000
Drills	4,200	4,300	4,100
Sanders	11,500	7,500	7,200
Metal buffers	9,700	5,300	5,100

CASE STUDY ACTIVITY

Advise Herbert Staley, sales manager for the Northern New Jersey manufacturing Company.

Robertshaw Controls Company

Robertshaw Controls Company could be traced back to a thermostat device invented by Frederick W. Robertshaw in Pittsburgh in 1899. A prolific inventor who obtained forty-one patents, Robertshaw guided the early growth of the organization. Soon after World War II the Grayson Company, based upon the inventions of John H. Grayson in California, and the Fulton Company, based upon the inventions of Weston M. Fulton in Tennessee, merged with Robertshaw to form the present corporation.

A major participant in the industrial controls industry, Robertshaw manufactured automatic controls and control systems for industry, commercial buildings, and the home. The product line included controls for regulating and measuring temperatures and pressure, for heating and cooling, for appliances, for transportation, and for industrial processes and systems, and instrumentation for other precise control requirements. The company specialized in the applications of the physical sciences, i.e., electronics, pneumatics, hydraulics, mechanics, and electromagnetics, to control energy and to enable products to work automatically. It also made a line of clocks and timers for household use, but this represented a very small part of the company's sales. In total, the company manufactured over ten thousand different products.

The company distributed its industrial products to original equipment manufacturers, contractors, replacement parts wholesalers, governmental agencies, the military, automotive and aircraft manufacturers, shipbuilding yards, public utility service departments, and various other industrial users. The clocks and timers for household use were sold to wholesalers, retailers, and trading stamp companies.

The demand for industrial goods, is, of course, derived; i.e., the demand depends completely on the demand for the consumer goods produced by the particular industry. For example, there is little need for a new temperature and pressure control system on the production line of a fruit canning factory unless a viable demand exists for the canned fruit.

Manufacturing plants owned and operated by the company included three in Pennsylvania, two in Ohio, four in California, two in Connecticut, one in Tennessee, and one in New Hampshire. In addition, Robertshaw leased and operated two plants in Tennessee and one each in Michigan, Pennsylvania, Georgia, and Virginia. Foreign subsidiary plants were located in Toronto and Oakville, Ontario, Canada; Sydney, Australia; Skelmersdale, England; Reims, France; Amsterdam, The Netherlands; Tokyo, Japan; and Caxias do Sul, Brazil. An affiliate plant was located in Mexico City, Mexico. There were ninety-nine hundred employees. Plant size varied from fifty to fifteen hundred employees. Selling efforts extended to fifty-one nations.

Justifiably proud of its technological expertise and its long tradition of inventions, Robertshaw continued to have a strong commitment to technological advancement. In the latest year inventors in the company were issued eighty-eight patents, compared with sixty-four the previous year and ninety-nine the year before that. The company was consistently among the most prolific firms in the number of patents obtained. Although each manufacturing division conducted some product research and development and was expected to do so, the company operated three facilities devoted exclusively to research and development, one in California and two in Pennsylvania. To permit a more coordinated approach and a cross-fertilization of ideas, the Advanced Technology Forecast Committee was formed in 1974 to monitor advanced technological developments that might be utilized in the controls industry and suggest potential new products. This committee consisted of representatives from the research and development, marketing, manufacturing, and patent departments.

In the most recent year the company's sales were $247,145,000, up 27.9 per cent from the previous year's $193,280,000. Sales for each of the five most recent years broken down by type of market are presented in Exhibit 1. A five-year summary operating statement of the company is presented as Exhibit 2.

EXHIBIT 1 **Robertshaw Controls Company, Five-Year Sales by Markets**

(To nearest million)		Temperature Controls for Homes and Commercial Buildings	Controls for Home Appliances	Industrial Controls and Instrumentation	Transportation, Consumer, and Other	Total
Latest year:	Volume	$92	$82	$37	$36	$247
	Per cent of total	37%	33%	15%	15%	100%
Two years ago:	Volume	$73	$55	$34	$31	$193
	Per cent of total	38%	28%	18%	16%	100%
Three years ago:	Volume	$64	$60	$34	$32	$190
	Per cent of total	34%	31%	18%	17%	100%
Four years ago:	Volume	$65	$65	$31	$32	$193
	Per cent of total	34%	34%	16%	16%	100%
Five years ago:	Volume	$62	$59	$27	$24	$172
	Per cent of total	36%	34%	16%	14%	100%

EXHIBIT 2 **Robertshaw Controls Company, Five-Year Summary of Operations (amounts in thousands, except per share data) Year ended December 31**

	Latest Year	Two Years Ago	Three Years Ago	Four Years Ago	Five Years Ago
Net sales	$247,145	$193,280	$189,899	$193,335	$172,459
Cost of products sold	194,443	156,701	155,292	150,007	129,217
Equity income (loss)	352	(85)	1,511	2,253	1,245
Other revenue	1,481	871	1,184	1,077	909
Interest expense	1,834	1,963	2,337	1,690	910
Taxes on income	7,607	2,157	1,399	6,780	7,940
Net income	9,382	2,943	5,020	10,438	9,798
Earnings per share of common stock based on average shares outstanding	2.42	.76	1.30	2.70	2.55
Cash dividends per share	.90	.75	.90	.83	.72
Average shares outstanding	3,876,591	3,871,726	3,871,709	3,871,525	3,838,504

In earlier years Robertshaw Controls Company was organized strictly by product type. There was a manufacturing division for a cluster of related products, and a sales department and an advertising department for the same cluster of products. Manufacturing was still organized by type of product into twelve divisions, but marketing was now organized by type of customer into eight groups. For example, the Industrial Instrument Marketing Group was in Richmond, Virginia, but the products that the customers of this group needed might come from the Grayson Manufacturing Division in Long Beach, California, the Simicon Manufacturing Division in Holland, Michigan, the Milford Manufacturing Division in Milford, Connecticut, or the Sylphon Manufacturing Division in Knoxville, Tennessee. Without this organizational structure a particular customer or potential customer might be called on by four different Robertshaw sales representatives.

Robertshaw spent $500,000 annually for space purchases for its advertising. Like most other industrial goods firms, the company exhibited a preference for personal selling efforts over advertising. The corporation had used the same advertising agency for ten years and was satisfied with it. Robert W. Pendergast, Robertshaw's corporate director of Public Relations and Advertising, noted that an agency's cooperative attitude was as important as its professional competence.

Perhaps the central difficulty in meeting Robertshaw's advertising needs was that most of the company's products were not highly visible. Most of the time the products were completely hidden, and thus unseen by nearly everyone. The company had not engaged in consumer advertising until late in the past year, when it launched a small, limited campaign in selected newspapers and do-it-yourself type magazines to support its automatic setback thermostat. This was a home control device that had the ability to adjust the temperature at times programmed by the residents.

Some advertising effort was decentralized to the eight marketing groups. In addition, each marketing group could retain its own advertising agency. The groups had been using their present agencies for periods of time varying from one to several years. The director of Public Relations and Advertising explained as follows:

As an arm of marketing, advertising of products and systems now follows the same group approach. Advertising strategies are keyed to portraying Robertshaw as a single source for a variety of controls and systems. Advertising to the chemical process industry, for example, is programmed to present Robertshaw's total instrumentation capability. In the appliance field, advertising backs up the marketing approach wherein an appliance maker looks to a single Robertshaw representative to supply all his control needs.

Decisions on marketing group advertising objectives, plans, media, and budgets generally are made by the groups themselves. In most cases, however, these plans are formulated only after discussion and consultation with the corporate director of advertising. Budgets are prepared by the groups and submitted to the corporate advertising director for approval. Written permission must be obtained for all additional programs not previously budgeted.

Each marketing group had additional promotional responsibilities, such as participation in appropriate trade shows and exhibitions. The total for all marketing groups combined was usually ten shows-exhibitions per year. Moreover, each marketing group prepared its own product catalog, which required approval from Pendergast.

A sizable amount of the advertising effort was centralized at corporate headquarters. The director of Public Relations and Advertising summarized corporate advertising, media selection, and copy themes in the following manner:

Corporate Advertising

For several years now, Robertshaw's prime corporate objectives have continued to be building a favorable awareness in the financial and investment community. Advertising strategy has centered on creating an understanding among target audiences of our involvement in many and diverse markets. Corporate messages are directed to the decision makers who influence investment decisions, and they also reach individual investors.

Media Choices

To make the most efficient use of our corporate budget, advertising has been concentrated in the *Wall Street Journal*, acknowledged leader in financial circles. Its readership also includes a broad reach among business executives. This provides a "bonus" in awareness among this audience because they are also decision makers in purchasing Robertshaw products as well as potential personal investors. Smaller campaigns are used in *Business Week* to reinforce the message to the general business community, and in *Institutional Investor* to reach their audience of major investors.

Copy Themes

Each ad in the campaign spotlights a Robertshaw product and its benefits to the user. Generally the headlines name one or more well-known customers for this Robertshaw control or control system. A closing paragraph points out Robertshaw's diversity, including its international involvement . . . and asks for action by offering more information. Separately and together, these messages convey a picture of leadership in a basic field—controls . . . diversity of markets for broad base of sales . . . R&D capability . . . proven performance record for blue chip companies. For several years, the ads have also pointed up our ability to perform as the Energy Control Company.

Results

This campaign has fulfilled its objective of contributing to a wider awareness of Robertshaw's total corporate capability. Because the ads talk about specific products, they produce inquiries—particularly on new products and controls that function to provide energy savings.

CASE STUDY ACTIVITY

Advise Robertshaw Controls Company.

Source: Reprinted with permission of Macmillan College Publishing Company from *Cases In Marketing: Orientation, Analysis and Problems*, 2nd Edition, by Thomas V. Greer.

Part Six

Trends in Business-to-Business Marketing

13 Marketing of Business Services

Learning Objectives

After reading this chapter, you should be able to:

- Identify the external environments facing the marketing manager for business services.
- Understand the important characteristics of business services.
- Appreciate the challenges and opportunities found in the marketing of business services:
- Differentiate among various methods of classifying business services.
- Comprehend the role and importance of international markets for business services.
- Discuss likely future trends in the marketing of business services.

Chapter Outline

Learning Objectives

The Marketing of Business Services: An Overview

The Environments for Business Service Firms
- The Economic Environment
- The Societal-Cultural Environment
- The Competitive Environment
- The Technological Environment
- The Political-Legal Environment

Important Characteristics of Business Services
- Intangibility
- Perishability and Fluctuating Demand
- Simultaneity
- Heterogeneity

Business Service Marketing—Challenges and Opportunities
- Service Marketing versus Product Marketing
- Positioning Strategy
- Bundling of Services
- Service Strategy and the Marketing Mix
  - Product
  - Price
    - The planned market position for the service product
    - The stage of the life cycle of the service product
    - The elasticity of demand
    - The competitve situation
    - The strategic role of price
  - Place
  - Promotion
- New-Service Development
  - Share building
  - Market extension
  - Line extension
  - New business

Classification of Services
- Seller-Related Bases
- Buyer-Related Bases
- Service-Related Bases
- Classifying Services by Clusters
- People-Based versus Equipment-Based Services

International Marketing of Business Services
- The Risks of International Marketing for Service Organizations
- Problems of Adaptation to and Operation in Overseas Markets
- Barriers to Trade in Services
  - Restrictions on foreign competition
  - Exchange control
  - Constraints on choice of factor input mix

The Future for Business Services

Summary

Key Terms

Review Questions

Cases

Case 13-1

Case 13-2

Suggested Additional Readings

Endnotes

THE MARKETING OF BUSINESS SERVICES: AN OVERVIEW

Many marketing textbooks devote little, if any, attention to program development for the marketing of business services; and for the most part, the entire area of business service marketing remains undefined or ill defined. Managers of service businesses can be forgiven for feeling that the entire service sector has been going through extensive change in recent years. There is an old Chinese curse that wishes its recipient, "May you live in a time of change." Caught up in the turmoil of changes, many managers must yearn for the good old days, when the behavior of competitors was more predictable (even implicitly agreed upon), when customers or clients were less demanding and more loyal, when employees could be relied on to spend their entire careers within the same organization, when government regulations and professional standards discouraged both new market entrants and service innovations, and when established ways of creating and delivering services remained just that: established.[1] Compared to consumer services research, few published sources exist on the benefits sought from and the performance of business services.[2]

Marketing, however, is slowly coming of age in the service sector, as it becomes obvious that the most basic trend of the last half of the twentieth century is the transformation from a product-oriented economy to a service-oriented one. Providers of professional business services (for example, management consultants, engineering consultants) are becoming more convinced of the need to adopt a greater marketing orientation when conducting their business activities.[3] The topical omission from textbooks is usually based on the assumption that the marketing of goods and the marketing of services are the same; so the techniques described for goods must apply to the marketing of services as well. In a sense this is true, as the marketer in both cases is concerned with developing a marketing strategy centered around the four controllable decision variables that comprise the marketing mix: the product (or service), the price, the distribution system, and the promotional program. Because the marketing of services usually requires a different treatment of the marketing mix ingredients, business marketers will be increasingly expected to respond to the unique challenges posed by service marketing. The purpose of this chapter is to acquaint the reader with some of the special problems and opportunities of service marketing. The problems of service firms are so distinct from those of tangible-goods firms that a separate chapter is needed to help the reader appreciate both the differences and their effects on business marketing strategy.

THE ENVIRONMENTS FOR BUSINESS SERVICE FIRMS

The diversity of the environment within which the business service marketer must work is reflected in its multiple sectors. There are a number of classification theories, but for our purposes, and as is shown in Figure 13-1, the environment will be viewed in five sectors: the economic environment, the societal-cultural environment, the competitive environment, the technological environment, and the political-legal environment.

FIGURE 13-1 **Marketing Environment for Business-to-Business Firms**

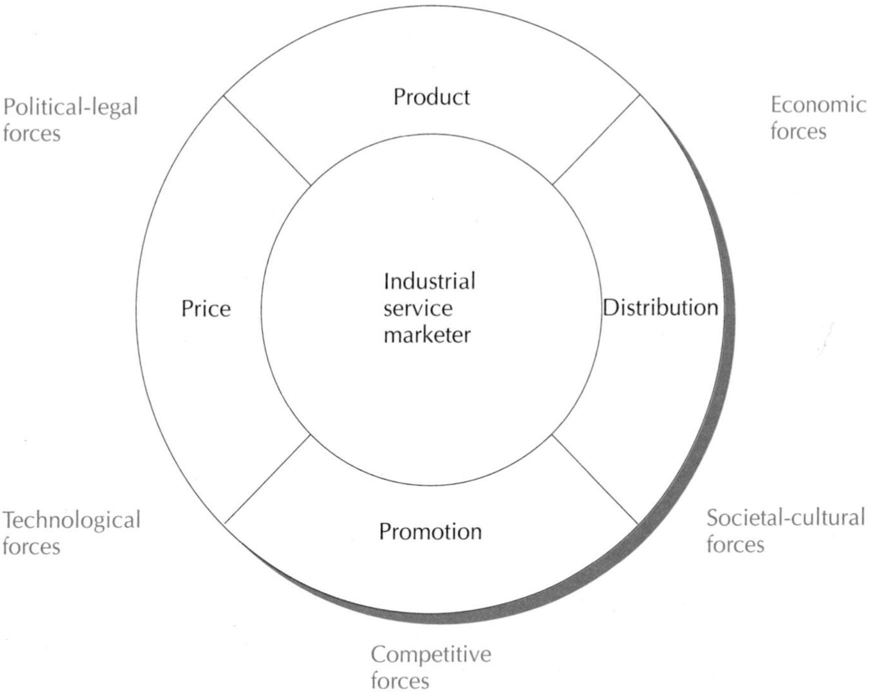

The Economic Environment

The *economic environment* includes forces associated with the macroenvironment, including factors such as inflation, interest rates, and gross national product (GNP). The sharp increase in spending for business services and the development of service industries have been among the most significant economic trends in the post–World War II economy. Most explanations for this trend have looked at it as the result of a maturing economy, along with the by-products of rapid economic growth. Rapid technological advances, coupled with the "knowledge explosion" of recent years, have made the servicing of the business sector very profitable; companies in this field range from suppliers of temporary help to highly specialized management-consulting firms. Many times the service provider can perform a specialized service more efficiently and at a lower cost than the buying firm can do itself. (See the "make-or-buy" decision in Chapter 3.)

The growth of business services and the increased spending for business services over the last decade have been spectacular. In recent years, business service firms have prospered primarily for two reasons. First, they are frequently able to perform a specialized function more efficiently than would the buying firm itself. Second, many companies are unable to perform certain services for themselves. Marketing research studies, for example, often require the knowledge that outside experts, such as Judson Rees and Associates, Limited, and Telecommunications Marketing Resource can provide. Temporary employment needs and employment counseling can often be better supplied by service firms such as Accountemps, Kelly Services, and Options, Incorporated. Technical recruitment can often be more productive by using firms such as Technical Procurement Service Incorporated, and SAT Recruitment and Placement, Incorporated. Legal and financial services are all represented, with service firms such as Kennedy Personnel Consultants and Schattle Personnel Consultants providing expertise in these areas.

The Societal-Cultural Environment

The *societal-cultural environment* contains the forces emanating from society as a whole; it includes both informal forces (the values of society) and more formally organized forces (some growing out of the result of the consumerism movement). The societal-cultural environment has a significant impact on the marketing of business services. A variety of social-cultural trends are relevant to the increased marketing of business services, such as the growing emphasis on safety and environmental considerations that has widened the market for several business services. The movement toward protecting the physical environment has provided new markets for energy-preserving consultation and products. The demand for on-site monitoring of dust, solvents, metals, asbestos, and noise for both federal and state requirements has increased the demand for testing specialists and consulting firms such as New England Testing Laboratory, Incorporated, and Enviro-Sciences, Incorporated. Additionally, the need for protection specialists such as Burns International Security Services and First Security Services Corporation has soared. As mentioned above, most of these firms will provide the specialized service more efficiently and at a lower cost than if the buying firm tried to perform these services itself.

The Competitive Environment

The *competitive environment* consists of all other service providers who are vying for the patronage of the same customer. A major influence on competitive intensity is the threat of new entrants. If entrance barriers are low, competitors can easily enter the market and intensify competition. Opportunities within the competitive environment include such things as (1) acquiring competing firms; (2) offering demonstrably better value, thus attracting prospective customers away from competitors; and (3) driving competitors out of the industry. The primary constraints in this environment are demand-stimulation activities of competing service providers and the number of prospects who cannot be lured away from the competition.[4]

Historically, many forms of competition have been almost nonexistent in some service industries:[5]

- Price competition has been severely limited by regulation and trade practices in transportation, telecommunications, the law, and medicine.
- Many service industries are difficult to enter (health care facilities, educational institutions, and the like).
- A major financial investment may be necessary (utilities).
- Special education or training may be required (professions).
- Government regulations may restrict operations (telecommunications, banking).

The entry of manufacturers into service markets has also increased the intensity of competition for the business service dollar. Some large manufacturers have begun to offer spin-off business services to other organizations. For instance, DuPont, Dow, Alcoa, and other companies noted for their technical expertise market analytical services and facilities, pollution control systems, and related products or services to other companies. These firms see the special needs of other businesses as an opportunity to profit from their own investments in research and development.[6] The problem of increased competition is the primary impetus for strategy change.

The Technological Environment

The vast majority of the economic growth in the United States has resulted from the *technological environment*, through increases in productivity (the output produced by each worker). Technological developments have accounted for tremendous increases in productivity, and this trend should not change in the foreseeable future. How will future increases in productivity be accomplished in a service economy? Theodore Levitt argues that service providers should assume a *manufacturing attitude*. "Instead of looking to service workers to improve results by greater exertion of animal energy, managers must see what kinds of organizations, incentives, technology, and skills could improve overall productivity."[7] The introduction of wide-bodied jets by some airlines enables them to serve twice as many passengers, using the same number of pilots and flight engineers. A major challenge to marketers during the 1990s is to implement gains in productivity, while not sacrificing the quality of service. This goal will most likely be realized through improved marketing.[8]

The Political-Legal Environment

The *political environment* would include the attitudes and reactions of the general public, business critics, and external organizations such as the Better Business Bureau. The *legal environment* would include local, state, and federal legislation (both real and envisioned), directed at protecting both business competition and the consumer (through the principle of "derived demand"). Political and legal forces are closely interrelated because, as legislation is enacted, legal decisions are interpreted by the courts, and regulatory agencies are created and operated mostly by people who occupy government positions. When political officials have positive feelings about particular firms or industries, they are less likely to create or rigidly enforce highly restrictive pollution control laws—at least not for the present. Additionally, another reason why business organizations need to be concerned about making a favorable impression on political officials is that these officials may play key roles in securing foreign markets.[9]

IMPORTANT CHARACTERISTICS OF BUSINESS SERVICES

There are a number of characteristics that not only distinguish goods and services but also impact business marketing program development. Four characteristics are unique to services and influence the way they are marketed: intangibility, perishability and fluctuating demand, simultaneity, and heterogeneity.

Intangibility

Services are intangible, and therefore, abstract. Most business services cannot appeal to the buyer's sense of taste, touch, smell, sight, or hearing before buying, which places some strain on the seller's marketing organization. Proven strategies of product marketing cannot be applied when the "product" being marketed cannot be seen, felt, or guaranteed to provide specific and measurable results. Because of the lack of tangibility, business service marketers find it difficult to differentiate their offerings, and as a result, services must be made tangible by visual representation and symbolism. Marketing promotion, through the sales force and the advertising department, becomes critical in service marketing, since the product itself is incapable of communicating its benefits.[10] Intangible products such as freight forwarding, consulting, repair, brokerage, or education can seldom be tried out or tested in advance of purchase. Buyers are forced to view advertising copy, listen to a sales presentation, or consult current users to determine how well a service will perform. Even the most tangible of products cannot be reliably tested prior to purchase. Inspecting an automatic order-picking installation in advance and studying, in advance, the vendor's design and quote with other members of the buying center still cannot guarantee satisfaction in most buying situations. The process of getting precisely what was ordered; having it built, delivered, and installed on time; and then having the installation run smoothly involves more than the tangible product itself. Intangibles can and will make or break the installation's success in most situations. So, it is logical to assume that all products are in some respects intangible. The use of nouns ("hotel" when we mean "lodging rental") obscures the fundamental nature of services, which are processes, not objects.[11]

Perishability and Fluctuating Demand

Services are perishable; they cannot be stored; and the markets for most business services fluctuate by the day, week, or season. Unused electric power, an empty airplane seat, and an idle machinist in a factory all represent business that is lost forever. This combination of perishability and fluctuating demand has created some very special problems with regard to strategy implementation for marketers of business services. Key decisions must be made on what maximum amount of capacity should be available to cope with surges in demand before service levels suffer. Furthermore, decisions must be made in times of low levels of usage on whether spare capacity will be idle, or whether short-term policies (differential pricing, special promotions, and the like) will be adopted to even out fluctuations in demand. Business service marketers thus lose the valuable buffer function of inventory that allows a producer to manufacture for inventory during slow periods and to draw on inventory during periods of peak demand. This unique combination of perishability and fluctuating demand offers exciting challenges and opportunities to business service marketers in the areas of product planning, pricing, and promotional strategy. For most service businesses, sales and mass promotional activities must be used extensively to increase sales volume during slack periods and thereby spread sales out more evenly over time.

Simultaneity

Production and consumption of services are inseparable: selling comes first, followed by production and consumption simultaneously. Services are used at the same time at which they are produced, which typically puts the business marketer of services in very close contact with the customer. As a result of this situation, service customers tend to perceive relatively greater risk when they are shopping for a service. They rely more heavily on the recommendations of others.[12] Word of mouth is a significant factor in generating new business for complex, hard-to-evaluate services.[13] In the marketing of many business services, a client relationship exists between the buyer and the seller, as opposed to the more typical customer-supplier relationship found in the marketing of tangible products. Physical proximity is essential to the successful delivery of services. An example of this type of relationship would be the business consulting relationship. The buyer considers the suggestions or advice provided by the seller, and the relationship is of an ongoing nature. In addition, since many business service firms are client-serving organizations, the marketing function is very professional, as seen in financial, legal, and educational services.

Heterogeneity

It is difficult to standardize services, and as a result, output can vary widely in quality. A major problem created by heterogeneity is quality control, whereby the provider of the business service can control the production but not the quality or the consumption of the service. The service marketer tries to control quality; some go to great lengths to standardize their services, in addition to investing in high-quality employees. However, even services of the same firm are remarkably dissimilar. Although standardization of some services (for example, insurance, transportation, and utilities) has increased, it is improbable that services will ever become as standardized as most tangible goods.

In addition to the above, the quality of service performance varies from one business service provider to another. Not all consulting firms, airlines, or insurance companies offer the same level of service. The quality of the service provided will also vary for the same provider from one occasion to another. A group seminar held by a psychological consulting firm, such as Nordlie Wilson, Incorporated, will achieve varying results, depending on client response and cooperation. The variability of business service output makes it difficult for the service firm to establish, maintain, and guarantee quality continuously.

CONCEPT QUESTIONS

1. Why is marketing coming of age in the service sector?
2. Why will business marketers increasingly be called upon to respond to the unique challenges of service marketing?
3. What does the presence of multiple environments say about the macroenvironment that business service marketers face?

BUSINESS SERVICE MARKETING—CHALLENGES AND OPPORTUNITIES

Although marketing functions are basically the same for many services and products, there is a difference in the organization and implementation for gaining a competitive advantage in business service marketing. American industry is changing. Honeywell Corporation estimates that 30 percent of its revenue comes from services, yet most of us think of the firm as a high-tech manufacturing company. General Telephone and Telegraph has earned over half of its revenue from services since 1974. The growing significance of business service marketing is just starting to be understood. It has been only in the last few years, thanks to a few scholars and practitioners, along with the American Marketing Association's Services Marketing Division, that the subject is now being addressed.

Service Marketing versus Product Marketing

As noted earlier, a distinctive feature about business service marketing is that production occurs at the point of sale.[14] This decentralization of service performance puts a different perspective on the role of a centralized business staff marketing department. A major function of the centralized staff is to get everyone else in the organization to practice marketing. Their role is to facilitate good marketing, because with a business service provider, everybody is responsible for the customer.

Service marketing is different from product marketing, but only to a certain extent. While some services differ from some goods, certain kinds of services actually have a great deal in common with certain tangible products. Whether service marketing is different depends on a person's perspective. Once this is determined, the question is whether to focus on the differences, the similarities, or both. It is perhaps incorrect to ask whether service marketing is different or whether it requires a special marketing approach. A more appropriate way of looking at things would focus on how to market a service successfully. Service marketers are not more marketing oriented because of their preoccupation with the unique characteristics of services. This preoccupation is somewhat myopic because it encourages service providers to ignore successful marketing techniques that have worked well for many products and could work just as well in the area of services.[15]

With a business product, the unit is usually well defined. This is not necessarily so in service marketing. A product can be measured objectively against specifications by checking tolerances and comparing weight, color, shape, and so on. Measuring a service such as an office building cleaning service or a new-product consulting service is not so easy. What is clean? What is efficient, feasible, and marketable?

In product marketing, once the need is defined, the manufacturing process takes over. With business service marketing, the "product" is not created until the service is performed. With an office building cleaning service, delivery occurs when the vendor employees arrive to do the work. Did they do a good job? Is the office clean? Did they arrive on time?

With a business product, there is no need for a distribution channel until after a product is manufactured, packaged, priced, and ready to ship. With a business service, the channel of distribution and delivery are one and the same. The employees of the office building cleaning service are at the same time manufacturing and distributing the product. With a business product, little change can be made without substantial costs of time and money, in most cases. However, with a service provider, the product can be altered quite easily. The office building cleaning service can provide additional services such as window washing and carpet cleaning on very short notice.

Finally, in business product development, time is required to develop, test, introduce, and provide an inventory buildup. With a business service, the provider distributes the product, usually within a twenty-four-hour period. Again, the office building cleaning service would provide an appropriate example.

Positioning Strategy

While differentiation and positioning strategies are of major concern to service marketers, an understanding of the relative durability of these strategies is limited.[16] Since a differentiated position generates superior returns only until competitive imitation takes place, business service marketers must recognize the need to formulate and implement durable strategies.[17] The image that a business service has in the mind of the user, especially in relation to competitive offerings, follows naturally after identification of the market segment sought. Business-to-business firms that have most successfully positioned themselves have answered these questions: To what extent do competitors provide a like service? To what extent are customer expectations met? To what extent does the company, the customer, and the competitor (the "Three Cs") relate to one another on dimensions considered important to the customer? When the service provider establishes and maintains a distinctive place for itself and its offerings in the market, it is said to be successfully positioned. In the increasingly competitive service sector, effective positioning is one of marketing's most critical tasks.[18]

Competitive positioning with both services and products is the key to success in today's marketplace. Success depends on a marketer's ability to clearly differentiate the service from its competition in a way that is meaningful to the customer.[19] Effective positioning requires marketing research, something foreign to nearly all but the best-managed business service firms. It is more complicated to research reactions to a service than to a product, because potential customers find it harder to put themselves into the role of using a prospective service than of using a product that they can hold and see. One of the regional telephone companies, in preparing for industry deregulation, learned from its major business users that some firms that used phone lines for data-processing purposes were interested in contracts providing twenty-four-hour repair service. Its retail customers, however, who were heavily dependent on phone service only during business hours, wanted a guaranteed minimum response time for service interruptions only during those hours. In the past, the company offered a single service contract that treated all business customers alike. Company management concluded that there was a great risk of losing business to competitors who tailored their telephone service to specific industries' needs. They, in turn, repositioned their service offering accordingly, establishing and maintaining a distinctive place for themselves and their offerings in the market. In the increasingly competitive service sector, effective positioning will be one of the business marketer's most critical tasks.

Bundling of Services

Broadly defined, *bundling* is the practice of marketing two or more products and/or services in a single "package" for a special price.[20] It is most often used by a firm with a broad line of complementary products, with its effectiveness being a function of the degree to which it stimulates demand in a way that achieves cost economies. Examples of bundling would include the sale of a maintenance contract with computer hardware, with the lease of a truck, or with a piece of machinery. The rationale for bundling is based primarily on the reality that the cost structure of most business service businesses is characterized by a high ratio of fixed to variable costs and by a high degree of cost sharing (such that the same facilities, equipment, and personnel are used to provide multiple services).[21] The objective of bundling is to add value while keeping cost increments small and thus not to increase price for the added value. Price bundling is a special form of discount pricing where two or more services are combined into a single package and sold at a special price. As a marketing strategy, bundling can impact a business-to-business firm's short-term success or failure. We will see an increased use of this marketing tool in the years ahead.

Service Strategy and the Marketing Mix

Since Jerome McCarthy popularized the Four Ps in 1964, marketing plans have incorporated these elements as key building blocks for marketing programs.[22] The controllable variables of product, price, place, and promotion have been the key in the development of strategy that involves identifying a target market segment and then developing a marketing program to deliver that product to members of the segment. All these elements must be combined into a cohesive package by the astute business service marketer.

Product. The development of new services is as important to a business service provider as new products are to a product-marketing firm. Also, the improvement of existing services and the elimination of unprofitable services are key strategies that must be employed. The development of a product line, involving the design and introduction of new service offerings, has been cited as one of the more difficult challenges of managers in the service sector.[23] The future long-term growth of major business-to-business corporations is more likely to result from service businesses than from the products they sell. While a service orientation may not be right for all manufacturers, chief executives who ignore it run the risk of limiting their companies' growth opportunities and of losing their market position to more farsighted rivals. The growth of the service sector will not displace industry, but it will add to the economy by leveraging manufacturers' resources in a whole new way. Service businesses usually require considerably less investment of time and money than manufacturing. However, it is more difficult to recruit, train, and manage employees who perform services. The transition from a product-marketing to a service-marketing orientation is difficult to make. Management should anticipate strong resistance.[24] According to those who have provided consulting services both to manufacturing and service firms:

> New product development is inherently more difficult, messier, and less successful in the service sector. In industry, research and development labs can usually come up with new designs that incorporate certain predictable functions and characteristics. On the other hand, when a service firm correctly, if subjectively, perceives a need, it cannot have the same confidence in its ability to deliver all the ingredients that comprise successful new service products. As a result, service organizations are more likely to be conservative about innovations. They focus most of their attention on geographical extensions of their service, or on minor modifications to the primary service package. True inventiveness is rare...innovation in the service sector is frequently the result of trial and error...original or imitative ideas exist in abundance. Yet, new ideas often ignore the deep and subtle linkages among the variables in the service package. Between imagination and execution lies a dark gulf that has swallowed up many a bright new product.[25]

Despite the difficulties involved, every service industry has companies and managers noted for their ability to foster new-product development or the design and implementation of new internal processes. In banking, Citicorp is often mentioned, along with Basic One and VISA, as those providing cash transfer service systems. In financial services, Merrill Lynch is often the first to produce new products that are later imitated by others, and Dun and Bradstreet relies on new-product development for a significant share of its revenue. In communications, Dow Jones and Gannett are frequently mentioned; in lodging, the Marriott Corporation.[26]

Some subelements of the controllable-variable product that the service firm's management must also be concerned with in selecting appropriate strategy development would include product-line width-and-depth adjustment, product-line warranties, and product-line naming, logos, and trademarks. Additionally, the strategies for individual product items must be aggregated into marketing plans for individual product lines, product and market domains, and total corporate marketing strategy.[27]

Price. A second controllable variable of the mix is price, which is important in business service marketing because profitability is more related to the respective net margin of a large number of services than to total revenues. The price of a service should be related to the achievement of marketing and organizational goals and should be appropriate for the service firm's overall marketing programs. In setting price objectives for services, a number of factors must be considered.[28] The more significant of these are as follows:

(1) The planned market position for the service product
(2) The stage of the life cycle of the service product
(3) The elasticity of demand
(4) The competitive situation
(5) The strategic role of price

The planned market position for the service product. How the service product is "seen" in relation to other like services available will clearly influence price strategy. Price is an important element in the marketing mix and, as noted earlier in the chapter, influences position; services are often "positioned" on the basis of intangible attributes. Price will influence market position.

The stage of the life cycle of the service product. The price of a service will relate to its life cycle, much the same as the price of a tangible product will fluctuate as the product moves through the stages of its life cycle. At introduction, management may opt to use a skimming or a penetration strategy, adjusting prices either upward or downward as competitive pressure dictates. Identifying a company's position in the life cycle, and the major objectives, decisions, problems, and organizational transitions needed for the future, can be anticipated.

The elasticity of demand. *Elasticity of demand* refers to the responsiveness of demand to changes in price. It is important for a business service provider to understand how elastic or inelastic demand for its service is in response to price changes. If the firm reduces its price, and demand is elastic, then the effect would be to reduce margins with no compensating increase in demand. Elasticity will impose limitations on certain price options.

The competitive situation. In situations where there is little differentiation between business service products and where competition is intense, price discretion is limited. In other settings, tradition and custom may influence the prices charged (for example, advertising agencies' commission system).

The strategic role of price. Pricing policies have a strategic role aimed at achieving organizational objectives, so the pricing decision on any particular business service should fit in with the firm's strategic objectives. Additionally, any pricing strategy must fit in with the way in which other elements of the marketing mix are manipulated to attain strategic ends. Also, the service price decision is uniquely constrained by environmental and product characteristics. A pricing procedure for services involves: (1) identifying the target market, (2) selecting an image for the firm that is compatible with the image of the target, (3) collecting data about the range of prices that segment members are willing to pay for the service, (4) determining price positions of major competitors, and (5) selecting the service pricing strategy.[29]

In the business service sector, the marketer must consider the demand for the services; production, marketing, and administrative costs; and the influence of competition. Price negotiation also forms an important part of many business service transactions, such as financial and legal assistance, equipment rental, insurance, and maintenance and protection services. Variable pricing may also be a viable pricing option.[30] Quantity discounts, payment terms, cash discounts, price bidding, trade discounts, adjustments in price that reflect peak-load pricing (seasonal, yearly, fluctuations in demand and/or supply), and bundling arrangements must also be considered when determining business strategy development with the price element of the marketing mix.

Place. The function of distribution channels for business services is to make the service available and convenient to the buyer. Services (unlike tangible goods) cannot be transported, so the channel is usually simpler and shorter. An attorney will work directly with a client; insurance will usually be purchased through an agent; and a business loan will be obtained through a bank officer. These are short, direct channels and exist, in large part, because of the intangibility of services, along with the need for continuing personal relationships between providers and users of many services. The objective of channel selection decisions is the same for the marketers of both goods and services—that is, to select channels that will maximize the firm's profit position over the long run.[31] For marketers of business services, this involves providing optimum service and coverage at minimum cost. Business marketers must clearly delineate their markets and understand the buying patterns for their services—when, where, and how the service is purchased and by whom.

Historically, in business service marketing, little attention has been paid to distribution. However, as competition grows, the value of convenient distribution is being recognized—hospitality firms like the Hyatt chain and accounting firms like Touche-Ross use multiple locations for the distribution of services. The use of a channel intermediary is another way to broaden distribution. It is now quite common for companies to deposit employees' paychecks into their bank accounts, thereby becoming an intermediary in distributing a bank's service. We have all seen vending machines set up at airports whereby insurance firms have attempted to expand their distribution network. Travel agents, tourist boards, hotel representatives, and centralized reservation systems are all examples of the use of intermediaries to expand on the place element of the marketing mix.

Promotion. As noted earlier in the chapter, the fact that many business services cannot appeal to the buyer's sense of touch, taste, smell, sight, or hearing before purchase places a heavy burden on the business marketing organization in general, and on the promotion element of the marketing mix in particular. Since the business-to-business firm is selling an idea, not a product, it must tell the buyer what the service will do, since it is often unable to illustrate, demonstrate, or display the service in use. Managers can expect to have greater market responsiveness to advertising programs when the company's reputation is positive and consistent with company information regarding its service offering.[32] For example, "information retailing," as described in the box entitled "Business-to-Business Marketing in Action," is an underused service with incredible opportunity for growth. MacFarlane and Company, Incorporated, of Atlanta, and Find S. V. P., Incorporated, of New York, are two of the better-known information retailers. This potential will only be recognized if information retailers can persuade prospective clients that the service provides them with a competitive advantage. Such a situation obviously points out the need for the effective promotion of services.

Service marketing uses many of the same promotional tools as product marketing; advertising, personal selling, publicity, and sales promotion are all available for developing an overall promotion plan. The use of publicity and sales promotion corresponds well with strategy implementation in product marketing, so the emphasis must be on the personal selling and advertising elements of the overall promotion mix. The inseparability of production and consumption will usually require face-to-face interaction between the buyer and seller of business services. As one executive put it, "In a service business, you're dealing with something that is primarily delivered by people to people. Your people are as much a part of your product as any other attribute of that service."[33] What the customer is really purchasing is the quality of those who provide the services. Business marketers need to be concerned with their workers, before that essence of quality can be produced and maintained.[34]

The use of advertising by business service providers is not new; it has been used for years in fields such as transportation and insurance. What is new is its use by firms in the professional services industries, such as attorneys and accountants, among others. For years, the use of advertising by professional service providers was considered unethical. Such is not the case today. The creative task is to attempt to create and convey a distinct image for the business service provider.

New-Service Development

Services comprise all economic activity in which the primary output is neither a product nor a construction. Services substitute directly for manufactured products across a wide spectrum. Few customers care whether a computer accomplishes a function by a hardware circuit or by its software. If anything, they may prefer the software approach, especially when, as with CAD/CAM, it substitutes for production machinery at a fraction of the cost.[35] New services are

BUSINESS-TO-BUSINESS MARKETING IN ACTION

INFORMATION RETAILERS: A POTENTIAL NOT YET REALIZED

Information retailing is an underused service with incredible opportunity for growth. Yet, this potential will only be realized if information retailers can persuade prospective clients that the service provides them with a competitive advantage.

Lack of awareness is understandable. Information retailing is fragmented and evolving so rapidly that even a precise definition is hard to develop. An acceptable one appears in "The Information Industry," a report by Paine Webber and the Information Industry Association. They define information retailing as the "activities of companies which search computer and manual information sources for their clients, and may provide document fulfillment services as stand-alone profit centers."

Moreover, many businesspeople aren't sure who information retailers are or what they do.

One important and growing segment consists of information brokers. This group searches electronic data bases and sometimes augments findings with telephone and/or personal interviews. Firms that provide training, software packages, or help establish an in-house library are included in this group.

Information retailers frequently offer several or all these services, and many do not fit into an identifiable segment. Customers are often able to work with one vendor and select from a menu of services designed to satisfy diverse information needs.

About 28 percent of information users use data bases that are business- or economics-oriented, according to the *1985 Survey of On-Line Professionals.* One representative business data base, ABI/Inform, is very comprehensive and widely used by business professionals. Anyone with a personal computer, modem, and telephone can access such information, but there are several good reasons to use outside sources. Information vendors can provide needed information quickly, analyze data rapidly and accurately, and create an interpretative report when required. They can also be objective.

Many businesses already realize these advantages. The proof is in the profits. Dominated by companies with annual sales of less than $1 million, the Paine Webber report estimated total 1987 information retailing revenues at $197 million, with 1990 revenues projected at $238 million, a 21 percent increase.

However, this represents less than 1 percent of the total information industry, which has an estimated worth of $24 billion. With such well-established and easily identified segments as document delivery and computer-based information services accounting for about three-quarters of this market, it's not surprising that the still emerging information retail segment is not clearly focused.

Needless to say, enormous potential exists for information retailers, but it will undoubtedly require educating nonusers regarding the benefits of on-line information services.

Source: L. Lyne Smith, III, "Information Retailers Must Educate Nonusers about the Service's Value," *Marketing News,* 22 (March 14, 1988), p. 10. Used with permission.

the lifeblood of any business service organization, with growth requiring a steady flow of new services. The best way, if not the only way, to generate service marketing ideas is to remain close to customers.[36] If the business service industry is properly nurtured, it will grow and generate much of America's future wealth.

In the past, there has been a tendency to develop new business services in a haphazard fashion, reacting to emergency conditions with little thought to long-term growth and true market needs. Strategy options for service businesses have been discussed elsewhere in this book and include market segmentation and positioning, among other things. In the context of this chapter, however, it is useful to highlight strategic choices by depicting the alternative directions that business service firms can take in their new-service efforts. They can choose to pursue newness either in terms of markets or offerings, or a combination of both. There are accordingly four basic avenues available in this framework:

(1) Sell more existing services to current buyers—a share-building strategy (also called market penetration).

(2) Sell existing services to market segments not previously served—a market-extension strategy (also called market development).

(3) Offer new services to current markets—a line-extension strategy (also called product development).

(4) Offer new services to market segments not previously served—a new-business strategy (also called diversification).[37]

Share building. When this avenue is used, the business marketer becomes aggressive, promoting discount pricing or aggressive promotion. There have been "accounting wars" between the "Big Six" public accounting firms; and many professionals, such as business marketing consultants, are aggressively promoting, mostly through direct mail, to attract more clients. This approach is appropriate in growing markets, but is expensive; and the effort may be futile in mature markets where market share has stabilized.

Market extension. This strategy seeks new groups of buyers with the firm's current business service offering. A firm such as Blue Cross/Blue Shield may go beyond group plans offered through employers to individual coverage sold to self-employed business people. Other firms, such as banking institutions, may decide to take their services abroad.

Line extension. This strategy is appropriate in mature business service industries where growth is not likely to come from established services. An example would be the hospitality industry, where hotels in popular vacation spots develop special packages for business groups during the off-season.

New business. Where a new-product department, new-product manager, or a business marketing research department has been established, it is within the duties of these units to provide a steady flow of new business service ideas. Although risky, the contemplation of new service offerings allows the business marketer to explore gaps and desires in the marketplace. Competitors are an excellent source of new service ideas.

Without a steady flow of new service offerings, the business service firm is not likely to survive over the long run. Too many service firms are slow to invest in new market opportunities and research facilities. They have stayed with old concepts and have concentrated on cost cutting rather than providing customers with services they want and need. Those businesses that are diversifying or segmenting have a strong grasp of how their operations should change over time.

CONCEPT QUESTIONS

1. What is a prerequisite to the effective positioning of a business service?
2. What are the two primary objectives in the bundling of business services?

CLASSIFICATION OF SERVICES

While there are a variety of models that attempt to classify services, some believe that classifications are not very helpful because they might misdirect marketing thinking and perpetuate a product orientation. Other scholars and practitioners believe that classification is helpful because it serves as a first step in obtaining an understanding of the ways in which markets operate. A classification model should be helpful to many in developing business marketing strategies for services and for evaluating current strategies and tactics used by service marketing organizations. Many models for services are derived from those used in the marketing of tangible goods, and some are based on assumptions about what is or is not a service. Figure 13-2 shows an illustration of three ways of classifying services: seller-related bases, buyer-related bases, and service-related bases.[38]

Seller-Related Bases

Seller-related bases is a common method of classification whereby the marketing organization may be classified according to whether it is "private" or "public"; and within each grouping, whether it is "profit" motivated or "not-for-profit" motivated. The "function performed" by the organization may also be used as a basis of classification, as can the "income source."

FIGURE 13-2 **An Illustration of Some Current Ways of Classifying Services**

Seller-Related Bases

Nature of enterprise	Functions performed	Income source
Private, for profit Private, nonprofit Public, for profit Public, nonprofit	Communication Consulting Educational Financial Health Insurance	Derived from market Market plus donations Donations only Taxation

Buyer-Related Bases

Market type	Way in which service is bought	Motives
Consumer market Industrial market Government market Agricultural market	Convenience service Shopping service Specialty service Unsought service	Instrumental— means to an end Expressive; i.e., an end in itself

Service-Related Bases

Service form	Human or machine based	High or low contact
Uniform service Custom service	Human-centered service Machine-centered service	High-contact service Low-contact service

Source: Donald Cowell, *The Marketing of Services,* Heinemann, London, 1985, pp. 28–30. Used with permission.

Buyer-Related Bases

Buyer-related bases would include the type of market, the way in which the service is bought, and the motives for purchase. The Swan and Pruden model for classifying business services suggests that establishing whether the motives for purchase are "instrumental," with the service being a means to an end, or "expressive," with the service being an end in itself, may also provide a useful framework for classifying some services.[39]

Service-Related Bases

Service-related bases is a classification in terms of whether service is human based or equipment based, or whether it involves high or low levels of personal contact.

It would seem that there is no one classification for a particular service, with different people viewing the same service in different ways at the same time. The bases shown in Figure 13-2 can be further developed to add additional dimensions to those suggested, such as temporal or spatial categories; rational or emotional motives; and high-urgency or low-urgency services. Such additional categories may be determined by judgment or through marketing research.

Classifying Services by Clusters

It has also been argued that development of greater sophistication in business service marketing will be aided if we can find new ways to group services other than by current industry classifications. Christopher H. Lovelock has suggested that a more useful approach would be to segment services into clusters that share certain relevant marketing characteristics—such as the nature of the relationship between the service organization and its customers, or patterns of demand relative to supply—and then to examine the implications for marketing action.[40] His article summarizes several past proposals for classifying services, as identified in Table 13-1. These proposals represent an attempt to answer one or more of the following questions:

(1) What is the nature of the service act?

(2) What type of relationship does the business service organization have with its customers?

(3) How much room is there for customization and judgment on the part of the business service provider?

TABLE 13-1 **Summary of Models for Classifying Services**

Author	Proposed Classification Schemes	Comment
Judd (1964)	1. Rented goods services (right to own and use a good for a defined time period) 2. Owned goods services (custom creation, repair or improvement of goods owned by the customer) 3. Nongoods services (personal experiences or "experiential possession")	First two are fairly specific, but third category is very broad and ignores services such as insurance, banking, legal advice and accounting.
Rathmell (1974)	1. Type of seller 2. Type of buyer 3. Buying motives 4. Buying practice 5. Degree of regulation	No specific application to service—could apply equally well to goods.
Shostack (1977)* Sasser et al.* (1978)	Proportion of physical goods and intangible services contained within each product "package"	Offers opportunities for multi-attribute modeling. Emphasizes that there are few pure goods or pure services.

continued on next page

TABLE 13-1 **Summary of Models for Classifying Services (continued)**

Author	Proposed Classification Schemes	Comment
Hill (1977)	1. Services affecting persons vs. those affecting goods 2. Permanent vs. temporary effects of the service 3. Reversibility vs. nonreversibility of these effects 4. Physical effects vs. mental effects 5. Individual vs. collective services	Emphasizes nature of service benefits and (in 5) variations in the service delivery/consumption environment.
Thomas (1978)	1. Primarily equipment-based a. Automated (e.g., car wash) b. Monitored by unskilled operators (e.g., movie theater) c. Operated by skilled personnel (e.g., airline) 2. Primarily people-based a. Unskilled labor (e.g., lawn care) b. Skilled labor (e.g., repair work) c. Professional staff (e.g., lawyers, dentists)	Although operational rather than marketing in orientation, provides a useful way of understanding product attributes.
Chase (1978)	Extent of customer contact required in service delivery a. High contact (e.g., health care, hotels, restaurants) b. Low contact (e.g., postal service, wholesaling)	Recognizes that product variability is harder to control in high contact services because customers exert more influence on timing of demand and service features, due to their greater involvement in the service process.
Kotler (1980)	1. People-based vs. equipment-based 2. Extent to which client's presence is necessary 3. Meets personal needs vs. business needs 4. Public vs. private, for-profit vs. nonprofit	Synthesizes previous work, recognizes differences in purpose of service organization.
Lovelock (1980)	1. Basic demand characteristics —Object served (persons vs. property) —Extent of demand/supply imbalances —Discrete vs. continuous relationships between customers and providers 2. Service content and benefits —Extent of physical goods content —Extent of personal service content —Single service vs. bundle of services —Timing and duration of benefits 3. Service delivery procedures —Multisite vs. single site delivery —Allocation of capacity (reservations vs. first come, first served) —Independent vs. collective consumption —Time defined vs. task defined transactions —Extent to which customers must be present during service delivery	Synthesizes previous classifications and adds several new schemes. Proposes several categories within each classification. Concludes that defining object served is most fundamental classification scheme. Suggests that valuable marketing insights would come from combining two or more classification schemes in a matrix.

*These were two independent studies that drew broadly similar conclusions.

Source: Christopher H. Lovelock, "Classifying Services to Gain Strategic Marketing Insights," *Journal of Marketing,* 47 (Summer 1983), pp. 9–20. Used with permission.

(4) What is the nature of demand and supply for the service?

(5) How is the service delivered?

By addressing each of the five questions posed, marketing managers can obtain a better understanding of their product, of customer relationships, of factors underlying variations in business demand, and of the characteristics of their service delivery systems. By recognizing characteristics that their service shares with other service providers, business marketing managers will look to new ideas as to how to resolve marketing problems shared in common with firms in other industries.

People-Based versus Equipment-Based Services

A final classification of services explored in this chapter, as diagrammed in Figure 13-3, is based on determining whether the service is people based or equipment based.[41] Within *people-based services*, we can distinguish between those involving professionals (accountants, consultants), skilled labor (plumbers, tool makers), and unskilled labor (janitors). In *equipment-based services*, we can distinguish among those involving automated equipment (vending machines), equipment operated by unskilled labor (taxis, motion picture projectors), and equipment operated by skilled labor (airplanes, computers).[42] Questions must be asked, such as, Is the client's presence necessary to the service (business psychology versus truck repair)? What about the service provider's motives (profit or not-for-profit) and form (private or public)? These characteristics, when crossed, produce four quite different types of service organizations.[43]

Regardless of which classification scheme is used, a problem in classifying a business service is the fact that many services are directly tied to a tangible product. An example of this would be a consultant's services. This service provider would produce a report (a tangible good) as a result of the service provided. The quality of the service is judged both by the actions of the consultant and by the report produced. Other business services are less tied to goods, such as an extermination service, which does not produce a tangible product and whose quality cannot be judged in the short term. Evaluating business service quality is difficult because of the number of people involved in the evaluation and because many services have a goods component.[44]

Interest in the study of marketing business services is a relatively recent phenomenon. Marketing expertise in the service sector has significantly lagged behind marketing efforts in the manufacturing sector despite the fact that the service sector is becoming increasingly competitive.[45] This is changing rapidly and reflects such developments as the partial or complete deregulation of several major service industries in recent years, the removal of professional association restrictions on using marketing techniques (particularly advertising), and the growth of new electronic delivery systems.[46] With increased competitive intensity, the understanding and use of a strong marketing effort will be essential to survival.

FIGURE 13-3 **Types of Service Businesses**

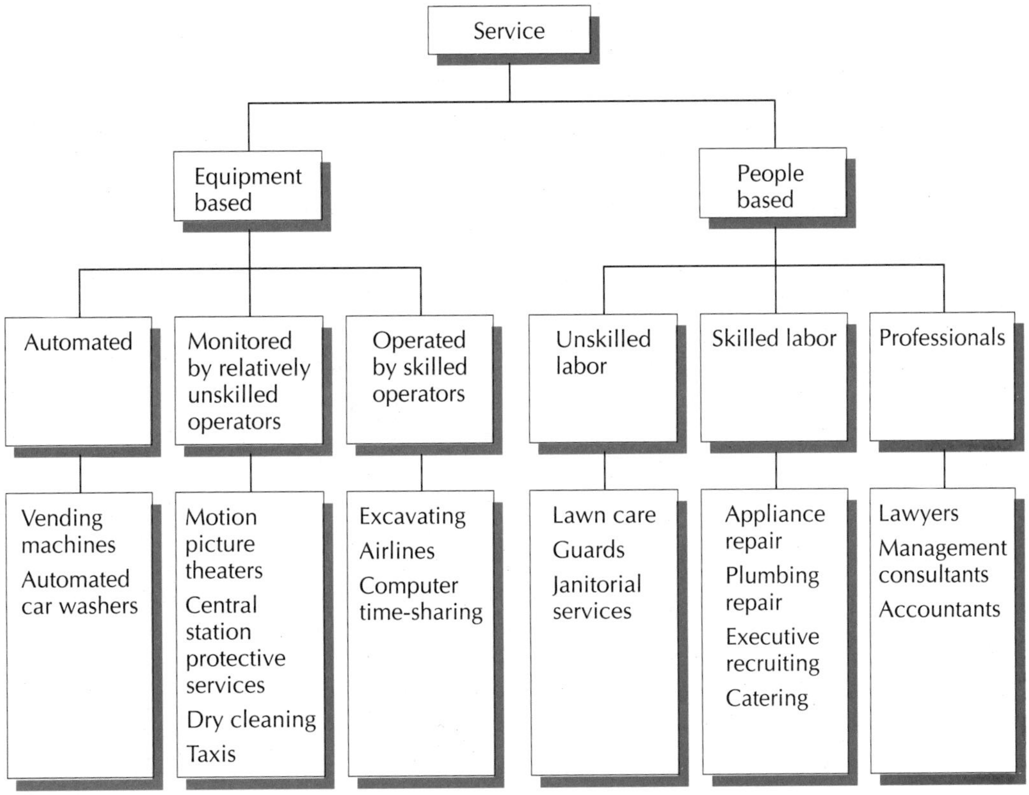

Source: Reprinted by permission of the *Harvard Business Review.* An exhibit from "Strategy Is Different in Service Businesses," by Dan R. E. Thomas (July/August 1978).

INTERNATIONAL MARKETING OF BUSINESS SERVICES

Service marketers are battling for foreign as well as domestic markets. Price Waterhouse (accounting), Hertz (car rental), J. Walter Thompson (advertising), Donovan, Newton, and Leisure (legal), and Bechtel (construction engineering) have had a history of aggressively competing for customers in global markets. Other U.S. service firms are expanding their operations. Holiday Inn has negotiated the purchase of property in 140 cities in Western Europe; where, by 1996, it will build hotels, most of which will have 250 to 300 rooms. Ramada Inn and Marriott Hotels each plan to add twenty more facilities by the mid 1990s, and

Sheraton is attempting to double its holdings to fifty hotels in Europe by the mid 1990s.[47] Although the United States is experiencing a large international trade deficit, such published data can be deceptive because the deficit is only reported in merchandise or tangible products. The United States actually exports more services than it imports. Future growth in the business service sector should help to offset the large merchandise deficits that the United States has been experiencing.[48] World trade in services is growing rapidly, and in spite of stringent restrictions placed on some aspects of this trade, its growth has been irrepressible and of strategic importance to many major service firms.

The principles of marketing services internationally are similar, in many respects, to those that apply to the marketing of services domestically. The strategies associated with the setting of clear objectives, of defining and selecting target markets, and of developing appropriate and specific marketing strategies and marketing mixes are much the same. What is very different, and what business service providers need to adjust to, are external environmental factors, such as the social, political, economic, legal, and cultural climates. The nature of these types of environmental forces facing international marketing managers are treated in detail in most international marketing textbooks (albeit in product marketing settings, in most cases); therefore, they will not be covered here. Their absence is in no way a measure of their importance. There are, however, few illustrations of how such influences affect service organizations specifically. Three strands of evidence relate to the following: (1) the risks of international marketing for service organizations; (2) the problems of adaptation to and operation in overseas markets; and (3) the barriers to trade in services.[49]

The Risks of International Marketing for Service Organizations

Carman and Langeard have suggested that while internationalization represents a growth strategy for service firms, the following are also true:

(1) Out-of-country expansion is a riskier strategy for a service firm than, for example, concentric diversification or new-service development in existing markets.

(2) Out-of-country expansion is riskier for a service business than it is for a manufacturer of physical items.[50]

They base their argument for the greater risk involved for service-related businesses on the fact that foreign expansion by product manufacturers can be undertaken more gradually; whereas service providers must go to the country, face the customer, and produce the service. The seller must produce on foreign soil and must deal directly with the customer. This situation, in addition to providing on-site quality control and coping with personnel and know-how difficulties, produces potential problems for service providers that might be minimized by tangible goods producers.

Problems of Adaptation to and Operation in Overseas Markets

It has also been suggested that service marketers may have a more difficult time with the host government than product marketers. They typically provide little capital inflow into the country, little or no technological transfer, and do little to upgrade the training of workers. This is an interesting but perhaps controversial view and would require more empirical evidence to substantiate such a claim.

Barriers to Trade in Services

Service marketers must become familiar with the barriers to international marketing that are unique to services. They must also become more familiar with management options available to work around those barriers. Barriers to the international marketing of services are due mainly to the close cultural relationships between a society and the services offered in it. These include tariff and nontariff barriers. The General Agreement on Tariffs and Trade (GATT) talks are an important multilateral approach toward reducing barriers to marketing in services. Nontariff barriers such as "buy-national" policies prove particularly problematic for international marketing managers of services.[51]

The barriers to services marketing with which we are also concerned here are those that relate specifically to foreign-produced services and cover discriminatory measures in the fields of banking, insurance, transport, consulting services, and so forth. For example, restrictions on capital movements may deter a service company from setting up a service operation in an overseas country in the first place, just as they may deter a manufacturer from building a factory. In a major study that examined the barriers to trade in services and other invisibles, the following general restrictions were identified.[52]

Restrictions on foreign competition. A service organization may be excluded by law, by a restrictive licensing system, by tariffs (that is, taxes), by takeover, or by nationalization. An example would be the limitation in many countries where internal routes are reserved for domestic airlines.

Exchange control. Limitations might be exercised over the purchase of foreign exchange for buying foreign-produced services. An example would be restrictions on the amount of foreign currency allowed for overseas travel.

Constraints on choice of factor input mix. The amount of capital or local labor that must be employed may be specified. An example would be in the employment of local nationals in a service such as banking.

Governments around the world have played a significant role in restricting the growth of multinational services. Many services have been considered critical to the well-being of a nation's citizens and to its own development, and some governments have seen fit to guarantee the delivery of some quality of services at low prices. National chauvinism, sometimes clothed in words such as "national defense," has at times been involved.[53] For whatever reasons, a variety of service trade barriers can be found around the world. Additional barriers would be discrimination against shippers wishing to transport foreign cargo, restraints on the international flow of information, the banning of operations by foreign insurance firms, and administrative delays that hinder licensing agreements. Of course, there are many more. Perhaps these potential impediments help to explain why services make up so small a share of international trade.

THE FUTURE FOR BUSINESS SERVICES

Today, service industries have assumed the mantle of economic leadership. These industries, encompassing trade, communications, transportation, food and lodging, financial and medical services, education, government, and technical services to industry, account for about 70 percent of the national income and 75 percent of the nonfarm jobs in the United States. In generating forty-four million new jobs in the past thirty years, service industries have absorbed most of the influx of women and minorities into the work force, softened the effects of every post–World War II recession, and fueled every recent economic recovery.[54] This trend will continue, because the demand for business services expands as business becomes more complex and as management further recognizes its need for business-service specialists.

For the next several years, the marketing of services will continue to receive attention from practitioners and academics alike, as the forces of deregulation and continued technological change will have a remarkable impact on our economy. Practitioners have learned that many of the ideas and approaches that were developed for the marketing of tangible goods fit uneasily and uncomfortably into their needs. Academics, seeking new fields in which to develop marketing ideas, will give increased attention to nongoods sectors like not-for-profit and service entities. There seems to be common agreement that the broad principles of marketing management are applicable to both these areas.

Finally, the future success and well-being of service marketing organizations will largely be a function of their understanding and reaction to the following propositions:

- There are greater opportunities for growth and expansion in the future in the areas of services than in those of goods.
- Mass production, industrial design, and systems engineering are being increasingly implemented and adapted to service businesses.

- Use of mass production and systems engineering increases productivity but leads to increased depersonalization of service marketing.
- The whole range of strategic marketing activities are relevant for service marketing, and their use will tend to satisfy the growing demand for diversity in service market offerings.[55]

The biggest increases in terms of share of output are likely to be in the areas of insurance, banking, finance, and communications. Many factors will influence the continuing development of the service sector in the 1990s, including the attitude of government toward services and technological innovation.

CONCEPT QUESTIONS

1. How is classifying services helpful to the business marketer?
2. How is the marketing of services internationally similar to the marketing of services domestically?
3. In what service areas will the greatest increase in share of output occur?

SUMMARY

1. For the most part, the entire area of service marketing remains ill defined. Marketing, however, is slowly coming of age in the service sector, as it becomes obvious that the last half of the twentieth century represents the transformation from a product-oriented economy to a service-oriented economy.
2. The major environments for business service firms include the economic, societal-cultural, competitive, technological, and political-legal environments. Each of these will impact upon a business service firm's sales and profits; the nature, role, and importance of each should be studied carefully in developing marketing objectives and accompanying strategies.
3. Four characteristics are unique to services and influence the way they are marketed: intangibility, perishability and fluctuating demand, simultaneity, and heterogeneity. Services are intangible in that they cannot appeal to the senses. Promotion, through the sales force and advertising department, must communicate the benefits of various business service offerings. Services are perishable and cannot be stored. Key decisions must be made on what maximum capacity level should be available to cope with surges in demand before service levels suffer. Production and consumption of services are inseparable; selling comes first, followed by production and consumption at the same time. It is difficult to standardize services; and as a result, output can vary widely in quality.
4. Although marketing functions are basically the same for many services and products, there is a difference in the organization and implementation for gaining a

competitive advantage in business service marketing. With business service marketing, the product is not created until the service is performed. When the service firm establishes and maintains a distinctive place for itself and its offerings in the market, it is said to be successfully positioned. The marketing mix can be applied to business services, just as it can to business products. The strategies for different services must be incorporated into the entire corporate strategy, and the development of new services is just as important as the development of new products. Business service companies can expand their service offerings through share building, market extension, line extension, and cultivating new business.

5. Classifications of services can be helpful in understanding the ways in which markets operate. They can also be an aid in developing marketing strategies for services and for evaluating current strategies and tactics used by business service organizations. A number of classifications have been offered, to include those that are seller related, buyer related, and service related; classification by clusters and by people and equipment bases are also possible. There seems to be no one classification for a particular service, with different people viewing the same service in different ways.
6. Service marketers are battling for foreign, as well as domestic, markets. Yet, governments around the world have played a significant role in restricting the growth of multinational services. Business service marketers must be alert to new opportunities in international markets, but they must also be aware of the many problems and pitfalls if they are to succeed in such markets.
7. For the next several years, the marketing of services will continue to receive great attention from both business practitioners and academicians. The biggest increases in terms of share of output are likely to be in the areas of insurance, banking, finance, and communications. Many factors will influence the continuing development of the service sector in the 1990s, including technological innovation and the attitude of government toward services.

KEY TERMS

Bundling
Buyer-related bases
Competitive environment
Economic environment
Elasticity of demand
Equipment-based services
Legal environment
Manufacturing attitude
People-based services
Political environment
Seller-related bases
Service-related bases
Societal-cultural environment
Technological environment

REVIEW QUESTIONS

1. Identify and discuss the six major environments that face the marketing manager for business services.

2. Identify and discuss four important characteristics of services. Provide an example of each one.
3. How does business service marketing differ from business product marketing? When is a business service properly positioned? What is meant by the bundling of services?
4. How does each element of the marketing mix contribute to the overall strategy used for a particular business service? Identify and discuss four methods by which a business-to-business firm can expand its service offerings.
5. What is the value of classifying services to the business services marketer? Describe three major models of classifying services according to Cowell. Distinguish between people-based and equipment-based services.
6. How are the principles of marketing services internationally similar to those of marketing services domestically? How are they different? Identify the risks and problems associated with the marketing of services abroad.
7. On what four propositions will the future well-being and success of services marketing depend? In what fields will the largest growth of services marketing occur?

Cases

CASE 13-1 SAS: A Leader in Profitable Customer Service

We led off the 1980s promising to become Europe's best airline for the frequent business traveler. Our priorities were safety, punctuality, and excellent service, in that order.

We promised to become the most punctual airline in Europe, and we have been for eight years running. We said that we would make Copenhagen Airport the best hub in Europe; the airport since won wide international acclaim as one of the best in the world. We pledged more frequent nonstops for business travelers; we have more than doubled them. And so on.

Our business strategies for the 1990s will be to make it easier for our customers—mainly European business travelers—to do good business. We've also outlined a course of action: to create a global travel service for the frequent business traveler.

The airline is stronger than ever. In the early 1980s our customers could fly to some 50 points outside Scandinavia with SAS. We can now offer our customers efficient nonstops and one-stops to more than 250 points worldwide.

We went from 26 hotels of our own to 130, gaining worldwide presence when we bought into Inter-Continental Hotels, a top-quality chain.

In tough competition, SAS Service Partner has become the leading airline caterer in Europe and a major player in international airport operations.

Our SAS Trading unit has blossomed as the market leader in duty-free sales in just the past couple of years. Thirty shops at Copenhagen Airport have helped make our main hub the most attractive in all of Europe. SAS Trading is now applying the same winning service recipe to other key airports we and our partners serve.

Diners Club, with our Nordic franchise, has been winning droves of business travel accounts as we add more and more value to the Card, which can now be used at more than 1.3 million establishments in 165 countries.

Our commitment for the 1990s is to make it easier and more fun to travel, and 36,000 SAS colleagues have now pledged our customers that the coming decade will be one of trust, simplicity, and care.

We shall be the first in the world to guarantee the service we give our customers on the ground, and in the air, in our hotels, shops and restaurants, and that there will be a money-back guarantee—generous compensation on the spot—to back up our commitments.

For simplicity's sake, we pledge curb-side check-in and telephone check-in (starting in Scandinavia), and EuroClass check-in at our hotels. If we said our goal for the

1980s was to slash time you have to stand in line, then the 1990s will be the decade we'll get rid of the lines altogether.

That we care for our customers will be obvious enough. All 36,000 of us will participate in a new round of quality service training this year.

We kept our promises in the 1980s. We'll do it again in the 1990s. We'll be there when you need us.

DISCUSSION QUESTIONS

1. In what ways are the services of competing airlines homogeneous, and in what ways are they heterogeneous?
2. What are some ways that an airline can differentiate itself from the competition and develop customer loyalty?
3. Describe SAS's targeting strategy and marketing mix.

Source: C. Lamb, J. Hair, and C. McDaniel, *Principles of Marketing*, 1st Edition (Cincinnati, OH: South-Western Publishing Company, 1992) p. 702.

CASE 13-2 The Case of the Squealing Tax Accountant

Don't snicker. Consider the plight of St. Louis restauranteur Steve Noles, thirty-three years old.

Mr. Noles says he relied on his trusted accountant, James Checksfield, to keep him out of trouble with the IRS. That was a serious mistake. Accountant Checksfield *was* the IRS—or, at least, a "controlled informant" for one of its special agents. The accountant helped turn up evidence that Mr. Noles skimmed untaxed income from receipts of his pizza restaurant.

The hapless Mr. Noles was indicted by a federal grand jury in St. Louis on six counts of income tax evasion. He faces up to twenty-four years in prison and $900,000 in fines if he is convicted.

Says Mr. Noles: "Jim Checksfield often sat in my living room with my wife and two children. We treated him like family. I trusted him. Why, I even gave him power of attorney to represent me before the Internal Revenue Service. This is the cruelest and most devious thing anyone could do to me."

Accountants are even more distressed. Mr. Checksfield's actions "deserve condemnation by all professionals," says Donald H. Skadden, the taxation vice president of the 290,000 member American Institute of Certified Public Accountants. He says the accountant's job is to point out errors to the client—not to the IRS. "The accountant is not allowed to inform the IRS of any such matters without the client's permission," he says.

Maybe that's the way it's supposed to be. But the IRS's toleration of its agents' practice of employing undercover informants whose identities are normally concealed—even from some IRS officials—has made it possible for agents to use accountants. The agency argues that with its limited budget, it needs all the help it can get to catch the country's tax evaders.

"We don't recruit informants," says Michael Orth, an IRS assistant regional commissioner. "They generally come to us on their own initiative because they're upset someone is avoiding their share of taxes. Why should we discourage this form of patriotism?"

DISCUSSION QUESTIONS

1. Do you think that it is ethical for a tax accountant to report a client to the IRS for income tax evasion?
2. Should the Institute for Certified Public Accountants or some other group take action against Mr. Checksfield? If so, what type of action?
3. Should professional organizations have power to sanction members for violating implied or expressed codes of ethics?

Source: C. Lamb, J. Hair, and C. McDaniel, *Principles of Marketing*, 1st Edition (Cincinnati, OH: South-Western Publishing Company, 1992) p. 709.

Suggested Additional Readings

Adams, Ronald J., and M. Reza Vaghefi. "The Application of Environmental Management Concepts to Hospital Strategic Planning." In *Marketing in a Dynamic Environment*, edited by Michael H. Morris and Eugene E. Teeple, 503–510. Atlantic Marketing Association, 2 (October 1986). **Current position of hospitals in the United States is described in the context of Porter's model of competitive strategy.**

Bharadwaj, Sundar, G. P. Rajan Varadarajan, and John Fahy. "Sustainable Competitive Advantage in Service Industries: A Conceptual Model and Research Proposition," *Journal of Marketing* (October 1993): 83–99.

Cespedes, Frank V. "Once More: How Do You Improve Customer Service?" *Business Horizons* 35 (March/April 1992): 58–67. **Discussion of management responsibility to provide the type of customer service that will result in customer retention.**

Day, Ellen, and Hiram C. Barksdale. "How Firms Select Professional Services." *Industrial Marketing Management* 21 (May 1992): 85–91. **Survey of both executives and clients pertaining to the important ingredients in a good relationship between the service provider and the client.**

Evans, Kenneth R., and Richard F. Beltramini. "Physician Acquisition of Prescription Drug Information." *Journal of Health Care Marketing* 6 (December 1986): 15–25. **Survey of specialists and general practitioners as to their sources of prescription drug information.**

Guiltinan, Joseph P. "The Price Bundling of Services: A Normative Framework." *Journal of Marketing* 51 (April 1987): 74–85. **Discussion of marketing strategy and complementary relationships in the price bundling of services.**

Heskett, James L. "Lessons in the Service Sector." *Harvard Business Review* 65 (March/April 1987): 118–126. **Discussion of organizational structure, target markets, quality, and economies of scale in the service sector.**

Hill, Donna J., and Nimish Gandhi. "Service Advertising: A Framework to Its Effectiveness." *Journal of Services Marketing* 6 (Fall 1992): 63–76. **Presentation of a classification scheme delineating services along organizational structures.**

Kastiel, Diane Lynn. "Service and Support: High Tech's New Battleground." *Business Marketing* 72 (June 1987): 54–66. **Study of marketing strategy, profitability, and contracts in the computer service industry.**

Lynn, Susan A. "Identifying Business Influences for a Professional Service: Implications for Marketing Efforts." *Industrial Marketing Management* 16 (May 1987): 119–130. **Survey of CPA firm selection, including marketing strategies used by CPA firms.**

McKee, Daryl, G. P. Rajan Varadarajan, and John Vassar. "The Marketing Planning Orientation of Hospitals: An Empirical Inquiry." *Journal of Health Care Marketing* 6 (December 1986): 50–60. **Survey of marketing strategies in hospitals, with a performance measurement using statistical analysis.**

Olszewski, Agnes Pauline, Hubert D. Hennessey, Philip Harris Monchar, and Arthur Boudin. "Corporate Culture: A Strategy to Enter Entrenched Markets." *The Journal of Business and Industrial Marketing* 2 (Summer 1987): 5–16. **Research illustrates a methodology to segment business markets on the basis of corporate culture. Application made to the corporate purchase of a financial service.**

Pesmen, Sandra. "Bring'em Along." *Business Marketing* 77 (July 1992): 52–53. **Discussion of the use of niche marketing in business customer travel.**

Raffield, Barney T., III. "Creating Promotional Synergism in the Marketing of Non-Credit, Continuing Education Programs." *Issues in Higher Education* 13 (October 1984), Division of Continuing Education, Kansas State University, Manhattan, Kansas. **Discussion of and guidelines for promoting continuing education programs to both business and consumer markets.**

Samli, A. Coskun, Laurence W. Jacobs, and James Willis. "What Presale and Postsale Services Do You Need to Be Competitive?" *Industrial Marketing Management* 21 (February 1992): 32–41. **Report on the types of important customer services that should be offered both prior to and following a sale.**

Shostack, G. Lynn. "Service Positioning through Structural Change." *Journal of Marketing* 51 (January 1987): 34–43. **Within service systems, structural process design can be used to "engineer" services on a more scientific, rational basis.**

Showalter, Michael A., and Judith A. Mulholland. "Continuous Improvement Strategies for Service Organizations." *Business Horizons* 35 (July/August 1992): 82–87. **A discussion of the role of top management in involving all employees in learning how to provide better service to the client base.**

Stern, Aimee. "One-Stop Shopping for Market Services." *Business Month* 129 (March 1987): 60–62. **Discussion of consulting, merchandising, and sales promotion services at one location.**

Turnbull, Peter W., and Michael L. Gibbs. "Marketing Bank Services to Corporate Customers: The Importance of Relationships." *International Journal of Bank Marketing* (UK), 5, No. 1 (1987): 19–26. **Discussion of segmentation and profitability in marketing bank customers to corporate clientele.**

Webster, Cynthia. "What Kind of Marketing Culture Exists in Your Service Firm?" *Journal of Services Marketing* 6 (Spring 1992): 54–67. **Discussion of how to utilize the marketing concept in the provision of services to business clients.**

ENDNOTES

[1]Christopher H. Lovelock, *Managing Services, Marketing Operations, and Human Resources* (Englewood Cliffs, N.J.: Prentice-Hall, 1988), xv.

[2]Arch G. Woodside, R. Hedley Sanderson, and Roderick J. Brodie, "Testing Acceptance of a New Industrial Service," *Industrial Marketing Management* (February 1988): 65–71.

[3]Philip L. Dawes, Grahame R. Dowling, and Paul G. Patterson, "Determinants of Pre-Purchase Information Search Effort for Management Consulting Services," *Journal of Business-to-Business Marketing* 1, no. 1 (1993): 31–61.

[4]J. Paul Peter and James H. Donnelly, Jr., *A Preface to Marketing Management*, 6th ed. (Plano, Tex.: Business Publications, 1993), 20.

[5]Eugene M. Johnson, Eberhard E. Scheuing, and Kathleen A. Gaida, *Profitable Service Marketing* (Dow Jones-Irwin, 1986), 45.

[6]*Ibid.*, 47.

[7]Theodore Levitt, "The Industrialization of Service," *Harvard Business Review* (September/October 1976): 63–75.

[8]For an analysis of the industrialization of service via hard, soft, and hybrid technologies, see Theodore Levitt, *The Marketing Imagination* (Glencoe, Ill.: Free Press, 1986) 50–71.

[9]From William M. Pride and O. C. Ferrell, *Marketing: Basic Concepts and Decisions*, 6th ed. (New York: Houghton Mifflin, 1988), 476–477.

[10]For suggestions on how to offset the marketing problems created by intangibility in services, see Theodore Levitt, "Marketing Intangible Products and Product Intangibles," *Harvard Business Review* (May/June 1981): 94–102. Also see Betsy D. Gelb, "How Marketers of Intangibles Can Raise the Odds for Consumer Satisfaction," *Journal of Consumer Marketing* (Spring 1985): 55–61. Also, Angela Rushton and David J. Carson, "Services Marketing with a Difference," *Marketing Intelligence and Planning* 17 (1989): 12–17.

[11]G. Lynn Shostack, "Service Positioning through Structural Change," *Journal of Marketing* 51 (January 1987): 34–43. Also see Scott Burton, "The Framing of Purchase for Services," *Journal of Services Marketing* 4 (Fall 1990): 55–67.

[12]William J. Winston, "Topic: Internal Marketing—Key to a Successful Professional Service Marketing Program," *Journal of Professional Services Marketing* (Winter 1986): 15–18.

[13]Karen Maru File, Ben B. Judd, and Russ Alan Prince, "Interactive Marketing: The Influence of Participation on Positive Word-of-Mouth and Referrals," *Journal of Services Marketing* 6 (Fall 1992): 5–14.

[14]The discussion in this section is from Thomas J. Fitzgerald, "Understanding the Differences and Similarities between Services and Products to Exploit Your Competitive Advantage," *Journal of Business and Industrial Marketing*, 2 (Summer 1987): 29–34.

[15]Sak Onkvisit and John J. Shaw, "Is Services Marketing 'Really' Different?" *Journal of Professional Services Marketing* 7, (1991): 3–17.

[16]The discussion in this section is from James L. Heskett, *Managing in the Service Economy* (Cambridge, Mass.: Harvard Business School Press, 1986), Chapter 2.

[17]Robert J. Fisher, "Durable Differentiation Strategies for Services," *Journal of Services Marketing* (Winter 1991): 19–28.

[18]G. Lynn Shostack, "Service Positioning through Structural Change."

[19]Carolyn R. Fryer, "What's Different about Services Marketing?" *Journal of Services Marketing* 5 (Fall 1991): 53–58.

[20]Joseph P. Guiltinan, "The Price Bundling of Services: A Normative Framework," *Journal of Marketing* 51 (April 1987): 74.

[21]John Dearden, "Cost Accounting Comes to Service Industries," *Harvard Business Review* 56 (September/October): 132–140.

[22]E. Jerome McCarthy, *Basic Marketing: A Managerial Approach*, 2d ed. (Homewood, Ill.: Richard D. Irwin, 1964): 38–40.

[23]Heskett, *Managing in the Service Economy*, 84.

[24]Irving D. Canton, "Managers Ignore the Service Option at Their Peril," *Business Month* 133 (March 1989): 85–86.

[25]"Service Management: The Toughest Game in Town", *Management Practice* (Fall 1984): 8.

[26]Heskett, *Managing in the Service Economy*, 85.

[27]For a model that management can follow in service (product) development, see G. Lynn Shostack, "Designing Services That Deliver," *Harvard Business Review* (January/February 1984): 133–139.

[28]This discussion follows M. G. Christopher, M. M. McDonald, and G. S. C. Wills, *Effective Marketing Management* (Gowers Aldershot, 1980), 108–109; and is adapted from Donald Cowell, *The Marketing Services* (London: Institute of Marketing and the CAM Foundation), 147–161. See also Martin R. Schlissel and Joseph Chasin, "Pricing of Services: An Interdisciplinary Review," *Services Industries Journal* 11 (July 1991): 271–286.

[29]Schlissel and Chasin, "Pricing of Services."

[30]Also see Stephen W. Brown, "New Patterns Are Emerging in Services Marketing Sector," *Marketing News* (June 7, 1985): 2.

[31]Victor P. Buell (ed.), *Handbook of Modern Marketing*, 2d ed (New York: McGraw-Hill, 1986), Chapter 24.

[32]Eunsang Yoon, Hugh J. Guffey, and Valerie Kijewski, "The Effects of Information and Company Reputation on Intentions to Buy a Business Service," *Journal of Business Research* 27 (July 1993): 215–228.

[33]Gary Knisely, "Comparing Marketing Management in Package Goods and Service Operations," in *Service Marketing*, ed. Christopher H. Lovelock (New York: Prentice-Hall, 1984), 21.

[34]John C. Crawford and Juliet M. Getty, "The Marketing of Services: A Quality Perspective," *Journal of Professional Services Marketing* 8 (1991): 5–15.

[35]James Brian Quinn and Christopher E. Gagnon, "Will Services Follow Manufacturing into Decline?" *Harvard Business Review* (November/December 1986): 95–103.

[36]Simon Hall, "A Framework for Generating Viable New Services," *Business Marketing Digest* 16 (Fourth Quarter 1991): 11–16.

[37]Based on Eugene M. Johnson, Eberhard E. Scheuing, and Kathleen A. Gaida, "New Service Development and Management," *Profitable Service Marketing* (Dow Jones-Irwin, 1986): 159–182.

[38]Donald Cowell, *The Marketing of Services*, 28–30.

[39]John E. Swan and H. O. Pruden, "Marketing Insights from a Classification of Services," *American Journal of Small Business* 2, no. 1 (July 1977).

[40]Christopher H. Lovelock, "Classifying Services to Gain Strategic Marketing Insights," *Journal of Marketing* 47 (Summer 1983): 9–20.

[41]Dan R. E. Thomas, "Strategy Is Different in Service Businesses," *Harvard Business Review* (July/August 1978). Also see Sak Onkvisit and John J. Shaw, "Is Services Marketing 'Really' Different?" *Journal of Professional Services Marketing* 7 (1991): 3–17.

[42]Philip Kotler, *Principles of Marketing*, 5th ed. (Englewood Cliffs, N.J.: Prentice Hall, 1991), 683.

[43]*Ibid.*

[44]Philip D. Cooper and Ralph W. Jackson, "Applying a Services Marketing Orientation to the Industrial Services Sector," *Journal of Business and Industrial Marketing* (Summer 1988): 51–54.

[45]Lovelock, "Classifying Services," 19. Also see Cynthia Webster, "What Kind of Marketing Culture Exists in Your Service Firm?" *Journal of Services Marketing* 6 (Spring 1992): 54–67.

[46]Lovelock, 19.

[47]"U.S. Hotel Chains Are Following the Tourists to Europe," *Business Week*, 19 August 1985, 75–77.

[48]From Robert F. Lusch and Virginia N. Lusch, *Principles of Marketing* (Boston, Mass.: Kent Publishing, 1987): 591–593.

[49]This section is largely based on Cowell, *Marketing of Services*, 265–275.

[50]M. Carman and E. Langeard, "Growth Strategies for Service Firms" (paper presented to the Eighth Annual Meeting of the European Academy for Advanced Research in Marketing, Groningen, the Netherlands, April 1979).

[51]Lee D. Dahringer, "Marketing Services Internationally: Barriers and Management Strategies," *Journal of Services Marketing* 5 (Summer 1991): 5–17.

[52]Much of this material is based upon Professor B. Griffith's small but valuable book, *Invisible Barriers to Invisible Trade* (New York: Macmillan, for Trade Policy Research Center, London, 1975).

[53]Heskett, *Managing in the Service Economy*, Chapter 8.

[54]James L. Heskett, "Lessons in the Service Sector," *Harvard Business Review* 65 (March/April 1987).

[55]R. Markin, *Marketing: Strategy and Management* (New York: John Wiley and Sons, 1982).

14 International Business Marketing

Learning Objectives

After reading this chapter, you should be able to:

- Appreciate the scope and challenge of international business marketing.
- Understand the international business environment.
- Recognize the complexities and significance of international law.
- Describe the impact of domestic laws in foreign markets.
- Differentiate among various methods of entry into international business markets.
- Discuss the development of global marketing mixes for international business markets.

Chapter Outline

Learning Objectives

The Scope and Challenge of International Business Marketing
- The Market
- Stages of Economic Development

The International Business Environment
- The Buying Process
- Cultural Dynamics
  - Required adaptations
  - Cultural imperatives
  - Cultural adiaphora
  - Cultural exclusives
- The Political and Legal Environment
  - The political environment
  - The legal environment
    - U.S. laws
    - Export controls
    - Antitrust laws
    - Webb-Pomerene associations
    - Foreign sales corporations
    - The Export Trading Company Act
    - The Foreign Corrupt Practices Act

International Law
- Tax Treaties and Treaties of Friendship, Commerce, and Navigation
- IMF and GATT
- UNCITRAL
- International Standards Organization

Domestic Laws in Foreign Markets
- Differing Legal Systems
- Foreign Laws and the Product
- Foreign Laws and Pricing
- Foreign Laws and Promotion

Entry Strategies for the International Business Market
- Exporting
- Licensing
- Joint Ventures
- Manufacturing
- Assembly Operations
- Franchising
- Turnkey Operations

Product Strategy in the International Business Market
- International Product and Service Positioning Strategy
- Adaptation versus Standardization
- Marketing Services Internationally

Managing the International Promotion Effort
- Global Sales Promotion
- Global Publicity
- Global Trends in Direct Marketing

Managing the International Distribution System

Pricing in the International Business Market
- Company Factors Affecting Pricing
  - Global corporate objectives
  - Cost-based approaches
  - Transfer price policies
- Market Factors Affecting Pricing
  - Income levels and market segments
  - Competitive structure
  - Channel structure
  - Grey markets
- Environmental Factors Affecting Pricing
  - Foreign exchange rates
  - Inflation rates
  - Price controls

Summary

Key Terms

Review Questions

Cases
- Case 14-1
- Case 14-2

Suggested Additional Readings

Endnotes

THE SCOPE AND CHALLENGE OF INTERNATIONAL BUSINESS MARKETING

Between the years 1988 and 1992, exports accounted for only 2.2 percent of economic growth in the United States, in an economy that otherwise would have declined 0.4 percent. Only 7.4 percent of the U.S. economy, compared with an average of 19 percent among our major trading partners, is derived from exports.[1] Additionally, the rate of growth of exports continued to decline, from 16 percent in 1988 to 4 percent in 1992. The United States ranks last among major trading partners in per capita government expenditures on export promotion. The United States must make trade a national priority.

What determines how well a company does in global markets? How should performance in global markets be measured? With the globalization of markets and industries, discovering the answers to these questions has become imperative.[2] To successfully compete in today's foreign markets requires a reevaluation of marketing programs in light of current trends. The successful business manufacturing firm or service provider cannot expect to be sought out by potential foreign customers; instead, the firm must effectively and actively compete in foreign and domestic markets, selling to increasingly demanding customers. It is not uncommon for those domestic firms that do export to derive over one-third of their revenues from foreign operations. For example, IBM's foreign earnings are about 40 percent of total revenue.[3] The growing perception of the world as one marketplace hopefully will encourage more business product and service marketers to change their orientation toward the market to a global one.

The Market

Two fundamental factors account for greater market similarities among business customers than consumer customers. First is the inherent nature of the product; business products are those goods and services used in the process of creating other goods and services. Consumer goods are in their final form and are consumed by individuals. Second is the motive or intent of the users; business customers are seeking profit while the ultimate consumer is seeking self-satisfaction. These factors manifest themselves in specific buying patterns, demand characteristics, and selling techniques for business goods. A marketing approach to a business goods or services customer is generally different from the marketing approach to a consumer because each is buying for a different reason.[4]

In addition to problems created by cultural, legal, political, and other environmental differences among countries, two significant trends to consider in the marketing of business goods and services are (1) rapidly growing demand for business goods and services throughout the world, and (2) global competition from Western Europe, Japan, and a host of developing countries from Asia to Latin America.[5] As noted earlier, the firm cannot expect to be sought out by buyers; instead, it must compete with the many eager and relatively new competitors actively selling to increasingly demanding customers.

Stages of Economic Development

Perhaps the most significant factor affecting the business goods marketer seeking to do business abroad is the differing degrees of industrialization among countries. Although generalizing about particular countries, and indeed specific parts of the world, can be a foolhardy practice, the stage of economic development in a particular country (or part of the world) can be used as a rough gauge in ascertaining demand, relative risk involved, and quality of goods sought. It is logical to assume that there is a relationship between the degree of economic development and the projected demand for business goods or services found within a country or particular part of the world.

Every country goes through five stages of economic development and each stage relates to the extent of production capability. (See Exhibit 14-1.) A production orientation allows broad generalizations to be made about the level of development and projected demand within a particular country or part of the world. However, the marketer must be cognizant of the fact that many countries are in a state of change and can overlap two stages at a time. For example, a Third World country in the first stage may purchase advanced technology like telecommunication satellites, computer systems, or nuclear power to speed up its industrialization.[6]

EXHIBIT 14-1 **Stages of Economic Development**

Stage 1. The Traditional Society

One with limited production functions, primarily agricultural. The level of productivity in manufacture as in agriculture is limited by the inaccessibility of modern science, its applications, and its frame of mind.

Stage 2. The Pre-Conditions for Take-Off

Societies in transition toward modernization. Some investment in infrastructure occurs and there is a widening scope of internal and external commerce. Some modern manufacturing appears but the society is still mainly characterized by the old social structure and values.

Stage 3. The Take-Off

Resistance to change lessens and the forces for economic growth come to dominate the society. Industries expand rapidly, requiring new investment. New techniques spread in agriculture as well as industry.

Stage 4. The Drive to Maturity

Continuing growth extends modern technology over the whole range of economic activity. The make-up of the economy changes unceasingly as technique improves, new industries grow and older ones level off. The economy extends its range into more complex technologies.

Stage 5. The Age of High Mass Consumption

The leading sectors shift toward durable consumers' goods and services. The structure of the working force changes with more employed in offices or in skilled factory jobs. The extension of modern technology as an objective is joined with a desire to improve social welfare and security.

Source: Walt W. Rostow, *The Stages of Economic Growth*, 2nd ed., Cambridge University Press, 1971. Reprinted with permission of Cambridge University Press.

The firm seeking to enter the international market might not be successful unless its product or service is matched to the particular stage of economic development in a particular country or part of the world.

The objective of this chapter is to identify some of the most common problems encountered when a firm begins to market business goods (and services) internationally and to make the student aware of the implications of the competitive and demand factors encountered when a firm enters this market. Companies can indeed capture new markets with good potential for growth by developing a product or introducing a service that meets worldwide requirements and positioning that product or service to capitalize on local needs.[7] To be most successful in the global marketplace, a company must view itself in a global context rather than just as a U.S. company doing business abroad. Yet, just as is the case in domestic markets, creating a market overseas involves identifying a previously unidentified need and satisfying it.

THE INTERNATIONAL BUSINESS ENVIRONMENT

Many U.S. firms are not aware of the potential market that lies abroad. Trading internationally is not an easy task. You need information. You need to know the wants and needs and the problems and opportunities of business in other countries. You need contacts. You need to know who to talk to and how they negotiate business deals. Various environmental factors can influence your international marketing strategy. Marketers should be as aware of the complex buying process, the social-cultural dynamics, the political-legal environment, and the economic environment in foreign markets as they are of those in domestic ones.

The Buying Process

As studied in Chapter 3, people involved in the buying process are members of what is referred to as the "buying center." The size of the buying center can vary from one, or a very few people, to groups of fifteen to twenty (or more) individuals. The initial major task of the marketer is to determine who is involved in the buying process so that communications (mail, media, or salesperson) can be aimed at the appropriate people within the prospect's firm. The size of the buying center varies with the complexity and importance of a purchase decision; and the composition of the buying group will usually change from one purchase to another, or even during various stages of the buying process. (Review Exhibit 3-1, "Roles of Buying Center Members in the Purchasing Process," Chapter 3.) Although the objectives of purchasing personnel may be universal, the makeup of the buying center and the interactions between members of the buying center will vary by country.[8]

In international marketing, it is often more difficult to (1) identify the members of the buying center, (2) determine their role in the buying process, and (3) communicate the appropriate information to them. Less-developed countries may not have well-developed staff functions, such as engineering and purchasing, so buying decisions may be made by a line supervisor, such as the plant manager. In Japan, the decision maker may appear to be a senior-level, older person, but the real decision may be made by a younger, lower-level manager. These differences in the decision process from country to country should be well understood by the international marketer. It should also be understood that the level of purchasing expertise and efficiency varies from country to country and will change over time.

Although it is often assumed that business buyers are completely rational people, seldom letting emotion creep into a buying situation, research has shown that professional purchasers are also influenced by the country of origin, even when all other variables are held constant.[9] The international marketer must recognize the country of origin's stereotypes and use this information when developing a marketing strategy. Highly nationalistic countries tend to encourage economic self-sufficiency, even at the expense of economic efficiency, which could have a negative effect on the international firm. Given the results of this research and analysis, the international marketer should pay close attention to the level of nationalism in a country, the country of origin's stereotypes, and the competence level of the purchasing function of the prospect firm.

Cultural Dynamics

The global environment is characterized by diverse and deep-rooted cultural norms and value systems. Considering the increasing economic interrelationships worldwide, today's marketers need to be aware of the importance of social-cultural differences in the process of adjusting and adapting a marketing strategy to foreign markets.[10]

Before entering a foreign market, business firms must study all aspects of a nation's culture, including language, education, social values, material culture, attitudes and values, and religious attitudes. Culture reflects the human aspect of a person's environment; it consists of beliefs, morals, customs, and habits learned from others. Attitudes and values often present potential or real obstacles to inexperienced marketers. Consider:

> Attempting to close a sale or even transact business over lunch in Switzerland would provoke the loss of a sale, as the Swiss never discuss business over lunch. Salespeople in Germany must be very respectful of their customers by calling them "Herr Doktor Schmidt," even if it sounds redundant. In Brazil, a salesperson has to dress the same as the customer, whether it's formal or informal. In India, contracts are seldom signed by the third meeting. In Switzerland and Germany, it's rude to shake hands across desks; instead, executives walk around their desks. French business people appreciate whenever a foreigner attempts to speak French, even if it's a few poorly spoken phrases. Japanese dislike immodesty and any salesperson who boasts or oversells their accomplishments is considered distasteful.[11] Pride and dignity are important anyplace in the world, but nowhere as important as in Asia. To speak or act in a way that may cause an Asian to lose face is tantamount to a physical assault in the West. "Frank" Americans may complain loudly about the defects they perceive in a host country, hence taking "face" away from the Asians standing by.[12]

Because culture deals with a group's design for living, it is pertinent to the study of international marketing.[13] When a promotional message is written (business advertisement, catalogue, and the like), symbols recognizable and meaningful to the market (the culture) must be used. In fact, culture is pervasive in all marketing activities; pricing, promotion, channels of distribution, product, and packaging. The marketer's efforts are often judged in a cultural context for acceptance, resistance, or rejection.

As global businesses interact, executives are exposed to differences in business practices that, in turn, change business behavior, just as cultures change when exposed to the ways of others. Some suggest a world business culture is evolving and, indeed, that may be the case. However, to assume that the trend toward similarities means that differences in business behavior do not still exist is to court disaster![14] A lack of understanding of the differences in business customs can create insurmountable barriers that prevent an otherwise acceptable product from ever reaching the final business user. A knowledge of the business culture, management attitudes, and business methods existing in a country and a willingness to accommodate the differences are important to success in an international market. Unless business marketers remain flexible in their own attitudes by accepting differences in basic patterns of thinking, local business tempo, religious practices, political structure, and family loyalty, they are hampered, if not prevented, from reaching satisfactory conclusions to business transactions.

Required Adaptations. Adaptation is a key concept in international marketing, and willingness to adapt is a crucial attitude. Adaptation, or at least accommodation, is required on small matters as well as large ones. As a guide to adaptation, Cateora tells us that there are ten basic criteria that all who wish to deal with individuals, firms, or authorities in foreign countries should be able to meet. They are (1) open tolerance, (2) flexibility, (3) humility, (4) justice and fairness, (5) adjustability to varying tempos, (6) curiosity and interest, (7) knowledge of the country, (8) liking for others, (9) ability to command respect, and (10) ability to integrate oneself into the environment. (See Figure 14-1.) Add the quality of adaptability to the other qualities of a good executive for a composite of the ideal international marketer.

The key to adaptation is to remain American while at the same time developing an understanding and willingness to accommodate differences that exist. Foreign businesspeople do not necessarily expect you to act like one of them. However, when different cultures meet, open tolerance and a willingness to accommodate each other's differences are necessary. Fortunately, among the many obvious differences that exist between cultures, only a few are troubling. They are:

Cultural imperatives. *Cultural imperatives* are the business customs and expectations that must be met and conformed to if relationships are to be successful. Successful business marketers know the Chinese word "Quan-xi," the Japanese "nigen kankei," or the Latin American "compadre." All refer to friendship, human relations, or attaining a level of trust. They also know that there is no substitute for establishing friendship in some cultures before effective business negotiations can begin.

Cultural adiaphora. *Cultural adiaphora* consists of the areas of behavior or customs that cultural outsiders may wish to conform to or participate in but that are not required. One need not adhere to local dress, greet another man with a kiss (a custom in some countries), or eat foods that disagree with the digestive system (so long as the refusal is gracious). On the other hand, a symbolic attempt to participate in adiaphora is not only acceptable but may also help to establish rapport. It demonstrates that the marketer has studied the culture.

Cultural exclusives. *Cultural exclusives* are customs or behavior from which the foreigner is excluded. A marketer needs to be perceptive enough to know when he or she is dealing with an imperative, an adiaphora, or an exclusive and have the adaptability to respond to each. There are not many imperatives or exclusives, but most offensive behavior results from not recognizing them. When in doubt, marketing managers should rely on good manners and respect for those with whom they are associating.

FIGURE 14-1 **Profile of the Ideal International Marketer**

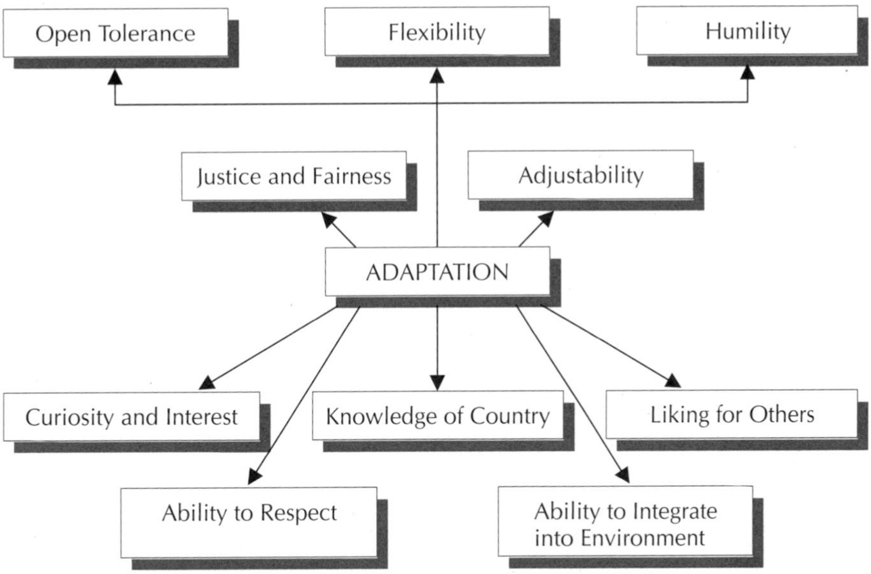

The Political and Legal Environment

As much as most managers would like to ignore them, political and legal factors often play a critical role in international marketing activities. Unfortunately (or fortunately), business and governments need each other. Business can only prosper when there are stable economic and political environments. These are prerequisites for business planning and risk taking. Even the best marketing plans can go bad as a result of unexpected political or legal influences. Today's political tumult, from the massacre in Tiananmen Square to the fall of the Berlin Wall, the collapse of the Soviet Union, and the bloodshed in Bosnia, has prompted growing ranks of international marketers to consider political risk, whether they operate manufacturing plants, participate in joint ventures, or simply export to foreign countries. Risk is the chance a company will lose money, property, even lives, because of events beyond its control, such as a revolution or political changes in regime or ideology, policy changes such as currency devaluations, or altered profit repatriation rules.

The political environment. Besides the business marketer, the principal players in the political arena are the host country governments, the home country governments, and the transnational bodies or agencies. The respective interactions of these groups result in a given political climate that may positively or negatively affect the operations of a business marketer trying to do business in the international arena. The task of the marketing manager is to assess the political forces that comprise the firm's political environment and to analyze their impact on marketing strategy. Exhibit 14-2 presents a checklist of questions that can guide this process.[15]

A company doing business across national boundaries should understand that no nation allows goods to flow across national borders unregulated. When the firm decides to import a product from its home country, it may quickly discover that the host country's political environment is not always hospitable. However, the host country's political atmosphere tends to improve if the company decides to invest in local production facilities, instead of importing finished products from outside to sell in the host country. Local production facilities improve the host country's balance of payments and create jobs. But a company should not assume that the host country will always welcome foreign capital. When IBM proposed building a computer plant in Mexico, the plan was rejected by the Mexican government. The government's principal objection involved IBM's policy of 100 percent ownership of the company's foreign factories.[16]

The climate for foreign investment varies greatly from country to country. An investment climate depends on both the type of investment involved and the political mood at the time. In general, local manufacturing is preferred over imports and over exports of natural resources for manufacturing elsewhere. Business investment in economic sectors with high unemployment rates are usually

EXHIBIT 14-2 **Checklist for Analyzing the Political Environment**

1. What is the country's political structure?
2. How do citizens, political parties, and special-interest groups participate in political decision making?
3. What is the current government's political philosophy? How is it implemented?
4. What are the philosophies of opposing political forces?
5. What role does the current government see for foreign business?
6. Is foreign business treated differently from local firms in public policy? If so, how?
7. What is the country's history in dealing with foreign businesses?
8. What is the process whereby changes in public policy are made?
9. What are the current and foreseeable trends in the relationship between the government in this country and in my home country?
10. What general role does government see for private business in this country's economic life?
11. What restrictions on international transfers of resources will affect my firm's operations in this country?
12. What are the major trends in the regulatory environment?
13. What incentives does the government give to private business and foreign investors?
14. What are the trigger points for increased nationalistic feelings in the host country?
15. How does the government assert its economic sovereignty?
16. What are the specific risks of loss of ownership or control of assets?
17. What are the chances of political harassment and what forms is it likely to take?
18. What tools can be used to build a mutually beneficial relationship with this country's government? Will they survive a possible change of government?
19. What are the possibilities of a change in government or other expressions of political instability?
20. Are my firm, my industry, and/or my products likely to be politically vulnerable?

welcomed, as is the introduction of sophisticated technologies, provided that those technologies do not displace existing jobs.

One problem often encountered with foreign politics is the conflicting signals sent by the host country to foreign firms. On one hand, the host country actively woos investment. To win foreign capital and new technology, the country pledges cooperation and various tax and financial incentives. On the other hand, the host country is often quick to accuse foreign firms of not providing the latest technology and expertise in local operations. It may also criticize these companies for making excessive profits and draining the nation of its wealth. To indicate displeasure, the host government may restrict the repatriation of profits to corporate headquarters abroad.

When discussing the international political environment, domestic politics must also be considered. Domestic politics are the politics that exist in the company's home country. Domestic criticism of a business product firm's international activities comes largely from labor and political organizations, which may accuse the company of exporting capital and jobs. These organizations feel that imports and direct investment abroad create unemployment at home. In some cases, this opposition is based on moral principle. For example, the citizens of many nations wanted to prohibit the importation of gold from South Africa, and they pressured companies in their countries not to invest in South Africa because of apartheid. Instead of providing support for international trade, the government of the home country can turn out to be a significant hindrance.

Finally, international politics must be considered. This involves the interaction of the overall environmental factors of two or more countries. The complexity of the political environment increases significantly when the interests of the company, the host country, and the home country do not coincide. Dresser, a U.S. corporation, became involved in such a problem when trying to supply materials for a Soviet gas pipeline. Because of the Reagan administration's ban on American firms' participation in the project, Dresser was threatened by the United States with a civil suit and a loss of export license if it allowed Dresser-France (its French subsidiary) to ship three compressors to the Soviet Union. France, on the other hand, was just as adamant in its decision to go ahead with the project. Calling upon its 1983 war emergency rules to override corporate decisions to protect national interests, the French government threatened Dresser-France with fines, jailing of executives, and seizure of the items in question. Dresser-France was put in the position of abiding by French laws that would cause its parent company to violate U.S. law.

The legal environment. From the political environment is generated the legal environment for business; that is, the nation's laws and regulations pertaining to business. A firm must know the legal environment in each market because these laws constitute the "rules of the game." The legal environment of international business marketing is complicated, having three dimensions. For an American firm these are (1) U.S. laws, (2) international law, and (3) domestic laws in each of the firm's foreign markets.[17]

The legal principles governing today's international arena result from centuries of commercial transactions between different nations. For the most part, the framework of the international trading system is based upon straightforward concepts of contract law. There are, however, important nuances. The best preparation for understanding the legal requirements governing international commerce begins at home, with a solid understanding of U.S. export enforcement and foreign corrupt practices policies.[18]

U.S. laws. A variety of laws and restrictions are relevant for international marketing and relate to exporting, antitrust, and organization and ownership arrangements.

Export controls. Like other countries, the United States has a variety of controls on export trade. (The United States has more than most countries.) One kind of control pertains to "country destinations." As of 1989, there were prohibitions on exports to Cambodia, Cuba, Libya, North Korea, and Vietnam, and severe restrictions for several other countries. Another relates to the "nature of the products" exported. For products having national security or foreign policy significance, there are controls or even prohibitions (terrorism equipment, missile technology, and nuclear technology, for example).

Antitrust laws. It might seem strange that U.S. antitrust laws would affect the foreign business activities of American companies. However, that is a fact of life for international business marketers. The opinion of the U.S. Justice Department is that even if an act is committed abroad, it falls within the jurisdiction of American courts if the act produces consequences for the United States. When an American firm expands abroad by acquiring a foreign company, the Justice Department will be concerned about the possible impact on competition in the United States. Remington Arms Company tried to acquire Sweden's AB Norma Projektilfabrik in an effort to get a foothold in the European Community, where high tariffs on third-country ammunition were nearly pricing Remington out of the market. The Justice Department said that acquiring Norma would allow Remington to increase its U.S. market share, as Norma was selling 10 percent of its output in the United States already. Remington gave up its efforts in the face of the challenge by the Justice Department.

Webb-Pomerene associations. *Webb-Pomerene associations* (The Export Trade Act) permit the cooperation of competing firms in export trade. Firms that compete domestically can collaborate in exporting. The intent was that American exporters be given countervailing power to enable them to compete against foreign oligopolies or cartels and to prevent them from playing off one exporter against another.

Foreign sales corporations. Most governments use the power of taxation to encourage or discourage different kinds of activity. The United States does not have value-added taxes, so it has sought other tax devices to encourage exports. A *foreign sales corporation* (FSC) is a sales company set up in a foreign country or a U.S. possession that can obtain a tax exemption on a portion of export earnings.

Export volume of firms in some of the early shared FSCs ranged from $500,000 to $16 million.

The Export Trading Company Act. In 1982, President Reagan signed the *Export Trading Company Act*, which permitted banks to invest in export trading companies (ETCs) and eased antitrust restrictions on export activities. Though ETCs may offer promise for the future, progress has been slow.

The Foreign Corrupt Practices Act. In the 1970s, there was a lot of publicity about the practice of bribery by American firms abroad. Payoffs to high government officials have often been the most effective promotional tool in international business. The most sensational cases involved United Brands and the president of Honduras, and Lockheed and the Japanese prime minister. As a result, the U.S. government passed the *Foreign Corrupt Practices Act* to prohibit U.S. firms from engaging in such payoffs abroad.

CONCEPT QUESTIONS

1. Why is a country's stage of economic development a key consideration for the international business marketer?
2. Why should the international business marketer carefully study cultural dynamics in overseas markets?
3. What is the difference between domestic politics and international politics?

INTERNATIONAL LAW

International law can be defined as the collection of treaties, conventions, and agreements between nations that more or less have the force of law. International law involves some mutuality, with two or more countries participating in the drafting and execution.

Tax Treaties and Treaties of Friendship, Commerce, and Navigation

The United States has signed *treaties of friendship, commerce, and navigation* (FCNs) with many countries. FCN treaties cover commercial relations between the two signing nations. They commonly identify the nature of the right of American companies to do business in those nations with which the United States has such a treaty and vice versa. FCN treaties usually guarantee "national treatment" to the foreign subsidiary; that is, it will not be discriminated against by the nation's laws and judiciary.

IMF and GATT

The *International Monetary Fund* (IMF) and the *General Agreement on Tariffs and Trade* (GATT) are part of the limited body of effective international law. Both agreements identify acceptable and nonacceptable behavior for the member nations. The international business marketer is interested in both IMF and GATT because of a shared concern in the maintenance of a stable environment conducive to international trade.

UNCITRAL

The United Nations established a commission on International Trade Law, UNCITRAL, with a goal to promote a uniform commercial code for the whole world. It bridges the communications gap between countries having different legal systems. It should minimize contract disputes and facilitate the task of selling goods between countries.

International Standards Organization

The *International Standards Organization* (ISO) is working toward the development of uniform international standards. Differing national standards are a major hindrance to international trade, and American industry has been less active in ISO than other exporting nations. This lack of interest may be costly in the long run, with the possibility of the United States finding itself closed out of many markets.

DOMESTIC LAWS IN FOREIGN MARKETS

The importance for foreign laws to the business marketer lies primarily in domestic marketing in each foreign market. The problem arises from the fact that the laws in each market tend to be somewhat different from those in every other market.

Differing Legal Systems

Before considering national peculiarities in marketing law, the business marketer should look at the basic legal systems that underlie individual national law. The differences among national legal systems are important to the international business marketer. Because the legal systems of no two countries are exactly the same, each foreign market must be studied individually and appropriate local legal talent hired where necessary.

Foreign Laws and the Product

The international business marketer will find many regulations affecting the product. Local laws often constrain the marketer's freedom as to other product features, such as package, label, and warranty. Labelling is subject to more legal requirements than the package. Brand names and trademarks are product attributes that also face different national requirements.

Foreign Laws and Pricing

Price controls are pervasive in the world economy. Many nations have some legal provisions for "resale price maintenance" (RPM), but there are many variations. Another variable is the fact that some countries allow price agreements among competitors.

Foreign Laws and Promotion

Advertising is one of the more controversial elements of marketing and is subject to more control than some of the others. Most nations have some law regulating advertising, and advertising groups in many nations have self-regulatory codes. New Zealand has no fewer than thirty-three laws relating to advertising. Also, sales promotion techniques encounter greater restrictions in some markets than in America. In the United States, there is often no constraint on contests, deals, premiums, and other sales promotion techniques. The situation is quite different elsewhere.

ENTRY STRATEGIES FOR THE INTERNATIONAL BUSINESS MARKET

Many business marketers have learned that it is not a practical strategy to enter all markets with a single-entry method. Even large multinational corporations such as IBM have to formulate multiple-entry strategies. IBM, once known for following a policy of doing business only through its subsidiaries, now uses a portfolio of entry strategies. In Europe, it uses joint ventures, cooperative projects with governments and competitors, and long-term supply relationships.[19]

The general tendency for most business firms is to enter the international market slowly, cautiously, and through exporting (either directly or indirectly through a third party). As they adopt long-term perspectives, they tend to move away from exporting and toward other entry strategies that provide more permanence, more competitive power, more control, and greater long-run profits. There are many entry strategies for foreign markets, from those with little risk and minimum control to those with maximum risk and maximum control. A sampling of these strategies will be discussed below.

Exporting

Exporting is a strategy in which a company, without any marketing or production organization overseas, exports a product from its home base. The product is basically the same as the one marketed in the home market. The leading U.S. exporters (with export sales and exports as percent of sales in parentheses) are General Motors ($8.3 billion, 8.14 percent), Boeing ($7.3 billion, 44.86 percent), Ford ($7.2 billion, 11.55 percent), General Electric ($4.3 billion, 12.35 percent), and IBM ($3.0 billion, 5.97 percent).[20] Risk is minimal, and the marketing effort is casual.

Licensing

Licensing is an agreement that permits a foreign company to use industrial property (that is, patents, trademarks, and copyrights), technical know-how and skills (for example, feasibility studies, manuals, technical advice, and the like), architectural and engineering designs, or any combination of these, in a foreign market. A licensor allows a foreign company to manufacture a product for sale in the licensee's country. Licensing is the fastest way to enter a market that is difficult for outsiders to enter. It requires a minimum investment, as the licensee already has a sales and distribution organization and has experience in dealing with the local government. Finally, there is no danger of being expropriated or nationalized.

Joint Ventures

A *joint venture* is simply a partnership. An international joint venture is one in which the partners are from more than one country. Each partner agrees to a joint venture to gain access to the other partner's skills and resources. Caterpillar has a joint venture with a South Korean company to produce Caterpillar's forklift trucks for Asian markets. Caterpillar also has a joint venture in Japan with Mitsubishi, enabling it to compete with Komatsu, a major competitor, in the Japanese home market. John Deere and Hitachi have a joint venture that assembles small-sized and medium-sized hydraulic excavators in Great Britain.[21]

Manufacturing

The manufacturing process can be employed as a strategy involving all or some manufacturing in a foreign country. IBM, for example, has sixteen plants in the United States and eighteen more in other countries. As starting from scratch can be a slow process, some business firms acquire a local company. However, historically, one U.S. acquisition in three has failed![22] Others will use local personnel in management positions. However, as Union Carbide learned in its operations in Bhopal, India, problems can occur. Local Indian personnel were inadequately trained in safety procedures, leading to one of the worst industrial accidents in the twentieth century.

Assembly Operations

An *assembly operation* is a variation on a manufacturing strategy. In this strategy, parts or components are produced in various countries in order to gain each country's comparative advantage. Capital-intensive parts may be produced in advanced nations, and labor-intensive assemblies may be produced where labor is abundant and labor costs are low. This strategy is common among manufacturers of electronics.

Franchising

Franchising provides exporters with a close and tight relationship to international markets. Franchising grants to the franchisee the right to carry on a certain manufacturing process and to use the brand name. The franchisee generally has a small but exclusive territory and is bound by the terms of the franchise contract. The contract provides for close supervision by the American franchiser, to assure adherence to standards and specified marketing practices.[23] Service companies such as Holiday Inn, Hertz, and Manpower have successfully used franchising to enter foreign markets.

Turnkey Operations

A *turnkey operation* is an agreement by the seller to supply a buyer with a facility fully equipped and ready to be operated by the buyer's personnel, who will be trained by the seller. In international business marketing, the term is usually associated with giant projects that are sold to governments or government-run companies. Large-scale plants requiring technology and large-scale construction processes unavailable in local markets commonly use this strategy. Such large-scale projects include building steel mills, cement, fertilizer, and chemical plants, and those related to such advanced technologies as telecommunications.

One would be naive to believe that a single-entry strategy would be suitable for all products or in all countries. A significant change in the investment climate can make a particular strategy ineffective, even though it worked well in the past.

PRODUCT STRATEGY IN THE INTERNATIONAL BUSINESS MARKET

Just because a product is successful in one country is no guarantee that it will be successful in other markets. A business marketer must always determine local needs and take them into account.

A product is often considered in a narrow sense as something tangible that can be described in terms of physical attributes, such as shape, dimension, components, form, color, and so on. A student of marketing, however, should realize that this definition of product is misleading since many products are intangible (for example, services). Actually, intangible products are a significant part of the American export market.[24]

In many situations, both tangible and intangible products must be combined to create a single, total product. This is clearly illustrated by the Klockner Group of Germany, which packages turnkey projects in the United States and exports them to Latin America and Third World countries. The tangible aspect of this product is the heavy input of U.S. equipment, which is well regarded and thus utilized on projects in Latin America. The intangible aspect of the package is the management expertise provided by Klockner.

The question of what products to sell in foreign markets is the essence of product policy in international marketing. Should we sell the same products we sell domestically, or should they be adapted to local conditions? Will our product line be the same abroad as at home, or should we sell a different mix of products in foreign markets? For each company and industry, the answers may be somewhat different. When firms first go multinational, they usually market their domestic products with minimal adaptation to foreign conditions. As noted earlier, another approach is to acquire a foreign firm that has products designed for its own market. Each of these approaches may be satisfactory as an initial method of getting business products for the international market. For the long run, however, a more sophisticated business and product development plan is desirable. In its planning process, the business firm must decide what businesses and what markets it wants to pursue.

International Product and Service Positioning Strategy

Product positioning is a marketing strategy that attempts to occupy an appealing space in customers' minds in relation to the spaces occupied by other competitive products. It has been said that the ability to successfully position products in domestic markets is the mark of a good marketer, and the ability to successfully position products in the international market is the mark of a great marketer! Successfully positioning a product internationally is a sophisticated process that requires awareness and sensitivity to the needs of many markets. While one of the important ingredients in establishing a positioning strategy is the inputs from marketing research, intuition, timing, and a marketing sense also play important parts in developing this strategy.

When we discuss positioning a product in the marketplace, we are referring to filling a void in a demand environment. The niche in which we position the product is a benefit separation between products available in that market. The position a product fills might be based on unique functional benefits that satisfy a need of a market segment of demand.

Much like market segmentation, product positioning is frequently ignored by American marketers in selling abroad. In the international marketplace, there appears to be no serious effort to position products in any meaningful way. When American products occupy attractive positions at all, it is usually by chance, and not by design. How a product is positioned could be determined by local regulations. This was the problem experienced by Pfizer in marketing Mecadox, a feed supplement-plus-antibiotic for hogs in Europe. The product was approved only as a feed supplement in certain countries, as an antibiotic in others, and as both in yet others.

Adaptation versus Standardization

A controversial issue in international marketing is the issue of product adaptation (localization) versus product standardization. Frequently debated in the international marketing literature, this issue centers on whether a business should pursue a strategy that is standardized across national markets or adapted to individual national markets.[25] *Product adaptation* means simply changing the product to meet local needs, while *product standardization* means that a product originally designed for a local market is exported to other countries with virtually no change, except perhaps for the translation of words and other cosmetic changes. The goals of reducing costs and complexity lead companies to consider standardization, while a customer orientation sways them toward product adaptation.

The attractions of standardization are obvious. It will usually result in lower costs and economies of scale in manufacturing, product development, and marketing. Managerial complexity is reduced, and export marketing is facilitated when the same product is exported to several countries. One study found that the majority (81 percent) of the U.S. respondents exported their business product without any modification.[26]

The greater argument for product adaptation is that by doing this the firm can realize greater profits. The economies referred to earlier represent cost minimization, not necessarily profit maximization. Modifying products for national or regional markets may raise revenues by more than the costs of adaptation.[27]

Lotus 1-2-3, the best-selling spreadsheet software package, underwent a major revision so as to serve the needs of the Japanese market. The adaptation took two years and involved a Japanese software developer as a partner. Lotus practically rebuilt the product from the ground up. The result was that the Japanese version was given a special Nikkei International Award for Creative Excellence, Lotus being the only international company to receive such an award in 1986. More practically, the Japanese version of Lotus immediately became the best selling business software product after its introduction in 1986.[28] It is clear that adaptation was crucial to Japanese success.

Marketing Services Internationally

The fastest-growing U.S. export during the past decade has been business services, with U.S. services trade estimated to be in excess of $120 billion today.[29] Accounting services, advertising, consulting, construction, insurance, auto rentals, hotel services, financial services, and others are included in the category of business services.[30]

The primary competition for American service firms comes from Western Europe, with Latin American and East Asian companies getting in on the act. India views the service business as an infant industry that must be nurtured and protected. As a result, direct and indirect trade barriers have been imposed to restrict foreign companies from domestic markets. Every reason, from the protection of infant industries to national security, has been used to justify some of the restrictive practices. A list of more than two thousand instances of barriers to the free flow of services among nations was recently compiled by the U.S. government.[31] The United States is stressing the elimination of trade barriers and market access for service industries.[32]

CONCEPT QUESTIONS

1. By what manner do most U.S. firms enter the international business market?
2. How can the manufacturing process be utilized as a market entry technique?
3. What is the value of franchising to international business exporters?

MANAGING THE INTERNATIONAL PROMOTION EFFORT

Advertising and promotion are important parts of the international marketing program of firms competing in the global marketplace. While more than $130 billion is spent on advertising in the United States each year, advertising expenditures outside the United States have increased dramatically over the past decade and are nearing $300 billion.[33] More and more companies are recognizing that an effective promotional program is important for business products and services firms competing in foreign markets, and many of these organizations are utilizing advertising agencies for their global advertising efforts. (See the "Business-to-Business Marketing in Action" box).

In addition to the importance of international business advertising and promotion, many firms have finally realized the challenge and difficulties that must be overcome in developing and implementing programs for the international market. An unfamiliar marketing environment coupled with customers who have different sets of values and customs as well as different purchase motives and abilities add to the challenge. In addition to different languages encountered from country to country, many different languages may be spoken within a particular country, such as in India or Switzerland. Many U.S. business marketers also find that media options are much more limited in many foreign countries owing to lack of availability or limited effectiveness. As a result of all these factors,

BUSINESS-TO-BUSINESS MARKETING IN ACTION

ADVERTISING AGENCIES ADJUST TO DEMANDS OF GLOBAL CLIENTS

In 1990, companies assigned more than $1.4 billion in pan-European business to advertising agencies, according to a survey by *Advertising Age*'s Euromarketing newsletter. The figure comprises 106 accounts worth more than $3 million each. Of the total, at least 80 accounts were new assignments. Several multinational agencies have adjusted their structure in response to increased globalization.

In an effort to bring together specialists within key disciplines from around the world, and to ensure horizontal communications within the agency, Lintas: Worldwide has created the Worldwide Creative Council, the Worldwide Media Council, and the Worldwide Integrated Communications Council. Pitching for pan-European business is complex and expensive, but agencies do benefit because a client is much less likely to change agencies once it has gone to the trouble of selecting one. Language barriers and national restrictions, such as laws that allow only television advertisements shot in a particular country, also present challenges.

Source: Julie Skur Hill, "A Brave New World of Brands: Agencies Adjust to Demands of Global Clients," *Advertising Age*, 62, Issue 36 (September 2, 1991), pp. 25–35.

different creative and media strategies as well as changes in other elements of the advertising and promotion program are often required for foreign markets.[34]

The issue of standardization is also a factor that must be considered when determining the type of advertising that will be used in global markets. A 1983 article by Theodore Levitt reignited the argument about standardized products and marketing programs in international business marketing. Levitt argued that companies should globalize their marketing strategies, marketing the same product the same way in all markets, foreign and domestic.[35] The desirability of global marketing has been widely debated, and an important part of the argument concerns the desirability of standardizing advertising worldwide.[36]

A policy of *global advertising* attempts to standardize advertising programs across international markets. Global advertising can be contrasted to *localized advertising*, in which different advertising programs are used in each international market. In practice, completely global advertising and completely localized advertising represent the extreme ends of a continuum.[37] In practice, most advertising programs fall somewhere between the two extremes. Within business markets, the opportunities for global appeals are more easily identifiable since the buying motives and purchase decisions are often similar across markets and are made explicit by established industry purchasing procedures. Many business products, including raw materials and technologically sophisticated products, are being marketed to an increasingly concentrated set of business buyers. Within these markets, standardized advertising in carefully selected trade media is more likely to play an information role, supplementing the efforts of a company's personal sales force.

Global Sales Promotion

The basic purposes of gaining attention and interest, and motivating a behavioral response within a target market, remain the same for sales promotion whether a business firm is operating domestically or globally. Business-to-business firms increasingly rely on trade-oriented sales promotion to help sell their products in foreign markets. The challenge for global business marketing managers is to assess the effectiveness of sales promotion efforts across different cultures and markets. This assessment of effectiveness needs to take into account the varying cultural, economic, social, and legal aspects of different markets.

Unlike advertising, which often can be done on a global basis, sales promotions must often be adapted to local markets. Kamran Kashani and John Quelch noted several important differences among countries that must be considered in developing a sales promotion program.[38] These include the stage of economic development, market maturity, customer perceptions of promotional tools, trade structure, and legal restrictions and regulations.

A discussion (however short) of global sales promotion would not be complete without touching on business (industrial) trade shows abroad. As American firms seek business markets abroad, a stumbling block confronting many new entrants concerns quickly gaining access to market information and decision makers. The business trade show is one vehicle that can serve the business marketer well in this regard.

It is estimated that there are over six hundred trade shows annually in seventy countries. Approximately 3,300 American companies participated in overseas trade fairs in 1989, a 25 percent increase over 1988, according to the U.S. Department of Commerce. West German trade fairs attracted 312 U.S. exhibitors in 1989.[39]

European trade fairs offer an excellent opportunity for business marketers to develop contacts for the emerging Eastern European market. According to Richard Humbert of the International Trade Association, "Participation in a trade fair is one of the best ways to test the potential of Europe and may be the most important step in a U.S. exporter's European marketing plan."[40] These shows are also a fertile ground for cultivating new customers for small- and medium-sized businesses. The entry time for exporting can be cut from six years to six months by regularly attending foreign trade fairs.[41] While nearly 60 percent of American visitors to trade fairs expect to purchase an exhibited product within two months of attending the fair, nearly 100 percent of businesspersons at foreign fairs are buyers with order books in hand or distributors looking for products that can be sold abroad.

Global Publicity

Incidents like Exxon's Valdez oil spill or Union Carbide's tragic accident at its plant in Bhopal, India, create situations that impact a company's image worldwide. Usually, companies have less control over global publicity relative to a domestic situation, and no firms are powerful enough to control a host country's media. At best, attempts are made to provide positive information about the company that is directed at influential targets, such as members of the broadcasting media, editors, or journalists.[42] For example, to reduce the trend of "Japan bashing" in the early 1990s in the United States, Japanese corporations have made use of public relations firms that assist in developing positive publicity regarding the companies' philanthropic activities in the United States.

Global Trends in Direct Marketing

The United States has a market environment and the skills for direct marketing that are unmatched in any other country in the world. Japan has the technological and cultural prerequisites to evolve into a key market for direct marketing, but its long tradition of distribution via multilayered channels still dominates the market. Estimates are that Europe, the other leading region in the world for direct marketing activities, is running about twenty years behind developments in the United States, although the gap is closing.

Postal regulations, unreliable postal service, and lack of telecommunication services (for instance, the concept of toll-free, or 800, numbers) have somewhat restricted direct marketing opportunities for U.S. firms. Nonetheless, direct marketing is quickly becoming a major force in developed economy markets. Market forces such as the introduction of the EUC (Europe's proposed common currency, the European Currency Unit), the gradual decline of customs and tariff barriers, and the increased reach of global media will all have a positive effect on the direct marketing of goods and services globally.

MANAGING THE INTERNATIONAL DISTRIBUTION SYSTEM

When the business-to-business firm considers entering the international market, it has to make two important decisions. First, will the new market for the product provide greater returns than would other options? Second, what is the most suitable market entry mode or type of channel structure to use? The development and maintenance of a global distribution system requires a tremendous commitment of time, money, and managerial energy that typifies the development of a global channel system. Firms may be using international channels that are not the most preferred, but they may not be able to change. Firms are not always able to obtain the best channel structure for their purposes. Foreign government restrictions, the dictates of corporate parents, resource scarcity, and contractual commitments all play a part in constraining decisions.[43]

A multitude of channel alternatives are available to the foreign marketer of business goods.[44] American firms distribute basically in three ways: through American-based export intermediaries; through foreign-based intermediaries; and through company-managed, direct-sales forces. Business products firms can use any combination of these three distribution systems or only one, depending on the extent of their involvement in foreign marketing and their organization, production facilities, and financial status. The type used depends on company size, level of market commitment, and market conditions (finance, intermediaries, political climate, and so forth). The use of domestic-based exporters is recommended for small- and medium-sized firms without extensive acumen in foreign operations, or for a firm that prefers a minimum of involvement in foreign sales. Most are concentrated in cities with major ports, carry a number of related but noncompetitive product lines, receive compensation in the form of commission on goods sold, and typically do not take title to, or possession of, the goods. Benefits provided to their clients include:[45]

Credit Assistance—Export middlemen often do their own financing, paying the business products manufacturer in dollars before the export order leaves the United States; thus, they relieve the client of foreign exchange risk.

Licensing—When local competition, import barriers, or transportation charges make the effective distribution of the exporter's products impractical or impossible, the export middlemen can help arrange for local production via joint ventures, or via a royalty license arrangement.

Shipping Expenses—By consolidating shipments from several clients to one overseas destination, and shipping under one bill of lading, export middlemen can provide savings to all their clients.

Demonstrations—Export middlemen can arrange overseas demonstrations and technical support training to foreign users or foreign sales representatives.

Specialization—Because export middlemen specialize in related product lines, they help the sales for each individual line.

To explain how a typical export middleman provides the needed global distribution services, suppose that this person handles electrical components and small machinery for construction. An overseas contractor asks for a price quote on compressors but also needs other equipment for field operations. The export middleman is in a position to offer related product and price information from various clients for the project, thereby benefiting all concerned, including the overseas customer who has the opportunity to deal with a single source of supply.

The use of foreign-based middlemen (independent local distributors) is often the only route for most who want to compete in Europe and elsewhere.[46]

Although successful exporting involves many factors, one key is how well an American firm is able to identify good international distributors. A leading manufacturer of farm and earth-moving equipment changed from direct distribution through company-owned sales subsidiaries to the use of independent local distributors. It was decided that independent local distributors would provide the company with a stronger, more economical organization that was far more stable for its products, which were sensitive to economic shifts. A local distributor often can weather economic ups and downs by carrying complementary products, along with exploiting markets considered too small to support a company sales organization but needing the services available from locally based distribution points.

The use of direct distribution through company-managed sales forces can be a viable option for some firms. A leading manufacturer of machine tools established its own sales distribution points throughout Europe. The decision was based on the competitive need to provide rapid service for its equipment and on a desire to participate in the lucrative parts market associated with the use of its products. This method of distribution was the most suitable for the company's circumstances. Business products and services are often sold directly through professional sales staffs throughout the world, since specialized knowledge and service may be requirements that remain constant across markets.

PRICING IN THE INTERNATIONAL BUSINESS MARKET

Pricing considerations in international business operations are not only more numerous than those in strictly domestic ones but also more ambiguous and risky. A selling firm must consider at least two different sets of laws, two competitive markets, the reactions of two sets of competitors, and two governments. It is not surprising that determining prices for international sales is such a difficult problem, even for the occasional exporter. Successful pricing is a key element in the profitability of any business operation, domestic or international.

Pricing is one area of international business marketing that has been largely overlooked. Of all the Four Ps of marketing, pricing is probably the one that receives the least attention, especially in the international business context. As competition for the world's markets becomes more intense, price will be increasingly more important as a competitive tool. The international business marketer is ultimately responsible for establishing price policies for a company's international operations.

Pricing for the international business products market can be influenced by a wide variety of factors, with only a few under the direct control of the firm. Figure 14-2 identifies the most common variables that can influence international pricing strategy.[47] While the groupings of company factors, market factors, and environmental factors are separated for discussion, we should keep in mind that

FIGURE 14-2 **Common Variables That Influence International Pricing Strategies**

Source: Richard J. Semenik and Gary J. Bamossy, *Principles of Marketing: A Global Perspective,* Cincinnati: South-Western Publishing Co., 1993, p. 292. Used with permission.

they are, in fact, interrelated. In addition, the more uncontrollable market and environmental forces are usually the most disruptive elements that affect international pricing. Taken together, these two sets of factors are often the best explanation as to why an otherwise well-conceived marketing strategy ends up as unprofitable.

Company Factors Affecting Pricing

Global corporate objectives. The increased emphasis by firms on global marketing, the deregulation of the European market in the early 1990s, and the shift to overseas production have all contributed to the development of pricing policy within globally oriented firms. By understanding the strategic emphasis on price in the marketing mix of the firm, and by appreciating other marketing mix influences in global markets (such as advertising, personal selling, and promotion differentiation), a business products marketer can, hopefully, make decisions based on company global objectives.

Cost-based approaches. The basis for any effective pricing policy is a clear understanding of the cost and profit variables involved. A clear definition of relevant costs and profits is often difficult to achieve. Understanding the various cost elements is a prerequisite for a successful international pricing strategy.

Transfer price policies. A substantial amount of international business takes place between subsidiaries of the same company. The price charged to all these subsidiaries is known as *transfer pricing*. Transfer pricing policies tend to be strictly under the control of the parent company. To pursue a strategy of profit maximization, a company may lower transfer prices for products shipped from some subsidiaries while increasing prices for products shipped to others. The company will then try to accumulate profits in subsidiaries where it is advantageous and keep profits low in others.

Market Factors Affecting Pricing

Income levels and market segments. Prices need to reflect the realities of each market in which the business products firm competes. The firm must take into account local market conditions and the realities of the marketplace. The challenge is to meet successfully the large number of local economic situations and market segments to be considered.

Competitive structure. The unique competitive structure in each market must be considered. If the company is a sole supplier of a particular business product or service, it will enjoy great pricing flexibility. If it has to compete against either local firms or other international companies, the opposite will be true. Cost structures may also be quite different for local competitors, which may affect their pricing structure.

Channel structure. The final price to the customer may be influenced by channel structure, including the length of the channel. As a general rule, most foreign countries tend to operate with longer channels than we do. This can significantly increase end-user prices, as an astute business products marketer will pick up on.

Grey markets. A major problem that international firms face is the phenomenon of different prices between countries. If price differences are large enough, entrepreneurs step in and buy products in low-price countries and re-export the products to high-price countries. Experts call this the *grey market* because these dealings take place outside the regular trade channels. This is often caused by currency fluctuations.

Combatting this problem is an endless battle for many companies, and most often a losing one at that. By 1999, European companies will all change over to a common currency, which will remove many of the market imperfections that currently encourage grey markets.

Environmental Factors Affecting Pricing

Foreign exchange rates. Currency swings are considered to be a major trade barrier. Movements in exchange rates, which can be 50 percent or more over a period of years, directly influence a firm's ability to compete on price. Exchange rate fluctuations are extremely critical with long-term contracts. The longer the time between the signing of an order and the actual delivery, the greater the exposure to foreign exchange risk. Firms can try to manage foreign exchange fluctuations, but they have no control over them. Table 14-1 summarizes a number of possible export strategies under varying currency conditions.

Inflation rates. When a company sells its products in a country that has a high rate of inflation, the risk is that once the constantly devaluing local currency

TABLE 14-1 **Factors Affecting Price under Varying Global Currency Conditions**

When Domestic Currency is WEAK...	When Domestic Currency is STRONG...
Stress price benefits	Engage in nonprice competition by improving quality, delivery and after-sale service
Expand product line and add more costly features	Improve productivity and engage in vigorous cost reduction
Shift sourcing and manufacturing to domestic market	Shift sourcing and manufacturing overseas
Exploit export opportunities in markets	Give priority to exports to relatively all strong-currency countries
Conduct conventional cash-for-goods trade	Deal in countertrade with weak-currency countries
Use full-costing approach, but use marginal-cost pricing to penetrate new/competitive markets	Trim profit margins and use marginal-cost pricing
Speed repatriation of foreign-earned income and collections	Keep the foreign-earned income in host country, slow collections
Minimize expenditures in local, host country currency	Maximize expenditures in local, host country currency
Buy needed services (advertising, insurance, transportation, etc.) in domestic market	Buy needed services abroad and pay for them in local currency
Minimize local borrowing	Borrow money needed for expansion in local market
Bill foreign customers in domestic currency	Bill foreign customers in their own currency

Source: S. Tamur Cavusgil, "Unraveling the Mystique of Export Pricing." *Business Horizons,* May–June 1988. Used with permission.

is converted to the seller's currency, the resulting amount will not even cover product costs. In countries with extremely high inflation rates, companies may price their products in a stable currency, such as the U.S. dollar, and translate prices into the local currency on a daily basis, or if possible, insist on payment in another currency.

Price controls. A company's pricing strategy in a particular market can be influenced by the government. Price control, in one form or another, can be found in every corner of the world. In the effort to control prices, governments have a number of options open to them, including dictating the price that is to be used in the market, dictating the margins allowed to intermediaries, establishing upper and lower limits of markups (creating price floors and ceilings), and using government subsidy. Overall, global pricing is one of the most complex decisions that business products marketing strategists must make.

CONCEPT QUESTIONS

1. Why is standardization a factor to consider in developing global advertising?
2. What is the purpose of global sales promotion?
3. Why should the international business marketer understand the role of inflation rates in conducting business overseas?

SUMMARY

1. To be successful in today's foreign markets requires a reevaluation of marketing programs in light of current trends. The firm must effectively compete with the competitors (foreign and domestic) actively selling to demanding customers. In addition to the problems created by cultural, legal, political, and other environmental differences among countries, there is a rapidly growing demand for business goods and services throughout the world; global competition is coming from western Europe, Japan, and a host of developing countries from Asia to Latin America. The U.S. firm desiring to market its products and/or services abroad must match them to the stage of economic development present in the countries in which they wish to do business.
2. Many U.S. firms are not aware of the potential market that lies abroad. International business marketers should be as aware of the complex buying process, social-cultural dynamics, the political-legal environment, and the economic environment in foreign markets as they are in domestic markets.
3. International law is the collection of treaties, conventions, and agreements between nations that more or less have the force of law. International law involves some mutuality, with two or more countries participating in the drafting and execution. International law includes treaties of friendship, commerce, and navigation, tax treaties, the International Monetary Fund, the General Agreement on Tariffs and Trade, UNCITRAL, and the International Standards Organization.
4. The importance of foreign laws to the business marketer lies primarily in domestic marketing in each foreign market. The problem arises from the fact that the laws in each market tend to be somewhat different from those in every other market. International business marketers must become familiar with laws in each country, because these individually affect the components of the company's marketing mix for each product or service marketed abroad.

5. The general tendency for most business firms is to enter the international market slowly, cautiously, and through exporting. As the companies adopt long-term perspectives, they tend to turn to other entry modes, such as licensing, joint ventures, manufacturing, assembly operations, franchising, and turnkey operations.
6. An international business marketer must always determine the local needs of a particular country in developing product strategies. Product positioning is a sophisticated process that requires awareness and sensitivity to the needs of many markets. Some firms may have to adapt some of their products to meet a particular country's needs, while other products in their mix can be sold exactly as they are being sold in the firm's domestic market.
7. Advertising and promotion are important parts of the international marketing programs of firms competing in the global marketplace. Often, U.S. marketers desiring to promote products and services abroad must contend with different languages, different customs and values, and various media options as they target their efforts in a multiple number of countries. Global sales promotion, global publicity, and global direct mail are all available as effective promotional tools for the astute international business marketer to utilize.
8. International business firms may be using channels that are not the most preferred, but they may not be able to change. Firms are not always able to obtain the best channels for their purposes. Foreign government restrictions, the dictates of corporate parents, resource scarcity, and contractual commitments all play a part in constraining decisions. However, a multitude of channels are available to the international business marketer to include American-based export middlemen; foreign-based middlemen; and company-managed, direct-sales forces. The type used depends on company size, level of market commitment, and market conditions.
9. Pricing considerations in international business markets are numerous, ambiguous, and risky. Pricing for the international business products market can be influenced by a wide variety of factors. Company factors affecting pricing include global corporate objectives, cost-based approaches, and transfer price policies. Market factors affecting pricing are income levels among market segments, competitive structure, channel structure, and grey markets. Environmental factors affecting pricing include foreign exchange rates, inflation rates, and price controls.

KEY TERMS

Assembly operation
Cultural adiaphora
Cultural exclusives
Cultural imperatives
Exporting
Export Trading Company Act
Foreign Corrupt Practices Act
Foreign Sales Corporation
Franchising
General Agreement on Tariffs and Trade
Global advertising
Grey market
International law
International Monetary Fund
International Standards Organization

Joint venture
Licensing
Localized advertising
Product adaptation
Product positioning
Product standardization
Transfer pricing
Treaties of friendship, commerce, and navigation
Turnkey operation
UNCITRAL
Webb-Pomerene associations

REVIEW QUESTIONS

1. What two factors account for greater market similarities among business customers than consumer customers? Identify and briefly describe five stages of economic development through which virtually every country goes.
2. Why is it more difficult to identify the members of the buying center in international business marketing than in domestic marketing? Why is a thorough understanding of cultural dynamics among countries important to the international business marketer? Why is adaptation such a key concept in international business marketing? Distinguish between the political and the legal environments involved in international business marketing.
3. What is meant by the term international law? What are treaties of friendship, commerce, and navigation? What are the respective roles of the International Monetary Fund, the General Agreement on Tariffs and Trade, UNCITRAL, and the ISO in international law?
4. Identify and briefly explain four areas in which domestic laws impact foreign trade. Identify and discuss the use of seven major modes of entry into international business markets. What is the most common way companies first enter international business markets?
5. What should be the essence of product policy in international business marketing? What is the role of product positioning in international business marketing efforts? When would an international business company utilize product adaptation, and when would it be better to employ product standardization?
6. Distinguish between global and local advertising. Briefly discuss the importance of sales promotion, publicity, and direct mail in global promotion.
7. Identify and explain the three basic ways in which most American companies distribute their products on an international basis.
8. Briefly describe three company factors, four market factors, and three environmental factors that affect pricing in international business markets. Why do you think that pricing has historically been given so little attention by international business marketers?

Cases

CASE 14-1 Trading Again with the Iranians?

Gillette Company pulled out of Iran over a decade ago. At the time, Gillette believed that a country that promoted three-day stubble didn't have much need for disposable razors. Now, the clean-shaven look is back, and the Boston-based manufacturer has returned. Business is much more successful than the company expected. "The amount of success we're having is as if we'd never left," says Middle East manager Mohammed Subieh. Iranian students are even learning English. In a school where "Down with America" banners grace the hall, Janet Mamoudzadeh, who married an Iranian, teaches English to her first-grade class. "They haven't had English here for twelve years, and now they have an American teacher," says the transplanted Missourian.

Ali Akbar Hashemi, president of Iran, seems to teeter between moderation and tradition. Religious revolutionaries praise Hashemi for following in the footsteps of the revered Ayatollah Ruhollah Khomeini. The people of Iran seem more concerned with the country's welfare than with the religious and nonreligious arguments. The Islam religion dictates that women should cover themselves. This custom was at one time enforced by revolutionaries who assaulted improperly clad women on the streets. Today, women are encouraged to adhere to the religion, but not through force. In the shrine of the Ayatollah, Islamic rules regarding women's attire are strictly enforced. Conversely, on the streets of Tehran, the dress code is not enforced.

Iran is even encouraging tourists to return to the country. At one time, foreigners arriving in Iran were thoroughly searched for non-Islamic videos, too-sheer stockings, and banned alcohol. Today, many passengers may travel through a green "nothing-to-declare" line. During the Iran-Iraq war, many buildings crumbled from lack of repair as much as from Iraqi Scud missiles. The city has also been given a facelift. Now the fountains are working again. The trash is being picked up, and flowers grow in new parks. Sidewalks are being repaired, and renovating of hotels continues. New trade delegations to Iran arrive in increasing numbers. The country is even considering changing the Iranian weekend of Thursday and Friday to Friday and Saturday to facilitate business communications.

Westerners in Iran see the country as much more moderate than in the past. The new government is looking into the practice of paying commissions (considered bribes by some people) to local government officials on government contracts. However, not all Iranians see this moderation movement as desirable. Since the Gulf War, Iran has restored ties with many of its Persian Gulf neighbors. Revolutionaries fear that these renewed relationships will lead to a greater dependence on the West. Iran spent ten years breaking ties with the West to forge a more religious nation. A former member of the Revolutionary Guard summarizes these feelings when he says, "A lot of people are asking themselves why they wasted all those years." Other radicals don't have problems with the change as long as Iran's Islamic character is preserved.

DISCUSSION QUESTIONS

1. If you were the marketing manager for a U.S. company, would you want to market your products in Iran? Why or why not?
2. What cultural factors are important to companies selling products in Iran?
3. If you had to enter the Iranian market, what method of entry would you prefer?

Suggested Reading

Brooks, Geraldine. "Iran Takes Some Steps Toward Moderation: Radicals Wait and See." *Wall Street Journal*, 29 April 1991, A1, A6.

Source: C. Lamb, J. Hair, and C. McDaniel, *Principles of Marketing,* 1st Edition (Cincinnati, OH: South-Western Publishing Company, 1992) p. 753.

CASE 14-2 International Trade without Direct Pricing

Recently, Lockheed Corporation sold maritime aircraft to Korea and took Hyundai personal computers as a payment. Lockheed plans to use the PCs in its far-flung organization.

On the other hand, if the American company accepts the goods with the intent of resale, it best have a solid estimate of demand. Coherent Communications Systems, based in Hauppauge, New York, sold a $1 million telephone switching system to Colombia and agreed to two tons of ginger as payment. Coherent then hired a commodity broker to help sell the spice. The government of Peru owes hundreds of millions of dollars to First Interstate, a twenty-one-bank holding company. With little chance of payment in hard currency, First Interstate decided to resort to bartering. Banks cannot take title to goods, so the holding company established First Interstate Trading Corporation. So far, the trading company has accepted wire, fish meal, frozen fish, shellfish, garments, fresh asparagus, garlic, onions, and wood products. First Interstate claims that bartering will enable it to reduce its outstanding loans to Peru by 50 percent by 1994.

The first priority of First Interstate is to ensure that it is not buying goods and then finding markets. The firm tackles the problem the other way around. Since the bank and the trading company are directly linked, this process is made easier. Available product lists are distributed to each of Interstate's twenty-one banks. The bank officers peruse the list and then contact likely prospects who are currently bank customers. The trading company will accept the Peruvian product only after ensuring that demand is there.

Midland Bank, which is owed approximately $300 million by Peru, watched First Interstate's success and decided to try bartering itself. Its first shipment netted Midland $22 million through the sale of iron pellets, fish meal, steel balls, coffee, cotton thread, alpaca cloth, zinc and lead oxides, and copper sulphate.

DISCUSSION QUESTIONS

1. Is there an implicit price in the countertrade process? What is it?
2. Why isn't there more bartering between firms in the United States?
3. What are the advantages to buyers who pay in goods and services instead of cash?

Source: C. Lamb, J. Hair, and C. McDaniel, *Principles of Marketing*, 1st Edition (Cincinnati, OH: South-Western Publishing Company, 1992) p. 551.

Suggested Additional Readings

Baker, Stephen, Elizabeth Weiner, Geri Smith, Ann Charters, and Ken Jacobson. "Latin America: The Big Move to Free Markets." *Business Week,* 15 June 1992, 50–55. **A discussion of the market potential, advantages, problems, and future implications for trade with Latin America.**

Briggs, Jean A. "A Political Miracle." *Forbes,* 11 May 1992, 108–110. **A case study of economic conditions, democracy, privatization, natural resources, foreign investments, and free-trade agreements in Chile.**

Chan, Peng S., and Peter T. Justis. "Franchising in the EC: 1992 and Beyond." *Journal of Small Business Management* 30 (January 1992): 83–88. **A discussion of the current trends, problems, and regulations involved in franchising in the European Community.**

Demaree, Allan T. "What Now for the U.S. and Japan?" *Fortune,* 10 February 1992, 80–82, 86, 90, 94–95. **A discussion of trade negotiations, protectionism, open markets, and quotas in regard to current trade relations between Japan and the United States.**

Donaldson, Thomas. "Can Multinationals Stage a Universal Morality Play?" *Business and Society Review* 81 (Spring 1992): 51–55. **A discussion of global ethics to include politics, culture, traditions, human rights, discrimination, legal issues, and environmental concerns.**

Dooley, Arch R., Miguel Leon, and Michael R. Wood. "The North American Free-Trade Agreement." *Business Quarterly* (Canada), 56 (Autumn 1991): 93–99. **A discussion of the advantages, problems, implementation, and managerial implications of the North American Free-Trade Agreement.**

Engardio, Pete, Amy Borrus, Chuck Hawkins, Dori Jones Yang, and Russ Mitchell. "Good Morning, Vietnam!" *Business Week,* 22 June 1992, 48–50. **A report on the economic conditions, market potential, and diversity of business opportunities in Vietnam.**

Fuhrman, Peter. "Getting in Bed Together." *Forbes,* 11 May 1992, 86–87. **Trends in joint ventures, diversification, and mergers and acquisitions among Europe's leading business-to-business companies.**

Gross, Neil, and Kathy Rebello. "Apple? Japan Can't Say No." *Business Week,* 29 June 1992, 32–33. **A case study of Apple's sales of PCs in the Japanese market.**

Gugler, Philippe. "Building Transnational Alliances to Create Competitive Advantages." *Long-Range Planning* (UK), 25 (February 1992): 90–99. **Examples of successes and problems in creating and implementing international business partnerships to gain competitive advantage.**

Kilburn, David. "How Unilever's South Korean Partnership Fell Apart." *Advertising Age* 63 (August 31, 1992): 3, 39. **A case study of the business marketing problems encountered by Unilever in its cooperative venture with South Korea.**

Kindel, Stephen. "Staying Competitive in a Shrinking World." *Financial World* 160 (October 15, 1991): 22–25. **A study of the marketing strategies, niche marketing, and methods of market entry utilized currently by multinational organizations.**

Konrad, Walecia, and Igor Reichlin. "The Real Thing Is Thundering Eastward." *Business Week,* 13 April 1992, 96, 98. **A report on trading possibilities in Eastern Europe, with particular emphasis on the beverage industry.**

Kraar, Louis. "Korea's Tigers Keep Roaring." *Fortune,* 4 May 1992, 108–110. **A report of U.S. trading involvement with the Republic of South Korea.**

Levine, Robert. "Why Isn't Japan Happy." *American Demographics* 14 (June 1992): 58–60. **A comparison between Japan and the United States as regards quality of life, economic growth, personal satisfaction, leisure time, housing, and the like.**

Liesse, Julie. "Kellogg Chief to Push Harder for International Growth." *Advertising Age,* 24 August 1992, 4, 26. **A discussion of the efforts of Kellogg's CEO to enter international markets with Kellogg's product lines.**

Louter, Pieter J. "An Inquiry into Successful Exporting," *European Journal of Marketing* (UK), 25, no. 6 (1991): 7–23. **A survey of small- and medium-sized Dutch exporters in regard to product quality, service after the sale, timely delivery, packaging, and reliability.**

Morais, Richard, and Michael Schuman. "Hong Kong Is Just around the Corner." *Forbes*, 12 October 1992, 50, 54, 58. **A discussion of the advantages for small- and moderate-sized businesses in the Hong Kong market.**

Oikawa, Naoko, and John F. Tanner, Jr. "The Influence of Japanese Culture on Business Relationships and Negotiations." *Journal of Services Marketing* 6 (Summer 1992): 67–74. **A discussion of the methods employed by the Japanese in conducting negotiations and business activities, with particular emphasis on their impact on U.S. businesses that trade with Japan.**

Perry, Nancy J. "What's Powering Mexico's Success?" *Fortune*, 10 February 1992, 109–110, 114–115. **A report on positive economic conditions in Mexico that have been created through trade, government programs, newly created demand, and social reforms.**

Raffield, Barney T., III. "The Impact of South Korea's Economy, Labor Unions, and Political Agenda on Its Trade Relations with the United States." In *Globalization of Business: Annual Conference Proceedings*, 250–260. New England Business Administration Association, November 1988. **A discussion of the impact of the westernization of South Korea on its trade relations with the United States.**

Schilit, W. Keith. "The Globalization of Venture Capital." *Business Horizons* 35 (January/February 1992): 17–23. **A discussion of various modes of entry for companies seeking to become multinational organizations.**

Toy, Stewart, John Templeman, Richard A. Melcher, John Rossani, and Stanley Reed. "Europe's Shakeout." *Business Week*, 14 September 1992, 44–46,51. **A discussion of the privatization of industries in the European community.**

Tseng, Jow-Ying, and Chwo-Ming Joseph Yu. "Export of Industrial Goods to Europe: The Case of Large Taiwanese Firms." *European Journal of Marketing* (UK), 25, no. 9 (1991): 51-63. **A report on the successes of Taiwanese companies in exporting business goods to Europe.**

ENDNOTES

[1]Paul Magnusson, "Grabbing the World Orders," *Business Week*, 1992, 110–118.

[2]Tyzoon Tyebjee, "Globalization Challenges Facing Fast-Growth Companies," *Journal of Business and Industrial Marketing* (December 1993): 58–64.

[3]Lexis F. Higgins, Scott C. McIntyre, and Cynthia G. Raine, "Design of Global Marketing Information Systems," *Journal of Business and Industrial Marketing* 6 (Summer/Fall 1991): 49–58.

[4]Philip R. Cateora, *International Marketing*, 7th ed. (Homewood, Ill.: Richard D. Irwin: 1990), 430–431.

[5]Stuart Gannes, "Organizing for International Success," *Distribution* (October 1988): 48–54.

[6]Norman W. McGuiness and Blair Little, "The Influence of Product Characteristics on the Export Performance of New Industrial Products," *Journal of Marketing* (Spring 1981): 110–122.

[7]Edward R. Koepfler, "Strategic Options for Global Market Players," *Journal of Business Strategy* 10 (July/August 1989): 46–50.

[8]This section is largely from Jean-Pierre Jeannet and Hubert D. Hennessey, *Global Marketing Strategies*, 2d ed. (Boston: Houghton Mifflin, 1992): 202–204.

[9]Phillip D. White and Edward W. Cundiff, "Assessing the Quality of Industrial Products," *Journal of Marketing* (January 1978): 80–86.

[10]Alma T. Mintu and Roger J. Calantone, "A Comparative Approach to International Marketing Negotiations," *Journal of Applied Business Research* 7 (Fall 1991): 90–97. See also Sudher H. Kale and Roger P. McIntyre, "Distribution Channel Relationships in Diverse Cultures," *International Marketing Review* 8 (1991): 31–45.

[11]Brian H. Flynn, "Homing in on Foreign Sales Customs," *Business Marketing* (June 1987): 91–92.

[12]John A. Reeder, "When West Meets East: Cultural Aspects of Doing Business in Asia," *Business Horizons* (January/February 1987): 69–74.

[13]This section is largely from Cateora, *International Marketing*, 66–68, 99ff.

[14]James S. Mortellaro, "Business across a Cultural Void," *Business Marketing* (February 1989): 62–66. See also Vasco Knotts, "Cross-Cultural Management: Transformations and Adaptations," *Business Horizons* (January/February 1989): 29–33.

[15]Edward W. Cundiff and Marge Tharp Hilger, *Marketing in the International Environment*, 2d ed. (Englewood Cliffs, N.J.: Prentice-Hall, 1988), 201.

[16]This section is largely from Sak Onkvisit and John J. Shaw, *International Marketing: Analysis and Strategy*, 2d ed. (New York: Macmillan, 1993), Chapters 4 and 5. See also Michael R. Czinkota and Iikka A. Ronkainen, *International Marketing* (New York: Dryden Press, 1993), Chapter 4.

[17]This section is largely from Vern Terpstra and Ravi Sarathy, *International Marketing*, 5th ed. (New York: Dryden Press, 1991), Chapter 5. See also Cundiff and Hilger, *Marketing in the International Environment*, 212–220.

[18]William A. Delphos, *The World Is Your Market: An Export Guide for Small Business* (Washington, D.C.: Braddock Communications, 1990), 75.

[19]This section is largely from Onkvisit and Shaw, *International Marketing*, Chapter 9.

[20]"America's Leading Exporters," *Fortune*, 20 July 1987, 72–73.

[21]Kathryn Rudie Harrigan, *Strategies for Joint Ventures* (Lexington, Mass.: D. C. Heath, 1985), 288–289.

[22]William H. Davidson, *Global Strategic Management* (New York: John Wiley and Sons, 1982), 63.

[23]Coskun A. Samli, Richard Still, and John S. Hill, *International Marketing: Planning and Practice* (New York: Macmillan, 1993), 196.

[24]This section is largely from Onkvisit and Shaw, *International Marketing*, Chapter 10; Cundiff and Hilger, *Marketing In the International Environment*, Chapter 11; and Cateora, *International Marketing*, Chapter 13.

[25]David M. Szmanski, Sungar G. Bharadwaj, and P. Rajan Varadarayan, "Standardization versus Adaptation of International Marketing Strategy: An Empirical Investigation," *Journal of Marketing* (October 1993): 1–17.

[26]Anthony C. Koh, "An Evaluation of International Marketing Research Planning in United States Export Firms," *Journal of Global Marketing* 4 (1991): 7–25.

[27]Terpstra and Sarathy, *International Marketing*, 254.

[28]See "Lotus Announces No. 1 Ranking and Design Award for Its Japanese Version of 1-2-3," and "Lotus Announces Shipment of Release 2J, a Japanese Version of 1-2-3," Lotus Development Corporation News Releases, February 24, 1987, and September 10, 1986.

[29]"Service Exports: The Silent Revolution," *Export Today* (April 1989): 5–8.

[30]"Expansion of Global Output and Trade Continued in 1990, According to GATT," *IMF Survey* (December 10, 1990): 376–377.

[31]Merriam Mashatt, "The FTA Sets International Precedent in Service Trade," *Business America* (January 30, 1989): 8–9.

[32]C. William Verity, "Uruguay Round," *Business America* (June 20, 1988): 2–7.

[33] *Survey of World Advertising Expenditures: Twenty-Fourth Edition* (New York: Starch INRA Hooper and the Roper Organization, 1991).

[34] George E. Belch and Michael A. Belch, *Introduction to Advertising and Promotion*, 2d ed. (Homewood, Ill.: Richard D. Irwin, 1993), 739.

[35] Theodore Levitt, "The Globalization of Markets," *Harvard Business Review* (May/June 1983): 92–102.

[36] This section is largely from David W. Nylen, *Advertising*, 4th ed. (Cincinnati, Ohio: South-Western Publishing, 1993), Chapter 20.

[37] Sandra E. Moriarty and Thomas R. Duncan, "Global Advertising: Issues and Practices," *Current Issues and Research in Advertising* 30 (1990): 313–341.

[38] Kamran Kashani and John A. Quelch, "Can Sales Promotion Go Global?" *Business Horizons* (May/June 1990): 37–43.

[39] Brad O'Hara, Fred Palumbo, and Paul Herbig, "Industrial Trade Shows Abroad," *Industrial Marketing Management* 22 (August 1993): 233–237.

[40] Richard R. Humbert, "Trade Fairs Are an Excellent Way to Take Advantage of the Growing Opportunities in Western Europe," *Business America* (December 21, 1987): 3–5.

[41] Steven Golob, "Sell Overseas at Trade Fairs," *Nation's Business* (March 1988): 57–60.

[42] This section is largely from Richard J. Semenik and Gary J. Bamossy, *Principles of Marketing: A Global Perspective* (Cincinnati, Ohio: South-Western Publishing, 1993), Chapter 11.

[43] Saul Klein and Victor J. Roth, "Satisfaction with International Marketing Channels," *Journal of the Academy of Marketing Science* 21 (Winter 1993): 39–44.

[44] This section is largely from Cateora, *International Marketing*, Chapter 13.

[45] Semenik and Bamossy, *Principles of Marketing*, 431–432.

[46] Eugene H. Frem, "We Can Do a Better Job of Selecting International Distributors," *Journal of Business and Industrial Marketing* 7 (Spring 1992): 61–70.

[47] This section is largely from Semenik and Bamossy, *Principles of Marketing*, 292–302. Also see Jeannet and Hennessey, *Global Marketing Strategies*, Chapter 13.

15 Ethical Considerations in Business-to-Business Marketing

Learning Objectives

After reading this chapter, you should be able to:

- Identify the major changes that impact business-to-business marketing strategy in the future.
- Explain the role of ethics in business-to-business marketing research.
- Differentiate among various types of ethical issues in business pricing.
- Distinguish among ethical issues faced by business salespeople in dealing with both their customers and their employers.
- Speak about the ethical problems that can arise in implementing business-to-business marketing strategy.
- Realize the complexities and ramifications of ethical issues in the international business environment.

Chapter Outline

Learning Objectives

Business-to-Business Marketing Ethics and The Future: An Overview
- Examples of Corporate Social Responsibility
- The Individuality of Ethical Standards

Strategy and Ethics in the Business-to-Business Marketing Environment

An Ethical Issue: The Organizational Buying Function and Buyer-Seller Relationships
- Business Ethics Is Not a One-Sided Proposition

Ethical Issues in Business-to-Business Marketing Research
- Society's Rights
- Clients' Rights
- Researchers' Rights

Ethics and the Management of the Business Pricing Function
- Setting a Fair Price
- Altering Product Quality without Changing Price
- Practicing Price Discrimination with Smaller Accounts
- Price Fixing
- Using a Competitor's Quote to Requote or Rebid
- Reciprocity

Ethics and the Management of the Business Sales Force
- Ethics in Dealing with Customers
  - Bribes
  - Gifts
  - Entertainment
  - Reciprocity
- Ethics in Dealing with Employers
  - Moonlighting
  - Changing jobs
  - Expense accounts
  - Contests

Ethics and Business Advertising Strategy
- Truth in Advertising
- Comparative Advertising

Ethics and International Business-to-Business Marketing
- Ethics from Country to Country
- The Complexity of International Ethical Issues

Summary

Key Terms

Review Questions

Cases
- Case 15-1
- Case 15-2

Suggested Additional Readings

Appendix 15-1 Future Trends in Business-to-Business Marketing

Endnotes

BUSINESS-TO-BUSINESS MARKETING ETHICS AND THE FUTURE: AN OVERVIEW

The quantity of discussion on social responsibility and ethics in marketing has increased tremendously in recent years, as marketing is the functional area most closely related to ethical abuse. There are various areas of marketing that can raise ethical questions about appropriate marketing practice. The current perception of business and marketing is anything but flattering. Most studies confirm that between 65 percent and 75 percent of all marketing managers face an ethical dilemma at some point in their careers.[1] Marketing ethics involves inquiring into the nature and grounds of moral judgments, standards, and rules of conduct relating to marketing decisions and marketing situations.[2]

Ethics implies a standard of behavior by which conduct is judged; but standards that may be legal may not always be ethical. Standards or beliefs about what is right and proper change over time; this question becomes more important as our economy becomes more competitive and our technology more complex. Furthermore, the factors that affect people's propensity to make ethical or unethical decisions are not fully understood. There is speculation that three general sets of factors influence the ethics of one's decisions.[3] First, individual factors such as values, knowledge, attitudes, and intentions are believed to influence a person's decision. Second, opportunity resulting from the absence of professional codes of ethics, of corporate policies regarding ethics, or of punishment, may encourage unethical decision making. Third, the values, attitudes, and behavior of significant others such as peers, supervisors, and top management affect the ethics of one's decisions. Because it is an organized discipline, business ethics provides a solid foundation from which to operate. Even so, the study of ethics is not without problems of interpretation, as major philosophies are sometimes in conflict with one another as to how a single issue may be resolved.[4]

What should be the guiding philosophy with regard to ethical considerations as we approach the twenty-first century? Business and marketing ethics have come to the forefront in recent years.[5] Marketing people are often suspected of attempting to get people to want things they do not need. Ironically, the driving force of modern marketing is the marketing concept, the basic principle of which is that business succeeds by giving customers what they truly want. The social discontents and ethical issues associated with marketing stem not necessarily from greed and deception but from functional limitations on the implementation of the marketing concept.[6] In a recent interview, Herbert Chao Gunther, executive director of the Public Media Center (San Francisco), said that much of corporate social responsibility is a matter of public relations. Gunther said that business cannot be trusted because corporations aim entirely to maximize profits, without any real accountability. Corporate executives who make decisions that lead to tremendous harm are protected under the corporate shield. Society needs a system that holds them accountable.[7] For many years there has been uncertainty within some industries regarding the position that corporate management should take. Three different views of corporate responsibility have been subscribed to:[8]

(1) *The Invisible Hand*. Under this philosophy, "the true and only social responsibilities of business organizations are to make profits and obey the laws...the common good is best served when each of us and our economic institutions pursue not the common good or moral purpose...but competitive advantage. Morality, responsibility, and conscience reside in the invisible hand of the free market system, not in the hands of the organizations within the system—much less in the hands of managers within the system."

(2) *The Hand of Government*. Under this philosophy, "the corporation would have no moral responsibility beyond political and legal obedience... corporations are to seek objectives which are rational and purely economic. The regulatory hands of the law and the political process, rather than the invisible hand of the marketplace, turn these objectives to the common good."

(3) *The Hand of Management*. This philosophy "encourages corporations to exercise independent, noneconomic judgment over matters of morals and ethics which face them in their short and long-term plans and operations." It seeks "Moral reasoning and intent" from the corporation, and for managers to "apply...individual morality to corporate decisions."

Examples of Corporate Social Responsibility

In companies today, examples of all three philosophies can be found. Some firms are totally profit oriented and leave social results to the marketplace. Others operate within the letter of the law but provide no moral or ethical leadership. Some managers, however, are going beyond the narrow goals of profit to act as social citizens and ethical leaders, as the trend today is for society to demand moral and ethical leadership from business. The findings of a recent study present evidence that a well-communicated code of ethics may be related to ethical sales-force behavior. It appears that a sales force that is employed in such an environment can be profiled as being relatively high in job performance and equally high in job satisfaction.[9] As is shown in Exhibit 15-1, the American Marketing Association published a code of ethics in 1988. This is an example of many similar codes being proposed by business organizations. Many large corporations—such as Caterpillar Tractor, IBM, Johnson Wax, ITT, Security Pacific

Corporation, Primerica Corporation, Chemical Banking Corporation, and Champion International Corporation—have adopted formal codes of ethics. More are sure to follow.

EXHIBIT 15-1 The American Marketing Association Code of Ethics

Members of the American Marketing Association (AMA) are committed to ethical professional conduct. They have joined together in subscribing to this Code of Ethics embracing the following topics:

Responsibilities of the marketer

Marketers must accept responsibility for the consequence of their activities and make every effort to ensure that their decisions, recommendations, and actions function to identify, serve, and satisfy all relevant publics: customers, organizations and society.

Marketers' professional conduct must be guided by:

1. The basic rule of professional ethics: not knowingly to do harm.
2. The adherence to all applicable laws and regulations.
3. The accurate representation of their education, training and experience.
4. The active support, practice and promotion of this Code of Ethics.

Honesty and fairness

Marketers shall uphold and advance the integrity, honor, and dignity of the marketing profession by:

1. Being honest in serving consumers, clients, employees, suppliers, distributors and the public.
2. Not knowingly participating in conflict of interest without prior notice to all parties involved.
3. Establishing equitable fee schedules, including the payment or receipt of usual, customary and/or legal compensation for marketing exchanges.

Rights and duties of parties in the marketing exchange process

Participants in the marketing exchange process should be able to expect that:

1. Products and services offered are safe and fit for their intended uses.
2. Communications about offered products and services are not deceptive.
3. All parties intend to discharge their obligations, financial and otherwise, in good faith.
4. Appropriate internal methods exist for equitable adjustment and/or redress of grievances concerning purchases.

It is understood that the above would include, *but is not limited to*, the following responsibilities of the marketer:

In the area of product development and management

- Disclosure of all substantial risks associated with product or service usage.
- Identification of any product component substitution that might materially change the product or impact on the buyer's purchase decision.
- Identification of extra-cost added features.

In the area of promotions:

- Avoidance of false and misleading advertising.
- Rejection of high-pressure manipulations, or misleading sales tactics.
- Avoidance of sales promotions that use deception or manipulation.

In the area of distribution:

- Not manipulating the availability of a product for purpose of exploitation.
- Not using coercion in the marketing channel.
- Not exerting undue influence over the resellers choice to handle a product.

In the area of pricing:

- Not engaging in price fixing.
- Not practicing predatory pricing.
- Disclosing the full price associated with any purchase.

In the area of marketing research:

- Prohibiting selling or fund raising under the guise of conducting research.
- Maintaining research integrity by avoiding misrepresentation and omission of pertinent research data.
- Treating outside clients and suppliers fairly.

continued

EXHIBIT 15-1 **The American Marketing Association Code of Ethics (continued)**

Organizational relationships:

Marketers should be aware of how their behavior may influence or impact on the behavior of others in organizational relationships. They should not demand, encourage or apply coercion to obtain unethical behavior in their relationships with others, such as employees, suppliers or customers.

1. Apply confidentiality and anonymity in professional relationships with regard to privileged information.
2. Meet their obligations and responsibilities in contracts and mutual agreements in a timely manner.
3. Avoid taking the work of others, in whole, or in part, and represent this work as their own or directly benefit from it without compensation or consent of the originator or owner.
4. Avoid manipulation to take advantage of situations to maximize personal welfare in a way that unfairly deprives or damages the organization or others.

Any AMA members found to be in violation of any provision of this Code of Ethics may have his or her Association membership suspended or revoked.

Source: American Marketing Association, Chicago, Ill., 1988. Reprinted with permission.

As we approach the next century, many firms are recognizing that ethical issues and social responsibility find their expression in the daily decisions of marketers, rather than in abstract ideals. Consider the following:

- Arthur Anderson and Company launched a $5 million project to teach ethics to business students. This project "will train college professors to use case studies that emphasize ethics in their courses on management, accounting, economics, finance, and marketing." The project stems from Anderson's desire to instill ethical decision-making standards in its forty thousand U.S. employees, according to Duane Kullberg, managing partner of Chicago-based Anderson.[10]
- DuPont Company, the world's leading producer of chlorofluorocarbons (CFCs), has called for a total phaseout of the chemicals to prevent destruction of the earth's protective ozone layer. The company "is convinced that an international treaty calling for 50 percent cuts in CFC production over the next decade is not stringent enough to prevent serious damage to the ozone layer." DuPont invented CFCs and sells $600 million worth of them annually, about a fourth of the world's supply.[11]
- Two-thirds of upper-level executives think people are "occasionally" unethical in their business dealings, while another 15 percent believe people are "often" unethical; 16 percent consider people "seldom" without ethics. These are among the findings of a survey of one thousand corporate executives on ethical behavior commissioned by McFeely-Wacherle Jett, a Chicago-based executive-recruiting firm. Nearly one in four executives believes ethical standards can impede successful careers, while 68 percent agree younger executives are driven to compromise their ethics "by the desire for wealth and material things." Still, 54 percent think that business executives and managers have higher ethical standards and behavior than the general population.[12]

The Individuality of Ethical Standards

Every marketing manager must work out his or her own philosophy of socially responsible and ethical behavior, looking beyond what is legal and allowed and developing standards based on personal integrity and corporate conscience. Business-to-business marketing executives of the 1990s will face many challenges, not the least of which will be ethical considerations in their decision-making process. Those marketers who are able to practice socially responsible behavior in carrying out the day-to-day decision-making process should be in a position to promote legality, fairness, and decency among organizations in the years ahead, as they realize that responsive corporate policy within this area makes good business sense.

STRATEGY AND ETHICS IN THE BUSINESS-TO-BUSINESS MARKETING ENVIRONMENT

Comparing the marketing strategies and tactics of business-to-business firms today versus ten or so years ago, the most striking impression is one of general marketing strategy obsolescence. Just a few short years ago, computer companies were introducing ever more powerful hardware for more sophisticated uses. Today, these same companies emphasize mini- and microcomputers and software; competitors launch new products, and customers switch their business; distributors lose their appeal; promotion costs skyrocket; new government regulations are announced and old ones are being enforced; and consumer groups attack. While all this is going on, and at a time when more than half the American public believes that the level of business ethics has declined significantly in the past decade, it might be the time for both academics and marketers (at least those who have stood idly by) to become involved. While we cannot deemphasize the importance of training, research and development, market development, and other disciplines that are central to our business system, we must start sensitizing managers to the interface of ethical values and the implementation of business-to-business marketing strategy. Questions should be asked such as: What laws are being proposed that might affect future marketing strategy? Which government agencies should we be working with in our quest for improved social and ethical behavior? What can the marketer expect in the areas of pollution control, product safety, advertising, price controls, and other areas relevant to present and future marketing strategy development? What is the attitude of the public toward the firm and the firm's products? In short, what major changes are occurring that will impact the implementation of future marketing strategies across several disciplines within the business marketing firm in the short, the intermediate, and the long term?

AN ETHICAL ISSUE: THE ORGANIZATIONAL BUYING FUNCTION AND BUYER-SELLER RELATIONSHIPS

Business buyers and sellers are engaged in activities that come under the continuing scrutiny of superiors, associates, prospective suppliers, the public, and the press. The National Association of Purchasing Management, mindful of the key problems often faced by professional buying individuals, codified many potential problems into its code of ethics. This code is as follows:[13]

(1) Interests of the firm are foremost in all dealings. This concept implicitly indicates that personal gain from business suppliers in the form of "commissions" (for example, gifts,) cloud the objectivity necessary in making the best decision for the buying firm.

(2) Buy without preference or prejudice. This calls for objectivity in vendor selection and avoiding conflict of interest when the buyer might have a financial interest in one particular vendor.

(3) Seek maximum value in purchases. This statement reinforces the objective of receiving the maximum value at the lowest overall price to the buying firm.

(4) Maintain a sound policy with regard to gifts. The cost of any gift is a marketing expense to the vendor that must be recaptured through higher prices.

(5) Strive for knowledge about materials, processes, and practical methods. This is a reminder that the buyer should not merely process requisitions and purchase orders.

(6) Be receptive to competent counsel from colleagues. This is a reminder to be open to new ideas and anything that might improve performance and further the goals of the employer.

(7) Counsel and assist other buyers. This means seeking improvements, aiding others, and so forth.

(8) Avoid "sharp practice." This includes misrepresentations in order to gain an unfair advantage over a vendor.

(9) Subscribe to honesty and truth in dealings. This is similar to the sharp-practice point and emphasizes that honesty and truth will benefit the buyer in the future with like action from vendors.

(10) Respect obligations. Obligations can range from contractual obligations to verbal understandings.

(11) Provide prompt and courteous reception to vendors. A seller's time is as valuable as the buyer's, so a prompt reception of salespeople is encouraged.

Although the typical buying organization has developed the methods of a science, its decisions remain largely a matter of personal judgment. The purchasing manager, through contacts and dealings with business salespeople, is the custodian of the firm's reputation for courtesy and fair dealing. The opposite is also true—the business salesperson is also expected to retain his or her firm's reputation for courtesy and fair dealing. A high ethical standard of conduct is essential for both parties. Courtesy and fair dealing beget confidence and cooperation on the part of both the buyer and seller. This is something intangible; something that will frequently spell the difference between a merely adequate buying or selling performance, with a major contribution to efficiency and profitability.

Business Ethics Is Not a One-Sided Proposition

The subject of business ethics is certainly not one-sided, as noted above. Buying personnel are faced from time to time with unethical sales practices; practices that might include (1) collusive bidding, (2) restrictive conditions in specifications, (3) artificial stimulation of demand, (4) verbal or actual sabotage of competitive products, (5) padding of orders and shipments, (6) the use of highly technical and/or other unfamiliar trade terms and metric measurements, (7) supposedly sample orders that are magnified into excessive quantities, and (8) obscure contract clauses buried in small type.[14] Furthermore, salespeople are not under direct, continuous supervision; rather, they are under constant pressure to produce sales and are faced with additional temptations offered by the myriad opportunities for unethical behavior that the position invites. Some of the most common areas of misconduct are as follows:[15]

- *Overselling.* Some customers are easily persuaded to buy more or costlier items than they should through the use of sharp practices.
- *Promising more than can be delivered.* Some salespeople are tempted to promise delivery when such a promise is unrealistic. They hope for the best and give excuses when pressured.
- *Lying.* This may range from exaggerated claims for a product or service to lying about a competitor's situation with regard to delivery, quality, price, and the like.
- *Failing to keep confidences.* Some salespeople may reveal information of value to their customer's competitors that should have been kept confidential.
- *Bribes.* Some bribery and the existence of some unscrupulous purchasing people are a fact of life. Bribery, kickbacks, and payoffs are illegal and can get both salespeople and their companies into serious trouble.
- *Gifts.* Many buying firms prohibit employees from accepting any gifts whatsoever. Perhaps more should do the same.

- *Entertainment*. Some entertainment is important and is a necessary part of doing business, as it might serve to strengthen a relationship and build rapport. However, caution is advised.

Bribes, gifts, and the use of entertainment are treated in more detail later in the chapter.

In the buyer-seller relationship, the best opportunity to maintain ethical standards is competent buying, supported by training, insistence on purchase contract performance, acceptance testing, and the like. Most sellers respect the buyer who is thorough and honest in the conduct of the buying office or buying center, and they will usually respond in kind.

CONCEPT QUESTIONS

1. How can marketing managers become more sensitized to the interface of ethical values and the implementation of marketing strategy?
2. How is the purchasing manager the custodian of his or her firm's reputation for courtesy and fair dealing?
3. What is the best opportunity for maintaining ethical standards in the buyer-seller relationship?

ETHICAL ISSUES IN BUSINESS-TO-BUSINESS MARKETING RESEARCH

The area of marketing research has been identified as involving activities that pose significant ethical problems.[16] It is important that not only marketing research students but also practitioners and professors of marketing research develop an awareness and concern for the ethical issues of the profession. Ethics in this context is concerned with the proper conduct of the marketing research process in business inquiry. Marketing research practices that deceive undermine the whole enterprise. Specific manifestations of such practices involve incomplete reporting, misleading reporting, and nonobjective research. Corporate intelligence gathering has earned a bad name because of certain dubious and illegal tactics employed by some firms.[17] As business-to-business marketing research grows as a form of marketing intelligence, researchers will be forced to examine the ethical aspects of their activities. People engaged in business-to-business marketing research may unknowingly use techniques and practices that the general public might consider unethical. Because of this, researchers should examine the profession for activities that may be questionable; that examination should lead to research activities that are appropriate to the general ethical expectations of society in general. This approach is not only "good" in an absolute sense, it is also self-serving.[18] Self-regulation guided by a vision of advertising and business in the service of society, as well as the marketer's own sense of integrity, address the problems better than external regulation.[19] Most marketing researchers would prefer to maintain high standards of conduct voluntarily, rather than have standards set and enforced by governmental action.

Society's Rights

Business is a social phenomenon that coexists with many other organizations and entities in society; as do these other organizations, business has certain responsibilities to society to honor certain rights. These rights include the following: (1) the right to be informed of research results that may impact society as a whole; and (2) the right to expect objective research results. The right to be informed is a very basic right and expresses the fundamental belief that if business discovers something, accidentally or otherwise, that may affect the general health and well-being of society in general, then the general public deserves to be informed of this finding. Consider the following:

- DuPont Company has vowed to stop making chlorofluorocarbons by the end of the 1990s. The chemicals, widely used in refrigerants and styrofoam, are suspected of eating away the Earth's protective ozone layer.
- Monsanto Company promised, and did, reduce all its hazardous air emissions by 90 percent by 1992 though the company previously met federal guidelines.
- Dow Chemical Company and the Sierra Club have jointly endorsed a proposed federal law that would sharply reduce hazardous-waste production. Dow itself has adopted an aggressive waste-reduction program.
- The Chemical Manufacturers Association has proposed for the first time to set operating and safety standards that its 170 members would have to meet to retain membership.[20]

The right to expect objective research results implies that if research results are made public, then the general public has a right to expect that the research was objective, complete, unbiased, and scientifically sound. If the results are used to deny a claim, then this behavior is unethical and violates a basic right of society.

Clients' Rights

For the sake of simplicity, the word "client" will be used to denote either an actual client in the case of a professional research firm, or the researcher's actual employer within the business sector. Clients' rights include the following: (1) the right of confidentiality of the working relationship; and (2) the right to expect quality research. The right of confidentiality is basic, as it may benefit competitors if they know that a study is being done. The anonymity of the client must be preserved, whether it is an internal study or a study commissioned by an outside research firm. The right to expect quality is again a very basic demand, as overly technical jargon, the failure to round numbers properly, unnecessary use of complex analytic procedures, or incomplete reporting can make good research difficult to understand and can cloud faulty research. Recently, and as reported in the *Wall Street Journal*, two groups of graduate students polled competitors of H. O. Penn Machinery Company in Armonk, New York, and Yancy Brothers in Atlanta, both Caterpillar dealers. These dealerships wanted the students to conduct competitive analyses on actual competitors, with the dealers providing names of competitors and even suggesting what questions to ask. The students were able to obtain and analyze information on competitors' inventory levels, sales volume, advertising expenditures, and even potential new-product introductions. The students identified themselves only as university students working on a class project, and when corresponding with the dealers, used university marketing department stationery. Said one of H. O. Penn's competitors: "I wouldn't give out that type of stuff if I knew it were going to someone other than students."[21] Can such practices be eliminated? Probably not. Can they be reduced? We think so.

Researchers' Rights

Several issues can arise in which the researcher, department, or firm needs protection, as shown in the researchers' rights. The right for protection against improper solicitation of proposals could refer to "sharp practices" mentioned earlier in this chapter. Proposals should not be solicited for the specific purpose of driving down prices, nor should a proposal from an outside research firm be given to an in-house research department for implementation. The right to expect accurate presentation of findings again refers to a possible distortion of findings. This not only misleads the client but is potentially damaging to other involved parties as well. The right to expect confidentiality of proprietary information on techniques is included to help researchers who develop special techniques for dealing with certain types of problems encountered. Examples would be proprietary modeling and simulation techniques.

ETHICS AND THE MANAGEMENT OF THE BUSINESS PRICING FUNCTION

Pricing is perhaps the most difficult of all the areas of marketing to examine from an ethical viewpoint because of the complexity of the price variable.[22] There is an expansive realm of ethical issues in pricing; issues that may be raised at all levels of the distribution channel, across different market structures and competitive situations, and across industry types. The following is an overview of some of the more important areas of ethical issues in pricing.[23]

Setting a Fair Price

Generally speaking, new products should be priced to gain experience and market share, which if done correctly, should meet stated company objectives in terms of profit and return on investment. As market share increases, lower costs should be the result. If a skimming price strategy is initially used, is the business firm under any moral obligation to lower prices without a clear market-oriented reason for doing so (such as competitive entry, competitive price move, and the like)? None of us is in a position to make a judgment on this question, and the question is raised only to point out that if profit goals are overemphasized, line management may perceive that profit should be placed above ethical considerations. Hopefully, competitive forces will keep prices and demand for the company products or product lines on an even keel.

Altering Product Quality without Changing Price

As noted in Chapter 3, product quality will usually determine price, as business buyers are reluctant to pay for unnecessary product quality. Also as noted in Chapter 3, an overanxious line manager may be tempted to reduce quality standards as part of a value analysis effort. Assume that a large equipment manufacturer initiates a major cost reduction effort, substituting plastic for steel in several subassemblies. Though realizing that the life of the equipment may drop slightly, the manufacturer does not point this out to prospective customers and does not reduce the price of the finished product to reflect the cost savings. (It must also be assumed that price exhibits an inelastic demand curve in this situation.) Is this ethical? Should the possibility of a shortened useful product life be brought to the attention of prospective business buyers? Will this decision depend on competitive forces, stage in the product life cycle, profitability of the product line, or pressure exerted by top management for increased profitability? Glib answers might be easy to generate here; however, in reality, ready answers to such questions are not easy to produce.

Practicing Price Discrimination with Smaller Accounts

Although the *Robinson-Patman Act* makes it unlawful to discriminate in price between commodities of like grade and quality and prohibits unfair competition (among other things), would someone be naive enough to think that price discrimination against smaller accounts does not happen occasionally with some business-to-business companies? In an effort to please, or because of a long-standing business (or even personal) relationship, in addition to both internal and external pressures, it is very probable that the business marketer will at least be tempted to treat some customers better than others when price is at issue. In most cases, this marketer would be shocked to learn of a potential violation of the law here, and in all probability, is doing what he or she thinks is best for the company given the realities of the situation. Although understandable, serious ethical and legal questions and issues can be raised here.

Price Fixing

A way of controlling competition is for a small group of producers to collude for their common good, agreeing on the prices to charge. This practice, known as *price fixing*, is illegal because it undermines the competitive system to the detriment of the buyer; it is also immoral. If firms join together and use their combined power to fix prices, drive out competitors, or to earn excessive profits at the expense of not only the business buyer but also the ultimate consumer, the market ceases to be competitive; the result is a decline in, or restriction of, a buyer's freedom to make economic choices. The courts have consistently held that agreements between firms to set prices are *per se violations* of Section 1 of the Sherman Act. This means that there is no defense on economic grounds, and the government only has to prove that there was intent to fix prices to obtain a conviction. Criminal penalties for those convicted of collusive price activity may include a fine, a prison term, or both. Antitrust penalties have become more severe since the enactment of a *federal antitrust statute* that makes it a felony to violate federal antitrust laws. The statute, which took effect on January 1, 1975, increases the maximum penalty that can be imposed against a company from $50,000 to $1 million and that can be imposed on an individual defendant from one year in prison and a $50,000 fine to three years in prison and a $100,000 fine. In view of the potential fines, jail terms, legal fees, damages, and loss of goodwill that may result from this practice, there would appear to be no valid justification for a firm to engage in this activity.

Using a Competitor's Quote to Requote or Rebid

When competitive bidding is used in the business sector, requests for bids are usually sent to from three to six potential vendors, depending on the dollar size of the purchase. Bidding is a morally justifiable procedure, providing it is fair. However, keeping it fair is not always an easy task. If the bidding process is too secret, then a violation of secrecy by any of the parties in the process violates the fairness condition of the bidding process. Obviously, the leaking of information to other potential suppliers is unfair, immoral, and unethical and could be the result of bribery or offers of a cash kickback. Although used fairly in the vast majority of cases, bidding is open to abuses and must be controlled if it is to be kept fair.

Reciprocity

Many business buyers often select suppliers who also buy from them. An example of the use of *reciprocity* would be a packaging manufacturer who buys needed chemicals from a chemical company that is buying a considerable amount of its packaging. Reciprocity, by itself, is not illegal. However, the Justice Department and the Federal Trade Commission monitor reciprocity because it may substantially lessen competition. Another example of reciprocity is the way the Canadian government purchased military aircraft from McDonnell Douglas (a U.S. firm). Canada agreed to buy $2.4 billion worth of aircraft; in return, McDonnell Douglas promised to find $2.9 billion of business for Canadian companies.[24] Reciprocity is forbidden if it eliminates competition in an unfair manner. As long as the buyer can show that competitive prices, quality, and service are being supplied, then reciprocity probably just makes good business sense. However, if those conditions are not being met, then perhaps the question of ethical standards should be addressed.

CONCEPT QUESTIONS

1. Why should marketing researchers examine their profession for activities that might be questionable?
2. Why is pricing such a difficult area to examine from an ethical viewpoint?

ETHICS AND THE MANAGEMENT OF THE BUSINESS SALES FORCE

As key links between their organizations and the business buyer, business salespeople encounter situations that, on occasion, lead to ethical conflict. Marketing ethics, in general, and selling ethics, in particular, have experienced increasing research attention.[25] For this discussion, ethical issues confronting sales personnel will be categorized into two broad areas: (1) ethics in dealing with customers; and (2) ethics in dealing with employers.[26] But first, consider the following vignettes:

Scenario 1: A business machinery salesperson faced the following problem. When a newly installed milling machine continued to malfunction, the customer demanded that the piece of equipment be immediately replaced with another new machine. Management within the selling firm decided to replace the machine with a slightly used demo that looked new. The salesperson did not know whether or not to inform the customer of the replacement with the obvious risk of losing the sale, or to defer to management's action, thus not only salvaging the sale, but perhaps even his or her job.

Scenario 2: A business real estate salesperson was attempting to sell a building to a client who finally had decided to make an offer on the building. The offer was several thousand dollars below not only the asking price but also the appraised value of the property. Knowing that the seller would decline such an offer, the salesperson considered telling the potential buyer that the seller was considering an offer extended by another potential buyer, even though no such offer existed.

Scenario 3: A business salesperson was attempting to sell cleaning supplies to a large, multiplant manufacturer of business widgets. The business buyer bluntly told the salesperson that for a private "fee" of $500, the contract could be signed very quickly. The salesperson, being fairly new in the position, told the sales manager what had happened. The sales manager, in turn, told the salesperson to do whatever was necessary to get the order, even if that included the payment of a $500 "fee" (bribe!).

These situations are very real for many people in the business sales force. Now, as mentioned earlier, we shall return to the two broad areas confronting sales personnel with regard to ethical considerations.

Ethics in Dealing with Customers

Occasionally, business salespeople will find themselves in the position of being tempted to compromise their ethical standards when dealing with some customers because the customer or a competitor is engaged in an unethical strategy. A half-truth or misrepresentation, a subtle demand for a gift or extraordinary entertainment, or some other unethical trick might tempt the salesperson to relax standards, especially when a large order is at stake. The major problem areas involved would be bribes, gifts, entertainment, and reciprocity.

Bribes. The use of bribes, although widespread and considered very acceptable behavior within some cultures, should be refused tactfully, allowing salespeople to act in the best interests of their employers and in fairness to all customers. Bribery not only is unethical but can also be illegal. A few years ago, a large American steel company was fined $325,000 for paying $400,000 in bribes to obtain ship repair business for their domestic shipyards.[27] In addition, it is often difficult to distinguish between a bribe, a gift to show appreciation, and a reasonable commission for services rendered, as bribery today is done in a more sophisticated manner and is less easy to identify. Bribery as we know it erupted as an international scandal in the middle to late 1970s, when there were revelations of payoffs to foreign officials by American companies selling abroad. The resultant political sensitivity in the United States and in several foreign countries did much to clean up a bad situation.[28] Bribery distorts the operation of fair bargaining, and salespeople should resist efforts for bribes from the occasional member of the business buying center who might want to engage in such activity.

Gifts. Accepting or giving gifts may or may not be ethical, but the practice of gift giving is under careful scrutiny within many business-to-business firms. If the giving of a gift is done as a condition of doing business (subtle or otherwise), then clearly the act is immoral and unethical; and it causes prejudice against those who fail to give a gift. Many firms have stopped the practice of giving Christmas gifts to customers, offering instead to contribute to a customer's favorite charity. Some common sense and social intelligence should be good guides in keeping the business selling firm within ethical boundaries.

Entertainment. Although the entertainment of customers and potential customers is quite common and may even be expected today, it too can pose ethical questions. Is taking a customer to lunch or to a ball game fair, reasonable, and expected? If that is deemed to be acceptable, then how about a few days at the company resort or fishing lodge, or a trip to view an equipment installation near Disneyland, with the buyer's spouse? Many times, members of the buying center resent attempts to influence them unduly and find efforts to obligate them to buy from a particular seller quite offensive. As a general rule, lavish entertainment can become unethical if the attempt is to substitute it for good selling techniques.

Reciprocity. As referred to earlier in this chapter, this phenomenon occurs when a buyer gives preference to a supplier who is also a customer; it is usually found in industries where products are homogeneous and/or there is not a high degree of price sensitivity. The buyer of business goods thus has the opportunity to use purchases to generate sales by a threat, overt or implied, or to withdraw patronage unless it is reciprocated. This practice obviously has ethical, and perhaps even legal, implications. Chemical Bank, the New York–based financial institution, with some 270 branches in the United States and 55 offices abroad, has long been noted for its innovative approach both to business ethics and to corporate responsibility. Its purchasing department has procedures to ensure fair and equitable treatment of the bank's suppliers; and, in order to avoid even the appearance of reciprocity, there is no review to determine which suppliers are Chemical customers before the bank awards contracts. Chemical's own printing subsidiary is expected to compete against other companies for most of the bank's printing orders.[29]

Ethics in Dealing with Employers

In dealing with their own employers, business salespeople encounter situations that may lead to unethical conduct. The major problem areas involved would be moonlighting, relationships with fellow salespeople, and expense accounts.

Moonlighting. Salespeople who waste or misuse time (especially those who work on a straight salary compensation plan) are in a sense stealing profits from the employing company. *Moonlighting*, the holding of more than one job, may be construed as a misuse of company time and therefore raises some potential ethical and moral questions. Employers have a right to expect full-time work from salespeople employed to sell their product, and those who work another job in the evening or have a side business of their own may violate the principle of time accountability. A salesperson who handles another product line (even if it is noncompetitive) is engaged in the unethical practice of *kiting*. The key here is disclosure; informing the employer that extra hours are being spent doing something else. If the employer agrees that the salesperson may engage in other work, or can carry the line of another company, then the salesperson's obligations with regard to ethical behavior have been satisfied.

Changing jobs. Another area in which salespeople face ethical responsibility is in changing jobs. An active effort by sales managers to "pirate" salespeople away from competitors is likely to be seen as unethical. Companies invest considerable money in training salespeople, in addition to the fact that over a period of time they build up customer knowledge and goodwill, of which they may take advantage if they change jobs and accept a position with a competitor. Job switchers have generally had access to confidential information, and perhaps competitive secrets, which if used as a ploy to gain new employment would be considered unethical of both the prospective employer and the recruiting sales manager.

Expense accounts. Most companies provide the sales force with sufficient travel and entertainment expense money to cover all justified expenses of doing business, and it is the responsibility of the salespeople and the sales managers to allocate expense dollars effectively. *Expense accounts* present special temptations and present the most frequent area for ethical abuse within a sales organization. The fine line that the sales manager must walk with regard to the element of expense account control can be trying. A tight control might cause the salesperson to curtail travel and necessary entertainment to the detriment of the company; loose control may result in selling expense ratios that are higher than they should be.

Contests. Contests are designed to motivate sales representatives to make more sales of all products, or to make more sales of specific products within a product line. The pressure to win can result in the "stockpiling" of orders until the contest begins, the selling of unneeded product to "friends" for later return for credit, or the overselling of unneeded products to good customers. All these practices are easy to rationalize, and all are unethical.

ETHICS AND BUSINESS ADVERTISING STRATEGY

When Winston Churchill took his entrance examination to get into Sandhurst in 1880, he was given a choice of three essay questions: Riding versus Rowing; Advertisements, Their Use and Abuse; and the American Civil War. (He chose the American Civil War.)[30] That the use and abuse of advertising tools and techniques were up for discussion more than a century ago reveals that today's criticisms of advertising are not new. Indeed, the manager overseeing the firm's promotional strategy has a primary responsibility to create profitable sales for the business unit, along with responsibilities toward the customers themselves. Advertising techniques have often been criticized by those outside the field as a dubious practice involving the use of questionable methods to accomplish nefarious ends. No business discussion of ethics would be complete without a section of study devoted to ethics and advertising strategy.

Truth in Advertising

Truth in advertising is a complex issue. Advertisements make statements with the purpose of trying to persuade buyers to purchase the product advertised. But statements supported solely by a reference to a scientific study would probably be very dull and may or may not be effective. Persuasion may take place by making statements, or by simply creating associations in the mind of the buyer. Some business advertisements simply show a picture of the product, with the belief being that when the buyer sees the name, it has an effect on purchasing. A statement made about a product may be true, may not mislead, and may not deceive; but may nevertheless be morally and ethically objectionable. Sometimes what the advertisement does not say is as important as what it does say. It is wrong to advertise and to sell a hazardous product without indicating its dangers.[31] General rules concerning truth in advertising can be summarized in the following way: It is immoral to lie, mislead, and deceive in advertising. It is immoral to fail to indicate dangers that are not normally expected. It is not immoral to use a metaphor or other figure of speech if these will be normally understood as the figurative use of language; nor it is immoral to persuade as well as to inform.[32]

Comparative Advertising

Comparative advertising is an advertisement or sales promotional piece that actually names the competitors and proceeds to compare one product to another. It can present both potential ethical and legal problems. Because of this, some business-to-business marketing managers prohibit or at least discourage such practices within their own firms, feeling that such practices serve no real purpose. The business customer has to make comparisons in selecting products, and most business copy can provide enough comparative and accurate information to aid that process. If comparisons are made, then clearly the standard should insist on accurate comparisons, as there might be a temptation to imply that a product that is superior to the competition in one characteristic is therefore superior overall. It might be recommended that a more ethical and responsible course of action would be to point out competitive differences, leaving the business customer to judge the superiority of the product offering (or its lack thereof).

Inherent in the semantics of advertising and promotion in general are the notions of lying, misrepresentation, deception, manipulation, and other questionable practices. Those that are unethical, immoral, or illegal should be labelled as such. Peers or members of top management influence most ethical decisions related to advertising in particular and promotion in general. Ethical decision making within this area is conceptually complex, and a multiplicity of factors can influence the final outcome. To implement and monitor ethical decision making in advertising in particular, and in other promotional activities in general, both the philosophical and organizational dimensions of ethics should be examined.[33]

ETHICS AND INTERNATIONAL BUSINESS-TO-BUSINESS MARKETING

In the mid 1970s, public shock over disclosures of bribery, kickbacks, and illegal campaign contributions by various corporations led to the development of the *Foreign Corrupt Practices Act* (FCPA), which was signed into law in 1977. (One of the more notable cases was the Lockheed involvement in payments made to the Japanese in connection with the sale of its L1011 Tri-Star and its F-104 Starfighter jets.) Recent past happenings in our global economy are filled with cases wherein large multinational enterprises have used their power in ways that seemed to hurt others. For example, the history of chemicals, metals, and oil contains numerous examples in which a few large firms dominating the market have extracted a heavy rent from their hosts. There have also been cases in which the power of the multinational enterprise has been manifested by its decisions to open or close plants, with powerful effects upon the communities in which such enterprises have operated. Still other cases, such as the chemical tragedy in Bhopal, India, have involved the pollution of the environment or the manufacture of harmful products.[34] Some multinationals have also used their power in the political arena, helping to elect candidates and shape legislation. The history of British Steel, Petroleos Mexicanos, Electricite de France, Montedison, and dozens of other large foreign national entities provide ample illustrations of the exercise of power in all the dimensions that have been mentioned so far.[35] It is perfectly clear that Union Carbide made a serious error of judgment; and that the Foreign Corrupt Practices Act has attacked, and will continue to attack, a rising tide of extortion and bribery in international business. It is also clear that our legal standards are not necessarily a reliable guide to overseas conduct.

Ethics from Country to Country

The ethical practices of business tend to vary from country to country. In one study, marketers in the United States, Germany, and France were asked to evaluate the ethical standards in marketing of the following countries: the United Kingdom, France, the Federal Republic of Germany, Greece, India, Israel, Italy, Japan, Mexico, and the United States.[36] The results, shown in Table 15-1, reveal a significant variation in the perceptions of the various countries. The data shown are the median

TABLE 15-1 **Perceptions of Ethical Standards in Marketing Provided by French, German, and U.S. Marketers**

	Respondents			
Country Ranked	**French Median**	**German Median**	**U.S. Median**	**Average Median**
United Kingdom	3	3	3	3
France	3	5	5	4*
Germany	2	2	2	2
Greece	8	7	7	7*
India	8	9	8	8
Israel	6	7	6	6
Italy	7	8	8	8*
Japan	5	5	4	5
Mexico	8	9	9	9*
United States	3	7	1	4*

Note: The data were obtained from respondents' ranking of the countries, with 1 representing the most ethical.
•Significance at the .05 level.

values of the ranked data from marketers in the three countries. The Federal Republic of Germany is perceived to be the most ethical country by marketers from all three of the countries, followed by the United Kingdom, and then the United States and France. Mexico was ranked lowest, with India and Italy not much higher. While some nationalism is evident, other factors were significant, as evidenced by the French ranking the West Germans as high as the West Germans ranked themselves. If this data is representative of the actual ethical practices being followed, then it would seem that the level of ethical behavior tends to increase with the level of economic development of the country. Whether this increase is caused by developments in the legal system of the country, or by society's expectations and the needs of the participants, is unknown. What is clear is that the United States was not ranked as the most ethical or unethical country in the survey. This result could mean different things to different people.

On the international scene, what is legal and what is ethical are not necessarily uniform worldwide. As noted earlier, in several countries the payment of *grease money* to high-level military officials to sell weapons to their government is not illegal, is common practice, and is expected. However, as far as some companies such as Whirlpool are concerned, this practice is both unethical and illegal. As Mr. Robert Gunts of Whirlpool Corporation stated in a recent address:

> Whirlpool will forego business opportunities if it takes unethical payments to acquire new business. We make that commitment with eyes wide open, knowing

> full well that we will lose some business opportunities, particularly when competing against businesses from nations which do not subscribe to our principles.[37]

It would seem that the types of payoffs mentioned earlier tend to feed on themselves, and there may be no end in sight once the word is out that a company will barter on its principles.

The Complexity of International Ethical Issues

Finally, when operating in the international environment, ethical issues in business-to-business marketing become somewhat more complex than when operating solely within the home country. As is described in the box entitled "Business-to-Business Marketing in Action," U.S. companies doing business in South Africa were repelled by the common practice of apartheid in that country. Many Americans wanted all U.S. business activity with South Africa halted until this situation was completely corrected. However, many Black South Africans were dependent upon U.S. business concerns in South Africa for employment. Therefore, a unilateral withdrawal of U.S. companies from South Africa, although honorable in intention, could have had a disastrous effect on the very people the action was intended to assist. While the following is not an exhaustive list, some important issues should be addressed when contemplating operations abroad:[38]

Product. Could the product cause damage to the people or the environment of the host country? What safeguards are in place to ensure that the product will not do this, or will lessen the impact if the unexpected does happen?

Promotion. Will the promotion be viewed as a bribe or a payoff by the host country?

Distribution. Is a bribe or payoff required to enter a foreign market? If so, is the company willing to engage in such activity? Will this violate ethical norms as presently set up and in place? Will disclosure impact domestic business?

Price. Will the price charged in the foreign market be viewed as "dumping" by the host country? Could the price charged in a foreign market have political, ethical, or moral implications in the domestic market?

CONCEPT QUESTIONS

1. What is the most ethical way to approach comparative advertising?
2. What led to the development of the Foreign Corrupt Practices Act?
3. What is Whirlpool management's view about making unethical payments to acquire international business?

BUSINESS-TO-BUSINESS MARKETING IN ACTION

AN ETHICAL PROBLEM IN SOUTH AFRICA FOR U.S. MARKETERS

The one situation in the 1980s that perhaps best illustrated ethical decision making on an international level was that of South Africa. The government of South Africa had long practiced apartheid, separation of the races. The blacks in South Africa protested apartheid throughout the 1980s, and hundreds of people were killed in clashes between blacks who had differences of opinion about the apartheid system and between blacks and the white ruling government.

Virtually all nations of the world, including the government of South Africa, felt that something had to be done about the system of apartheid. Some small steps were made to change some of the rules, but the changes were few and slow. Protestors in the United States demanded that American organizations, such as universities, stop investing in firms that did business in South Africa. The idea was to pressure the South African government to end apartheid more quickly. The protests grew more insistent when increased violence erupted in South Africa. Soon, protestors called for U. S. firms to pull out of South Africa entirely.

In 1986, an advertisement sponsored by eighty American companies operating in South Africa, including Citibank, IBM, Coca-Cola, and Union Carbide, called for a complete end of all forms of apartheid. One possibility was that all such U.S. firms would pull their subsidiaries out of South Africa. Many people proposed that very solution. The problem was that U.S. firms employed many black employees and were some of the fairest and most liberal employers in the country. If they had pulled out, it would have hurt the economy of South Africa badly. That meant both whites and blacks would suffer, and other nations would have been less likely to lend money to businesses in the area. The government might have fallen, but what would have remained would be a country with a weaker business base to build on. This would have hurt blacks more than whites in the long run, because blacks are in the majority.

American businesses with subsidiaries in South Africa faced a serious ethical problem. Should they stay in South Africa and try to get the government to be more liberal with blacks? They do have a significant influence. Or should they pull out in protest and potentially hasten the end of apartheid, but increase black unemployment and remove a source of pressure on other businesses to be as fair as U.S. businesses are with blacks? American businesses have subsidiaries in many countries with poor race relations or suppressive governments. Should they pull out of all such countries or stay and try to promote change? What is the moral and ethical position for businesses to take relative to other governments? These are the kinds of international ethical questions that will have to be answered in the next decade.

SUMMARY

1. Ethics means the standards by which behavior is judged. Standards that may be legal may not be ethical. Standards and beliefs about what is right and proper change over time. This question is becoming more important as our economy becomes more competitive and our technology more complex.
2. Comparing the marketing strategies and tactics of business-to-business firms today versus a decade ago, the most striking impression is one of general marketing strategy obsolescence. Business marketers must become sensitized to the interface of ethical values and the implementation of business-to-business marketing strategy. They must learn to recognize the major changes that will impact the implementation of future marketing strategies.
3. Through contacts and dealings with business salespeople, the purchasing manager is the custodian of his or her firm's reputation for courtesy and fair dealing. The subject of business ethics applies equally to both the business buyer and seller. In the buyer-seller relationship, the best opportunity for maintaining ethical behavior is competent buying supported by training, insistence of purchase contract performance, and acceptance testing. Most business salespeople respect the buyer who is thorough and honest in his or her purchase transactions.
4. People engaged in business marketing research may unknowingly use techniques and practices that the general public might consider unethical. Because of this, researchers should examine their profession for activities that may be questionable, in order to avoid such practices. Business marketing researchers should be aware of society's rights, clients' rights, and researchers' rights in discharging their professional duties.
5. Business pricing is perhaps the most difficult of all the areas of marketing to examine from an ethical perspective because of the complexity of the price variable. Common areas of ethical concern in business pricing include setting a price that meets company objectives while not taking advantage of the customer, altering product quality without changing price, practicing price discrimination with smaller accounts, price fixing, obtaining information on a competitive price quotation in order to requote or rebid, and reciprocity.
6. As key links between their organizations and the business buyer, business salespeople encounter situations that, on occasion, lead to ethical conflict. Business salespeople may be tempted to lower their ethical standards in dealing with their customers in such areas as bribes, gifts, entertainment, and reciprocity. They may be likewise tempted in their dealings with employers in such areas as moonlighting, changing jobs, expense accounts, and bribes.
7. A statement made about a product may be true, may not mislead, may not deceive, but may nevertheless be morally and ethically objectionable. What the advertisement does not say may be more important than what it does say. In comparative advertising, the business marketer should carefully point out competitive differences, leaving the customers to judge the superiority of the product offering.

8. What is considered to be ethical practice can vary from country to country. Ethical issues can become much more complex when operating in international markets rather than in domestic markets. The international business marketer must adapt each of the elements of the marketing mix to the particular customer and to the particular country where the marketing mix is to be used.

KEY TERMS

Comparative advertising
Ethics
Expense accounts
Federal antitrust statute
Foreign Corrupt Practices Act
Grease money
Kiting
Moonlighting
Per se violations
Price fixing
Reciprocity
Robinson-Patman Act
Truth in Advertising

REVIEW QUESTIONS

1. What are the three sets of factors that influence the ethics of an individual's decisions? Identify and describe three different views of corporate social responsibility. Provide a business example for each one.
2. What kinds of questions should business marketers ask in order to sensitize themselves to the interface of ethical values and the implementation of business marketing strategy?
3. How can the purchasing manager be the custodian of his or her firm's reputation for courtesy and fair dealing? What types of unethical sales practices are likely to face business buyers from time to time? What types of ethical misconduct are more appropriate to the business salesperson?
4. Of what three sets of rights should all professional marketing researchers be aware in the discharge of their activities? How can ethics be applied to the business-to-business marketing research function?
5. Why is pricing perhaps the most difficult of all the marketing areas to examine from an ethical perspective? Discuss six types of potential unethical conduct in business pricing.
6. What are four types of ethical problems that business salespeople might encounter in dealing with their customers? What are four types of ethical problems that business salespeople might encounter in dealing with their employers?
7. What are two ways in which persuasion may take place in business promotion? How can comparative advertising be used in an unethical manner?
8. What led to the establishment of the Foreign Corrupt Practices Act of 1977? What is its primary purpose? What is the Whirlpool Corporation's policy on making unethical payments to acquire new international business?

Cases

CASE 15-1 Coke Battles for French Bottling Contracts

No market better tests Coca-Cola's newfound European aggressiveness than France, which has the lowest per capita consumption of Coke in the European community. Pernod-Ricard, the largest spirits producer, controlled Coke's bottling there for forty years. Coke management figured the poor performance stemmed largely from Pernod's relationship with retail customers: Coke worried that the French company sold to retailers at a high price and promoted its own Orangina brand at the expense of Coke and Coca-Cola's other products, including orange Fanta and lemon-lime Sprite. A two-year legal battle over bottling contracts finally ended last year in Coke's favor, forcing Pernod to sell certain operations for $140 million. Even Thierry Jacquillat, Pernod's chief, thinks Coke was smart: "Behind this is something quite understandable for a company controlling a brand."

Now France is the only major market in the world where Coke owns the bottling business outright. Says one soft-drink buyer from a major French hypermarket, "Every one of our stores realizes it is much better now than with Pernod-Ricard. There's more contact with the bottler, more promotions, and more money to spend."

DISCUSSION QUESTIONS

1. Should a company like Coca-Cola have the right to end a forty-year relationship with a distributor? Why or why not?
2. What impact do you think this decision will have on other European bottlers?
3. What other alternatives might Coca-Cola management have considered? What are the pros and cons of each one?

Source: C. Lamb, J. Hair, and C. McDaniel, *Principles of Marketing*, 1st Edition (Cincinnati, OH: South-Western Publishing Company, 1992) p. 130.

CASE 15-2 Phoenix Laser Systems, Incorporated

Laser technology seems to be the answer for nearsighted people. Three companies—Summit Technology, Incorporated, Visx, Incorporated, and Taunton Technology, Incorporated—are currently testing high-powered ultraviolet lasers called excimers. The excimer process removes excess tissue from the cornea of the eye. In reshaping the cornea, the lasers allow the unaided eye to focus correctly. Two new entries into the laser eye surgery business are Intelligent Surgical Lasers, Incorporated, and Phoenix Laser Systems, Incorporated.

Phoenix Laser Systems is challenging the excimer companies with a different type of machine. Instead of shaving layers of tissue from the surface, Phoenix uses a solid-state laser to remove tissue from inside the cornea. The harmless beam of light focuses behind the eye's surface and can vaporize tiny pockets of cells forty times smaller than those treated with excimer technology. The Phoenix system uses a tracking device, similar to that used in surface-to-air missiles, to follow movements of the eye. The system shuts off if it loses track of the target. This capability replaces the skilled hands of the surgeon. The excimer machines use a clamp to keep the eye from moving.

The Phoenix system offers two main advantages over the excimer technology. First, the Phoenix machines are substantially cheaper. Prototypes of the excimer machines cost as much as $450,000, while the Phoenix laser should sell for $125,000. Second, the Phoenix machines emit harmless light. In contrast, the excimer lasers emit ultraviolet light that can cause a slight cloudiness on the surface of the cornea and may be linked to cancer. The excimer manufacturers maintain that the little hazing that may occur can be treated with medication. Responding to the cancer issue, these companies contend that federal regulators have shown no concern.

Opthamologists say it is too early to tell which technology is better. More test results are needed. Phoenix has had some success experimenting with rabbits but has yet to perform any testing on humans. In this area, the excimer technology has a head start. Currently, the excimer technology is being tested on humans.

Phoenix Laser Systems recently shipped machines to Bogota, Colombia, and Paris, France, for testing on human subjects. All of the laser technology companies expect regulators to take a full two years before approving any of these machines for clinical use.

DISCUSSION QUESTIONS

1. Do you think companies like Phoenix Laser Systems should conduct tests on animals and humans? What are the ethical implications of your answer?
2. Do you think it is acceptable to test these types of products outside the United States in countries where fewer legal restrictions exist? Why or why not?
3. Should companies like Phoenix be allowed to report findings based on preliminary studies before significant testing is done? Why or why not?

Source: C. Lamb, J. Hair, and C. McDaniel, *Principles of Marketing*, 1st Edition (Cincinnati, OH: South-Western Publishing Company, 1992) p. 722.

Suggested Additional Readings

Behof, Kathleen. "The Right Way to Snoop on the Competition." *Sales and Marketing Management* 136 (May 1986): 46–48. **Guidelines on how to acquire competitive information legally and ethically.**

Caywood, Clarke L., and Gene R. Laczniak. "Ethics and Personal Selling: Death of a Salesman as an Ethical Primer." *Journal of Personal Selling and Sales Management* 6 (August 1986): 815–827. **Guidelines for and discussion of ethical issues and problems in personal selling.**

Farmer, Richard N. "Would You Want Your Granddaughter to Marry a Taiwanese Marketing Man?" *Journal of Marketing* 51 (October 1987): 111–116. **Reexploration of marketing ethics in contemporary times, with an emphasis on Taiwan as a newly industrialized country.**

Felch, Robert I. "Standards of Conduct: The Key to Supplier Relations." *Journal of Purchasing and Materials Management* 21 (Fall 1985): 16–18. **Discussion of unethical conduct in negotiations and other purchasing activities.**

Fraedrich, John Paul. "The Impact of Perceived Risk and Moral Philosophy: Type of Ethical Decision-Making in Business Organizations." *Journal of Business Research* 24 (June 1992): 283–295. **Discussion of ethically impactive business decisions, including a survey of retail managers.**

Halcomb, Ruth. "Incentives and Ethics." *Incentive Marketing* 160 (October 1986): 36–39, 67. **Trends in salespeople's abuse of incentives.**

Hoffman, Carl C., and Kathleen P. Hoffman. "Does Comparable Worth Obscure the Real Issues?" *Personnel Journal* 66 (January 1987): 83–95. **Survey of the perceptions of wage differentials and sex roles among dual career couples.**

Kirkpatrick, Jerry. "A Philosophic Defense of Advertising." *Journal of Advertising* 15, No. 2 (1986): 42–48, 64. **Theoretical discussion of social issues and the moral basis of capitalism and egoism.**

Lantos, Geoffrey P. "An Ethical Base for Marketing Decision-Making." *Journal of Business and Industrial Marketing* 2 (Spring 1987): 11-16. **Discussion of the use of ethics in marketing decision making, with particular emphasis on the roots of ethical philosophies.**

Laroche, Michael, K. L. McGown, and Joyce Rainville. "How Ethical Are Professional Marketing Researchers?" *Business Forum* 11 (Winter 1986): 21–25. **Canadian survey of researchers' attitudes and behavior and of common industry practices.**

Murray, Keith B., and John R. Montahari. "Strategic Management of the Socially Responsible Firm: Integrating Management and Marketing Theory." *Academy of Management Review* 11 (October 1986): 815–827. **Normative model of corporate social responsibility, and guidelines for moral expectations of target publics.**

Painter, Tony. "Sales Promotion: Deciphering the Codes." *Marketing* (UK), 24 (February 13, 1986): 43–45. **Self-regulation codes for advertising and sales promotion in the United Kingdom.**

Peattie, Ken, and Moira Ratnayaka. "Responding to the Green Movement." *Industrial Marketing Management* 21 (May 1992): 103–110. **Study of the trends in business environmental performance.**

Raffield, Barney T., III. "Student Evaluations of the Ethics of Marketing Practices: A Replication with a New Generation and Further Implications for the Role of Marketing Education." In *Marketing in a Dynamic Environment*, edited by Michael H. Morris and Eugene E. Teeple, 290–298. Atlantic Marketing Association, 2 (October 1986). **Comparison of 1960s and 1970s students with 1980s students in regard to their perceptions of the ethics of common marketing practices.**

Robin, Donald P., and R. Eric Reidenbach. "Social Responsibility, Ethics, and Marketing Strategy: Closing the Gap between Concept and Application." *Journal of Marketing* 51 (January 1987): 44–58. **Study of ethical values and objectives in organizational behavior, corporate culture, and market planning.**

Savage, J. A., and J. M. Majot. "Industry Preaches Green but Is Far from Clean." *Business and Society Review* 83 (Fall 1992): 39–42. **Discussion of business participation in conferences about environmental concerns.**

Singhapakdi, Anusorn and Scott J. Vitell. "Marketing Ethics: Sales Professionals versus Other Marketing Professionals." *Journal of Personal Selling and Sales Management* 12 (Spring 1992): 27–38. **Study of the differences in ethical values between salespeople and other marketing professionals.**

Springer, Robert F., and H. E. French III. "Determining Fraud: The Role of Resale Price Maintenance." *Journal of Business* 59 (July 1986): 443–459. **Study of recent antitrust cases, with a discussion of the disadvantages of free pricing and misleading markups.**

Stundza, Tom. "You and the Environment." *Purchasing* 112 (April 16, 1992): 49, 51, 53. **Study of industry waste reduction to include costs, impacts, and regulations.**

Trevisan, Richard E. "Developing a Statement of Ethics: A Case Study." *Journal of Purchasing and Materials Management* 22 (Fall 1986): 8–14. **Study of ethics in purchasing policies and practices and in vendor relations.**

APPENDIX 15-1 Future Trends in Business-to-Business Marketing

The decade of the 1990s promises to be a significant one for business marketers as they try to anticipate trends, deal with technological breakthroughs, and plan long-term strategies. The decade ahead promises continued advances in technological capabilities, expanding worldwide markets, greater deregulation of industry, along with many other challenges and opportunities. The firm that does not anticipate and plan for anticipated change will probably fall into Levitt's marketing myopia trap and lose ground to more astute marketers.[39] According to a 1985 survey of chief executive officers and other top managers, 64 percent believe that marketing is now the most important functional area for their companies.[40] Obviously, top management will be looking toward the marketing group for direction as we proceed through this decade.

What will the practice of business-to-business marketing be like in the late 1990s? A careful assessment of some of the factors that will affect future marketing performance should be helpful in trying to answer this question, since it is these factors that will, to a large extent at least, influence and guide the firm as it moves through this decade.

Technology

Major changes are occurring in the energy, materials, transportation, information, and genetic (bioengineering) fields. Industries that are not strong on the technology dimension will be particularly vulnerable to competition, both from new industries and from foreign competitors that have made the necessary investment. Most major steel firms still use the blast furnace technology developed in the 1800s. Foreign steel firms and those domestic companies who invested in modern manufacturing technology have been highly successful in the past decade.[41] Those that did not invest in such technology will continue to fall behind and become less competitive. A major implication of the so-called *knowledge explosion* will be the introduction of new types of products and services. A majority of American manufacturing facilities will move to significantly greater automation through computerized machine tools, robotic systems, and computer-aided design and manufacturing (CAD/CAM). Because of the anticipated increased use of *CAD/CAM*, business manufacturing firms will be able to modify and design products more quickly. Also, because of the growth projected in the area of information- and computer-based technology, firms selling computer hardware and software will witness a major growth opportunity. American success in high-tech marketing is too essential to the nation's future to give it the marketing-as-usual treatment. Who marvels now over the automobile, or the light bulb? Likewise, future generations will not be impressed with today's technological breakthroughs.

Competition

The last decade has been perhaps the most turbulent period ever faced by business-to-business marketing managers because of increased foreign competition, dramatic changes in technology and rates of innovation, and large shifts in interest rates and inflation. A by-product of the mounting international competition that American companies will continue to face here and abroad has been, and in all probability will continue to be, the recent trend toward the formation of *research consortia*. Encouraged by relaxed antitrust restrictions and favorable actions by Congress, companies have been banding together to form research and development organizations that, hopefully, will speed the development and use of technologies so necessary to making American industry more competitive in the future. An example of one of these research and development consortia is Microelectronics and Computer Technology Corporation, based in Austin, Texas. Since opening in 1983, membership has grown from twelve to twenty-one firms, including firms such as Honeywell, Control Data, RCA, NCR, Boeing, National Semiconductor, and Eastman Kodak. In 1988, MCC spent $65 million pioneering new technologies in such areas as advanced computer design and semiconductor packaging.[42] The hoped-for result of these efforts will be that business-to-business firms will better understand their competitors' possible future strategies, thus giving them an advantage over those which tend to be inner oriented. There seems to be no doubt that marketing executives generally agree that competition, both foreign and domestic, will intensify and that firms will be spending more of each sales dollar on marketing because of this increased competition.

Finally, there has been a trend toward larger firms, a trend that should continue as we move through the 1990s. By the year 2000, it is expected that 90 percent of all U.S. communications facilities will be owned by fifteen firms.[43] If small firms are to compete successfully, personal service, better segmentation, and flexibility will, out of necessity, be major differential advantages. Large firms will also continue to diversify, being able to develop and apply expensive new technology more easily. Again, smaller firms will be forced to find their niche.

Government

Domestic political trends foreshadow what the economic environment will be like for business; they also indicate what legal-regulatory approach government will most likely take toward the private sector. One of the most relevant government actions facing business marketers in the years ahead is continued deregulation of the marketplace. Banks are almost fully deregulated, and the Federal Communications Commission is deregulating FM radio stations. The success of deregulation could spur the federal government to sell such assets as the Tennessee Valley Authority to private industry. Deregulation might force greater price competition, putting the burden of success or failure on the marketing manager, rather than on government supports and restraints.[44]

Global Events

As we close in on the year 2000, business marketers will be exposed to exciting opportunities and risks, as trade barriers continue to fall while worldwide per capita income increases, heightened literacy is experienced, and standardization in measures makes overseas investment even more attractive than it is now. Political disruptions, nationalism, improved capabilities of foreign companies, and countries' interest in self-sufficiency all pose risks and potential opportunities for firms contemplating entering and/or increasing international involvement.

Telemarketing

The use of telephone selling will continue to expand as business marketers continue to discover that it is a productive, yet low-cost method of selling. According to the Direct Marketing Association, more money is spent annually in the United States on telemarketing than on direct mail. In addition to its use as a selling tool, the use of the telephone in marketing will continue to expand by handling reorders, following up on customer orders, and providing customer services. Products that will continue to be important to a telemarketing effort would be standardized, relatively low-priced industrial products, such as small tools, wire, cable, nuts and bolts, screws, and other basic MRO (maintenance, repair, and operating) supplies. Telemarketing designed to sell products almost always operates in a straight-rebuy situation. This is not likely to change. In some companies, telemarketing will make the order-taking sales representative virtually obsolete. For example, American Hospital Supply, through computer usage, can determine product availability, shipping dates, and can even place an order. Ford,

Chrysler, and GM are jointly developing a system where a manufacturer and its larger suppliers will communicate electronically, eliminating the personal sales call and reducing paperwork. Future telemarketing advances are expected to increase the operating efficiency and time responsiveness of participating industries.

Materials Management

Other techniques—such as just-in-time (JIT) inventory, materials requirements planning (MRP), optimal production technology (OPT), and flexible manufacturing systems (FMS)—will greatly impact business strategies as we move through the decade of the 1990s toward the twenty-first century. Efficiency and competitive advantage will present the marketer with both challenges and opportunities.

Few would doubt that domestic manufacturing processes and materials management techniques have changed dramatically during the 1980s and will continue to do so during the 1990s. Computer technology has enabled manufacturers to operate their production lines and corresponding purchasing operations more efficiently and effectively. Marketers may well find that the utilization of such techniques by customer organizations necessitates fundamental changes in the way in which they do business.[45] When marketing to firms using the production operations techniques listed above, the selling firm that is able to guarantee delivery in direct response to production requirements, or that can work with an on-line inventory ordering system, will have a strategic competitive advantage.

Pricing will also be a strategic option of the marketing mix in the struggle for survival as we approach the year 2000. A recent study clearly shows that profitability and maximization of profit have surpassed market share and growth as major pricing objectives and tactics.[46]

Continued Development of the Buyer-Seller Relationship

In the future, business marketers can look forward to increased sophistication on the part of the business buyer and other members of the industrial buying center. Personal relationships have played an important part in business relations in the past, and this trend will continue as the expertise of both buyers and sellers will rise to new levels in the immediate years ahead. More business-to-business firms will hire engineers for the buying assignment so that they will be able to perform technical buying and analytical work on a comparable plane with the seller. Most of the routine clerical tasks of the past are in management information form, which enables the buyer to devote more time and effort working with the seller on value-analysis projects, make-or-buy decisions, and the like. In brief, it is safe to assume that both buyer and seller will find it to their mutual benefit to expand the base upon which their business relationship is built. Formulation of pricing strategies should be a fundamental goal of firms looking to increase effectiveness in the 1990s and beyond.

Promotion, distribution, customer targeting, and segmentation strategy must also be studied as changes in the field are dramatically affecting strategies and operational decisions within these areas. The advent of the computer-integrated database, relationship marketing, the "total quality" philosophy, and electronic data interchange will allow both buyers and sellers to operate more as a team. All the elements of the marketing mix will be affected.

ENDNOTES

[1]Gene R. Laczniak and Patrick E. Murphy, "Fostering Ethical Marketing Decisions," *Journal of Business Ethics* 10 (April 1991): 259–271.

[2]Anusorn Singhapakdi and Scott J. Vitell, "Marketing Ethics: Factors Influencing Perceptions of Ethical Problems and Alternatives," *Journal of Macromarketing* 10 (Spring 1990): 4–18.

[3]O. C. Ferrell and Larry G. Gresham, "A Contingency Framework for Understanding Ethical Decision-Making in Marketing," *Journal of Marketing* 49 (Summer 1985): 87–96.

[4]Donald P. Robin and Eric R. Reidenbach, "Social Responsibility, Ethics, and Marketing Strategy: Closing the Gap between Concept and Application," *Journal of Marketing* 51 (January 1987): 44–58.

[5]Scott J. Citell and James Muncy, "Consumer Ethics: An Empirical Investigation of Factors Influencing Ethical Judgements of the Final Consumer," *Journal of Business Ethics* 11 (August 1992): 585–597.

[6]Steven H. Star, "Marketing and Its Discontents," *Harvard Business Review* 67 (November/December 1989): 148–154.

[7]Milton Moskowitz, "The Corporate Responsibility Shell Game," *Business and Society Review* (Spring 1992): 73–76.

[8]Kenneth E. Goodpaster and John B. Matthews, Jr., "Can a Corporation Have a Conscience?" *Harvard Business Review* (January/February 1982): 132–141.

[9]William A. Weeks and Jacques Nantel, "Corporate Codes of Ethics and Sales Force Behavior: A Case Study," *Journal of Business Ethics* 11 (October 1992): 753–760.

[10]Lee Berton, "Arthur Anderson Launches Program to Teach Ethics," *Wall Street Journal*, 11 March 1988, 31.

[11]Mary Lu Carnevale, "DuPont Plans to Phase Out CFC Output," *Wall Street Journal*, 25 March 1988, 2, 11.

[12]Timothy D. Schellhardt, "What Bosses Think about Corporate Ethics," *Wall Street Journal*, 6 April 1988, 27.

[13]Adapted from Joseph L. Cavinato, *Purchasing and Materials Management* (St. Paul, Minn.: West, 1984) 409–411. Also see Edward J. O'Boyle and Lyndon E. Dawson, "The American Marketing Association Code of Ethics: Instructions for Marketers," *Journal of Business Ethics* 11 (December 1992): 921–932.

[14]Stuart F. Heinritz and Paul V. Farrell, "Ethics of Purchasing," in *Purchasing Management: Selected Readings*, ed. Victor P. Gravereau and Leonard J. Konopa (Columbus, Ohio: Grid Publishing, 1973), 223–233.

[15]Ronald D. Balsley and E. Patricia Birsner, *Selling: Marketing Personified* (New York: Dryden Press, 1987), 421–423.

[16]Ishmail P. Akaah, "Attitudes of Marketing Professionals toward Ethics in Marketing Research: A Cross-National Comparison," *Journal of Business Ethics* 9 (January 1990): 45–53.

[17]Patrick E. Murphy and Gene R. Laczniak, "Emerging Ethical Issues Facing Marketing Researchers," *Marketing Research* 4, (June 1992): 6-11.

[18]Much of the following is drawn from Donald S. Tull and Del I. Hawkins, *Marketing Research: Measurement and Method*, 4th ed. (New York: Macmillan, 1987), Chapter 19; and Duane Davis and Robert M. Cosenga, *Business Research for Decision Making* (Boston: Kent Publishing, 1985), 433–437. These two sources provide excellent treatments of the major ethical issues in the conduct of business research. Also see Michael A. Mayo and Lawrence J. Marks, "An Empirical Investigation of a General Theory of Marketing Ethics," *Journal of the Academy of Marketing Science* 18 (Spring 1990): 163–171.

[19]Paul F. Camenisch, "Marketing Ethics: Some Dimensions of the Challenge," *Journal of Business Ethics* 10 (April 1991): 245–248.

[20]Laurie Hays, "Chemical Firms Press Campaign to Dispel Their 'Bad Guy' Image," *Wall Street Journal*, 20 September 1988, 1.

[21]Clare Ansberry, "For These M.B.A.s, Class Became Exercise in Corporate Espionage," *Wall Street Journal*, 22 March 1988, 37.

[22]William J. Kehoe, "Ethics, Price Fixing, and the Management of Price Strategy," in *Marketing Ethics: Guidelines for Managers*, ed. Gene R. Laczniak and Patrick E. Murphy (Lexington, Mass.: Lexington Books, 1985), 71–83.

[23]Adapted from Patrick E. Murphy and Gene R. Laczniak, "Marketing Ethics: A Review with Implications for Managers, Educators and Researchers," in *Review of Marketing*, ed. Ben M. Enis and Kenneth J. Roering (Chicago: American Marketing Association, 1981), 251–266.

[24]"New Restrictions on World Trade," *Business Week*, 19 July 1982, 119.

[25]Alan J. Dubinsky, Marvin A. Jolson, Masaaki Kotabi, and Jim Un Chal, "A Cross-National Investigation of Industrial Salespeople's Ethical Perceptions," *Journal of International Business Studies* 22 (Fourth Quarter 1991): 651–670.

[26]Adapted from Alan J. Dubinsky, "Studying Field Salespeople's Ethical Problems: An Approach for Designing Company Policies," in Laczniak and Murphy, *Marketing Ethics*, 41–53. See also Anusorn Singhapakdi and Scott J. Vitell, "Marketing Ethics: Sales Professionals versus Other Marketing Professionals," *Journal of Personal Selling and Sales Management* 12 (Spring 1992): 27–38; and Tony L. Henthorne, Donald P. Robin, and Eric R. Reidenbach, "Identifying the Gaps in Ethical Perceptions between Managers and Salespersons: A Multidimensional Approach," *Journal of Business Ethics* 11 (November 1992): 849–856.

[27]*Wall Street Journal*, 25 July 1980, 5.

[28]Thomas Griffith, "Payoff Is Not 'Accepted Practice,'" *Fortune*, August 1976, 122–125.

[29]"Chemical Bank Programs in Business Ethics and Corporate Responsibility," Ethics Resource Center, Inc., in *Corporate Ethics: A Prime Business Asset*, The Business Roundtable, February 1988, 31–40.

[30]Randolph S. Churchill, *Winston S. Churchill*, Vol. 1 (Boston: Houghton Mifflin, 1966) 129.

[31]Richard T. DeGeorge, *Business Ethics*, 2d ed. (New York: Macmillan, 1986), 279.

[32]*Ibid.*, 280.

[33]Laczniak and Murphy, *Marketing Ethics*, 27–39.

[34]Raymond Vernon, "Ethics and the Multinational Enterprise," in *Ethics and the Multinational Enterprise*, ed. W. Michael Hoffman, Ann E. Lange, and David A. Fedo, Proceedings of the Sixth National Conference on Business Ethics, Bentley College (Waltham, Mass.: University Press of America, 1985), 61–69.

[35]*Ibid.*

[36]David J. Fritzsche and Helmut Becker, "Linking Management Behavior to Ethical Philosophy—An Empirical Investigation," *Academy of Management Journal* (March 1984), 166–175, adapted from David J. Fritzsche, "Ethical Issues in Multinational Marketing," in Laczniak and Murphy, *Marketing Ethics*, 85–96.

[37]Robert Gunts, "Ethics as A Way of Life," in Hoffman, Lange, and Fedo, *Ethics and the Multinational Enterprise*, 101–106.

[38]Adapted from Fritzsche, *Ethical Issues in Multinational Marketing*, 85–96.

[39]Theodore Levitt, "Marketing Myopia," *Harvard Business Review* 53 (September/October 1975): 26–44.

[40]Coopers and Lybrand, "Strategic Marketing Top Priority of Chief Execs," *Marketing News* (January 31, 1986): 1, 17.

[41]Donald R. Lehmann and Russell S. Winer, *Analysis for Marketing Planning* (Plano, Tex.: Business Publications, 1988), 50.

[42]"Additional Perspectives: Can Consortia Keep Us Competitive?" An interview with MCC's Bobby Inman, reprinted from *World* (March/April 1986): 40–42; and presented in *Essentials of Marketing High Technology*, William L. Shanklin and John K. Ryans, Jr. (Lexington, Mass.: Lexington Books, 1987), 70–74.

[43]"The Revival of Productivity," *Business Week*, 13 February 1984, 92–100.

[44]See Jeanne Saddler, "In Rush to Deregulate, FCC Outpaces Others, Pleases the Industry," *Wall Street Journal*, 7 December 1983, 1, 21. Also see James Cook, "Profits over Principle," *Forbes*, 25 March 1985, 148–154.

[45]For an expanded discussion of these potential changes, see Michael H. Morris and Jere L. Dailey, "Implications of Trends in Materials Management for the Industrial Marketer," *AMA Educators Proceedings* (1986), 212–217.

[46]For an expanded discussion of future strategic pricing activity, see Barbara J. Coe, "Shifts in Industrial Pricing Objectives," *AMA Educators Proceedings* (1986), 9–12.

Case Study

National Peach Council

Among the several pesticides used on agricultural crops was dibromochloropropane, usually termed DBCP. This chemical was widely used on fruit trees, cotton, and soybeans to combat wormlike nematodes and some other pests that imperil these crops. A total of about thirty million pounds of this pesticide was produced and marketed annually by several companies. The three main suppliers were Dow Chemical Company, Shell Oil Company, and Occidental Chemical Company. Dow sold this product under the trade name Fumazone, Shell under the trade name Nemagon Soil Fumigant, and Occidental under the trade names Green Light, Garden Fume, and CHA-KEM-CO.

Evidence of the effect of DBCP on people working closely with it came to light in at least three locations in August. In Dow Chemical Company's DBCP plant at Magnolia, Arkansas, there was evidence of sterility in twelve male workers, whereas in Shell's installations in Denver and Mobile sixteen of twenty-one male workers tested after exposure to the chemical showed abnormally low sperm counts. The Oil, Chemical, and Atomic Workers Union filed complaints with the government, especially the Occupational Safety and Health Administration (OSHA), a unit of the Department of Labor, and the Environmental Protection Agency. These agencies imposed emergency restrictions on the handling of the substance and began studying the imposition of permanent restrictions or banning of the product. The manufacturers of the product voluntarily halted its production.

Following the reaction of OSHA to the DBCP health threat, the executive secretary of the National Peach Council, Robert K. Phillips, sent the letter reproduced as Exhibit 1 and dated September 12 to Dr. Eula Bingham, assistant secretary of labor for Occupational Safety and Health. A few days later the National Cancer Institute, a federal agency, released the results of a research project in which it was shown that large doses of DBCP caused cancer in laboratory rats and mice. Philips did not have advance knowledge of these research results. According to Phillips, someone employed by OSHA gave a copy of his September 12 letter to a *New York Times* reporter on September 26. That newspaper and news wire services carried portions of the letter on September 27.

There followed considerable news coverage about the product, the manufacturers, the workers, and the proposal from the National Peach Council. Phillips stated that the suggestion was made in good faith and with sincerity. He noted further that people might think he was speaking tongue in cheek but he definitely was not. Phillips

EXHIBIT 1 **Letter from National Peach Council to O.S.H.A.**

National Peach Council

Dr. Eula Bingham
Assistant Secretary for Occupational Safety and Health
U.S. Department of Labor
Washington, D.C. 20210

Recently we received the interesting DOL news release concerning worker exposure to DBCP.

It appears to us that you and Secretary Marshall may have overreacted, or at least that is your public posture.

While involuntary sterility caused by a manufactured chemical may be bad, it is not necessarily so. After all, there are many people who are now paying to have themselves sterilized to assure they will no longer be able to become parents.

How many of the workers who have become sterile were of an age that they would have been likely to have children anyway? How many were past the age when they would want to have children? These, too, are important questions.

If possible sterility is the main problem, couldn't workers who were old enough that they no longer wanted to have children accept such positions voluntarily? They would know the situation, and it wouldn't matter. Or could workers be advised of the situation, and some might volunteer for such work posts as an alternative to planned surgery for a vasectomy or tubal ligation, or as a means of getting around religious bans on birth control when they want no more children.

We do believe in safety in the work place, Dr. Bingham, but there can be good as well as bad sides to a situation.

Above all, please don't try to get a ban on the manufacture and sale of the chemical DBCP, because that would cause some losses of agricultural production which would be serious.

Sincerely,

Robert K. Phillips
Executive Secretary

stated to the press: "All these government agencies overdo everything. I know they carry things to extremes. They should at least consider alternatives to banning this material." He added that, "after all, people take some kind of chance every day."

In mid-November Phillips made the following statement:

> It is . . . only in the last few years that peach producers, and many others in agriculture, have come to the somewhat belated realization that Congress can and will pass laws which allow Federal *bureaucrats* powers which would have been undreamed of only a few years ago.

> The situation which has developed in Washington requires more checking and more direct contact than ever before, and it seems the situation will build more in that direction.
>
> That is just one of the reasons that National Peach Council, as an organization which speaks only for the nation's peach industry, is so important to each and every peach grower.

Eula Bingham replied to Phillips on November 21, ten weeks after Phillips had written her. Her letter arrived on November 25 and is reproduced as Exhibit 2.

On December 13 Phillips added the following:

> It [Bingham's letter] is a nice enough letter, but does not, in my opinion, serve as an answer to the letter I wrote to her on September 12.
>
> Dr. Bingham certainly deserves praise for the recent moves to wipe out a large number of trivial job-safety standards and loosen enforcement standards. At least there is progress in that direction.

THE NATIONAL PEACH COUNCIL

The National Peach Council was an agricultural federation representing the interest of growers of fresh market peaches throughout the United States. Established in 1942, it was the only peach farmers trade association of national scope in the United States, and had sixty-three hundred members and associate members. The latter were manufacturers of equipment and supplies needed by this industry, sales agencies, and other interested firms. Production and per capita consumption of fresh peaches had exhibited small decreases for several years.

The council had various activities. For example, it published a monthly newspaper and employed a professional home economist to assist in its educational public relations efforts to increase the use of fresh peaches. The Council also held a large national convention lasting four days once a year at which there were speeches, panels, and technical papers on horticulture and the economics of the industry. The latest convention, held in San Antonio, included sessions on peach tree disease control, nursery certification, use of computers and aerial photography in orchard management, chemical and mechanical thinning of fruit, evaporative cooling to delay blooming, herbicides in orchard floor management, peach varieties by production area, peaches and competitive fruits around the world, and wholesale and retail marketing. Another activity of the Council was the preparation and dissemination of news releases and direct contact with the United States Department of Agriculture. For example, many growers found that their peaches were not selling one mid-August. When these growers notified the National Peach Council, that organization Mailgrammed factual but promotional information to the major networks. The organization also contacted the Plentiful Foods section at the Department of Agriculture, which prepared a radio news release and got it out immediately rather than using the regular release system, which would have required seven to ten days.

One recent interesting activity of the National Peach Council was participation in the planning of proposed legislation known as the Freestone Peach Research and Education Act. This proposed statute called for a plan of action and a nongovernmental board to oversee the resulting program of research and promotional education.

EXHIBIT 2 **Letter from O.S.H. A. to National Peach Council**

Office of the Assistant Secretary

Mr. Robert K. Phillips
Executive Secretary
National Peach Council
Post Office Box 1085
Martinsburg, West Virginia 25401

Dear Mr. Phillips:

In response to your letter of September 12 regarding the sterilization of workers, I can think of no situation where the material impairment of an employee's health or reproductive capacity as a result of exposure to a toxic substance could be regarded as beneficial. The right to have children is a fundamental human right entitled to serious protection under the Occupational Safety and Health Act of 1970. There is no comparison between involuntary sterilization resulting from exposure to a chemical in the workplace and voluntary sterilization achieved by a medical procedure. Voluntary sterilization involves a conscious, deliberate choice by a man or woman to end one's reproductive capability. Instead, the Occupational Safety and Health Admininstration (OSHA) must set standards which assure that no employee will suffer material impairment of health or functional capacity during the entire lifetime.

Sterility is only one hazard of exposure of 1,2-Dibromo-3-Chloropropane ("DBCP"). Degenerative changes occur in several organs of the body, and there is also a cancer hazard. OSHA intends to treat DBCP as a carcinogen because well-designed studies have demonstrated the carcinogenicity of DBCP in both sexes of two mammalian species at multiple dose levels. Therefore, the Agency's decision to issue an emergency temporary standard is based not only on the sterilant effects of DBCP but also on other serious health effects, including the carcinogenicity of DBCP.

In light of serious health effects from worker exposure to DBCP, I believe that the issuance of an emergency temporary standard was necessary and appropriate to protect employees from this grave danger.

Please be assured that your letter has been included in the official record of the permanent standard for DBCP.

Sincerely,

Eula Bingham
Assistant Secretary
Occupational Safety and Health

Research would be on all phases of the production and marketing of freestone peaches. The promotional education would consist of preparation and dissemination of materials to households, institutional food buyers, restaurant chains, teachers, and others. Costs would be met by assessments on fresh peaches marketed. Rates of half a cent per bushel to several cents per bushel were being considered. Under the proposed legislation the plan of action would have to go to a referendum among freestone peach farmers. The federal government would only monitor that the resulting work adhered to the statutes and the guidelines established by the plan of action that had been approved by a vote of the growers.

OCCUPATIONAL SAFETY AND HEALTH ADMINISTRATION

The Occupational Safety and Health Administration was a relatively new agency, but it had quickly established itself as an activist group. It was considered unreasonable, arbitrary, capricious, and indifferent to cost by much of the business community. A survey of [congressional members'] opinions of OSHA conducted by the White House revealed several criticisms, including harassment of business organizations, too many forms, and unnecessary paperwork. Even the highly liberal Senator George McGovern (Democrat, South Dakota) attacked OSHA for "overregulation of small business [and] nitpicking enforcement."

CASE STUDY ACTIVITY

Advise the National Peach Council.

Source: Reprinted with permission of Macmillan College Publishing Company from *Cases In Marketing: Orientation, Analysis and Problems*, 2nd Edition, by Thomas V. Greer. Copyright © 1979 by Thomas V. Greer.

Part Seven

Comprehensive Cases

Case Studies

Branford and Sons, Inc.

Raising his wineglass toward his son, Felix Branford launched into a toast, proudly proclaiming the first hundred years in the family business an unqualified success, and looking forward as the next generation takes the reins. "Here is to you, Robert, the next in the Branford line; may the business we have worked so hard to cultivate and grow be as prosperous in your hands as it has been in mine, my father's, and his father's before—to your future!"

As the glasses clinked, Felix's mind wandered back through time and into the years ahead with a mixture of satisfaction and concern. It's difficult, he thought, to turn all of this over to Robert, even with his engineering degree and shiny new MBA. I have experienced many difficulties and see many more to come. Ah, it is no easy thing, this new world with all of the changes, customers demanding more and more, old markets being replaced by new ones, dealing with many different countries—it makes my head spin. My grandfather would not believe the changes in his clock gear business, and I wonder what my son's children will see when they take the company. Oh, well, this is a happy occasion, not a time for worry. "Robert, pour me another; the next hundred years have only just begun, as have you, so tonight we enjoy—tomorrow, it's back to work!"

HISTORY OF THE COMPANY

In 1881, Alexander Branford and his wife began what was to become a lasting institution in the Hudson River Valley of upstate New York, starting out machining movements for the New England clock industry. Within five years, Branford Clockworks was established, consisting of a small workshop and a staff of four, growing to a work force of thirty with the first modern industrial building in the town of Westfield by the turn of the century. As technology progressed and electricity moved into the countryside, business and productivity increased. By the outbreak of World War I, the work force had increased to sixty, including twenty employees who worked at home on their own pivoting operations in neighboring villages. As was the case throughout America, the war effort depleted the male population and production in the clock gear industry slowed.

The years immediately following the war saw many changes in the Branford business. With the return of his sons, a new firm was established, Branford and Sons, which began to look beyond New England clocks for business expansion, eventually building a broader domestic customer base. As post-war expansion occurred, so grew Branford, investing heavily in the highest quality Swiss gear-cutting machines. By 1920, the manufacturing facility was equipped with batteries of lathes and automatic pinion-cutting machines. With this expanded capacity and versatility, Alexander's sons, Albert, Emile, and Philip, moved into the domestic automobile, electrical appliance, and timing equipment businesses utilizing their combined experience in small shaft/gear production.

The 1920s and 1930s saw steady growth with the workforce peaking at seventy by 1940. World War II, however, saw a replay of earlier events and employment fell back once again. Nevertheless, as the 1940s began to unfold, the three brothers recognized a need to upgrade plant and equipment, and reorganized to increase financial and marketing flexibility, in preparation of anticipated growth in new markets. Thus was formed three separate smaller companies, one of which was Phillip Branford and Sons, the direct precursor of today's ongoing concern.

Phillip held the reins during the 1950s, with son Felix responsible for the technical, production, and marketing function. During this time, their largest customers began moving gear-cutting operations in-house, forcing Branford to search for new business, while at the same time, revitalizing their physical operations. Those years were difficult times, with Phillip and Felix struggling to maintain their existing business while developing new contacts. The decade took its toll and in 1960, Phillip, in ill health, turned over the company to Felix, with the charge to build the new facility which would take them into the future. In 1963, Felix and his work force of forty-seven moved into their new factory in the Westfield Industrial Park.

Still restricting their business to U.S. customers, Felix decided in 1969 to make a major technological move into high-speed multispindle automatic lathes in order to lengthen runs and develop economies of scale. With the growth of the European consumer market throughout the 1960s and 1970s, and the rapid growth in the number of small electric motors in domestic and imported automobiles, Branford saw an increase in the potential demand for his products in the auto and electronics industries. By the early 1980s company sales totaled $4 million, produced with a work force of 105. With Felix still guiding the company, his only son, Robert, joined the company in 1982, having completed his engineering and business studies as well as military service. Not content with a strictly domestic market, Robert, with his multilingual capabilities (English, Italian, German), began to seek foreign markets, with the vision of a multinational customer base, and a worldwide market for expansion. By 1988, results of Robert's efforts were evident, with sales tripling to $13 million, and a work force growing to 150 people. During this six-year period, approximately 75 percent of the growth was due to exports, with export sales currently accounting for a full 50 percent of total business.

CURRENT OPERATIONS

"I know we are a small family business, but I believe we can grow to a much larger company if we hire the right people to manage our business. We now have many more employees and markets and you and I cannot be everywhere at once!" Robert, in his efforts to expand the business, approached his father, Felix, explaining his position and desire to bring in outside managers to help operate the business. "When we had thirty, forty, and sixty people, you could concentrate on the technical side as well as generate new business, but then we dealt only in the United States, and today we export to eight other countries and are planning on even more."

"Robert, I have seen how you have brought in new customers and demand for new products, but I handle the technical side of the business and am not comfortable with outsiders moving into Branford. This is not their family, this is not their business, and this is not their life. I do not like the idea of someone else telling me what is good for Branford. Let me think about it, Robert, this is not a simple matter."

THE ORGANIZATION

With the addition of Robert to the family business, the organization expanded to accommodate the new export business and resulting increased sales (see Figure 1). In addition to increasing the production work force, management now included Felix, the president and general manager; Robert handling marketing and the export business; a separate export office with two bilingual secretaries (English/Italian and English/German); and a manager for each of the functional areas: quality, purchasing, domestic sales, accounting, and production. Under the production manager were four production supervisors and one technical specialist who assisted in design, estimating, and troubleshooting. Although nominally the head of the organization, Felix remained closely involved in the engineering and production aspects of the business but as time passed, the scent of transition grew stronger and the signs of change became more apparent.

THE MARKET

As recently as 1982, the market was confined to the United States; by the end of 1988, 50 percent of the company's sales came from export business. Table I shows the breakdown by country.

While sales have been historically and continue to be concentrated in the automotive industry, Branford has been active in product development, capitalizing on the trend toward upscale cars and all of the automated features that have become standard; i.e., power windows, power seats, multiple windshield wipers, etc. Another development since 1982 includes a joint venture with a high-impact plastics molding house, combining Branford's gear-cutting expertise with precision plastic parts to produce plastic gear/metal shaft assemblies. Also, due to his high-precision reputation, a French subsidiary of a U.S.-based medical device manufacturer contracted Branford to become a supplier of high-quality threaded nickel-plated brass fittings, thus entering the French market. Table II breaks out sales by general product category and Table III lists customers by country.

In most of the market segments in which Branford is competing, the 1980s saw a steady increase in share as well as overall growth; Table IV traces this growth for three selected lines.

MARKET PROFILES

The automotive industry continues to be the mainstay of Branford's business and the company foresees a strong future in this area for electric motors, citing BMW,

FIGURE 1 **Branford and Sons, Inc.**

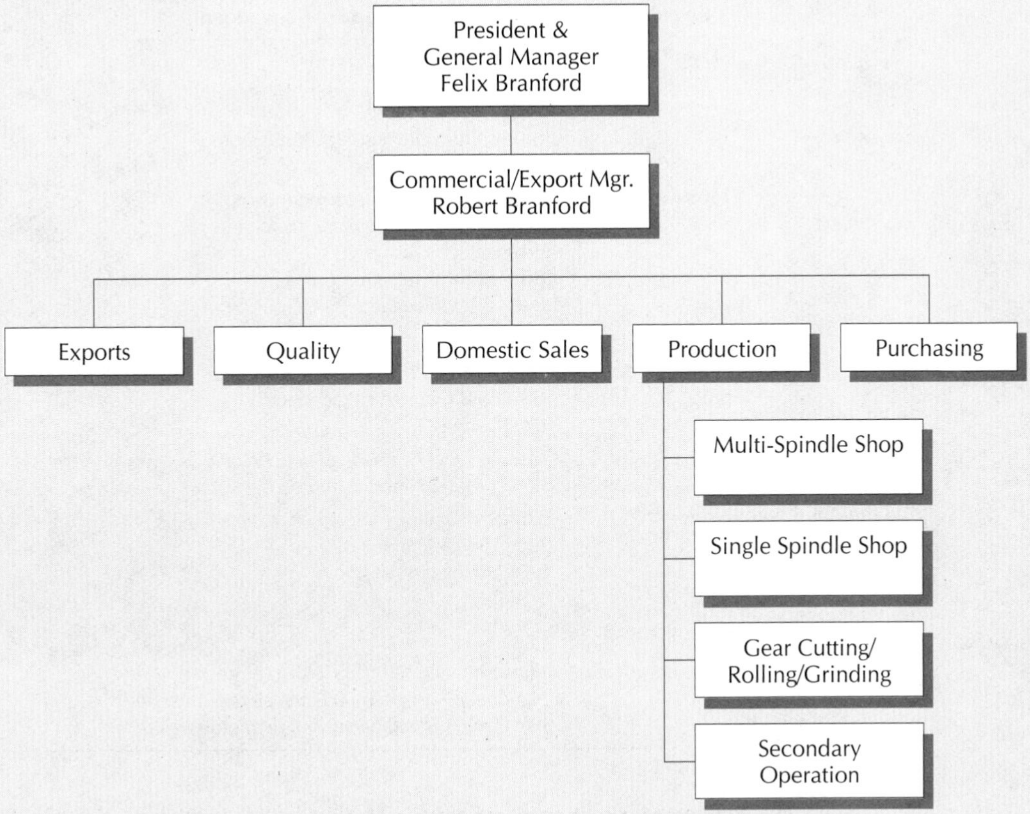

TABLE I **Sales by Country**

Country	Percent of Total Sales
United States	50
Italy	14
Germany	12
Hong Kong	7
Sweden	5
France	4
The Netherlands	4
Canada	2
Taiwan	2
Japan	N.A. (New Entry)

TABLE II **Sales by Product Category**

Product Category	Percent of Total Sales
Automotive	65
Household appliances	12
Electronic	8
Medical	8
Munitions	5
Misc.	2

TABLE III **Foreign Customers/Products by Country**

Country	Customer/Product Components
Italy	Magnetti Marelli (auto parts)
	Ciaramella (electronic motors)
	Weber (carburetors)
	United Technologies (electronic motors)
	Unus (electric motors)
Germany	Bosch (turned parts, electric motors)
	SWF (turned parts, electric motors)
	Brose (electric-powered seat components)
	AB Elektronik (electronics)
	Rockwell Golde (auto parts)
	Stihl
Hong Kong	Johnson Electrical (electric motors)
France	Medico Lyon (medical connectors)
	Eli Lilly (twist caps)
Canada	Medico Quebec (medical connectors)
	Power Motion (electric motors)
Taiwan	Taigeme (electric motors)
	Adlee (electric motors)
	Shin Lin (electric motors)
Sweden	Electrolux
The Netherlands	Phillips
Japan	Matsushita (turned parts; electric motors)
	National Motors (turned parts; electric motors)
	Panasonic (turned parts; electric motors)

TABLE IV **Percent Market Share in Selected Markets, 1981–1989**

	'81	'82	'83	'84	'85	'86	'87	'88	'89
Automotive parts	2	5	8	10	15	20	30	35	45
Appliance parts	—	—	1	3	5	6	8	11	13
Medical connectors	—	—	—	9	18	36	70	71	72

Mercedes, and Honda as using up to approximately 40 motors in each vehicle. Even if auto sales weaken by 5–10 percent, Branford feels that the number of motors per vehicle will increase at such a rate as to offset that decline. In household appliances, Italy is their strongest market, with one of the largest private manufacturers in Europe, Ciaramella, their largest customer. The munitions business is declining primarily due to individual countries' national security concerns; Branford is expending no resources on foreign business in this line and is concentrating on maintaining domestic business only.

The medical business has grown rapidly over the past five years but is leveling out, due both to saturation of the metal connector market as well as a desire by

Branford to keep production at current levels, at least for the foreseeable future. With a decline in the electronics market for small machines parts, Branford intends to focus on the four major lines, i.e., auto, home appliance, electric motors, and medical.

RISK THREATS

Fully 50 percent of Branford's business is perceived as nearly risk-free, that part being their U.S. customers. However, the export business is thought to be not so secure. Germany, Switzerland, and Spain are strong European competition. In Japan, a new market, as well as Hong Kong, the Japanese, Taiwanese, and even the Chinese are considered serious or potential threats. In general, Branford feels that in most of their export countries, the strongest competition is from local suppliers, and while few in number, they are often large, well-organized companies or subsidiaries of very large corporations, i.e., Nippondenso/Honda.

Problem areas include price pressure from Asian competition and strong financial capabilities of larger competitors. Although competitors attempt in some markets to sell on price, Branford quality stands the test, even against the well-known Asian standard. In terms of financing, Branford acknowledges that a strong desire to remain a private family business prevents their taking advantage of equity markets available to public companies, and may place them at a disadvantage relative to their better heeled competitors.

As with any multinational, large or small, foreign currencies present varying degrees of risk. For Branford, this aspect of international business has seen both good and not so good times. For example, when the company first entered the foreign markets in 1982, the dollar was trading at 7ff; during the high U.S. interest rate period from 1983–1985, the dollar rose to 10.5ff which seriously diminished their exports to France. However, as the interest rates declined, so did the ff/U.S.$ exchange rate, settling in at approximately 6ff/U.S.$. The values of Deutsche marks and yen have also fluctuated during this time, approximately 10 percent and 30 percent, respectively. Table V lists the currencies of payments for each export country.

Branford sees exchange rates as an important factor in their overall strategy, impacting decisions such as types of technologies, products, markets, and even company philosophy. By setting the quality standard in their industry, they hope to overcome rate fluctuations, increase share, increase production, and lower costs and

TABLE V **Export Payment Currencies**

Exports to:	Payment in:
Italy	U.S.$
Germany	Deutsche marks
Hong Kong	U.S.$
France	French francs
Canada	U.S.$
Taiwan	U.S.$
Japan	Yen
Sweden	Swedish krona
Netherlands	French francs

prices, further increasing sales. Although speculating in the currency markets is an alternative, Branford avoids this tactic, stating that the company is too small and isn't structured to handle that type of business. In general, Branford considers the French franc to be the highest risk currency; annual purchases in the forward market with monthly settlements has been the only way this problem has been addressed. Other arrangements with French customers have been discussed but none have been found to be satisfactory to both parties.

DISCUSSION QUESTIONS

1. What is the company's current strategy? Should it be modified for the future?
2. What markets should Branford consider for growth potential?
3. What organization and human resource issues face Branford and how should they be resolved?
4. What impact will the departure of F. Branford have on training needs?
5. List alternatives related to all of the strategic issues and recommend a course of action.

Source: Case submitted by Raymond Cheser, Nova Southeastern University—Doctoral Candidate.

Leykam Mürztaler

In February 1989, Dr. Gertrude Eder, Marketing Manager for Leykam Mürztaler AG, was reviewing a problem that had occupied her thoughts a great deal during the past few months. Although Leykam Mürztaler, like the paper industry in general, had been doing well in recent years, it was her opinion that it was time to think about ways to strengthen the company's ability to prosper as industry growth inevitably began slowing down. In particular, she was considering what recommendations to offer the Executive Board regarding the firm's branding strategy.

LEYKAM MÜRZTALER AG

The past few years had been good for the Leykam Mürztaler Group. Paralleling the industry's increased sales, the firm's total sales had risen from ASch4,842 million[1] in 1983 to ASch7,100 million in 1988, an increase of 47 percent. For Leykam Mürztaler AG, the principal operating component of the Group, 1988 revenues had reached ASch6,300 million, an increase over 1986 of 41 percent, enhanced by the successful start-up of a new production line and by above average growth in demand for high-grade coated woodfree printing papers, the firm's main sales segment.

Leykam Mürztaler AG, together with its predecessor companies, had been a producer of paper for over four hundred years. Headquartered in Gratkorn, Austria, the firm produced coated woodfree printing paper and newsprint, with integrated pulp production. Principal mills and offices were located at Gratkorn and Bruck, Austria. Export sales offices for coated woodfree paper were headquartered in Vienna.

In 1988, woodfree papers represented approximately 80 percent of sales, newsprint 13 percent and pulp 7 percent. Twenty-two percent of revenues came from Austria, 56 percent from Western Europe and 22 percent from exports to the rest of the world (including Eastern Europe). The highest share of exports was for coated woodfree papers at approximately 90 percent.

(Production volumes in 1987 and 1988 are shown in Exhibit 1.) The large increase in production of printing and writing paper in 1988 (to 340,900 tonnes) reflected successful selling of the output of the new coated woodfree paper machine at Gratkorn, with a capacity of 138,000 tonnes per year. The decline in pulp production reflected a change in product mix. External sales of pulp were declining as the company's pulp production was further integrated into the company's own paper production.

With the addition of the new production line, the company had become the European market leader in coated woodfree papers, with a market share of 8–10 percent. In December 1987 the Supervisory Board approved a project to establish a new production line at Bruck to produce mechanical coated printing papers (LWC) for magazines, catalogues and printed advertising materials. Planned capacity was 135,000 tonnes, to be put into operation at the end of 1989.

Despite the increased level of investment, financial results were very good. In 1987, the last year for which complete financial details were available, profit was down slightly from the previous year (see Exhibit 2), reflecting the greatly increased depreciation charges associated with the new paper machine and the decision to use the reducing-balance method of depreciation for it and some other equipment. Cash flow, however, was close to an all-time record, results were "clearly better than originally forecast," and operating profits were near the top of the European woodfree paper

***EXHIBIT 1* Highlights of the Development of the Leykam-Mürztaler Group**

		1987	1988	%
Production (in tons)	Printing and writing papers	272,900	340,900	+24.9
	Newsprint (Bruck)	98,200	99,200	+ 1.0
	Paper total	371,100	440,100	+18.6
	Chemical pulp	209,500	204,500	– 2.4
	Mechanical pulp	30,900	32,100	+ 3.9
	Deink pulp	58,900	62,700	+ 6.4
Total sales (gross, in ASch mn)	Leykam Mürztaler AG	5,234	6,300	+20.4
	Export share	4,056	5,100	+25.7
	Exports in %	78	81	—
	Leykam Mürztaler Group	5,906	7,100	+20.2
Capital expenditure and prepayments for fixed assets	(in ASch mn)	1,418	1,500	+ 5.8
Cash flow	(in ASch mn)	1,020	1,500	+47.1
Employees (excluding apprentices)	as of 31 December	2,825	2,865	+ 1.4

Source: Annual Report.

EXHIBIT 2 **Financial Results**

	1983	1984*	1985**	1986	1987
Total sales (gross, in AS m)	4,842	5,367	5,420	5,187	5,906
Export Sales (AS m)	2,973	3,413	3,537	3,331	4,062
Export shares of Leykam-Mürztaler AG (%)	69	72	74	74	78
Capital investment (AS m)	313	253	444	2,461	1,518
Total depreciation (AS m)	374	344	337	476	1,064
thereof: reducing-balance depreciation (AS m)	—	—	—	125	674
Cash flow (AS m)	373	1,025	959	871	1,020
Profit for the year (AS m)	1	422	81	101	67
Personnel expenditure (AS m)	1,096	993	1,046	1,076	1,231
Number of employees (excluding apprentices) as of 31 December	2,918	2,424	2,364	2,578	2,825
Dividend and bonus (AS m)	—	54	81	101	67
(%)	—	4+4	4+8	4+8	8

*Excluding Niklasdorf Mill.
**Excluding Frohnierten Mill from 1 April 1985.

Source: Annual Report.

producers, on a percent of sales basis. Preliminary indications were that financial results for 1988 would be still better.

The company marketed its coated products under its MAGNO series brand (e.g., MAGNOMATT, MAGNOPRINT, MAGNOMATT K) principally through wholly owned merchants in Austria and other merchants throughout Western Europe. In addition, it sold to other kinds of merchants in Austria as well as to some printers and publishers directly. Paper merchants were contacted by sales representatives in Vienna and Gratkorn, sales subsidiaries in Germany, Italy and France, and sales agents in other European countries. Some of its products were sold on a private brand basis to certain large merchants.

Although Leykam Mürztaler served paper markets on a worldwide basis, and planned to enter the LWC market, this case focuses on coated woodfree papers for printing applications in Western Europe.

THE PULP AND PAPER INDUSTRY IN WESTERN EUROPE[2]

Despite its maturity, the pulp and paper industry was undergoing major change. Characterized by high breakeven volumes, small fluctuations in demand could significantly impact profits, and there was some evidence that capacity was outgrowing demand. Despite the sophistication of paper-making technology, product differentiation was increasingly difficult to achieve. Some paper makers were integrating backwards to control the cost or assure the supply of pulp. Others were integrating forward, buying paper merchants in order to have better control of marketing. Still others were integrating horizontally to have a more complete product line.

Other changes were affecting the industry as well. Customers were being merged, acquired or reorganized, thus changing established purchasing patterns. Changes in advertising were impacting traditional usage patterns. Paper merchants were merging to gain economies of scale. Some were emphasizing private brands to reduce their dependence on paper makers. Markets were fragmenting as new, small businesses were forming at a record rate. Consumption patterns were changing. In Europe, consumption ranged from 233kg per capita in Sweden to 60 in Portugal, but growth rates ranged from a high of 29.4 percent in Greece to a low of 2.4 percent in Denmark. There was some uncertainty about the implications of Europe's move toward a true common market in 1992, although trade barriers were not a significant factor in the industry.

PRINTING AND WRITING PAPER

In the pulp and paper industry, the major and high growth segment was printing and writing papers. Both coated and uncoated papers were produced from mechanically or chemically processed pulp to form four broad categories: coated woodfree, mechanical coated,[3] uncoated woodfree and mechanical uncoated. To be defined as coated, a paper had to have a surface coating of at least 5 grams per square meter (gsm).

Coated woodfree papers represented the highest quality category, in terms of printability, gloss, feel, ability to reproduce color and many other characteristics. Grades of coated woodfree papers were not precisely specified, but the industry had established further categories such as cast coated, art paper, standard and low coated. (See Exhibit 3 for categories and prices.) The standard grade represented the bulk of sales. Within this category, however, there were many gradations—the amount of whiteness, brightness, stiffness and other characteristics. Leykam Mürztaler competed principally at the high end of the standard grade, but was planning to enter the art paper segment also.

EXHIBIT 3 **Prices per Tonne (in $) of Woodfree Printing and Writing Papers in Western Europe (2nd Quarter 1987 delivered)**

Grade	West Germany	UK	France	Netherlands
Cast coated, sheets	2734	2324	2588	2480
Art paper, sheets	1897	1660	1837	1736
Standard, sheets	1283	1212	1235	1166
Standard, reels	1199	1145	1169	1091
Low coated, sheets	1172	1130	1136	1066

Note: Cast coated paper was estimated to represent 5% of the coated woodfree market, Art paper 7–8%, Standard coated 70% and Low coated less than 20%. Within the standard coated category, actual transaction prices could vary as much as 25% as a function of quality and as much as 10% due to competitive or other factors.

Source: EKONO Strategic Study, September 1988.

Coated woodfree was the smallest printing and writing paper segment (17.8 percent) of total consumption, but it was also the most dynamic, with an average growth rate of 8.4 percent from 1980 to 1987. Expectations were that 1988 consumption would exceed three million tonnes.

MARKETS FOR PRINTING AND WRITING PAPER

Principal markets for printing and writing paper were magazines (33 percent), direct mail (17 percent), brochures and general print advertising (15 percent), copy paper (11 percent), other office paper (9 percent) and books (5 percent). For coated woodfree papers, it was estimated that advertising, direct and indirect, accounted for 85–90 percent of consumption.[4]

On a country by country basis, there was significant variation in the mix of advertising expenditures, however. In the UK, for instance, the bulk of advertising expenditures went to newspapers and TV, whereas in Germany advertising expenditures were split somewhat evenly among newspapers, magazines, catalogues and direct mail.[5] Major uses for coated woodfree papers were direct mail, brochures, annual reports, etc. The dynamic growth of coated woodfree papers in recent years was largely fueled by the rapid increases in "non-classical" advertising. Changes in this mix could significantly affect country consumption patterns for coated woodfree papers.

Despite cost pressures and shifts in individual markets and end uses, coated woodfree papers were benefiting from demand for more and better four-color printing as advertisers sought ways to improve the impact of their messages.

THE PRINTING INDUSTRY

The vast majority of orders for coated woodfree paper were placed by printers, either on the merchant or directly on the mill. In some instances, however, for very large orders, the order would be placed by either the printer or the publisher, depending on which seemed to have the strongest negotiating position with the supplier.

Selection of paper grade and manufacturer was a complex process that varied significantly according to end use, size of order, and sophistication of both the printer and the specifier or user. Almost without exception, the printer had the final say in the selection of paper make and could significantly influence the grade of paper as well. The specifier (ad agency) or user (advertiser, publisher, mail order house, etc.) influenced paper selection, particularly with respect to grade, and could also influence selection of make, subject to final agreement by the printer.

For the printer, key paper characteristics were printability and runability. Surface characteristics, whiteness and brightness were also important. Price was always important, especially when deciding between two suppliers with similar offerings or where paper costs represented a significant portion of the total cost of the printed product. Complaint handling, emergency assistance, speed and reliability of delivery were key service components. Sales representative knowledge was also important. Within limits, relative importance of decision criteria varied from one country to another. In Italy and the UK, for instance, price and quality tended to be equally important, whereas quality and service factors tended to predominate importance rankings in Switzerland. There was some favoritism given producers for patriotic reasons, but seldom at the expense of quality or price.

The user or specifier considered many of the same characteristics as the printer. Printability and delivery were usually at the top of the list, but the major concern was the paper's suitability for the particular advertising message, within the constraints of the overall advertising budget.

Despite the apparent similarity of products offered by different mills, there was substantial variation in runability, which could only be determined by actual trial. According to one printer:

> The final test is how well the paper prints on our presses. This is a matter of "fit" between paper, ink and press characteristics. We find there are variations between papers that meet the same specifications, which can only be determined by actual trial. This is not cheap as a trial involves printing three thousand sheets. Because the paper characteristics cannot be completely specified, we like the idea of a mill brand. One time we tested two merchant brands that we thought were different. Then we found out that the paper came from the same mill, so we really wasted our time on the second test.
>
> The merchant's sales representative is important, but we don't need him to call all that frequently. We like to talk to him about trends or problems we're having, but when we need something quickly, we call the merchant.
>
> Once we have selected a paper, it is critically important that its quality be consistent. Most suppliers are pretty good. Except for obvious flaws, however, we find they tend to want to blame problems on the ink or the press.

Over the past several years, the number of printers remained relatively constant, at about fifteen to twenty thousand with decreases from mergers and acquisitions offset by a growth in instant print outlets. In the last ten years, the number of commercial print customers doubled to over five hundred thousand, half of whom used instant print outlets.

As the number of small businesses and the use of desktop publishing continued to grow, it was suggested that within ten years traditional printers would perhaps only handle longer-run full color work. Monochrome and spot color work would be produced in customers' offices, with the paper buying decision being made by people with little knowledge about paper or printing.[6] In-plant printing, however, was not expected to have a significant impact on the coated woodfree market.

PAPER MERCHANTS

Printers and publishers were reached in two principal ways: direct sales from the mill and sales from the mill through merchants, either independent or mill-owned. Direct sales were more common for high volume products sold in reels, such as newsprint and LWC magazine paper. The pattern of distribution was influenced by characteristics of the transaction (see Exhibit 4) and the pattern varied significantly from one country to another (see Exhibit 5). For coated woodfree papers it was estimated that 70–80 percent of sales went through merchants.

As with all wholesalers, stocking to provide quick delivery in small quantities was a principal merchant function. Fragmentation of the fastest growing market segments (business and small printer) had decreased the average order size and increased demand for a wide choice of paper grades, making it more difficult for mills to directly access these customers.

EXHIBIT 4 **Transaction Characteristics: A Comparison of the Roles of Manufacturers and Merchants**

Characteristics	Manufacturer	Merchant
Order size (kg)	>1,500	200–500
Items carried	Small	2,500–5,000
Fixed costs	High	Low
Stock level (kg)	>2,000/item	500–1,750
Delivery	Often slow	24 hours
Service	None	Possible
Cash flow	Low	Low

Source: The European Printing and Writing Paper Industry—1987.

EXHIBIT 5 **Market Shares per Distribution Channel (%)**

	Country			
Form of Distribution	*UK*	*France*	*Germany*	*Italy*
Paper mills	48	50	59	80
Mill-owned merchants	52	50	—	20
Independent Merchants	52	—	41	20

Source: The European Printing and Writing Paper Industry—1987.

In warehousing, larger merchants had introduced expensive computer-controlled logistical systems, which reduced delivery times and the cost of preparing orders for delivery. Predictions were made that electronic interchange of information between merchants and their suppliers and larger customers would be the norm within the next few years. Merchants in the UK were spearheading an initiative to achieve industry standards for bar codes throughout Europe.

Changes in end user profiles and new customer needs had forced merchants to expand the scope of their activities and customer support functions. As a result, the merchants' role broadened to include a number of additional services, including technical advice on paper choice and broader printing problems.

Private branding, supported by advertising, had long been used by some merchants to differentiate their products and service. Some large merchants had also invested in testing apparatus, similar to that found in mills, to check conformance to specifications and to support their desire to become principals, with full responsibility for product performance.

Merchant margins varied with location, type of sale and nature of the transaction. For sales from stock, margins ranged from a low of 12 percent in Italy and 15 percent in Germany to 25 percent in France and Switzerland. Margins reduced to about 5 percent, or less, when a merchant acted as the intermediary solely for invoicing purposes.[7] (A typical income statement for a paper merchant is shown in Exhibit 6.)

EXHIBIT 6 Typical Income Statement: Paper Merchant

	%
Sales	100
Cost of goods sold	75
Contribution	25
Other costs	23
Net profit	2
Depreciation	.5
Cash flow	2.5

Source: The European Printing and Writing Paper Industry—1987.

EXHIBIT 7 Paper Merchants: Ownership and Concentration per Country

Country	Merchants totaling 80% of country sales	Ownership
Sweden	2	mill-owned
Denmark	3	mostly mill-owned
Netherlands	5	mill-owned
Belgium	5	mill-owned
Switzerland	5	mostly mill-owned
Austria	2 (70%)	mill-owned
France	6	mill-owned
West Germany	7	all independent
UK	few big and many small ones	partly mill-owned mostly independent

Source: Paper Merchanting, the Viewpoint of Independent Merchant.

Patterns of merchant ownership also varied from one country to another (see Exhibit 7). In the UK, for example, Wiggins Teape, a paper producer established in 1780, became a merchant in 1960 when existing merchants resisted introducing carbonless copy paper in the market. The company opened a network of offices to stimulate demand and provide technical support for the product. Between 1969 and 1984, the company acquired control of several major merchants operating in the UK, France, Belgium, Italy and Finland. In 1984, sales of $480 million made Wiggins Teape the largest merchant in Europe.

On the other hand, Paper Union, one of the two largest merchants in Germany (turnover of $142 million and market share of 12 percent in 1984), was an independent merchant. It was formed in the early 1960s, from three smaller merchants, in an attempt to reach the critical size of one hundred thousand tonnes per year. Due to low margins in Germany, Paper Union had emphasized reducing operating costs and consistently fast delivery. Plans were being made, however, to introduce further services and advertising in an attempt to add value and increase customer awareness.

The move toward company-owned merchants was not without controversy. According to one independent merchant:

> We believe that independent merchants are very much in the best interest of paper mills. We're aware, of course, that many mills are integrating forward, buying merchants in order to maintain access to distribution. It is our view, however, that this will cause a number of problems. No one mill can supply all the products that a merchant must offer. Hence, even mill-owned merchants must maintain relations with a number of other mills, who will always want to supply their full range of products to the merchant, including those which compete with the parent mill. This will create serious tensions and frequently will put the merchant in the position of having to choose between corporate loyalty and offering the best package to the customer. The parent can, of course, impose restrictions on the merchant with respect to selling competing products, but the sales force would have serious problems with this.
>
> Our strong preference is for exclusive representation of a mill. This is particularly important where there are strong influencers, such as advertisers, to whom it is important for us to address considerable promotional effort. Also when we are an exclusive merchant, we provide the mill with extensive information on our sales, which allows the mill to do market analysis that both we and the mill find very valuable. We certainly would not provide this kind of information if the mill had intensive distribution. In a country like Switzerland, we can give the mill complete geographic and account coverage, so it's not clear to us why the mill needs more than one merchant. In our view, intensive distribution creates a situation where there is much more emphasis on price. While this first affects the merchant, it inevitably affects the mill as well.
>
> If we do sell for a mill that has intensive distribution, we prefer to sell it under our brand, although we identify the mill, in small print. This is somewhat an historical artifact, going back to the days when mills did not attempt to brand their products, but if we're going to compete for business with another merchant, selling for the same mill, we feel having our name on the product helps us differentiate ourselves from the competitor.
>
> At the same time, we should point out that we don't sell competing brands. There are about five quality grades within standard coated woodfree, and we handle two to three brands.

One industry expert predicted significant changes in distribution patterns.[8]

> Looking to the future, it is predicted that there will be an increase in the number of paper grade classifications, moving from four just a few years ago to twenty or more. There will be an increasing number of different types of middlemen and distributors, and merchants will move into grades traditionally regarded as mill direct products (e.g., newsprint and mechanical grades) to bring these grades to the smaller customers.
>
> Just as we have seen a technological revolution hit the traditional printing industry, we must now see a marketing revolution hit the traditional paper industry. Selection of the correct channel of distribution and the development of an active working relationship with that channel will be vital.

COMPETITION IN COATED WOODFREE PAPERS

In varying degrees, Leykam Mürztaler encountered at least ten major European firms in the markets it served in Europe. Some, like KNF and Zanders, competed principally in coated woodfree papers. Others, like Stora and Feldmühle, produced a wide range of products, from coated woodfree papers to tissue to newsprint.

There was considerable variation in competitive emphasis among producers. Zanders, for instance, generally regarded as the highest quality producer, mostly produced cast coated and premium art paper, competed only at the top end of the standard coated range and was relatively unusual in its extensive use of advertising. Hannover Papier was particularly strong in service, offering fast delivery. PWA Hallein, which had tended to emphasize price over quality, had recently improved its quality but was keeping prices low in an apparent effort to gain market share. Arjomari, the biggest French producer, owned the largest merchant chain in France and had recently purchased merchants in the UK and Southern Europe. It had recently entered the premium art paper segment, generally regarded as difficult to produce for. Burgo, a large Italian conglomerate, concentrated principally on the Italian market. (See Exhibit 8 for a report on the image of selected suppliers.)

Rapid growth in the coated woodfree market had stimulated capacity additions by existing producers and was also stimulating conversion of facilities from uncoated to coated. Nordland of Germany, for instance, switched one hundred thousand tonnes of capacity from uncoated to coated by adding a coater in October 1988. Excellent in service, there was, however, some question about is ability to produce high quality.

Branding was a relatively new aspect of the industry. All the major producers had established brand names for major products or grades. To date, however, only Zanders had actively promoted its brand to the trade or to advertisers.

EXHIBIT 8 **Major Mill Reputation**

Company	Comments on Reputation
Zanders (Germany)	• Mercedes Benz in coated woodfrees • Excellent service • Strong promotion • Marketing activities have also been directed to advertising agencies, who can influence on choice of brand
Leykam Mürztaler	• Reliable supplier • Good service
Arjomari (France)	• Strong positions in France due to its own merchants
Condat (France)	• Good and stable quality
Feldmühle (Germany)	• Stable quality • Rapid deliveries and good stocking arrangements
KNP (Netherlands)	• Flexible supplier, also accepts small orders • Good service
PWA Hallein (Germany)	• Competes with price
Scheufelen (Germany)	• Good and stable quality • Reliable deliveries
Stora Kopparberg (Sweden)	• Reliable deliveries • Quality and service OK

Source: EKONO Strategic Study, September 1988.

MARKETING AT LEYKAM MÜRZTALER AG

Marketing activities at Leykam Mürztaler were divided between the Sales Director, Wolfgang Pfarl, and the Marketing Manager, Gertrude Eder. Pfarl, a member of the Executive Board, was responsible for pricing as well as all personal selling activities, both direct and through merchants. Eder was responsible for public relations, advertising and sales promotion, and marketing research. As a staff member, she reported to Dr. Siegfried Meysel, the Managing Director.

COATED WOODFREE PRODUCTS AND MARKETS

In coated woodfree papers, Leykam Mürztaler offered a comprehensive product line of standard coated papers under the MAGNO brand, for both sheet and web offset printing. These were produced in a wide variety of basis weights, ranging from eighty–three hundred grams per square meter depending on the particular application. The firm targeted the high quality end of the standard coated category by offering higher coat weights, better gloss and print gloss, and better printability.

Using Austria as its home market, Leykam Mürztaler focused its principal efforts on countries in Europe. The majority of sales revenues came, in roughly similar amounts, from Austria, Italy, France and the UK, with somewhat higher sales in Germany. Belgium, Holland, Switzerland and Spain were important but smaller markets.

The firm also sold in a number of other countries, including the United States. Penetration of the U.S. market by the European paper industry had been assisted by the favorable exchange rates during the early 1980s. The firm's policy, however, was to maintain it position in different countries despite currency fluctuations. As Gertrude Eder explained:

> We believe our customers expect us to participate in their markets on a long-term basis and to be competitive with local conditions. This may cost us some profits in the short term, as when we maintained our position in the UK despite the weak pound, but now that the pound is strong again, this investment is paying off. If we had reduced our presence when the exchange rate was unfavorable, it would have been very difficult to regain our position.

CHANNELS OF DISTRIBUTION

Over the years, Leykam Mürztaler had sold most of its output through merchants. To some degree the method of distribution was influenced by the country served as the firm tended to follow the predominant trade practice in each country. In Switzerland, Germany and the UK, all its business was done through merchants. In France, Italy and Austria, there was a mixed pattern of distribution, but with a strong merchant orientation.

Merchants were carefully selected, and the firm did business only with stocking merchants who competed on service rather than price. In some countries (e.g., Holland) it used exclusive distribution, but this was not the normal pattern. Gertrude Eder explained:

> As a large producer, we have a volume problem. In the larger countries, one merchant simply can't sell enough product for us, plus we believe it is risky to commit completely to one merchant.

Similarly, Wolfgang Pfarl commented:

> In Germany, for instance, we could go to one merchant only, but to get the volume of business we need would require going into direct business with some non-stocking merchants, and that is something that neither we nor our stocking merchants want to happen.

To date, the trend toward mill ownership of merchants had not adversely affected the firm's ability to get good merchant representation. There was some concern, however, that with changing patterns of mill ownership, some merchants might be closed off to firms like Leykam Mürztaler in the future.

Service was also seen as a key to merchant relations. In this connection, the firm felt its computerized order system and new finishing facilities at the Gratkorn mill, highly automated, permitting flexibility in sheeting and packaging, and able to handle the total output of the new paper machine, provided great service capability and gave it a competitive advantage. As the mill superintendent put it:

> From a production standpoint, the ideal scenario is one in which we can run one grade of paper all year and ship it to customers in large reels. Reality is that meeting customer needs is critical, and I believe we have "state-of-the-art competence" in our ability to meet a tremendous variety of customer requirements efficiently.

PRICING

Pricing practices in the paper industry had a strong commodity orientation and, for coated woodfree papers, industry prices tended to serve as the basis for arriving at transaction prices. (See Exhibit 3 for information on industry prices and paper grades.) For sales to merchants, Leykam Mürztaler negotiated price lists, using the industry prices as a starting point, with final prices taking paper quality and other relevant factors into account. Price lists then remained in effect until there was a change in industry price levels. Routine orders were priced from the established price list. Large requirements, however, usually involved special negotiation.

According to one Leykam Mürztaler sales manager:

> We have some interesting discussions with our merchants about price. The customer knows we make a high quality product, so his principal interest is in getting it at the lowest possible price. In Europe there is no uniform classification of coated papers, as there is in the USA and Japan, so a standard approach is to try to get me to reclassify my product to a lower grade, and so a lower price. To some extent, though, my customer's preoccupation with price simply reflects price pressures he is experiencing from his customers. Still, it is frustrating because we believe we offer a lot more than just price and a good product. But I think we do a good job for the firm in getting the highest price possible.

BRANDING

In recent years, Leykam Mürztaler had followed the industry practice of branding its principal products. It did, however, supply products to certain merchants for private branding, a practice that was established when mill branding was not the norm. In 1988, some 30 percent of sales carried a merchant brand, largely reflecting the volume from Germany and the UK, where private branding was customary. Recently, however, the firm had started to identify most of its products by using a typical Leykam Mürztaler packaging, even for private labels.

Brands had been promoted primarily by the sales force, in direct contact with customers, using brochures and samples and by packaging. More recently, a series of superb visual messages was commissioned, using the theme "Dimensions in Paper" to suggest ways that high quality paper combined with printing could produce more effective communication. The script accompanying the visual messages was designed to appeal to both the advertisers, with emphasis on communication, and printers with emphasis on paper finish, touch, color, absorption, contrast and other key paper characteristics. On a limited basis, these messages had appeared in selected magazines and in brochures for customers.

There was general agreement within the firm that more emphasis needed to be placed on branding as a way to achieve product differentiation and convey the desired high quality image. There was less agreement on how much to spend promoting the brands or how to deal with merchants who were now buying Leykam Mürztaler products for sale under the merchants' labels. According to Gertrude Eder:

> Over the past few years we designed the corporate logo and corporate graphics and established blue, black and white as the colors for all corporate communication. We have worked hard to establish a consistent presentation of our corporate identity. Feedback from customers and the sales department indicated that this has helped improved our visibility and image. Nevertheless, we are currently spending considerably less than 1 percent of sales on advertising. Zanders, on the other hand, a firm of about our size, has been spending a lot of money on advertising for years and as a result has better visibility than we do, particularly with advertising agencies, as well as an enviable reputation for quality and service.
>
> I don't know what the right number is for us, but we will need to spend substantially more if we are to establish the kind of brand awareness and image we desire. I think that to have any significant impact would take a minimum of ASch3–4 million for classical advertising (i.e., advertising in trade publications, in various languages) and ASch8–10 million for promotions, including brochures, leaflets and trade fairs. In Western Europe we have to advertise in at least four to five languages, and sometime more. In addition, the nature of the ads varies. In private brand countries, our ads emphasize the company name and focus on the Dimensions in Paper theme as well as the company's experience and modern production facilities. In other countries we emphasize the MAGNO brand.
>
> We are convinced that printers want to know what mill brand they are buying. Also, we believe that there is some subjectivity in selecting paper, particularly by the advertiser, and we want to convince the advertiser that his message will come across better on Leykam Mürztaler paper.

The decision on supplying Leykam Mürztaler products for private branding was even more complex. As Wolfgang Pfarl commented:

> I understand the position of the merchants who want to offer a private brand. The fact remains, however, that it is the mill that determines product characteristics and is responsible for meeting specifications. It is really a question of who is adding the value. In my view the merchant ought to emphasize those things which he controls,

> such as local stocks, good sales representation and service. Putting a merchant label on paper produced by Leykam Mürztaler misrepresents the value added picture. Don't get me wrong. Our firm strongly believes in merchants. In fact, we avoid direct business whenever there are strong stocking merchants. It's just that we think mills and merchants have distinct roles to play, and they should not be confused.
>
> Currently, we will still produce for a merchant's label, but we have started to insist that it also is identified as Leykam Mürztaler. The merchants aren't very happy about this, but we think it's the right thing to do.

Nevertheless, the situation with respect to existing merchants was difficult. As one of the senior sales managers said:

> We have been supplying some of our merchants with paper to be sold under a private label for a long time, and they have invested substantial sums of money in establishing their own brands. I completely support the company's position on this, but I don't know how we can get the practice to change. If we insist on supplying products only under our own brand, there are alot of competitors who would, I think, be happy to step in and take our position with some merchants. If we can't convince a merchant to switch over to our brand, we could lose a lot of business, in one or two instances as much as 6,000 tonnes. On the other hand, if we aren't uniform on this, we will be unable to really exploit the potential of developing our own brands.

In addition to questions about branding policy, it was not clear how to capitalize on increased brand preference, if indeed it were achieved. As Wolfgang Pfarl said:

> We might want to think in terms of higher prices or increased share, or some combination. Exactly what we would do could vary from market to market.

PERSONAL SELLING

Contact with merchants and with large, directly served accounts in Europe was mainly made by the company's own sales force headquartered in Vienna, by sales representatives in subsidiary companies in Germany, Italy and France, and by sales agents in other markets (e.g., the UK). Direct sales representatives numbered twenty. Including clerical staff, Leykam has some sixty individuals in its sales department, most of whom had direct contact with customers.

The major activity of the sales force was making direct calls on large customers and on merchants. In addition, sales representatives made occasional calls on merchant's customers, generally accompanied by the merchant's sales representative. Objectives usually included negotiating long-term contracts, "selling" the existing product line, new product introduction, and a review of customer requirements for products and service.

It was the firm's belief that its sales force was a major asset and that sales representatives could significantly influence relations with merchants. A major objective for all Leykam Mürztaler representatives was to do everything possible to develop close relations with assigned merchants. According to Wolfgang Pfarl:

> The average age of our sales force is between thirty-five and forty, and most of the individuals have spent their entire career in sales with Leykam Mürztaler. They are

> really committed to serve the customer, with on-time deliveries or any other aspect of our relationship, and the customer really respects their high level of service. In addition, they are good negotiators and represent Leykam effectively during contract negotiations. They do not need to be technical experts, but they make sure that our technical people provide technical information as required. Also, they monitor shipping performance, make presentations to merchants and may make joint customer calls with merchant sales representatives.

Mathias Radon, one of the Vienna-based sales managers, made the following comments:

> In total we call on about one hundred merchants in Europe. I work with our sales offices in Italy, France and Belgium and handle five merchants personally in the UK, in cooperation with our representative there. I call on the merchants two to three times a year and have extensive phone contact with our sales offices and representatives from Vienna.
>
> In general, the customer wants to talk about quantity, price and service. We have conversations about private labelling. The new merchants would like us to give them private labels, but I think they know they can't get it. On the other hand, the ones to whom we are currently providing private labels don't want to give it up. The problem varies from country to country. In France, for instance, it's not such a big problem.
>
> One of my objectives is to encourage more stock business versus indent (merchant orders for direct mill shipment to the customer). This means we have to give them better service and provide back-up stocks.
>
> Some merchants handle mill brands that compete directly with Leykam Mürztaler, but most tend to do this under a private label.
>
> From time to time we work to develop a new merchant, but generally we work on building long-lasting relationships with existing merchants. We encourage trips by merchant personnel to the mill. I will make short presentations to merchant sales representatives when I call on the merchant, but generally they are pretty knowledgeable about paper. We've tried contests and other incentives with merchants and are still thinking about it, but I'm not sure if that's what we should do.
>
> From a quality standpoint, I try to stress whiteness, opacity, printability/runability and consistency. Lots of customers ask for lab figures, but I don't think you can rely just on lab reports. We have trial print runs every week by an independent printer to check our consistency. I think most printers feel the same way.
>
> We tend to have lots of small problems rather than any one large problem. Branding, for instance, pricing, friction when we appoint a new merchant and country variations with regard to ways of doing business. I think branding will be important in all countries, but how we capitalize on it may have to vary.

AFTER SALES SERVICE

Problems in printing could arise due to a number of circumstances. There might be variations or flaws in the paper or in the ink. Presses could develop mechanical problems. Even changes in temperature and humidity could negatively affect printing quality. Because of the complexity of the printing process, the cause of a problem was not always clear, and reaching an equitable settlement could be difficult.

When problems did arise, the printer turned to the merchant or mill for technical advice and frequently wanted financial compensation for lost production. According to Wolfgang Pfarl:

> When the printer encounters a production problem, it is important for us to be able to give him technical advice and work with him to solve the problem. Sometimes the sales representative can do this. More often, we have to involve one of our technical people from the mill. All too often, however, the printer is just looking for someone to compensate him financially, and we have to be very tough or we're likely to find ourselves paying for a lot other people's mistakes.

FUTURE ISSUES

Looking to the future, the firm was focusing its attention on managing "through the business cycle." As Wolfgang Pfarl put it:

> Our real challenge is to strengthen our market position in Western Europe. Most of our coated woodfree paper goes into advertising. We have seen extraordinary growth in this market in the last few years, but we have to expect there will a significant downturn in one or two years and that advertiser will then look intensely at their costs. In many cases this means the printer will suggest a lower cost grade as a substitute for coated woodfree. Our task is to differentiate MAGNO from the generic category and position it a "a paper for all seasons," so the speak. In other words, we want our customers to think of MAGNO as the "right" paper for high quality advertising, separately from woodfree.
>
> In general, this means strengthening our corporate identity, being partners of the strongest merchants and encouraging our merchants to support the MAGNO brand.

In a similar vein, Gertrude Eder commented:

> This is a business where the impact of the business cycle is made worse by the tendency of merchants to overstock in good times and destock in bad times. Our objective, I think, should be to position Leykam as the last mill the merchant or printer would think of canceling in a downturn.

ENDNOTES

This case was written by Professor H. Michael Hayes as a basis for class discussion rather than to illustrate either effective or ineffective handling of an administrative situation.

[1]ASch12.48 = $1.00 in December 1988.

[2]Western Europe included the countries in the European Community plus Finland, Norway, Sweden, Austria and Switzerland.

[3]Designated LWC or MWC, depending on the weight, although the dividing line was not precise.

[4]ECC International, Limited, 1987.

[5]Papis Limited.

[6]By BIS Marketing Research Limited.

[7]The European Printing and Writing Paper Industry - 1987, IMEDE Case No. GM 375.

[8]From a paper presented by BIS Marketing Research Limited.

Index

Abbott Laboratories, 255–56
ABC analysis of inventory items, 100
Academic publications, 151
Acceleration principle, 13
Accessory equipment, 16
Accountability, in forecasting, 196
Account executive, 411 table
Account representatives, 408 table
Accuracy, forecasting, 196
Action close, 423 table
Adaptability, in interview, 465 table
Adaptations
  required, 570
  versus standardization, 581
Adaptive control, 201, 202 table
Administrative concerns, and research, 146
Administrative costs, 173–74
Adoption-diffusion process
  business product, 242–44
  factors influencing rate of, 243–44
Adoption process, stages in, 242–43
Advantage, perceived, 243
Advertising, 478
  business, 483–95
  comparative, 619–20
  content of business, 494
  contribution of expenditures on to profit, 482 fig.
  differences between business and consumer, 484 table
  foreign controls on, 577
  of global clients, 583
  goals of business, 484–87
  how to ruin business, 489
  in-house, 496–97
  international, 507–08
  localized, 583
  responses to business, 506–07
  use of by service providers, 541
  value of, 506
Advertising agencies, 496–97
  use of, 494–95
Advertising Research Foundation (ARF), 506
Advertising specialties, 504–05
Advertising strategy, ethics and business, 618–20
Aerojet General, 105
Affordable technique, for setting budget, 481
Agencies
  advertising, 496–97
  international advertising, 507, 508 table
  use of advertising, 494–95
Agent, 67, 314–17
Air transport, 346 table, 348, 368
Alcoa, 266, 531
Allied Signal, 250
Alternate proposal close, 423 table
American Cancer Society, 513
American Cyanimid, 361
American Excelsior, 294
American Home Products Corporation, 255
American Hospital Supply, 191, 320, 631
American Marketing Association, 137, 604
  code of ethics of, 605–06 table
Analysis
  conjoint, 281
  cost-benefit, 274
  of market research, 144–45
Answering the objection, 421 table
Antitrust laws, 574
A-P-A Transport Corporation, 373–74
Apple Computer, 238, 239
Arlington Chamber of Commerce, 163–64
Armstrong World Industries, 320
Arthur Anderson and Company, 606
Arthur D. Little, 350
Assembly operations, 578–79
Assets, return on, 108
Asset turnover, 108
Assumptive close, 423 table
AST Research, Inc., 207
Atkinson, Bill, 238–39
Audio-visual aids, 418
Autocratic leadership style, 459 fig.
Autopsies, 225
Awareness, 242
  creating product, 484
  increasing through business advertising, 485
  research studies in, 159–60

Balance-sheet close, 423 table
Ball Corporation, 351
Banks, 318
Bargaining power, of buyers and sellers, 184
Bartering, 595
BASF Wyandotte, 249
Bechtel, 549
Bendix, 362
Benefits, of trade shows, 501
Benefit segmentation, 403
Benefit selling, 403
Bias
  in data, 156
  in sequence, 157
Bidding, 280
Bids, soliciting, 37
Birdybacking, 348
Blanket-order system, 101
Boeing, exporting by, 578
Boston Consulting Group, 245
Bottom-up method of forecasting, 197
Box-Jenkins, 201, 202 table
Brand preference, weakening in, 277
Branford and Sons, Inc., 642–48
Break-even analysis, 271
Breaking of bulk, 304
Bribes, 609, 616

Bristol-Myers, 255
Broadcast media, 488–89
Brokers, 317–18
Brown and Bigelow, 415
Budget
 developing promotional, 480–83
 trade show, 503
Build-up method of forecasting, 197, 446
Bundling, 285, 537
Business activity, changes in levels of, 241
Business analysis, 226
Business buyers
 objectives of, 81
 seven rights of, 81–82
Business buying
 price in, 90–91
 quality in, 85–88
 service in, 88–89
 situations of, 62–66
 who participates in, 400 table
Business channel strategy, 302
Business customers, 17–19
Business demand, characteristics of, 13–14
Business forces, 48
Business life cycles, 234–37
Business market
 difference from consumer market, 7–12
 increasing size of, 5
 leasing in, 285–87
 personal selling in, 396–97
 physical distribution in, 342–45
 segmenting, 178–80
Business marketing
 opportunities in, 6
 overview of, 4–5
 product strategy in, 220–21
 reasons for studying, 5–7
Business marketing research, 132–34
 major tasks of, 134–37
 process of, 143–45
Business pricing, 263
Business product portfolio classification, 244–48
Business products distributors, 309–14
Business publications, 488
Business purchasing, roles of buying center members in, 83 table
Business sale, cost to close, 402
Business sales titles, 411 table
Business schools, 455
Business selling
 career paths in, 410 fig.
 closing techniques of, 423 table
Business selling (*cont.*)
 international, 424–25
 seven deadly sins of, 424 table
 styles of, 412 table
 trends in, 412–18
Business services, 17
 characteristics of, 532–34
 marketing of, 528–29
Business-to-business organizations, 4
Buyer behavior, understanding, 402–06
Buyer needs
 methods to uncover, 404–05
 understanding, 403
Buyer-related bases, 544, 545
Buyers, 83 table, 182, 400 table
 advantages of leasing for, 286
 analyzing strengths of, 98–99
 bargaining power of, 184
 behavioral styles of, 405 table
 business, 8–9, 81–82
 changing role of, 47–50
 considerate, 405
 profile of business-to-business, 49–50
 understanding of technology by, 106–07
Buyer-seller relationship, 48, 405, 608–10
Buying
 in channel strategy, 303
 knowledge of motives for, 485–86
 motives of business, 50–53
 multiple influences on, 11
 professional, 10–11
 total cost of, 45
Buying behavior, nature of business, 14
Buying center, 82–85
 decisions makers in, 86 table
 variation in members of, 85
Buying decisions, environmental forces and, 102–07
Buying-decisions model, 406–07
Buying influences, 84 table
Buying personnel, and unethical sales practices, 609
Buying power, determinants of, 183 fig.
Buying process, 568
 business, 35–39

Capacity, 40–41
Career paths, in business selling, 410 fig.
Career planning, in interview, 466 table
Carle Instruments, 479
Cash cows, 245 fig., 246 table
Cash discounts, 289
Cash quadrant, 245
Catalogues, business, 490
Categorical plan, 41–42
Caterpillar Tractor, 91, 360, 578
Causal forecasting techniques, 201–03, 203 table
Census studies, 147
Centralization, 54–55
Centralized organization, versus decentralized, 441–42
Centralized purchasing, advantages of, 55
Centralized responsibility, 61
Centralized-stores system, 100–101
Central Maintenance and Welding, 89
Certified Purchasing Manager, 11
Chainco, 268
Channel alternatives, for foreign marketing, 586
Channel communication, 305
Channel conflict, 321–27
 legal perspective on, 324
Channel decisions
 international, 329–31
 nature of, 306
Channel intermediary
 functions of, 302–06
 use of, 540
Channel management, 305
Channel members, cooperative relationship with, 398
Channels
 combining direct and indirect, 318–19
 cooperation in, 319–21
 direct, 307–08
 indirect, 18, 308–18
 methods of cooperation, 320–21
Channels of distribution, 10
Channel structure, 589
Charity, 513
Chemical Bank, 617
Chemical Manufacturers Association, 611
Chrysler Corporation, 224
 and just-in-time, 362
Ciba Consumer Pharmaceuticals, 513
Cincinnati Milacron, 254–55
Citicorp, 538
Claims processing, 349
Clarifying the objection, 421 table
Clemson Meat Company, 428–29
Clients' rights, 611–12
Close, 419, 422
Closed bidding, 280

Closing techniques, 423 table
Clusters, classifying services by, 546–48
Coca-Cola Company, 190
  in Europe, 471
  in France, 626
Code of ethics, 604
Codependency, between buyers and sellers, 360
Coding, 144
Coherent Communications Systems, 595
Columbus-McKinnon Corporation, 327
Combination organizations, 444
COMDEX, 500, 501
Commercial enterprises, 18
Commercial sources, 151
Communication
  channel, 305
  management of, 399–400
Company knowledge, 451–52
Comparative advertising, 619–20
Compensation, 461–62
  of international salespeople, 466–67
Competing merchandise, 326
Competition, 181
  changes in product mix of, 240–41
  getting clues on from customers, 138
  impact on in U.S., 574
  in marketing, 630–31
  methods to counter price, 90
  and price, 264
  restrictions on foreign, 551
Competitive bidding, 279–84
Competitive environment, 104, 529, 531
Competitive knowledge, 453
Competitive parity technique, for setting budget, 481
Competitive situation, 539
Competitive structure, 589
Competitors, industry, 182
Computers, 234
  use of laptop, 417–18
Concept generation, 224–25
Conduct, unseemly, 424 table
Conference Board, The, 136
Confidences, failure to keep, 609
Confidentiality, and research, 146
Conflict management, 323
Conjoint analysis, 281
Conner Peripherals, 114–15
Considerate buyer, 405
Consultative selling, 412 table
Consulting firms, private, 454–55
Consultive leadership style, 459 fig.
Consumer marketing research, 132–34
Consumer markets
  differences from business markets, 7–12
  personal selling in, 396–97
Contests, 504–05, 618
Contract, 34, 66, 68
  issuing, 38–39
Contribution pricing, 268
Controller, 83
Cooperation, buyer-seller, 9–10
Corporate objectives, global, 588
Corporate responsibility, 604
Cost-based approaches, 588
Cost-benefit analysis, 274
Cost minimization, 581
Cost-ratio plan, 45–47
Costs
  administrative, 173–74
  to close business sale, 402
  inventory, 174
  of personal selling, 401–02
  per potential customer of trade shows, 501
  and price, 264–65
  production, 173
  promotion, 174
  reducing overall selling, 485
  reducing selling through advertising, 486
  total, 85
  total of purchasing decision, 90
  trade-offs against, 352–55
Country destinations, 574
Crafford Tool and Die Corporation, 194
Creative selling, 409
Credit assistance, 586
Crinshaw Company, 388–91
Cultural adiaphora, 570
Cultural dynamics, 568–71
Cultural exclusives, 570
Cultural imperatives, 570
Culture, dissimilarities in, 424
Cumulative discounts, 288
Currency
  fluctuations in, 290, 589
  restrictions on foreign, 551
Customer knowledge, 452–53
Customers
  business, 17–19, 566
  close contact with, 534
  ethics in dealing with, 616–17
  international, 19–20
  understanding buying behavior of, 82
Customer service, 351–56
  follow-up as, 422
  policy checklist, 354 table
Customer service (*cont.*)
  typical complaints, 353 table
Customer-size segments, 171
Customer specialization, 444
Custom Wheel Lights, Inc., 470–71

Dale Carnegie, 455
Data bank, 139
Database marketing system, 137
Database sources, 151–54
Data sheets, 490
Data sources
  primary, 156–58
  secondary, 146–56
Davis and Geck, 361
Dealer display rooms, 228
DeBeer's, 184
Decentralization, 54–55
Decentralized organization, versus centralized, 441–42
Deciders, 83 table, 400 table
Decision makers, in buying centers, 86 table
Decision making, 399
  unethical, 603
Decision process, differences in, 568
Decline phase, 278
Defense industry, 174
Delivery
  in just-in-time, 58
  reliability of, 89
Delphi method, 198–99, 200 table
Demand
  elastic, 273
  elasticity of, 539
  fluctuating, 13–14, 533
  inelastic, 273
  and price, 265
  price elasticity of, 272–74
  projection of, 193–96
  unitary, 273
Demand assessment, 272–74
Demand estimation, 170
Democratic leadership style, 459 fig.
Demonstrations, 586
Dependability, lack of, 424 table
Deregulation, 349–51
Derived demand, 13
Differentiation, through service, 88–89
Diffusion index, 201, 203 table
Diffusion process, 243
Direct channels, 307–08
Direct close, 423 table
Direct-financing lease, 287
Direct mail, 489
Direct marketing, 489–94
  global trends in, 585
Directories, industrial trade, 488
Direct-sales force, 586, 587

Distribution, 540, 622
exclusive, 329
intensive, 327–28
international, 368
physical in the business market, 342–45
positioning by, 188, 191
selective, 328–29
Distribution Centers, Inc., 359
Distribution channels, for business services, 540
Distribution element, of marketing mix, 305
Distribution system, managing international, 585–87
Distributor, business products, 309–14
District sales manager, 411 table
Diversification, 543
Divestment strategy, 249–50
Dogs, 245 fig., 246 table
Domestic agents, 330
Domestic laws, in foreign markets, 576–77
Domestic merchants, 330
Donovan, Newton, and Leisure, 549
Dow Chemical Company, 277, 368, 531, 636
and Sierra Club, 611
Dow Jones, 538
Down payment, 286
Dresser, 573
Drucker, Peter, 343
Dun and Bradstreet, 538
DuPont, 181, 249, 444, 531
and chlorofluorocarbons, 606, 611
partnership with advertising agencies, 498 table
and price skimming, 275
sales training by, 451

Eaton Corporation, 250
Econometrics, 201, 203 table
Economic activity, type of, 178
Economic development, stages of, 566–67
Economic environment, 103, 529, 530
Economic order quantity model, 364–65
Economic value, 270–71
Economies of scale, 235
Economy, borderless, 180
Effectiveness, measuring of promotion campaign, 506–07
80/20 axiom, 360, 399, 478
Elanco Products, 228 table
Elastic demand, 273
Elasticity of demand, 539
Electronic Data Interchange (EDI), 360–61
Electronic-ordering system, 101–02
Electro-Scientific Industries, 461
Emotional need, 403
Employees, ethics in dealing with, 617–18
Employment needs, temporary, 530
End use, of business goods, 14
Engineering
development of value, 92
and new-product development, 222
Engineers, 83, 84 table
sales, 408 table
Entertainment, 610, 617
Entrants
potential, 182
threat of new, 184
Entry, barriers to, 183 fig.
Entry strategies, for international business market, 577–79
Environmental analysis, 102, 103
Environmental factors
affecting pricing, 589–91
and buying decisions, 102–07
emphasis on, 530
Environmental scanners, 103
Environments
analysis of changing, 20–21
for business service firms, 529–32
competitive, 104, 529, 531
economic, 103, 529, 530
ethical, 105–07
international business, 567–75
legal, 532, 571–75
marketing, 102, 607
physical, 103–04
political, 532, 571–75
E.O.Q. model, 364–65
Epson Corporation, 311, 312
Equal Employment Opportunity Act, 415
Equipment, special for research, 145
Establishing readiness, 421 table
Ethical environment, 105–07
Ethics
and business advertising strategy, 618–20
in buyer-seller relationships, 608–10
complexity of international, 622
in dealing with customers, 616–17
in dealing with employees, 617–18
individuality of, 607
and international marketing, 620–22
and management of business pricing function, 612–15
and management of business sales force, 615–18
marketing, 603–07
Ethics (*cont.*)
in marketing research, 610–12
and strategy in marketing environment, 607
Europe, 585
Coca-Cola in, 471
Evaluation, 225–26, 243
Ex-Cell-O Corporation, 501
Exchange control, 551
Exchange rates, foreign, 589
Exclusive distribution, 329
Exclusive feature, 497, 499 table
Expected profit, 283
Expenditures
prioritizing promotional, 481–82
purchasing cost as percentage of, 82
Expense accounts, 618
Experience curves, 234–37
Expertise, 145
Expert power, 407, 408
Exponential smoothing, 200–201, 202 table
Export controls, 574
Exporting, 330, 577–78
Export intermediates, 586
Exports, 565
Export Trading Company Act, 575
Exxon Valdez, 585

Fabricated and component parts, 16
Fabric Studio, The, 25–26
Face-to-face activities, 419–22
Facilitating agencies, 318
Family considerations, in interview, 465 table
Farmland Industries, 285
Federal antitrust statute, 614
Federal Express
and distribution, 191
and service positioning, 191–92
television advertising by, 489
Feedback, 325–26
Females, increasing number as buyers, 49
Field operations, for marketing research, 144
Field sales training, 454
Financial, in interview, 466 table
Financial services, 530
Financing, in channel strategy, 304
Find S.V.P. Incorporated, 541
First Interstate Trading Corporation, 595
Fishybacking, 348
Five-force model, 182
Fluctuating demand, 13–14, 533
F.O.B. destination, 348
F.O.B. origin, 348
Follow-up, 145, 422–24

Ford Motor Company, 225
  exporting, 578
Forecasting, 136–37
  accountability in, 196
  build-up method of, 197, 446
  causal, 201–03
  common problems in, 195–96
  for decision making, 193–94
  implementation of, 196
  mystique of, 196
  qualitative approaches to, 197–99, 200 table
  quantitative approaches to, 199–203
  selecting methods of, 196–203
Foreign Corrupt Practices Act, 575, 620
Foreign investment, climate for, 572
Foreign markets, domestic laws in, 576–77
Foreign sales corporations, 574–75
Formularized (AIDA) model, 406
Forum Company, 455
France, Coca-Cola in, 626
Franchising, 579
Fruehauf Trucking Company, 126–27
Functional organization, 440, 441 fig.

Gallo Wine Company, 208
Games, 504
Gannett, 538
Gatekeepers, 83 table, 400 table
General Agreement on Tariffs and Trade (GATT), 551, 576
General Dynamics, 174
General Electric, 442
  and Electronic Data Interchange, 361
  exporting, 578
  and telemarketing, 413
  and trade directories, 488
  use of computers by, 417
  and value analysis, 91
General Foods, 444
Generalists, 307
General-line distributors, 309
General Motors, 10
  exporting, 578
  and just-in-time, 362
  and rate of return, 266
  Saturn Division of, 430–31
  and shipping for just-in-time, 363 table
General purchasing department, 53
General sales manager, 411 table
General Telephone and Telegraph, 535
General Trailer Company, 123–24
Geographical price adjustments, 289
Geographic location, 40, 178
Geographic segments, 171
Geographic specialization, 442, 443 fig.
Gift close, 423 table
Gifts, 609, 617
Gillette Company, in Iran, 594–95
Global events, in marketing, 631
Goals
  of business advertising, 484–87
  influencing buying decisions, 53 fig.
  of salespersons versus sales manager, 438
Goods and services, classification of business, 14–17
Government
  hand of, 604
  home country, 571
  in marketing, 631
  in restricting growth of services, 552
Governmental organizations, 18–19
Governmental sources, 147, 151
Grease money, 621
Grey markets, 589
Growth, 445
Growth phase, 277
Growth rate matrix, 245

Hard bargainer, 405
Harper Group, The, 361
Harvesting strategy, 249
Health, in interview, 465 table
Henderson, Bruce, 244
Hertz, 549
  franchising, 579
Heterogeneity, 534
Hewlett-Packard, 234
  television advertising by, 489
  and value-based strategy, 270
High mass consumption, age of, 567 table
Hitachi, 578
Holiday Inn, 549
  franchising, 579
Home country government, 571
Home office sales training, 454
Honeywell Corporation, 535
Horizontal publications, 487–88
Host country government, 571
House accounts, 325
Hudson Valley Tree Company, 295–96
Humor, as sales tool, 420
Hunt-Wesson Foods, 34–35
Hyatt, 540
HyperCard, 238–39

IBM, 51, 442
  and bundling strategy, 285
IBM (*Cont.*)
  and compensation, 467
  effects of advertising on selling efforts, 486 table
  entry strategies of, 577
  exporting, 578
  foreign earnings of, 566
  and foreign sales training, 466
  image of, 191
  manufacturing by, 578
  marketing strategy of, 173
  in Mexico, 159, 572
  and price leadership, 278
  and product life-cycle model, 234
  television advertising by, 489
  use of Delphi method by, 199
Iceberg pricing, 285
Idea generation, 224–25
Image
  improving advertiser's, 485
  positioning by, 188, 190–91
Implementation, of forecasting, 196
Income levels, 589
Inconsistency, in forecasting, 196
Incremental method, 446–47
Indirect channel intermediaries, 330–31
Indirect channel members, 18
Indirect channels, 308–18
Industrial distributor, 309–14
Industrialization, differing degrees of, 566
Industrial traffic function, 342
Industry structure, elements of, 183 fig.
Inelastic demand, 13, 273
Inflation rates, 589–90
Influencers, 82, 83 table, 400 table
Information flow, 451
Information retailers, 541, 542
Information sources, developing, 146–58
Ingersoll-Rand, 309
Inmac, 185, 186
Input-output analysis, 202, 203 table
Inspection, of delivered goods, 39
Installations, 15
Institutions, 19
Intangibility, 532–33
Intensive distribution, 327–28
Interdependence, of business-to-business firms, 6
Interest, 242
Intermediaries, indirect-channel, 330–31
Intermodal transport, 346 table, 348
International business environment, 567–75
International business market
  entry strategies for, 577–79

International business market (*cont.*)
pricing in, 587–91
product strategy in, 579–82
International business selling, 424–25
International channel decisions, 329–31
International customers, 19–20
International distribution, 368
International law, 575
International marketer, profile of ideal, 571 fig.
International marketing
of business services, 549–52
ethics and, 620–22
managing U.S. salespeople in, 464–67
promotional strategy for, 507–09
risks for service organizations, 550–51
scope and challenge of, 565–67
International Monetary Fund (IMF), 576
International positioning strategy, 580–81
International promotion effort, managing, 582–85
International salespeople, interview for, 465–66 table
International Standards Organization, 576
International trade, without direct pricing, 595–96
Interpretation, of market research, 144–45
Interviews
adaptability in, 465 table
for international candidates, 465–66 table
personal, 156
selection, 448
Introduction phase, 275–77, 419
Inventory
ABC analysis of, 100
control of, 360–65
under just-in-time, 60
lack of in business service, 533
techniques to control, 364
Inventory costs, 174
Inventory levels, 325
Invisible hand, 604
Iran, Gillette Company in, 594–95
Itel Distribution Systems, 372–73

Japan, 585, 620
dealing with media in, 512
expectation of salespeople in, 464
Job analysis, 447
Jobbers, 309
Job description, written, 447–48
Jobs, changing, 618
Job skill requirements, of sales manager, 439
Job specification, 447
John Deere and Company, 360, 578
Joint demand, 14
Joint ventures, 578
Jury of executive opinion, 197–98, 200 table
Just-in-time (JIT), 9, 40, 57–61, 361–64
location in, 58
planning shipping for, 363 table
J. Walter Thompson, 549

Kanban, 61
Kiting, 618
Klockner Group, 580
Knowledge
company, 451–52
competitive, 453
customer, 452–53
product, 452
Knowledge explosion, 104, 630
Kodak, and foreign sales training, 466

Laboratory of Advertising Performance, 401
Laissez-faire leadership style, 459 fig.
Language, differences in, 424
Language ability, in interview, 465 table
Language barrier, 164
Laptop computers, use of, 417–18
Law of agency, 66, 67
Laws
domestic in foreign markets, 576–77
international, 575
Leadership
deadly sins of, 460 table
golden rules of, 460 table
providing, 458–59
by sales manager, 437
Leading indicators, 201, 203 table
Learning curve analysis, 234–35
Learning International, 454, 455, 456
Leasing, 12
in business market, 285–87
Legal considerations, 146
in pricing, 267–68
Legal environment, 532, 571–75
Legal-political environment, 105
Legal services, 530
Leykam Mürztaler, 648–66
Licensing, 578, 586
Life cycle
business, 234–37
of service product, 539
Life-cycle analysis, 202, 203 table
Life-cycle costing, 275–78
Limited-line distributors, 309
Lincoln Electric, 90
Line and staff organization, 440, 441 fig.
Line-extension strategy, 543
Line organization, 440
Line simplification strategy, 249
Links, 139
Local sales training, 454
Location, in just-in-time, 58
Lockheed Corporation, 225, 595, 620
Loctite Corporation, 83
Logistical management, 343
Logistical service levels, 356
Logistics services, third-party, 372
Lotus, 239, 581
Lovelock, Christopher H., 546
Loyalty, 51
Lying, 609

McDonnell Douglas, 615
negative publicity, 499
MacFarlane and Company, Inc., 541
McGraw-Hill Research Department, 402
McIlhenny Company, 380–87
Macroeconomic forces, 180
Macro/micro segmentation, 175
Mail, direct, 489
Mail order, marketing view of business, 491
Mail surveys, 157
Maintenance, repair, and operating (MRO) supplies, 16–17
Maintenance selling, 409
Major equipment, 15
Make-buy decision, 36
Make-or-buy analysis, 94–96
in research, 145–46
Management
conflict, 323
hand of, 604
logistical, 343
Management consultant, 321
Manpower, franchising, 579
Manufacture, reasons to, 95–96
Manufacturer-intermediary relationship, problem areas in, 324–27
Manufacturers Hanover Corporation, 72
Manufacturers' representative, 314–17
Manufacturing, 578
Manufacturing attitude, 532
Marginal pricing, 268–70
Margins, higher, 189
Market aggregation, 172

Market characteristics, 136
Market competitive analysis, 182–84
Market demand, 195
Market development, 543
Market-extension strategy, 543
Market factor, 194, 241–42
Market forecast 195
Market growth, 236
Market index, 194
Market information, in channel strategy, 305
Marketing
  business, 4–7, 220–21
  of business services, 528–29, 535–44
  competition in, 630–31
  direct, 489–94
  ethics in, 603–07
  future trends in, 629–33
  government in, 631
  international business services, 549–52
  international and ethics, 620–22
  management of, 171
  partnership in, 313
  product strategy in business, 220–21
  promotional strategy for international, 507–09
  scope and challenge of international, 565–67
  service versus product, 535–36
Marketing environment, 102
  strategy and ethics in, 607
Marketing expertise, in service sector, 548
Marketing information systems, 325–26
  basic elements of future, 139–40
  versus marketing research, 137–42
  primary uses of, 140–42
  sources of input to, 141 fig.
Marketing managers, and new-product development, 222
Marketing mix
  for business buyers and consumers, 396
  service strategy and, 537–41
Marketing planning and strategy, 20–21
Marketing pricing policy, international, 289–90
Marketing promotion, 533
Marketing research
  conducting international, 159–60
  differences between business and consumer, 132–34
  ethics in, 610–12
  major tasks of business, 134–37
  organization of business, 158–59
Marketing research (*cont.*)
  versus marketing information system, 137–42
  process of business, 143–45
Marketing strategy
  and buyer perceptions of problems, 89
  concentrated, 174
  in different buying situations, 65 fig.
  differentiated, 173–74
  undifferentiated, 172–73
Marketing vice president, 411 table
Market maturity, 236–37
Market penetration, 275, 543
Market-penetration pricing, 276–77
Market position, planned for service product, 539
Market potential, 134, 194–95
Market-price level, 279
Market profitability analysis, 182
Market pull, 223
Markets
  analysis of, 171
  consumer, 7–12, 396–97
  creating a promotional plan for, 479
  domestic laws in foreign, 576–77
  international business, 577–82, 587–91
  segmenting business, 178–80
  similarity of, 181
  strategies for segmentation of, 172–74
Market sales manager, 411 table
Market saturation, 277
Market segmentation, approaches to, 174–77
Market segments, 589
  evaluating potential, 181–84
Market share, 195
  as objective, 266
Market-share analysis, 134–36
Market skimming, 275
Markup percentages, traditional, 263
Marriott Corporation, 538, 549
Massey-Ferguson, 181, 360
Materials acqusition-retention cycle, 81
Materials management, 56–61
Maturity, drive to, 567 table
Maturity phase, 277
Mayflower Moving and Storage, 124
Mazda Motor Corporation, 104
Media
  broadcast, 488–89
  options in foreign countries, 582
  print, 487–88
  selection of, 487–94
Media mix, 487
Medtronic, 226
Mentally formulating the order, 421 table
Merck-DuPont joint venture, 26–27
Merisel, Incorporated, 335–36
Merrill Lynch, 538
Mexico, IBM in, 159, 572
Microelectronics and Computer Technology Corporation, 630
Micro Motion, 362, 363 table
Microsales analysis, 136
Middlemen, use of foreign-based, 586
Midland Bank, 596
Missionary sales, 320, 409
Mixed distribution system, 318
Models, 139
Modified-rebuy buying, 66
Monsanto, 611
Moonlighting, 617–18
Morale, improving, 451
Moral principle, 573
Morlock Manufacturing Company, 71
Motivation
  in interview, 465 table
  of sales force, 458–62
  satisfaction as, 462
Motivator, financial incentive as, 461
Motives
  of business buying, 50–53
  knowledge of buying, 486
Motor Carrier Act, 351
Motorola, 88
Motor transport, 346–47
Moving average, 199–200, 202 table
Muffco, 238, 240
Multidimensional scaling (MDS), 186
Multiple sourcing, 52
Mystique, of forecasting, 196

National account sales manager, 411 table
National Association of Purchasing Management, 49, 608
National Cash Register Corporation, 95, 185, 444
  and compensation, 467
  and foreign sales training, 466
National chauvinism, 552
National income, service industries as percent of, 552
National Peach Council, 636–40
National sales manager, 411 table
National Semiconductor, 316
NEC Corporation, 207
Need, recognizing, 36
Negotiation, 96–99, 412 table
  complex, 11
  fundamentals of successful, 98 fig.

Nested approach, to market segmentation, 175–77
New-business strategy, 543, 544
New-product committee approach, 230–31
New-product department approach, 231–32
New-product development, 220, 221 fig., 221–29
  ideas for from autopsies, 225
  important attributes of, 223–24
  in service industry, 538
New-product effort, organization by, 230–32
New-product pricing strategies, 275–77
New-product venture team, 232
New-service development, 541–44
New-task buying, 63–65
New Zealand, 577
Niche, 185
Noncumulative discounts, 288
Nondisclosure rule, 149
Nonprice factors, 90
Northern Chemical Company, 112–14
Northern New Jersey Manufacturing Company, 518–20
Not-for-profit marketing organization, 544

Objectives
  global corporate, 588
  setting, 455
  setting for promotional plan, 479–80
  trade show, 503
Obsolescence, of secondary data, 154
Occidental Chemical Company, 636
Occupational Safety and Health Administration, 640
OEMs, 18
Ohno, Taüche, 60
One-more-yes close, 423 table
On-line vendor, 152, 153
Open bidding, 280
Operating capacity, 241
Operating economies, 174
Operating lease, 287
Optimism, unlimited, 424 table
Optimization, 139
Order processing, 366–68
Organizations
  business-to-business, 4
  centralized, 441–42
  combination, 444
  functional, 440, 441 fig.
  governmental, 18–19
  size of, 178

Orientation, of international salespeople, 466
Overselling, 609
Ownership, avoiding risk of, 286

Paccar, 190
Paper Mate, 7
Partnered selling, 313
Partnership marketing, 313
Partnershipping, 47
Peat-Marwick, 490
Peerless Trucking Company, 126
PepsiCo Incorporated, 190
Perceived value, 90–91
Percentage of sales, technique for setting budget, 481
Perceptual mapping, 185–87
Performance considerations, 40
Perishability, 533
Perrier Limited, 334–35
Per se violations, 614
Persoft, 239
Personal selling, 418–24
  in business and consumer markets, 396–97
  cost of, 401–02
  profile of, 397–400
Persuader, 205, 459 fig.
Petty cash system, 101
Pfizer, 580
Phoenix Laser Systems, Inc., 627
Physical distribution
  in business market, 342–45
  management of, 305, 343
Physical environment, 103–04
Physical supply, 343
Piggybacking, 348
Pipeline transport, 346 table, 348
Place, 537, 540
Planning, 399
  poor, 424 table
Planning function, of channel members, 320
Plantations Plastics, 450
Plant controller, 84 table
Plant manager, 83, 84 table
Plant visits, 40
Playing the odds, 52
Political conditions, 181
Political considerations, 146
Political environment, 532, 571–75
Political-legal environment, 529, 532
Political risks, 159, 571
Politics, 573
Positioning, 170
  of business products, 187–93
  by image, 188, 190–91
Positioning strategy, 536–37
  getting started on, 192–93
  international, 580–81

Posttesting, 506
Precision Industries, 412
Pre-conditions for take-off, 567 table
Predatory pricing, 268
Preliminary activities, 419
Preparation, for marketing research, 144
Presentation stage, 419
Press conference, 497, 499 table
Press kits, 497, 499 table
Press release, 497, 499 table
Pretesting, 506
Price, 537, 539–40, 622
  in business buying, 90–91
  competition and, 264
  conflict in regard to, 323
  costs and, 264–65
  demand and, 265
  exchanging information on, 267
  positioning by, 188, 189–90
  practicing discrimination with smaller accounts, 613–14
  relationship with quality, 190
  setting fair, 613
Price adjustments, geographical, 289
Price controls, 590–91
Price elasticity, of demand, 272–74
Price fixing, 267, 614
Price leadership strategy, 278–79
Price planning, 263
Price positioning, 189
Price skimming, 275–76
Price strategy, factors influencing, 264–68
Price Waterhouse, 549
Pricing
  business, 263
  company factors affecting, 588
  contribution, 268
  environmental factors affecting, 589–91
  foreign laws and, 577
  iceberg, 285
  in international business market, 587–91
  legal considerations in, 267–68
  marginal, 268–70
  market factors affecting, 589
  market-penetration, 276–77
  methods of, 268–72
  predatory, 268
  return-on-investment, 271–72
  target return-on-investment, 271–72
Pricing function, ethics and management of business, 612–15
Pricing objectives, 265–66
Pricing policies
  in business pricing strategy, 288–89
  international marketing, 289–90

Primary data, 146
Print media, 487–88
Prioritizing
  promotional expenditure, 481–82
  target audience, 482
Private marketing organization, 544
Private transportation, 349
Private warehouse, 358–59
Prizes, use of, 505
Probabilistic bidding model, 281–84
Problem recognition and definition, 143
Problems, buyer perceptions of, 89
Problem-solving model, 407–08
Processing, of market research, 144
Process materials, 16
Procurement function, 180
Product adaptation, 581
Product commercialization, 229
Product development, 226, 543
Product introduction, 236
Production capability, extent of, 566
Production costs, 173
Production manager, 83, 84 table
Production schedules, in just-in-time, 59
Productivity, increases in, 531
Product knowledge, 452
  lack of, 424 table
Product management approach, 230
Product manager, 230
  duties of, 231 table
Product marketing, versus service marketing, 535–36
Product mix, determinants of, 237–42
Product modification costs, 173
Product portfolio, 244–46
  strategies of, 246–48
Product positioning strategy, 185–93
Product promotions, 498
Products, 537–39, 622
  adoption-diffusion process of, 242–44
  breakdown of logistical cost for, 357 fig.
  deletion strategy of, 248–50
  development of new, 220, 221 fig., 221–29
  foreign laws and, 576–77
  improving knowledge of, 451
  life-cycle analysis of, 233–37
  nature of exported, 574
  positioning of business, 187–93
  pricing across life cycle of, 275–78
  supplying information about through advertising, 485
Product sales manager, 411 table
Product segments, 171
Product specialization, 442–44
Product standardization, 581
Product strategy
  in business marketing, 220–21
  international, 250
  in international business market, 579–82
Product testing, 228
Product usage, 180
Product-use tests, 228
Professional publications, 488
Professionals, 548
Professional trainers, 454–55
Profit
  contribution of advertising expenditures to, 482 fig.
  expected, 283
  impact of purchasing on, 107–09
  as percentage of sales, 107
Profitability
  ascertaining, 94–95
  effect of training on, 455
Profit marketing organization, 544
Profit maximization, 265, 581
  over entire relationship, 59
Promotion, 537, 541, 622
  business sales, 499–505
  cause-related, 513
  creating a plan for business markets, 479
  determining and implementing mix of, 483–505
  developing budget for, 480–83
  following up and modifying, 507
  foreign laws and, 577
  global sales, 584
  international sales, 508–09
  marketing, 533
  measuring effectiveness of, 506–07
  overview of, 478–79
  prioritizing expenditures for, 481–82
  product, 498
  setting objectives for, 479–80
  strategy for international markets, 507–09
Promotional aid, 321
Promotional considerations, 146
Promotion costs, 174
Promotion effort, managing international, 582–85
Publications, 151, 487–88
Publicity, 478
  business, 495–99
  global, 585
  international, 508–09
  techniques to secure, 497–99
Public marketing organization, 544
Public warehouse, 358–59
Purchase decision, 37
Purchase phase, 82
Purchase responsibilities, segmentation by, 177
Purchase situation, 82
Purchase volume, 8
Purchasing
  basic policies and procedures of, 34–35
  costs of, 82
  functions that report to, 50 fig.
  impact of on company profit, 107–09
  and the law, 66–68
  reasons for separate department for, 54
  responsibilities of, 87–88
  who it reports to, 51 fig.
Purchasing agent, 84 table
Purchasing decision, total cost of, 90
Purchasing executive, profile of, 49
Purchasing organization, 53–55
Purchasing personnel, performance of, 48
Purchasing-sales interchange, 66
Pushiness, 424 table

Qualifications, sales job, 448
Qualitative approaches to forecasting, 197–99, 200 table
Quality
  altering without changing price, 613
  in business buying and selling, 85–88
  positioning by, 188, 190
  product, 90
  relationship with price, 190
  of service, 534
Quality control department, 39, 534
  in just-in-time, 58
Quality positioning, 190
Quantitative approaches to forecasting, 199–203
Quantity discounts, 288–89
Question marks, 245 fig., 246 table
Questionnaire construction, 144
Quick response, 360
Quote, using competitor's, 614

Rail transport, 346 table, 347, 368
Ramada Inn, 549
Rand Corporation, 198
Rating, factors in, 42 fig.
Raw materials, 17
Reciprocity, 11, 614–15, 617
Recruitment, 447–48
  technical, 530
Referent power, 408
Regional integration, 180
Regional sales manager, 411 table
Regression, 201, 203 table

Relationship
in just-in-time, 59
of sales manager, 439
Relationship marketing, 47–48, 59
Remington Arms Company, 574
Replacement parts, availability of, 88
Reporting, of marketing research, 145
Reputation, positive, 541
Reputation research studies, 159–60
Resale price maintenance, 577
Research
analysis of market, 144–45
business marketing, 132–37, 143–45
conducting international marketing, 159–60
confidentiality and, 146
consumer marketing, 132–34
ethics in marketing, 610–12
organization of business marketing, 158–59
preparation for market, 144
process of business marketing, 143–45
right to be informed of results of, 611
using inside specialists for, 145–46
using outside specialists for, 145–46
Research consortia, 630
Research design, planning, 143
Researchers' rights, 612
Research studies, marketing, 530
Residual value, 287
Resourcefulness, in interview, 465 table
Responsibility
corporate social, 604–06
of sales manager, 438–39
Return on assets, 108
Return on investment, 265–66
Return-on-investment pricing, 271–72
Rhode Island Hospital, 344
RIBCO Industries, 441
Risks
of international marketing for service organizations, 550–51
perceived, 243
political, 159, 571
spreading, 52
Risk taking, in channel strategy, 305
Rivalry, 184
determinants of, 183 fig.
Robertshaw Controls Company, 520–24
Robinson-Patman Act, 267, 288, 613
Rockwell International, 307
Routing, 348
Rules and regulations, 105
Ryder, 350

Safety, growing emphasis on, 530
Sales
cost to close business, 42
decline in, 237
increased, 286
missionary, 409
profit as percentage of, 107
promotion for business, 499–505
support, 409
Sales activities, specialization by, 442
Sales agents, 317–18
Sales analysis, 136
Sales branch, 307
Sales calls, scheduling of, 399
Sales development, 409
Sales force
costs of, 401 table
determining size of, 444–47
directing and motivating, 458–62
ethics and management of business, 615–18
evaluation of, 462–64
staffing, 444–49
training and developing, 450–58
Sales-force composite, 198, 200 table
Sales forecast, 195
Sales function
promotion to assume the, 479
promotion to support, 478
Sales job facilitator, 405
Sales job qualifications, 448
Sales management
leadership by, 437
selecting, 437–39
Sales organizations, basic types of, 439–44
Salespeople, 408 table, 411 table
characteristics of, 406 table
international, 465–66
managing in international markets, 464–67
missionary, 320
perspective on selling process, 418–24
Sales positions, types of, 408–12
Sales potential, 195, 446
Sales presentation, approaches to business, 406–08
Sales promotion. *See* Promotion.
Sales quotas, 459–61
Sales resistance, handling, 421 table
Sales staff, building into a team, 457
Sales tasks, 409
Sales team, 396
Sales territory, 453
Sales training
evaluating, 455–58
purposes of, 450–51
Sales training department, 454
Sales vice president, 411 table
Sales volume, 8
Sales-volume base, 307–08
Saleswoman, emergence of, 414–16
Sample size, 144
Sandia National Laboratories, 88, 234
SAS, 556–57
Satisfaction
as motivator, 462
of sales manager, 439
Saturn Division, 430–31
Say's Law, 223
Screening, 225–26
Sealed Air Corporation, 92
Secondary data
evaluating, 155 fig.
sources of, 146–56
Segmentation, 170
approaches to market, 174–77
benefit, 403
general market strategy for, 171–72
international, 180–81
macro/micro, 175
nested approach to, 175–77
strategies for business market, 172–74
variables for organizational markets, 179 fig.
Selection, of salespeople for international markets, 464
Selection process, 447, 448–49
Selective distribution, 328–29
Self-regulation, 611
Seller
advantages of leasing for, 286
analyzing strengths of, 98–99
Seller-related bases, 544, 545 fig.
Selling, 398
benefit, 403
business, 410 fig., 412 table, 424–25
in channel strategy, 303
consultative, 412 table
cost of personal, 401–02
creative, 409
emphasis on personal, 12
international business, 424–25
maintenance, 409
partnered, 313
personal, 418–24
personal in business and consumer markets, 396–97
profile of personal, 397–400
service, 409
systems, 412 table

Selling (*cont.*)
team, 412 table
trends in business, 412–18
Selling process, personal, 418–24
Selling spectrum, 406–12
Selling styles
contemporary, 410
types of, 408–12
Selling techniques, 452
Service, 324–25
availability of, 90
as competitive effort, 89
differentiation through, 88–89
marketing of business, 535–44
positioning by, 188, 191–93
quality of, 534
types of businesses, 549 fig.
Service firms, environments for business, 529–32
Service industry, new-product development in, 538
Service marketing, versus product marketing, 535–36
Service-related bases, 544, 545–46
Services
barrers to trade in, 551–52
bundling of, 537
business, 17
in business buying and selling, 88–89
characteristics of business, 532–34
classification of, 544–49
classifying by clusters, 546–48
financial, 530
future for business, 552–53
international marketing of, 549–52
legal, 530
marketing of, 552
marketing of business, 528–29
marketing internationally, 581–82
people-based versus equipment-based, 548–49
production and consumption of, 533–34
summary of models for classifying, 546–47 table
supplying information about through advertising, 485
Service salespeople, 408 table
Service sector, 528
importance of, 6
marketing expertise in, 548
Service selling, 409
Service strategy, and marketing mix, 537–41
SHANEX, 136
Share-building strategy, 543
Share/growth matrix, 245
Shell Oil Company, 636
Sheraton, 550
Sherman Antitrust Act, 267, 614
Sherman Brothers Trucking, 124–25
Shipping expenses, 586
Sierra Club, and Dow Chemical Company, 611
Signode Industries, 232
Simultaneity, 533–34
Single sourcing, in just-in-time, 59
Size, of company, 53–54
Skilled labor, 250, 548
Small-order problem, 99–102
Smith-Kline Diagnostics, 96
Social-cultural differences, 569
Socialize, 405
Social unrest, potential, 159
Societal-cultural environment, 529, 530–31
Society's rights, 611
Sorting, in channel strategy, 304
South Africa, 159, 623
Specialists, 307
Specialization, 586
geographic, 442, 443 fig.
organizing by, 442–44
trend toward, 313
Specialties, advertising, 504–05
Specifications, developing product, 37
Sperry Univac, 223
Squibb, 466
Stake Fastener Company, 317
Standard Industrial Classification (SIC) Code, 147, 149, 178
Standardization, adaptation versus, 581
Standard Oil of New Jersey, 489
Stars, 245 fig., 246 table
Statistical Abstract of the United States, 153 table
Steelcase, 191
Steiger Tractor Company, 104
Storage, in channel strategy, 304
Straight rebuy buying, 65–66
Straight shooter, 405
Strategic business unit, 244
Strategic partnerships, 47
Strategy
advertising, 618–20
business product deletion, 248–50
concentrated marketing, 174
entry, 577–79
and ethics in marketing environment, 607
factors influencing price, 264–68
harvesting, 249
international positioning, 580–81
Strategy (*cont.*)
international product, 250
line-extension, 543
line simplification, 249
market-extension, 543
marketing, 65 fig., 89, 172–74
new-business, 543, 544
new-product pricing, 275–77
positioning, 192–93, 536–37
price leadership, 278–79
product, 220–21
product in international business market, 579–82
product positioning, 185–93
Strategy development, 224
Strong Tool Company, 457
Style, management, 458–59
Substitute products, threat of, 184
Substitutes, 182
Substitution threat, determination of, 183 fig.
Supplier-customer relationship, 9–10
Supplier involvement, in just-in-time, 59
Supplier power, determinants of, 183 fig.
Suppliers, 182
bargaining power of, 184
Support sales, 409
Support services, 326
Survey of buyer intentions, 198, 200 table
Surveys
comparing methods of, 157 table
mail, 157
telephone, 156
Sweepstakes, 504
Sylvania, 104
Systems interrogation, 139
Systems selling, 412 table, 413

Tabulation, of market research, 144–45
Take-off, 567 table
Target audiences
identifying, 483 fig.
prioritizing, 482
Task and objective technique, for setting budget, 481
Taxation, power of, 574
Tax benefits, of leasing, 286
Tax treaties, 575
Tax treatment of business goods, 14
Team selling, 412 table
Technical assistance, 88, 324–25
Technical recruitment, 530
Technological environment, 104–05, 529, 531–32

Technological uncertainty, 244
Technology, 237–40
  advances in, 180
  in marketing, 629–30
  positioning by, 188, 189
  understanding of by buyers, 106–07
Technology push, 222–23
Telecommunication, in just-in-time, 58–59
Telemarketing, 413–14, 491
  in the future, 631–32
Telephone surveys, 156
Temporary employment needs, 530
Test marketing, 228
Texas Instruments, 189, 277
Thomas Register of American Manufacturers, 488
3M Corporation, 225, 233, 470
  and intensive distribution, 327
  and value-based strategy, 270
Time, management of, 453
Time-series techniques, 199–201, 202 table
Time wasting, 424 table
Timken Roller Bearing Company, 489
Top-down method of forecasting, 197
Total cost, 85
  of purchasing decision, 90
Touche-Ross, 540
Toyota, 60
Trade, barriers to in international market, 551–52
Trade deficit, 550
Trade directories, industrial, 488
Trade discounts, 288, 309
Trade-off analysis, 352
Trade-offs, cost, 352–55
Trade publications, 151
Trade Show Bureau, 502
Trade shows, 228, 499–503
  abroad, 584
  benefits of, 501
  selecting, 503
Traditional approach, to materials management, 57
Traditional society, 567 table
Traffic management, 345–49
Training, 326
  evaluating sales, 455–58
  of international salespeople, 466
  purposes of, 450–51
  sales force, 450–58
  what it should cover, 451–53
  who should do, 453–55
Transactional process, 323
Transfer price policies, 588
Transnational agencies, 571
Transportation
  in channel strategy, 304
  modes of, 345–48
Treaties of friendship, commerce, and navigation, 575
Trend fitting, 199, 202 table
Trial, 243
Truck, 368
Trus Joist Corporation, 119–28
Truth in advertising, 619
Turnkey operations, 579
Turnover, expected, 445–47
Tuttle Corporation, 213–15

Uncertainty, reducing, 51
UNCITRAL, 576
Union Carbide, 620
  in Bhopal, 578, 585
  negative publicity, 499
Uniroyal, 103
Unitary demand, 273
Unskilled labor, 548
Upjohn, 513
U.S. and Foreign Commercial Service, 330
User-customers, 18
Users, 83 table, 400 table
User segments, 171
U.S. laws, 574
U.S. Steel, 278

Vallen Corporation, 368
Valmont Industries, 417
Value, perceived, 90–91
Value analysis, 91–94
  in just-in-time, 59
Value-based strategy, 270
Value engineering, development of, 92
Vendor analysis, 37
Vendor performance, evaluating, 39
Vendor rating approaches, 41–47
Vendor rating sheet, 37, 38 fig.
Vendors, evaluating potential, 40–47
Vendor stocking, 368
Vendor visitation form, 43 fig.
Vertical integration, 330
Vertical publications, 488

Wang Laboratories, 92
Warehouse, internal, 362
Warehousing, 356–59
Water transport, 346 table, 347–48, 368
Webb-Pomerene associations, 574
Weighted-point plan, 43–45
Westinghouse International, 160, 442
Whirlpool, 621
Wilson Learning Corporation, 454
Word of mouth, 534
Workload method, 446
W.W. Grainger, 357

Xerox, 48, 415, 442, 452
  television advertising by, 489

Yarway Corporation, 315

Zenith Data Systems, 418